Lecture Notes in Computer Science   12819

Antonio Cerone · Peter Csaba Ölveczky (Eds.)

Theoretical Aspects of Computing – ICTAC 2021

18th International Colloquium
Virtual Event, Nur-Sultan, Kazakhstan, September 8–10, 2021
Proceedings

 Springer

Editors
Antonio Cerone
Nazarbayev University
Nur-Sultan, Kazakhstan

Peter Csaba Ölveczky (iD)
Department of Informatics
University of Oslo
Oslo, Norway

ISSN 0302-9743   ISSN 1611-3349 (electronic)
Lecture Notes in Computer Science
ISBN 978-3-030-85314-3   ISBN 978-3-030-85315-0 (eBook)
https://doi.org/10.1007/978-3-030-85315-0

LNCS Sublibrary: SL1 – Theoretical Computer Science and General Issues

This Springer imprint is published by the registered company Springer Nature Switzerland AG
The registered company address is: Gewerbestrasse 11, 6330 Cham, Switzerland

Preface

This volume contains the proceedings of the 18th International Colloquium on Theoretical Aspects of Computing (ICTAC 2021), which was held during September 8–10, 2021. The event was supposed to take place in Nur-Sultan, Kazakhstan, but due to the pandemic it had to be held as a fully virtual event, organized by Nazarbayev University.

The conference concerns all aspects of theoretical computer science and aims at bringing together researchers and practitioners from academia, industry, and government to present research and exchange ideas and experience, addressing challenges in both theoretical aspects of computing and the exploitation of theory through methods and tools for system development. ICTAC also aims to promote research cooperation between developing and industrial countries.

ICTAC 2021 received 55 paper submissions. Almost all papers received at least three reviews. Based on the reviews and extensive discussions, the program committee decided to accept 20 papers. This volume contains the revised versions of these 20 papers, which cover a wide variety of topics, including: getting the best price for selling your personal data; attacking Bitcoin; optimizing various forms of model checking; synthesizing and learning algorithms; formalizing and verifying contracts, languages, and compilers; analyzing the correctness and complexity of programs and distributed systems; and finding connections from proofs in propositional logic to quantum programming languages.

The conference also featured invited talks by Wil van der Aalst (RWTH Aachen University, Germany), Alan Dix (Swansea University, UK), Kim Guldstrand Larsen (Aalborg University, Denmark), and Grigore Rosu (University of Illinois at Urbana-Champaign, USA). An abstract of the invited talk by Larsen and full papers accompanying those by van der Aalst and Dix are included in this volume.

Many colleagues and friends contributed to ICTAC 2021. We thank the invited speakers for accepting our invitations to give invited talks and the authors who submitted their work to ICTAC 2021. We are grateful to the members of the program committee and the external reviewers for providing timely and insightful reviews, as well as for their involvement in the post-reviewing discussions. We would also like to thank the regional publicity chairs for their work attracting submissions and Springer for sponsoring the Best Paper Award.

July 2021

Antonio Cerone
Peter Csaba Ölveczky

Organization

Program Chairs

Antonio Cerone   Nazarbayev University, Kazakhstan
Peter Csaba Ölveczky   University of Oslo, Norway

Steering Committee

Frank de Boer	CWI, The Netherlands
Martin Leucker (Chair)	University of Lübeck, Germany
Zhiming Liu	Southwest University, China
Tobias Nipkow	Technical University of Munich, Germany
Augusto Sampaio	Federal University of Pernambuco, Brazil
Natarajan Shankar	SRI International, USA
Tarmo Uustalu	Tallinn University of Technology, Estonia

Program Committee

Erika Ábrahám	RWTH Aachen University, Germany
Bernhard K. Aichernig	Graz University of Technology, Austria
Musab A. Alturki	Runtime Verification Inc., USA, and King Fahd University of Petroleum and Minerals, Saudi Arabia
Étienne André	Université de Lorraine, France
Ebru Aydin Gol	Middle East Technical University, Turkey
Kyungmin Bae	Pohang University of Science and Technology, South Korea
Maurice ter Beek	ISTI-CNR, Italy
Dirk Beyer	Ludwig-Maximilian University Munich, Germany
Simon Bliudze	Inria Lille, France
Roberto Bruni	University of Pisa, Italy
Antonio Cerone	Nazarbayev University, Kazakhstan
Manuel Clavel	Vietnamese-German University, Vietnam
Adrian Francalanza	University of Malta, Malta
Rob van Glabbeek	Data61, CSIRO, Australia
Sergey Goncharov	Friedrich-Alexander University Erlangen-Nürnberg, Germany
Jan Friso Groote	Eindhoven University of Technology, The Netherlands
Stefan Gruner	University of Pretoria, South Africa
Osman Hasan	National University of Sciences & Technology, Pakistan
Klaus Havelund	Jet Propulsion Laboratory, USA
Kim G. Larsen	Aalborg University, Denmark

Axel Legay	Université catholique de Louvain, Belgium
Martin Leucker	University of Lübeck, Germany
Manuel Mazzara	Innopolis University, Russia
Catherine Meadows	Naval Research Laboratory, USA
Larissa Meinicke	The University of Queensland, Australia
Hans de Nivelle	Nazarbayev University, Kazakhstan
Kazuhiro Ogata	JAIST, Japan
Peter Csaba Ölveczky	University of Oslo, Norway
Catuscia Palamidessi	Inria, France
Elaine Pimentel	Federal University of Rio Grande do Norte, Brazil
José Proença	Polytechnic Institute of Porto, Portugal
Riadh Robbana	INSAT, Carthage University, Tunisia
Gwen Salaün	University of Grenoble Alpes, France
Davide Sangiorgi	University of Bologna, Italy, and Inria, France
Lutz Schröder	Friedrich-Alexander University Erlangen-Nürnberg, Germany
Volker Stolz	Western Norway University of Applied Sciences, Norway
Georg Struth	The University of Sheffield, UK

Regional Publicity Chairs

Stefan Gruner	University of Pretoria, South Africa
Kazuhiro Ogata	JAIST, Japan
Elaine Pimentel	Federal University of Rio Grande do Norte, Brazil
Riadh Robbana	INSAT, Carthage University, Tunisia
Nikolay Shilov	Innopolis University, Russia

Additional Reviewers

Yehia Abd Alrahman	Karam Kharraz
Mario S. Alvim	Michalis Kokologiannakis
Tomer Ashur	Sandeep Kulkarni
Giorgio Bacci	Frédéric Lang
Marco Bernardo	Thomas Lemberger
Laura Bussi	Anders Miltner
Guillermina Cledou	Carlos Olarte
Khanh Huu The Dam	Renato Neves
Guillaume Dupont	Andrea Pferscher
Rick Erkens	Johannes Åman Pohjola
Lorenzo Gheri	Danny Bøgsted Poulsen
Imen Ben Hafaiedh	Adnan Rashid
Andreas Hülsing	Jose Ignacio Requeno
Peter Gjøl Jensen	Martin Sachenbacher

Wendelin Serwe   Adele Veschetti
Francesco Sica   Olivier Verdier
Flip van Spaendonck   Nico Weise
Daniel Thoma

Sponsor

 NAZARBAYEV
UNIVERSITY

Model Checking and Machine Learning Joining Forces in UPPAAL (Invited Paper)

Kim Guldstrand Larsen

Department of Computer Science, Aalborg University, Denmark

In the talk we offer a detailed presentation on how the symbolic model checking techniques of Uppaal has joined forces with machine learning during the last 10 years.

The first step towards exploiting the efficiency of machine learning in UPPAAL was made in the branch UPPAAL SMC. Here [5], UPPAAL SMC offers highly efficient statistical model checking capabilities in order to provide performance analysis for a rich class of stochastic hybrid automata [10], and in a manner that consistently refines the Boolean verdicts of the model checking capability of classical UPPAAL. During the last 10 years this effort includes development of a sound theoretical foundation (e.g. the underlying stochastic semantics of timed automata [2]), the supporting algorithmic analysis (e.g. sequential testing a'la Wald), the efficient tool implementation as well as a long range of applications.

Most recently the SMC engine of UPPAAL has been considerably accelerated by exploiting independencies of system components during generation of random runs. In UPPAAL SMC , as in Gillespie's algorithm for biochemical systems, components are repeatedly racing against each other, calling for a resampling of all components after each step. A challenge is to prove that resampling only step-dependent components leave the probability distribution on runs unchanged. Another challenge is to develop static analysis methods for identifying independencies. This in turn has significantly reduced the complexity of run-generation (from quadratic to – in practice – linear), allowing UPPAAL SMC to scale to millions of components, as witnessed by recent applications to so-called Agent-based models for COVID19 analysis with millions of components, e.g. one per citizen of Denmark [9]. In addition, using the SMC engine may be used to generate synthetic data from stochastic hybrid automata in order to learn Bayesian networks for infering beliefs of key observable and unobservable properties in settings with scares data [8].

In the most recent branch UPPAAL STRATEGO [4, 3], symbolic techniques are combined with reinforcement learning to efficiently obtain near-optimal yet safe strategies for hybrid Markov decision processes. Taking as inputs 1) a hybrid Markov decision process H, 2) a safe constraint ϕ and 3) an objective function O to be optimized, UPPAAL STRATEGO first provides a most permissive safety strategy guaranteeing that ϕ is fullfilled using a timed game abstraction of H. Here well-known symbolic model checking techniques are used. Next, applying various learning methods, sub-strategies (thus still safe) optimizing O are subsequently obtained. The talk will present new (Q-, M-, ..) learning methods developed [7], preliminary results on their convergence [6], the ability to learn and output small and explainable strategies using decision trees

[1], and the approach for taking partial observability into account. In addition the talk will provide a demonstration of the new UPPAAL STRATEGO on the Smart Farming Challenge of the Dagstuhl seminar "Analysis of Autonomous Mobile Collectives in Complex Physical Environments" (October 2019). Also on-going applications of UPPAAL STRATEGO on water-management, traffic-light control, energy-aware building ao will be pointed out.

During the next five-year period the effort on combining model checking and machine learning will continue in the newly granted Villum-Investigator Center S4OS[1] of the speaker.

References

1. Ashok, P., Křetínský, J., Larsen, K. G., Le Coënt, A., Taankvist, J. H., Weininger, M.: SOS: Safe, optimal and small strategies for hybrid markov decision processes. In: Parker, D., Wolf, V. (eds.) Quantitative Evaluation of Systems. QEST 2019. LNCS, vol. 11785, pp. 147–164 Springer, Cham (2019). https://doi.org/10.1007/978-3-030-30281-8_9
2. Bertrand, N., et al.: Stochastic timed automata. Log. Methods Comput. Sci., **10**(4), 2014
3. David, A., et al.: On time with minimal expected cost!. In: Cassez, F., Raskin, J. F. (eds.) Automated Technology for Verification and Analysis. ATVA 2014. LNCS, vol. 8837, pp. 129–145. Springer, Cham (2014). https://doi.org/10.1007/978-3-319-11936-6_10
4. David, A., Jensen, P. G., Larsen, K. G., Mikučionis, M., Taankvist, J. H.: UPPAAL STRATEGO. In: Baier, C., Tinelli, C. (eds.) Tools and Algorithms for the Construction and Analysis of Systems. TACAS 2015. LNCS, vol. 9035, pp. 206-211. Springer, Berlin, Heidelberg (2015). https://doi.org/10.1007/978-3-662-46681-0_16
5. David, A., Larsen, K. G., Legay, A., Mikucionis, M., Poulsen, D. B.: UPPAAL SMC tutorial. Int. J. Softw. Tools Technol. Transf. **17**(4), 397–415 (2015)
6. Jaeger, M., Bacci, G., Bacci, G., Larsen, K. G., Jensen, P. G.: Approximating euclidean by imprecise markov decision processes. In: Margaria, T., Steffen, B. (eds.) Leveraging Applications of Formal Methods, Verification and Validation: Verification Principles. ISoLA 2020. LNCS, vol. 12476, pp. 275–289. Springer, Cham (2020). https://doi.org/10.1007/978-3-030-61362-4_15
7. Jaeger, M., Jensen, P. G., Guldstrand L. K., Legay, A., Sedwards, S., Taankvist, J. H.: Teaching stratego to play ball: optimal synthesis for continuous space MDPs. In: Chen, Y.F., Cheng, C. H., Esparza, J. (eds.) Automated Technology for Verification and Analysis. ATVA 2019. LNCS, vol. 11781, pp. 81–97. Springer, Cham (2019). https://doi.org/10.1007/978-3-030-31784-3_5
8. Jaeger, M., Larsen, K. G., Tibo, A.: From statistical model checking to run-time monitoring using a bayesian network approach. In: Deshmukh, J., Ničković, D. (eds.) Runtime Verification. RV 2020. LNCS, vol. 12399, pp. 517–535. Springer, Cham (2020). https://doi.org/10.1007/978-3-030-60508-7_30

---

[1] S4OS: Scalable analysis and Synthesis of Safe, Small, Secure and Optimal Strategies for CPS.

9. Jensen, P. G., Jørgensen, K. Y., Larsen, K. G., Mikučionis, M., Muñiz, M., Poulsen, D. B.: Fluid Model-Checking in UPPAAL for Covid-19. In: Margaria, T., Steffen, B. (eds.) Leveraging Applications of Formal Methods, Verification and Validation: Verification Principles. ISoLA 2020. LNCS, vol. 12476, pp. 385–403. Springer, Cham (2020). https://doi.org/10.1007/978-3-030-61362-4_22

10. Larsen, K. G.: Statistical model checking, refinement checking, optimization, … for stochastic hybrid systems. In: Jurdziński, M., Ničković, D. (eds.) Formal Modeling and Analysis of Timed Systems. FORMATS 2012. LNCS, vol. 7595, pp. 7–10. Springer, Berlin, Heidelberg (2012). https://doi.org/10.1007/978-3-642-33365-1_2

Contents

Quantum Computing

Security and Privacy

Synthesis and Learning

Systems Calculi and Analysis

Invited Papers

Concurrency and Objects Matter! Disentangling the Fabric of Real Operational Processes to Create Digital Twins

Wil M. P. van der Aalst[1,2(✉)]

[1] Process and Data Science (Informatik 9), RWTH Aachen University,
Aachen, Germany
`wvdaalst@pads.rwth-aachen.de`
[2] Fraunhofer-Institut für Angewandte Informationstechnik (FIT),
Sankt Augustin, Germany

Abstract. Process mining dramatically changed the way we look at process models and operational processes. Even seemingly simple processes like Purchase-to-Pay (P2P) and Order-to-Cash (O2C) are often amazingly complex, and traditional hand-made process models fail to capture the true fabric of such processes. Many processes are inherently concurrent and involve interaction between different objects (customers, suppliers, orders, items, shipments, payments, machines, workers, etc.). Process mining uses event data to construct process models that can be used to diagnose performance and compliance problems. If such models reflect reality well, they can be used for forward-looking forms of process mining, including predictive analytics, evidence-based automation, and what-if simulation. The ultimate goal is to create a "digital twin of an organization" that can be used to explore different improvement actions. This paper provides a high-level overview of the different process mining tasks followed by a more detailed discussion on concurrency and object-centricity in process mining.

Keywords: Process mining · Event data · Concurrency · Digital twins

1 Towards a Digital Twin of an Organization

The desire to adequately describe operational processes has been around since the 1890-ties when the field of *scientific management* emerged. Scientific management is also known as Taylorism, named after its pioneer Frederick Winslow Taylor (1856–1915) who tried to systematically improve economic efficiency, especially labor productivity. Taylor systematically observed how people work and can be seen as the "first process miner" using pen and paper (see Fig. 1). In 1950 computers started to influence business processes. However, the systematic use of data about operational processes is much more recent [1].

© Springer Nature Switzerland AG 2021
A. Cerone and P. C. Ölveczky (Eds.): ICTAC 2021, LNCS 12819, pp. 3–17, 2021.
https://doi.org/10.1007/978-3-030-85315-0_1

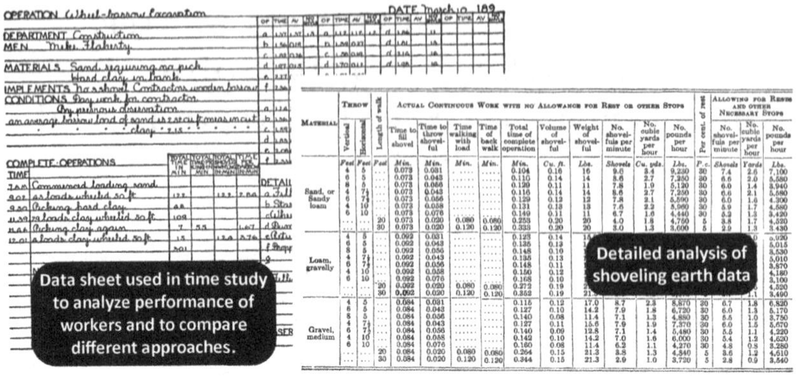

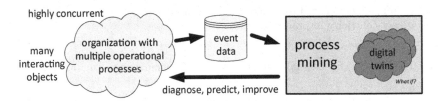

Fig. 1. Analyzing event data to improve operational processes is not that new. This is illustrated by some of the tables in [33]. Frederick Winslow Taylor can be seen as the first "process miner" using manually collected event data.

The desire to build computer models that mimic organizations and processes is also not that new. Since the 1960-ties so-called *discrete event simulation* tools have been available with SIMULA [11] as one of the first influential examples. In discrete event simulation it is common to estimate parameters and distributions based on observed data (e.g., service times and arrival rates). However, one still needs to model the process by hand. The first comprehensive approaches to automatically learn complete simulation models from event data became available around 2008 [30,31]. Based on event logs, it is possible to learn a control-flow model (transition system, Petri net, of BPMN model) that is enriched with information about resources, data, and time using replay or alignment techniques [30,31].

Fig. 2. Process mining provides a concrete approach to create a digital twin of an organization and its operational processes. A key element is the creation of a model based on event data that is able to mimic reality as well as possible. Such a model needs to be able to capture concurrency and interacting objects (customers, workers, products, orders, payments, shipments, etc.).

The notion of a *digital twin* is part of the Industry 4.0 development facilitated through advanced data analytics (machine learning, process mining, etc.) and the Internet of Things (IoT) connectivity [15,20]. The notion can be described as an effortless integration of the "real reality" and a "modeled reality" in both directions. The "modeled reality" is based on the "real reality", but may also influence the "real reality". This is one of the key concepts in the *Internet of Production* (IoP) developed at RWTH Aachen University [6]. In IoP, *process mining* plays a key role. Gartner coined the term *digital twin of an organization* to indicate that the desire to create a digital twin is not limited to specific Industry 4.0 applications [19]. The goal is to create a virtual representation of an organization and its operational processes (including assets such as architectures, infrastructures, roles, responsibilities, products, etc.) to assess the impact of change in a controlled environment. Note that this is only a vision that is still far away from reality. However, it illustrates the role that models will need to play in the future.

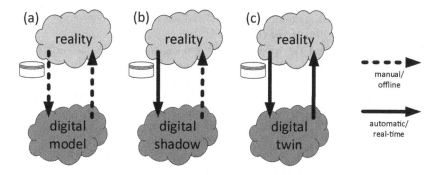

Fig. 3. The difference between a digital model, a digital shadow, and a digital twin.

Figure 3 illustrates the difference between (a) a digital model, (b) a digital shadow, and (c) a digital twin. Building a discrete event simulation model (using e.g. Arena, AnyLogic, CPN Tools, FlexSim, Vensim, or Simul8) in a classical way corresponds to the *digital model* notion in Fig. 3(a). The dashed lines show that the model is created by hand. There is no automated connection between reality and the digital model. Moreover, insights generated by the simulation model do not automatically lead to concrete actions. The *digital shadow* notion in Fig. 3(b) uses a model, driven by data automatically extracted from reality. If such a connection is automated, it is often possible and desirable to update the model continuously. If reality changes, also the model changes. However, insights and diagnostics still need to be translated into actions manually. The *digital twin* notion in Fig. 3(c) shows that there is an automated and real-time connection between reality and the model(s) in both directions. As a result, the digital twin directly influences reality, possibly without human intervention.

It is important to note that many of these ideas have been realized in the context of process mining, albeit with a focus on individual processes in isolation [1]. Most process mining techniques aim to create a digital shadow, as indicated in Fig. 3(b). This ranges from control-flow discovery (from mining directly follows graphs [2] to scalable inductive mining [23]) to automatically creating simulation models (e.g., [30,31]). However, under the umbrella term of "operational support" [1], process mining also aims to impact the process automatically in real-time. An early example is the work presented in [32], where workflow technology is connected to process mining. In [32] YAWL is used as a workflow management system, ProM as a process mining system, and CPN Tools as the simulation engine. ProM is used to learn a faithful simulation model from the event data of YAWL and/or the models in YAWL. At any point in time, the current state of the YAWL workflow system can be loaded into the simulation model and simulated using CPN Tools. This concept is termed *short-term simulation* because rather than focusing on the steady-state behavior, the focus is on transient behaviors and answering what-if questions. Commercial process mining tools increasingly support what we call "action-oriented process mining". This means that diagnostics are turned into actions. The recent release of the Celonis EMS (Execution Management System), which embeds a low-code workflow management system, illustrates this trend.

The above shows that the idea of creating a digital twin was already realized in the field of process mining long before the term became "in vogue". However, existing approaches typically focus on well-defined processes that are considered in isolation. We are still far away from creating a realistic "digital twin of an organization". In this paper, we focus on two of the many challenges to create such digital twins:

- *Concurrency.* Organizations are like distributed systems or social systems. The different parts operate autonomously but need to synchronize at selected points in time. Although most organizations and systems are highly concurrent, the dominant paradigm is still the highly sequential Turing machine model created in 1936 which does not allow for concurrency. The von Neumann architecture defined in 1945 is based on the Turing machine and also views computation as a sequential process. Moreover, automata, transition systems, Markov chains, and many other representations of behavior do not support concurrency. If concurrency is supported, it is often added as an afterthought. Representations that start from concurrency, like Petri nets, are still the exception. Consider for example a Petri net without places and just transitions. Even people familiar with Petri nets have difficulties to accept that such a Petri net allows for any behavior (and that Petri nets are much more declarative than commonly assumed). Although organizations are highly concurrent, event logs are viewed as sequential (i.e., events are assumed to be totally ordered). This complicates the creation of a digital twin from event data.
- *Object-centricity.* Most of the modeling notations used (e.g., BPMN, Workflow Nets, UML activity diagrams, etc.) assume a single case notion. However, events may involve a variety of objects. Consider for example batching where in one event many objects are affected or an assembly step where a collection of objects is transformed into a new composite object. When drawing for example a BPMN model one needs to pick one case notion (the process

instance). In many applications this is not so easy. Consider for example the hiring process of new employees. Is the vacancy the case or the application? One can also consider the classical example of ordering books from Amazon. One order may include multiple books, a shipment may contain books of different orders, and an order may involved multiple shipments. Possible case notions are order, book, and shipment. It is impossible to create a digital twin of an organization without being able to represent the different objects and their interactions.

For example, imagine a car factory producing hundreds of cars per day with each car assembled from thousands of components. Process models that do not allow for concurrency and object-centricity are clearly unable to describe such a factory as a digital twin.

The remainder of this paper is organized as follows. Section 2 present a short high-level introduction to process mining. Section 3 discusses event logs and the importance of concurrency and object-centricity. Section 4 concludes this short paper.

2   Process Mining: A Top-Down View

In recent years, we could witness an uptake in process mining. There used to be a gap between *process science* (i.e., tools and techniques to improve operational processes) and *data science* (i.e., tools and techniques to extract value from data). Mainstream machine learning and data mining techniques do not consider operational processes. Business Process Management (BPM) and Operations Research (OR) tend to start from models rather than data. Process mining bridges this gap [1].

Currently, there are over 35 commercial process mining vendors (ABBYY Timeline, ARIS Process Mining, BusinessOptix, Celonis Process Mining, Disco/Fluxicon, Everflow, Lana, Mavim, MPM, Minit, PAFnow, QPR, etc.) and process mining is applied in most of the larger organizations in countries such as Germany and The Netherlands. Example application domains include: finance (Rabobank, Hypovereinsbank, etc.), telecom (Deutsche Telekom, Vodafone, etc.), logistics (Vanderlande, etc.), production (BMW, Siemens, Fiat, Bosch, etc.), food (Edeka, etc.), fashion (Zalando, etc.), energy (E-on, etc.), transport (Uber, DB, Lufthansa, etc.), healthcare (AstraZenica, Medtronic, etc.), consulting (Deloitte, EY, KPMG, etc.), and IT systems (Dell, IBM, ServiceNow, etc.).

Figure 4 shows a high-level overview of process mining. Event data need to be extracted from information systems. Such data can be explored, filtered, and cleaned. Process discovery tools transform event data into process models (e.g., BPMN, Petri nets, and UML activity diagrams). There are simple approaches like creating so-called Directly-Follows-Graphs (DFGs) that do not discover concurrency thus having obvious problems [2]. The Alpha algorithm was the first to discover concurrent processes [7]. This approach provides some guarantees, but most processes do not satisfy the assumptions described in [7]. After

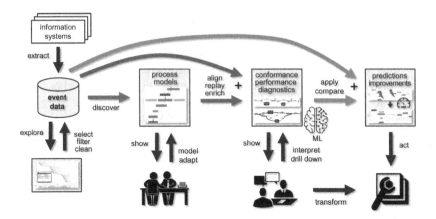

Fig. 4. Overview of the process mining pipeline.

the Alpha algorithm, dozens of more sophisticated algorithms were proposed [1,9,21–23,34]. Using replay and alignment techniques it is possible to relate process models (hand-made or discovered) with event data. This can be used to discover differences between reality and model [1,10,29]. Moreover, the model can be extended with additional perspectives, e.g., organizational aspects, decisions, and temporal aspects. This way, detailed performance analyses are possible. Root-cause analysis can be performed for both conformance and performance problems. It is always possible to relate observations to the original event data. Such evidence-based diagnostics aid discussions about root-causes and possible improvements. The right-hand side of Fig. 4 refers to forward-looking techniques aimed at improving the processes. Process models extended with additional perspectives (organizational aspects, decisions, and temporal aspects) can be used to predict conformance and performance problems. As described in [1], predictions can be used to generate recommendations. Figure 4 shows that Machine Learning (ML) techniques can be used in this step. These may range from novel deep learning approaches (e.g., artificial recurrent neural networks like LSTM) to more traditional approaches like logistic regression and decision-tree learning.

It should be noted that process mining techniques are different from mainstream Machine Learning (ML) techniques. However, as Fig. 4 shows, process mining can be used to generate ML problems. The current trend is to make process mining techniques more action-oriented, e.g., automatically trigger a corrective workflow when a problem emerges.

The process mining manifesto [17] published a decade ago lists 11 challenges. Most of these challenges still exist and are still relevant. Figure 5 maps eight challenges onto the overview used before (Fig. 4). These are partly overlapping with the challenges listed in [17], e.g., basic tasks like data extraction and process discovery remain challenging. The reader interested in applications of process mining is recommended to read [26] with experience reports from Siemens, BMW, Uber, ABB, Bayer, and several other organizations.

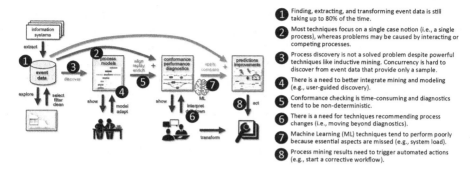

Fig. 5. Some of the challenges encountered when applying process mining.

The top-left corner and bottom-right corner show the interface between the real systems and organization on the one hand and process mining technology on the other hand. These correspond to the solid arrows in Fig. 3(c) used to explain the notion of a digital twin. Using state-of-the-art process mining tools it is possible to create a digital twin with limited scope (e.g., a single process). Process mining is probably the most concrete technology available to create digital twins. Most of the proposals are merely visions or application specific.

3   Process Mining: A Bottom-Up View

After providing a high-level view on process mining, we focus on concurrency and object-centricity. These are essential to create digital twins that properly reflect real organizations. To illustrate these concepts, we use Petri nets. However, it is good to note that the ideas are generic and not notation-specific.

3.1   Petri Nets

Figure 6 shows an accepting labeled Petri net eight places $(p1, p2, \ldots, p8)$ and seven transitions $(t1, t2, \ldots, t7)$ with initial marking $[p1]$ and final marking $[p8]$. We assume that the reader is familiar with the semantics of Petri nets [5,13,25,27,28]. However, to make the paper more self-contained, we informally explain the behavior of an accepting labeled Petri net. A transition t is *enabled* in a marking if each of its input places contains at least one token. An enabled transition t may *fire*, i.e., one token is removed from each of the input places •t and one token is produced for each of the output places t•. This way the Petri net can move from one marking to the next. For example, in the marking shown in Fig. 6 (with a token in $p1$) only $t1$ is enabled. Firing $t1$ means the consumption of one token and the production of three tokens. The resulting marking is $[p2, p3, p4]$. In this marking, four transitions are enabled: There is a choice between $t5$ or $t6$ because both compete for the token in $p4$. The ordering of $t2$, $t4$, and $t5$ or $t6$ is not fixed. The transitions in Fig. 6 are labeled, e.g., executing $t6$ correspond to taking an X-ray. Moreover, next to the initial marking indicated by the black token in place $p1$, there is also a final target marking with just a token in $p8$. We are interested in firing sequences leading from $[p1]$ to $[p8]$. Three examples are: $\sigma_1 = \langle t1, t2, t4, t5, t7 \rangle$, $\sigma_2 = \langle t1, t2, t4, t6, t7 \rangle$, and $\sigma_3 = \langle t1, t2, t3, t2, t3, t2, t4, t6, t7 \rangle$. There are infinitely many firing sequences due to the loop. If we block the loop and do not fire transition $t3$, there are 12 possible firing sequences.

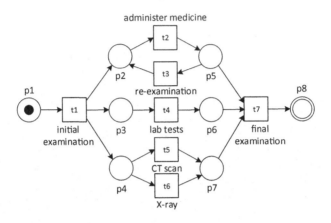

Fig. 6. An accepting labeled Petri net eight places $(p1, p2, \ldots, p8)$ and seven transitions $(t1, t2, \ldots, t7)$.

Figure 7 shows three example *runs* of the accepting labeled Petri net. Places in Fig. 7 correspond to tokens in Fig. 6, and transitions in Fig. 7 correspond to transition firings in Fig. 6. A run of a Petri net corresponds to a partial order. For example, $r1$ in Fig. 7 does not impose an ordering on the three middle activities. The transition labels in Fig. 7 refer to the transitions in Fig. 6, e.g., $t21$, $t22$, and $t23$ in run $r3$ refer to transition $t2$ (administer medicine). For a formal definition of the runs of a Petri net, we again refer to standard literature [12, 14, 27]. Typically, the number of runs is much smaller than the number of firing sequences. For example, if we block the loop and do not fire transition $t3$, then there are only two runs ($r1$ and $r2$) whereas there where 12 possible firing sequences (e.g., σ_1 is one of the six firing sequences corresponding to run $r1$). Run $r3$ corresponds $7 * 6 = 42$ firing sequences.

The fact that run $r3$ corresponds to 42 firing sequences illustrates the challenge of discovering concurrency. If we assume that $t3$ is executed at most 5 times, then there are $2(1 + 1 + 1 + 1 + 1 + 1) = 12$ runs and $2(13 * 12 + 11 * 10 + 9 * 8 + 7 * 6 + 5 * 4 + 3 * 2) = 812$ firing sequences. Even when our event log has information about thousands of traces, it is extremely unlikely that one can witness all 812 variants (especially when not all variants have an equal probability). This illustrates that one cannot ignore concurrency, because it will lead to an explosion of possible interleavings of which just a fraction will be witnessed.

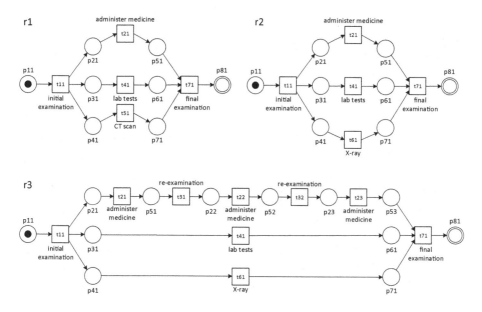

Fig. 7. Three example runs of the accepting Petri net: $r1$, $r2$, and $r3$. Run $r3$ corresponds to 42 firing sequences.

3.2   Object-Centric Partially-Ordered Event Logs

Next to the problem of concurrency, we also need to deal with events referring to collections of objects. This is analogous to moving from a classical Petri net to a Colored Petri Net (CPN) [5,18]. In a CPN, tokens have values and can present different objects. In a classical Petri net, tokens are indistinguishable and transitions cannot consumer or produce a variable number of tokens.

Techniques to discover Petri nets from event data assume precisely one case identifier per event [3,4]. These case identifiers are used to correlate events, and the resulting discovered Petri net aims to describe the life-cycle of individual cases. In reality, there are often multiple intertwined case notions, and it is impossible to pick a single case notion to describe the whole process. For example, events may refer to mixtures of orders, items, packages, customers, and products. A package may refer to multiple items, multiple products, one order, and one customer. Therefore, we need to assume that each event refers to a collection of objects, each having a type (instead of a single case identifier). Such *object-centric event logs* are closer to data in real-life information systems (e.g., SAP, Salesforce, Oracle, etc.). From an object-centric event log, we want to discover an *object-centric Petri net* with places that correspond to object types and transitions that may consume and produce collections of objects of different types. Such object-centric Petri nets visualize the complex relationships among objects of different types.

In the remainder, we present object-centric event logs as defined in [3,4]. Note that this is a simplified version of the later *OCEL standard* (see ocel-standard.org) which also adds attributes to objects [16]. OCEL also provides JSON/XML serializations of object-centric event logs and intends to overcome the limitations of the XES standard [8]. Recall that is the official IEEE standard for storing and exchanging event data assuming a single case notion.

Definition 1 (Universes). *We define the following universes (based on [3,4]):*

- $\mathbb{U}_{ei}$ *is the universe of event identifiers,*
- $\mathbb{U}_{act}$ *is the universe of activity names (also used to label transitions in an accepting Petri net),*
- $\mathbb{U}_{time}$ *is the universe of timestamps,*
- $\mathbb{U}_{ot}$ *is the universe of object types (also called classes),*
- $\mathbb{U}_{oi}$ *is the universe of object identifiers (also called entities),*
- $type \in \mathbb{U}_{oi} \to \mathbb{U}_{ot}$ *assigns precisely one type to each object identifier,*
- $\mathbb{U}_{omap} = \{omap \in \mathbb{U}_{ot} \nrightarrow \mathcal{P}(\mathbb{U}_{oi}) \mid \forall_{ot \in dom(omap)} \forall_{oi \in omap(ot)} type(oi) = ot\}$ *is the universe of all object mappings indicating which object identifiers are included per type,[1]*
- $\mathbb{U}_{att}$ *is the universe of attribute names,*
- $\mathbb{U}_{val}$ *is the universe of attribute values,*
- $\mathbb{U}_{vmap} = \mathbb{U}_{att} \nrightarrow \mathbb{U}_{val}$ *is the universe of value assignments,[2] and*
- $\mathbb{U}_{event} = \mathbb{U}_{ei} \times \mathbb{U}_{act} \times \mathbb{U}_{time} \times \mathbb{U}_{omap} \times \mathbb{U}_{vmap}$ *is the universe of events.*

An event $e = (ei, act, time, omap, vmap) \in \mathbb{U}_{event}$ is characterized by a unique event identifier ei, the corresponding activity act, the event's timestamp $time$, and two mappings $omap$ and $vmap$ for respectively object references and attribute values.

Definition 2 (Event Projection). *Given* $e = (ei, act, time, omap, vmap) \in \mathbb{U}_{event}$, $\pi_{ei}(e) = ei$, $\pi_{act}(e) = act$, $\pi_{time}(e) = time$, $\pi_{omap}(e) = omap$, *and* $\pi_{vmap}(e) = vmap$.

$\pi_{omap}(e) \in \mathbb{U}_{ot} \nrightarrow \mathcal{P}(\mathbb{U}_{oi})$ maps a subset of object types onto sets of object identifiers for an event e. An *object-centric event log* is a collection of *partially ordered events*. Event identifiers are unique, i.e., two events cannot have the same event identifier.

Definition 3 (Object-Centric Event Log). $L = (E, \preceq_E)$ *is an event log with* $E \subseteq \mathbb{U}_{event}$ *and* $\preceq_E \subseteq E \times E$ *such that:*

- $\preceq_E$ *defines a partial order (reflexive, antisymmetric, and transitive),*
- $\forall_{e_1,e_2 \in E} \ \pi_{ei}(e_1) = \pi_{ei}(e_2) \ \Rightarrow \ e_1 = e_2$, *and*
- $\forall_{e_1,e_2 \in E} \ e_1 \preceq_E e_2 \ \Rightarrow \ \pi_{time}(e_1) \leq \pi_{time}(e_2)$.

---

[1] $\mathcal{P}(\mathbb{U}_{oi})$ is the powerset of the universe of object identifiers, i.e., object types are mapped onto sets of object identifiers. $omap \in \mathbb{U}_{ot} \nrightarrow \mathcal{P}(\mathbb{U}_{oi})$ is a partial function. If $ot \notin dom(omap)$, then we assume that $omap(ot) = \emptyset$.

[2] $\mathbb{U}_{att} \nrightarrow \mathbb{U}_{val}$ is the set of all partial functions mapping a subset of attribute names onto the corresponding values.

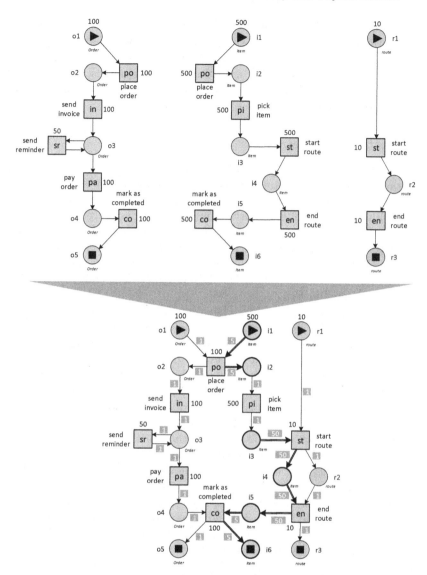

Fig. 8. An Object-Centric Petri Net (OCPN) can be learned by first learning a classical Petri net per object type and then merging the nets while correcting the multiplicities using variable arcs (a detailed derivation of the process model was presented in [4]).

Definition 3 allows for partially ordered event logs. Many process mining techniques require a total order, e.g., events are ordered based on timestamps and when two events have the same timestamp we assume some order. However, there are process discovery techniques that take into account causalities [3,24]. These can exploit such partial orders. There may be many reasons to use partially ordered event logs: efficiency, imprecise timing information, uncertainty, and explicit partial order information (e.g., based on data flow analysis). As argued before, it is unreasonable to assume that all possible interleavings will indeed be present in the event log. Instead of a partial order one can also use the stricter notion of a weak order. This is particularly suitable when one has imprecise timestamps (e.g., events on the same day cannot be ordered).

3.3   Object-Centric Petri Nets

In this paper, we argued that concurrency and objects matter. To progress the field of process mining, we cannot assume that events are totally ordered and can be correlated using a single case notion. Hence, we need process mining techniques and process model representations handling concurrency and object-centricity as first-class citizens. In [4], we presented an approach to automatically learn a so-called *Object-Centric Petri Net* (OCPN) given an object-centric event log (e.g., in OCEL format [16]). A detailed explanation of the approach to discover OCPNs is beyond the scope of this short paper. Therefore, we only show the example depicted in Fig. 8.

Let $L = (E, \preceq_E)$ be an event log. The events in E refer to objects. Therefore, given a specific object o of type ot, it is possible to create a partial order of all events that refer to o. $(E_o, \preceq_{E_o})$, with $E_o = \{e \in E \mid o \in \pi_{omap}(e)(ot)\}$ and $\preceq_{E_o} = \preceq_E \cap (E_o \times E_o)$, defines the corresponding partial order. Hence, we can group all partial orders of events corresponding to objects of a given type ot to get the required input for a standard process discovery algorithm. Note that the same event may appear in multiple partial orders. Next, we can learn a process model per object type. For simplicity, we assume that we discover a labeled accepting Petri net per object type satisfying the constraint that labels of visible transition are unique. There may be silent transitions (i.e., transitions that do not refer to an activity). However, there cannot be two transitions referring to the same activity.

The top part of Fig. 8 shows three labeled accepting Petri nets discovered for 100 orders, 500 items, and 10 routes. These three models happen to be sequential, but could have been concurrent. The initial and final markings are denoted by the places with the play and stop symbol. Next, the three labeled accepting Petri nets are merged into an OCPN. Since the visible transitions are unique, merging is trivial. However, the annotations need to be modified. In an OCPN there is a one-to-one correspondence between transition firings and events. A single event (i.e., transition occurrence) may involve a *variable number of objects* (e.g., one order may have any number of items). This is indicated by the double arcs in the lower part of Fig. 8. For example, on average one execution of *place order* corresponds to five items and one order. On average one execution of *start route* corresponds to 50 items and one route. For more details, we refer to [4].

The discovery Object-Centric Petri Nets (OCPNs) from object-centric event logs in OCEL format is still in its infancy. However, the topic is important because in most applications of process mining one faces the problem of one-to-many and many-to-many relations between different types of objects relevant for an organization. Processes are intertwined and difficult to separate. Figure 8 shows that it is possible to create one, more holistic, process model that is showing the interactions between the different types of objects. Actually, the term "process model" may be misleading in the context of OCPNs that may represent collections of interacting processes.

4   Conclusion

To create a "digital twin of an organization" we need to disentangle the fabric of real operational processes. Process mining provides many of the ingredients to make such a step. In this paper, we provided a high-level overview of process mining and linked it to historical developments in the field of scientific management and simulation. As shown, there have been early examples of digital twins (or at least digital shadows) in the field of process mining. We mentioned, for example, the work combining the process mining framework ProM, the workflow management system YAWL, and CPN Tools as the simulation engine [32]. This enabled new forms of "short-term simulation" that can be used to see the effects of decisions given the current state and historic information.

However, we are far away from fully capturing the fabric of real operational processes in a single model. An important prerequisite is the proper handling of concurrency and entangled objects. One event may refer to many objects and organizations are highly concurrent. It is unrealistic to assume that one can witness all interleavings of highly concurrent processes. Therefore, we elaborated on Object-Centric Petri Nets (OCPNs) and OCEL as a format for exchanging object-centric event logs [16].

Future research needs to address the challenges described in this paper. Compared to the pen-and-paper analyses done by Frederick Winslow Taylor and colleagues more than a century ago, we have booked tremendous progress. The detailed event data available today provide unprecedented opportunities to create digital twins (provided we are able to concurrency and object-centricity properly).

Acknowledgments. The author thanks the Alexander von Humboldt (AvH) Stiftung for supporting his research.

References

1. van der Aalst, W.M.P.: Data science in action. In: Process Mining. Springer, Heidelberg (2016). https://doi.org/10.1007/978-3-662-49851-4_1
2. van der Aalst, W.M.P.: A practitioner's guide to process mining: limitations of the directly-follows graph. In: International Conference on Enterprise Information Systems (Centeris 2019). Procedia Computer Science, vol. 164, pp. 321–328. Elsevier (2019)
3. van der Aalst, W.M.P.: Object-centric process mining: dealing with divergence and convergence in event data. In: Ölveczky, P.C., Salaün, G. (eds.) SEFM 2019. LNCS, vol. 11724, pp. 3–25. Springer, Cham (2019). https://doi.org/10.1007/978-3-030-30446-1_1

4. van der Aalst, W.M.P., Berti, A.: Discovering object-centric Petri nets. Fund. Inform. **175**(1–4), 1–40 (2020)

5. van der Aalst, W.M.P., Stahl, C.: Modeling Business Processes: A Petri Net Oriented Approach. MIT Press, Cambridge (2011)

6. van der Aalst, W.M.P., Brockhoff, T., Ghahfarokhi, A.F., Pourbafrani, M., Uysal, M.S., van Zelst, S.J.: Removing operational friction using process mining: challenges provided by the Internet of Production (IoP). In: Hammoudi, S., Quix, C., Bernardino, J. (eds.) DATA 2020. CCIS, vol. 1446, pp. 1–31. Springer, Cham (2021). https://doi.org/10.1007/978-3-030-83014-4_1

7. van der Aalst, W.M.P., Weijters, A.J.M.M., Maruster, L.: Workflow mining: discovering process models from event logs. IEEE Trans. Knowl. Data Eng. **16**(9), 1128–1142 (2004)

8. Acampora, G., Vitiello, A., Di Stefano, B., van der Aalst, W., Günther, C., Verbeek, E.: IEEE 1849: the XES standard - the second IEEE standard sponsored by IEEE Computational Intelligence Society. IEEE Comput. Intell. Mag. **12**(2), 4–8 (2017)

9. Augusto, A., Conforti, R., Marlon, M., La Rosa, M., Polyvyanyy, A.: Split miner: automated discovery of accurate and simple business process models from event logs. Knowl. Inf. Syst. **59**(2), 251–284 (2019)

10. Carmona, J., van Dongen, B., Solti, A., Weidlich, M.: Conformance Checking: Relating Processes and Models. Springer, Cham (2018). https://doi.org/10.1007/978-3-319-99414-7

11. Dahl, O.J., Nygaard, K.: SIMULA: an ALGOL based simulation language. Commun. ACM **1**, 671–678 (1966)

12. Desel, J.: Validation of process models by construction of process nets. In: van der Aalst, W., Desel, J., Oberweis, A. (eds.) Business Process Management. LNCS, vol. 1806, pp. 110–128. Springer, Heidelberg (2000). https://doi.org/10.1007/3-540-45594-9_8

13. Desel, J., Esparza, J.: Free Choice Petri Nets. Cambridge Tracts in Theoretical Computer Science, vol. 40. Cambridge University Press, Cambridge (1995)

14. van Dongen, B.F., Desel, J., van der Aalst, W.M.P.: Aggregating causal runs into workflow nets. In: Jensen, K., van der Aalst, W.M., Ajmone Marsan, M., Franceschinis, G., Kleijn, J., Kristensen, L.M. (eds.) Transactions on Petri Nets and Other Models of Concurrency VI. LNCS, vol. 7400, pp. 334–363. Springer, Heidelberg (2012). https://doi.org/10.1007/978-3-642-35179-2_14

15. Fuller, A., Fan, Z., Day, C., Barlow, C.: Digital twin: enabling technologies, challenges and open research. IEEE Access **8**, 108952–108971 (2020)

16. Ghahfarokhi, A.F., Park, G., Berti, A., van der Aalst, W.M.P.: OCEL Standard (2021). www.ocel-standard.org

17. van der Aalst, W., et al.: Process mining manifesto. In: Daniel, F., Barkaoui, K., Dustdar, S. (eds.) BPM 2011. LNBIP, vol. 99, pp. 169–194. Springer, Heidelberg (2012). https://doi.org/10.1007/978-3-642-28108-2_19

18. Jensen, K.: Coloured Petri Nets. Basic Concepts, Analysis Methods and Practical Use. Monographs in Theoretical Computer Science An EATCS Series, Springer, Heidelberg (1997). https://doi.org/10.1007/978-3-642-60794-3

19. Kerremans, M., Kopcho, J.: Create a digital twin of your organization to optimize your digital transformation program. Research Note G00379226 (2019). www.gartner.com

20. Kritzinger, W., Karner, M., Traar, G., Henjes, J., Sihn, W.: Digital twin in manufacturing: a categorical literature review and classification. IFAC-PapersOnLine **51**(11), 1016–1022 (2018). 16th IFAC Symposium on Information Control Problems in Manufacturing INCOM 2018

21. Leemans, S.J.J., Fahland, D., van der Aalst, W.M.P.: Discovering block-structured process models from event logs - a constructive approach. In: Colom, J.-M., Desel, J. (eds.) PETRI NETS 2013. LNCS, vol. 7927, pp. 311–329. Springer, Heidelberg (2013). https://doi.org/10.1007/978-3-642-38697-8_17

22. Leemans, S.J.J., Fahland, D., van der Aalst, W.M.P.: Discovering block-structured process models from event logs containing infrequent behaviour. In: Lohmann, N., Song, M., Wohed, P. (eds.) BPM 2013. LNBIP, vol. 171, pp. 66–78. Springer, Cham (2014). https://doi.org/10.1007/978-3-319-06257-0_6

23. Leemans, S.J.J., Fahland, D., van der Aalst, W.M.P.: Scalable process discovery and conformance checking. Softw. Syst. Model. **17**(2), 599–631 (2018)

24. Lu, X., Fahland, D., van der Aalst, W.M.P.: Conformance checking based on partially ordered event data. In: Fournier, F., Mendling, J. (eds.) BPM 2014. LNBIP, vol. 202, pp. 75–88. Springer, Cham (2015). https://doi.org/10.1007/978-3-319-15895-2_7

25. Murata, T.: Petri nets: properties, analysis and applications. Proc. IEEE **77**(4), 541–580 (1989)

26. Reinkemeyer, L.: Process Mining in Action: Principles, Use Cases and Outlook. Springer, Berlin (2020). https://doi.org/10.1007/978-3-030-40172-6

27. Reisig, W.: Petri Nets: Modeling Techniques, Analysis, Methods, Case Studies. Springer, Berlin (2013). https://doi.org/10.1007/978-3-642-33278-4

28. Reisig, W., Rozenberg, G. (eds.): Lectures on Petri Nets I: Basic Models. Lecture Notes in Computer Science, vol. 1491. Springer, Berlin (1998). https://doi.org/10.1007/3-540-65306-6

29. Rozinat, A., van der Aalst, W.M.P.: Conformance checking of processes based on monitoring real behavior. Inf. Syst. **33**(1), 64–95 (2008)

30. Rozinat, A., Mans, R.S., Song, M., van der Aalst, W.M.P.: Discovering colored petri nets from event logs. Int. J. Softw. Tools Technol. Transf. **10**(1), 57–74 (2008)

31. Rozinat, A., Mans, R.S., Song, M., van der Aalst, W.M.P.: Discovering simulation models. Inf. Syst. **34**(3), 305–327 (2009)

32. Rozinat, A., Wynn, M., van der Aalst, W.M.P., ter Hofstede, A.H.M., Fidge, C.: Workflow simulation for operational decision support. Data Knowl. Eng. **68**(9), 834–850 (2009)

33. Taylor, F.W.: The Principles of Scientific Management. Harper and Bothers Publishers, New York (1919)

34. van Zelst, S.J., van Dongen, B.F., van der Aalst, W.M.P., Verbeek, H.M.W.: Discovering workflow nets using integer linear programming. Computing **100**(5), 529–556 (2018)

Qualitative–Quantitative Reasoning: Thinking Informally About Formal Things

Alan Dix[(✉)] [iD]

The Computational Foundry, Swansea University, Wales, UK
alan@hcibook.com
https://alandix.com/academic/papers/ICTCS-QQ-2021

Abstract. Qualitative–quantitative reasoning is the way we think informally about formal or numerical phenomena. It is ubiquitous in scientific, professional and day-to-day life. Mathematicians have strong intuitions about whether a theorem is true well before a proof is found – intuition that also drives the direction of new proofs. Engineers use various approximations and can often tell where a structure will fail. In computation we deal with order of magnitude arguments in complexity theory and data science practitioners need to match problems to the appropriate neural architecture or statistical method. Even in the supermarket, we may have a pretty good idea of about how much things will cost before we get to the checkout. This paper will explore some of the different forms of QQ–reasoning through examples including the author's own experience numerically modelling agricultural sprays and formally modelling human–computer interactions. We will see that it is often the way in which formal and mathematical results become useful and also the importance for public understanding of key issues including Covid and climate change. Despite its clear importance, it is a topic that is left to professional experience, or sheer luck. In early school years pupils may learn estimation, but in later years this form of reasoning falls into the gap between arithmetic and formal mathematics despite being more important in adult life than either. The paper is partly an introduction to some of the general features of QQ-reasoning, and partly a 'call to arms' for academics and educators.

Keywords: Informal reasoning · Estimation · Mathematical models · Order of magnitude · Covid models · Monotonicity

1 Motivation

When I first read Hardy and Wright's Number Theory [15] I was captivated. However, as much as the mathematics itself, one statement always stood out for me. In the very first chapter they list a number of "questions concerning primes", the first of which is whether there is a formula for the nth prime.

© Springer Nature Switzerland AG 2021
A. Cerone and P. C. Ölveczky (Eds.): ICTAC 2021, LNCS 12819, pp. 18–35, 2021.
https://doi.org/10.1007/978-3-030-85315-0_2

Hardy and Wright explicitly say that this seems "unlikely" given the distribution of the series is "quite unlike what we should expect on any such hypothesis." I think most number theorists would still agree with this assertion, indeed many cryptographic techniques would collapse if such a formula were discovered. Yet what is this sense that the structure of primes and the structure of formulae are so different? It is not formal mathematics itself, else it would be a proof.

In engineering, computation, physics, indeed any quantitative or formal domain, the precise and provable sits alongside an informal grasp of the nature of the domain. This was certainly true in my own early and more recent work on formal modelling of human computer interaction: sometimes, as in the case of undo, one can make exact and faithful statements and proofs, but more often in order to achieve formal precision, one resorts to simplistic representations of real-life. However, despite their gap from the true phenomena, these modes, however lacking in fidelity, still give us insight.

I'm sure this will be familiar to those working in other areas where theoretical models are applied to practical problems. There is a quantum-like tension between the complexity of the world and our ability to represent it, between accuracy and precision, between fidelity and formality. Yet, we do learn about real phenomena from these simplified models, and in many contexts, from primary school estimation to scientific research we use these forms of thinking – I call this qualitative–quantitative reasoning.

This has become particularly important during Covid, when both simple formulae and massive supercomputing models offer precise predictions of the impact of specific interventions. However, even the most complex model embodies simplifications and it is when the different models lead to qualitatively similar behaviours that they are most trusted. Similar issues arise for climate change, international economics and supermarket shopping.

Qualitative–quantitative reasoning is ubiquitous, but not often discussed – almost a dirty secret for the formalist and yet what makes theory practical. There are lessons for science and for schools, challenges for visualisation and argumentation. I don't know all of the answers, but by bringing this to the surface I know there are exciting questions.

In the rest of this paper we'll first move through a series of examples that each exhibit different forms of QQ-reasoning. The final section will outline practical and theoretical challenges.

2 Informal Insights from Formalism – The PIE Model

My first work as an academic centred on creating formal models of interactive systems [9], notably the PIE model [8], a simple input–output model of interaction (see Fig. 1). Whilst cognitive models try to model the mental behaviour of humans, the intention here was to model the systems that people use and to formalise key properties that lead to a system being usable.

Some aspects of this are amenable to strong proofs. Notably undo, which is expected to have predictable properties (really important it works!) but which also has a relatively straightforward algebraic definition:

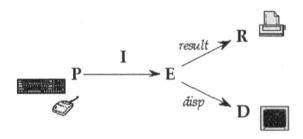

Fig. 1. The PIE model, a simple input–output model of interactive systems

$$\forall c \in Commands : c \frown undo \sim null \tag{1}$$

(Here $\frown$ means performing the commands one after each other and $\sim$ means "has the same effect in all contexts".)

There are slight nuances to this, occasionally commands (such as typing) are clumped, and some purely presentation-level commands (such as scrolling) are ignored. However, this is pretty solid. One core question though is whether undo itself is undoable; that is:

$$undo \frown undo \sim null \tag{2}$$

Some systems *appear* to have this property, doing undo twice acts as a single-step redo. This is often called *flip undo*. However, one of the early proofs in the area showed that this was impossible for all but trivial systems [9]. To see this consider two commands c_1 and c_2:

$$
\begin{aligned}
c_1 &\sim c_1 \frown (undo \frown undo) \\
&= (c_1 \frown undo) \frown undo \\
&\sim null \frown undo \\
&\sim (c_2 \frown undo) \frown undo \\
&= c_2 \frown (undo \frown undo) \\
&\sim c_2
\end{aligned}
\tag{3}
$$

That is all commands have the same effect, which can only happen if the system has no more than two states.

As well as being a theoretical result it had the practical application that one should not attempt to 'debug' pure forms of flip undo to attempt to make undo just like any other command – this is impossible. Instead we have to accept that undo commands (undo, redo, etc.) have to be treated as a separate kind of command. In later work, Mancini's thesis used category theory to show that with fairly minimal assumptions, there are only two kinds of consistent undo system: forms of flip undo (but where undo is treated as a special command) and stack-based undo–redo [6,18].

However, these cases of complete proofs were comparatively rare. Many aspects of interaction are far more complex.

The initial impetus for the PIE model came from Harold Thimbleby's quest for 'Generative User-Engineering Principles' (GUEPs) [25] and also the desire for systems that were 'what you see is what you get'. This was used to formalise various forms of *predictability* and *reachability* properties, the former regarding whether it was possible to infer the state of the system, and the effect of commands from its display, and the latter how easy it was to get to desired states (undo is related to this) (Fig. 2).

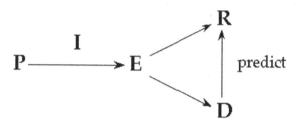

Fig. 2. A simple formulation of *predictability* in the PIE model – require a function from the display to the final result.

In relatively simple cases, such as medical devices, these properties can be verified by model checking [2], but this is impossible for larger systems. Even more critical issues such as the special undo commands become increasingly frequent: models that accurately model real systems rapidly become Baroque and those that are clean enough to reason with do not model reality.

This is not just a problem for interactive systems, but a general issue for modelling – complexity and simplicity at odds However, anyone who has created a formal specification of a substantial system will tell you that it is usually not so much the final specification that matters, but the understanding you gain through the *process*. Similarly many theoretical treatments of issues are so far from the real system that they cannot in any way be used to predict precise behaviours, but nevertheless, the insights gained through theoretical analysis and proofs yield understanding that may help in more practical situations.

3   Making Decisions – Electrostatically Charged Agricultural Crop Sprays

Before modelling humans I modelled agricultural crop sprays.

Factory paint sprays often use electrostatically charged spray droplets, which are then attracted to an earthed object, such as a car, ensuring a full coating and less waste. By a similar principle if an agricultural spray is charged it is attracted to the crop potentially leading to better coverage, less waste and less environmentally damaging spray drift. The main centres researching this in the early 1980s were ICI and the National Institute for Agricultural Engineering. At the latter we created numerical simulations of the movement of charged sprays in order to understand their behaviour and improve design choices [7].

Given computer speeds then were measured in KHz rather than GHz and memory in 10 s of Kb, the models were, perforce, simple! However, even today the complexity of a field of swaying wheat would challenge a super computer. To make this tractable, the modelling was performed in two parts.

The first stage was to model the transport from crop sprayer to the top of the crop (Fig. 3). Note that this has been flattened to two dimensions (effectively assuming a infinitely long spray boom!) to make the computation tractable. This is relatively simple, a point source for the spray, with an area held at high voltage (to represent the sprayer itself) and the crop top treated as a flat earthed surface, ignoring the fine structure. The output from this stage is the speed and density of the drops as they enter the top of the crop.

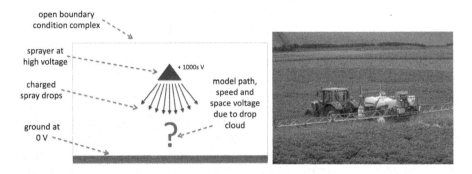

Fig. 3. Agricultural spray above the canopy (left) model of electrostatic spray (right) real sprayer (image right: Pauline Eccles (CC BY-SA 2.0); https://commons.wikimedia. org/wiki/File:Crop_spraying,_Bromsash_-_geograph.org.uk_-_1367703.jpg)

As is evident there are already several simplifications here. However, the within canopy modelling is far more difficult. In reality crops have leaves, seed heads and are different sizes. In the model these are treated as flat vertical lines (Fig. 4). Furthermore this is also a 2D model, so the crop is effectively modelled as infinitely long parallel metal plates. Indeed, for some experiments with real spray, such plates were used with paper collectors in order to obtain physical spray coverage data.

The speeds and density of drops entering the canopy from the above crop model could be used to match the relevant within-crop model in order to create an end-to-end model of how initial flow rates, drop size, charge etc. affect spray deposition. The output data was copious, but was categorised into three classes (Fig. 5):

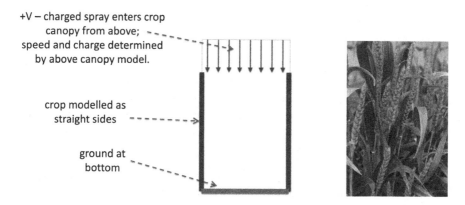

+V – charged spray enters crop
canopy from above;
speed and charge determined
by above canopy model.

crop modelled as
straight sides

ground at
bottom

Fig. 4. Within the crop canopy (left) model of electrostatic spray (right) real wheat (image right: Stephencdickson (CC BY-SA 2.0); https://commons.wikimedia.org/wiki/File:Green_wheat.jpg)

Class I – great penetration: spray misses crop and mostly ends up in the earth

Class II – uniform deposit: spray creates a relatively even coverage

Class III – little penetration: spray ends up mostly at the top of the crop

Of these, it is (2) we want; both (1) and (3) effectively waste spray and may leave untreated portions of crop.

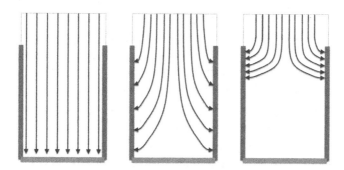

Fig. 5. Electrostatic spray coverage (left, Class I) misses crop and ends on the ground; (middle, Class II) good coverage of the crop; (right, Class III) too concentrated at the top of the crop.

In rough terms looking at the inputs to the *within canopy* model, the first class corresponds to fast or low charge droplets, and the last to slow or high charge particles, but this simple correspondence is more complex when looking at the complete above and within canopy models. High charge on small drops can lead to high space charge of 10s of thousands of volts (rather like the way

a rain cloud builds up charge to create lightning) and this can then accelerate
the drops as they enter the canopy so counter intuitively mean they end on the
ground (Class I).

This knowledge itself was useful as it was hard to measure space charge.
However, part of the aim was to go beyond the scientific knowledge to practical
design advice. The mathematical model allowed one to make precise predictions
as to which class a particular set of input parameters would yield, but of course
the model was very far from reality. Instead dimensional analysis was used to
reduce the input set to two main dimensionless features (π_1, π_2), the modelling
runs were then plotted into the two dimensional design space and a map produced of how the input parameters corresponded to the classes, rather like the
phase space of a gas–liquid–solid for water (Fig. 6).

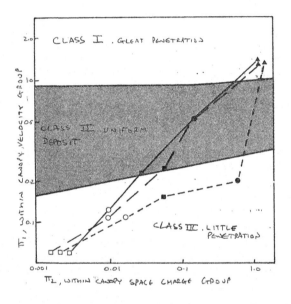

Fig. 6. 'Phase space' of different classes of spray pattern

While we had little confidence in the precise values of the modelling, the
overall shape of this map was useful. For example, if we were getting too much
spray on the ground (Class III), we might either try to increase dimensionless
parameter π_1 or to reduce parameter π_2, either of which could be manipulated
using different concrete parameters.

Note how the very precise, but massively over simplified numerical model
was used to create a qualitative understanding of the design space, which could
then be used to make useful engineering interventions.

4   Orders of Magnitude – Climate Change and Complexity

4.1   Infinitesimals and Limits

I recall reading Conway's "On numbers and games" [4] while still at school and being transported by the sheer exuberance of the text. There can be a tendency to skip to the second half (part one) a joyous exploration of the odd arithmetic properties of games. However, the first half (part zero) is equally exciting dealing with, what has become known as, 'surreal numbers' – both transfinite ordinal arithmetic (fairly commonly taught in maths courses), but also (less commonly taught) the way this can also give a formal treatment of infinitesimals.

Even if you've not come across these formal infinitesimals, you will have been taught calculus using lots of ϵs and limit proofs:

$$f'(x) \;=\; \lim_{\epsilon \to 0}(f(x+\epsilon) - f(x))/\epsilon \qquad (4)$$

Crucially we learn that we can often ignore order of magnitude smaller terms: ϵ terms when dealing with 'ordinary' sized numbers, or ϵ^2 terms when dealing with ϵs:

$$f(x+\epsilon) - f(x) \;\approx\; \epsilon f'(x) \qquad (5)$$

4.2   Day-to-Day Reasoning

In everyday life we also understand this, we may say "it's only a drop in the ocean". Formally we may use 'much greater than' ($\gg$) or 'much less than ($\ll$), but also informally we effectively use rules such as:

$$A \gg b \,\wedge\, b > c \;\implies\; A \gg c \qquad (6)$$

and:

$$A \gg b \;\implies\; A + b \approx A \qquad (7)$$

Unfortunately, less well understood in day-to-day logic is that the ocean is made up of drops, that is:

$$A \gg b_i \,\wedge\, N \, is \, very \, large \;\implies\; A \not\approx A + \sum_{i=1}^{N} b_i \qquad (8)$$

In fact, there are 'thrifty' sayings that capture this: "many a mickle makes a muckle', or "mind the pennies and the pounds look after themselves". However, despite our best environmental or fair trade intentions, it is too easy when deciding on purchases in the supermarket, or choosing whether to walk or jump in a car, to simply think "it won't make a difference". For ten thousand years, humanity was able to think like that, assuming that our individual impact would be absorbed by the vastness of land, sea and air. This underpins Locke's "as much and as good" proviso for the fair acquisition of land [17, Chap. V, para. 27], effectively assuming that nature's bounty is inexhaustible.

Of course, we now face the imminence of climate change, the ubiquity of plastics in the oceans and, with Covid, the critical nature of thousands of personal precautions, each insignificant in themselves, yet between them allowing or preventing the spread of disease. Looking back, we are also able to see that these impacts, while ever-accelerating, are not entirely new; for example, it is possible that the desertification of central Australia was due to slash-and-burn farming by early settlers thousands of years ago [19].

4.3   Algorithmic Complexity

In complexity theory, we argue formally about such order of magnitude relations using big and little 'O' notation. At a practical level we also get used to effectively counting the levels of directly or indirectly embedded loops to get an idea of the exponent r in $O(N^r)$.

Just like with plastic waste, we can sometimes forget that these are about theoretical limits and that in practice an $O(N^2)$ algorithm with a small constant K, may actually be faster than an $O(N \log N)$ with large K.

An extreme example of this is the linear programming simplex algorithm [5], one of the most successful early examples of operational research. Simple linear programming problems consist of N linear constraints over M variables $(N > M)$. The optimal value of a linear objective function must lie at one of the vertices (Fig. 7). The simplex algorithm is basically a form of hill–climbing optimisation, moving from vertex to neighbouring vertex following the direction of maximum gain.

Given a linear objective function, the simplex algorithm is guaranteed to terminate after a finite number of steps, and in practice is linear in the number of constraints N. I say 'in practice', because in theory it can be much worse. Indeed it is possible to create Byzantine examples where the simplex algorithm visits all C_M^N vertices. That is its *worst case* behaviour is $O(N^{N-M})$.

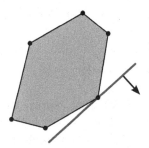

Fig. 7. Linear programming – the linear constraints create a polytope feasible region, the optimal value of a linear objective is on one of the vertices (image https://commons. wikimedia.org/wiki/File:Linear_optimization_in_a_2-dimensional_polytope.svg)

In fact there are alternative algorithms for linear programming that have better worst case behaviour (I once heard of one that was $O(N \log N)$, but not been able to track it down). However, in practice they are all far slower in terms of *average case* complexity.

4.4   Sorting

Furthermore, the real world is finite. For some graph/network problems, where algorithms are often exponential or multiple-exponential, N more than five or six is enough to end up in the theory 'limits'. However, for other problems practical limits may be more significant.

We all know that sorting is $O(N \log N)$, but in fact every real sorting algorithm works on finite sized keys within a computer with finite disk space. When sorting finite keys, in principle bucket-sorts give algorithms with time linear in N. See, for example, the IBM Punch Card Sorter in action [23] – this required just W passes to sort W-character keys, that is effectively an $O(N\,W)$ algorithm.

You might wonder how this squares with the well-known information-theory-based $O(N \log N)$ lower bound for sorting algorithm. First, the theoretical bound depends on it being necessary to compare sufficient items to determine a *total order* on the items. If $W < \log N$ there will be many equally placed items. Second, the information theory bound is incredibly broad, even working with magical oracles that tell you where to put items – effectively it is lower bound on the time taken to *read the result*. Even with bucket sorts you need to output the items! Finally, if there are N items the memory has to be at least big enough for these and hence both memory accesses and addresses are $(O(\log N)$, pushing real behaviour back into the $O(N \log N)$ territory (although note that by similar arguments Quicksort is really $O(N\,(\log N)^2)$!

If you feel that these practical bit-twiddling examples feel a little contrived, there is the story of a Google employee giving a talk at Cambridge. During the presentation one of the eminent computer scientists in the audience did some quick complexity calculations in their head, and at the end stood up and said, "I like your algorithm, but unfortunately it doesn't scale". The Google employee responded, "well it works for 10 billion web pages".

4.5   What is Computation?

The lower bound result for sorting is relatively rare, and, as noted, is based on information theory measures and hence works for oracles as well as 'real' computation. One of the reasons for this is that while we have had an abstract measure of information content dating back more than 70 years [21,22], our computational metrics are, in comparison, weak.

One of my own intuitions (albeit not as informed as Hardy and Wright's!) is that some variant of Galois theory may be a way to get traction. Of course, this may simply be because the story of Évariste Galois is one of the great romances of mathematics – writing in his garret, the night before the fatal duel "there is no time, there is no time ...".

Galois theory is about what numbers it is *possible* to construct using the solution to particular equations [24] (for example square roots in geometric constructions). This is rather like non-existence proofs in computability such as the halting problem.

Of course in computing we also want to know *how many* steps it takes. While standard Galois theory does not address this, one can have variants where you are allowed only finite numbers of extension operations. The resulting sets form a tower (see Fig. 8) and have some nice mathematical properties:

$$\forall a \in \mathbb{Q}_n(\sqrt{2}), b \in \mathbb{Q}_m(\sqrt{2}) \; : \; \{a+b, a-b, a*b, a/b\} \subset \mathbb{Q}_{n+m}(\sqrt{2}) \qquad (9)$$

That is the sets are homomorphic to the semigroup of positive integers. If one looks at more complex Galois extensions with multiple radicals, such as $\mathbb{Q}_{n,m,s}(\sqrt{p}, \sqrt{q}, \sqrt{r})$; one ends up with a simple product semigroup if p, q and r are co-prime, but may yield more complex semigroups if they have common factors (e.g. 12, 50, 30).

As is evident this feels rather like counting computational steps of different kinds, so may be a fruitful path. I have never moved beyond this stage myself; perhaps a reader will be inspired to dig further!

5   Knowing What to Model – Covid Serial Interval

During the summer of 2020 an estimate I made of the potential impact of university re-opening on Covid-19 deaths [10] was publicised and criticised as overstating the problem. In hindsight both later estimates by the UK Government SAGE group and actual case data in September and October showed that in fact

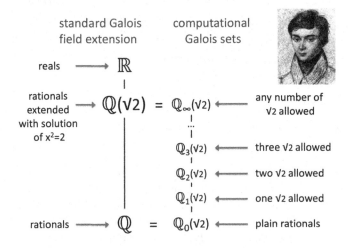

Fig. 8. Computational Galois theory

I had been optimistic. At one point in the summer, in a BBC Radio interview, Kit Yates (University of Bath academic and popular science writer) had stated that the time between infections (called the *serial interval*) used in the paper of 3.5 days was too short and the real figure should be 5.5 days. In fact the actual modelling was independent of this figure (it just changes the time scale), but this did bring my attention to the wide variation in estimates of the serial interval.

Yates was absolutely correct in that the WHO Covid-19 information at the time used a 5.5 day estimate, however, at the same time the growth graphs used by the BBC used a 3.5 day figure. Furthermore SAGE estimates of UK R factor, when compared with the doubling time, were *effectively* using a 3.5 day period (although this will have arisen out of detailed models). If one then looks further at meta-analysis papers reviewing large numbers of studies, the range of estimates varies substantially [20]. Why the discrepancy?

In part this may be due to the fact that, while R_0 and the serial interval are often stated as if they were fundamental parameters of the disease, they both depend critically on many social and environmental factors: how many contacts people have, whether indoors or outdoors, etc. In particular, R_0 tends to be higher and the serial interval shorter in densely populated areas in cold and damp climates – as is typical in the UK, but R_0 is lower and the serial interval longer in more thinly populated areas as is the case in many parts of Africa and the USA outside major cities (and even in the suburbs).

The above statement is already a qualitative–quantitative argument, but one that is perhaps so obvious it doesn't appear to be so.

A little less obvious is the complex, but comprehensible, way in which the serial interval changes when either individual caution or statutory control measures modify the spread of disease.

1. If, when infected people become symptomatic, they take substantial self-quarantining actions, this will mean less post-symptomatic contagion, but have no impact on pre-symptomatic contacts. This therefore *reduces* the serial interval.
2. For asymptomatic cases, some contacts are sporadic such as fellow passengers on public transport. For these contacts the likelihood of contagion is lower, but the average timing of those infected unlikely to be affected.
3. For asymptomatic cases, some contacts are frequent such as work colleagues and family members. For these contacts, they will have some reduction in the eventual probability of catching the disease, but crucially if they do catch it, they are likely to take longer to do so. That is, for this group the serial interval *increases*.

Note that effect (1) decreases the serial interval, effect (3) reduces it and effect (2) makes no difference. This interplay of positive and negative effects is not uncommon. One might be prompted to use further QQ-reasoning to compare the effects – it is assumed that for Covid-19 asymptomatic infections are a major driver of growth, so that might suggest (3) will be more significant than (1). Alternatively one might use the analysis to perform more detailed and precise modelling.

Finally there is a third sampling-based influence on the serial interval. Figure 9 shows the distribution of serial times for 468 infection pairs from [12]. Note the large variation: once someone is infected they may pass it on to some people straight away, but others only after a considerable period. It is the average period that is usually quoted, but this hides considerable variation.

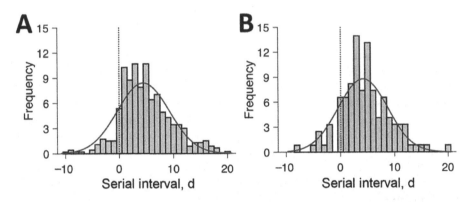

Fig. 9. Distribution of the serial interval from [12]. A is based on 468 pairs of cases and B is a subset of the 122 most reliable infection pairs. Note the negative serial intervals will be due to pre-symptomatic infections as the time measured is between the onset of symptoms of the pair.

Imagine we have perfect retrospective knowledge so that we know who caught the disease, from whom and when. There are two ways we could measure the distribution.

1. Forward – consider each infectious person (source), who they infect and when. This is the canonical serial interval.
2. Backward – consider each infected person, who they were infected by (source) and how far into that source's infection.

During a period of disease growth ($R > 1$), the number of infectious people increases with time, meaning method (2) will encounter more people infected recently and hence create a shorter estimate of the serial interval than method (1). Similarly during a period of disease decline ($R < 1$) the serial interval calculated by (2) will be longer than by (1).

The serial interval combines with R to give the exponential rate of growth. If one uses the 'true' serial interval from (1) this ends up a little too large (when $R > 1$), but estimate (2) is too short. The value that gives the exponential approximation, the *effective serial interval*, is between the two.

If we wish to work out exactly how these estimates differ, we will need more precise modelling. However, the QQ-reasoning suggests what we should be modelling and directs us towards what we should be looking for in the modelling.

6   Monotonic Reasoning – Change at the Shops and the Impact of Automation

Some years ago I was in a charity shop, probably buying books, I usually am. I gave the woman who was serving a ten pound note and she started to count out change – more than ten pounds of change. I told her and we worked out the right sum for the change. I think she had simply mistyped a figure into the till, but the thing that surprised me was that she hadn't noticed. This was probably due to what is often called 'automation bias', the tendency to believe what a computer tells us, even when patently wrong. Of course, automation errors, when they happen, are often gross hence the importance of being able to have a broad idea of what is a reasonable answer. In this case I was using a simple form of monotonic reasoning:

$$b > 0 \implies A - b < A \tag{10}$$

We may also do similar reasoning in two dimensions using the Poincaré property – every closed non-self intersecting line in 2D space has an inside and an outside. If you have crossed a city ring road going into the city and have not re-crossed it, then you must still be inside. However, whether this is a logical argument or more of a 'gut' knowledge about the world depends on spatial ability ... or perhaps learnt skill.

Many economic issues depend on more or less complex chains of monotonic reasoning. Figure 10 shows two arguments for and against the value of automation. On the left hand side there is the 'pro' argument: automation leads to increased productivity, hence increases overall prosperity and this makes people better off. However, on the right-hand side is the counter argument that increased automation leads to less need for labor, hence unemployment and poverty.

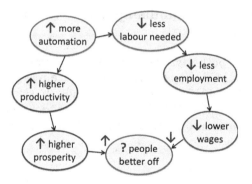

Fig. 10. Positive and negative impact of automation

Rather like the Covid examples, different arguments lead to positive and negative effects. We might resolve this by estimating (more QQ-reasoning!) the size of the effects. Perhaps more pertinently we might ask, "who benefits?"

Laying out an argument in this way also makes it easier to debate the steps in the inferences, rather like argumentation systems such as IBIS (issue-based information system) [3,16]. For example, the link that suggests that automation leads to less labour has been questioned using the example of Amazon, which in 2016 installed 15,000 robots, but instead of reducing labour in fact also increased their employees by 46% [13]. This has then been used to argue that robots increase employment [14]. However, it is likely that the growth is due to the left hand thread in Fig. 11: robots, improved competitiveness, helped the company grow its sales and hence increased employment *at Amazon*. Seeing this immediately brings to mind the right hand arc of the same figure, that the growth of Amazon has probably shrunk other businesses and hence decreased employment elsewhere.

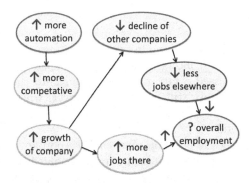

Fig. 11. Does automation create jobs?

7   Formalising and Visualising QQ – Allen's Interval Calculus

Figures 10 and 11 are both a visualisation of the argument and also a type of formal representation of the qualitative–quantitative reasoning about automation. It is a form of high-level argumentation, similar to safety cases used in the nuclear and aviation industry. While the validity of each judgement step ('this increases that') is a human one, given such lower-level judgements, the overall reasoning can be verified:

given
    increase in A leads to an increase in B   (human judgement)
and
    increase in B leads to an increase in C   (human judgement)
conclude
    increase in A leads to an increase in C   (formal inference)

We can find other examples of formalisation of QQ in the literature. Some force you to make the informal judgements very precise, for example fuzzy logic demands a precise shape for the uncertainty function and Bayesian statistics require that you encode your belief as if it were a probability [11]. Other methods embrace the human-like reasoning more wholeheartedly, including various representations of naïve physics or informal reasoning used in cognitive science and artificial intelligence such as Allen's Interval Calculus [1] for reasoning about temporal events (see Fig. 12).

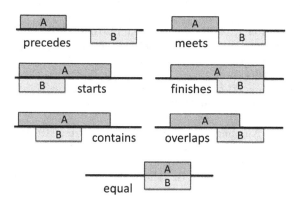

Fig. 12. Different temporal relations (from [1])

8   Discussion and Call to Action

We have seen a variety of examples of qualitative–quantitative reasoning. Some were about gaining informal understanding from formal or theoretical models; some were about rough sizes: monotonicity and orders of magnitude; and some were about numerical modelling: how to guide what we model and how to turn idealised or simplified models into representations that are useful for decision making. While many of the examples were about academic or professional use, others were about the general populace. Indeed, in a data-dominated world, understanding numerical arguments is essential for effective citizenship.

We have also seen that there are existing methods and representations to help with qualitative–quantitative reasoning, but relatively few given the criticality in so many walks of life.

There are three lessons I'd like the reader to take away:

– recognise when you are using qualitative–quantitative reasoning so that you can think more clearly about your own work, and perhaps make it more accessible or practically useful.

– realise that it is a potential area to study theoretically in itself – are there ways to formalise or visualise some of the informal reasoning we use about formal things!
– seek methods and tools to help others think more clearly about this: in universities, industry and schools.

References

1. Allen, J.F.: Maintaining knowledge about temporal intervals. Commun. ACM **26**(11), 832–843 (1983). https://doi.org/10.1145/182.358434
2. Campos, J.C., Fayollas, C., Harrison, M.D., Martinie, C., Masci, P., Palanque, P.: Supporting the analysis of safety critical user interfaces: an exploration of three formal tools. ACM Trans. Comput.-Hum. Interact. **27**(5), 1–48 (2020). https://doi.org/10.1145/3404199
3. Conklin, J., Begeman, M.L.: GIBIS: a hypertext tool for exploratory policy discussion. ACM Trans. Inf. Syst. **6**(4), 303–331 (1988). https://doi.org/10.1145/58566.59297
4. Conway, J.H.: On Numbers and Games. Academic Press (1976)
5. Dantzig, G.B.: Origins of the Simplex Method, pp. 141–151. Association for Computing Machinery, New York (1990). https://doi.org/10.1145/87252.88081
6. Dix, A., Mancini, R., Levialdi, S.: The cube - extending systems for undo. In: Proceedings of DSVIS 1997, pp. 473–495. Eurographics (1997). https://alandix.com/academic/papers/dsvis97/
7. Dix, A.J., Marchant, J.A.: A mathematical model of the transport and deposition of charged spray drops. J. Agric. Eng. Res. **30**, 91–100 (1984)
8. Dix, A.J., Runciman, C.: Abstract models of interactive systems. In: Johnson, P., Cook, S. (eds.) People and Computers: Designing the Interface, pp. 13–22. Cambridge University Press (1985). https://alandix.com/academic/papers/PIE85/PIE-paper.html
9. Dix, A.: Formal Methods for Interactive Systems. Academic Press (1991). https://alandix.com/books/formal/
10. Dix, A.: Impact of a small number of large bubbles on COVID-19 transmission within universities (2020). https://arxiv.org/abs/2008.08147
11. Dix, A.: Bayesian Statistics, chap. 2, pp. 141–151. Cambridge University Press (2021)
12. Du, Z., Xu, X., Wu, Y., Wang, L., Cowling, B.J., Meyers, L.A.: The serial interval of COVID-19 from publicly reported confirmed cases. medRxiv (2020). https://doi.org/10.1101/2020.02.19.20025452. https://www.medrxiv.org/content/early/2020/03/13/2020.02.19.20025452
13. González, A.: Amazon's robot army grows by 50 percent. The Seattle Times (2016). https://www.seattletimes.com/business/amazon/amazons-robot-army-grows/
14. Hamid, O.H., Smith, N.L., Barzanji, A.: Automation, per se, is not job elimination: how artificial intelligence forwards cooperative human-machine coexistence. In: 2017 IEEE 15th International Conference on Industrial Informatics (INDIN), pp. 899–904 (2017). https://doi.org/10.1109/INDIN.2017.8104891
15. Hardy, G.H., Wright, E.M.: An Introduction to the Theory of Numbers, 4th edn. Oxford (1975)

16. Kunz, W., Rittel, H.W.J., Messrs, W., Dehlinger, H., Mann, T., Protzen, J.J.: Issues as elements of information systems. Technical report, University of California, Berkeley (1970). https://citeseerx.ist.psu.edu/viewdoc/summary?doi=10.1.1. 134.1741
17. Locke, J.: Second Treatise of Government (1689). https://gutenberg.org/ebooks/ 7370
18. Mancini, R.: Modelling Interactive Computing by Exploiting the Undo. Dottorato di ricerca in informatica, ix–97-5, Università degli Studi di Roma "La Sapienza" (1997). https://hcibook.net/people/Roberta/
19. Pearce, F.: Earth's most important rivers are in the sky - and they're drying up. New Sci. **3254** (2019). https://www.newscientist.com/article/mg24432540-600-earths-most-important-rivers-are-in-the-sky-and-theyre-drying-up/
20. Rai, B., Shukla, A., Dwivedi, L.: Estimates of serial interval for COVID-19: a systematic review and meta-analysis. Clin. Epidemiol. Glob. Health 157–161 (2021). https://doi.org/10.1016/j.cegh.2020.08.007
21. Shannon, C.E.: A mathematical theory of communication. Bell Syst. Tech. J. **27**(3), 379–423 (1948). https://doi.org/10.1002/j.1538-7305.1948.tb01338.x
22. Shannon, C.E., Weaver, W.: The Mathematical Theory of Communication. University of Illinois Press, Urbana (1949)
23. Shirriff, K.: IBM punched card sorter type 83, from 1955. https://www.youtube. com/watch?v=AyO3n20SpoI
24. Stewart, I.N.: Galois Theory, 4th edn. Chapman and Hall/CRC (2015). https:// doi.org/10.1201/b18187. (First ed. 1973)
25. Thimbleby, H.: Generative user-engineering principles for user interface design. In: INTERACT 1984, pp. 661–666 (1984)

Databases and Distributed Transactions

Some Aspects of the Database Resilience

Luis Henrique Bustamante[1,2]([✉]) [iD] and Ana Teresa Martins[2]

[1] Federal University of Paraíba, Rio Tinto, Brazil
`henrique@dcx.ufpb.br`
[2] Federal University of Ceará, Fortaleza, Brazil
`ana@dc.ufc.br`

Abstract. The resilience problem for a Boolean query in a database is the task of finding a minimum set of tuples that, when deleted from the database, turns the query evaluation false. We examine the parameterized complexity of a particular version of this problem for fixed queries. A natural parameter for this problem is the number of tuples needed to be deleted. For this, we use a formal characterization of the solution set that proves the W[1] membership for this parameter and a fixed-parameter tractable result when considering the database treewidth.

Keywords: Database resilience · Parameterized complexity · Conjunctive query

1 Introduction

This work was motivated by the recent interest in the complexity of database resilience problem [4,5,8,9]. The resilience problem for a boolean query in a database is the task to find a set of tuples that, when deleted from the database, turns the query evaluation on the database false.

"*The resilience problem of a query*" was formulated in [4] as a decision problem that simplifies and extends the analysis of previously studied research problems in the area of database theory like "deletion propagation" and "casual responsibility". These problems, for example, operate changes on input and consider some expected behavior for query evaluation. In [4], for queries without self-join (repetition of a relation symbol, named *self-join-free queries*), a dichotomy result was obtained for tractability when a "cycle structure" (*a triad*) is absent from the query. The presence of a triad in a self-join-free query implies NP-completeness. The previous study allowed a better understanding of the complexity of the related problems (deletion propagation etc.), while the antecedent results for these problems characterized all as NP-complete problems.

In [5], they improve the analysis for conjunctive queries with single self-joins (just one relation can be repeated) with two atoms with the same relation symbol. For this case, some new structural properties were identified to classify

This research was supported by the Brazilian National Council for Scientific and Technological Development (CNPq) under the grant number 424188/2016-3.

A. Cerone and P. C. Ölveczky (Eds.): ICTAC 2021, LNCS 12819, pp. 39–46, 2021.
https://doi.org/10.1007/978-3-030-85315-0_3

the resilience problem as NP-complete, and, again, a dichotomy complexity result was obtained. They also consider a second case for queries with three atoms with the same relation symbol. For this second case, they present a sequence of complexity results that establish the NP-completeness for some particular queries.

These results of increasing complexity motivate a more fine-grained study of all parameters of the problem and a reflection of other possible sources of hardness for resilience.

Parameterized complexity [3] is a subarea of computational complexity where the analysis considers an additional term called parameter. A problem that admits an algorithm with an arbitrary running time concerning the parameter and polynomial in terms of the input size is called a fixed-parameter tractable problem. This notion is one of the main concepts in the area with many essential consequences and applications. However, many other problems cannot be classified in this way and, for these, there are a wide variety of intractable parameterized classes. The most representative of these classes is W[1] which has many problems with natural parameterizations. Some examples of complete problems for W[1] are the Clique problem when parameterized by the size of the clique and evaluating conjunctive queries with the size of the query as a parameter.

In [8,9], the resilience problem for conjunctive queries was proved to be co-W[1]-complete. To prove that the problem is in co-W[1], they reduce the problem to a canonical W[1]-complete problem, the weighted satisfiability. For a negative instance of the resilience problem, they constructed a k-satisfiable propositional formula if and only if D does not have a contingency set. For hardness, they obtained a reduction from the k-clique problem. In [8,9], the problem was stated with three inputs: the database, the query, and a natural number that corresponds to the size of the solution. The parameterized analysis of this problem considers the query size $|\varphi|$ and the natural number k.

By taking a different perspective, we aim to identify the source of the complexity of the resilience problem. Here, we explore the parameterized complexity of the resilience problem for a conjunctive query in terms of the size of the solution set Γ and the treewidth of the database (Sect. 4). These results follow a model theoretical approach (Sect. 3). For a fixed conjunctive query φ, we denote the resilience problem for φ by Res_φ, and we can conclude that the problem is in W[1] when parameterized by the size $|\Gamma|$. This result drives a formal characterization of the contingency set in monadic second-order logic, leading to an FPT algorithm due to Courcelle's Theorem.

There is a important aspect in locate a problem within W[1], and it is related to an algorithmic solvability faster than the exhaustive search over all $\binom{n}{k}$ subsets. For example, p-Clique, a W[1]-complete problem, has an algorithm that runs in time $\mathcal{O}(n^{(\omega/3)k})$ [10], achieved with the use of a $n \times n$ matrix multiplication algorithm with running time in $\mathcal{O}(n^\omega)$ (best known value for ω is 2.3728639 [7]). For p-Dominating-set, a W[2]-complete problem, we cannot do anything better than an algorithm running in $\mathcal{O}(n^{k+1})$ unless CNF satisfiability has an $2^{\delta n}$ time algorithm for some $\delta < 1$ [12].

2   Preliminaries

We assume the reader has some knowledge in Mathematical Logic, Computational Complexity, Parameterized Complexity (see for example [1,3,11]). In the following subsections, we give some basic definitions.

2.1   Conjunctive Query

Let τ be a relational vocabulary[1] $\{R_1,\dots,R_\ell\}$ each relation R_i, $1 \leq i \leq \ell$, has some natural number r_i as its arity. The class of *conjunctive queries* is the set of first-order formulas over τ of the form

$$\varphi(y_1,\dots,y_p) := \exists x_1 \dots \exists x_q (g_1(\overline{z_1}) \wedge \dots \wedge g_m(\overline{z_m})),$$

where, each x_i with $1 \leq i \leq q$ is an existential variable, the y are free variables, and each g_j, $1 \leq j \leq m$, is an *atom* using a relation symbol from τ and variables from $\overline{z_i} \subseteq \{x_1,\dots,x_q\} \cup \{y_1,\dots,y_p\}$. However, we restrict our attention to the class of *boolean conjunctive queries*, conjunctive queries without free variables.

As usual, these queries are evaluated into a database D, denoted here by a relational τ-structure $D = \langle \{a_1,\dots a_d\}, R_1^D,\dots,R_\ell^D \rangle$ for some relational vocabulary $\tau := \{R_1,\dots,R_\ell\}$. The domain or universe of D, $\{a_1,\dots a_d\}$, is also called the *active domain*, and the elements of the relations are called *tuples* of D.

2.2   Parameterized Complexity

A *parameterized problem* is a pair (Q,κ) over the alphabet Σ, such that $Q \subseteq \Sigma^*$ is a decision problem and κ is a polynomial time computable function from Σ^* to natural numbers $\mathbb{N}$, called the *parameterization*. For an *instance* $x \in \Sigma^*$ of Q or (Q,κ), $\kappa(x) = k$ is the *parameter* of x.

We say that a problem (Q,κ) is *fixed-parameter tractable* if there is an algorithm that decides for all $x \in Q$ in time $f(\kappa(x)) \cdot |x|^{O(1)}$ for some computable function f. The class of all fixed-parameter tractable problems is called FPT. We can extend the notion of polynomial-time reductions to FPT-reductions, and, in the same way, we can handle the notions of hardness and completeness.

The set of quantifier-free formulas is denoted by Σ_0 and Π_0. For $t > 0$, we define Σ_{t+1} as the class of formulas in the form $\exists x_1 \dots \exists x_k \varphi$, such that $\varphi \in \Pi_t$; and Π_{t+1} as the class of all formulas of the form $\forall x_1 \dots \forall x_k \varphi$, where $\varphi \in \Sigma_t$.

We define $\varphi(X_1,\dots X_l)$ as a first-order logic (FO) formula with $X_1,\dots X_l$ as second-order free variables. Given a vocabulary τ of φ, and for all $i \in [l]$, s_i corresponds to the arity of X_i. A solution for φ in $\mathcal{A}$ is a tuple $\bar{S} = (S_1,\dots,S_l)$, where, for each $i \in [l]$, $S_i \subseteq A^{s_i}$, such that $\mathcal{A} \models \varphi(\bar{S})$. Thus, $\varphi(X)$ corresponds to a formula in FO with a unique relation variable X. *The weighted definability problem* for a formula φ, p-WD$_\varphi$, considers a structure $\mathcal{A}$ and $k \in \mathbb{N}$ as inputs, and decides if exists $S \subseteq A^s$ with $|S| = k$ such that $\mathcal{A} \models \varphi(S)$.

---

[1] Constants are allowed for relational vocabulary.

For a class of formulas $\Phi \subseteq$ FO, we define p-WD-Φ as the class of all problems p-WD$_\varphi$ such that $\varphi \in \Phi$. Then, we characterize the W-Hierarchy in terms of p-WD-Φ for fragments Π_t. For all $t \geq 1$, we define $W[t] = [p\text{-WD-}\Pi_t]^{\text{fpt}}$.

Due to the closure of the W-hierarchy classes, to show the membership within some finite level, one has to produce[2] a structure and a formula that satisfies it.

Monadic second-order logic (MSO) is an extension of FO with a quantification over second-order variables $\exists X$ and $\forall X$. The Courcelle's Theorem says that model checking for properties expressed in MSO has an algorithm in polynomial time when parameterized by the treewidth of the graph. We can use the generalized version of this theorem to any mathematical structure [2]. For these definitions and results, consider [3].

2.3   Resilience Revisited

Let D be a database, and φ be a conjunctive query in some fixed vocabulary τ. As stated in [4], the resilience problem takes D and φ and decides whether there exists a minimum set Γ of tuples in D (a set of $(a_{i_1} \ldots a_{i_{r_j}}) \in R_j^D$ for some $j \in [\ell]$ and $i_1, \ldots, i_{r_j} \in [d]$) that can be removed to make the query φ false, i.e. $D \nvDash \varphi$. The set Γ is called a *contingency set*. A *k-contingency set* is a contingency set of size k.

We denote different versions of the resilience problem that take the conjunctive query as fixed or not. The first version of the resilience problem takes a fixed conjunctive query φ, a database D, and a natural number k as its inputs.

---

p-RES$_\varphi$

Instance: A relational database D, and $k \in \mathbb{N}$.

Parameter: k.

Problem: Decide whether D has a k-contingency set w.r.t φ.

The second version of the resilience problem is similar to what we know as the "combined complexity" of model checking and considers a relational database D, a conjunctive query φ, and a natural number k as inputs. We denote it by p-Resilience.

---

p-RESILIENCE

Instance: A relational database D, a conjunctive query φ, and $k \in \mathbb{N}$.

Parameter: k.

Problem: Decide whether D has a k-contingency set w.r.t φ.

---

[2] This is the strategy applied in Theorem 2.

Each different parameterization function κ can define a different problem p-κ-Resilience. For example, a function that combines k and $|\varphi|$ will define p-$[k, |\varphi|]$-Resilience. In [8], the p-$[k, |\varphi|]$-Resilience problem for a conjunctive query was proved to be co-W[1]-complete.

Theorem 1 [8]. *p-$[k, |\varphi|]$-Resilience is co-W[1]complete.*

3   Formal Characterization of the Contingency Set

For a more suitable description of the contingency set, we use another structure to represent a database where the domain becomes a set of tuples and the active domain. This new structure is similar to what a hypergraph does to a graph.

Let D be a relational database in $\tau = \{R_1, \ldots, R_\ell\}$ with maximum arity $s = \text{ar}(\tau)$. We introduce an auxiliary structure called the **extended database** $\mathfrak{D}$ of the database D in a different vocabulary σ, which is a relational σ-structure with an universe constructed by the union of the elements of D, the tuples of D (all $t \in R_i^D$ for all $i \in [\ell]$), and the natural numbers in $[s]$ with a different vocabulary $\sigma = \{T_{R_1}, \ldots, T_{R_\ell}, \text{Adom}, \text{Inc}\}$ consisting of unary relation symbols, but Inc, a ternary relation symbol.

An *extended database* $\mathfrak{D}$ is a three-sorted σ-structure

$$\langle \{a_1, \ldots, a_d\} \cup \{b_1, \ldots, b_n\} \cup [s], T_{R_1}^{\mathfrak{D}}, \ldots, T_{R_\ell}^{\mathfrak{D}}, \text{Adom}^{\mathfrak{D}}, \text{Inc}^{\mathfrak{D}} \rangle,$$

where $d := |D|$, n is the number of tuples of D. Each b_i is an element in

$$\{t_{R, \bar{a}} \mid R \in \tau, \text{ and } \bar{a} \in R\}.$$

It follows that the number of tuples n is bounded by d^s.

Proposition 1 (Extended Database) *There exist polynomial time transformations that convert the database D in τ into an extended database $\mathfrak{D}$ in σ, and a first-order formula φ (conjunctive query) in τ to another first-order formula φ' (conjunctive query) in σ such that*

$$D \vDash \varphi \Leftrightarrow \mathfrak{D} \vDash \varphi'.$$

The proof consists of a construction of an extended database $\mathfrak{D}$ in $\sigma = \{\text{Adom}, T_{R_1}, \ldots, T_{R_\ell}, \text{Inc}\}$

Proof Let D be a relational database with universe $\{a_1, \ldots, a_d\}$, in the vocabulary $\tau = \{R_1, \ldots, R_\ell\}$, and φ, a conjunctive query in τ, in the form $\exists x_1 \ldots \exists x_q (g_1(\overline{z_1}) \wedge \ldots \wedge g_m(\overline{z_m}))$ such that $\overline{z_i} \subseteq \{x_1, \ldots x_q\}$ and each g_i is an atom.

We construct an extended database $\mathfrak{D}$ in $\sigma = \{\text{Adom}, T_{R_1}, \ldots, T_{R_\ell}, \text{Inc}\}$ from the relational database D.

To construct the universe of $\mathfrak{D}$, we add all elements of $|D|$, the tuples of D represented by $\{t_{R, \bar{a}} \mid R \in \tau, \text{ and } \bar{a} \in R^D\}$ and a set of naturals $[s]$. All elements are pairwise distinct. So, the cardinality of the universe of $\mathfrak{D}$ is essentially $\|D\|$. This process takes $O(d + n)$ where n is the number of tuples.

To define the unary relations of $\mathfrak{D}$, we directly construct $\text{Adom}^{\mathfrak{D}} := |D|$ and $T_{R_i}^{\mathfrak{D}} := \{t_{R,\bar{a}} \mid \bar{a} \in R^D\}$ for every $R \in \tau$. Secondly, we construct the incidence relation in terms of the following definition

$$\text{Inc}^{\mathfrak{D}} := \{(a, i, t_{R,\bar{a}}) \mid R \in \tau, \bar{a} = (a_1, \dots, a_r) \in R^D, \text{ and } a = a_i\}.$$

To construct φ', we will relativize all existential and universal quantifiers to Adom, i.e., we will inductively replace, from the inner most quantifier, the $\exists x \psi$ by $\exists x (\text{Adom}(x) \wedge \psi)$, and the $\forall x \psi$ by $\forall x (\text{Adom}(x) \rightarrow \psi)$. After that, we replace every atomic subformula $R_{\bar{x}}$ for $R \in \tau$ by $\exists z (T_R(z) \wedge \bigwedge_{i=1}^r Inc(x_i, i, z))$ where z is a new variable.

Assuming that $D \vDash \varphi$, we can proof by induction on φ that $\mathfrak{D} \vDash \varphi'$.

If we restrict our attention to conjunctive queries, we do not increase the alternation of quantifiers. Then, after the translation of a conjunctive query φ, the obtained formula φ' is also a conjunctive query.

*Example 1 (**Translating a Conjunctive Query**).*

Let D be a database over a vocabulary $\tau = \{R_1, \dots, R_\ell\}$, and let φ be a conjunctive query over the same vocabulary τ in the form $\exists x_1 \dots \exists x_q (R_{i_1}(\overline{z_1}) \wedge \dots \wedge R_{i_m}(\overline{z_m}))$ for $i_1, \dots, i_m \in [\ell]$. If $D \vDash \varphi$, we can apply the previous conversions for φ to obtain a different conjunctive query. First, we inductively relativize the existential quantifiers to achieve the sentence

$$\exists x_1 \dots \exists x_q \left(\bigwedge_{i=1}^q \text{Adom}(x_i) \wedge \psi \right),$$

where $\psi := R_{i_1}(\overline{z_1}) \wedge \dots \wedge R_{i_m}(\overline{z_m})$. Then we can replace each R_{i_j} in ψ by $\exists y_j (T_{R_{i_j}}(y_j) \wedge \bigwedge_{p=1}^{r_{i_j}} Inc(x_p, p, y_j))$, and our final formula in the prenex normal form is

$$\exists x_1 \dots \exists x_q \exists y_1 \dots \exists y_m \left(\bigwedge_{i=1}^q \text{Adom}(x_i) \wedge \bigwedge_{j=1}^m T_{R_{i_j}}(y_j) \wedge \bigwedge_{j=1}^m \bigwedge_{p=1}^{r_{i_j}} Inc(x_{j_p}, p, y_j) \right).$$

Using the construction in Proposition 1, we can prove the following equivalence:

Lemma 1. *p-Resilience is fpt-equivalent to the p-Resilience over the extended vocabulary.*

For a fixed φ and a corresponding formula φ' with respect to Proposition 1, we have the following consequence.

Corollary 1. *p-Res$_\varphi \equiv^{fpt}$ p-Res$_{\varphi'}$.*

For the next section, we both use the database D or an extended database of D interchangeable.

4   The "Data Complexity" of the Resilience Problem

In this section, we describe a universal sentence ψ that characterizes Γ in the problem p-Res_φ using the previous definition and results.

We can then state that p-Res_φ is in W[1] when parameterized by the size k of the contingency set Γ.

Theorem 2. *For all conjunctive query φ, p-Res_φ is in W[1].*

The proof of the Theorem 2 is the construction of the following sentence

$$\psi_{res}(X) := \forall x_1 \ldots \forall x_q \forall y_1 \ldots \forall y_m$$

$$\left(\left(\bigwedge_{i=1}^m \neg X(y_i) \wedge \bigwedge_{i=1}^q \mathrm{Adom}(x_i) \wedge \bigwedge_{j=1}^m \bigwedge_{p=1}^{r_{i_j}} \mathrm{Inc}(x_{j_p}, p, y_j) \right) \rightarrow \bigvee_{j=1}^m \neg T_{i_j}(y_j) \right),$$

and that we can conclude that p-Res_φ is in p-WD-Π_1.

For some conjunctive queries φ such that the resilience problem is in PTIME [4,5], p-Res_φ is trivially fixed-parameter tractable. However, the Theorem 2 gives us a good upper bound for all φ.

By adding an existential quantifier, the contingency set Γ can be defined in MSO by $\exists X \psi_{res}(X)$. Using the Courcelle's Theorem, we can check in FPT-time if there is a contingency set of size at most k in a database with bounded treewidth.

Theorem 3. *p-Res_φ is in FPT when parameterized by the treewidth of the database D.*

Proof. Using the monadic formula, $\exists X \varphi_{res}(X)$ such that $\varphi_{res}(x)$ was previously defined, we can evaluate it over the extended database $\mathfrak{D}$ as input by an algorithm that runs in FPT-time considering the treewidth of $\mathfrak{D}$ and the size of the formula [2].

5   Conclusion

By fixing the conjunctive query, we prove an upper bound within W[1] for p-Res_φ when parameterized by the size of the contingency set. We do not know yet whether the problem is hard for W[1].

We present a formal description of the problem, and we consider a particular version of the resilience problem that differs from the analysis proposed by [8,9]. Then, we conjecture some further directions that could refine both views:

1. Can we use the formal description adopted here in this paper to improve the analysis of p-Resilence? Is this problem fixed-parameter tractable considering the tree-width of the underlying graph of the conjunctive query?
2. Can we show some optimally in the sense of [6] in terms of the tree-width? Maybe by saying that the resilience problem becomes tractable for those queries that have bounded tree-width structure?

References

1. Ebbinghaus, H.D., Flum, J., Thomas, W.: Mathematical Logic. Springer, New York (2013)
2. Flum, J., Frick, M., Grohe, M.: Query evaluation via tree-decompositions. J. ACM (JACM) **49**(6), 716–752 (2002)
3. Flum, J., Grohe, M.: Parameterized Complexity Theory. Springer, Heidelberg (2006). https://doi.org/10.1007/3-540-29953-X
4. Freire, C., Gatterbauer, W., Immerman, N., Meliou, A.: The complexity of resilience and responsibility for self-join-free conjunctive queries. Proc. VLDB Endow. **9**(3) (2015)
5. Freire, C., Gatterbauer, W., Immerman, N., Meliou, A.: New results for the complexity of resilience for binary conjunctive queries with self-joins. In: Suciu, D., Tao, Y., Wei, Z. (eds.) Proceedings of the 39th ACM SIGMOD-SIGACT-SIGAI Symposium on Principles of Database Systems, PODS 2020, Portland, OR, USA, 14–19 June 2020, pp. 271–284. ACM (2020). https://doi.org/10.1145/3375395.3387647
6. Grohe, M., Schwentick, T., Segoufin, L.: When is the evaluation of conjunctive queries tractable? In: Proceedings of the Thirty-Third Annual ACM Symposium on Theory of Computing, pp. 657–666 (2001)
7. Le Gall, F.: Powers of tensors and fast matrix multiplication. In: Proceedings of the 39th International Symposium on Symbolic and Algebraic Computation, pp. 296–303. ACM, New York (2014)
8. Miao, D., Cai, Z.: Parameterized complexity of resilience decision for database debugging. In: Duan, Z., Ong, L. (eds.) ICFEM 2017. LNCS, vol. 10610, pp. 332–344. Springer, Cham (2017). https://doi.org/10.1007/978-3-319-68690-5_20
9. Miao, D., Li, J., Cai, Z.: The parameterized complexity and kernelization of resilience for database queries. Theoret. Comput. Sci. **840**, 199–211 (2020). https://doi.org/10.1016/j.tcs.2020.08.018
10. Nešetřil, J., Poljak, S.: On the complexity of the subgraph problem. Comment. Math. Univ. Carol. **26**(2), 415–419 (1985)
11. Papadimitriou, C.H.: Computational Complexity. Wiley, New York (2003)
12. Pătraşcu, M., Williams, R.: On the possibility of faster sat algorithms. In: Proceedings of the Twenty-First Annual ACM-SIAM Symposium on Discrete Algorithms, pp. 1065–1075. SIAM, Austin (2010)

On the Correctness Problem
for Serializability

Jürgen König[1]([⊠]) and Heike Wehrheim[2]

[1] Paderborn University, Paderborn, Germany
jkoenig@mail.upb.de
[2] Carl von Ossietzky University of Oldenburg, Oldenburg, Germany

Abstract. Concurrent correctness conditions formalize the notion of "seeming atomicity" in concurrent access to shared object state. For different sorts of objects (databases, concurrent data structures, software transactional memory) different sorts of correctness conditions have been proposed (serializability, linearizability, opacity). Decidability of concurrent correctness conditions studies two problems: the *membership problem* asks whether a single execution is correct; the *correctness problem* asks whether all executions of a given implementation are correct.

In this paper we investigate decidability of Papadimitrious's notion of serializability for database transactions. Papadimitriou has proved the membership problem for serializability to be NP-complete. For correctness we consider a stricter version also proposed by Papadimitriou, which requires an additional real time order constraint. We show this version to be decidable given that all transactions are live.

1 Introduction

The purpose of concurrent correctness conditions is the definition of correct concurrent access to shared state. Correctness therein typically means that concurrent accesses behave as though these were happening *atomically*. Technically, this "seeming atomicity" is formalized by comparing concurrent executions (histories) to serial ones. Today, several such correctness conditions exist for varying sorts of objects, for example serializability [19] for database transactions, linearizability [16] and quiescent consistency [6] for concurrent data structures and opacity [14] for software transactional memories.

Implementations of such objects often employ intricate algorithms with fine-grained concurrency and without explicit locking. Hence, research often works towards finding model checking techniques to automatically check concurrent correctness of implementations. The quest for such techniques starts with determining the decidability and complexity of concurrent correctness conditions. Research in this area revolves around two problems: the *membership problem* and the *correctness problem*. The membership problem studies the correctness

The authors are supported by DFG grant WE2290/12-1.

A. Cerone and P. C. Ölveczky (Eds.): ICTAC 2021, LNCS 12819, pp. 47–64, 2021.
https://doi.org/10.1007/978-3-030-85315-0_4

of single executions, whereas the correctness problem looks at all executions generated by some implementation. In both cases, executions are compared to the behaviour of serial specifications.

In this paper, we are concerned with the correctness problem for *serializability*, the most frequently employed correctness condition for databases. Serializability was first defined by Papadimitriou [19]. Papadimitiriou has shown the membership problem to be NP-complete. For the correctness problem, Alur and McMillan [1] have studied a variant of serializability, called *conflict serializability* [10], and have shown it to be decidable and in PSPACE. Later, Bouajjani et al. [3] have shown the correctness problem for conflict serializability for an unbounded number of processes to be in EXPSPACE. Conflict serializability is based on a notion of conflict between events and (semi-)commutatibility of non-conflicting events in histories. This differs from Papadimitriou's original definition of serializability.

Here, we study decidability of the correctness problem for a definition of serializability following Papadimitriou's original idea (without a notion of conflict). More precisely, we focus on a variant of serializability, called *SSR* in [19]. *SSR* requires the reads-from relation of live transactions to be the same when comparing concurrent and serial histories as in the original definition proposed by Papadimitriou. In addition it requires the real-time order of transactions to be preserved. We prove *SSR* to be decidable under the assumption that all transactions are live. In the further we present the related work in Sect. 2, present the necessary notations and definitions in Sect. 3, our decidability result in Sect. 4, and finally give a conclusion in Sect. 5.

2 Related Work

A number of works study decidability questions for concurrent correctness conditions. A frequently studied correctness condition is conflict serializability [10]. Conflict serializability is different from (view) serializability as defined by Papadimitriou, as its equivalence definition is expressed via conflicts between events which is not possible for view serializability. Several works are concerned with the complexity of the membership and correctness problem for conflict serializability [1, 3, 10, 19]. The correctness problem for conflict serializability is in PSPACE for a finite amount of threads [1], while for an unbounded number of threads it is EXPSPACE-complete [3]. Notably the proof for the latter result uses the fact that only a finite amount of information, independent of history length, is necessary to determine conflict serializability. Hence the basic idea to prove decidability is similarly to ours. Furthermore, multiple model checking approaches for conflict serializability have been published [5, 9, 11, 13].

For sequential consistency, Alur and McMillan [1] have shown the correctness problem to be undecidable; a result which we used for showing undecidability of serializability. Automatic model checking techniques therefore typically work on subclasses only [15, 20].

For linearizability [16], there are again results both for the membership and correctness problem [1, 3, 12]. Notably, the correctness problem for a bounded

$$\mathbf{R}_{t_1}^{1}(y)\mathbf{R}_{t_2}^{2}(x)\mathbf{W}_{t_2}^{2}(x)\mathbf{W}_{t_1}^{1}(x,y)\mathbf{R}_{t_1}^{3}(x)\mathbf{W}_{t_1}^{3}(z)$$

$$\mathbf{R}_{t_1}^{tr_w}()\mathbf{W}_{t_1}^{tr_w}(x,y,z)\mathbf{R}_{t_1}^{1}(y)\mathbf{R}_{t_2}^{2}(x)\mathbf{W}_{t_2}^{2}(x)\mathbf{W}_{t_1}^{1}(x,y)\mathbf{R}_{t_1}^{3}(x)\mathbf{W}_{t_1}^{3}(z)\mathbf{R}_{t_1}^{tr_r}(x,y,z)\mathbf{W}_{t_1}^{tr_r}()$$

$$\mathbf{R}_{t_2}^{2}(x)\mathbf{W}_{t_2}^{2}(x)\mathbf{R}_{t_1}^{1}(y)\mathbf{W}_{t_1}^{1}(x,y)\mathbf{R}_{t_1}^{3}(x)\mathbf{W}_{t_1}^{3}(z)$$

Fig. 1. Example histories. From top to bottom: $h_e, \overline{h_e}, h_s$.

number of threads is in EXSPACE, while the unbounded case is undecidable. Bouajjani et al. proved that for the unbounded case linearizability is still decidable for a subclass of programs that are data independent [4]. There are furthermore multiple works targeting automatic model checking of linearizability [17,21–23].

Finally, for other correctness conditions like opacity or quiescent consistency additional model checking approaches and theoretical results exist (see e.g. [2, 7,8,13,18]).

3   Background

We start by defining the correctness problem for serializability. Like other concurrent correctness conditions, serializability is based on the notion of *histories*. Histories are sequences of events (reading of or writing to shared state by threads) grouped into transactions. In the sequel, we mainly follow the original definition by Papadimitriou [19].

A history is an interleaving of read and write events of a fixed number of threads. Each read and write operates on a number of variables. The events of a thread are grouped into *transactions*. A thread can execute several transactions. Thus a history is a sequence of read and write events indexed both by their threads and their transactions and parametrized by the set of accessed variables. For readability, we omit the set brackets of variable sets in examples. We let T be the finite set of threads, Var be the finite set of shared variables and Tr the set of transactions.

Definition 1 (History). *A history is a sequence of events $ev_0 \ldots ev_n$, where for all i, $0 \leq i \leq n$, either $ev_i = \mathbf{W}_t(V)$ or $ev_i = \mathbf{R}_t(V)$ with $t \in T, V \subseteq Var$.*

Notation. The definition does not mention transactions since given a sequence of events indexed by threads there is – up to isomorphism – only one way to assign transaction identifiers to events – when transactions are well-formed (see below). We let $\mathcal{H}$ be the set of all histories. The set of events Ev is divided into read events Ev_{rd} and write events Ev_{wr}. The set of all transactions of a history h is $tr(h)$, and we write $tr \in h$ if a transaction tr occurs in h. Events can be indexed by their transaction tr which makes them unique, e.g. the event $\mathbf{R}_t^{tr}(V)$ is a read by thread t of all variables in V within the transaction tr. If an event occurs in a history $h \in \mathcal{H}$, we write $ev \in h$. If the event ev is ordered before another event ev' in history h, we write $ev <_h ev'$. For two histories (or more generally sequences of events) h and h', we write $h \cdot h'$ for the concatenation of h and h', $h \preceq h'$ if h is a prefix of h', and $h \sqsubseteq h'$ if h is a subsequence of h'.

Histories have to be *well-formed* in the following sense:

1. A transaction consists of one or two events. If one, it is a read event. If two, one is a read and the other a write event.
2. Both events are executed by the same thread.
3. The write event (if it exists) is ordered after the read event, and no event of the same thread occurs in between the read and the write event.

The history h_e shown in Fig. 1 (top) is such a well-formed history.

The thread t of a transaction tr is denoted as $t(tr)$, which without loss of generality we assume to be identical for all histories, i.e., a fixed transaction tr is always executed by the same thread. We say a transaction is *unfinished* whenever it only has a read event in a history, and call it *finished* when it has two events in a history. For a transaction tr and history h we denote the first case as $unfin(tr, h)$.

For serializability we furthermore need to define real time orders as well as equivalence of histories. Two transactions tr_1, tr_2 are *real time ordered* in a history h, $tr_1 \prec_h tr_2$, when tr_1 is finished and the write event of tr_1 occurs before the read event of tr_2. The real time order of h, $h.RT \subseteq Tr \times Tr$, contains all pairs (tr_1, tr_2) such that $tr_1 \prec_h tr_2$. In h_e we for example have $1 \prec_{h_e} 3$ but $1 \not\prec_{h_e} 2$.

To define the notion of equivalence and finally serializability, we furthermore need to define (a) the reads-from relation in a history, (b) the augmentation of a history, and (c) liveness of transactions. A transaction tr_1 *reads* $v \in Var$ *from* transaction tr_2 in h whenever there exists a write event $ev = \mathbf{W}_t^{tr_2}(V)$ and a read event $ev' = \mathbf{R}_{t'}^{tr_1}(V')$ $(t, t' \in T, V, V' \subseteq Var)$ in h and $v \in V \cap V'$ such that $ev <_h ev'$ and no other event writing to v exists in between ev and ev'. The reads-from relation of h is denoted as $h.RF \subseteq Tr \times Tr \times Var$. For $tr, tr' \in tr(h)$ and $v \in Var, (tr, tr', v) \in h.RF$ means that tr' reads v from tr in h. In our example we have $(1, 3, x) \in h_e.RF$ and $(2, 3, x) \notin h_e.RF$.

To ensure that all transactions can read from some writes and all variables are read at the end, histories get augmented with additional transactions. The *augmented history* $\overline{h}$ for a history h is the history where two transactions are added, tr_w at the start and tr_r at the end of the history. The transaction tr_w writes to each variable and reads from none, and tr_r reads all variables and writes to none. For an example see the augmentation $\overline{h_e}$ of history h_e in Fig. 1 (additional transactions in grey). Then, a transaction tr in an augmented history $\overline{h}$ is called *live* whenever it either is tr_r or for a live transaction tr' and $v \in Var$, $(tr, tr', v) \in \overline{h}.RF$. A transaction is live in a non-augmented history h if it is live in its augmented version $\overline{h}$. In the example history h_e transaction 2 is not live since the only variable x it writes to is never read in $\overline{h_e}$. Note that this notion of liveness is slightly different from the notion of transaction liveness in software transactional memory (which corresponds more to being finished).

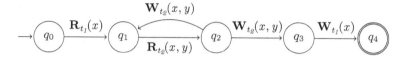

Fig. 2. Implementation Automaton Example: I_{ex}

Definition 2. *Two well-formed histories* $h, h' \in \mathcal{H}$ *are equivalent* $(h \equiv h')$ *iff*

- *they have the same set of transactions and*
- *for any live* $tr \in h$ *and any* $tr' \in h$, $(tr', tr, v) \in h'.RF \Leftrightarrow (tr', tr, v) \in h.RF$.

In the example we have $h_e \equiv h_s$. As noted by Papadimitriou [19], it is actually sufficient for equivalence that both histories have the same set of *live* transactions, but w.l.o.g. this is equivalent to assuming their transactions overall are identical.

A history is *serial* whenever each read event either belongs to an unfinished transaction or is directly followed by the write of its transaction. We let $\mathcal{H}_S$ be the set of serial histories. History h_s in Fig. 1 is serial. We can now define strict serializability for histories with multiple transactions per thread. The definition mainly follows the one given by Papadimitriou[1]. Note it differs from the serializability definition employed by Alur et al. which is *conflict serializability* [10].

Definition 3 (SSR^+). *A history* h *is* serializable under SSR^+ *(or strictly serializable) iff there exists a serial history* h_s *such that*

1. $h \equiv h_s$, *and*
2. $h.RT \subseteq h_s.RT$ *(real time order preservation)*.

Note that the real time order contains the thread order. In our example, h_s has the same real time order as h_e. Thus overall h_e is serializable under SSR^+.

Whenever for history h, a history h_s as required by the above definitions exists, we say h is *serializable to* h_s *under* SSR^+ or call h_s an *s-witness* of h. Let h_s be a serial history and S be a set of serial histories. The set of histories serializable to h_s under SSR^+ is denoted $SSR^+(h_s)$. Additionally, $SSR^+(S)$ denotes the set of histories h such that there exists a $h_s \in S$ such that h is serializable to h_s under SSR^+.

Correctness Problem. With these definitions at hand, we can define the actual problem we are interested in. The *correctness problem* is the problem of checking whether each of the generated histories of an implementation I is serializable to some serial history generated by a specification S. We assume that both I and S – as common in the related literature [1,8] – are given as finite state automata, and let $L(A)$ be the language accepted by an automaton A. Figure 2 is

---

[1] The difference lays in our introduction of transaction identifiers and the accompanying requirement of thread order preservation, which is often assumed for traditional memory models.

an example of an implementation automaton. It generates (accepts) the language $L(I_{ex}) = \mathbf{R}_{t_1}(x)\left(\mathbf{R}_{t_2}(x,y)\mathbf{W}_{t_2}(x,y)\right)^+\mathbf{W}_{t_1}(x)$. Transaction identifiers can be freely assigned to the events of the transactions of each word in this language. We assume that both specification and implementation automaton only generate well-formed histories.

Then the correctness problem for strict serializability is defined as follows.

Problem 1 (Correctness Problem for Strict Serializability). Given an implementation I and a specification S, determine whether $L(I) \subseteq SSR^+(L(S))$ is true.

Assuming S to be an automaton producing every serial history (for given threads T and variables Var), the automaton I_{ex} is not correct according to the above definition. It accepts the history $\mathbf{R}_{t_1}^1(x)\mathbf{R}_{t_2}^2(x,y)\mathbf{W}_{t_2}^2(x,y)\mathbf{W}_{t_1}^1(x)$. This history is not serializable under SSR^+.

4   The Correctness Problem for SSR^- Is Decidable

We look at the decidability of the correctness problem for strict serializability. Here, we show decidability for a subclass of SSR^+ (called SSR^-) where the assumption is that all transactions in a history are live or unfinished.

The decidability follows from the fact that we can construct a finite automaton whose language is empty if and only if all histories generated by the implementation automaton are strictly serializable. The states of this automaton are (approximations of) equivalence classes of histories where the equivalence captures the strict serializability of histories and their extensions.

The assumption of all transactions being live or unfinished guarantees prefix-closedness of strict serializability and thus allows us to incrementally construct the states of the equivalence class automaton.

Proposition 1. *Let $\mathcal{H}_{live}$ be the set of histories with live[2] transactions only, $\mathcal{H}_{un,live}$ be the set of histories where all transactions are either unfinished or live and $h \in \mathcal{H}_{live}$. If h is not strictly serializable, so are all $h' \in \mathcal{H}_{un,live}$ such that $h \preceq h'$.*

In the following we assume (1) all histories to contain live or unfinished transactions only and (2) an implementation automaton to only accept words (histories) in which all transactions are finished. We can therefore employ a notion of equivalence of histories meaning (a) same set of transactions and (b) same reads-from relation (for all transactions, not just live ones). This is important for the construction below because it allows us to directly check for the correctness of reads-from relations when observing the next read, not needing to wait for the transaction of this read to become finished. The notion of s-witness used in the sequel is based on this adapted equivalence definition.

We furthermore assume checking strict serializability against the *most general specification automaton*. The most general specification automaton generates *all*

---

[2] Note that all live transactions have to be finished.

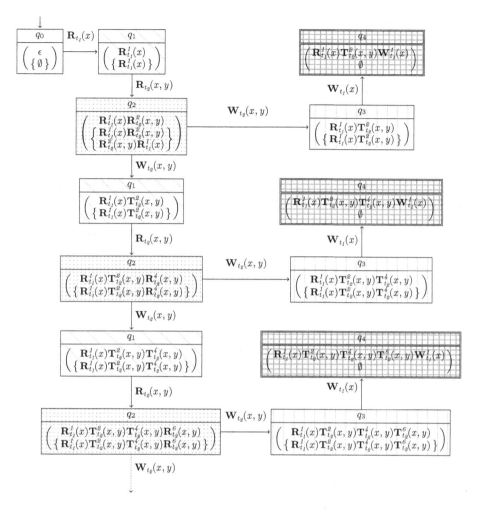

Fig. 3. Excerpt of histories of I_{ex} (of Fig. 2) and their s-witnesses

serial histories. Thus the specification automaton S does not play a role in the following. Deciding strict serializability for specific automata S would require additional tracking of states of S in the below given construction.

4.1 Compact Representation

We start by looking at a naive approach for generating all histories of an implementation automaton and explain how to compact these infinitely many histories to some finite structure. Given an implementation automaton, a naive approach would simply try to explore the entire state space of the implementation, i.e. to generate all of its histories and check them for strict serializability. An excerpt of the state space of implementation automaton I_{ex} as a graph can be seen in

Fig. 3. The upper half of each node shows the current state of the automaton and the lower half the history of the events executed so far and its set of s-witnesses. Note that an entire transaction of the form $\mathbf{R}_{t_i}^j(x)\mathbf{W}_{t_i}^j(x)$ is for brevity denoted as $\mathbf{T}_{t_i}^j(x)$.

The obvious problem with this approach is that the state space of implementations can be infinite, as there are infinitely many histories. Our approach is now to reduce the state space by *merging* nodes which behave similarly. In the graph in Fig. 3, these are marked with the same filling pattern. For example, consider the striped states (second column, second, fourth and sixth state): Whenever we execute $\mathbf{W}_{t_2}(x,y)\mathbf{W}_{t_1}(x)$ from a striped node, we end up in a node with implementation state q_4 and an empty s-witness, i.e. the current history is not strictly serializable. Whenever we execute $\mathbf{W}_{t_2}(x,y)$, we either end up in a node with implementation state q_3 or q_2 where in both cases the corresponding history is strictly serializable. So summarizing we consider two nodes as behaving similarly whenever

- they contain the same implementation automaton state, and
- when appending identical events, both either keep or loose their strict serializability.

Merging these two nodes into one does not change the accepted language of the automaton. We show decidability by proving that such a graph with merged nodes has (a) a finite number of nodes (and thus is representable as a finite automaton) and (b) this automaton is effectively constructable.

We start by formalizing the above similarity on histories.

Definition 4 (SSR-extension equivalence). *Two histories $h, h' \in \mathcal{H}$ are SSR-extension equivalent ($h \equiv_{ext} h'$) iff $\forall n \in \mathbb{N}, \forall ev_0 \ldots ev_n \in Ev^n$ either*

- *$h \cdot ev_0 \ldots ev_n$ and $h' \cdot ev_0 \ldots ev_n$ are both strictly serializable,*
- *or $h \cdot ev_0 \ldots ev_n$ and $h' \cdot ev_0 \ldots ev_n$ are both not strictly serializable.*

The question is how to determine whether two histories are SSR-extension equivalent. The general idea is to reduce a history to the essential information needed to determine whether appending events keeps the history strictly serializable or not. This information is called *SSR-data*. Whenever two histories have the same SSR-data, they are SSR-extension equivalent. Below we will show that there are only finitely many different (valid) SSR-data which is key to our decidability result.

Witness Extensions. Before we formalize SSR-data, we take a look at some properties of histories, their s-witnesses and extensions with events. Figure 4 shows the first such property in a diagram. The upper level is a history h and its extension h' by one read event. The read event is (and can only be) appended at the end. The lower level depicts one s-witness (h_s) for h and one for h' (h'_s). Here, we see that the new read event is inserted in the middle of h_s. What is important, however, is that the new s-witness h'_s needs to be a *supersequence* of h_s, i.e. we cannot reorder events already occurring in h_s. This is due to the requirements of strict serializability (equality of reads-from relation and subset on real-time ordering). The same applies to extensions with write events. Hence, we only have a limited amount of candidate s-witnesses when extending a history.

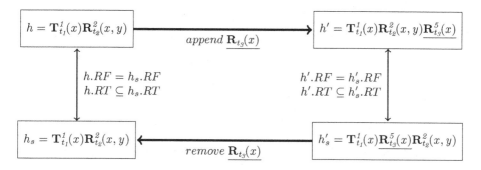

$$h = \mathbf{T}_{t_1}^1(x)\mathbf{R}_{t_2}^2(x, y) \xrightarrow{\text{append } \underline{\mathbf{R}_{t_3}(x)}} h' = \mathbf{T}_{t_1}^1(x)\mathbf{R}_{t_2}^2(x, y)\underline{\mathbf{R}_{t_3}^5(x)}$$

$$\begin{array}{cc} h.RF = h_s.RF & h'.RF = h'_s.RF \\ h.RT \subseteq h_s.RT & h'.RT \subseteq h'_s.RT \end{array}$$

$$h_s = \mathbf{T}_{t_1}^1(x)\mathbf{R}_{t_2}^2(x, y) \xleftarrow{\text{remove } \underline{\mathbf{R}_{t_3}(x)}} h'_s = \mathbf{T}_{t_1}^1(x)\mathbf{R}_{t_3}^5(x)\mathbf{R}_{t_2}^2(x, y)$$

Fig. 4. Supersequence property for extensions of s-witnesses

$$h = \mathbf{T}_{t_1}^1(x)\mathbf{R}_{t_1}^3(x)\mathbf{R}_{t_2}^2(x, y) \xrightarrow{\underline{\mathbf{W}_{t_1}(x)}} h' = \mathbf{T}_{t_1}^1(x)\mathbf{R}_{t_1}^3(x)\mathbf{R}_{t_2}^2(x, y)\underline{\mathbf{W}_{t_1}^3(x)}$$

$$h_{s_1} = \mathbf{T}_{t_1}^1(x)\mathbf{R}_{t_2}^2(x, y)\mathbf{R}_{t_1}^3(x) \xrightarrow{\text{insert } \underline{\mathbf{W}_{t_1}(x)}} h'_{s_1} = \mathbf{T}_{t_1}^1(x)\mathbf{R}_{t_2}^2(x, y)\mathbf{R}_{t_1}^3(x)\underline{\mathbf{W}_{t_1}^3(x)}$$

$$h_{s_2} = \mathbf{T}_{t_1}^1(x)\mathbf{R}_{t_1}^3(x)\mathbf{R}_{t_2}^2(x, y) \xrightarrow{\text{insert } \underline{\mathbf{W}_{t_1}(x)}} h'_{s_2} = \mathbf{T}_{t_1}^1(x)\,\mathbf{R}_{t_1}^3(x)\mathbf{W}_{t_1}^3(x)\mathbf{R}_{t_2}^2(x, y)$$

Fig. 5. A history and its s-witnesses extended with a write event

Next, we need to be able to compute s-witness extensions (or at least, a compact form of them). To this end, we need to determine which of the supersequence candidates can be kept and which are to be eliminated because they are no valid s-witnesses for the extended history. For this, consider Fig. 5. The history h (top) is strictly serializable and both the histories h_{s_1} and h_{s_2} are s-witnesses. When history h is extended by event $\mathbf{W}_{t_1}^3(x)$, this event gets appended at the end of the history. Similarly, we need to insert $\mathbf{W}_{t_1}^3(x)$ into the s-witnesses to find a witness for h'.

As this is a write event, all serial candidates must have the write by transaction 3 directly follow the read event of 3. In Fig. 5 the write is thus inserted directly after the last event of its thread in both cases. The resulting histories are obviously serial. Second, we need to check whether h'_{s_1} and h'_{s_2} preserve the real time order of h'. This is the case. Third, we need to check if the reads-from orders of h' and h'_{s_1}, h'_{s_2}, respectively, are identical. For h'_{s_1} this is the case as well. For h'_{s_2} they are different: In h_{s_2} transaction 1 writes to x which transaction 2 reads with transaction 3 occuring in between. We say that x belongs to the *write-before-read-after* (short, *wbra*) *variables* of 3. Thus in h'_{s_2} the write of transaction 3 is read (by transaction 2) which it is not in h'. Hence h'_{s_2} is not an s-witness of h' and this candidate needs to be eliminated.

The elimination can be determined by looking at the write-before-read-after variables formalized with the help of the last-writer function.

Definition 5 (Last Writer). *Given a history* $h = ev_0 \ldots e_n$, *the* last writer function *for an event ev,* $lw_{ev,h} : Var \rightarrow Tr \cup \{tr_{ini}\}^3$, *determines the last writer to a variable v, i.e.* $lw_{ev,h}(v) = tr$ *iff*

- $tr \in h$ *and tr contains a write event w writing to v,*
- $w <_h ev$ *(the write occurs before ev),*
- *and there is no write* w' *to v such* $w <_h w' <_h ev$.

Note that it is not possible to use the reads-from relation here, as the last writer function returns the last writer of a variable at arbitrary specified event of the history, which does not have to be a read, reading that variable. When the event ev is the last event in a history, we elide the index to lw.

The *write-before-read-after variables* of a transaction are all variables that get written to before and read from after that transaction.

Definition 6 (Write-Before-Read-After Variables). *Given a serial history* h_s *with unfinished transaction tr and read event ev, the* write-before-read-after *function* $wbra_h : Tr \rightarrow 2^{Var}$ *of h determines the variables written before and read after a transaction, i.e.* $v \in wbra_h(tr)$ *holds iff*

- *there exists a transaction* tr_1 *s.t.* $lw_{ev,h}(v) = tr_1$ *and*
- *a transaction* tr_2 *with a read event* ev' *s.t.* $ev <_h ev'$ *and* $lw_{ev',h}(v) = tr_1$.

If tr is finished, then $wbra_h(tr) = \emptyset$.

Summarizing, for extensions with write events we get the following property: an s-witness h_s can be extended with a write event $\mathbf{W}_t^{tr}(V)$ if

$$wbra_{h_s}(tr) \cap V = \emptyset . \tag{1}$$

Next we look at extensions with read events. For a read the preservation of the serial nature of an s-witness is trivial, as a new read does not violate it no matter where it is added. Still all feasible candidates must have the additional read located after the last write of the old s-witness. Otherwise the real time order of the extended history is trivially not preserved. In Fig. 6 there are two s-witnesses for h with different orders for the writing transactions. Note that in every history except h we removed all empty reads for brevity. For h_{s_1} two successor candidates exist, h'_{s_1} where the read is added after $\mathbf{R}_{t_1}^3(x)$ and h'_{s_2} where it is added before. Similary for h_{s_2} two candidates exist. For both s-witnesses both successor candidates preserve the real time order of h'.

---

[3] We assume tr_{ini} to be the transaction initializing all variables.

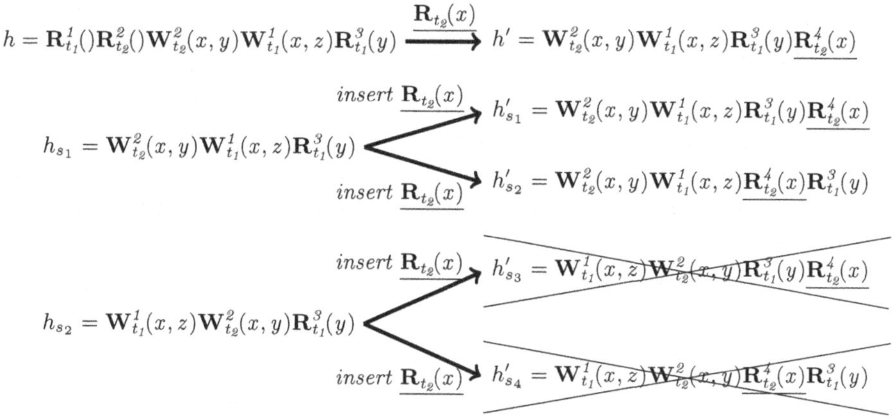

$$h = \mathbf{R}^1_{t_1}()\mathbf{R}^2_{t_2}()\mathbf{W}^2_{t_2}(x,y)\mathbf{W}^1_{t_1}(x,z)\mathbf{R}^3_{t_1}(y) \xrightarrow{\mathbf{R}_{t_2}(x)} h' = \mathbf{W}^2_{t_2}(x,y)\mathbf{W}^1_{t_1}(x,z)\mathbf{R}^3_{t_1}(y)\underline{\mathbf{R}^4_{t_2}(x)}$$

$$h_{s_1} = \mathbf{W}^2_{t_2}(x,y)\mathbf{W}^1_{t_1}(x,z)\mathbf{R}^3_{t_1}(y) \begin{cases} \xrightarrow{insert\ \mathbf{R}_{t_2}(x)} h'_{s_1} = \mathbf{W}^2_{t_2}(x,y)\mathbf{W}^1_{t_1}(x,z)\mathbf{R}^3_{t_1}(y)\underline{\mathbf{R}^4_{t_2}(x)} \\ \\ \xrightarrow{insert\ \mathbf{R}_{t_2}(x)} h'_{s_2} = \mathbf{W}^2_{t_2}(x,y)\mathbf{W}^1_{t_1}(x,z)\underline{\mathbf{R}^4_{t_2}(x)}\mathbf{R}^3_{t_1}(y) \end{cases}$$

$$h_{s_2} = \mathbf{W}^1_{t_1}(x,z)\mathbf{W}^2_{t_2}(x,y)\mathbf{R}^3_{t_1}(y) \begin{cases} \xrightarrow{insert\ \mathbf{R}_{t_2}(x)} h'_{s_3} = \mathbf{W}^1_{t_1}(x,z)\mathbf{W}^2_{t_2}(x,y)\mathbf{R}^3_{t_1}(y)\underline{\mathbf{R}^4_{t_2}(x)} \\ \\ \xrightarrow{insert\ \mathbf{R}_{t_2}(x)} h'_{s_4} = \mathbf{W}^1_{t_1}(x,z)\mathbf{W}^2_{t_2}(x,y)\underline{\mathbf{R}^4_{t_2}(x)}\mathbf{R}^3_{t_1}(y) \end{cases}$$

Fig. 6. A history and its s-witnesses extended with a read event

For the reads-from relation both successor candidates for h_{s_1} are valid as the new read event reads from transaction 1 in both cases. The candidates for h_{s_2} differ in reads-from order, as the read event reads from transaction 2. This is the case since in h_{s_1} the last writer on x is transaction 1 which is identical to that of h, but for h_{s_2} transaction 2 is the last writer which is different from h. The summary in such and similar cases is thus: an s-witness h_s can be extended with a read event $\mathbf{R}^{tr}_t(V)$ if for all variables $v \in V$, the last writer of v in h and h_s is the same:

$$\forall v \in V : lw_{h_s}(v) = lw_h(v). \tag{2}$$

These considerations lead us to keeping both the last writer and the wbra variables in the SSR-data.

SSR-Data. We can now take a look at the SSR-data and its extension for events for an example (Fig. 7). Note that in the full state space of an implementation automaton we would need to store a complete history and its set of s-witnesses. Here we now apply two compression functions to the history and to each s-witness, and only store their compressed versions together with the wbra variables. The compression works as follows: For each s-witness we remove every finished transaction that is not a last writer; for the history we remove each transaction that is finished and not a last writer in any (compressed) s-witness of the history. The first compression function is denoted as sub ($sub : \mathcal{H} \rightarrow \mathcal{H}$), the latter as $suball$ ($suball : \mathcal{H} \times 2^{\mathcal{H}} \rightarrow \mathcal{H}$). In $suball(h, H)$, the set H is some set of (possibly already compressed) s-witnesses. Both compression functions generate strings which are subsequences of their (first) argument.

In the given example history $\mathbf{T}^2_{t_2}(x)\mathbf{T}^1_{t_1}(x)$ (Fig. 7, top node) the first transaction is not the last writer of any variable, it is also finished, so it is removed when extracting SSR-data. The *wbra* variables are shown as "$-$" as there is no unfinished transaction. In the one s-witness, transaction 1 is removed as it is finished. Then we see a number of extensions with events (transitions from left to right) followed by compression steps (diagonal arrows from right to left). These show how the SSR-data is first extended and then again compressed. When a new event is appended to the history each compressed s-witness is expanded like a normal s-witness, as discussed above. As all last writers are known (can be seen from compacted s-witnesses and history) we can compare them. We can also check whether a write is in conflict with the *wbra* variables of its transaction (condition (1)). For each new s-witness the wbra set is generated from the previous s-witness. After each extension the resulting tuple is compressed again.

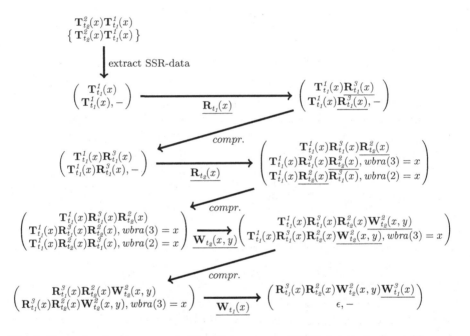

Fig. 7. Examples for the computation of successors of SSR-data; *wbra* variables only shown if non-empty.

In general SSR-data are elements of the form $\mathcal{H} \times 2^{\mathcal{H}_S \times W}$, where W is the set of all functions $wbra : Tr \rightarrow Var$. We store a (compressed) history together with a set of pairs containing (compressed) s-witnesses and their wbra functions.

Definition 7 (Validity of SSR-data). *Let $h \in \mathcal{H}$ be a history and H_s its set of s-witnesses. A pair $(h_c, HW) \in \mathcal{H} \times 2^{\mathcal{H}_S \times W}$ is valid SSR-data for h iff*

- $h_c = suball(h, H_s)$ *(compressed history), and*
- $HW = \{(sub(h_s), wbra_{h_s}) \mid h_s \in H_s\}$ *(pairs of compressed s-witnesses and their wbra functions).*

Proposition 2. *Let $h \in \mathcal{H}$ not be strictly serializable. Then its valid SSR-data is $(suball(h, \emptyset), \emptyset)$ where $suball(h, \emptyset) \neq \epsilon$.*

Key to decidability is the fact that we only have a finite amount of different valid SSR-data.

Lemma 1. *The number of SSR-data valid for some history is bound in size by $O((|Var| \cdot 2^{2|Var|} + |T| \cdot 2^{|Var|})!)$.*

We next formally define the successor computation (as in Fig. 7). The extension and compression step are unified into one function, which is composed out of a function for appending a write and one for appending a read event ev.

$$ext((h_c, HW), ev) = \begin{cases} ext_r((h_c, HW), ev) & \text{if } ev \in Ev_{rd}, \\ ext_w((h_c, HW), ev) & \text{if } ev \in Ev_{wr}. \end{cases}$$

We next define ext_w and ext_r starting with write extensions. For each compressed s-witness of the input SSR-data, we need to check whether the writing thread's *wbra* variables contain any of the variables written to by the write event (Condition (1)). If not, then both (compressed) s-witness and (compressed) history need to be extended with the write event and the wbra variables of all transactions updated. Let $ev(tr)$ denote the last element of transaction tr in the context of a history.

Definition 8 (Extension with write). *Let (h_c, HW) be some SSR-data and $ev = \mathbf{W}_t^{tr}(V)$ a write event.*
Then $ext_w((h_c, HW), ev) = (h'_c, HW')$ where $(h'_s, wb_{h'_s}) \in HW'$ iff there exists some pair $(h_s, wb_{h_s}) \in HW$ such that $h_s = ev_0 \dots ev(tr) \dots ev_n$ and

- $wb_{h_s}(tr) \cap V = \emptyset$ *(no writing of wbra variables)*,
- $h'_s = sub(ev_0 \dots ev(tr)ev \dots ev_n)$ *(compression of extended s-witness)*,
- $wb_{h'_s}(tr) = \emptyset$ *(wbra variables of finished transaction emptied)*,
- $\forall tr' \neq tr \in Tr : wb_{h'_s}(tr') = wb_{h_s}(tr')$ *(wbra variables of other transactions kept)*

and $h'_c = suball(h_c \cdot ev, HW')$ (history compressed w.r.t. new s-witnesses).

This write extension preserves validity of SSR-data.

Lemma 2. *Let h be a history, (h_c, HW) its valid SSR-data and ev a write event. Then the SSR-data $ext_w((h_c, HW), ev)$ is valid for $h \cdot ev$.*

Next we define the extension with read events. For each s-witness we check if its last writers for the variables read are identical with that of the compressed history (condition (2)); if yes we generate all candidates where the new read is placed after the last write. We then compress these and update the *wbra* variables. Finally the compressed history is expanded and again compressed using the information from the new s-witness set. Let $lwr(h)$ denote the last write event of history h.

Definition 9 (Extension with reads). *Let (h_c, HW) be some SSR-data and $ev = \mathbf{R}_t^{tr}(V)$ a read event.*
Then $ext_r((h_c, HW), ev) = (h_c', HW')$ where $(h_s', wb_{h_s'}) \in HW'$ iff there exists some pair $(h_s, wb_{h_s}) \in HW$ such that $h_s = ev_0 \ldots lwr(h_s) \ldots ev_n$ and

- $\forall v \in V : lw_{h_s}(v) = lw_{h_c}(v)$ *(last writers of history and s-witnesses agree)*,
- $h_s' = sub(ev_0 \ldots lwr(h_s) \ldots ev \ldots ev_n)$ *(compression of extended s-witness, read inserted somewhere after last write)*,
- $\forall tr' \in Tr : wb_{h_s'}(tr') = wb_{h_s}(tr') \cup wbra_{h_s'}(tr')$ *(wbra variables of all transactions updated)*

and $h_c' = suball(h_c \cdot ev, HW')$.

This read extension preserves validity of SSR-data.

Lemma 3. *Let h be a history, (h_c, HW) its valid SSR-data and ev a read event. Then the SSR-data $ext_r((h_c, HW), ev)$ is valid for $h \cdot ev$.*

For a sequence seq and some SSR-data (h_c, HW), we write $ext((h_c, HW), seq)$ for the consecutive extension of the SSR-data with the events of seq. Now given an event sequence h, we can simply apply ext consecutively for each event, and if none of the thus computed SSR-data contains $\emptyset$ as the second element of the pair, the history h is strictly serializable.

SSR-Data and SSR-Extension Equivalence. As a last step in the definition of SSR-data, we show the desired property about SSR-extension equivalence: if two histories h and h' have the "same" valid SSR-data, then they are SSR-extension equivalent. Here we employ similarity up to transaction renamings, i.e. transaction identifiers can be arbitrarily renamed via a bijective function $r : Tr \rightarrow Tr$ when r preserves threads (for all tr, $t(tr) = t(r(tr))$). We write $(h_c, HW) \equiv_{data} (h_c', HW')$ if the two SSR-data are the same up to renaming of transactions.

Theorem 1. *Let $h, h' \in \mathcal{H}$ be two histories and (h_c, HW) and (h_c', HW') their valid SSR-data. If $(h_c, HW) \equiv_{data} (h_c', HW')$, then $h \equiv_{ext} h'$.*

The reverse implication does not hold: SSR-data is only approximating SSR-extension equivalence. For the correctness of the automaton construction given next this direction of the implication suffices.

4.2   Construction of Finite Automaton

In our decision procedure, we generate a finite automaton where the states are pairs of implementation automaton states and SSR-data of histories. The infinite state space obtained via the naive exploration strategy is thus collapsed into a finite automaton. This automaton can be constructed by starting with the SSR-data of an empty history and then generating new SSR-data according to the events in the implementation automaton using the above given extension

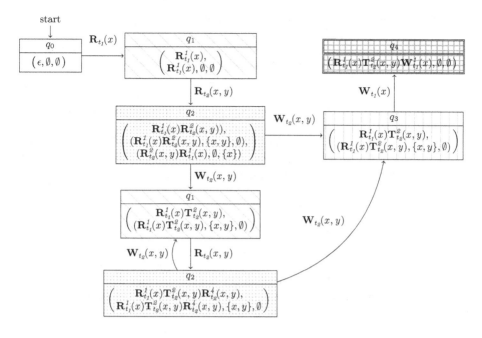

Fig. 8. SSR-automaton of I_{ex} (of Fig. 2)

function. As we only have a finite number of different SSR-data (as of Lemma 1) such a construction terminates.

To formalize this construction, we let $SSR_{T,Var}$ be the set of all SSR-data with thread identifiers from T and variables from Var. We furthermore let $SSR\emptyset_{T,Var}$ be the set of all SSR-data of the format $(h_c, \emptyset)$, where $h_c \neq \epsilon$.

Definition 10. *Let* $I = (Q, \delta, q_0, F)$ *be an implementation automaton. The* SSR-automaton of I $(E(I))$ *is the automaton* $(Q_E, \delta_E, q_{0,E}, F_E)$ *such that*

- $Q_E = Q \times SSR_{T,Var}$,
- $q_{0,E} = (q_0, (\epsilon, \emptyset))$,
- $F_E = F \times SSR\emptyset_{T,Var}$

and $((q, ssr), ev, (q', ssr')) \in \delta_E$ *iff* $(q, ev, q') \in \delta$ *and* $ext(ssr, ev) = ssr'$.

The thus constructed automaton is a finite automaton since by Lemma 1 we only have finitely many different valid SSR-data. Furthermore, we can derive strict serializability of the implementation automaton from the language of the SSR-automaton.

Theorem 2. *Let* I *be an implementation automaton. Then* I *is strictly serializable iff* $L(E(I)) = \emptyset$.

This finally gives us the decidability of SSR^-.

Corollary 1. *The correctness problem for SSR⁻ is decidable.*

Figure 8 shows the result of the construction for our running example. The diagram only depicts the reachable states. Note that the standardized naming of transactions can lead to a "renaming" of transactions and does so for transaction 3 in one case. We see that the language of the SSR-automaton is non-empty (the state with the grid pattern is accepting), and hence not all histories of the implementation automaton are strictly serializable. We also see that equivalence of SSR-data only implies SSR-extension equivalence: there are still two striped and two dotted states which are SSR-extension equivalent but have different SSR-data, and thus could not be compacted to a single state.

5   Conclusion

In this paper we have studied the decidability of the correctness problem of serializability. We have proven a strenghtening of serializability with an additional requirement of real-time order preservation to be decidable. As future work we plan to investigate whether our assumption of liveness of transactions can be removed while keeping the decidability result.

References

1. Alur, R., McMillan, K.L., Peled, D.A.: Model-checking of correctness conditions for concurrent objects. Inf. Comput. **160**(1–2), 167–188 (2000). https://doi.org/10.1006/inco.1999.2847
2. Armstrong, A., Dongol, B., Doherty, S.: Reducing opacity to linearizability: a sound and complete method. CoRR abs/1610.01004 (2016). http://arxiv.org/abs/1610.01004
3. Bouajjani, A., Emmi, M., Enea, C., Hamza, J.: Verifying concurrent programs against sequential specifications. In: Felleisen, M., Gardner, P. (eds.) ESOP 2013. LNCS, vol. 7792, pp. 290–309. Springer, Heidelberg (2013). https://doi.org/10.1007/978-3-642-37036-6_17
4. Bouajjani, A., Emmi, M., Enea, C., Hamza, J.: On reducing linearizability to state reachability. Inf. Comput. **261**(Part), 383–400 (2018). https://doi.org/10.1016/j.ic.2018.02.014
5. Cohen, A., O'Leary, J.W., Pnueli, A., Tuttle, M.R., Zuck, L.D.: Verifying correctness of transactional memories. In: Formal Methods in Computer-Aided Design, 7th International Conference, FMCAD 2007, Austin, Texas, USA, 11–14 November 2007, Proceedings, pp. 37–44. IEEE Computer Society (2007). https://doi.org/10.1109/FAMCAD.2007.40
6. Derrick, J., Dongol, B., Schellhorn, G., Tofan, B., Travkin, O., Wehrheim, H.: Quiescent consistency: defining and verifying relaxed linearizability. In: Jones, C., Pihlajasaari, P., Sun, J. (eds.) FM 2014. LNCS, vol. 8442, pp. 200–214. Springer, Cham (2014). https://doi.org/10.1007/978-3-319-06410-9_15
7. Doherty, S., Groves, L., Luchangco, V., Moir, M.: Towards formally specifying and verifying transactional memory. Formal Aspects Comput. **25**(5), 769–799 (2013). https://doi.org/10.1007/s00165-012-0225-8

8. Dongol, B., Hierons, R.M.: Decidability and complexity for quiescent consistency. In: Grohe, M., Koskinen, E., Shankar, N. (eds.) Proceedings of the 31st Annual ACM/IEEE Symposium on Logic in Computer Science, LICS '16, New York, NY, USA, 5–8 July 2016, pp. 116–125. ACM (2016). https://doi.org/10.1145/2933575. 2933576

9. Emmi, M., Majumdar, R., Manevich, R.: Parameterized verification of transactional memories. In: Zorn, B.G., Aiken, A. (eds.) Proceedings of the 2010 ACM SIGPLAN Conference on Programming Language Design and Implementation, PLDI 2010, Toronto, Ontario, Canada, 5–10 June 2010, pp. 134–145. ACM (2010). https://doi.org/10.1145/1806596.1806613

10. Eswaran, K.P., Gray, J., Lorie, R.A., Traiger, I.L.: The notions of consistency and predicate locks in a database system. Commun. ACM **19**(11), 624–633 (1976). https://doi.org/10.1145/360363.360369

11. Farzan, A., Madhusudan, P.: Monitoring atomicity in concurrent programs. In: Gupta, A., Malik, S. (eds.) CAV 2008. LNCS, vol. 5123, pp. 52–65. Springer, Heidelberg (2008). https://doi.org/10.1007/978-3-540-70545-1_8

12. Gibbons, P.B., Korach, E.: The complexity of sequential consistency. In: Proceedings of the Fourth IEEE Symposium on Parallel and Distributed Processing, SPDP 1992, Arlington, Texas, USA, 1–4 December 1992, pp. 317–325. IEEE Computer Society (1992). https://doi.org/10.1109/SPDP.1992.242728

13. Guerraoui, R., Henzinger, T.A., Singh, V.: Model checking transactional memories. Distrib. Comput. **22**(3), 129–145 (2010). https://doi.org/10.1007/s00446-009-0092-6

14. Guerraoui, R., Kapalka, M.: On the correctness of transactional memory. In: Chatterjee, S., Scott, M.L. (eds.) Proceedings of the 13th ACM SIGPLAN Symposium on Principles and Practice of Parallel Programming, PPOPP 2008, Salt Lake City, UT, USA, 20–23 February 2008, pp. 175–184. ACM (2008). https://doi.org/10. 1145/1345206.1345233

15. Henzinger, T.A., Qadeer, S., Rajamani, S.K.: Verifying sequential consistency on shared-memory multiprocessor systems. In: Halbwachs, N., Peled, D. (eds.) CAV 1999. LNCS, vol. 1633, pp. 301–315. Springer, Heidelberg (1999). https://doi.org/ 10.1007/3-540-48683-6_27

16. Herlihy, M., Wing, J.M.: Linearizability: a correctness condition for concurrent objects. ACM Trans. Program. Lang. Syst. **12**(3), 463–492 (1990). https://doi. org/10.1145/78969.78972

17. Liu, Y., Chen, W., Liu, Y.A., Sun, J.: Model checking linearizability via refinement. In: Cavalcanti, A., Dams, D.R. (eds.) FM 2009. LNCS, vol. 5850, pp. 321–337. Springer, Heidelberg (2009). https://doi.org/10.1007/978-3-642-05089-3_21

18. O'Leary, J.W., Saha, B., Tuttle, M.R.: Model checking transactional memory with spin. In: 29th IEEE International Conference on Distributed Computing Systems (ICDCS 2009), Montreal, Québec, Canada, 22–26 June 2009, pp. 335–342. IEEE Computer Society (2009). https://doi.org/10.1109/ICDCS.2009.72

19. Papadimitriou, C.H.: The serializability of concurrent database updates. J. ACM **26**(4), 631–653 (1979). https://doi.org/10.1145/322154.322158

20. Qadeer, S.: Verifying sequential consistency on shared-memory multiprocessors by model checking. IEEE Trans. Parallel Distrib. Syst. **14**(8), 730–741 (2003). https:// doi.org/10.1109/TPDS.2003.1225053

21. Vafeiadis, V.: Automatically proving linearizability. In: Touili, T., Cook, B., Jackson, P. (eds.) CAV 2010. LNCS, vol. 6174, pp. 450–464. Springer, Heidelberg (2010). https://doi.org/10.1007/978-3-642-14295-6_40

22. Vechev, M., Yahav, E., Yorsh, G.: Experience with model checking linearizability. In: Păsăreanu, C.S. (ed.) SPIN 2009. LNCS, vol. 5578, pp. 261–278. Springer, Heidelberg (2009). https://doi.org/10.1007/978-3-642-02652-2_21
23. Zhang, S.J.: Scalable automatic linearizability checking. In: Taylor, R.N., Gall, H.C., Medvidovic, N. (eds.) Proceedings of the 33rd International Conference on Software Engineering, ICSE 2011, Waikiki, Honolulu, HI, USA, 21–28 May 2011, pp. 1185–1187. ACM (2011). https://doi.org/10.1145/1985793.1986037

Efficient Model Checking Methods

A Set Automaton to Locate All Pattern Matches in a Term

Rick Erkens$^{(\boxtimes)}$ and Jan Friso Groote

Mathematics and Computer Science, Eindhoven University of Technology,
Eindhoven, The Netherlands
`r.j.a.erkens@tue.nl`

Abstract. Term pattern matching is the problem of finding all pattern matches in a subject term, given a set of patterns. Finding efficient algorithms for this problem is an important direction for research [21]. We present a new set automaton solution for the term pattern matching problem that is based on match set derivatives where each function symbol in the subject pattern is visited exactly once. The algorithm allows for various traversal patterns over the subject term and is particularly suited to search the subject term in parallel.

Keywords: Pattern matching · Set automaton · Parallel algorithm

1 Introduction

Given a set of term patterns and a subject term, we are interested in the *subterm matching problem*, which is to find all locations in the subject term where a pattern matches. We restrict ourselves to linear patterns, that is, patterns in which no variable occurs more than once. In term rewriting the subterm matching problem corresponds to finding all redexes, given a left-linear rewrite system. Typically, the matching operation must be performed for many subject terms using the same pattern set, which makes it desirable that matching is efficient. The costs of preprocessing the pattern set is less important as it is only done once.

The subterm pattern matching problem should not be confused with the *root (pattern) matching problem*. In the latter, only the matches at a specific position in the subject term are needed. There are many solutions to the root matching problem that are designed to efficiently deal with sets of patterns [21]. Moreover these solutions have been compared in the practical setting of theorem proving [20]. A solution for the root matching problem can be applied to solve the subterm matching problem by applying it to every position in a subject term. But this solution can be expensive as many function symbols in the subject term will be inspected multiple times.

In contrast to the root matching problem, efficient solutions to the subterm matching problem are generally restricted to only a single pattern, and not to a set as is common in term rewriting. They do not use an automaton and

A. Cerone and P. C. Ölveczky (Eds.): ICTAC 2021, LNCS 12819, pp. 67–85, 2021.
https://doi.org/10.1007/978-3-030-85315-0_5

process both the pattern and the subject term, which is expensive if the matching problem needs to be solved for a huge number of subject terms. Existing solutions for pattern sets are reductions from stringpath matching, which requires the resulting stringpaths to be merged in order to yield a conclusive answer. The algorithm that we propose is a mixture of an automaton and the match set approach. It is explicitly formulated for an arbitrary number of patterns, operates directly on the subject term in a top-down fashion, and directly outputs pattern-position pairs instead of stringpath matches.

We present a solution using a so-called *set automaton*. In a set automaton intermediate results are stored in a set and these stored results can be processed independently using the same automaton. This is similar to a pushdown automaton where intermediate results are stored on a stack to be processed at a later moment. A set automaton allows for massive parallel processing. This is interesting given the prediction that the next boost in computing comes from developing algorithms that are more parallel in nature [19].

Given a pattern set $\mathcal{L}$, we construct a deterministic automaton that prescribes a traversal of subject terms t. The automaton is executed at some position p in t, initially at the root. In each state a next transition is chosen based on the function symbol f in t at a prescribed position, which is a sub-position of p. Every function symbol of t is only inspected once. Each transition is labelled with zero or more outputs of the form $\ell@p'$, announcing a match of pattern ℓ at some position p' in the subject term.

Each transition ends in a set of configurations (state/position pairs) that must be processed further. In case the resulting set always consists of one single configuration, the set automaton behaves as an ordinary deterministic automaton. The order in which the resulting configurations need to be processed is undetermined, hence the name *set* automaton. In a sequential implementation a stack or queue could be used to store these pairs giving depth-first or breadth-first strategies. But more interestingly, the new state/position pairs can be taken up by independent processors, exploring the subject term t in parallel. Note that also when running in parallel the algorithm adheres to its main asset, namely that every function symbol of t will only be inspected once.

The set automaton is generated by taking function symbol/position derivatives of match goal sets, similar to how Brzozowski derivatives work for regular expressions [2]. The derivatives are partitioned into independent classes, giving rise to the set of next states. By shifting the match goal sets back, the relative displacement through the subject term is derived allowing to calculate the position where the next state must be evaluated. This keeps the automaton finite.

The paper is organized as follows. After some preliminaries we informally discuss an example set automaton that matches associativity patterns in Sect. 3. Section 4 is dedicated to the set automaton construction. In Sects. 5 we show that the construction is a well-defined and terminating procedure, and in Sect. 6 we prove that the obtained set automaton is indeed a correct and efficient solution to the subterm matching problem. The details of the proofs can be found in [12]. In Sect. 7 we discuss the complexity of applying a set automaton and briefly discuss some preliminary experiments on the size of set automata. Lastly in Sect. 8 we share our thoughts on future work.

1.1 Related Work

Many solutions for the subterm pattern matching problem focus on the time complexity or benchmarking of matching *one* pattern against *one* subject term. See for example [4,8,10,24]. These methods are typically inefficient if there is a large pattern *set*, and the subject terms that need to be matched against the pattern set outnumber the subject term size and pattern size by orders of magnitude. Especially in model checking tools that use term rewriting to manipulate data [3,11], the pattern set size is usually a fixed parameter whereas the amount of terms that need to be rewritten blows up according to state space explosion. A better solution is to preprocess the pattern set into an automaton-like data structure. Even though the preprocessing step is usually expensive, the size of the pattern set does not appear as a parameter in the time complexity of the matching time, as opposed to applying aforementioned solutions for every pattern. This makes the subterm matching problem efficiently solvable against a vast number of subject terms. To our knowledge, our approach is the first top-down deterministic automata-based solution, that achieves this efficiency.

A literature study on related solutions is found in the taxonomy of [5,6]. Hoffmann and O'Donnell [18] convert a pattern into a set of stringpaths, after which they create an Aho-Corasick automaton [1] that accepts this set of string-paths. Cleophas, Hemerik and Zwaan report that this algorithm is closely related to their algorithm, which constructs a tree automaton from a single pattern [7]. In [5], Algorithm 6.7.9, there is a version of this algorithm that supports multiple patterns. The disadvantage of both approaches is that a subject term is scanned for matching stringpaths, rather than term pattern matches. In order to yield a conclusive answer to the term pattern matching problem, it is required to keep track which stringpaths match for every pattern, at every position in the subject term. Our set automata are built directly on the pattern set, which allows us to output pattern-position pairs directly and avoid the postprocessing step of merging stringpath matches.

Flouri et al. create a push-down automaton in [13] from a single pattern. This approach is very similar to the construction of our set automaton in the sense that match-sets are used in the automaton construction. Using such a push-down automaton requires a bottom-up evaluation, and takes linear time in the size of the subject term. Both traits are shared with Hoffman and O'Donnell's bottom-up algorithm [18].

Tree automata theory is a well-studied generalisation of string automata theory [9]. It is known that subterm matching can be done with a nondeterministic *bottom-up* tree automaton. Such automata can be made deterministic by means of a powerset construction. It is also well-known that subterm matching can be done with a nondeterministic *top-down* tree automaton, but using a determin-istic top-down automaton is not possible. Intuitively, top-down tree automata do not allow look-ahead. Upon taking an f-transition, all children of the f-node

continue in a exactly one new configuration, which causes problems when there
are overlapping patterns. Formally one can show that every deterministic top-
down tree automaton that accepts the trees $f(a,b)$ and $f(b,a)$, will also accept
$f(a,a)$ and $f(b,b)$. Set automata are constructed by encoding the look-ahead in
the states, and only descend the subject term when it is allowed.

The notation and the fact that set automaton states are labelled with positions, have much in common with Adaptive Pattern Matching Automata [23],
which form a solution to the root pattern matching problem.

2   Preliminaries

A signature is a sequence of disjoint, finite sets of function symbols $\mathbb{F}_0, \mathbb{F}_1, \ldots, \mathbb{F}_n$
where $\mathbb{F}_i$ consists of function symbols of arity i. We denote the arity of f by
$\#f$. The set of constants is $\mathbb{F}_0$, the entire signature is defined by $\mathbb{F} = \bigcup_{i=0}^{n} \mathbb{F}_i$
and the set of non-constants is denoted by $\mathbb{F}_{>0} = \bigcup_{i=1}^{n} \mathbb{F}_i$ Let $\mathbb{T}(\mathbb{F})$ be the
set of terms over $\mathbb{F}$, defined as the smallest set that contains the variable ω,
every constant, and for all $f \in \mathbb{F}_{>0}$, whenever $t_1, \ldots, t_{\#f} \in \mathbb{T}(\mathbb{F})$, then also
$f(t_1, \ldots, t_{\#f}) \in \mathbb{T}(\mathbb{F})$. The set of closed terms $\mathbb{T}_C(\mathbb{F})$ is defined similarly, but
without the clause $\omega \in \mathbb{T}_C(\mathbb{F})$. Since we only deal with linear patterns, that
is, patterns in which no variable occurs twice, it is unnecessary to distinguish
between the terms $f(x)$ and $f(y)$. Therefore we only use one variable ω.

A pattern over the signature $\mathbb{F}$ is a term in $\mathbb{T}(\mathbb{F}) \backslash \{\omega\}$. We use ℓ to range
over patterns. A pattern is typically the 'left-hand side' of a rewrite rule. Given
a pattern $\ell = f(t_1, \ldots, t_n)$, its head symbol is given by $\mathsf{hd}(\ell) = f$. A pattern set
is a finite, non-empty set of patterns. We use $\mathcal{L}$ to denote pattern sets.

A position is a list of non-zero natural numbers. We use $\mathbb{P}$ to denote the set
of all positions and we use ϵ to denote the empty list; it is referred to as the
root position. Given two positions p, q their concatenation is denoted by $p.q$. The
root position acts as a unit with respect to concatenation.

To alleviate the notation, we often denote a pair (x, p) in some set $X \times \mathbb{P}$ by
$x@p$ so that the pair may be read as 'x at position p'. The term domain function
$\mathcal{D} : \mathbb{T}(\mathbb{F}) \rightarrow \mathcal{P}(\mathbb{P})$ maps a term to a set of positions. That is, $\mathcal{D}(\omega) = \{\epsilon\}$,
for all $a \in \mathbb{F}_0$ we have $\mathcal{D}(a) = \{\epsilon\}$, and for all $f \in \mathbb{F}_n$ with $n > 0$ we have
$\mathcal{D}(f(t_1, \ldots, t_n)) = \{\epsilon\} \cup \bigcup_{i \leq n} \{i.p \mid p \in \mathcal{D}(t_i)\}$.

Given a term t and a position $p \in \mathcal{D}(t)$, the subterm of t at position p is
denoted by $t[p]$. A pattern ℓ matches term t on position p iff for all $p' \in \mathcal{D}(\ell)$
such that $\ell[p'] \neq \omega$ we have that $\mathsf{hd}(t[p.p']) = \mathsf{hd}(\ell[p'])$.

Let $\mathsf{sub}(t)$ be the subpatterns of t, given by $\{t[p] \mid p \in \mathcal{D}(t) \text{ and } t[p] \neq \omega\}$.
Since ω is not a pattern, it is excluded from this set on purpose. We extend $\mathcal{D}$
and sub to sets of terms by pointwise union. That is, $\mathcal{D}(\mathcal{L}) = \bigcup_{\ell \in \mathcal{L}} \mathcal{D}(\ell)$, and
similarly for sub.

3   An Example Set Automaton

In this section we informally discuss the example set automaton in Fig. 1. It
can be used to solve the term matching problem for the associativity patterns

$\ell_1 = f(f(\omega, \omega), \omega)$ and $\ell_2 = f(\omega, f(\omega, \omega))$. We work in a setting with one binary function symbol f and one constant a.

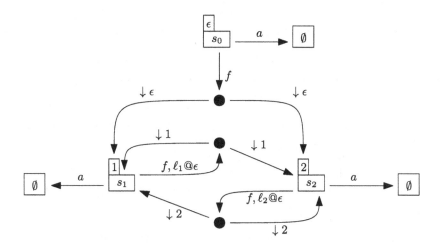

Fig. 1. A set automaton for the associativity patterns.

We explain this automaton by applying it to the term $t = f(f(a, f(a, a)), a)$. The evaluation is done in a top-down fashion. That is, in order to inspect position $p.i$ we need to have inspected position p before. A *configuration* is a state paired with a position. We start at (s_0, ϵ), the initial state paired with the root position. The automaton tells us which position in t to inspect, which pattern matches are given as an output at which positions, and it tells at which configurations the evaluation of the automaton must be continued.

The initial state s_0 is labelled with the root position in the box on top of it. This means that we have to inspect the function symbol in t at position ϵ relative to the position p of the configuration. Since $p = \epsilon$ for the initial configuration, we inspect the head symbol at $t[\epsilon.\epsilon]$ which is f. There are two f-transitions from state s_0 in the automaton, which have been depicted graphically as an f-labelled arrow, going to a black dot with two outgoing arrows. If a match is found, the transition is labelled with $\ell@p'$ to indicate that pattern ℓ matches at position p' relative to the position p. In this case, no such label is present on the f-labelled transition. Therefore no pattern match is reported. Furthermore, the arrows from the black dots are labelled with a relative displacement p'' indicating that the new configuration must have the position $p.p''$. In this case, the displacement annotation $\downarrow \epsilon$ prescribes that we continue the evaluation at position $\epsilon.\epsilon$. The two transitions for f go to states s_1 and s_2 indicating that both states must be evaluated independently, resulting in the configurations (s_1, ϵ) and (s_2, ϵ). This can be done in parallel, but for simplicity we do a sequential traversal and continue in state s_1.

We are in configuration (s_1, ϵ). The state label of s_1 is 1, so we look at position $\epsilon.1$. In term $t = f(f(a, f(a, a)), a)$ we observe $\mathsf{hd}(t[\epsilon.1]) = f$, so we take *both* f-transitions from s_1. The arrow labelled by f, is accompanied by the label $\ell_1@\epsilon$. This means that we announce a match for pattern ℓ_1 at position ϵ relative to the configuration position. Since that position is still ϵ, we announce that ℓ_1 matches t at position ϵ. From the black dot there are two outgoing arrows with the label $\downarrow 1$. This means that we continue in configurations $(s_1, \epsilon.1)$ and $(s_2, \epsilon.1)$.

Continuing the evaluation in configuration $(s_2, 1)$, we find the state label 2 on top. So, we inspect t at position 2 relative to position 1 and find that $\mathsf{hd}(t[1.2]) = f$. We again follow both outgoing f-transitions. First we announce a match for pattern ℓ_2 at position ϵ relative to position 1, so we get that t matches ℓ_2 at position 1. Following the arrows from the bottom black dot, we continue in configurations $(s_1, 1.2)$ and $(s_2, 1.2)$.

Now the configurations (s_2, ϵ), $(s_1, 1)$, $(s_1, 1.2)$ and $(s_2, 1.2)$ still remain. Inspecting t at each position $p.L(s)$ where p is the configuration position and $L(s)$ is the state label, we find the constant a. Following any a-transition, the evaluation ends up in the final state, denoted by $\emptyset$, which means that no new configurations must be added for evaluation.

The algorithm provides the following answer to the question "at which positions do the patterns $\ell_1 = f(f(\omega, \omega), \omega)$ and $\ell_2 = f(\omega, f(\omega, \omega))$ match the term $t = f(f(a, f(a, a)), a)$?". The pattern ℓ_1 matches t at the root position and ℓ_2 matches t at position 1. Observe that the algorithm inspected every position of t exactly once. The construction of the automaton guarantees this efficiency, even though at every inspection occurrence of a symbol f two independent evaluations of the automaton were started.

4   Automaton Construction

We describe how to create a set automaton based on *position-/function symbol derivatives*. To this end we first formally define the automaton, and in particular, what kind of information should be encoded by states.

The sets of *match obligations MO* and *match announcements MA* are respectively defined by

$$MO = \mathcal{P}(\mathsf{sub}(\mathcal{L}) \times \mathbb{P}) \backslash \{\emptyset\} \quad MA = \mathcal{L} \times \mathbb{P}.$$

A *match goal* is a match obligation paired with a match announcement. To limit the amount of parentheses, we often denote a match goal, i.e. a pair in $MO \times MA$, by $\ell_1@p_1, \ldots, \ell_n@p_n \to \ell@p$. Such a match goal should be read as: "in order to announce a match for pattern ℓ at position p, we are obliged to observe the (sub)pattern ℓ_i on position p_i, for all $1 \leq i \leq n$". We denote the positions of a match obligation *mo* by $\mathsf{pos}(mo)$, defined by $\mathsf{pos}(mo) = \{p \in \mathbb{P} \mid (t, p) \in mo\}$.

A set automaton for the pattern set $\mathcal{L}$ is a tuple $(S, s_0, L, \delta, \eta)$ where

- $S \subseteq \mathcal{P}(MO \times MA) \backslash \{\emptyset\}$ is a finite set of states;
- $s_0 \in S$ is the initial state;
- $L : S \to \mathbb{P}$ is a state labelling function;

- $\delta : S \times \mathbb{F} \to \mathcal{P}(S \times \mathbb{P})$ is a transition function;
- $\eta : S \times \mathbb{F} \to \mathcal{P}(\mathcal{L} \times \mathbb{P})$ is an output function.

The empty set serves as a final state, but it has no outgoing transitions and no output. Furthermore, a match goal of the form $\ell@p \to \ell@p$ is called *fresh*, and a match goal of the form $mo \to \ell@\epsilon$ is called a *root goal*.

Example 1. Consider the pattern $\ell = f(f(\omega, g(\omega)), g(\omega))$. Figure 2 is a set automaton for the singleton pattern set $\{\ell\}$. It serves as a running example throughout this section and the next. The state labels are given in the small boxes on the top left of every state, and on the top right of every state there is an identifier. We have $L(s_0) = \epsilon$ and $L(s_3) = 1.2$. Formally we have $\delta(s_3, f) = \{(s_0, 1.1), (s_1, 1.2)\}$, which is depicted graphically as an f-labelled arrow going to the black dot, with two outgoing position-labelled arrows to s_0 and s_2. The only non-empty output set is $\eta(s_3, g) = \{\ell@\epsilon\}$. For all other state/symbol pairs (s, h) we have $\eta(s, h) = \emptyset$. The final state $\emptyset$ has two incoming transitions. For graphical purposes it is displayed twice.

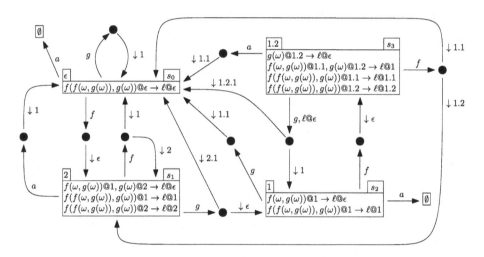

Fig. 2. A set automaton for $\ell = f(f(\omega, g(\omega)), g(\omega))$.

4.1 Initial State

Let $\mathcal{L}$ be a pattern set. We construct the automaton $M = (S, s_0, L, \delta, \eta)$ by starting with the initial state. It is labelled with the root position and its match goals are all possible fresh root goals:

$$s_0 = \{\ell@\epsilon \to \ell@\epsilon \mid \ell \in \mathcal{L}\} \quad \text{and} \quad L(s_0) = \epsilon.$$

4.2 Function-Symbol-Position Derivatives

To define the transition relation, we introduce function-symbol-position derivatives. This terminology is borrowed from Brzozowski derivatives of regular expressions [2]. From a state s with $L(s) = p$, and a symbol f, we determine the f-p-derivative of s by computing the reduced match obligations of s and adding the fresh match goal $\ell@p.i \to \ell@p.i$ for every argument i of f and every pattern $\ell \in \mathcal{L}$. Based on observing function symbol f at position p, the match obligation $\ell_1@p_1, \ldots, \ell_n@p_n$ can be altered in one of four ways.

- $p = p_1$, $n = 1$ and $\ell_1 = f(\omega, \ldots, \omega)$. Then $f@p$ is the last observation that was needed, so the obligation is fulfilled. The match announcement paired with this obligation is presented as a pattern match.
- $p = p_i$ for some i and $\mathsf{hd}(\ell_i) \neq f$. Then $f@p$ contradicts with an expected observation, so the match obligation is discarded.
- $p \neq p_i$ for all i. Then $f@p$ is unrelated, so the obligation remains unchanged by this observation.
- otherwise $p = p_i$ for some i and $\mathsf{hd}(\ell_i) = f$, but $f@p$ is only one of the many expected observations. Then $\ell_i@p_i$ is removed and the arguments of ℓ_i are added as new match obligations.

Formally, the mapping $\mathsf{reduce} : MO \times \mathbb{F} \times \mathbb{P} \to MO \cup \{\emptyset\}$ alters the match obligation mo after the observation $f@p$ by

$$\mathsf{reduce}(mo, f, p) = \{\ell@q \in mo \mid q \neq p\} \cup$$
$$\{\ell[i]@p.i \mid \ell@p \in mo \wedge 1 \leq i \leq \#f \wedge \ell[i] \neq \omega\}.$$

Using the mapping reduce, we can define the f-derivative of state s by

$$\mathsf{deriv}(s, f) = unchanged \cup reduced \cup fresh, \text{ where}$$
$$unchanged = \{mo \to ma \in s \mid L(s) \notin \mathsf{pos}(mo)\}$$
$$reduced = \{\mathsf{reduce}(mo, f, L(s)) \to ma \mid mo \to ma \in s \wedge$$
$$\exists \ell[\ell@L(s) \in mo \wedge \mathsf{hd}(\ell) = f] \wedge \mathsf{reduce}(mo, f, L(s)) \neq \emptyset\}$$
$$fresh = \{\ell@L(s).i \to \ell@L(s).i \mid \ell \in \mathcal{L} \wedge 1 \leq i \leq \#f\}$$

Example 2. Recall the pattern $\ell = f(f(\omega, g(\omega)), g(\omega))$ and the set automaton in Fig. 2. Consider state s_1. The parts of $\mathsf{deriv}(s_1, g)$ are computed as follows:

$$unchanged = \{f(f(\omega, g(\omega)), g(\omega))@1 \to \ell@1\}$$
$$reduced = \{f(\omega, g(\omega))@1 \to \ell@\epsilon\}$$
$$fresh = \{f(f(\omega, g(\omega)), g(\omega))@2.1 \to \ell@2.1\}.$$

Note that the goal $f(f(\omega, g(\omega)), g(\omega))@2 \to \ell@2$ disappears completely since there is a mismatch with the expected symbol g at position 2.

4.3   Derivative Partitioning

One application of deriv creates new match obligations with strictly lower positions. Repeated application of deriv therefore results in an automaton with an infinite amount of states. To solve this problem we take two more steps after computing the derivative. First, we partition the derivative into independent equivalence classes. Then, in every equivalence class, we lower the positions of all match goals as much as possible. These two measures suffice to create a finite set automaton.

Note from Example 2 that the derivative has two match obligations at position 1, and one match obligation at position 2.1. To obtain an efficient matching algorithm, it is important that goals with overlapping positions stay together to obtain an efficient matching algorithm. Conversely, sets of goals that are independent from each other can be separated to form a new state with fewer match goals. When evaluating a set automaton this creates the possibility of exploring parts of the subject term independently.

Given a finite subset of match obligations $X \subseteq MO$, define the *direct dependency relation* R on X for all $mo_1, mo_2 \in X$ by $mo_1 \ R \ mo_2$, iff $\mathsf{pos}(mo_1) \cap \mathsf{pos}(mo_2) \neq \emptyset$. Note that R is reflexive (since MO excludes the empty set) and symmetric. But R is not transitive, since for the obligations

$$mo_1 = \{t_1@1\} \quad mo_2 = \{t_1@1, t_2@2\} \quad mo_3 = \{t_2@2\}$$

we have $mo_1 \ R \ mo_2 \ R \ mo_3$, but not $mo_1 \ R \ mo_3$. Denote the *dependency relation* on X by $\sim_X$, defined as the transitive closure of R. Two match obligations are said to be *dependent* iff $mo_1 \sim_X mo_2$. We extend $\sim_X$ to match goals by $(mo_1 \to ma_1) \sim_X (mo_2 \to ma_2)$ iff $mo_1 \sim_X mo_2$. The subscript X is mostly omitted if the set is clear from the context, but note that it is necessary to define this relation separately on every state. Defining it on the set of all match obligations will simply result in the full relation $MO \times MO$.

To determine the outgoing transitions we partition $\mathsf{deriv}(s, f)$ into equivalence classes with respect to dependency $\sim$ on the match obligations. Each equivalence class then corresponds to a new state. The set of equivalence classes of the derivative is denoted by $[\mathsf{deriv}(s, f)]_\sim$. We use the letter K to range over equivalence classes.

Example 3. Consider the g-derivative of Example 2. Partitioning yields

$$K_1 = \{f(f(\omega, g(\omega)), g(\omega))@1 \to \ell@1 f(\omega, g(\omega))@1 \to \ell@\epsilon\}$$
$$K_2 = \{f(f(\omega, g(\omega)), g(\omega))@2.1 \to \ell@2.1\}$$

Example 4. Consider the f-derivative of s_2, which is exactly s_3. Note that the goals $g(\omega)@1.2 \to \ell@\epsilon$ and $f(f(\omega, g(\omega)), g(\omega))@1.1 \to \ell@1.1$ are not directly dependent, but the goal $f(\omega, g(\omega))@1.1, g(\omega)@1.2 \to \ell@1$ is directly dependent to both goals. Therefore we obtain a singleton partition.

4.4   Lifting the Positions of Classes

Partitioning into smaller states is not enough to obtain a finite state machine since the positions of match goals are increasing. As the last part of the construction, we shorten the positions of every equivalence class. This can be done due to the following observation. Suppose that we are looking at term t on position ϵ. If all match goals say something about position 1 or lower, we can remove the prefix 1 everywhere, and start to look at term t from position 1. Inspecting position $1.p$ from the root is the same as inspecting p from position 1.

Let $\mathsf{pos}_{MA}(K)$ denote the positions of the match announcements of K. We want to 'lift' every position in every goal of K by the greatest common prefix of $\mathsf{pos}_{MA}(K)$, which we denote by $\mathsf{gcp}(\mathsf{pos}_{MA}(K))$. To ease the notation we write $\mathsf{gcp}(K)$ instead of $\mathsf{gcp}(\mathsf{pos}_{MA}(K))$. Since all positions in a state are of the form $\mathsf{gcp}(K).p'$, we can replace them by p'. Define $\mathsf{lift}(s)$ by $\mathsf{lift}(s) = \{(\mathsf{lift}(mo), \ell@p') \mid (mo, \ell@\mathsf{gcp}(s).p') \in s\}$ where $\mathsf{lift}(mo) = \{\ell@p' \mid \ell@\mathsf{gcp}(s).p' \in mo\}$.

This concludes the construction of the transition relation. For a state s and a function symbol f, we fix $\delta(s, f) = \{(\mathsf{lift}(K), \mathsf{gcp}(K)) \mid K \in [\mathsf{deriv}(s, f)]_\sim\}$. Note that $\mathsf{gcp}(K)$ is also recorded in each transition since it tells us how to traverse the term.

Example 5. Continuing in Example 3, we compute the greatest common prefix and corresponding transition for the two equivalence classes. For K_1 we have $\mathsf{gcp}(K_1) = \mathsf{gcp}(\{1, \epsilon\}) = \epsilon$. Then $\mathsf{lift}(K_1) = K_1 = s_2$, and therefore $(s_2, \epsilon) \in \delta(s_1, g)$. Class K_2 has one goal with $\mathsf{gcp}(K_2) = \mathsf{gcp}(\{2.1\}) = 2.1$. Then $\mathsf{lift}(K_2) = \{f(f(\omega, g(\omega)), g(\omega))@\epsilon \to \ell@\epsilon\}$, which yields the transition $(s_0, 2.1) \in \delta(s_1, g)$.

4.5   Output Patterns

The output patterns after an f-transition are simply the match announcements that accompany the match obligations that reduce to $\emptyset$:

$$\eta(s, f) = \{ma \in MA \mid f(\omega, \ldots, \omega)@L(s) \to ma \in s\}.$$

Example 6. Consider state s_3 in Fig. 2. The goal $g(\omega)@1.2 \to \ell@\epsilon$ can be completed upon observing g at position 1.2, so we fix $\eta(s_3, g) = \{\ell@\epsilon\}$.

4.6   Position Labels

For every state s there must be a position label $L(s)$ in order to construct the transitions from s. It makes sense to only choose a position from one of the match obligations. We demand the extra constraint that this position should be part of a root match goal. The construction guarantees that every state has a root goal, which we prove in detail in the next section. Similar to Adaptive Pattern Matching Automata [23], there might be multiple positions available to choose from. Any of such positions can be chosen in the construction of the automaton, but this position needs to be fixed when s is created.

4.7   Summary

The following is a summary of the construction of a set automaton.

- $s_0 = \{\ell@\epsilon \rightarrow \ell@\epsilon \mid \ell \in \mathcal{L}\}$;
- $\delta(s, f) = \{(\mathsf{lift}(K), \mathsf{gcp}(K)) \mid K \in [\mathsf{deriv}(s.f)]_\sim\}$;
- $\eta(s, f) = \{ma \in MA \mid f(\omega, \ldots, \omega)@L(s) \rightarrow ma \in s\}$; and
- $L(s)$ can be any $p \in \mathsf{pos}(mo)$ for some root match goal $mo \rightarrow \ell@\epsilon \in s$.

5   Validity of the Construction

In order to see that the construction algorithm of the set automaton works we need to know whether the following two properties hold. Firstly, it is necessary that $L(s)$ is a position in the match obligation of some root goal, but it is not immediately clear that every state has a root goal. Secondly, the algorithm needs to terminate. In this section we show that these properties are valid.

First we need some extra preliminaries. In the previous section we used $\mathsf{gcp}(P)$ to denote the greatest common prefix in a set of positions. This is a lattice construct that requires more elaboration to do proofs.

Definition 1 (Position join-semilattice). *Position p is said to be below position q, denoted by $p \leq q$, iff there is a position q' such that $p = q.q'$. Position p is strictly below q, denoted by $p < q$, if in addition $q' \neq \epsilon$. This definition makes the structure $(\mathbb{P}, \leq)$ a join-semilattice. That is, $\leq$ is reflexive, transitive and antisymmetric, and for each finite, non-empty set of positions P there is a unique join $\bigvee P$, which satisfies $p \leq \bigvee P$ for all $p \in P$ and whenever $p \leq r$ for all $p \in P$ then also $\bigvee P \leq r$. We call this join the greatest common prefix $\mathsf{gcp}(P)$. We denote the join of two positions p and q by $p \vee q$. Two positions p, q are comparable if $p \leq q$ or $q \leq p$.*

Proposition 1. *The following properties hold for (sets of) positions.*

- *For all $p, q, r \in \mathbb{P}$ we have $p.q \leq p.r \Leftrightarrow q \leq r$;*
- *For all $p \in \mathbb{P}$, for all $i \in \mathbb{N}^+$ we have $p \not\leq p.i$;*
- *For all $p, q, r \in \mathbb{P}$, if $p \leq q$ and $p \leq r$ then q and r are comparable;*
- *For all $p, q \in \mathbb{P}$, if p and q are comparable then $p \vee q = p$ or $p \vee q = q$; and*
- *For all finite $P, Q \subseteq \mathbb{P}$ we have $\mathsf{gcp}(P \cup Q) = \mathsf{gcp}(P) \vee \mathsf{gcp}(Q)$.*

Lastly, consider the straightforward notion of reachable state. A state s is reachable if there is a sequence of transitions to it from s_0. That is, s_0 is reachable and whenever s is reachable and $(s', p) \in \delta(s, f)$, then s' is also reachable. The following claims are useful in many places of the correctness proof.

Proposition 2. *Let s be a reachable state.*

- *For all goals $\ell_1@p_1, \ldots, \ell_n@p_n \rightarrow \ell@p$ in s we have that $p_i \leq p$ for all i.*
- *For all distinct $p, q \in \mathsf{pos}_{MO}(s)$ the positions p and q are incomparable.*

– *For all distinct $p, q \in \text{pos}_{MO}(\text{deriv}(s, f))$ the positions p and q are incomparable.*

First, we show that every reachable state always has an available root goal. By definition of the transition function, the positions of all match goals in a class K get shortened by $\text{gcp}(K)$ after partitioning. The partitioning allows us to show that $\text{gcp}(K)$ is always in $\text{pos}_{MA}(K)$.

Lemma 1. *Let s be a reachable state. Then for all $f \in \mathbb{F}$, if $K \in [\text{deriv}(s, f)]_{\sim}$ then there is a goal $mo \to \ell@\text{gcp}(K)$ in K.*

Proof (Sketch). By induction on the size of K. The base case is trivial, and if $|K| \geq 2$ then K can be split into two non-empty classes with a dependency between them. By using Propositions 1 and 2, and the induction hypothesis we can show that one of the two smaller classes has a goal of the right form. □

Corollary 1. *Every reachable state has a root goal.*

Next, we show that the construction terminates. There are two key observations to termination. Firstly, the lift operation always shortens the positions of derivative partitions with respect to $\leq$. Secondly, every state label is a match obligation position of some root goal in that state. This allows us to prove that reachable states can only have match positions in some finite set.

Lemma 2. *Let N be the largest arity of any function symbol in $\mathbb{F}$, and define the set of reachable positions by $\mathcal{R} = \{p \in \mathbb{P} \mid \exists q, r, i : q \in \mathcal{D}(\mathcal{L}) \wedge r \in \mathbb{P} \wedge 1 \leq i \leq N \wedge r.p = q.i\}$. Then for all reachable states s we have that $\text{pos}_{MO}(s) \subseteq \mathcal{R}$.*

Intuitively, since there are only finitely many state labels, the longest position in any match obligation is of the form $L(s).i$ where i is bounded by N.

Corollary 2. *There are finitely many reachable states.*

6   Correctness of the Evaluation

The informal evaluation that was discussed in Sect. 3 describes how to apply an automaton M to a subject term. Formally this procedure can be defined by the mapping $\text{eval}_M : S \times \mathbb{P} \times \mathbb{T}(\mathbb{F}) \to \mathcal{P}(\mathcal{L} \times \mathbb{P})$ given by

$$\text{eval}_M(s, p, t) = \{\ell@p.q \mid \ell@q \in \eta(s, f)\} \cup \bigcup_{(s', p') \in \delta(s, f)} \text{eval}(s', p.p', t)$$

where $f = \text{hd}(t[p.L(s)])$. Finding all pattern matches in a term t is the invocation of $\text{eval}_M(s_0, \epsilon, t)$. The desired correctness property can then be stated as follows:

$$\text{eval}_M(s_0, \epsilon, t) = \{\ell@p \in \mathcal{L} \times \mathbb{P} \mid \ell \text{ matches } t \text{ at } p\}.$$

This property cannot be shown by a straightforward structural induction on t. The set automaton does not necessarily allow every top-down traversal, as opposed to tree automata. In this section we take a detour and prove an equivalent correctness claim. The proof is sketched as follows. First, we add explicit structure to the evaluation by computing an evaluation tree $ET_M(t)$ of a term t. We prove a one-to-one correspondence between the nodes of $ET_M(t)$ and t. It follows that this method of pattern matching is efficient in the sense that every position of t is inspected exactly once. Soundness and completeness are shown at the end of the section.

6.1   Evaluation Trees

Definition 2. *An* evaluation tree *for an automaton* $M = (S, s_0, L, \delta, \eta)$ *is a tuple* $(N, \rightarrow)$ *where* $N \subseteq S \times \mathbb{P}$ *is a set of nodes, and* $\rightarrow \subseteq N \times N$ *is a set of directed edges. With a closed term* t *we associate an evaluation tree* $ET_M(t) = (N, \rightarrow)$ *defined as the smallest evaluation tree such that*

- *there is a root* $(s_0, \epsilon) \in N$; *and*
- *whenever* $(s, p) \in N$ *and* $\mathsf{hd}(t[p.L(s)]) = f$ *then for every* $(s', p') \in \delta(s, f)$ *there is an edge* $(s, p) \rightarrow (s', p.p')$ *with* $(s', p') \in N$.

The successors of a node n *are given by* $Suc(n) = \{n' \in N \mid n \rightarrow n'\}$.

Example 7. Figure 3 shows the term $t = f(g(a), f(f(a, g(a)), g(a)))$ and its evaluation tree $ET_M(t)$, given the set automaton M of Fig. 2. There is a one-to-one correspondence between the positions of t and the nodes of the evaluation tree.

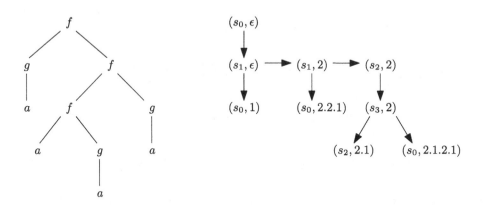

Fig. 3. The term $t = f(g(a), f(f(a, g(a)), g(a)))$ on the left and its evaluation tree $ET_M(t)$ on the right.

We prove that $ET_M(t)$ indeed corresponds to t in general. To this end, we define for every node the set of positions that still has to be inspected. That is, the set of work that still has to be done.

Definition 3. *Define the mapping $W : N \to \mathcal{P}(\mathcal{D}(t))$ by*

$$W(s,p) = \{p.q \in \mathcal{D}(t) \mid \exists r : r \in pos_{MO}(s) \wedge q \leq r\}.$$

By definition of s_0 we have $W(s_0, \epsilon) = \mathcal{D}(t)$. Intuitively this makes sense, since at the beginning of the evaluation, no work is done and all the positions still have to be inspected. The mapping W fixes a correspondence between an evaluation tree and $\mathcal{D}(t)$. This follows from the following lemma.

Lemma 3. *Let $ET_M(t) = (N, \to)$ and consider an arbitrary node $(s, p) \in N$.*

1. *For all successors $(s', p.p') \in Suc(s,p)$ we have that $p.L(s) \notin W(s', p.p')$.*
2. *For all distinct successors $(s_1, p.p_1), (s_2, p.p_2) \in Suc(s,p)$ we have that the sets $W(s_1, p.p_1)$ and $W(s_2, p.p_2)$ are disjoint.*
3. *We have that $W(s,p) = \{p.L(s)\} \cup \bigcup_{n \in Suc(s,p)} W(n)$.*

By combining these properties, we get the following two corollaries.

Corollary 3. *For all terms t, we have that $ET_M(t) = (N, \to)$ is a finite tree.*

Corollary 4. *Define $\varphi : N \to \mathcal{D}(t)$ by $\varphi(s,p) = p.L(s)$. Then φ is a bijection.*

It follows that the evaluation of a term terminates, and every position is inspected exactly once. Whenever an evaluation tree node has multiple outgoing edges, it means that parallellism is possible. This parallellism preserves the efficiency of no observation being made twice.

6.2   Soundness and Completeness

First, consider the following evaluation function that takes an evaluation tree node and traverses it until a leaf node is reached.

Definition 4. *Given $ET_M(t) = (N, \to)$, define $\mathsf{eval}_M : N \to \mathcal{P}(\mathcal{L} \times \mathbb{P})$ by*

$$\mathsf{eval}_M(s,p) = \{\ell@p.q \mid \ell@q \in \eta(s, \mathsf{hd}(t[p.L(s)]))\} \cup \bigcup_{(s',p.p') \in Suc(s,p)} \mathsf{eval}_M(s', p.p').$$

By Corollary 4, applying eval on the initial state from the root position is the same as retrieving the output at every level of the evaluation tree.

$$\mathsf{eval}_M(s_0, \epsilon) = \bigcup_{(s,p) \in N} \{\ell@p.q \mid \ell@q \in \eta(s, \mathsf{hd}(t[p.L(s)]))\}. \tag{1}$$

In Theorem 1 we show that $\mathsf{eval}_M(s_0, \epsilon)$ yields exactly all pattern matches of a closed term. This correctness theorem consists of two claims. The soundness claim is that whenever the evaluation yields an output, then it is indeed a correct match. The completeness claim is that whenever some pattern matches at some position, then the evaluation will output it at some point.

To understand soundness, consider that match goals carry history. Intuitively, a match goal $a@1, b@2 \to f(a,b)@\epsilon$ has a history of having seen f already. A state with this goal can only be reached by evaluating a term with symbol f. This notion can be formalised as follows.

Definition 5. *The history of an evaluation tree node (s, p) respects t iff for all goals $mo \to \ell@q \in s$, for all $r \in \mathcal{D}(\ell)$ such that $\ell[r] \neq \omega$, if there is some $r' \in pos(mo)$ with $r \not\leq r'$ then $hd(t[p.r]) = hd(\ell[r])$.*

With this definition, the following invariant is the key to soundness.

Lemma 4. *Let $ET_M(t) = (N, \to)$. The history of every node (s, p) respects t.*

To understand completeness, observe that upon taking derivatives a fresh match obligation is added for every new position. The partitioning then takes care of grouping the fresh goals with other goals that have the same positions.

Proposition 3. *Whenever a state has a match obligation on position p, then it has the fresh match goal $\ell@p \to \ell@p$ for all $\ell \in \mathcal{L}$ as well.*

The following invariant connects to Proposition 3. Intuitively, if a term matches pattern ℓ at position $p.q$, and the evaluation tree reaches a state with some goal $mo \to \ell@q$ is a match announcement, then this announcement belongs to some goal in some state visited by eval, until it is given as an output.

Lemma 5. *If ℓ matches t at $p.q$ and there is a node (s, p) and a match goal $mo \to \ell@q \in s$ then either $\ell@q \in \eta(s, hd(t[p.L(s)]))$ or there is a node $(s', p.p') \in Suc(s, p)$ such that s' has some goal $mo' \to \ell@q'$ with $q = p'.q'$.*

Theorem 1 (Correctness). *For all closed terms t,*

$$eval_M(s_0, \epsilon) = \{\ell@p \in \mathcal{L} \times \mathcal{D}(t) \mid \ell \text{ matches } t \text{ at } p\}.$$

Proof. As mentioned before, we show soundness and completeness.

$\subseteq$ By Eq. 1 it suffices to show that for all nodes (s, p), whenever $\ell@q \in \eta(s, hd(t[p.L(s)]))$ then ℓ matches t at $p.q$. Consider that $hd(t[p.L(s)]) = f$. By definition of η, see Sect. 4.5, we have $f(\omega, \ldots, \omega)@L(s) \to \ell@q \in s$. By Lemma 4, the history of node (s, p) respects t. Then for all positions $r \in \mathcal{D}(\ell)$ with $\ell[r] \neq \omega$ and $r \neq L(s)$ we have that $hd(t[p.r]) = hd(\ell[r])$. From the additional observation $hd(\ell[L(s)]) = f = hd(t[p.L(s)])$ and Proposition 2 it follows that ℓ matches t at $p.q$.

$\supseteq$ Consider that ℓ matches t at p. By Corollary 4, consider the node $\varphi^{-1}(p) = (s, q)$. By definition of φ we have $q.L(s) = p$. Since $L(s) \in pos_{MO}(s)$, the fresh goal $\ell@L(s) \to \ell@L(s)$ is s by Proposition 3. Then the repeated application of Lemma 5 yields a node $(s', q.q')$ such that s' has some goal $mo' \to \ell@r$ with $L(s) = q'.r$ and $\ell@r \in \eta(s', hd(t[q.q'.L(s')]))$. Then $\ell@q.q'.r \in eval(s', q.q')$ by definition of eval. Since $q.q'.r = q.L(s) = p$ it follows that $\ell@p \in eval(s', q.q')$. By Eq. 1 we conclude $\ell@p \in eval(s_0, \epsilon)$. $\qquad\square$

7   Complexity and Automaton Size

Given an automaton M of pattern set $\mathcal{L}$, the matching algorithm $\mathsf{eval}_M(s_0, t)$ runs in $O(d(n + m))$ time where n is the number of function symbols in t, and m is the amount of pattern matches in t, and d is the maximal depth of any pattern in $\mathcal{L}$. The factor d is due to the fact that observing a function symbol on position $L(s)$ takes $|L(s)|$ time in general.

The size of a set automaton is exponential in the worst case, which is not surprising due to similar observations concerning the root pattern matching problem. Gräf observed that a left-to-right pattern matching automaton is exponentially large in the worst case [15]. Sekar et al. observed that adaptive pattern matching automata are exponentially big in the worst case as well, although a good traversal can reduce the automaton size exponentially in some cases [23].

A deterministic bottom-up finite tree automaton can be constructed for a pattern set that recognises whether *there is* a pattern match in a term. Such an automaton can have 2^{n-1} states, where n is the total amount of function symbols in the pattern set [9, Exercise 1.1.10].

However, practical experiments with pattern sets show that the set automaton size is small, which is in line with other forms of automata-based matching. We generated set automata to match the left hand sides of rewrite systems used in mCRL2 [16, Appendix B], see Table 1. In almost all cases the amount of states in the set automaton does not exceed the number of patterns.

Table 1. The set automaton sizes for parts of the default mCRL2 specification.

Specification	Signature size	Amount of patterns	Amount of states
int	22	50	27
pos	15	46	45
nat	37	91	117
fset	15	28	23
set	20	40	24
list	16	26	24
bool	9	27	14
bag	29	44	32
fbag	18	30	25
real	30	31	31

The degree of freedom in the choice of state labels strongly influences the set automaton size. Consider for example the set of terms $\{t_n\}_{n \in \mathbb{N}}$ given by $t_0 = \omega$ and $t_{n+1} = f(t_n, g(\omega))$. The set automaton in Example 1 is generated for pattern set $\{t_2\}$. We found that the choice of state labels influences the automaton size by a quadratic factor. By choosing the right-most available position one obtains an automaton of size $2n$ for the pattern set $\{t_n\}$. A left-most strategy yields an automaton of size $n^2 + n$ for $\{t_n\}$.

8   Future Work

The original motivation for this work is to construct a high performance term rewriter suited for parallel processing, which can both work on a single large term as well as on many small terms, repeatedly. This means that the matching effort must be minimal, which is provided by the automaton, and it also requires that the subject term is not transformed before matching commences. To enable term rewriting, our matching algorithm must still be extended with term rewriting along lines set out in [17]. We want to employ the knowledge that we have about the structure of the right-hand side of a rewrite rule, minimizing inspecting known parts of a newly constructed term. Fokkink et al. have a similar approach in [14], based on Hoffmann and O'Donnell's algorithm from [18].

Our algorithm has freedom in the position of the function symbol to be selected, as well as in the next state/position pair that the evaluator chooses. It is interesting to see whether with knowledge about the distribution of function symbols in subject terms, this freedom can be exploited to construct a most efficient set automaton. For instance, we may want to generate the first match as quickly as possible. This is particularly interesting in combination with rewriting where some sub-terms do not have to be inspected as they will be removed by the rewriting rules.

Observe that the algorithm as it stands does not employ non-linear patterns in line with matching algorithms such as [22]. But in term rewriting non-linear patterns do occur and therefore an extension to support them is desired. An extension that provides all matches in a setting where some symbols are known to be associative and/or commutative would also be interesting.

Acknowledgement. We would like to thank Bas Luttik for discussion, and the anonymous referees, whose comments led to improvements of this paper.

References

1. Aho, A.V., Corasick, M.J.: Efficient string matching: an aid to bibliographic search. Commun. ACM **18**(6), 333–340 (1975). https://doi.org/10.1145/360825.360855
2. Brzozowski, J.A.: Derivatives of regular expressions. J. ACM **11**(4), 481–494 (1964). https://doi.org/10.1145/321239.321249
3. Bunte, O., et al.: The mCRL2 toolset for analysing concurrent systems. In: Vojnar, T., Zhang, L. (eds.) TACAS 2019. LNCS, vol. 11428, pp. 21–39. Springer, Cham (2019). https://doi.org/10.1007/978-3-030-17465-1_2
4. Chauve, C.: Tree pattern matching for linear static terms. In: Laender, A.H.F., Oliveira, A.L. (eds.) SPIRE 2002. LNCS, vol. 2476, pp. 160–169. Springer, Heidelberg (2002). https://doi.org/10.1007/3-540-45735-6_15
5. Cleophas, L.G.: Tree algorithms: two taxonomies and a toolkit. Ph.D. thesis, Eindhoven University of Technology (2008)

6. Cleophas, L.G., Hemerik, K.: Taxonomies of regular tree algorithms. In: Holub, J., Zdárek, J. (eds.) Proceedings of the Prague Stringology Conference 2009, Prague, Czech Republic, 31 August–2 September 2009, pp. 146–159. Czech Technical University in Prague (2009). http://www.stringology.org/event/2009/p14.html

7. Cleophas, L.G., Hemerik, K., Zwaan, G.: Two related algorithms for root-to-frontier tree pattern matching. Int. J. Found. Comput. Sci. **17**(6), 1253–1272 (2006). https://doi.org/10.1142/S012905410600439X

8. Cole, R., Hariharan, R., Indyk, P.: Tree pattern matching and subset matching in deterministic $O(n \log^3 n)$-time. In: Tarjan, R.E., Warnow, T.J. (eds.) Proceedings of the Tenth Annual ACM-SIAM Symposium on Discrete Algorithms, Baltimore, Maryland, USA, 17–19 January 1999, pp. 245–254. ACM/SIAM (1999). http://dl.acm.org/citation.cfm?id=314500.314565

9. Comon, H., et al.: Tree automata techniques and applications (2007). http://www.grappa.univ-lille3.fr/tata. Accessed 12 Oct 2007

10. Dubiner, M., Galil, Z., Magen, E.: Faster tree pattern matching. J. ACM **41**(2), 205–213 (1994). https://doi.org/10.1145/174652.174653

11. Eker, S., Meseguer, J., Sridharanarayanan, A.: The Maude LTL model checker. Electron. Notes Theor. Comput. Sci. **71**, 162–187 (2002). https://doi.org/10.1016/S1571-0661(05)82534-4

12. Erkens, R., Groote, J.F.: A set automaton to locate all pattern matches in a term (2021)

13. Flouri, T., Iliopoulos, C.S., Janousek, J., Melichar, B., Pissis, S.P.: Tree template matching in ranked ordered trees by pushdown automata. J. Discrete Algorithms **17**, 15–23 (2012). https://doi.org/10.1016/j.jda.2012.10.003

14. Fokkink, W.J., Kamperman, J., Walters, P.: Within arm's reach: compilation of left-linear rewrite systems via minimal rewrite systems. ACM Trans. Program. Lang. Syst. **20**(3), 679–706 (1998). https://doi.org/10.1145/291889.291903

15. Gräf, A.: Left-to-right tree pattern matching. In: Book, R.V. (ed.) RTA 1991. LNCS, vol. 488, pp. 323–334. Springer, Heidelberg (1991). https://doi.org/10.1007/3-540-53904-2_107

16. Groote, J.F., Mousavi, M.R.: Modeling and Analysis of Communicating Systems. MIT Press (2014). https://mitpress.mit.edu/books/modeling-and-analysis-communicating-systems

17. Hoffmann, C.M., O'Donnell, M.J.: Interpreter generation using tree pattern matching. In: Aho, A.V., Zilles, S.N., Rosen, B.K. (eds.) Conference Record of the Sixth Annual ACM Symposium on Principles of Programming Languages, San Antonio, Texas, USA, January 1979, pp. 169–179. ACM Press (1979). https://doi.org/10.1145/567752.567768

18. Hoffmann, C.M., O'Donnell, M.J.: Pattern matching in trees. J. ACM **29**(1), 68–95 (1982). https://doi.org/10.1145/322290.322295

19. Leiserson, C.E., et al.: There's plenty of room at the top: what will drive computer performance after Moore's law? Science 368(6495) (2020). https://doi.org/10.1126/science.aam9744. https://science.sciencemag.org/content/368/6495/eaam9744

20. Nieuwenhuis, R., Hillenbrand, T., Riazanov, A., Voronkov, A.: On the evaluation of indexing techniques for theorem proving. In: Goré, R., Leitsch, A., Nipkow, T. (eds.) IJCAR 2001. LNCS, vol. 2083, pp. 257–271. Springer, Heidelberg (2001). https://doi.org/10.1007/3-540-45744-5_19

21. Ramakrishnan, I.V., Sekar, R.C., Voronkov, A.: Term indexing. In: Robinson, J.A., Voronkov, A. (eds.) Handbook of Automated Reasoning (in 2 Volumes), pp. 1853–1964. Elsevier and MIT Press (2001). https://doi.org/10.1016/b978-044450813-3/50028-x

22. Ramesh, R., Ramakrishnan, I.V.: Nonlinear pattern matching in trees. J. ACM **39**(2), 295–316 (1992). https://doi.org/10.1145/128749.128752
23. Sekar, R.C., Ramesh, R., Ramakrishnan, I.V.: Adaptive pattern matching. SIAM J. Comput. **24**(6), 1207–1234 (1995). https://doi.org/10.1137/S0097539793246252
24. Trávníček, J., Janoušek, J., Melichar, B., Cleophas, L.: On modification of Boyer-Moore-Horspool's algorithm for tree pattern matching in linearised trees. Theor. Comput. Sci. **830**, 60–90 (2020)

Accelerating SpMV Multiplication in Probabilistic Model Checkers Using GPUs

Muhammad Hannan Khan[1]([✉]), Osman Hassan[1], and Shahid Khan[2]

[1] School of Electrical Engineering and Computer Science,
National University of Sciences and Technology (NUST), Islamabad, Pakistan
{hkhan.msee17seecs,osman.hasan}@seecs.edu.pk
[2] Software Modeling and Verification, RWTH Aachen University, Aachen, Germany
shahid.khan@cs.rwth-aachen.de

Abstract. Probabilistic model checking is a prominent formal verification technique for analyzing stochastic systems. Probabilistic model checkers hinge upon the sparse matrix-vector (SpMV) multiplications to compute reachability probabilities, i.e., the probability of reaching a target state from a given initial state. Being compute- and memory-intensive task, SpMV is a bottleneck in using probabilistic model checking for analyzing scalable real-world case studies. This paper presents a methodology to accelerate SpMV multiplication in probabilistic model checkers using graphic processing units (GPUs). Since GPUs efficiently execute basic linear algebraic operations such as multiplication, one achieves improvements in computation times. These improvements, however, are not significant in the presence of memory transfer overheads. We apply traditional optimization techniques and hide the memory transfers from the host computer to the GPU inside the state-space-exploration stage. This hiding significantly reduces the latency caused by memory transfers during execution. We implemented the proposed acceleration approach with CUDA-based cuSPARSE API and asynchronous multiple copy algorithms in the probabilistic model checker STORM, with a focus on its SpMV multiplier. In our experiments, we observed 16 times speed up on average over the state-of-the-art.

Keywords: Probabilistic model checking · GPU · STORM · Sparse matrix-vector multiplication

1 Introduction

Model Checking [11] is a widely used formal verification technique [23] that exhaustively builds a behavioral model $\mathcal{M}$ of a given system for a given property ϕ, and automatically verifies if the system exhibits the property $\mathcal{M} \models \phi$. A model checker not only verifies the properties over a model but, in case of a failing property, also provides counterexamples. These counterexamples help developers in understanding and rectifying the non-conforming behavior. As real-world

© Springer Nature Switzerland AG 2021
A. Cerone and P. C. Ölveczky (Eds.): ICTAC 2021, LNCS 12819, pp. 86–104, 2021.
https://doi.org/10.1007/978-3-030-85315-0_6

systems pervasively exhibit stochastic behavior, probabilistic model checking (PMC) is an important extension of model checking [25]. PMC allows verifying stochastic systems, modeled as Markov chains (MCs) or Markov decision processes (MDPs), against probabilistic properties.

Scalability is a persistent issue for both steps of model checking: (1) model building and (2) property verification. The scalability issue in the former step leads to the infamous state-space explosion problem [38]. A promising technique to mitigate the state space explosion problem is the lazy verification approach where partial state space is explored to achieve the results of acceptable precision, see [28]. The scalability issue in the later step is equally important. Internally, the probabilistic model checkers represent the probabilistic behavioral model (state space) as a sparse matrix, and property verification leads to repeated sparse matrix-vector multiplication. As the size of the state-space is translated into the dimensions of the said matrix, the growing size of state space contributes to the complexity of performing arithmetic on such matrices. This increase in complexity results in large computation costs and memory requirements.

Parallel model checking algorithms [3,4,37] traditionally rely on CPU clusters to mitigate the property verification scalability issue, but GPUs have emerged in recent years as the primary compute resource for the application and acceleration of such mathematics. Bosnacki et al. [8] used the Jacobi method in the core sparse matrix and dense vector multiplication to speed up the Markov chain model checking and demonstrated their results on PRISM, a probabilistic model checker, running on GPUs. This was further improved in [9] by enhancing the parallelization of the algorithm, where the memory copying is identified as the main bottleneck for GPU-based algorithms. Cormie-Bowins et al. [12] implemented the matrix multiplication using the Jacobi and the BiCGStab method on GPUs. They compared their work with Bosnacki's advanced GPU-based PRISM. Wijs et al. [40] identified how the wrap-based segments and the modified sparse row (MSR) format matrices improved the sparse matrix-vector multiplication 4.5 times on average. Bylina et al. [10] identified multiple formats for storing sparse matrices to limit the memory footprint and discussed their applicability in GPU-based sparse matrix-vector multiplication. Berger et al. [7] utilized the CUSP library to obtain a significant speed-up when dealing with large models that require multiple iterations to overcome the initial memory copy overhead in STORM [17], a probabilistic model checker. They identified two main challenges: (1) the memory transfer overheads consuming up to 99.96% of time in extreme cases and (2) the lack of hardware support for double-precision floating-point arithmetic. Wijs et al. [39] provided a comprehensive tool, called the GPU-EXPLORE. This tool combines the maximum data inside the 32-bit integers and stores information in the texture memory to mitigate the uncoalesced access overheads. This approach targets only explicit-state model checking; hence, it cannot be utilized for probabilistic models. Bell et al. [5] presented a generic approach to SpMV multiplication on GPUs. They proposed fine-tuned kernels for different storage types of sparse matrices. Moreover, they proposed bypassing the memory latency and computing bottleneck by introducing large-scale GPU-based distributed systems. In all the above-mentioned works, we find latency—delay due to copying data from a host to device—as the primary bottleneck for GPU-based SpMV multiplication. This underscores the need for a generic multiplication kernel that fully utilizes the available hardware resources.

This paper presents a methodology to further speed up the SpMV multiplications. We investigate the SpMV multiplication in the context of probabilistic reachability probability for discrete-time Markov chains (DTMCs). The methodology (1) leverages upon the traditional optimization methods, (2) hides the memory transfers from the host to the GPU inside the state-space-exploration stage and (3) benefits from the STORM framework-specific algorithms. We use CUDA's native cuSPARSE API and compare the results with the existing CUSP and CPU-based implementations. We also identify some pitfalls and bottlenecks that we encountered when accelerating such algorithms on GPUs. Our selection of STORM is mainly motivated by its promising results [18,24] while maintaining the space for improvement in SpMV multiplication.

2   Preliminaries

2.1   Behavioral Model

Definition 1 (Discrete Time Markov Chains). *A discrete-time Markov chain (DTMC) is a tuple* $\mathcal{M} = (S, \mathbf{P}, s_{init}, AP, L)$ *[2], where: S is a set of states; $\mathbf{P} : S \times S \to [0,1]$ is the transition probability function such that $\forall s$: $\sum_{s' \in S} \mathbf{P}(s, s') = 1$; $s_{init} \in S$ is an initial distribution; AP is a set of atomic propositions; and $L : S \to 2^{AP}$ is a labeling function.*

2.2   Reachability Probability

Reachability probability amounts to computing the probability to reach a predefined set of states $B \subset S$ from any $s \in S \setminus B$. Let $x_s = Pr\{s \models \Diamond B\}$ denote the reachability probability for state s. x_s is computed as:

$$x_s = \underbrace{\sum_{t \in S \setminus B} \mathbf{P}(s, t) \cdot x_t}_{\text{reach } B \text{ via } t \notin B} + \underbrace{\sum_{u \in B} \mathbf{P}(s, u)}_{\text{reach } B \text{ in one step}} . \tag{1}$$

Equation 1 states that either a state $s \in B$ is reached within one step or first a state $t \in S \setminus B$ is reached from which B is reached. If B is not reachable from s, then $x_s = 0$. If $s \in B$, then $x_s = 1$, see [26] for details. For the vector $x = (x_s)_{s \in S}$, where all set of states have a valid path to B, we get from Eq. 1

$$x_s = Ax + b, \tag{2}$$

where the matrix A contains the transitional probabilities and b contains the probability of reaching B in one step. Using a (heterogeneous) linear equation system, we rewrite Eq. 2 as:

$$(I - A) \cdot x = b, \tag{3}$$

where I is an identity matrix. The probability distribution of $\mathcal{M}$ being in a state after n transitions, given that the computation starts with an initial state vector s_{init}, is denoted by $\theta_n^{\mathcal{M}}$ and computed as

$$\theta_n^{\mathcal{M}} = \mathbf{P} \cdot \mathbf{P} \cdot ... \cdot \mathbf{P} \cdot s_{\text{init}} = \mathbf{P}^n \cdot s_{\text{init}} \tag{4}$$

Since calculating the n power of the matrix is a computationally expensive operation [2], $\theta_n^{\mathcal{M}}$ is calculated by recursive matrix-vector multiplications.

2.3 Sparse-Matrix Representations

The general sparse matrix-vector multiplication equation is $y = \alpha \mathbf{A}x + \beta \mathbf{y}$, where: $\mathbf{A}$ is the sparse matrix of size $Cols \times Rows$; x (y) is a dense vector of size $Cols$ ($Rows$); and both α and β are scalars. The process of multiplication can, therefore, be summarized by the following equation

$$y_i = \sum_{A_{i,j} \neq 0} A_{i,j} \cdot x_j + \beta \cdot y_i \tag{5}$$

Equation 5 indicates that the operation to be performed at each Non-zero value (V_{NNZ}) of the sparse-matrix A results in an overall $(V_{NNZ} + Rows) \cdot 2$ floating point operations.

This paper utilizes the compressed sparse row (CSR) format due to (1) its wide utilization in STORM and (2) its ability to provide a balanced computation across matrices of different sizes and sparsity, as identified in [10,21]. The CSR format divides the matrix into 3 arrays: (1) non-zero data values, (2) their column indices, and (3) offsets of each row represented in the data.

2.4 GPU Programming

Graphical processing units (GPUs) are highly parallel programmable processors. They specialize in accelerating the low-level algorithms, which have large computational requirements and are parallelizable. GPUs follow the single instruction multiple data (SIMD) programming model, i.e., the GPU processes multiple data elements in parallel using the same instruction.

Next, we describe two of the most widely used GPU accelerators and their pros and cons. Both have their unique programming models and provide multiple tools to allow optimizations and computations of algorithms.

OpenCL. The OpenCL [32] provides a cross-platform environment that can be easily ported to multiple architectures like the CPUs, GPUs, digital signal processors (DSPs), and even field-programmable gate arrays (FPGAs). Unfortunately, due to this heterogeneous behavior, OpenCL is not device-specific; hence it does not specialize in any particular hardware.

CUDA. To cater for general-purpose computing on GPUs (GPGPU), NVIDIA has developed the compute unified device architecture (CUDA) [36]. As the scientific community is the primary user of this model, we have many off-the-shelf APIs available that target most of the complex and commonly used tasks.

A survey of existing work considers CUDA as a better option due to the availability of specialized APIs, like the CUBLAS and the cuSPARSE [13,34]. Our use of CUDA is mainly motivated by the following two reasons:

- Fang [19] shows that CUDA significantly outperforms OpenCL in arithmetic computations but lacks in data movement,
- CUDA provides us with multiple open-source tools that reduce the time and complexity of converting the existing code to the CUDA platform.

The GPU devices are typically mounted on the peripheral component interconnect express (PCIe) socket when connected as a co-processor. These devices act as slaves while relying mostly on of tiny applications called kernels. Figure 1a depicts this behavior of sequential executions in a CUDA application. All data, which needs to be processed, must be transferred to the GPU via the PCIe interface, as shown in Fig. 1b.

The CUDA programming model provides the user with an abstraction of this parallel architecture in the form of directives governing the systems ability to call the SIMD instructions, memory movement and thread synchronizations. At the lowest level of a CUDA subsystem, we have a simple thread that performs the task assigned by the kernel. A thread block is a batch of threads that share memory and perform a task either collectively or individually. The threads of multiple blocks do not co-operate and require extensive synchronizations. Figure 1a shows how various blocks can be combined to form a one, two, or three dimensional units called grids.

3   Proposed Optimization Flow

This section outlines a strategy, based on conventional and non-conventional methods, to reduce the compute requirements of a probabilistic model checker. The overall approach is to determine a set of pre-requisites rules along with system-specific techniques to optimize the SpMV multiplication, see Fig. 2.

Typically, in optimization problems, the whole system is kept intact and only the problem set is cherry-picked for acceleration. Likewise, we identify possible injection points in the system where we introduce the custom code. We introduce Algorithm 1 that describes the proposed optimization strategy along with key points of code injection.

3.1   Identification of the SpMV

As discussed in Sect. 2, the process of calculating the probabilities using the matrix-vector multiplication involves very high computation requirements. In the proposed approach, we identify algorithms that first build the model in

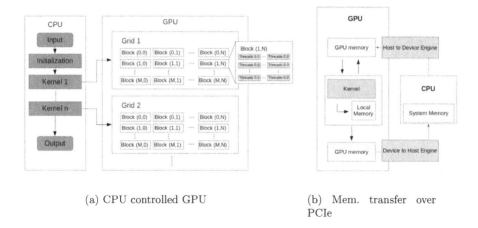

(a) CPU controlled GPU

(b) Mem. transfer over PCIe

Fig. 1. GPU programming model

terms of the sparse-matrix and then perform model checking. The approach is in line with the STORM's *sparse* and *hybrid* engine. This approach allows us to shift the relatively sequential operation of state exploration on the CPU along with a sparse matrix solver on the GPU. As the explored state of the model is sparse, we use different sparse storage formats to further reduce the memory footprint.

3.2 Introducing CUDA

We introduce a bottom-up technique where we first target and isolate the STORM multiplier and replace it with CUDA based cuSPARSE API. CUSP [6] is another open-source CUDA library that performs the SpMV multiplication. Our choice of using cuSPARSE over CUSP is primarily based on the fact that cuSPARSE has coalesced global memory accesses and provides better occupancy of GPUs. Moreover, it allows asynchronous executions with respect to the host and may return control back to the user before completion. Another reason is that, unlike CUSP, cuSPARSE has been integrated into the CUDA toolkit. Thanks to this integration, cuSPARSE is regularly updated and actively maintained with the support for the state-of-the-art drivers, technology and CUDA enhancements, such as using tensor cores [31], NVIDIA tool extension (NVTX), etc. We discuss, in the experimental results section, how cuSPARSE was observed to be faster than the CUSP implementation.

In Algorithm 1-Phase C, we create a multiplier that accepts the sparse-matrix A_{CSR} in the CSR format, initial vector x_{init} and N as the number of iterations of the multiplier. The copying of data to and from the GPU is required before processing any data. This is followed by calling the cuSPARSE's single or double precision SpMV function. Initially, we need to calculate the memory required for the GPU using the equation:

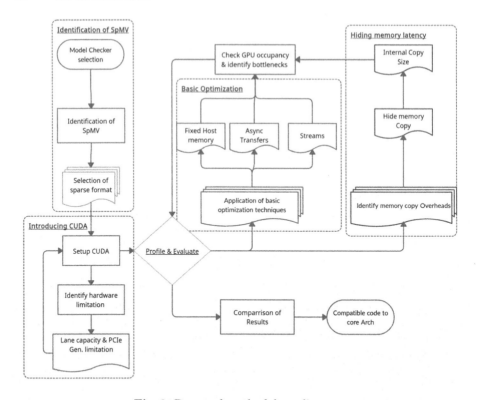

Fig. 2. Proposed methodology diagram

$$M_{Req} = (\mathcal{P}_{Val} \cdot (||V_{NNZ}|| + ||x_{init}|| \cdot 2) + (\mathcal{P}_{Ind} \cdot (||Offset_{Row}|| + ||V_{NNZ}||))) \quad (6)$$

where $\mathcal{P}_{Val}$ is the precision of V_{NNZ}, $Offset_{Row}$ is the row offset vector of A_{CSR} and V_{NNZ} is the vector of values in A_{CSR}. The M_{Req} is the maximum memory that the GPU can accommodate without dividing the matrix into a subset to compute the SpMV multiplication.

Another limiting factor is the PCIe interface of the GPUs. Table 1 presents an overview of different PCIe interfaces available and their theoretical performance.

Table 1. PCIe types and data rates [1,20]

Interface	Data-rate supported
PCIe x1 Gen 3	1 GB/s
PCIe x8 Gen 3	8 GB/s
PCIe x16 Gen 3	16 GB/s
PCIe x16 Gen 4	32 GB/s

Memory copy is the main source of latency in all GPU applications that are generated as a consequence of the type of PCIe slot selected. Figure 4 illustrates the ratio of the time spent on kernel compute vs memory transfers. We observed that in the mobile versions of GPUs, the x8 PCIe interface is commonly used due to the limited availability of space, and on the other hand, fast x16 interfaces based on Gen 3, or more recently Gen 4, are used in desktop computers.

Algorithm 1 Complete optimized algorithm

Phase-A

1: **procedure** BUILDING SPARSE MATRIX($\mathcal{M}$)
2:     ...
3:     **procedure** STATE EXPLORATION(s, Cp_{min})
4:         ToExplore = $\{s_0\}$
5:         Discovered = { }
6:         s_{old} = { }
7:         **while** $ToExplore \neq Null$ **do**
8:             $s_{picked} \in$ ToExplore
9:             s_x = FindSuccessors(s_{picked})
10:             Discovered = Discovered $\cup$ s_{picked}
11:             ToExplore = (ToExplore $\setminus$ s_{picked}) $\cup$ s_x
12:             **if** s_x is $\geq Cp_{min}$ **then**   ▷ 1st insertion of CUDA
13:                 Copy-Asynchronous($V_{Chunks}(i)$) = $s_x \setminus s_{old}$
14:                 $s_{old} = s_x$
15:                 $Cp_{min} = Cp_{min*1.75}$
16:             **end if**
17:         **end while**
18:     **end procedure**
19:     ...
20: **end procedure**

Phase B

21: **procedure** REASSEMBLE AND COPY(V_{Chunks}, x_{init})   ▷ 2nd insertion of CUDA
22:     Copy-Asynchronous(x_{init})$_{Host \rightarrow Device}$
23:     **for** each item i in V_{Chunks} **do**
24:         Copy-Optimized($V_{Chunks}(i) \rightarrow A_{CSR}$)$_{Device} \rightarrow$ Device
25:     **end for**
26: **end procedure**

Phase C

27: **procedure** CUDA MULTIPLIER(A_{CSR}, x_{init}, N)   ▷ 3rd insertion of CUDA
28:     **for** values of N **do**
29:         y = cuSPARSE SpMV($A_{CSR} \cdot x_{init}$)
30:         Swap pointers($x_{init} \leftarrow y$)
31:     **end for**
32: **end procedure**

3.3   Basic Optimizations

Several possible optimizations can be considered, and at various levels, ranging from overlapping data transfers with computation down to fine-tuning floating-point operation sequences. NVIDIA provides a best practice guide [14] that outlines all traditional optimization strategies. In our context, minimizing the transfer of data between the host and the device is essential. This minimization might lead to sacrificing the computations on GPU to run kernels that otherwise exhibit similar performance on the host CPU.

Pinned Memory. *Page-locked* or *pinned memory* transfers attain the highest bandwidth between the host and the device. Since the GPU is not able to access the data directly from the *pageable* host memory, the CUDA driver must first allocate a temporary page-locked, or "pinned" memory. The required data is first copied to the pinned array and then transferred from the pinned array to the device memory. On PCIe $x16$ Gen3 cards, for example, the pinned memory can attain transfer rates of about 12 GB/s.

Async-Transfer. *CudaMemcpy* provides the basic data transfer between the host and the device by blocking the execution control of the host thread until the data transfer is complete. The *asynchronous data transfer* function, *cudaMemcpyAsync*, is a non-blocking variant of the *cudaMemcpy* in which the control is returned immediately to the host thread. This allows the user to queue multiple copy commands to constantly engage the *Copy-engine* while the CPU is free to perform other tasks. Utilizing *async-transfers* along with *pinned memory* techniques, forms the "Copy-Asynchronous" procedure in Algorithm 1.

Stream is a pipeline within the CUDA API that allows a sequence of operations to be executed on the device in a given order, defined host-side. These streams, while maintaining the order within the context they run, allow the execution of multiple streams that can be interleaved or executed concurrently. Figure 3 shows how multiple streams can fully utilize hardware that remains unused when a sequential flow is implemented.

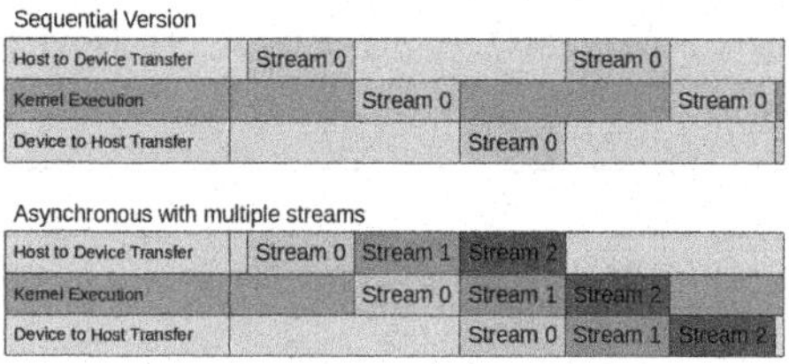

Fig. 3. Stream allowing sequential operation into concurrent operations

Some other optimization techniques include batching small transfers together in order to fully utilize the PCIe transfer speeds and handling of strided accesses using coalesced reads from the global memory.

3.4   Hiding Memory Latency

While traditional optimization techniques provide multi-fold speed-ups, most algorithms require custom optimizations that exploit the flow of the system to create room for specific code insertion. It can be observed form Fig. 4 that the bulk of memory latency comes from the copying of the three CSR vectors replacing the transitional matrix. Therefore, minimizing the time taken for this operation is of utmost importance.

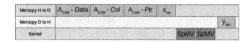

Fig. 4. Memory latency generated when computing SpMV multiplication.

For repeated $Y_i = Ax_i + b$, the value of x_i is equal to Y_{i-1}, this adds latency due to the transfer of vector from device to device. In cases where two variables of equal length within the CUDA environment needs to be copied, we swap their memory pointers followed by reassigning the context through the cuSPARSE API. Algorithm 1-C follows this logic in the "Swap pointers" procedure to remove the copy overhead between x_{init} and y.

STORM uses its sparse-matrix builder utility to create the transitional matrix $\mathbf{A}$ by state exploration for each successor state (s_x) and assigns it as a row of the matrix. Since these rows, depicting state transitions, are fixed, we propose Algorithm 1-A as an extension of the state exploration process. We introduce the variable $V_{Chunks}(i)$ where each i is a pointer to memory containing rows of matrix $\mathbf{A}$. Since all memory copying is asynchronous, the control is handed back to the API as soon as the command is executed, ensuring that the delay in the state exploration is minimal. Algorithm 1-B shows how we efficiently rearrange the pointers inside a contiguous memory, once all data is copied inside the memory at the multiplication point.

Recalling Fig. 1a, all instructions to the GPU are directed by the CPU. When the number of states and choices increase, the number of copy pointers and the instructions required to rearrange them also increases, as shown in Fig. 5a. This sequential execution is catered by utilizing the maximum streams, since there is no limitation on the parallel copy operation internally in the device.

To optimize the copying speeds over the PCIe, it is typically recommended to have large copy sizes [33] by batching small transfers together. We introduced a limit Cp_{min} in Algorithm 1-A to ensure that the copy process groups multiple rows of matrix $\mathbf{A}$ together. The number of rows is increased at every copy to ensure that the algorithm adapts as the state-space increases to accommodate the size of the end transitional matrix. Figure 5b shows a significant performance upgrade after the application of both of the optimization strategies.

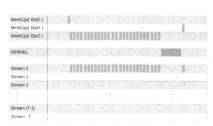
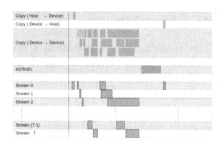

(a) Sequential reassemble and copy   (b) Reassemble and copy with multiple streams and batched data

Fig. 5. Illustration of Nvidia's Visual Profiler output showing memory copy and SpMV compute

3.5 Profile and Evaluate

Profiling and evaluation is an essential step after each optimization strategy is implemented. We use the NVIDIA Visual Profiler [16] for GPUs with compute capability of less than 8.0 and NVIDIA compute [15] for compute capability greater than or equal to 8.0. Another important factor in evaluating the quality of optimization is the occupancy of the GPU, i.e., the amount of processor usage by the hardware [22]. The quality of an optimization is proportional to the occupancy per streaming multiprocessors (SMs).

For our experiments, we selected the same test vectors that were previously used to evaluate the PRISM model checker [29]. We focus on the NAND and Herman case studies because they provide a wide range of test vectors with varying size.

4   Experimental Evaluation

The standard STORM multiplier $y = Multiplier(A, x_{init}, N)$ takes three parameters as input: (1) a sparse-matrix A, (2) a dense initial state vector x_{init} and (3) number of times to perform multiplication N. The multiplier returns a dense vector y depicting step-bounded readability probability of each state. For the implementation of the SpMV, we randomized the dense vectors in the range $[0, 1]$ and increased the value of N.

We introduce the term *"Complete CUDA"* to collectively represent the basic optimization techniques and hiding the memory transfers inside the state-space exploration. The experiments are performed on three different combinations of CPUs and GPUs each scaling in performance to accommodate technological advances within each generation. The combinations are as follows:

1. Intel i7-7700 CPU @ 2.8 GHz with GTX 1050 PCIe 3rd Gen x8 lane;
2. Intel i7-6700 CPU @ 3.4 GHz with GTX 1080 PCIe 3rd Gen x16 lane;

3. AMD RYZEN 3970x 32-core @ 3.7 GHz with RTX 3090 PCIe 4th Gen x16 lane.

We present the results of combination 2 here, and more details for 1 and 3 can be found in [27].

All systems run the standard Ubuntu 18.04 LTS with CUDA toolkit 11.2. We compare our SpMV implementation with the STORM built-in multiplier function, and the cuSPARSE implementation with the CUSP implementation. All tests are conducted assuming a double precision with the multiplier count = 2, making the worst-case scenario for GPUs due to such models' requirements for low latency. We provide the results for each benchmark as the value of N is increased. Finally, we illustrate the difference between the cuSPARSE and CUSP.

4.1 NAND Case Study

This case study [35] concerns NAND multiplexing, which is a technique for ensuring reliable computation using unreliable devices. There are two variables that change the dynamics of the model: (1) N is the number of inputs in each bundle and (2) K is the number of restorative stages. The experimental results are depicted in Table 2 and Fig. 6a.

Table 2. NAND: comparing optimizations with STORM multiplier

NAND constants		Size of Matrix	Sparsity	Basic CUDA	Complete CUDA	Storm	Speed-up Factor
N	K		%	MS	MS	MS	$\frac{\text{STORM}}{Complete}$
20	1	78332 × 78332	99.99802	0.382	0.27	3.1045	11.5
20	2	154942 × 154942	99.999001	0.69	0.424	4.019	10
20	3	231552 × 231552	99.99933	0.92	0.514	6.208	12
20	4	308162 × 308162	99.9995	1.21	0.69	8.2	11.9
40	1	1004862 × 1004862	99.99984	3.61	1.769	30.594	17.3
40	2	2003082 × 2003082	99.99992	6.91	3.391	54.716	16.1
40	3	3001302 × 3001302	99.99995	10.3	5.002	82.158	16.4
40	4	3999522 × 3999522	99.99996	13.68	6.66	112.76	17
60	1	4717592 × 4717592	99.99997	16.48	7.861	131.434	16.7
60	2	9420422 × 9420422	99.999983	43.33	15.614	265.969	17
60	3	14123252 × 14123252	99.999989	64.581	23.296	392.483	16.9
60	4	18826082 × 18826082	99.999992	79.22	31.142	528.142	17

The measurements against the STORM implementation show speed-up of 16 times on average with the *Complete CUDA* GPU implementation. In smaller matrices, we observe the basic optimization strategy giving similar results as the complete optimizations. This is expected since the latency is less significant with smaller matrices.

Table 3. Herman: comparing optimizations with STORM multiplier

Model Name	Matrix Size	Sparsity	Basic CUDA	Complete CUDA	Storm	Speed-up factor
		%	MS	MS	MS	$\frac{STORM}{Complete}$
Herman3	8 × 8	56.25	0.2	0.202	0.0015	0.007
Herman5	32 × 32	76.17	0.2	0.217	0.0025	0.012
Herman7	128 × 128	86.64	0.21	0.197	0.0070	0.036
Herman9	512 × 512	92.5	0.21	0.209	0.525	2.513
Herman11	2048 × 2048	95.8	0.31	0.242	4.624	19.11
Herman13	8192 × 8192	97.62	1.83	0.603	16.026	26.58
Herman15	32768 × 32768	98.66	15.19	3.573	125.495	35.12

4.2 Herman Case Study

The self-stabilizing algorithm Herman [30] operates synchronously in an oriented ring, where the communication is unidirectional in the ring. In this protocol, the number of processes in the ring must be odd. Our choice of Herman stems from the fact that it exhibits lower sparsity in comparison to other benchmark models and thus leads to a faster multiplication but this speed-up is compromised due to an increase in the memory copy operations from the host to the device. We also evaluate how using GPUs to solve small matrix-vector multiplication is counter-intuitive since the setup cost of matrix multiplication is greater than the complete multiplication on CPU. Execution times can be seen in Table 3 and comparisons are illustrated in Fig. 6b.

For the Herman model, the proposed approach initially performs worse than the original STORM multiplier. We observe a minimum time of 0.2 ms for all matrices and since the STORM multiplier can handle matrices of up to 512 × 512 in under 0.5 ms, it significantly decreases the speed-up factor but with models greater than 2048 × 2048 we see an up to 35 times increase in performance in the proposed approach.

Unlike the NAND model, which on average saw twice the performance gain when comparing the basic with *Complete CUDA* optimizations, as shown in Fig. 7a, we see a higher difference in favor of complete optimizations in the Herman model. This is due to lower sparsity, which creates a higher cost for memory copying if the transfer time is not included in the state-space exploration.

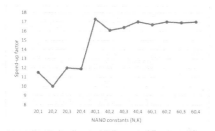

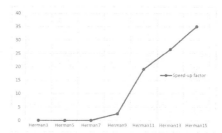

(a) Speed-up factor in NAND model.   (b) Speed-up factor in Herman model.

Fig. 6. Results from NAND and Herman model.

4.3   Increasing Value of N

All of the above observations have been made assuming a value of $N = 2$ denoting that the matrix-vector multiplication is performed twice before termination. With an increased value of N, the cost of performing SpMV multiplication once can be computed as

$$Ratio_n = \frac{Time_{N=1}}{Time_{N=n}} \cdot n \tag{7}$$

with n being the multiplication count. We observe from Table 4, that the time taken for a single SpMV multiplication instance reduces with an increased value of N in all models. This behavior, as illustrated in Fig. 7b, is expected since GPUs traditionally use such tactics to compensate for the initial latency caused by memory transfers [22].

Table 4. Execution time of SpMV multiplication for each value of N

| | Multiplication count - N | | | | | |
Name	1	4	6	10	50	100
Herman3	183	56.75	40.833	28.7	15.46	13.78
Herman5	180	55.5	41.667	29.9	15.96	14.24
Herman7	184	61	41.67	29.5	16.12	13.73
Herman9	188	62.5	40.167	29.2	15.66	13.84
Herman11	214	69	54.5	41.8	26.12	24.52
Herman13	467	207.5	177.3	155	127.34	122.92
Herman15	2633	1361	1219.67	1107.4	968.86	951.78

4.4   CUSP vs cuSPARSE

The CUSP vs cuSPARSE kernel comparison is performed for different matrices and Table 5 shows a steady lag that CUSP maintains behind the cuSPARSE library. We found that the resource utilization per streaming multiprocessor in the cuSPARSE API resulted in a lower time to compute a kernel of the same dimension and value as compared to the CUSP implementation.

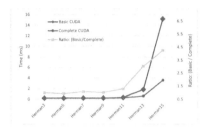
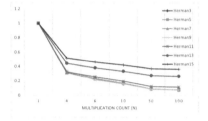

(a) Basic and complete optimizations with the ratio of Basic/complete.

(b) $Ratio_n$ of each model with increased value of N.

Fig. 7. Comparison results of optimizations and increased N.

Table 5. Kernel duration for the Herman model over CUSP and cuSPARSE

Model	CUSP time	cuSPARSE time	$\frac{CUSP}{cuSPARSE}$
Herman3	18.23	10.312	1.768
Herman5	24.29	10.27	2.365
Herman7	32.56	9.69	3.36
Herman9	107.2	10.03	10.69
Herman11	437.7	22.65	19.32
Herman13	2836	123.44	22.98
Herman15	19720	956.78	20.61

4.5   Comparing GPUs

We also compared hardware on the basis of generation with the RTX-3090 being the top-of-the-line GPU using PCIe 4.0 x16 lanes followed by the GTX-1080 and GTX-1050 (x8 lane). From Table 6, we find that the RTX-3090 performs up to 228% faster on matrices that require a higher memory bandwidth, similar to those of the Herman model, while on high sparsity matrices we see an improvement of 137.5%.

For our results, we compare the output probabilities with the ones obtained via STORM's multiplier and found both of them to be identical. The results identify that for small matrices, the GPU implementation is not recommended since the time taken for such SpMV multiplications on CPU was observed to be less than 100 ms. On the other hand, we see a significant performance gain of up to 80 times on high-end GPUs with models that have large matrices and high transitions per state, and up to 20 times on average in highly sparse matrices. Furthermore, when applying the multiplication on the sparse-matrices with only basic optimization techniques, we observe that, on average, 83% of the time is spent on memory transfers while this ratio reduces to 65% when memory copy latency is hidden inside the state-space exploration. This is due to CUDA's ability to allow multiple fast streams when copying data within the device as compared to copies from the host. Finally, we see that older GPU generations

Table 6. Speed-up factor over different generations on Nand and Herman model

Model	RTX-3090 (Gen.4–16 Lane)	GTX-1080 (Gen.3–16 Lane)	GTX-1050 (Gen.3–8 Lane)
NAND − 20,1	4.905	11.5	5.344
NAND − 20,2	9.871	10	6.205
NAND − 20,3	8.742	12	6.589
NAND − 20,4	15.75	11.9	7.059
NAND − 40,1	15.16	17.3	8.443
NAND − 40,2	17.56	16.1	8.352
NAND − 40,3	19.13	16.4	8.006
NAND − 40,4	19.16	17	8.090
NAND − 60,1	19.77	16.7	7.926
NAND − 60,2	21.60	17	7.846
NAND − 60,3	22.11	16.9	7.927
NAND − 60,4	22.63	17	8.249
Herman3	0.031	0.007	0.05
Herman5	0.061	0.012	0.108
Herman7	0.143	0.036	0.34
Herman9	0.73	2.513	2.67
Herman11	7.21	19.11	12.2
Herman13	37.49	26.58	16.08
Herman15	80.31	35.12	18.59

also provide speed-ups of up to 8 times in comparison to the STORM multiplier on CPU.

5   Conclusion

This paper has presented a GPU-based methodology to optimize sparse-matrix vector multiplications for probabilistic model checking. Significant improvements in performance are achieved by enabling optimizations on the memory transfer step and by using built-in CUDA APIs. Several aspects of the proposed approach are studied. Experiments revealed a speed up of 16 times over the state-of-the-art.

All GPU assisted applications are limited by their global memory utilization. As state-of-the-art hardware crams maximum 80 Gigabytes of memory, the next step towards the GPU aided model checkers will be to cater for matrix-vector multiplications where the size of the variables exceed the limit of the GPU memory. Abstraction techniques to reduce the size of model are generally applied to merge multiple states with indistinguishable behaviour. Techniques such as bisimulation minimization could either be applied in the GPU or output of the CPU-based implementation can be imported and merged in the GPU memory. Extension to a more generic problem set, such as nested bounded probabilistic model checking along with cross-platform comparison with other hardware accelerators and implementation of simulation algorithms such as statistical model checking can be explored as possible future avenues. Another interesting future direction will be to implement the state-space exploration inside the GPU. Since this pre-processing step takes a significant amount of time, GPU-based exploration can introduce a parallel implementation to find successor states. This approach will also avoid repeated memory movement between the host and the GPU; thus it will inherently preempt the primary latency factor.

References

1. Ajanovic, J.: PCI express 3.0 overview. In: Proceedings of Hot Chip: A Symposium on High Performance Chips, vol. 69, p. 143 (2009)
2. Baier, C.: Principles of Model Checking. MIT press, Cambridge (2008)
3. Barnat, J., et al.: Parallel model checking algorithms for linear-time temporal logic. In: Handbook of Parallel Constraint Reasoning, pp. 457–507. Springer, Cham (2018). https://doi.org/10.1007/978-3-319-63516-3_12
4. Barnat, J., Brim, L., Stříbrná, J.: Distributed LTL model-checking in SPIN. In: Dwyer, M. (ed.) SPIN 2001. LNCS, vol. 2057, pp. 200–216. Springer, Heidelberg (2001). https://doi.org/10.1007/3-540-45139-0_13
5. Bell, N., Garland, M.: Efficient Sparse Matrix-Vector Multiplication on CUDA. Tech. rep, Citeseer (2008)
6. Bell, N., Garland, M.: Cusp: Generic parallel algorithms for sparse matrix and graph computations. Version 0.3. 0 35 (2012)
7. Berger, P.: GPU-aided model checking of Markov decision processes (2014)
8. Bošnački, D., Edelkamp, S., Sulewski, D., Wijs, A.: GPU-PRISM: An extension of prism for general purpose graphics processing units. In: 2010 Ninth International Workshop on Parallel and Distributed Methods in Verification, and Second International Workshop on High Performance Computational Systems Biology, pp. 17–19. IEEE (2010)
9. Bošnački, D., Edelkamp, S., Sulewski, D., Wijs, A.: Parallel probabilistic model checking on general purpose graphics processors. Int. J. Softw. Tools Technol. Transfer **13**(1), 21–35 (2011)
10. Bylina, B., Bylina, J., Karwacki, M.: Computational aspects of GPU-accelerated sparse matrix-vector multiplication for solving Markov models. Theor. Appl. Inform. **23**, 127–145 (2011)
11. Clarke, E.M., Grumberg, O., Long, D.E.: Model checking and abstraction. ACM Trans. Program. Lang. Syst. (TOPLAS) **16**(5), 1512–1542 (1994)
12. Cormie-Bowins, E.: A comparison of sequential and GPU implementations of iterative methods to compute reachability probabilities. arXiv preprint arXiv:1210.6412 (2012)
13. Corporation, N.: The API reference guide for cuSPARSE (2021). https://docs.nvidia.com/cuda/cusparse/index.html
14. Corporation, N.: Cuda c++ best practices guide (2021). https://docs.nvidia.com/cuda/cuda-c-best-practices-guide/index.html

15. Corporation, N.: Nvidia nsight compute (2021). https://developer.nvidia.com/nsight-compute
16. Corporation, N.: Nvidia visual profiler (2021). https://developer.nvidia.com/nvidia-visual-profiler
17. Dehnert, C., Junges, S., Katoen, J.-P., Volk, M.: A storm is coming: a modern probabilistic model checker. In: Majumdar, R., Kunčak, V. (eds.) CAV 2017. LNCS, vol. 10427, pp. 592–600. Springer, Cham (2017). https://doi.org/10.1007/978-3-319-63390-9_31
18. Fabarisov, T., Yusupova, N., Ding, K., Morozov, A., Janschek, K.: The efficiency comparison of the prism and storm probabilistic model checkers for error propagation analysis tasks. Industry 4.0 3(5), 229–231 (2018)
19. Fang, J., Varbanescu, A.L., Sips, H.: A comprehensive performance comparison of CUDA and OpenCL. In: 2011 International Conference on Parallel Processing, pp. 216–225. IEEE (2011)
20. Gonzales, D.: PCI express 4.0 electrical previews. In: PCI-SIG Developers Conference (2015)
21. Greathouse, J.L., Daga, M.: Efficient sparse matrix-vector multiplication on GPUs using the CSR storage format. In: SC'14: Proceedings of the International Conference for High Performance Computing, Networking, Storage and Analysis, pp. 769–780. IEEE (2014)
22. Harris, M.: Optimizing cuda. SC07: High Performance Computing With CUDA 60 (2007)
23. Hasan, O., Tahar, S.: Formal verification methods. In: Encyclopedia of Information Science and Technology, 3rd Edition, pp. 7162–7170. IGI Global (2015)
24. Hensel, C., Junges, S., Katoen, J.P., Quatmann, T., Volk, M.: The probabilistic model checker Storm. arXiv preprint arXiv:2002.07080 (2020)
25. Hérault, T., Lassaigne, R., Magniette, F., Peyronnet, S.: Approximate probabilistic model checking. In: Steffen, B., Levi, G. (eds.) VMCAI 2004. LNCS, vol. 2937, pp. 73–84. Springer, Heidelberg (2004). https://doi.org/10.1007/978-3-540-24622-0_8
26. Katoen, J.: The probabilistic model checking landscape. In: LICS, pp. 31–45. ACM (2016)
27. Khan, H.: Storm-cuda (2021). https://github.com/khan-hannan/StoRM-CUDA
28. Khan, S., Katoen, J.-P., Volk, M., Bouissou, M.: Scalable reliability analysis by lazy verification. In: Dutle, A., Moscato, M.M., Titolo, L., Muñoz, C.A., Perez, I. (eds.) NFM 2021. LNCS, vol. 12673, pp. 180–197. Springer, Cham (2021). https://doi.org/10.1007/978-3-030-76384-8_12
29. Kwiatkowska, M., Norman, G., Parker, D.: The PRISM benchmark suite. In: 9th International Conference on Quantitative Evaluation of SysTems, pp. 203–204. IEEE CS press (2012)
30. Kwiatkowska, M., Norman, G., Parker, D.: Probabilistic verification of Herman's self-stabilisation algorithm. Formal Aspects Comput. 24(4), 661–670 (2012)
31. Markidis, S., Der Chien, S.W., Laure, E., Peng, I.B., Vetter, J.S.: Nvidia tensor core programmability, performance and precision. In: 2018 IEEE International Parallel and Distributed Processing Symposium Workshops (IPDPSW), pp. 522–531. IEEE (2018)
32. Munshi, A., Gaster, B., Mattson, T.G., Ginsburg, D.: OpenCL programming guide. Pearson Education (2011)
33. Nambiar, P.P., Saveetha, V., Sophia, S., Sowbarnika, V.A.: GPU acceleration using CUDA framework. Int. J. Innovative Res. Comput. Commun. Eng. 2(3), 200–205 (2014)

34. Naumov, M., Chien, L., Vandermersch, P., Kapasi, U.: Cusparse library. In: GPU Technology Conference (2010)
35. Norman, G., Parker, D., Kwiatkowska, M., Shukla, S.: Evaluating the reliability of NAND multiplexing with PRISM. IEEE Trans. Comput. Aided Des. Integr. Circuits Syst. **24**(10), 1629–1637 (2005)
36. Sanders, J., Kandrot, E.: CUDA by example: an introduction to general-purpose GPU programming. Addison-Wesley Professional (2010)
37. Stern, Ulrich, Dill, David L..: Parallelizing the murϕ verifier. In: Grumberg, Orna (ed.) CAV 1997. LNCS, vol. 1254, pp. 256–267. Springer, Heidelberg (1997). https://doi.org/10.1007/3-540-63166-6_26
38. Valmari, A.: The state explosion problem. In: Reisig, W., Rozenberg, G. (eds.) ACPN 1996. LNCS, vol. 1491, pp. 429–528. Springer, Heidelberg (1998). https://doi.org/10.1007/3-540-65306-6_21
39. Wijs, A., Neele, T., Bošnački, D.: GPUexplore 2.0: unleashing gpu explicit-state model checking. In: Fitzgerald, J., Heitmeyer, C., Gnesi, S., Philippou, A. (eds.) FM 2016. LNCS, vol. 9995, pp. 694–701. Springer, Cham (2016). https://doi.org/10.1007/978-3-319-48989-6_42
40. Wijs, A.J., Bošnački, D.: Improving GPU sparse matrix-vector multiplication for probabilistic model checking. In: Donaldson, A., Parker, D. (eds.) SPIN 2012. LNCS, vol. 7385, pp. 98–116. Springer, Heidelberg (2012). https://doi.org/10.1007/978-3-642-31759-0_9

A Divide & Conquer Approach to Conditional Stable Model Checking

Yati Phyo⑩, Canh Minh Do⑩, and Kazuhiro Ogata$^{(\boxtimes)}$⑩

School of Information Science, Japan Advanced Institute of Science
and Technology (JAIST), Nomi, Ishikawa 923-1211, Japan
{yatiphyo,canhdominh,ogata}@jaist.ac.jp

Abstract. We describe a stratified way to model check conditional stable properties expressed as $\varphi_1 \rightsquigarrow \Box\varphi_2$, where φ_1, φ_2 are state propositions, so as to alleviate the state space explosion problem. We prove a theorem that the proposed technique is correct and design an algorithm based on the theorem.

Keywords: Conditional stable properties · Linear temporal logic (LTL) · Model checking.

1 Introduction

It is still challenging to alleviate the state space explosion problem in model checking [2] reasonably well. To address the challenge, our research group came up with a divide & conquer approach to model checking leads-to properties [4] expressed as $\varphi_1 \rightsquigarrow \varphi_2$, where φ_1, φ_2 are state propositions, and eventual (or eventually) properties [1] expressed as $\Diamond\varphi$, where φ is a state proposition. Our research group also built a tool supporting the divide & conquer approach to model checking leads-to properties [5], has been building a tool for eventual properties and expanding the technique so as to handle other LTL properties.

This paper describes an ongoing work that extends the technique so as to handle conditional stable properties expressed as $\varphi_1 \rightsquigarrow \Box\varphi_2$, where φ_1, φ_2 are state propositions. Conditional stable properties informally say that whenever something is true, it will eventually happen that something else will be always true (or will be stable). The properties can be used to express desired properties self-stabilizing systems [3] should satisfy.

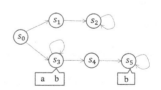

Fig. 1. SimpSys (or K)

Let us outline the proposed technique with a simple system (or Kripke structure) called SimpSys (or K) as depicted in Fig. 1 so that you can intuitively comprehend the technique. SimpSys has six states $s_0, \ldots, s_5$, where s_0 is the

This research was partially supported by JSPS KAKENHI Grant Number JP19H04082.

A. Cerone and P. C. Ölveczky (Eds.): ICTAC 2021, LNCS 12819, pp. 105–111, 2021.
https://doi.org/10.1007/978-3-030-85315-0_7

only initial state. There are eight transitions depicted as arrows in Fig. 1. Let us consider two atomic propositions a and b. The labeling function is defined as depicted in Fig. 1. Let us take a $\rightsquigarrow \Box$b as a property concerned. We can straightforwardly check that SimpSys satisfies the property, namely SimpSys $\models$ a $\rightsquigarrow$ $\Box$b, and then do not need to use the proposed technique for this model checking experiment. We, however, use this simple model checking experiment to sketch the technique.

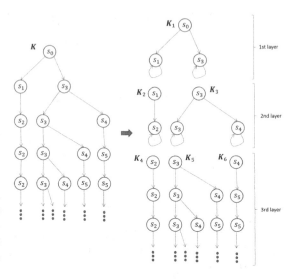

Fig. 2. Split of the state space of K into 3 layers

The left part of Fig. 2 shows the reachable state space of SimpSys, while the right part shows the six sub-state spaces $(K_1, \ldots, K_6)$ obtained by splitting the reachable state space into three layers. The proposed technique first checks $K_1 \models \Box\neg$a. There is one counterexample $s_0, s_3, s_3, \ldots$, and then no check is done for K_3. The technique checks $K_2 \models \Box\neg$a, which has no counterexample, and then checks $K_4 \models$ a $\rightsquigarrow \Box$b, which has no counterexample. The technique checks $K_5 \models \Diamond\Box$b and $K_6 \models \Diamond\Box$b, both of which have no counterexample. Therefore, the technique concludes that the property holds for SimpSys. The point is as follows: the number of different states in K is six, while those in $K_1, \ldots, K_6$ are 3, 2, 2, 1, 3 and 2, respectively. Because the number of different states in each sub-state space can be less than the one in the original reachable state space, the proposed technique may make it possible to check $\varphi_1 \rightsquigarrow \Box\varphi_2$ even if any existing LTL model checker cannot because of the state space explosion problem.

2   Preliminaries

Definition 1 (Kripke structures). *A Kripke structure $K \triangleq \langle S, I, T, A, L \rangle$ consists of a set S of states, a set $I \subseteq S$ of initial states, a left-total binary relation $T \subseteq S \times S$ over states, a set A of atomic propositions and a labeling function L whose type is $S \to 2^A$. An element $(s, s') \in T$ is called a (state) transition from s to s' and may be written as $s \to_K s'$.*

An infinite sequence $s_0, s_1, \ldots, s_i, s_{i+1}, \ldots$ of states is called a path of K iff for any natural number i, $(s_i, s_{i+1}) \in T$. Let π be $s_0, s_1, \ldots, s_i, s_{i+1}, \ldots$ and some notations on π are defined as follows: $\pi(i)$ is s_i; π^i is $s_i, s_{i+1}, \ldots$; π_i is

$s_0, s_1, \ldots, s_i, s_i, s_i, \ldots$; $\pi^{(i,j)}$ is $s_i, s_{i+1}, \ldots, s_j, s_j, s_j, \ldots$ if $i \leq j$ and $s_i, s_i, s_i, \ldots$ otherwise; $\pi^{(i,\infty)}$ is π^i, where i, j are natural numbers. A path π of K is called a computation of K iff $\pi(0) \in I$. Let P_K be the set of all paths of K. Let $P_{(K,s)}$ be $\{\pi \mid \pi \in P_K, \pi(0) = s\}$, where $s \in S$. Let $P^b_{(K,s)}$ be $\{\pi_b \mid \pi \in P_{(K,s)}\}$, where $s \in S$ and b is a natural number. Note that $P^\infty_{(K,s)}$ is $P_{(K,s)}$.

Definition 2 (Syntax of LTL). *The syntax of linear temporal logic (LTL) is as follows:* $\varphi ::= a \mid \top \mid \neg\varphi \mid \varphi \vee \varphi \mid \bigcirc\varphi \mid \varphi \, \mathcal{U} \, \varphi$, *where* $a \in A$.

Definition 3 (Semantics of LTL). *For any Kripke structure K, any path π of K and any LTL formula φ, $K, \pi \models \varphi$ is inductively defined as follows:*

- $K, \pi \models a$ *iff* $a \in \pi(0)$
- $K, \pi \models \top$
- $K, \pi \models \neg\varphi_1$ *iff* $K, \pi \not\models \varphi_1$
- $K, \pi \models \varphi_1 \vee \varphi_2$ *iff* $K, \pi \models \varphi_1$ *and/or* $K, \pi \models \varphi_2$
- $K, \pi \models \bigcirc\varphi_1$ *iff* $K, \pi^1 \models \varphi_1$
- $K, \pi \models \varphi_1 \, \mathcal{U} \, \varphi_2$ *iff there exists a natural number i such that $K, \pi^i \models \varphi_2$ and for each natural number $j < i$, $K, \pi^j \models \varphi_1$*

where φ_1 and φ_2 are LTL formulas. Then, $K \models \varphi$ iff $K, \pi \models \varphi$ for all computations π of K.

$\bot \triangleq \neg\top$ and some other connectives are defined as follows: $\varphi_1 \wedge \varphi_2 \triangleq \neg((\neg\varphi_1) \vee (\neg\varphi_2))$, $\varphi_1 \Rightarrow \varphi_2 \triangleq (\neg\varphi_1) \vee \varphi_2$, $\varphi_1 \Leftrightarrow \varphi_2 \triangleq (\varphi_1 \Rightarrow \varphi_2) \wedge (\varphi_2 \Rightarrow \varphi_1)$, $\Diamond\varphi_1 \triangleq \top \, \mathcal{U} \, \varphi_1$, $\Box\varphi_1 \triangleq \neg(\Diamond\neg\varphi_1)$ and $\varphi_1 \rightsquigarrow \varphi_2 \triangleq \Box(\varphi_1 \Rightarrow \Diamond\varphi_2)$. $\bigcirc, \mathcal{U}, \Diamond, \Box$ and $\rightsquigarrow$ are called next, until, eventually, always and leads-to temporal connectives, respectively. State propositions are LTL formulas such that they do not have any temporal connectives. This paper focuses on properties that can be expressed as $\varphi_1 \rightsquigarrow \Box\varphi_2$, where φ_1, φ_2 are state propositions. Such properties are called conditional stable properties. Although it is unnecessary to directly define the semantics for $\varphi_1 \rightsquigarrow \Box\varphi_2$, we can define it as follows:

- $K, \pi \models \varphi_1 \rightsquigarrow \Box\varphi_2$ iff there exists a natural number i $(\geq j)$ such that $K, \pi^i \models \Box\varphi_2$ if there exists a natural number j such that $K, \pi^j \models \varphi_1$.

3 Multiple Layer Division of Conditional Stable Model Checking

Lemma 1. *Let φ be any state proposition of K. Let k be any natural number. Then, $(K, \pi \models \Box\varphi) \Leftrightarrow (K, \pi_k \models \Box\varphi) \wedge (K, \pi^k \models \Box\varphi)$.*

Proof. Because φ is a state proposition, whether it holds only depends on the first state of a given path. If $(K, \pi \models \Box\varphi)$, then φ holds for $\pi(i)$ for all i, and vice versa. If $K, \pi_k \models \Box\varphi$ and $K, \pi^k \models \Box\varphi$, then φ holds for $\pi(i)$ for $i = 0, \ldots, k$ and φ holds for $\pi(i)$ for $i = k, \ldots$, respectively, and therefore φ holds for $\pi(i)$ for all i, and vice versa. $\qquad\square$

Lemma 2. *Let φ_1, φ_2 be any state propositions of K. Let k be any natural number. Then, $(K, \pi^k \models \Diamond\Box\varphi_2) \Rightarrow (K, \pi \models \varphi_1 \leadsto \Box\varphi_2)$.*

Proof. From the assumption, there exists i $(\geq k)$ such that $K, \pi^i \models \Box\varphi_2$. Thus, $K, \pi \models \varphi_1 \leadsto \Box\varphi_2$.   □

Lemma 3. *Let φ_1, φ_2 be any state propositions of K. Let k be any natural number. Then, $(K, \pi_k \models \Box\neg\varphi_1) \wedge (K, \pi^k \models \varphi_1 \leadsto \Box\varphi_2) \Rightarrow (K, \pi \models \varphi_1 \leadsto \Box\varphi_2)$.*

Proof. The case is split into two cases: (1) $K, \pi^k \models \Box\neg\varphi_1$ and (2) $K, \pi^k \not\models \Box\neg\varphi_1$. In (1), $K, \pi \models \Box\neg\varphi_1$ from the first conjunct of the assumption and Lemma 1. Hence, $K, \pi \models \varphi_1 \leadsto \Box\varphi_2$. In (2), from the second conjunct of the assumption, there exists i $(\geq k)$ such that $K, \pi^i \models \Box\varphi_2$. Thus, $K, \pi \models \varphi_1 \leadsto \Box\varphi_2$.   □

Lemma 4 (Two layer division of $\varphi_1 \leadsto \Box\varphi_2$). *Let φ_1, φ_2 be any state propositions of K. Let k be any natural number. Then,*

$$(K, \pi \models \varphi_1 \leadsto \Box\varphi_2)$$
$$\Leftrightarrow [(K, \pi_k \models \Box\neg\varphi_1) \Rightarrow (K, \pi^k \models \varphi_1 \leadsto \Box\varphi_2)] \wedge$$
$$[(K, \pi_k \not\models \Box\neg\varphi_1) \Rightarrow (K, \pi^k \models \Diamond\Box\varphi_2)]$$

Proof. (1) Case "only if" ($\Rightarrow$): The case is split into two cases: (1.1) $K, \pi \models \Box\neg\varphi_1$ and (1.2) $K, \pi \not\models \Box\neg\varphi_1$. In (1.1), $K, \pi^k \models \Box\neg\varphi_1$ from Lemma 1. Therefore, $K, \pi^k \models \varphi_1 \leadsto \Box\varphi_2$. In (1.2), there exists i such that $K, \pi^i \models \varphi_1$. Thus, from the assumption, there exists j $(\geq i)$ such that $K, \pi^j \models \Box\varphi_2$. Hence, $K, \pi^k \models \varphi_1 \leadsto \Box\varphi_2$ and $K, \pi^k \models \Diamond\Box\varphi_2$.

(2) Case "if" ($\Leftarrow$): The case is split into two cases: (2.1) $K, \pi_k \models \Box\neg\varphi_1$ and (2.2) $K, \pi_k \not\models \Box\neg\varphi_1$. In (2.1), $K, \pi \models \varphi_1 \leadsto \Box\varphi_2$ from Lemma 3. In (2.2), $K, \pi \models \varphi_1 \leadsto \Box\varphi_2$ from Lemma 2.   □

Definition 4 (CStable$_L$). *Let L be any non-zero natural number, k be any natural number and d be any function such that $d(0)$ is 0, $d(x)$ is a natural number for $x = 1, \ldots, L$ and $d(L+1)$ is ∞.*

1. $0 \leq k < L - 1$

$\text{CStable}_L(K, \pi, \varphi_1, \varphi_2, k)$
$\triangleq [(K, \pi^{(d(k),d(k+1))} \models \Box\neg\varphi_1) \Rightarrow \text{CStable}_L(K, \pi, \varphi_1, \varphi_2, k+1)] \wedge$
$[(K, \pi^{(d(k),d(k+1))} \not\models \Box\neg\varphi_1) \Rightarrow (K, \pi^{(d(L),d(L+1))} \models \Diamond\Box\varphi_2)]$

2. $k = L - 1$

$\text{CStable}_L(K, \pi, \varphi_1, \varphi_2, k)$
$\triangleq [(K, \pi^{(d(k),d(k+1))} \models \Box\neg\varphi_1) \Rightarrow (K, \pi^{(d(k+1),d(k+2))} \models \varphi_1 \leadsto \Box\varphi_2)] \wedge$
$[(K, \pi^{(d(k),d(k+1))} \not\models \Box\neg\varphi_1) \Rightarrow (K, \pi^{(d(k+1),d(k+2))} \models \Diamond\Box\varphi_2)]$

Theorem 1 ($L+1$ layer division of $\varphi_1 \leadsto \Box\varphi_2$). *Let L be any non-zero natural number. Let $d(0)$ be 0, $d(x)$ be any natural number for $x = 1, \ldots, L$ and $d(L+1)$ be ∞. Let φ_1, φ_2 be any state propositions of K. Then,*

$$(K, \pi \models \varphi_1 \leadsto \Box\varphi_2) \Leftrightarrow \text{CStable}_L(K, \pi, \varphi_1, \varphi_2, 0)$$

Proof. By induction on L.

- Base case ($L = 1$): It follows from Lemma 4.
- Induction case ($L = l + 1$): We prove the following:

$$(\boldsymbol{K}, \pi \models \varphi_1 \rightsquigarrow \Box \varphi_2) \Leftrightarrow \text{CStable}_{l+1}(\boldsymbol{K}, \pi, \varphi_1, \varphi_2, 0)$$

Let d_{l+1} be d used in $\text{CStable}_{l+1}(\boldsymbol{K}, \pi, \varphi_1, \varphi_2, 0)$ such that $d_{l+1}(0) = 0$, $d_{l+1}(i)$ is an arbitrary natural number for $i = 1, \ldots, l+1$ and $d_{l+1}(l+2) = \infty$. The induction hypothesis is as follows:

$$(\boldsymbol{K}, \pi \models \varphi_1 \rightsquigarrow \Box \varphi_2) \Leftrightarrow \text{CStable}_l(\boldsymbol{K}, \pi, \varphi_1, \varphi_2, 0)$$

Let d_l be d used in $\text{CStable}_l(\boldsymbol{K}, \pi, \varphi_1, \varphi_2, 0)$ such that $d_l(0) = 0$, $d_l(i)$ is an arbitrary natural number for $i = 1, \ldots, l$ and $d_l(l + 1) = \infty$. Because $d_{l+1}(i)$ is an arbitrary natural number for $i = 1, \ldots, l + 1$, we suppose that $d_{l+1}(1) = d_l(1)$ and $d_{l+1}(i + 1) = d_l(i)$ for $i = 1, \ldots, l$. Because π is any path of $\boldsymbol{K}$, π can be replaced with $\pi^{d_l(1)}$. If so, we have the following as an instance of the induction hypothesis:

$$(\boldsymbol{K}, \pi^{d_l(1)} \models \varphi_1 \rightsquigarrow \Box \varphi_2) \Leftrightarrow \text{CStable}_l(\boldsymbol{K}, \pi^{d_l(1)}, \varphi_1, \varphi_2, 0)$$

From Definition 4, $\text{CStable}_l(\boldsymbol{K}, \pi^{d_l(1)}, \varphi_1, \varphi_2, 0)$ is $\text{CStable}_{l+1}(\boldsymbol{K}, \pi, \varphi_1, \varphi_2, 1)$ because $d_l(0) = d_{l+1}(0) = 0$, $d_l(1) = d_{l+1}(1)$ and $d_l(i) = d_{l+1}(i + 1)$ for $i = 1, \ldots, l$ and $d_l(l + 1) = d_{l+1}(l + 2) = \infty$. Therefore, the induction hypothesis instance can be rephrased as follows:

$$(\boldsymbol{K}, \pi^{d_{l+1}(1)} \models \varphi_1 \rightsquigarrow \Box \varphi_2) \Leftrightarrow \text{CStable}_{l+1}(\boldsymbol{K}, \pi, \varphi_1, \varphi_2, 1)$$

From Definition 4, $\text{CStable}_{l+1}(\boldsymbol{K}, \pi, \varphi_1, \varphi_2, 0)$ is

$$[(\boldsymbol{K}, \pi^{(d_{l+1}(0), d_{l+1}(1))} \models \Box \neg \varphi_1) \Rightarrow \text{CStable}_L(\boldsymbol{K}, \pi, \varphi_1, \varphi_2, 1)] \wedge$$
$$[(\boldsymbol{K}, \pi^{(d_{l+1}(0), d_{l+1}(1))} \not\models \Box \neg \varphi_1) \Rightarrow (\boldsymbol{K}, \pi^{(d_{l+1}(L), d_{l+1}(L+1))} \models \Diamond \Box \varphi_2)]$$

which is

$$[(\boldsymbol{K}, \pi^{(d_{l+1}(0), d_{l+1}(1))} \models \Box \neg \varphi_1) \Rightarrow (\boldsymbol{K}, \pi^{d_{l+1}(1)} \models \varphi_1 \rightsquigarrow \Box \varphi_2)] \wedge$$
$$[(\boldsymbol{K}, \pi^{(d_{l+1}(0), d_{l+1}(1))} \not\models \Box \neg \varphi_1) \Rightarrow (\boldsymbol{K}, \pi^{(d_{l+1}(L), d_{l+1}(L+1))} \models \Diamond \Box \varphi_2)]$$

because of the induction hypothesis instance. From Lemma 4, this is equivalent to $\boldsymbol{K}, \pi \models \varphi_1 \rightsquigarrow \Box \varphi_2$. $\qquad \Box$

Algorithm 1. A divide & conquer approach to conditional stable model checking

---

input : K – a Kripke structure
φ_1, φ_2 – State propositions
L – a non-zero natural number
d – a function such that $d(x)$ is a non-zero natural number for $x = 1, \ldots, L$

output: Success ($K \models \varphi_1 \rightsquigarrow \Box\varphi_2$) or Failure ($K \not\models \varphi_1 \rightsquigarrow \Box\varphi_2$)

```
1  NCxS ← I
2  CxS ← ∅
3  forall the l ∈ {1, ..., L} do
4  │   NCxS′ ← {π(d(l)) | s ∈ NCxS, π ∈ P^(d(l))_(K,s)}
5  │   CxS′ ← {π(d(l)) | s ∈ CxS, π ∈ P^(d(l))_(K,s)}
6  │   forall the s ∈ NCxS do
7  │   │   forall the π ∈ P^(d(l))_(K,s) do
8  │   │   │   if K, π ⊭ □¬φ₁ then
9  │   │   │   │   NCxS′ ← NCxS′ − {π(d(l))}
10 │   │   │   │   CxS′ ← CxS′ ∪ {π(d(l))}
11 │   NCxS ← NCxS′
12 │   CxS ← CxS′
13 forall the s ∈ NCxS do
14 │   forall the π ∈ P_(K,s) do
15 │   │   if K, π ⊭ φ₁ ⤳ □φ₂ then
16 │   │   │   return Failure
17 forall the s ∈ CxS do
18 │   forall the π ∈ P_(K,s) do
19 │   │   if K, π ⊭ ◇□φ₂ then
20 │   │   │   return Failure
21 return Success
```

---

4   A Divide & Conquer Approach to Conditional Stable Model Checking Algorithm

An algorithm can be constructed based on Theorem 1, which is shown as Algorithm 1. Just after the first **forall** loop, $NCxS \cup CxS$ is the set of all states located at the bottom of the Lth layer (or the top of the $L + 1$st layer); if there exists a state s in a path fragment from an initial state to a state s_L located at the bottom of the Lth layer such that φ_1 holds for s, s_L is in CxS and CxS consists of all such states located at the bottom of the Lth layer; $NCxS$ consists of all the other states located at the bottom of the Lth layer. The code fragment at lines 13–16 checks $\varphi_1 \rightsquigarrow \Box\varphi_2$ for each path that starts with each state in $NCxS$. The code fragment at lines 17 – 20 checks $\Diamond\Box\varphi_2$ for each path that starts with each state in CxS. The first **forall** loop generates the two sets of states located at bottom of the Lth layer by checking $\Box\neg\varphi_1$ for some paths obtained from intermediate layers (1st to Lth layers).

5 Future Directions

We will build a tool supporting the proposed technique and conduct case studies demonstrating that the proposed technique and tool are useful. We will expand the technique in order to handle other properties.

References

1. Aung, M.N., Phyo, Y., Do, C.M., Ogata, K.: A divide and conquer approach to eventual checking. Mathematics **9**, 368 (2021). https://doi.org/10.3390/math9040368
2. Clarke, E.M., Henzinger, T.A., Veith, H., Bloem, R.: Handbook of Model Checking. Springer, Berlin, Heidelberg (2018). https://doi.org/10.1007/978-3-319-10575-8
3. Dolev, S.: Self-Stabilization. MIT Press, Cambridge (2000)
4. Phyo, Y., Do, C.M., Ogata, K.: A divide and conquer approach to leads-to model checking. Comput. J. (2021). https://doi.org/10.1093/comjnl/bxaa183
5. Phyo, Y., Do, C.M., Ogata, K.: A support tool for the L+1-layer divide and conquer approach to leads-to model checking. In: Proceedings of COMPSAC 2021. IEEE (2021). https://doi.org/10.1109/COMPSAC51774.2021.00118

Formalization and Verification in Coq and Isabelle

Certifying Choreography Compilation

Luís Cruz-Filipe$^{(\boxtimes)}$ ⓘ, Fabrizio Montesi ⓘ, and Marco Peressotti ⓘ

Department of Mathematics and Computer Science, University of Southern Denmark,
Campusvej 55, 5230 Odense M, Denmark
{lcfilipe,fmontesi,peressotti}@imada.sdu.dk

Abstract. Choreographic programming is a paradigm for developing concurrent and distributed systems, where programs are *choreographies* that define, from a global viewpoint, the computations and interactions that communicating processes should enact. *Choreography compilation* translates choreographies into the local definitions of process behaviours, given as terms in a process calculus.

Proving choreography compilation correct is challenging and error-prone, because it requires relating languages in different paradigms (global interactions vs local actions) and dealing with a combinatorial explosion of proof cases. We present the first certified program for choreography compilation for a nontrivial choreographic language supporting recursion.

Keywords: Choreographic programming · Formalisation · Compilation

1 Introduction

Choreographic programming is an emerging programming paradigm where the desired communication behaviour of a system of communicating processes can be defined from a global viewpoint in programs known as *choreographies* [25]. Then, a provably-correct compiler can automatically generate executable code for each process, with the guarantee that executing these processes together implements the communications prescribed in the choreography [5,7]. The theory of such compilers is typically called EndPoint Projection (EPP).

Choreographies are inspired by the "Alice and Bob" notation for security protocols [27]. The key idea is to have a linguistic primitive for a communication from a participant to another: statement `Alice.e → Bob.x` reads "`Alice` evaluates expression `e` and sends the result to `Bob`, who stores it in variable `x`". This syntax has two main advantages. First, the desired communications are syntactically manifest in a choreography, which makes choreographic programming suitable for making interaction protocols precise. Second, it disallows writing mismatched send and receive actions, so code generated from a choreography enjoys progress (the system never gets stuck) [7].

Work partially supported by Villum Fonden, grant no. 29518.

A. Cerone and P. C. Ölveczky (Eds.): ICTAC 2021, LNCS 12819, pp. 115–133, 2021.
https://doi.org/10.1007/978-3-030-85315-0_8

The potential of choreographic programming has motivated the study of choreographic languages and EPP definitions for different applications, including self-adaptive systems [15], information flow [21], system integration [16], parallel algorithms [10], cyber-physical systems [17,23,24], and security protocols [17].

EPP involves three elements: the source choreography language, the target language, and the compiler. The interplay between these components, where a single instruction at the choreographic level might be implemented by multiple instructions in the target language, makes the theory of choreographic programming error-prone: for even simpler approaches, like abstract choreographies without computation, it has been recently discovered that a few key results published in peer-reviewed articles do not hold and their theories required adjustments [28], raising concerns about the soundness of these methods.

In this article, we present a certified program for EPP, which translates terms of a Turing complete choreographic language into terms of a distributed process calculus. Our main result is the formalisation of the hallmark result of choreographic programming, the "EPP Theorem": an operational correspondence between choreographies and their endpoint projections. This is the first time that this result has been formalised in a theorem prover, increasing our confidence in the methodology of choreographies.

Structure and Related Work. Our formalisation is developed in Coq [4], and we assume some familiarity with it. We start from a previous formalisation [13] of a choreographic language (Core Choreographies [12]), which we recap in Sect. 2. This formalisation only deals with the choreographic language and its properties; in particular, the target calculus for EPP is not defined therein.

In Sect. 3, we define our target language: a distributed process calculus inspired by the informal presentation in [26]. The calculus has communication primitives that recall those commonly used for implementing choreography languages, e.g., as found in (multiparty) session types [20]. In Sect. 4, we define *merging* [5]: a partial operator that addresses the standard problem (for choreographies) of checking that each process implementation eventually agrees on the choice between alternative behaviours in protocols [3,5]. Building on merging, in Sect. 5, we define EPP. Then, in Sect. 6, we explore *pruning* [5]: a preorder induced by merging that plays a key role in the EPP Theorem, proved in Sect. 7.

Choreographies are used in industry for the specification and definition of web services and business processes [19,29]. These languages feature recursion or loops, which are not present in the only other formalisation work on choreographies that we are aware of [18]. We have validated the theory of EPP from [26], and made explicit several properties that are typically only implicitly assumed. Our results show that the ideas developed by researchers on choreographies, like merging, can be relied upon for languages of practical appeal.

2   Background

We use the choreographic language of [26], which is inspired by Core Choreographies (CC) [12]. So far, this is the only Turing complete choreographic language that has been formalised [13]. In this section, we recap this formalisation, which our work builds upon. We refer the reader to [13] for a discussion of the design options both behind the choreographic language and the formalisation. Some of these are relevant for our development, and we explain them when needed.

CC is designed to model communication protocols involving several participants, called processes, each equipped with memory cells, identified by variables. Communications are of two kinds: *value communications*, where a process evaluates an expression using the values stored in its memory and sends the result to a (distinct) process; and *(label) selections*, where a process selects from different behaviours available at another process by means of an identifier (the label). Selections are used to communicate local choices made by a process to other processes. Recursive and infinite behaviour is achieved by defining procedures.

Syntax. The formalisation of CC is parametric on the types of processes (`Pid`, ranged over by `p`), variables (`Var`, ranged over by `x`), expressions (`Expr`, ranged over by `e`), values stored in memory (`Value`, ranged over by `v`), Boolean expressions (`BExpr`, ranged over by `b`) and procedure names (`RecVar`, ranged over by `X`). Equality on these types must be decidable. Labels, ranged over by `l`, are either `left` or `right`, which is common in choreographies and session types [6,8,30].

The syntax of choreographies is defined by the following BNF grammar.

```
eta ::= p.e -> q.x | p -> q[l]
  C ::= eta; C | If p.b Then Ct Else Ce | Call X | RT_Call X ps C | End
```

An `eta` is a communication action, where `p.e -> q.x` is a value communication[1] and `p -> q[l]` is a label selection. `Eta` is the type of all communication actions.

Choreographies are ranged over by `C`. A choreography `eta; C`, can execute a communication `eta` and continue as `C`. A conditional `If p.b Then Ct Else Ce` evaluates the Boolean expression `b` in the memory of process `p` and continues as `Ct` or `Ce`, according to whether `b` evaluates to `true` or `false`. Choreography `Call X` is a call to a procedure `X`. Term `RT_Call X ps C` is a *runtime term*, discussed below. Term `End` is the terminated choreography. We write `Choreography` for the type of all choreographies.

This grammar is implemented as a Coq inductive type, e.g., `eta; C` stands for `Interaction eta C`, where `Interaction : Eta → Choreography → Choreography` is a constructor of type `Choreography`.

Example 1 (Distributed Authentication). The choreography `C1` below describes a multiparty authentication scenario where an identity provider `ip` authenticates a client `c`, to server `s` (we name subterms for later use).

```
C1 := c.credentials -> ip.x; If ip.(check x) Then C1t Else C1e
C1t := ip -> s[left]; ip -> c[left]; s.token -> c.t; End
C1e := ip -> s[right]; ip -> c[right]; End
```

---

[1] For readability, we use notations closer to the usual mathematical ones than in formalisation, where they are slightly different due to Coq's restrictions on overloading.

C1 starts with c communicating its credentials, stored in the local variable credentials, to ip, which stores them in x. Then, ip checks if the credentials are valid or not by evaluating the local expression check x, and signals the result to s and c by selecting left when the credentials are valid (C1t) and right otherwise (C1e). In the first case, the server communicates a token (stored in its local variable token) to the client, otherwise the choreography ends.

Because the guard of the conditional is evaluated by ip, only this process knows which branch of the choreography to execute. This is an instance of the *knowledge of choice* problem. Label selections propagate this information to processes whose behaviour depends on this choice (in this case, both s and c). ◁

A *program* is a pair (Procedures P,Main P):DefSet * Choreography. Elements of type DefSet (set of procedure definitions) map each X to a pair containing the processes used in X (Vars P X) and the choreography to be executed (Procs P X). These procedure definitions can then be called from each other and from Main P (using term Call X), allowing for the definition of recursive behaviour.

Executing procedure calls generates runtime terms. Choreography Call X can reduce by a process p entering X. It becomes RT_Call X ps C, where C is the definition of X and ps is the list of processes used in X (other than p). This term can then either reduce by another process entering the procedure (and being removed from ps), or by executing some action in C that does not involve processes in ps (and C is updated). When the last process in ps calls X, RT_Call X ps C reduces to C. The runtime term RT_Call X ps C is not meant to be used when writing a choreography, and in particular it should not occur in procedure definitions. A choreography that does not include any such term is called *initial*.

There are three kinds of restrictions when writing choreographies.

(i) Intended use of choreographies. Interactions must have distinct processes (no self-communication), e.g., p.e -> p.x is disallowed.
(ii) Intended use of runtime terms. All choreographies Procs P X must be initial. Main P may include subterms RT_Call X ps C, but ps must be nonempty and include only process names that occur in Vars P X.
(iii) Design choices in the formalisation. Informally, Vars X contains the processes that are used in Procs X. This introduces constraints that are encapsulated in the definition of well-formed program.

The constraints in the last category are particularly relevant for the proof of the EPP Theorem, so we discuss them in that context in Sect. 7.

Example 2. Let Defs:DefSet map FileTransfer to the pair consisting of the process list c :: s :: nil and the following choreography.

```
s.(file, check) -> c.x;                (* send file and check data      *)
If c.( crc(fst(x))== snd(x))           (* cyclic redundancy check       *)
  Then c -> s[left]; End               (* file received correctly, end  *)
  Else c -> s[right]; Call FileTransfer (* errors detected, retry        *)
```

FileTransfer describes a file transfer protocol between a server s and a client c using Cyclic Redundancy Checks (crc) to detect errors from a noisy channel. ◁

Semantics. The semantics of CC is defined as a labelled transition system using inductive types. It uses a *state*, which is a function mapping process variables to their values: State:Pid $\to$ Var $\to$ Value.

The semantics is structured in three layers. The first layer specifies transitions with the following relation, parameterised on a set of procedure definitions.

```
CCC_To : DefSet → Choreography → State
              → RichLabel → Choreography → State → Prop
```

Rules in this set include that p.e -> q.x;C in state s transitions to C in state s', where s' coincides with s except that s' q x now stores the value obtained by evaluating e at p in state s.[2] RichLabel includes information about the executed term – the above communication is labelled R_Com p v q x. There are also rules for out-of-order execution: interactions involving distinct processes can be executed in any order, reflecting concurrency. For example, p.e -> q.x;r -> s[left] can execute as a communication from p to q followed by a label selection from r to s, but also as the latter label selection followed by the former communication.

The second layer raises transitions to the level of programs, abstracting from unobservable details. It is defined by a single rule: if CCC_To Defs C s t C' s', then ({|Defs; C|}, s) —[forget t]⟶ ({|Defs; C'|},s'). Here, {|Defs; C|} denotes the program built from Defs and C, and forget removes unobservable details from transition labels (e.g., forget (R_Com p v q x) is L_Com p v q). Labels for conditionals and procedure calls all simplify to L_Tau p, denoting an internal action at p. The third layer defines the reflexive and transitive closure of program transitions.

Important properties of CC formalised in [13] include deadlock-freedom by design (any program P such that Main P $\neq$ End reduces), confluence (if P can execute two different sequences of actions, then the resulting programs can always reduce to a common program and state), and Turing completeness.

Example 3. Consider the program {|D; C1|} where C1 is the choreography in Example 1 and D:DefSet is arbitrary (there are no recursive calls in C1).

{|D; C1|}, st1) —[L_Com c ip v1]⟶ ({|D; If ip.(check x) Then C1t Else C1e|},st2)

where v1 is the evaluation of e at c in st1 and st2 updates the value of ip's variable x accordingly. If check x is true at ip in st2, then it continues as follows.

{|D; If ip.(check x) Then C1t Else C1e|}, st2) —[L_Tau ip]⟶ {|D; C1t|}, st2)
   —[L_Sel ip s left; L_Sel ip c left]⟶* {|D; s.token -> c.t; End|}, st2)
   —[L_Com s c v2]⟶ {|D; End|}, st3)

where v2 is the evaluation of token at s in st2 and st3 updates st2 accordingly. Otherwise, it continues as follows.

{|D; If ip.(check x) Then C1t Else C1e|}, st2) —[L_Tau ip]⟶ {|D; C1e|}, st2)
   —[L_Sel ip s right; L_Sel ip c right]⟶* {|D; End|}, st2)

---

[2] The semantics of CC only requires extensional equality of states, which is why s' is quantified over rather than directly defined from s.

In compound transitions, the actions in the label are executed in order.   ◁

Example 4. Let Defs as in Example 2 and C be the body of FileTransfer. Consider the program {|Defs; Call FileTransfer|}. The processes in the procedure FileTransfer can start a call in any order as exemplified by the transitions below.

{|Defs; Call FileTransfer|},st) —[L_Tau c]⟶
    ({|Defs; RT_Call FileTransfer s::nil C|},st) —[L_Tau s]⟶ ({|Defs; C|},st)

{|Defs; Call FileTransfer|},st) —[L_Tau s]⟶
    ({|Defs; RT_Call FileTransfer c::nil C|},st) —[L_Tau c]⟶ ({|Defs; C|},st)

The state st is immaterial.   ◁

3 Stateful Processes

Our first contribution is formalising SP (Stateful Processes), the process calculus for implementing CC [26], which is inspired by the process calculi in [11,12].[3]

3.1 Syntax

SP is defined as a Coq functor with the same parameters as CC. Its syntax contains three ingredients: behaviours, defining the actions performed by individual processes; networks, consisting of several processes running in parallel; and programs, defining a set of procedure definitions that all processes can use.

Behaviours. Behaviours are sequences of local actions – counterparts to the terms that can be written in CC – defined by the following BNF grammar.

B ::= End | p!e;B | p?x;B | p⊕l;B | p&mBl//mBr | If b Then Bt Else Be | Call X

This grammar is again formalised as a Coq inductive type, called Behaviour. Terms End, If b Then Bt Else Be and Call X are as in CC. Value communications are split into p!e; B, which evaluates e, sends the result to p, and continues as B, and by p?x; B, which receives a value from p, stores it at x, and continues as B.[4]

Label selections are divided into p⊕l; B – sending the label l to p and continuing as B – and p & mBl // mBr, where one of mBl or mBr is chosen according to the label selected by p. Both mBl and mBr have type option Behaviour (either None or Some B, where B is a behaviour): a process does not need to offer behaviours

---

[3] The choreography language CC is also inspired by the works [11,12], but formalising it in Coq benefitted substantially from adopting a labelled transition system semantics. This is discussed extensively in [13]. In this work, we made similar changes to the process calculus not only for similar reasons, but also to keep a close correspondence with the choreography language.

[4] Processes communicate by name. In practice, names can be either process identifiers (cf. actors), network addresses, or session correlation data.

corresponding to all possible labels. Informally, branching terms are partial functions from labels to behaviours; we capitalise on the fact that there are only two labels to simplify the formalisation.

Many results about `Behaviours` are proved by structural induction, requiring inspection of subterms of branching terms. The induction principle automatically generated by Coq is not strong enough for this, and our formalisation includes a stronger result that we use in later proofs.

Networks. Networks have type `Pid → Behaviour`. We define extensional equality of networks, `N== N'`, and show that it is an equivalence relation. To model practice, where networks are written as finite parallel compositions of behaviours, we introduce some constructions: `N|N'` is the parallel composition of `N` and `N'`; `p[B]` is the network mapping `p` to `B` and all other processes to `End`; and `N ~~ p` denotes network `N` where `p` is now mapped to `End`. The formalisation includes a number of lemmas about extensional equality, for example that updating the behaviours of two processes yields the same result independent of the order of the updates.

Programs. Finally, a `Program` is a pair (`Procs P,Net P`):`DefSetB * Network`, where `DefSetB = RecVar → Behaviour` maps procedure names to `Behaviours`.

Programs, networks and behaviours should satisfy well-formedness properties similar to those of CC. However, these properties are automatically ensured when networks are automatically generated from choreographies, so we do not discuss them here. They are included in the formalisation.

Example 5. Consider the network `N = c[Bc] | s[Bs] | ip[Bip]` composed by the behaviours below.

```
Bc := ip!credentials; ip & Some (s?t; End) // Some End
Bs := ip & Some (c!token; End) // Some End

Bip := c?x; Bip'
Bip' := If (check x) Then (s⊕left; c⊕left; End) Else (s⊕right; c⊕right; End)
```

This network implements the choreography in Example 1.   ◁

3.2 Semantics

The semantics of SP is defined by a labelled transition system. Transitions for communications match dual actions in two processes, while conditionals and procedure calls simply run locally. We report the representative cases – the complete definition can be found in the source formalisation [14]. For readability, we first present them in the standard rule notation.

$$\frac{\begin{array}{cc} \text{v} := \text{eval\_on\_state e s p} \quad \text{N p} = \text{q!e; B} \quad \text{N q} = \text{p?x; B'} \\ \text{N'} == \text{N} \sim\sim \text{p} \sim\sim \text{q} \mid \text{p}[\text{B}] \mid \text{q}[\text{B'}] \quad \text{s'} == \text{update s q x v} \end{array}}{(\{\mid \text{Defs}; \text{N}\mid\}, \ \text{s}) \ -[\text{L\_Com p v q}] \longrightarrow (\{\mid \text{Defs}; \text{N'}\mid\}, \ \text{s'})} \ \text{S\_Com}$$

$$\frac{\begin{array}{cc} \text{N p} = \text{q}\oplus\text{left; B} \quad \text{N q} = \text{p \& Some B1 // Br} \\ \text{N'} == \text{N} \sim\sim \text{p} \sim\sim \text{q} \mid \text{p}[\text{B}] \mid \text{q}[\text{B1}] \quad \text{s} == \text{s'} \end{array}}{(\{\mid \text{Defs}; \text{N}\mid\}, \ \text{s}) \ -[\text{L\_Sel p q left}] \longrightarrow (\{\mid \text{Defs}; \text{N'}\mid\}, \ \text{s'})} \ \text{S\_LSel}$$

$$\frac{\text{N p} = \text{If b Then B1 Else B2} \quad \text{beval\_on\_state b s p} = \text{true} \quad \text{N'} == \text{N} \sim\sim \text{p} \mid \text{p}[\text{B1}] \quad \text{s} == \text{s'}}{(\{\mid \text{Defs}; \text{N}\mid\}, \ \text{s}) \ -[\text{L\_Tau p}] \longrightarrow (\{\mid \text{Defs}; \text{N'}\mid\}, \ \text{s'})} \ \text{S\_Then}$$

$$\frac{\text{N p} = \text{Call X} \quad \text{N'} == \text{N} \sim\sim \text{p} \mid \text{p}[\text{Defs X}] \quad \text{s} == \text{s'}}{(\{\mid \text{Defs}; \text{N}\mid\}, \ \text{s}) \ -[\text{L\_Tau X p}] \longrightarrow (\{\mid \text{Defs}; \text{N'}\mid\}, \ \text{s'})} \ \text{S\_Call}$$

Functions `eval_on_state` and `beval_on_state` evaluate a (Boolean) expression locally, given a state, while `update s q x v` updates state s by changing the value of q's variable x to v. We write also $==$ for extensional equality of states.

As for choreographies, the formalisation of these rules is done in two steps. The first step defines a transition relation parameterised on the set of procedure definitions, and includes richer transition labels (necessary for doing case analysis on transitions). This relation is defined as an inductive type, whose first defining clause is shown below.[5]

```
Inductive SP_To (Defs : DefSetB) :
  Network → State → RichLabel → Network → State → Prop :=
  | S_Com N p e B q x B' N' s s' : let v := (eval_on_state e s p) in
    N p = (q!e; B) → N q = (p?x; B') → N' == N ~~ p ~~ q | p[B] | q[B'] →
    s' == (update s q x v) → SP_To Defs N s (R_Com p v q x) N' s'    (...)
```

This relation is then lifted to configurations just as for CC: if SP_To Defs N s t N' s', then $(\{\mid \text{Defs}; \text{N}\mid\}, \text{s}) -[\text{forget t}] \longrightarrow (\{\mid \text{Defs}; \text{N'}\mid\}, \text{s'})$. Closure under reflexivity and transitivity (with similar notation) is again defined as for choreographies.

Example 6. We illustrate the possible transitions of the network from Example 5. We abbreviate the behaviours of processes that do not change in a reduction to ... to make it more clear what parts of the network are changed. Furthermore, we omit trailing `Ends` in `Behaviours`.

The network starts by performing the transition

---

[5] Coq's type inference mechanism allows us to omit types of most universally quantified variables and parameters. We abuse this possibility to lighten the presentation.

{|D; c[Bc] | s[Bs] | ip[Bip]|}, st1) —[L_Com c ip v1]⟶
  {|D; c[ip & Some (s?t) // Some End] | s[...] | ip[Bip']|}, st2)

where v1 and st2 are as in Example 3. If eval_on_state (check x) st2 ip is true, it continues as follows

{|D; c[ip & Some (s?t) // Some End] | s[Bs] | ip[Bip'], st2)
  —[L_Tau ip]⟶   {|D; c[...] | s[...] | ip[s⊕left;c⊕left], st2)
  —[L_Sel ip s left]⟶ {|D; c[...] | s[c!token] | ip[c⊕left], st2)
  —[L_Sel ip c left]⟶ {|D; c[s?t] | s[...] | ip[End], st2)
  —[L_Com s c v2]⟶   {|D; c[End] | s[End] | ip[End], st3)

where v2 and st3 are again as in Example 3. Otherwise, it continues as follows.

{|D; c[ip & Some (s?t) // Some End] | s[Bs] | ip[Bip'], st2)
  —[L_Tau ip]⟶   {|D; c[...] | s[...] | ip[s⊕right;c⊕right], st2)
  —[L_Sel ip s right]⟶ {|D; c[...] | s[End] | ip[c⊕right], st2)
  —[L_Sel ip c right]⟶ {|D; c[End] | s[End] | ip[End], st2)

The labels in these reductions are exactly as in Example 3.   ◁

Transitions are compatible with network equality and state equivalence.

Lemma SPP_To_eq : ∀ P s1 tl P' s2 s1' s2',
  s1== s1' → s2== s2' → (P,s1) —[tl]⟶ (P',s2) → (P,s1') —[tl]⟶ (P',s2').

Lemma SPP_To_Network_eq : ∀ P1 P1' P2 s s' tl, (Net P1== Net P1') →
  (Procs P1 = Procs P1') → (P1,s) —[tl]⟶ (P2,s') → (P1',s) —[tl]⟶ (P2,s').

These results are instrumental in some of the later proofs, and are proven for the three levels of reductions. The following, related, result is also important.

Lemma SPP_To_Defs_stable : ∀ Defs' N N' tl s s',
  {|Defs N,s|} —[tl]⟶ {|Defs' N',s'|} → Defs = Defs'.

We also prove that transitions are completely determined by the label.

Lemma SPP_To_deterministic : ∀ P s tl P' s' P'' s'',
  (P,s) —[tl]⟶ (P',s') → (P,s) —[tl]⟶ (P'',s'') →
  (Net P'== Net P'') ∧ Procs P' = Procs P'' ∧ (s' == s'').

Finally, we show that the semantics of SP is confluent. Although this is not required for our main theorem, it is a nice result that confirms our expectations.

The formalisation of SP consists of 37 definitions, 80 lemmas, and 2000 lines.

4   Merging

Intuitively, process implementations are generated from choreographies recursively, by projecting each action in the choreography to the corresponding process action – for example, a value communication p.e -> q.x should be projected as a send action q!e at p, as a receive action p?x at q, and not projected to any other processes. However, this causes a problem with conditionals. Projecting a choreography If p.b Then Ct Else Ce for any process other than p, say q, requires combining the projections obtained for Ct and Ce, such that q can "react" to whichever choice p will make. This combination is called *merging* [5].

Merge is typically defined as a partial function mapping pairs of behaviours to behaviours that returns a behaviour combining all possible executions of the two input behaviours (if possible). For SP, two behaviours can be merged if they are structurally similar, with the possible exception of branching terms: we can merge branchings that offer options on distinct labels. For example, merging p & (Some B) // None with p & None // (Some B') yields p & (Some B) // (Some B'), allowing If p??b Then (p-> q[left];q.e -> p;End) Else (p-> q[right];End) to be projected for q as p & Some (p!e; End) // Some End.

Since functions in Coq are total, formalising merging poses a problem. Furthermore, assigning type Behaviour → Behaviour → option Behaviour to merging causes ambiguity, since branching terms have subterms of type option Behaviour.[6] Instead, we define a type XBehaviour of extended behaviours, defined as Behaviour with an extra constructor XUndefined : XBehaviour. Thus, an XBehaviour is a Behaviour that may contain XUndefined subterms.

The connection between Behaviour and XBehaviour is established by means of two functions: inject : Behaviour → XBehaviour, which isomorphically injects each constructor of Behaviour into the corresponding one in XBehaviour, and collapse : XBehaviour → XBehaviour that maps all XBehaviours with XUndefined as a subterm to XUndefined. The most relevant properties of these functions are:

```
Lemma inject_elim : ∀ B, ∃ B', inject B = B' ∧ B' ≠ XUndefined.
Lemma collapse_inject : ∀ B, collapse (inject B) = inject B.
Lemma collapse_char'' : ∀ B, collapse B = XUndefined → ∀ B', B ≠ inject B'.
Lemma collapse_∃ : ∀ B, collapse B ≠ XUndefined → ∃ B', B = inject B'.
```

Using this type, we first define XMerge on XBehaviours as below, where we report only representative cases. (Pid_dec and Expr_dec are lemmas stating decidability of equality on Pid and Expr, allowing us to do case analysis.)

```
Fixpoint Xmerge (B1 B2:XBehaviour) : XBehaviour := match B1, B2 with
| XEnd, XEnd ⇒ XEnd
| XSend p e B, XSend p' e' B' ⇒ if Pid_dec p p' && Expr_dec e e'
    then match Xmerge B B' with XUndefined ⇒ XUndefined
                              | _ ⇒ XSend p e (Xmerge B B') end
    else XUndefined
| XBranching p Bl Br, XBranching p' Bl' Br' ⇒ if Pid_dec p p'
    then let BL := match Bl with None ⇒ Bl' | Some B ⇒
      match Bl' with None ⇒ Bl | Some B' ⇒ Some (Xmerge B B') end end
    in let BR := match Br with None ⇒ Br' | Some B ⇒
      match Br' with None ⇒ Br | Some B' ⇒ Some (Xmerge B B') end end
    in match BL, BR with Some XUndefined, _ ⇒ XUndefined
      | _, Some XUndefined ⇒ XUndefined | _, _ ⇒ XBranching p BL BR end
    else XUndefined                                              (...)
```

Using XMerge we can straightforwardly define merging.

---

[6] Essentially because it is not possible to distinguish if the behaviour assigned to a label is None because it was not defined, or because a recursive call to merge failed.

Definition merge B1 B2 := Xmerge (inject B1) (inject B2).

We show `merge` to be idempotent, commutative and associative. This last proof illustrates the major challenge of this stage of the formalisation: it requires a triple induction with 512 cases, of which 84 cannot be solved automatically. These had to be divided in further subcases of different levels of complexity. The final case, when all behaviours are branching terms, requires six (!) nested inductions to generate the 64 possible combinations of defined/undefined branches, which had to be done by hand. The total proof is over 500 lines.

The largest set of lemmas about `merge` deals with inversion results, such as:

Lemma merge_inv_Send : ∀ B B' p e X, merge B B' = XSend p e X →
  ∃ B1 B1', B = p ! e; B1 ∧ B' = p ! e; B1' ∧ merge B1 B1' = X.

The similar result for branching terms is much more complex, since there are several cases for each branch (if it is `None`, then both `B` and `B'` must have `None` in the corresponding branch, otherwise it may be from `B`, from `B'`, or a merge of both), and its proof suffers from the same problems as the proof of associativity (thankfully, not to such a dramatic level). Automation works better here, and the effect of the large number of subcases is mostly felt in the time required by the `auto` tactic. Still, the formalisation of merging consists of 6 definitions, 43 lemmas, and 2550 lines – giving an average proof length of over 50 lines.

5 EndPoint Projection

The next step is defining EndPoint Projection (EPP): a partial function that maps programs in CC to programs in SP. The target instance of SP has the same parameters as CC, except that the set of procedure names is `RecVar * Pid` – each procedure is implemented from the point of view of each process in it.

Partiality of EPP stems from the problem of choreography realisability [3]. A choreography such as If p.b Then (q.e -> r.x) Else End cannot be implemented without additional communications between p, q and r, since the latter processes need to know the result of the conditional to decide whether to communicate (see also Example 1). We say that this choreography is not *projectable* [12].

We define EPP in several layers. First, we define a function `bproj : DefSet →` `Choreography → Pid → XBehaviour` projecting the behaviour of a single process. Intuitively, `bproj Defs C p` attempts to construct p's behaviour as specified by C; the parameter `Defs` is used for procedure calls, whose projections depend on whether p participates in the procedure. Returning an `XBehaviour` instead of an `option Behaviour` gives information about where exactly merging fails (the location of `XUndefined` subterms), which can be used for debugging, providing information to programmers, or for automatic repair of choreographies [2,12].

We show some illustrative cases of the definition of `bproj`.

```
Fixpoint bproj (Defs:DefSet) (C:Choreography) (r:Pid) : XBehaviour := match C with
| p.e -> q.x; C' ⇒
  if Pid_dec p r then XSend q e (bproj Defs C' r)
              else if Pid_dec q r then XRecv p x (bproj Defs C' r)
                        else bproj Defs C' r
```

```
| p -> q[left]; C' ⇒
  if Pid_dec p r then XSel q left (bproj Defs C' r)
                 else if Pid_dec q r then XBranching p (Some (bproj Defs C' r)) None
                                     else bproj Defs C' r
| If p.b Then C1 Else C2 ⇒
  if Pid_dec p r then XCond b (bproj Defs C1 r) (bproj Defs C2 r)
                 else Xmerge (bproj Defs C1 r) (bproj Defs C2 r)
| CCBase.Call X ⇒ if In_dec P.eq_dec r (fst (Defs X)) then XCall (X,r) else XEnd
(...)
```

The next step is generating projections for all relevant processes. We take the set of processes as a parameter, and collapse all individual projections.

```
Definition epp_list (Defs:DefSet) (C:Choreography) (ps:list Pid)
  : list (Pid * XBehaviour) := map (fun p ⇒ (p, collapse (bproj Defs C p))) ps.
```

A choreography C is projectable wrt Defs and ps if epp_list Defs C ps does not contain XUndefined, and Defs:DefSet is projectable wrt a set of procedure names Xs if snd (Defs X) is projectable wrt Defs and fst (Defs X) for each X in Xs. Projectability of programs is a bit more involved, and we present its Coq formalisation before discussing it.

```
Definition projectable Xs ps P :=
  projectable_C (Procedures P) ps (Main P) ∧ projectable_D Xs (Procedures P) ∧
  (∀ p, In p (CCC_pn (Main P) (fun _ ⇒ nil)) → In p ps) ∧
  (∀ p X, In X Xs → In p (fst (Procedures P X)) → In p ps) ∧
  (∀ p X, In X Xs → In p (CCC_pn (snd (Procedures P X)) (fun _ ⇒ nil)) → In p ps).
```

The first two conditions simply state that Main P and Procedures P are projectable wrt the appropriate parameters. The remaining conditions state that the sets ps and Xs include all processes used in P and all procedures needed to execute P. (These sets are not necessarily computable, since Xs is not required to be finite. However, in practice, these parameters are known – so it is easier to include them in the definition.) Function CCC_pn returs the set of processes used in a choreography, given the sets of processes each procedure call is supposed to use.

We now define compilation of projectable choreographies (epp_C), projectable sets of procedure definitions (epp_D), and projectable programs (epp). These definitions depend on proof terms whose structure needs to be explored, and are done interactively; afterwards, we show them to be independent of the proof terms, and that they work as expected. We give a few examples.

```
Lemma epp_C_wd : ∀ Defs C ps H H', (epp_C Defs ps C H)== (epp_C Defs ps C H').
Lemma epp_C_Com_p : ∀ Defs ps C p e q x HC HC', In p ps →
  epp_C Defs ps (p.e-> q.x;C) HC p = q!e; epp_C Defs ps C HC' p.
Lemma epp_C_Cond_r : ∀ Defs ps p b C1 C2 HC HC1 HC2 r, p ≠ r →
  inject (epp_C Defs ps (If p.b Then C1 Else C2) HC r)
  = merge (epp_C Defs ps C1 HC1 r) (epp_C Defs ps C2 HC2 r).
```

Projectability of C does not imply projectability of choreographies that C can transition to. This is due to the way runtime terms are projected: RT_Call X ps C' is projected as a call to (X,p) if p is in ps, and as the projection of C' otherwise. Our definition of projectability allows in principle for C to be unprojectable for a process in ps, which would make it unprojectable after transition. That this situation does not arise is a consequence of the intended usage of runtime terms: initially C' is obtained from the definition of a procedure, and ps is the set of processes used in this procedure. Afterwards ps only shrinks, while C' may change due to execution of actions outside ps. We capture these conditions in the notion of strong projectability, whose representative case is:

```
Fixpoint str_projectable Defs (C:Choreography) (r:Pid) : Prop :=
match C with | RT_Call X ps C ⇒ str_projectable Defs C r ∧
  (∀ p, In p ps → In p (fst (Defs X))
      ∧ Xmore_branches (bproj Defs (snd (Defs X)) p) (bproj Defs C p))  (...)
```

The relation Xmore_branches, explained in the next section, is a semantic characterisation of how the projection of bproj Defs snd (Defs X) p may change due to execution of actions not involving p in snd (Defs X).

Projectability and strong projectability coincide for initial choreographies. Furthermore, we state and prove lemmas that show that strong projectability of C imply strong projectability of any choreography that C can transition to.

6 Pruning

The key ingredient for our correspondence result is a relation on behaviours usually called *pruning* [5,7]. Pruning relates two behaviours that differ only in that one offers more options in branching terms than the other; we formalise this relation with the more suggestive name of more_branches (in line with [26]), and we include some illustrative cases of its definition.

```
Inductive more_branches : Behaviour → Behaviour → Prop :=
| MB_Send p e B B': more_branches B B' → more_branches (p ! e; B) (p ! e; B')
| MB_Branching_None_None p mBl mBr :
    more_branches (p & mBl // mBr) (p & None // None)
| MB_Branching_Some_Some p Bl Bl' Br Br' :
    more_branches Bl Bl' → more_branches Br Br' →
    more_branches (p & Some Bl // Some Br) (p & Some Bl' // Some Br')  (...)
```

The need for pruning arises naturally when one considers what happens when a choreography C executes a conditional at a process p. In the continuation, only one of the branches is kept. However, no process other than p knows that this action has been executed; therefore, if the projection of C executes the corresponding action, both behaviours are still available for all processes other than p. Given how merging is defined, this means that these processes' behaviours may contain more branches than those of the projection of the choreography after reduction.

Pruning is naturally related to merging, as stated in the following lemmas.

```
Lemma more_branches_char : ∀ B B', more_branches B B' ↔ merge B B' = inject B.
Lemma merge_more_branches :
  ∀ B1 B2 B, merge B1 B2 = inject B → more_branches B B1.
```

Pruning is also reflexive and transitive. Further, if two behaviours have an upper bound according to pruning, then their merge is defined and is their lub.

```
Lemma more_branches_merge : ∀ B B1 B2, more_branches B B1 →
    more_branches B B2 → ∃ B', merge B1 B2 = inject B' ∧ more_branches B B'.
```

Finally, two behaviours with fewer branches than two mergeable behaviours are themselves mergeable.

```
Lemma more_branches_merge_extend : ∀ B1 B2 B1' B2' B,
    more_branches B1 B1' → more_branches B2 B2' → merge B1 B2 = inject B →
    ∃ B', merge B1' B2' = inject B' ∧ more_branches B B'.
```

These two results are key ingredients to the cases dealing with conditionals in the proof of the EPP Theorem. They require extensive case analysis (512 cases for the last lemma, of which 81 are not automatically solved by Coq's `inversion` tactic even though most are contradictory). Analogous versions of some of these lemmas also need to be extended to `XBehaviours`, which is straightforward.

Pruning extends pointwise to networks, which we denote as N ≫ N'. The key result is that, due to how the semantics of SP is defined, pruning a network cannot add new transitions.

```
Lemma SP_To_more_branches_N : ∀ Defs N1 s N2 s' Defs' N1' tl,
    SP_To Defs N1 s tl N2 s' → N1' ≫ N1 → (∀ X, Defs X = Defs' X) →
    ∃ N2', SP_To Defs' N1' s tl N2' s' ∧ N2' ≫ N2.
```

The reciprocal of this result only holds for choreography projections, and is proven after the definition of EPP.

The formalisation of pruning includes 3 definitions, 25 lemmas, and 950 lines. Some of these results are used for defining of EPP (previous section), but we delayed their presentation as its motivation is clearer after seeing those definitions.

Example 7. The choreography C1 in Example 1 is projectable, yielding the network in Example 5: `bproj Defs C1 c = inject Bc`, `bproj Defs C1 s = inject Bs`, and `bproj Defs C1 ip = inject Bip`.

If we remove selections from C1, the resulting choreography is not projectable on process c: projecting the conditional requires merging the projections at c of the two branches (now simply `s.token -> c.t; End` and `End`), which fails since `bproj Defs C5 c = inject (s?t; End)` and `bproj Defs End c = inject End`, but `merge (s?t; End) End = XUndefined`. Likewise, merging would fail for s. ◁

7 EPP Theorem

We now prove the operational correspondence between choreographies and their projections, in two directions: if a choreography can make a transition, then its projection can make the same transition; and if the projection of a choreography can make a transition, then so can the choreography. The results of the transitions are not directly related by projection, since choreography transitions may eliminate some branches in the projection; thus, establishing the correspondence for multi-step transitions requires some additional lemmas on pruning.

Preliminaries. Both directions of the correspondence depend on a number of results relating choreography transitions and their projections. These results follow a pattern: the results for communications state a precise correspondence; the ones for conditionals include pruning in their conclusions; and the ones for procedure calls require additional hypotheses on the set of procedure definitions.

Lemma CCC_To_bproj_Sel_p : ∀ Defs C s C' s' p q l, str_projectable Defs C p →
    CCC_To Defs C s (CCBase.TL.R_Sel p q l) C' s' →
    ∃ Bp, bproj Defs C p = XSel q l Bp ∧ bproj Defs C' p = Bp.

Lemma CCC_To_bproj_Call_p : ∀ Defs C s C' s' p X Xs, str_projectable Defs C p →
    (∀ Y, In Y Xs → str_projectable Defs (snd (Defs Y)) p) →
    (∀ Y, set_incl_pid (CCC_pn (snd (Defs Y))) (fun X ⇒ fst (Defs X)))
                          (fst (Defs Y))) →
    In X Xs → CCC_To Defs C s (CCBase.TL.R_Call X p) C' s' →
    bproj Defs C p = XCall (X,p)
    ∧ Xmore_branches (bproj Defs (snd (Defs X)) p) (bproj Defs C' p).

These lemmas are simple to prove by induction on C. The tricky part is getting the hypotheses strong enough that the thesis holds, and weak enough that any well-formed program will satisfy them throughout its entire execution.

From these results, it follows that projectability is preserved by choreography reductions. This property is needed even to state the EPP Theorem, since we can only compute projections of projectable programs.

Lemma CCC_To_projectable : ∀ P Xs ps,
    Program_WF Xs P → well_ann P → projectable Xs ps P →
    (∀ p, In p ps → str_projectable (Procedures P) (Main P) p) →
    (∀ p, In p (CCC_pn (Main P) (Vars P)) → In p ps) →
    (∀ p X, In X Xs → In p (Vars P X) → In p ps) →
    ∀ s tl P' s', (P,s) —[tl]⟶ (P',s') → projectable Xs ps P'.

Some of the hypotheses from the previous lemmas are encapsulated in the first two conditions: well-formedness of P, which ensures that any runtime term RT_Call X qs C in Main P only includes processes in qs that are declared to be used by X (this trivially holds if Main P is initial, and is preserved throughout execution); and well-annotation of P, i.e., the processes used in any procedure are a subset of those it declares.[7] The remaining hypotheses state, as before, that Xs and ps include all processes and procedures relevant for executing Main P.

Similarly, we prove that strong projectability is preserved by transitions.

Completeness. In the literature, completeness of EPP is proven by induction on the derivation of the transition performed by the choreography C. For each case, we look at how a transition for C can be derived, and show that the projection of C can make the same transition to a network with more branches than the projection of C'. The proof is lengthy, but poses no surprises.

Lemma EPP_Complete : ∀ P Xs ps, Program_WF Xs P → well_ann P → ∀ HP,

---

[7] Equality is not necessary, and it would make this property harder to prove.

(∀ p, In p ps → str_projectable (Procedures P) (Main P) p) →
(∀ p, In p (CCC_pn (Main P) (Vars P)) → In p ps) →
(∀ p X, In X Xs → In p (Vars P X) → In p ps) →
∀ s tl P' s', (P,s) —[tl]⟶ (P',s') →
∃ N tl', (epp Xs ps P HP,s) —[tl']⟶ (N,s')
    ∧ Procs N = Procs (epp Xs ps P HP) ∧ ∀ H, Net N ≫ Net (epp Xs ps P' H).

By combining with the earlier results on pruning, we immediately obtain the generalisation for multi-step transitions.

Soundness. Soundness is proven by case analysis on the transition made by the network, and then by induction on the choreography inside each case. For convenience, we split this proof in separate proofs, one for each transition. We omit the statements of these lemmas, since they include a number of technical hypotheses (similar to those in e.g. SP_To_bproj_Com, which is used in the proof of the case of communication, but more complex). By contrast with completeness, all these lemmas are complex to prove: each case requires around 300 lines of Coq code. The proofs have similar structure, but are still different enough that adapting them can not be done mechanically.

The last ingredient is a lemma of practical interest on procedure names: each process only uses "its" copy of the original procedure names. This lemma is not only crucial in the proof of the next theorem, but also interesting in itself: it shows that the set of procedure definitions can be fully distributed among the processes with no duplications.

Lemma SP_To_bproj_Call_name : ∀ Defs Defs' ps C HC s N' s' p X,
    SP_To Defs' (epp_C Defs ps C HC) s (R_Call X p) N' s' →
    ∃ Y, X = (Y,p) ∧ X_Free Y C.

All these ingredients are combined in the proof of soundness of EPP.

Lemma EPP_Sound : ∀ P Xs ps, Program_WF Xs P → well_ann P → ∀ HP,
    (∀ p, In p ps → str_projectable (Procedures P) (Main P) p) →
    (∀ p, In p (CCC_pn (Main P) (Vars P)) → In p ps) →
    (∀ p X, In X Xs → In p (Vars P X) → In p ps) →
    ∀ s tl N' s', (epp Xs ps P HP,s) —[tl]⟶ (N',s') →
    ∃ P' tl', (P,s) —[tl']⟶ (P',s') ∧ ∀ H, Net N' ≫ Net (epp Xs ps P' H).

Generalising this result to multi-step transitions requires showing that pruning does not eliminate possible transitions of a network. This is in general not true, but it holds when the pruned network is the projection of a choreography.

Lemma SP_To_more_branches_N_epp : ∀ Defs N1 s N2 s' tl Defs' ps C HC,
    N1 ≫ epp_C Defs' ps C HC → SP_To Defs N1 s tl N2 s' →
    ∃ N2', SP_To Defs (epp_C Defs' ps C HC) s tl N2' s' ∧ N2 ≫ N2'.

The formalisation of EPP and the proof of the EPP theorem consists of 13 definitions, 110 lemmas, and 4960 lines of Coq code. The proof of the EPP Theorem and related lemmas make up for around 75% of this size.

8   Discussion and Conclusion

We have successfully formalised a translation from a Turing-complete choreographic language into a process calculus and proven its correctness in terms of an operational correspondence. This formalisation showed that the proof techniques used in the literature are correct, and identified only missing minor assumptions about runtime terms that trivially hold when these are used as intended.

To the best of our knowledge, this is the first time such a correspondence has been formalised for a full-fledged (Turing-complete) choreographic language. Comparable work includes a preliminary presentation on a certified compiler from choreographies to CakeML [18], which however deals only with finite behaviours [22]. In the related realm of multiparty session types (where choreographies do not include computation), a similar correspondence result has also been developed independently [9].

The complexity of the formalisation, combined with the similarities between several of the proofs, means that future extensions would benefit from exploiting semi-automatic generation of proof scripts.

Combining these results with those from [13] would yield a proof that SP is also Turing complete. Unfortunately, the choreographies used in the proof of Turing completeness in [13] are not projectable, but they can be made so automatically, by means of an amendment (repair) procedure [12]. In future work, we plan to formalise amendment in order to obtain this result.

References

1. Albert, E., Lanese, I. (eds.): Formal Techniques for Distributed Objects, Components, and Systems. LNCS, vol. 9688. Springer, Cham (2016). https://doi.org/10.1007/978-3-319-39570-8
2. Basu, S., Bultan, T.: Automated choreography repair. In: Stevens, P., Wąsowski, A. (eds.) FASE 2016. LNCS, vol. 9633, pp. 13–30. Springer, Heidelberg (2016). https://doi.org/10.1007/978-3-662-49665-7_2
3. Basu, S., Bultan, T., Ouederni, M.: Deciding choreography realizability. In: Field, J., Hicks, M. (eds.) Procs. POPL, pp. 191–202. ACM (2012). https://doi.org/10.1145/2103656.2103680
4. Bertot, Y., Castéran, P.: Interactive Theorem Proving and Program Development. Texts in Theoretical Computer Science, Springer (2004)
5. Carbone, M., Honda, K., Yoshida, N.: Structured communication-centered programming for web services. ACM Trans. Program. Lang. Syst. **34**(2), 8:1-8:78 (2012). https://doi.org/10.1145/2220365.2220367
6. Carbone, M., Lindley, S., Montesi, F., Schürmann, C., Wadler, P.: Coherence generalises duality: A logical explanation of multiparty session types. In: Desharnais, J., Jagadeesan, R. (eds.) Procs. CONCUR. LIPIcs, vol. 59, pp. 33:1–33:15. Schloss Dagstuhl - Leibniz-Zentrum für Informatik (2016)
7. Carbone, M., Montesi, F.: Deadlock-freedom-by-design: multiparty asynchronous global programming. In: Giacobazzi, R., Cousot, R. (eds.) Procs. POPL, pp. 263–274. ACM (2013). https://doi.org/10.1145/2429069.2429101
8. Carbone, M., Montesi, F., Schürmann, C.: Choreographies, logically. Distributed Comput. **31**(1), 51–67 (2018). https://doi.org/10.1007/s00446-017-0295-1

9. Castro-Perez, D., Ferreira, F., Gheri, L., Yoshida, N.: Zooid: a DSL for certified multiparty computation: from mechanised metatheory to certified multiparty processes. In: Freund, S.N., Yahav, E. (eds.) Procs. PLDI, pp. 237–251. ACM (2021). https://doi.org/10.1145/3453483.3454041

10. Cruz-Filipe, L., Montesi, F.: Choreographies in practice. In: Albert and Lanese [1], pp. 114–123. https://doi.org/10.1007/978-3-319-39570-8_8

11. Cruz-Filipe, L., Montesi, F.: Procedural choreographic programming. In: Bouajjani, A., Silva, A. (eds.) FORTE 2017. LNCS, vol. 10321, pp. 92–107. Springer, Cham (2017). https://doi.org/10.1007/978-3-319-60225-7_7

12. Cruz-Filipe, L., Montesi, F.: A core model for choreographic programming. Theor. Comput. Sci. **802**, 38–66 (2020). https://doi.org/10.1016/j.tcs.2019.07.005

13. Cruz-Filipe, L., Montesi, F., Peressotti, M.: Formalising a Turing-complete choreographic language in Coq. In: Cohen, L., Kaliszyk, C. (eds.) Procs. ITP. LIPIcs, vol. 193, pp. 15:1–15:18. Schloss Dagstuhl - Leibniz-Zentrum für Informatik (2021). https://doi.org/10.4230/LIPIcs.ITP.2021.15

14. Cruz-Filipe, L., Montesi, F., Peressotti, M.: A formalisation of a Turing-complete choreographic language in Coq. https://doi.org/10.5281/zenodo.4548709

15. Preda, M.D., Gabbrielli, M., Giallorenzo, S., Lanese, I., Mauro, J.: Dynamic choreographies: Theory and implementation. Log. Methods Comput. Sci. **13**(2) (2017). https://doi.org/10.23638/LMCS-13(2:1)2017

16. Giallorenzo, S., Lanese, I., Russo, D.: ChIP: a choreographic integration process. In: Panetto, H., Debruyne, C., Proper, H.A., Ardagna, C.A., Roman, D., Meersman, R. (eds.) OTM 2018. LNCS, vol. 11230, pp. 22–40. Springer, Cham (2018). https://doi.org/10.1007/978-3-030-02671-4_2

17. Giallorenzo, S., Montesi, F., Peressotti, M.: Choreographies as objects. CoRR abs/2005.09520 (2020)

18. Gomez-Londono, A., Aman Pohjola, J.: Connecting choreography languages with verified stacks. In: Procs. of the Nordic Workshop on Programming Theory, pp. 31–33 (2018)

19. Object Management Group: Business Process Model and Notation (2011). http://www.omg.org/spec/BPMN/2.0/

20. Honda, K., Yoshida, N., Carbone, M.: Multiparty asynchronous session types. J. ACM **63**(1), 9 (2016). https://doi.org/10.1145/2827695, also: POPL, pp. 273–284 (2008)

21. Lluch Lafuente, A., Nielson, F., Nielson, H.R.: Discretionary information flow control for interaction-oriented specifications. In: Martí-Oliet, N., Ölveczky, P.C., Talcott, C. (eds.) Logic, Rewriting, and Concurrency. LNCS, vol. 9200, pp. 427–450. Springer, Cham (2015). https://doi.org/10.1007/978-3-319-23165-5_20

22. Londoño, A.G.: Choreographies and cost semantics for reliable communicating systems (2020)

23. López, H.A., Heussen, K.: Choreographing cyber-physical distributed control systems for the energy sector. In: Seffah, A., Penzenstadler, B., Alves, C., Peng, X. (eds.) Procs. SAC, pp. 437–443. ACM (2017). https://doi.org/10.1145/3019612.3019656

24. López, H.A., Nielson, F., Nielson, H.R.: Enforcing availability in failure-aware communicating systems. In: Albert and Lanese [1], pp. 195–211. https://doi.org/10.1007/978-3-319-39570-8_13

25. Montesi, F.: Choreographic Programming. Ph.D. Thesis, IT University of Copenhagen (2013)

26. Montesi, F.: Introduction to choreographies (2021). Accepted for publication by Cambridge University Press

27. Needham, R.M., Schroeder, M.D.: Using encryption for authentication in large networks of computers. Commun. ACM **21**(12), 993–999 (1978). https://doi.org/10.1145/359657.359659

28. Scalas, A., Yoshida, N.: Less is more: multiparty session types revisited. Proc. ACM Program. Lang. **3**(POPL), 30:1–30:29 (2019). https://doi.org/10.1145/3290343

29. W3C: WS Choreography Description Language (2004). http://www.w3.org/TR/ws-cdl-10/

30. Wadler, P.: Propositions as sessions. J. Funct. Program. **24**(2–3), 384–418 (2014). https://doi.org/10.1017/S095679681400001X

A Mechanically Verified Theory of Contracts

Stéphane Kastenbaum[1,2(✉)], Benoît Boyer[2], and Jean-Pierre Talpin[1]

[1] Inria Rennes - Bretagne Atlantique, Rennes, France
stephane.kastenbaum@inria.fr
[2] Mitsubishi Electric R&D Centre Europe, Rennes, France

Abstract. Cyber-physical systems (CPS) are assemblies of networked, heterogeneous, hardware, and software components sensing, evaluating, and actuating a physical environment. This heterogeneity induces complexity that makes CPSs challenging to model correctly. Since CPSs often have critical functions, it is however of utmost importance to formally verify them in order to provide the highest guarantees of safety. Faced with CPS complexity, model abstraction becomes paramount to make verification attainable. To this end, assume/guarantee contracts enable component model abstraction to support a sound, structured, and modular verification process. While abstractions of models by contracts are usually proved sound, none of the related contract frameworks themselves have, to the best of our knowledge, been formally proved correct so far. In this aim, we present the formalization of a generic assume/guarantee contract theory in the proof assistant Coq. We identify and prove theorems that ensure its correctness. Our theory is generic, or parametric, in that it can be instantiated and used with any given logic, in particular hybrid logics, in which highly complex cyber-physical systems can uniformly be described.

1 Introduction

With the rise of cyber-physical systems with growingly critical functions, it becomes of the utmost importance to develop frameworks that support their sound design and guarantee their safety. Currently, to design such systems, engineers use informally specified tools such as Simulink [8]. Simulink is a very convenient toolbox to connect components to form systems. From atomic components, systems become components in larger systems that can be reused in multiple places in a given design. As an effort to verify Simulink systems, formal verification frameworks such as MARS translate Simulink design into a formal specification language [7,12]. This approach alters the native hierarchy of Simulink models in the specification but allows modularity to be reconstructed afterward in the target formal language. Ideally, however, we would like to conserve the intended component hierarchy for the verification process, in order to better support abstraction in places of the design. Contracts are a tool to support the abstraction of subsystems in such specification formalisms.

© Springer Nature Switzerland AG 2021
A. Cerone and P. C. Ölveczky (Eds.): ICTAC 2021, LNCS 12819, pp. 134–151, 2021.
https://doi.org/10.1007/978-3-030-85315-0_9

Contracts help to design and to verify complex systems by abstracting component models, using their assumptions and guarantees in place of their exact, internal specification. A contract being more abstract than the specification of a component makes the modular verification of large systems feasible.

In this paper, we first review the related works. We then give an overview of the contract theory proposed by Benveniste et al. [3,4]. The subsequent section presents the formalization of our theory in the proof assistant Coq. We then illustrate its instantiation with a simple propositional logic. This gives us the opportunity to discuss some design choices in the formalization. Finally, we outline future works and conclude.

2 Related Works

A recent interest in creating contract frameworks for cyber-physical systems is appearing. The complexity of such systems and their interconnections make the verification and validation process challenging, render traditional system design methods inadequate, and call for more powerful frameworks to design such complex systems [11,19].

Design by contracts was first proposed by Meyer for software programming [14]. Hence, specification by contracts traditionally consists of pre- and post-conditions, leaving the continuous timed variables extraneous of the specification. This is not practical when designing cyber-physical systems, where time is intrinsically linked to the continuous behavior of the system. In contracts for cyber-physical systems, we replace pre-conditions by assumption and post-condition by guarantee, the main difference being that the assumption and guarantee can express properties of continuous timed variables.

To design cyber-physical systems, numerous hybrid logics have been proposed. Differential dynamic logic (commonly abbreviated as $\mathbf{d\mathcal{L}}$) defines hybrid programs, a combination of discrete computation and differential equations to model cyber-physical systems [18]. It is equipped with a proof assistant, Keymaera X, to check and prove safety and reachability properties on the modeled systems [10]. While the verification process supports decomposition, it does not support parallelism hence modularity. Multiple approaches have therefore been investigated to define contracts in $\mathbf{d\mathcal{L}}$ [13,15]. Their goal is to define a composition theorem allowing to connect multiple components. Both approaches conceptualize components as a design pattern on hybrid programs and design contracts as abstract specifications around them.

Hybrid CSP is an extension of CSP with differential equations used to model cyber-physical systems [5]. A language to describe the trace of executions, the duration calculus, is used in conjunction with HCSP to verify properties of cyber-physical systems [6,22]. This is done in the proof assistant Isabelle [16]. Since CSP supports composition, work to define contracts in HCSP have focused on the composition of abstract specifications in the duration calculus [21].

Other approaches have been considered to define contracts for cyber-physical systems. For example, contracts defined with Signal Temporal Logic were used to ensure the safety of autonomous vehicles in [2].

While slightly different from one another, all these definitions of contracts have the same core ideas. Namely, a contract abstracts the specification of a component in the same logic. These definitions also support the same usual operators on contracts such as composition or refinement. A meta-theory of contracts has been defined, aiming at unifying all theories of contracts [4]. The theory of assume/guarantee contract instantiates the meta-theory and is generic enough to bridge the gap between related definitions of contracts [1,3]. It was used, for instance, to define contracts in heterogeneous logics and relate them together [17]. It is given an overview in Sect. 3.

Foster et al. have proposed a mechanized theory of contracts in Isabelle and the Unified Theory of Programming (UTP) using pre-, peri- and post-conditions to abstract discretely timed systems [9].

Yet the meta-theory of contracts and the theory assume/guarantee of contracts have, to the best of our knowledge, no formalized proof of correctness. In the following sections, we propose a formalization of both of them in the proof assistant Coq with the goal to instantiate them with a hybrid logic that could be defined using that theorem prover [20].

3   Overview of the Meta-theory and the Assume/Guarantee Theory of Contract

In this section, we recall the meta-theory of contracts introduced by Benveniste et al. [4]. Then the definition of one of its implementation: the set-theoretic assume/guarantee contract theory [3].

3.1   Meta-theory

In the meta-theory of contracts, there is only one notion, that of component. That notion is kept abstract, it is not defined. In practice, it is meant to represent an element of a system performing a specific task. In the remainder, components are noted by the letter σ.

Components are subject to a relation of compatibility which, in the meta-theory, is kept abstract as well. Two compatible components can be composed to create a larger component or subsystem. Composition is akin to connecting two elements of a system together. We note $\sigma_1 \times \sigma_2$ for the composition of components σ_1 and σ_2.

We call *environment* of σ any component that is compatible with σ. For example, when considering the motor of a car, the other components interacting with the motor form a sub-system: the environment of the motor. Conversely, when considering the gearbox, the other components of the car, including the motor, are the environment.

A contract is the specification of a task in a system. We model a contract with a pair $C = (\mathcal{E}, \mathcal{M})$ with $\mathcal{M}$ a set of components and $\mathcal{E}$ a set of environments compatible with every component in $\mathcal{M}$. Multiple components can perform that same task, all must respect its contract. We say that a component σ *implements* the contract C, if $\sigma \in \mathcal{M}$. We use the notation $\sigma \vdash C$ for σ implements C. A contract is also a specification of the environment. It describes any environment in which the task can be achieved by the components. Dually, we note $e \vdash_E C$ to say that e *provides* the contracts, meaning $e \in \mathcal{E}$.

The goal of a specification is to be an abstraction on actual components. Multiple contracts can be the specifications of the same component on different levels of abstraction. We introduce the *refinement* relation to describe that a contract is the abstraction of another. Here C_1 is the refined version of C_2. This means that any implementations of C_1 can be used in place of an implementation of C_2.

Definition 1 (Refinement). $C_1 \preccurlyeq C_2 \equiv \mathcal{M}_1 \subseteq \mathcal{M}_2 \wedge \mathcal{E}_2 \subseteq \mathcal{E}_1$

Sometimes, multiple specifications can be applied to the same component. For example, we want a component to be fast and correct. There is both a specification for the speed of the component and one for the correctness. Therefore, we want to regroup both specifications on the same contract. Any contract which refines both contracts can be used, though it is more desirable to use the most abstract contract. With this in mind, we define the conjunction of contracts as the greatest lower bound of refinement.

Definition 2 (Conjunction). $C_1 \sqcap C_2$ *is the greatest lower bound of contract on refinement.*

For now, we only have considered one component in its environment. Yet most of the complexity of systems comes from the composition of multiple components. The problem can be formulated as *"If we have the specification of two components, can we determine the specification of the composition of the components?"*. The subtlety is that each component is part of the environment for the other. So the result of their specifications takes into account this point.

Definition 3 (Composition).

$$C_1 \otimes C_2 \equiv \min \left\{ C \left| \begin{array}{ll} \forall M_1 \vdash C_1 & M_1 \times M_2 \vdash C \\ \forall M_2 \vdash C_2 \implies & E \times M_2 \vdash C_1 \\ \forall E \vdash_E C & E \times M_1 \vdash C_2 \end{array} \right. \right\}$$

The definition of quotient, lowest upper bound, compatibility, and consistency of contracts are not relevant for our purposes. The interested reader is directed toward their definitions in [4].

As much as this meta-theory gives us, it is not enough to be used. It only allows us to understand what are the necessary tasks needed to define a contract theory. The meta-theory is not constructive, for example, the min operator used in the definition of composition doesn't give us the actual contract. In the next section, we define an actually usable contract theory, without losing any generality.

3.2   Assume/Guarantee Contract Theory

This section defines a contract theory by instantiating the meta-theory with concrete definitions, starting with that of a component. We model a component by the properties it guarantees on the system.

In this state-centered theory, there is no clear demarcation between inputs and outputs. We note d the set of all variables. For simplification purposes, all variables hold value the same domain B.

A state is a valuation of all the variables, that is to say, it is a surjective function from d to B. The state space $S : d \rightarrow B$ is every configuration the system can be in.

In system design, an assertion is a property of the state the system is in. We use the duality of sets, it can be seen either as a collection of elements or as a property that every element satisfies. Here, we consider the assertion as every state that satisfies the property. This means, we define an assertion A as a subset of the state space, noted $A \subseteq S$. A component is not only viewed as a property it ensures on the variables but as every state satisfying this property. Which means a component is a set of states.

Here every component is compatible with every other component. Meaning every component can be composed, or connected, to any other component. The composition of two components is simply the intersection of their assertions. This means that every component can be seen as an environment for another. We should mention that if a component is an empty set, it is a non-implementable component.

Using contracts as defined in the meta-theory above is not practical, we use another definition and will prove later that they're equivalent. Here, contracts are associations of assumption and guarantee. The assumption is the input accepted by the component and the guarantee is properties ensured on the output of the component.

A contract is an abstract specification of a component. The goal is to define rules which restrain both the implementation of the component and the environment it needs to be in. Here, the assumption is the restriction on the environment whereas the guarantee is the restriction on the component.

Definition 4 (Assume/guarantee contract). *An assume/guarantee contract is the combination of two assertions, one for the assumption (A) one for the guarantee (G). For a contract $c = (A, G)$ we define projections to get the assumption and the guarantee*

$$A(c) = A \; ; \; G(c) = G$$

.

Now, we define what it means for a state to *satisfy* a contract. A state satisfies a contract if either it's a state excluded from the contract's assumption, or the contract's guarantee holds for the state.

Definition 5 (Satisfies).

$$s \vdash c \equiv s \in \overline{A(c)} \cup G(c)$$

We can lift this definition to components. A component σ implements a contract if every state in σ satisfies the contract.

Definition 6 (Implements).

$$\sigma \vdash c \equiv \forall s \in \sigma, \ s \vdash c$$

A environment e provides a contract if every state of e is included in the assumption of the contract.

Definition 7 (Provides).

$$e \vdash_E c \equiv \forall s \in e, \ s \in A(c)$$

This leads to a particular point in assume/guarantee contracts. With the above definition, we notice that multiple contracts can be implemented by the same components and provided by the same environments. So we have a class of contracts which are all equivalent, as they specify the same set of components and environment. We define *saturation* an idempotent operation which doesn't change the set of components satisfying the contract, nor the set of environment providing the contract. We then always use the saturated version of a contract.

Definition 8 (Saturation).

$$\text{saturate}(c) \equiv (A(c), \ \overline{A(c)} \cup G(c))$$

Next, we want to define the refinement relations between two contracts. There is a simple definition of refinement. The most refined contract needs to have stronger guarantee, and looser assumption. In the formalization, we prove that it is equivalent to Definition 1.

Definition 9 (A/G refinement).

$$c1 \preccurlyeq c2 \equiv A(c1) \supseteq A(c2) \wedge G(c1) \subseteq G(c2)$$

This definition is decidable if and only if $\subseteq$ is decidable. We do want the refinement relation to be decidable, hence we have to make sure that $\subseteq$ is decidable.

To find the conjunction of contracts, (or the greatest lower bound of refinement), we have the formula below. Contrary to Definition 2 in the meta-theory, this definition is constructive.

Definition 10 (A/G conjunction).

$$c1 \sqcap c2 \equiv (A(c1) \cap A(c2), G(c1) \cup G(c2))$$

Composition of contracts is defined as followed, this definition is constructive. It also is the min in the sens of refinement as expressed in Definition 3.

Definition 11 (A/G composition).

$$c1 \otimes c2 \equiv (A', G')$$

With

$$A' \equiv A(c1) \cap A(c2) \cup \overline{G(c1) \cap G(c2)}$$

$$G' \equiv G(c1) \cap G(c2)$$

We now have two definitions of contracts. The key difference is the definition of refinement, conjunction, and composition. The meta-theory has an intuitive definition, while the assume/guarantee theory has more interesting properties. In the next section, we formalize the assume/guarantee theory of contract and prove that it is equivalent to the above meta-theory of contract.

4   Formalization of Assumption/Guarantee Contract Theory

The meta-theory intends to provide a generic contract theory that can be instantiated by several logics. Each logic presents some features that enable or facilitate the verification of system properties. Proving that several logics implement the same meta-theory is a way to unify them. Here, we formalize the assume/guarantee contract theory and prove it to correspond to the definitions given in the meta-theory.

The contract theory relies on set-theoretic definitions. At this stage, we assume the abstract type `set : Type → Type` which is equipped with the usual set operators as $\cup$, $\cap$, $\neg$. We also assume the relations $\in$ and $\subseteq$ as well as the set equivalence `s1 == s2` which is extended to the standard equality `s1 = s2` by extensionality.

In this section, we give an overview of our formalization of the contract theory. First, we consider every component to be defined on the same variables, next, we see how to handle multiple variable sets.

4.1   Single Variable Set

For a given set of variables, the semantics of a contract is defined by the assertion of its assumption and guarantee, each represented by a set of states. A state is a valuation from variables to values, where the variables are a set of identifiers as in the following:

```
Variable vars : set ident.
Definition var := { v : ident | v ∈ vars }.
Definition state := var → B.
Definition assertion := set state.
Definition component := assertion.
Definition environment := component.
Record contract : Type := mkContract { A : assertion ; G : assertion }.
```

The types `ident` and `value` are parameters of our theory and kept abstract, but we require that identifiers must be discriminable and their membership to sets must be decided. `vars` is the set of identifiers used in the system, and `var` is the type of a variable, namely an identifier with the proof that it's in `vars`. At this stage of the development, we assimilate the concept of a component with its behavior as in Sect. 3.2.

We define assertions as state predicates using the duality of sets, namely, `s ∈ q` denotes that `s` satisfies the assertion `q`. Contracts are directly defined as pairs of assertions relating the behavior expected from the environment (assumption) with the behavior of the component (guarantee). The syntax c.A (and c.G) denotes the assumption (respectively guarantee) of the contract c in the rest of the paper[1].

The semantics of the contract relies on the implementation of a contract by a component. In order to define it, we first introduce the satisfiability of the contract by a single state and the saturation principle.

```
Definition satisfies (s : state) (c : contract) : Prop :=
    s ∈ ¬ c.A ∪ c.G.
```

Basically, a state satisfies a contract either if the state is discarded by the assumption and nothing is guaranteed by the contract, or the state satisfies both assumption and guarantee of the contract.

In the following code, we saturate contracts when necessary, indeed it's easier to saturate a contract than to check if it's already saturated. Whereas in the mathematical definition it is easier to consider every contract to be saturated than to saturate every time. In the code, we **saturate** contracts when needed, whereas in the mathematical definition we have considered contracts to be saturated.

```
Definition saturate (c : contract) : contract :=
    {| A := c.A ;
       G := ¬ c.A ∪ c.G |}.
```

The contract saturation is sound: the same states are characterized before and after the saturation of any contract.

```
Theorem saturate_sound : forall (s : state) (c : contract),
    satisfies s c ↔ satisfies s (saturate c).
```

We extend the contract satisfiability from states to components to define the implementation relation. Additionally, we also need to characterize the relationship between contract and environment.

```
Definition implements (σ : component) (c : contract) : Prop :=
    forall s, s ∈ σ → satisfies s c.
Notation "σ ⊢ c" := (implements σ c).
Definition provides (e : environment) (c : contract) : Prop :=
    e ⊆ c.A .
```

---

[1] The Coq's original syntax is c.(A) but we replaced it for the sake of readability.

Then, we can define the refine relation on contracts. Here, it is important to note that we are implementing the assume/guarantee theory of contracts. The refinement and composition relation are defined differently in the meta-theory and in the assume/guarantee theory.

```
Definition refines (c1 c2 : contract) : Prop :=
    let (c1' , c2') := (saturate c1 , saturate c2) in
    c2'.A ⊆ c1'.G ∧ c1'.G ⊆ c2'.G.
Notation "c1 ≼ c2" := (refines c1 c2).
```

Since refines is an order, we proved the usual properties: reflexivity, transitivity, and antisymmetry. We also demonstrated that this set-theoretic definition is equivalent to the more standard and meaningful Definition 1 of the refinement given by the meta-theory.

```
Theorem refines_correct : forall (c1 c2 : contract),
    c1 ≼ c2 ↔
    (forall σ: component, σ ⊢ c1 → σ ⊢ c2) ∧
    (forall e: environment, provides e c2 → provides e c1).
```

The conjunction of contracts corresponds to the multiple views, one can have on the same component. In the meta-theory, it is defined as the greatest lower bound of refinement. So, we prove that our set definition is equivalent to the meta-theoretical Definition 2.

```
Definition glb (c1 : contract) (c2 : contract) : contract :=
    let c1' := saturate c1 in let c2' := saturate c2 in
    mkContract (c1'.A ∪ c2'.A) (c1'.G ∩ c2'.G).
Notation "c1 ⊓ c2" := (glb c1 c2).
```

```
Theorem glb_correct : forall c1 c2 : contract,
    (c1 ⊓ c2) ≼ c1 ∧ (c1 ⊓ c2) ≼ c2 ∧
    (forall c, c ≼ c1 → c ≼ c2 → c ≼ (c1 ⊓ c2)).
```

The central operator in contracts algebra is the composition. Two contracts can be composed if they are defined on the same variables. The composition of components aims to construct a contract specifying the composition of components. We provide a set-theoretic definition and then show that it corresponds to the meta-theory Definition 3.

```
Definition compose (c1 c2 : contract) : contract :=
    let c1' := saturate c1 in
    let c2' := saturate c2 in
    let g := c1'.G ∩ c2'.G in
    let a := (c1'.A ∩ c2'.A) ∪ ¬ g in
    mkContract a g.
Notation "c1 ⊗ c2" := (compose c1 c2).
```

Here again, we give the proof that it corresponds to Definition 3 given in the meta-theory.

Theorem `compose_correct` :
    forall (c1 c2 : contract) ($\sigma1$ $\sigma2$: component) (e : environment),
    $\sigma1 \vdash$ c1 $\rightarrow$ $\sigma2 \vdash$ c2 $\rightarrow$ **provides** e (c1 $\otimes$ c2) $\rightarrow$
    ($\sigma1 \cap \sigma2 \vdash$ c1 $\otimes$ c2 $\wedge$ **provides** (e $\cap$ $\sigma2$) c1 $\wedge$ **provides** (e $\cap$ $\sigma1$) c2).

Theorem `compose_lowest` : **forall** (c1 c2 c : contract),
    (**forall** ($\sigma1$ $\sigma2$: component) (e : environment),
    $\sigma1 \vdash$ c1 $\rightarrow$ $\sigma2 \vdash$ c2 $\rightarrow$ **provides** e c $\rightarrow$
    ($\sigma1 \cap \sigma2 \vdash$ c $\wedge$ **provides** (e $\cap$ $\sigma2$) c1 $\wedge$ **provides** (e $\cap$ $\sigma1$) c2)) $\rightarrow$
    c1 $\otimes$ c2 $\preccurlyeq$ c.

The above definitions all consider every state to be defined on the same variables. Yet, it is highly improbable that every component needs every variable to be defined. Thus, some components are defined on different sets of variables. To define the composition of components defined on different sets of variables, we need to extend their definitions to larger sets. We may also want to eliminate variables out of contracts. If a component allows for every possible value of a variable and doesn't give any guarantee on it there is no need to have it in the specification.

4.2 Alphabet Equalization

This section considers the case when contracts are defined over different domains of variables. Two problems can occur in this situation. First, we may need to compose two contracts that are not defined on the same variables. In that case, we need a way to extend the two contracts on the union of their variables. Then, some variables in a contract may be useless. For example, if a component provides the input for another component, maybe the composition of the two contracts specifying the components doesn't need to specify this variable. In that case, we need the elimination of variables.

In [3], the authors defined elimination of variables and extension of contracts. The elimination of variables is defined in the following way.

Definition 12. *For a contract* $c = (A, G)$, *and a variable* v *in the contract. The contract without* v *is :*

$$[c]_v \equiv (\forall v \ A \ ; \ \exists v \ G)$$

This definition is not usable in our formalization. A and G are both sets, the quantifier has no meaning for sets. To define this elimination of variable, the authors consider assertions as logic formulas and bind free variables with quantifiers. However, this shortcut cannot be taken with a formal proof assistant. The definition of the extension of contracts was also eluded by considering assertion as logic formulas.

In the following, we give a set-theoretic definition in Coq of the elimination of variables in a contract and the definition of the extension of contracts. We assume d1 and d2 two variable sets, with H12 : d1 $\subseteq$ d2.

First, we define H'12 : var d1 $\rightarrow$ var d2, which takes a variable in d1 and shows that it is also a variable in d2.

Definition H'12 (v1 : var d1) : var d2 := let (i,H1) := v1 in exist _ i (H12 i H1).

Here, we use H12 to show that the ident i in d1 is also in d2. Indeed, the type of H12 is forall v : ident, v ∈ d1 → v ∈ d2. Hence, H12 i H1 is of type i ∈ d2, and exist _ v (H12 i H1) is of type var d2.

We define the projection of a single state on a smaller variable set.

Definition project (e2 : state d2) : state d1 :=
    fun v1 ⇒ e2 (H'12 v1).

We extend the definition of projection of state to the projection of assertion. Which is the projection of every state in it. If we consider the assertion as the property it holds on variables, the projection is similar to the existential quantifier. For example, the assertion $P(x, y)$ projected on the variables $\{y\}$ is $\exists x, P(x, y)$.

Definition project_assertion (a : assertion d2) : assertion d1 :=
    fun e1 ⇒ exists e2, e2 ∈ a ∧ project e2 = e1.

Then, we can define the inverse of the projection. Which for a state gives the set of states that project to it. Notice that the extension of a state gives an assertion. Multiple states defined on d2 have the same projection on d1.

Definition extend_state (e : state d1) : assertion d2 :=
    fun e2 ⇒ project e2 = e.

Similar to the extension of states, extending an assertion a1 is done by taking every state that projects to a state in a1.

Definition extend_assertion (a1 : assertion d1) : assertion d2 :=
    fun e2 ⇒ project e2 ∈ a1.

Next, we need to define the *strong projection* of an assertion. Which is the set of states where every extension of the states are in the assertion. The equivalent of the strong projection when viewing assertion as property is the ∀ quantifier. The strong projection of $P(x, y)$ on $\{y\}$ is $\forall x, P(x, y)$.

Definition project_assertion_forall (a : assertion d2) : assertion d1 :=
    fun e1 ⇒ extend_state e1 ⊆ a.

Finally, we can define the elimination of variables in a contract. Eliminating variables is the same thing as projecting onto the other variables. We reuse Definition 12 with the set definitions of projection.

Definition project_contract (c2 : contract d2) : contract d1 :=
    let c2' := saturate _ c2 in
    mkContract _ (project_assertion_forall c2'.A)
                (project_assertion c2'.G).

Extending a contract onto a bigger variable set is extending both the assumption and the guarantee. In the set theory, this part is implicit. With the proof assistant, we have to make it explicit.

Definition **extend_contract** (c1 : contract d1) : contract d2 :=
    let c1' := saturate _ c1 in
    mkContract _ (extend_assertion (c1'.A) (extend_assertion (c1'.G)).

We can now define composition on two contracts defined on different variables. We assume d1 d2 and d3, with H1 : d1 $\subseteq$ d2 and H2 : d2 $\subseteq$ d3.

Definition **extended_compose** (c1 : contract d1) (c2 : contract d2) :
    contract d3 :=
    compose _ (extend_contract H1 c1) (extend_contract H2 c2).

We can partially verify the correction of the extended composition, though we still need to find a satisfying correction theorem. For example, we verify that the composition of contracts implements the composition of components on different sets of variables.

Theorem **extended_compose_correct** : forall (c1 : contract d1) (c2 : contract d2)
    (σ1 : component d1) (σ2 : component d2),
    implements _ σ1 c1 $\rightarrow$ implements _ σ2 c2 $\rightarrow$
    implements _ (extend_assertion H1 σ1 $\cup$ extend_assertion H2 σ2)
       (extended_compose c1 c2).

5   Instantiating the Assume/Guarantee Contract Theory

Our goal is to have a formally verified generic theory for contracts. With this generic theory, one could define contracts with any propositional logic. The requirement to use the contracts theory is to give the alphabet of variables and the set of values. Three properties are also required: the set of values need to be inhabited, and both equality and the $\in$ relation must be decidable.

In a nutshell, one needs to instantiate this interface:

Class **Theory** := {
    B : Type ;
    ident : Type ;
    any_B : B ;
    eq_dec_ident : forall x y : ident, {x = y} + {x <> y} ;
    in_dec_ident : forall (v : ident) (d : set ident), {v $\in$ d} + {v $\notin$ d} ;
}.

Given these elements, the theory can be instantiated. The parameter ident is the type of identifier of the variables. The parameter B is the type of values the variables can yield. We need B to be inhabited, giving any value with any_B is sufficient to verify it. We require equality and the $\in$ relation to be decidable for identifiers. Hence eq_dec_ident, in_dec_ident are required. This class is used to define states, on which assertion, components, and contracts are defined.

When instantiating the class, the definitions provided suffice to define contracts and components for a given logic. Yet, defining contracts this way may be too tedious to be practical. Usually, a logic has a grammar to define formulas, and a "satisfy" relation saying if a state satisfies a formula. So the workflow is to define the assertion in the language of the logic, then create the set of states using the assertion and the satisfy function. We aim to simplify this workflow.

An idea is to define contracts and components in the logic, and then show their equivalence with the contracts defined in the meta-theory. The following example shows how to proceed.

5.1   Example with a Simple Propositional Logic

To demonstrate how this theory could be used to create a framework, we developed a simple propositional logic. We use Prop as the value type, and nat as the identifier of variables. We instantiate the class as the following:

```
Instance theo : Theory := {
    ident := nat ;
    B := Prop ;
    default_B := True ;
    eq_dec_ident := eq_dec_nat ;
    in_dec_ident := in_dec_nat ;
}.
```

Where eq_dec_nat and in_dec_nat are assumed. For this instance, we define our states.

```
Definition state (d : set ident) : Type := forall x : variable d, B.
```

Then we define a formula algebra, with standard connectors and natural numbers to identify variables. Notice that the formula type is dependent of the variables it is defined on. We need this to define states properly.

```
Inductive expr {d : set ident} : Type :=
    | f_tt : expr
    | f_var : var d → expr
    | f_not : expr → expr
    | f_and : expr → expr → expr.
```

```
Inductive sat {d : set ident} : state d → expr d → Prop := ...
```

To define a contract with two formulas a and g as assumption and guarantee, we do:

```
Variable d : set ident.
Definition formula_to_assert (formula : expr) : assertion d :=
    fun e ⇒ sat e formula.
Definition mkContractF (a g : expr d): contract d :=
    mkContract d (formula_to_assert a) (formula_to_assert g).
```

5.2   Logic Specific Contracts

We may want to define contracts that are only defined in the logic, with a formula as assumption and guarantee.

```
Record contractF :=
    ContractF {A : expr d ; G : expr d}.
```

We can define `refinesF`, `composeF` and `glbF`, which are the same as the set definitions, but we replace ∪, ∩ and ¬ by `f_or`, `f_and` and `f_not`. With the translation of logic contract to contract in set theory, we can check that the definition of the operators are correct.

```
Definition c2c (cf : contractF) : contract d :=
    mkContractF d (cf.A) (cf.G).
Theorem refinesF_correct : forall (cf1 cf2 : contractF),
    refines d (c2c cf1) (c2c cf2) ↔ refinesF cf1 cf2.
Theorem composeF_correct : forall (cf1 cf2 : contractF),
    c2c (composeF cf1 cf2) == compose d (c2c cf1) (c2c cf2).
Theorem glbF_correct : forall (cf1 cf2 : contractF),
    c2c (glbF cf1 cf2) == glb _ (c2c cf1) (c2c cf2).
```

Here, == is the equivalence of contracts, defined by:

```
Definition equiv (c1 : contract) (c2 : contract) : Prop :=
    refines c1 c2 ∧ refines c2 c1.
Notation "c1 == c2" := (equiv c1 c2).
```

We have now verified that our contracts are correctly instantiating the theory. We could use them to design a system and verify properties on it.

6 Discussion

In this section, we justify certain design choices. We explored different ways to define the theory, which we found inefficient for the reasons described below.

6.1 State as Function vs. State as Vector

A prior version of the formalization defined states as vectors of values. States were defined on a vector of variables, and the index allowed to determine which values corresponded to each variable.

```
Variable n : nat.
Definition state := Vector.t B n.
Definition vars := Vector.t ident n.
Definition assertion := sets state.
Record contract vars := Contract {
    A : assertion ;
    G : assertion ;
}.
```

The practical problem of this solution is that it is very difficult to add variables to a state. Vectors embed their length in the type, which makes composing two contracts defined on different variables impossible.

If we have a contract c1 defined on the variables d1, and c2 defined on the variables d2, the composed contract is defined on variables d3 = d1 ∪ d2. The size of d3 needs to be known before constructing the contract. But it is not possible, because we don't know the size of d1 ∩ d2.

Even though defining states as vector works on paper, it rises many problems when using a proof assistant. In definitive, functions are sufficient to model states. This is why we define states as functions in our formalization.

6.2 Variable Set as Type Parameter vs. Variable Set as Record Field

In our definitions, every state, assertion, or contract depends on the variables it is defined on. This is a situation where we use the power of dependent type theory. Another solution would have been to hold the variable in a field of the record.

```
Record contract := Contract {
    d : set ident ;
    A : assertion d ;
    G : assertion d ;
}.
```

But the problem occurs when defining operators on contracts. We need contracts to be defined on the same variables. If the contracts are defined on different variables, we don't have any definition of the operator. This means we should have a partial function, returning an option type, namely, it returns the result when it exists, and a default value when it does not. However, working with partial functions means we have to always verify that the result exists when proving theories about it. By parameterizing the type of contract we limit the use of the operator to only contracts defined on the same variables. This means the operator is a total function which is easier to work with, especially in proof activity.

6.3 Extending Assertion on Another Set of Variables

We first defined the extension of assertion by using the union of the variables it's defined on, and another set of variables.

```
Definition extend_assertion {d1 d2 : set ident} (a1 : assertion d1) :
    assertion (d1 ∪ d2) := ...
```

This definition adds a lot of problems when composing contracts defined on variable sets that are equal but constructed differently. This leads to an assertion defined on d1 ∪ d2, and another on d2 ∪ d1. The two sets are equal, thanks to the union being commutative, but for instance, the types d1 ∪ d2 and d2 ∪ d1 are not the same in Coq. Since we parameterize the contracts type with their variables of definition, the types contract (d1 ∪ d2) and contract (d2 ∪ d1) are also different. Our composition operator requires the two contracts to be of the same type, this means it is not possible to compose contracts that are not of the same types. Composing these contracts is impossible, we need to change their definitions.

One solution would be to define another extension function:

```
Definition extend_assertion_l {d1 d2 : set ident} (a2 : assertion d2) :
    assertion (d1 ∪ d2) := ...
```

But it seems quite inelegant, every function needs to be defined two times. Our solution is to use another set of variables as the final set.

```
Definition extend_assertion {H : d1 ⊆ d2} (a1 : assertion d1) :
    assertion d2 := ...
```

This removes the problem altogether but changes the way we have to think about the extension of assertion.

7 Conclusion

In this paper, we presented a formalization of the set-theoretical assume/guarantee contracts in the proof assistant Coq, and showed how to instantiate it with a given logic. To the best of our knowledge, it is the first mechanized formalization of a theory of assume/guarantee contracts for system design. The formalization gives us the assurance that the notion of assume/guarantee contract is a correct instance of the meta-theory of contract. We also gave a set-theoretic definition of extension and elimination of variables in a contract, which was not defined in the original works. Finally, we demonstrated how to construct contracts in a simple propositional logic and proved the refinement, conjunction, and composition rules correct. The complete implementation of our formalization in Coq is available **here**.[2]

Ideally, the theory of contracts should help engineers struggle with the specification of contracts during system design. In this aim, having a tool to detect contradictory contracts early could prove useful. For now, the composition operator does not certify that the resulting contract is compatible with any environment nor implementable by a component. This may lead to a problem in the design process should the contradictory contracts be composed and incorrect contracts be defined, leading to an unimplementable contract. We can detect that a contract is unimplementable but it could be useful for a more efficient process to be able to detect contradictory contracts before composing them.

While the formalization of the contract theory we made (in the proof assistant Coq) may be of cumbersome use for realistically scaled design systems, this work was not intended to provide a usable contract theory applicable to any logic. Each logic features specific design choices that hint at the proper way contracts should be combined with them. However, our formalization demonstrates that different contract definitions fit the same global (meta) theory. Our aim is to prove that their definitions of refinement, composition, and conjunction are equivalent. The first step of this future work would be to implement a hybrid logic such as differential dynamic logic or the duration calculus into the Coq proof assistant, then formalize their contract theory. Finally, by instantiating our contract theory,

---

[2] https://github.com/merce-fra/SKT-VerifedContractTheory.

we could show the equivalence of their contracts, or pinpoint their differences if they are not equivalent.

References

1. Abadi, M., Lamport, L.: Composing specifications. ACM Trans. Programm. Lang. Syst. **15**(1), 73–132 (1993). https://doi.org/10.1145/151646.151649
2. Aréchiga, N.: Specifying safety of autonomous vehicles in signal temporal logic. In: 2019 IEEE Intelligent Vehicles Symposium (IV), pp. 58–63 (2019). https://doi.org/10.1109/IVS.2019.8813875
3. Benveniste, A., Caillaud, B., Ferrari, A., Mangeruca, L., Passerone, R., Sofronis, C.: Multiple viewpoint contract-based specification and design. In: de Boer, F.S., Bonsangue, M.M., Graf, S., de Roever, W.-P. (eds.) FMCO 2007. LNCS, vol. 5382, pp. 200–225. Springer, Heidelberg (2008). https://doi.org/10.1007/978-3-540-92188-2_9
4. Benveniste, A., et al.: Contracts for systems design: theory. Report, INRIA, July 2015
5. Chaochen, Z., Ji, W., Ravn, A.P.: A formal description of hybrid systems. In: Alur, R., Henzinger, T.A., Sontag, E.D. (eds.) HS 1995. LNCS, vol. 1066, pp. 511–530. Springer, Heidelberg (1996). https://doi.org/10.1007/BFb0020972
6. Chaochen, Z., Ravn, A.P., Hansen, M.R.: An extended duration calculus for hybrid real-time systems. In: Grossman, R.L., Nerode, A., Ravn, A.P., Rischel, H. (eds.) HS 1991-1992. LNCS, vol. 736, pp. 36–59. Springer, Heidelberg (1993). https://doi.org/10.1007/3-540-57318-6_23
7. Chen, M., et al.: MARS: a toolchain for modelling, analysis and verification of hybrid systems. In: Hinchey, M.G., Bowen, J.P., Olderog, E.-R. (eds.) Provably Correct Systems. NMSSE, pp. 39–58. Springer, Cham (2017). https://doi.org/10.1007/978-3-319-48628-4_3
8. Dabney, J.B., Harman, T.L.: Mastering Simulink. Pearson, Upper Saddle River (2003)
9. Foster, S., Cavalcanti, A., Canham, S., Woodcock, J., Zeyda, F.: Unifying theories of reactive design contracts. Theor. Comput. Sci. **802**, 105–140 (2020). https://doi.org/10.1016/j.tcs.2019.09.017
10. Fulton, N., Mitsch, S., Quesel, J.-D., Völp, M., Platzer, A.: KeYmaera X: an axiomatic tactical theorem prover for hybrid systems. In: Felty, A.P., Middeldorp, A. (eds.) CADE 2015. LNCS (LNAI), vol. 9195, pp. 527–538. Springer, Cham (2015). https://doi.org/10.1007/978-3-319-21401-6_36
11. Graf, S., Quinton, S., Girault, A., Gössler, G.: Building correct cyber-physical systems: why we need a multiview contract theory. In: Howar, F., Barnat, J. (eds.) FMICS 2018. LNCS, vol. 11119, pp. 19–31. Springer, Cham (2018). https://doi.org/10.1007/978-3-030-00244-2_2
12. Liebrenz, T., Herber, P., Glesner, S.: Deductive verification of hybrid control systems modeled in simulink with KeYmaera X. In: Sun, J., Sun, M. (eds.) ICFEM 2018. LNCS, vol. 11232, pp. 89–105. Springer, Cham (2018). https://doi.org/10.1007/978-3-030-02450-5_6
13. Lunel, S., Mitsch, S., Boyer, B., Talpin, J.-P.: Parallel composition and modular verification of computer controlled systems in differential dynamic logic. In: ter Beek, M.H., McIver, A., Oliveira, J.N. (eds.) FM 2019. LNCS, vol. 11800, pp. 354–370. Springer, Cham (2019). https://doi.org/10.1007/978-3-030-30942-8_22

14. Meyer, B.: Applying 'design by contract'. Computer **25**(10), 40–51 (1992). https://doi.org/10.1109/2.161279
15. Müller, A., Mitsch, S., Retschitzegger, W., Schwinger, W., Platzer, A.: Tactical contract composition for hybrid system component verification. Int. J. Softw. Tools Technol. Transf. **20**(6), 615–643 (2018). https://doi.org/10.1007/s10009-018-0502-9
16. Nipkow, T., Paulson, L.C., Wenzel, M.: Isabelle/HOL: A Proof Assistant for Higher-Order Logic. Lecture Notes in Computer Science. Springer, Heidelberg (2002). https://doi.org/10.1007/3-540-45949-9
17. Nuzzo, P.: Compositional design of cyber-physical systems using contracts. Ph.D. thesis, UC Berkeley (2015)
18. Platzer, A.: Differential dynamic logic for hybrid systems. J. Autom. Reason. **41**(2), 143–189 (2008). https://doi.org/10.1007/s10817-008-9103-8
19. Sangiovanni-Vincentelli, A., Damm, W., Passerone, R.: Taming Dr. Frankenstein: contract-based design for cyber-physical systems*. Eur. J. Control **18**(3), 217–238 (2012). https://doi.org/10.3166/ejc.18.217-238
20. Team, T.C.D.: The Coq proof assistant, version 8.7.2. Zenodo, February 2018. https://doi.org/10.5281/zenodo.1174360
21. Wang, S., Zhan, N., Guelev, D.: An assume/guarantee based compositional calculus for hybrid CSP. In: Agrawal, M., Cooper, S.B., Li, A. (eds.) TAMC 2012. LNCS, vol. 7287, pp. 72–83. Springer, Heidelberg (2012). https://doi.org/10.1007/978-3-642-29952-0_13
22. Wang, S., Zhan, N., Zou, L.: An improved HHL prover: an interactive theorem prover for hybrid systems. In: Butler, M., Conchon, S., Zaïdi, F. (eds.) ICFEM 2015. LNCS, vol. 9407, pp. 382–399. Springer, Cham (2015). https://doi.org/10.1007/978-3-319-25423-4_25

A Complete Semantics of $\mathbb{K}$ and Its Translation to Isabelle

Liyi Li[1(✉)] and Elsa L. Gunter[2]

[1] Department of Computer Science, University of Maryland, College Park, USA
liyili2@umd.edu
[2] Department of Computer Science, University of Illinois at Urbana-Champaign,
Champaign, USA
egunter@illinois.edu

Abstract. $\mathbb{K}$ [46] is a rewrite-based executable semantic framework in which programming languages, type systems and formal analysis tools can be defined using configurations, computations and rules. Isabelle/HOL [41] is a generic proof engine which allows mathematical formulas to be built into a formal language and provides tools to prove those formulas in a logical calculus. In this paper we define **IsaK**, a reference semantics for $\mathbb{K}$, which was developed through discussions with the $\mathbb{K}$ team to meet their expectations for a semantics for $\mathbb{K}$. Previously, we defined the static semantics for $\mathbb{K}$ [28]; thus, this paper mainly focuses on its dynamic semantics. More importantly, we investigate a way to connect $\mathbb{K}$ and Isabelle by building a translation framework, **TransK**, to translate programming languages defined in $\mathbb{K}$ into theories defined in Isabelle, which can not only allow programmers to define their programming languages easily in $\mathbb{K}$ but also have the ability to reason about their languages in Isabelle. In order to show a well-established translation, we prove that the $\mathbb{K}$ specification is sound and relatively complete with respect to the translated Isabelle theory by **TransK**. To the best of our knowledge, **IsaK** is the first complete formal semantics defined for $\mathbb{K}$, while **TransK** is the first complete translation from a real-world, order-sorted algebraic system to a many-sorted one. All the work is formalized in Isabelle/HOL at https://github.com/liyili2/KtoIsabelle.

1 Introduction

$\mathbb{K}$ is a domain specific language that takes a language specification as an input and generates an interpreter for it, including an execution engine to show the trace behaviors of executing a program in the specification. There is a rich body of published work on $\mathbb{K}$ itself [44], and specifications given in $\mathbb{K}$, such as the work listed in Sect. 6. Despite the success of $\mathbb{K}$, there are issues. While there have been a number of papers published concerning theories about $\mathbb{K}$ [8,18,43,46,47,49], there is no source that sufficiently defines the complete syntax and semantics of $\mathbb{K}$ or allows for rigorous proofs of the properties of the languages defined in $\mathbb{K}$. In addition, while $\mathbb{K}$ supports specific tools for analyzing programs in

© Springer Nature Switzerland AG 2021
A. Cerone and P. C. Ölveczky (Eds.): ICTAC 2021, LNCS 12819, pp. 152–171, 2021.
https://doi.org/10.1007/978-3-030-85315-0_10

a language defined in $\mathbb{K}$, it provides very little support for formal reasoning about the language itself. Even though $\mathbb{K}$ has been used in the definitions of an impressive number of programming languages, the support it offers users for language definitions is still fairly limited. Other than an interpreter generator and a small tool to prove properties about a specific program, there are no built-in tools for doing inductive proofs about a language specification. Finally, because early versions of $\mathbb{K}$ had features that were dropped in intermediate versions, only to be reintroduced in later versions, and because different versions displayed different behaviors, it is clear that there is not a consensus among the $\mathbb{K}$ community on what $\mathbb{K}$ is.

Our contribution, a full, formal language specification of $\mathbb{K}$, called **IsaK**, addresses these concerns and forms the foundation of tools for the maintenance, revision, and expansion of $\mathbb{K}$. We also define a shallow embedding of $\mathbb{K}$ into Isabelle (Sect. 4), named **TransK**, and prove that the embedded $\mathbb{K}$ specification in Isabelle bi-simulates it original $\mathbb{K}$ specification in **IsaK** (Sect. 5) for any **IsaK** specification. From this, we now can define a language specification in $\mathbb{K}$ and prove theories about the specification in Isabelle. Previously, we defined the **IsaK** static semantics [28]. We focus on the **IsaK** dynamic semantics in this paper (Sect. 3).

Several benefits accrue from our work. To the best of our knowledge, **IsaK** is the *first complete semantics* of $\mathbb{K}$. Other than the two simple descriptions of $\mathbb{K}$ [46,49], there are no resources discussing its syntax or semantics. Indeed, all $\mathbb{K}$ implementations contain some undesirable behaviors, so it is hard for one to learn the exact meanings of $\mathbb{K}$ operators. In the process of defining $\mathbb{K}$, we needed to constantly interview the $\mathbb{K}$ team to understand the meanings of the $\mathbb{K}$ operators and look at the Java source code of the $\mathbb{K}$ implementation to understand how $\mathbb{K}$ was being defined. The definition of **IsaK** provides a $\mathbb{K}$ standard for users, and save their time of learning $\mathbb{K}$.

To the best of our knowledge, **TransK** is the *first translation implementation* from an order-sorted algebraic system ($\mathbb{K}$) to a many-sorted one (Isabelle). Previous work only defined the general and theoretical concepts for translating order-sorted terms into many-sorted ones [25,36]. The result of translating specifications defined in $\mathbb{K}$ into Isabelle theories introduces the ability to bring general theorem proving to the $\mathbb{K}$ language specifications. Now, we are able to define a formal language specification and learn about the formal meaning of the language in **IsaK**, then translate it into an Isabelle theory through **TransK** and prove properties about the whole language in Isabelle (currently $\mathbb{K}$ lacks such ability). Before **TransK**, no $\mathbb{K}$ tools were able to handle this job. We want to define language specifications in $\mathbb{K}$ because of the rapid prototyping concise nature in $\mathbb{K}$ than in Isabelle, extra tools that $\mathbb{K}$ offers, and the usage of several complete real-world specifications [5,13,14,17,40] in $\mathbb{K}$. We want to prove theorems about such specifications in the theory translated by **TransK** because it is a lot simpler and clearer than the representations of these specifications directly in the deep embedding system (**IsaK**). All **IsaK** and **TransK** programs and theorems have been formalized and proved in Isabelle, and the implementation of **TransK** is provided in Ocaml that is directly exported from Isabelle.

2   Overview

We briefly discuss $\mathbb{K}$'s current semantic layout. The formal semantics as it is presented in **IsaK** is divided into two parts: static and dynamic semantics. The static semantics takes as input the frontend-AST (FAST) representation of a user-defined language specification ($\mathbb{K}$/**IsaK** theory) or programs that are allowed by a specification. Through the translation process in the static semantics, which performs computations that can be done statically (referred to as compile-time operations), the $\mathbb{K}$/**IsaK** theory in FAST is processed and translated into a representation in backend-AST format (BAST) with validity and type checks. The **IsaK** static process is given in [28]. Here, we mainly introduce the **IsaK** dynamic semantics (based on BAST) in Sect. 3 and its translation to Isabelle in Sect. 4.

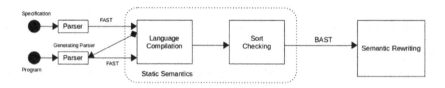

Fig. 1. The structure of **IsaK**

As indicated in Fig. 1, the operational behavior of the $\mathbb{K}$ specification contains four major steps: parsing, language compilation, sort checking, and semantic rewriting. Parsing itself comes in two phases: one to learn the grammar of the object language (the programming language being defined), and the other to incorporate that grammar into the grammar of $\mathbb{K}$ to parse the definitions of the rules and semantic objects defining the executable behavior of programs in the object language. The parsers translate the concrete syntax for $\mathbb{K}$ and the object languages that describe therein to FAST, eliminating mixfix syntax and other syntactic sugar in the process. Language compilation and sort checking are the steps in the static semantics, which is introduced in [28].

An example of specifications defined in the $\mathbb{K}$ BAST form is in Fig. 2. A more concrete example (FAST) is given in [27]. Here are some key points.

Syntax in a $\mathbb{K}$ Theory. In $\mathbb{K}$, the keyword SYNTAX introduces a finite set of syntactic definitions, separated by "|", such as the definition of the sort Exp. Each syntactic definition is a list of names. The names in Sans Serif font are non-terminals (sorts), while the names in TT font are terminals. A syntactic definition (e.g. Exp ::= Var) introducing only a singleton sort defines a relation that subsorts the singleton sort (Var) to the target sort (Exp). A definition that (syn) SYNTAX Exp ::= Exp / Exp [strict(1)] | Var | Int   (cof) $\left\langle \begin{matrix} \langle \$PGM : \text{KItem} \rangle_k \langle .\text{Map} \rangle_{env} \langle .\text{Map} \rangle_{heap} \\ \langle\langle\langle .K \rangle_{name} \langle .K \rangle_{body} \langle 0 \rangle_{key} \rangle_{class*} \rangle_{classes} \end{matrix} \right\rangle_T$

(heat) $x \ / \ y \curvearrowright tl \Rightarrow x \curvearrowright \square \ / \ y \curvearrowright tl$ when $\neg\text{isKResult}(x)$

(bagr) $\begin{aligned} &\langle B : \text{Bag} \ \langle X \curvearrowright \kappa \rangle_k \ \langle \rho_1, X \mapsto N, \rho_2 \rangle_{env} \ \langle \rho_3, N \mapsto E, \rho_4 \rangle_{heap} \rangle_T \\ &\Rightarrow \langle B : \text{Bag} \ \langle E \curvearrowright \kappa \rangle_k \ \langle \rho_1, X \mapsto N, \rho_2 \rangle_{env} \ \langle \rho_3, N \mapsto E, \rho_4 \rangle_{heap} \rangle_T \end{aligned}$

(fun)
SYNTAX Int ::= fresh(Set , Int) [function]
(a) fresh(.Set, n) $\Rightarrow n$ +Int 1
(b) fresh(SetItem($n::$Int) S, m) $\Rightarrow$ fresh(S, n) when m <Int n
(c) fresh(SetItem($n::$Int) S, m) $\Rightarrow$ fresh(S, m) when m >=Int n

Fig. 2. A briefing of $\mathbb{K}$

subsorts sorts to KResult (e.g. KResult ::= Int) defines the evaluation result sorts in a specification. Other kinds of syntactic definitions introduce user defined terms that express rules and programs. Every "real" syntactic definition (not subsorting) creates a prefix AST format like $\mathcal{KLabel}(\mathcal{KList})$, where the $\mathcal{KLabel}$ term acts as a constructor automatically generated by the terminals and the structure of the definition, and the $\mathcal{KList}$ term is the argument list generated from the non-terminals of the definition. The syntax definitions in a $\mathbb{K}$ theory are compiled by the **IsaK** static semantics into a sort set, a symbol table, a subsort relation and several heating/cooling rules as inputs for the **IsaK** dynamic semantics (Sect. 3).

$\mathbb{K}$ **Attributes in Syntax in FAST are Equal to Semantic Rules in BAST.** $\mathbb{K}$ allows users to define attributes in a syntactic definition (written in brackets e.g. [strict], in Fig. 2), some of which have semantic meanings. For example, a syntactic definition with a strict(1) attribute generates a pair of heating/cooling rules for the first non-terminal position in a term whose top-most constructor matches the definition. In $\mathbb{K}$, heating rules are to break down a term into subterms and let other semantic rules evaluate them, while the meaning of a cooling rule is to merge an evaluated subterm to the right position ($\square$) of the term. Rule (heat) in Fig. 2 is an example heating rule generated for the attribute in (syn). "$\curvearrowright$" is a list concatenation operator for connecting the computation sequence in a k cell, while "$\square$" is a special builtin operation in $\mathbb{K}$ representing the removal of a redex subterm from a term and the creation of a "hole" waiting to be filled.

$\mathbb{K}$ **Configurations.** Allowing users to define a global initial **configuration** for every $\mathbb{K}$ theory is a key $\mathbb{K}$ feature. The initial configuration of a specification is an algebraic structure of the program states, which are organized as nested, labeled **cells**. Cells are in XML formats (like $\langle...\rangle_T$) that hold semantic information, including the program itself (prefixed by the $ operator in Fig. 2). While the order of cells in a configuration is irrelevant, the contextual relations between cells are relevant and must be preserved by rules defined by users and subsequently "completely filled" in the compilation step in $\mathbb{K}$ according to the configuration. In a trace evaluation, each step of the computations should produce a result state (configuration) that "matches" the structure of the initial configuration, meaning that the names, sorts, and structural relations of the cells are preserved in the result and initial configuration. Leaf cells represent pieces of the program state, like computation stacks or continuations (e.g., k), environments (e.g., env), heaps (e.g., heap), etc. The content of each cell in an initial configuration has dual roles: it establishes the initial value of the computation and also defines the sort of the cell content. For example, the key cell in the configuration (Fig. 2) is defined as 0 and sort Int; during an evaluation, the cell's initial value is 0, and in every state of the evaluation, its content has a sort that subsorts to Int.

Semantic Rules in a $\mathbb{K}$ **Theory in BAST.** In this paper, we focus on the dynamic semantics of $\mathbb{K}$. All these unconventional configuration rules are assumed to be compiled to a standard form (BAST) by the **IsaK** static semantics [28], and the dynamic semantics definitions are based on the compiled format. Figure 2 also contains a set of BAST rules. The simplest form of the rules, such as rule (**heat**) (K rules), describe behaviors that can happen in a k cell (representing the computation list in a thread), without mentioning any other cells. They describe behaviors that can happen in a k cell, especially how the current executing expression is changed and the relationships among different positions in the computation list. The most complicated form of rules, such as rule (**bagr**), are typical configuration rules (Bag rules) in $\mathbb{K}$, and they describe interactions among different device/state components in a system. In $\mathbb{K}$, Bag rules are also powerful enough to manipulate language device resources. For example, since the class cell is marked as "*", one is allowed to write a rule to add a class data entry in the classes cell (details are in [27]). $\mathbb{K}$ also allows users to write equational rules, named *function rules*. The format is like the fresh definition in Fig. 2. Its syntactic definition (**fresh**) is labeled by an attribute function, and then the rules whose left-hand top-most constructor is the same as the $\mathcal{KLabel}$'s term syntactic definition are recognized by $\mathbb{K}$ to be the function rules under the function definition. The left-hand-side of a valid function rule has argument sorts that subsort to the argument sorts defined in the function definition, and the target sort of the right-hand-side subsorts to the target sort of the definition.

IsaK Static Semantics. The static semantics [28] is a process for translating an **IsaK** theory or a program belonging to the theory from FAST to BAST. It involves the compilation of syntactic definitions from an **IsaK** theory to a symbol table, which is for keeping syntactic information. Static semantics also gathers sort and subsort information, generates rules that users specify as attributes in the FAST syntactic definitions, and performs validity checks on the input **IsaK** theory. One of the most important steps it performs on a theory is sort checking. The type system we developed for **IsaK** is simple, similar to one in a simple typed lambda calculus, with additional subsorting relations. We have shown that the type preservation theorem in **IsaK** (see Sect. 3.2).

3   The IsaK Dynamic Semantics

Here we introduce the **IsaK** dynamic semantics, which is defined in Isabelle, based on the BAST terms transformed from the static semantics in [28]. Given an **IsaK** theory and a program belonging to the theory, the **IsaK** dynamic semantics produces the program execution trace according to the semantic rules in the theory. The development of $\mathbb{K}$ was based on the footprint of Rewriting Logic [22]. **IsaK** theories and programs are similar to Rewriting Logic theories and ground terms.

To facilitate the presentation, we have some relations derived from a relation (R), including the reflexive ($R^?$), transitive (R^+), and reflexive-transitive (R^*) closures. $[A]$ is the identity relation for a set A. $A \times B$ is the cross product of sets A and B, and $\times$ binds tighter than $\cup$. Some notational conventions in the paper are provided in Fig. 3 and [27]. For example, s ranges over sorts and c ranges over $\mathcal{KLabel}$, etc. In the figure, every name in $\mathcal{Chancery}$ font represents a type in Isabelle we defined for an **IsaK** component; every name in Sans-Serif font represents a sort or configuration (of type $\mathcal{CName}$) in an **IsaK** theory; everything in TT font is a construct (including program variables) programmers write in a program belonging to a theory, and everything in *Italics* is a meta-variable representing a term in **IsaK**.

Sorts

$\qquad SystemSort \triangleq \{\mathsf{K}, \mathsf{KItem}, \mathsf{KList}, \mathsf{List}, \mathsf{Set}, \mathsf{Map}, \mathsf{Bag}\}$

$\qquad BuiltinSort \triangleq SystemSort \cup \{\mathsf{Bool}\}$

$\qquad \mathcal{RName} \subseteq \mathcal{UsrSort} \qquad BuiltinSort \cap \mathcal{UsrSort} = \emptyset$

$\qquad ResultSort \triangleq \mathcal{RName} \cup \{\mathsf{Bool}\}$

$\qquad s \in \Psi \triangleq \mathcal{UsrSort} \cup BuiltinSort$

Subsorts

$(\Psi, \sqsubseteq)$ is a poset

$\sqsubseteq \supseteq (\mathcal{UsrSort} \times \{\mathsf{KItem}\}) \cup \{(\mathsf{KItem}, \mathsf{K})\}$

$\forall s_1 \, s_2. \; s_1 \in \{\mathsf{KList}, \mathsf{List}, \mathsf{Set}, \mathsf{Map}, \mathsf{Bag}\}$

$\qquad \wedge s_1 \sqsubseteq s_2 \Rightarrow s_1 = s_2$

Domains and Example Terms

$v \in \mathcal{CName} \triangleq \mathcal{BName} \cup \{\mathsf{k}\}$ Config Names

$c \in \mathcal{KLabel} \triangleq \mathcal{LName} \cup \{\mathtt{klabel}, \mathtt{isKResult}, \wedge, \neg, =\}$ KLabels (Constructors)

$k \in \mathcal{KItem} \triangleq \mathcal{KLabel}\,(\mathcal{KList})::s \mid \square::s$ KItem Terms

$k \in \mathcal{K} \triangleq \mathcal{KItem} \; list$ Associative and Identitive KItem Sequences

$kl \in \mathcal{KList} \triangleq \mathcal{K} \; list$ Associative and Identitive K Sequences

$\qquad \mathcal{MapItem} \triangleq \mathsf{mConstr}(\mathcal{K}, \mathcal{K})$ Singleton Map Terms

$M \in \mathcal{MapItem}' \triangleq \mathcal{Map} \mid \mathcal{KLabel}\,(\mathcal{KList})::\mathsf{Map} \mid \square::\mathsf{Map}$ Map Terms With Funs

$M \in \mathcal{Map} \triangleq \mathcal{MapItem}' \; list$ Idempotent, and Functional Map Terms

$\qquad \mathcal{BagItem} \triangleq \mathsf{bConstr}(\mathcal{CName}, \mathcal{Term})$ Singleton Configurations

$C \in \mathcal{Bag} \triangleq \mathcal{BagItem} \; list$ Associative, Commutative, and Identitive Configuration Terms

Allowed Terms: $t \in \mathcal{Term} \triangleq \mathcal{KItem} \cup \mathcal{K} \cup \mathcal{List} \cup \mathcal{Set} \cup \mathcal{Map} \cup \mathcal{Bag}$ Patterns/Expressions: $(\mathcal{Pat}|\mathcal{Exp}) \triangleq \mathcal{Term}$

Rule Format In BAST

$rl \in \mathcal{Rule} \triangleq \mathcal{K} \Rightarrow \mathcal{K}$ **when** $\mathcal{KLabel}\,(\mathcal{KList})::s_2$ (* K Transition Rules($s_2 \sqsubseteq \mathsf{Bool}$) *)

$\qquad \mid \mathcal{Bag} \Rightarrow \mathcal{Bag}$ **when** $\mathcal{KLabel}\,(\mathcal{KList})::s_2$ (* Configuration Transition Rules($s_2 \sqsubseteq \mathsf{Bool}$) *)

$\qquad \mid \mathcal{KLabel}\,(\mathcal{KList})::s \Rightarrow \mathcal{KLabel}\,(\mathcal{KList})::s_1$ **when** $\mathcal{KLabel}\,(\mathcal{KList})::s_2$

$\qquad\qquad$ (* Function Rules($s_1 \sqsubseteq s \sqsubseteq \{\mathsf{K}, \mathsf{List}, \mathsf{Map}, \mathsf{Set}\} \wedge s_2 \sqsubseteq \mathsf{Bool}$) *)

Fig. 3. Part of **IsaK** syntactic components in isabelle

3.1 Syntactic Component Highlights in BAST

We first briefly introduce some BAST syntactic features of an **IsaK** theory or program of the theory while the full BAST syntax is described in [27]. Every **IsaK** theory is expressed as a tuple of $(\Psi, \sqsubseteq, \Upsilon, \Delta)$, where Ψ is a set of sort names, $(\Psi, \sqsubseteq)$ is a poset representing sorts and subsorts for terms, Υ is a symbol table and Δ is a set of $\mathcal{R}ule$ terms. $\sqsubseteq$ is a subsort relation built on pairs of sorts in Ψ. We show restrictions on Ψ and $\sqsubseteq$ in Fig. 3.

Sorts and Subsorts. Every sort is disjointly either a user-defined sort ($\mathcal{U}sr\mathcal{S}ort$) or a built-in sort ($\mathcal{B}uiltin\mathcal{S}ort$). Each sort in $\mathcal{R}esult\mathcal{S}ort$ is either Bool, or a user-defined sort that can be the result sort of a computation, like Int. There are several restrictions on $\sqsubseteq$. For example, sort K is the upper bound of $\mathcal{U}sr\mathcal{S}ort$, while KItem is the supremum of the same set. The elements in {KList, List, Set, Map, Bag} do not have subsort relations other than reflexive relations in $\sqsubseteq$.

The reason to have these different kinds of sorts in **IsaK** is that terms with different sorts have different kinds of implicit equational properties in the pattern matching phase of a semantic evaluation step (see Sect. 3.2). Each term in **IsaK** is associated with exactly one kind of sort. Any user-defined sort term, like all valid terms for the Exp definition in Fig. 2, is subsorted to KItem and represented by the $\mathcal{K}Item$ term in Fig. 3, and has no implicit equational properties; while $\mathcal{B}uiltin\mathcal{S}ort$ terms have different representations (in Isabelle) and might be associated with implicit equational properties. For example, a $\mathcal{M}ap$ term, like the terms representing heap in the configuration and the rules in Fig. 2, has a set of equational rules that are associated for enforcing its idempotent property and also for being functional. Since all $\mathcal{B}uiltin\mathcal{S}ort$ terms have at least associative and identitive equational properties, **IsaK** implements them as lists in Isabelle, such as the $\mathcal{B}ag$ and $\mathcal{K}$ definitions in Fig. 3, to avoid the implementation of these two properties in the pattern matching algorithm.

Additionally, when a result sort is declared in the original $\mathbb{K}$, the sort is subsorted to the special sort KResult. This formalization causes a problem in the type (sort) soundness: a term with a result sort can be rewritten to another result-sorted term, but the position holding the term is only defined to hold the original sort. For example, assume that x has the value true in the heap, and we want to compute the expression $x/1$. This is ill-formed but the original $\mathbb{K}$ sort system cannot detect it, if we subsort both Bool and Int to KResult (Fig. 2). In **IsaK**, we discard the KResult sort and view the sorts subsorting to KResult as defining a Boolean predicate for a set of result sorts. We use the predicate isKResult, whose meaning is membership in $\mathcal{R}esult\mathcal{S}ort$. We replace every definition in a $\mathbb{K}$ theory that subsorts a term to KResult with an isKResult predicate for the term. Thus, the subsort relation of KResult in a $\mathbb{K}$ theory is replaced in **IsaK** by isKResult that checks a property on terms. An example is given as the heat rule in Fig. 2.

Syntactically Valid Terms, Rules, and Configurations. A syntactically valid term (with or without meta-variables) in **IsaK** is defined with the same term validity definitions as Rewriting Logic [22] (see [27]). In **IsaK**, a valid term is constructed through constructs whose syntactic information is stored as an entry in the symbol table Υ, which contains a constructor (symbol) name (a $\mathcal{K}Label$ term), a list of argument sorts, a target sort, and a flag of a construct. The flag indicates if the constructor is a function one. As we have mentioned in Sect. 2, an **IsaK** function is defined through a function constructor syntax definition and a set of rules for which the left-hand-side top-most constructor being the exact function constructor, such as the `fresh` function in Fig. 2. Moreover, **IsaK** adds a □ term, that represents an evaluation context hole (like the ones in ⟨heat⟩ in Fig. 2), for every sort (except sort KList and Bag).

The above description is for terms, but an **IsaK** theory usually contains syntactic definitions and semantic rules (Δ). The syntax for $\mathcal{Rule}$ terms is defined in Fig. 3. Every rule in BAST has the form ($\mathcal{Pat} \Rightarrow \mathcal{Exp}$ when $\mathcal{Exp}$). In a rule, the left-hand-side term (left of $\Rightarrow$) is called a pattern, while the right-hand-side and the condition term are called expressions. Like Rewriting Logic and the traditional functional programming languages, the terms that are allowed to be patterns are more restricted than those for expressions. Details are in [27]. As we mentioned in Sect. 2, there are only three kinds of rules in a theory: K, Bag, and function rules. K rules describe the transition behaviors in a k cell (a place for storing a sequence of instructions to be executed). Bag rules describe the interactions between program instructions in a k cell and other program state components (represented by $\mathcal{Bag}$ terms). We implement function terms for different sorts in Isabelle as separate syntactic definitions. Note, for example, the differences in the definitions for $\mathcal{MapItem}$ and $\mathcal{MapItem'}$ in Fig. 3.

Finally, an actual "program" that an **IsaK** theory (BAST) is interpreted/executed on is an initial configuration like the one in Fig. 2. It is a user-defined sequence of instructions (in a k cell) with the filling of the initial state components defined in the initial configuration.

3.2   The Definition of the Dynamic Semantics

Here we introduce the **IsaK** evaluation semantics on a configuration of an **IsaK** theory $\Theta = (\Psi, \sqsubseteq, \Upsilon, \Delta)$. Any initial configuration for Θ is represented as a ground term configuration (C_0) that has the type $\mathcal{Bag}$. The evaluation of an initial configuration (C_0) in Θ produces a set of traces, each of which contains a sequence of configurations, where the $(i+1)$-th configuration (C_{i+1}) is the result of applying a rule from Δ to the i-th configuration (C_i). We first introduce procedures that are common to every evaluation step.

Common Evaluation Procedures. There are three consecutive procedures that every evaluation step in **IsaK** needs. We introduce them separately. The first one is the pattern matching procedure (`match`). The pattern matching algorithm in **IsaK** is a normal top-most pattern matching procedure. Given a rule rl and ground term t, the procedure $\mathtt{match}(rl, t)$ pattern-matches the pattern side of rl (the left-hand side) with t, and generates a map from the meta-variables on the left side of rl to subterms in t or $\bot$ if there is no match. Pattern-matching here means that for a pattern of the form (p, t) with $p = c(p_1, ..., p_n)$ and ground term $t = c'(t_1, ..., t_m)$, we have $c = c'$, $n = m$, and σ_i is the result of matching p_i with t_i, then the result is $\bigcup_i \sigma_i$ so long as for all meta-variables $x \in (\mathtt{dom}(\sigma_i) \cap \mathtt{dom}(\sigma_j))$ we have $\sigma_i(x) = \sigma_j(x)$, and for a pattern that is a meta-variable x, the result of the match is $\{x \mapsto t\}$. For simplicity, we define $\mathtt{match}(\Theta, t)$ to find the rule rl in the rule set of Θ whose left-hand side matches term t and which generates a mapping. In Isabelle, we utilize its builtin pattern matching algorithm (with the list pattern matching). The second common procedure is the substitution procedure (subs). Given a term p with meta-variables $x_1, ..., x_n$ and map m from the meta-variables to ground terms, $\text{subs}(m, p)$ substitutes the ground term $m(x_i)$ for the occurrences of every meta-variable x_i ($1 \leq i \leq n$) in p. In Isabelle, we faithfully implement a substitution function, for any possible terms in **IsaK**, which can be extracted to Ocaml.

The third procedure is the term normalization procedure (norm). Normalization only applies to the whole ground term configuration C. $\text{norm}(C)$ searches every subterm in C and rewrites it to a canonical form. Mainly, there are two properties that a canonical form guarantees, and they both deal with implicit equational properties in *BuiltinSort* terms. First, for a *Set*, *Bag*, and *Map* term, which is implemented as a list in Isabelle, we give an order for elements in the list and ensure that every such list is sorted by this order during every step of computation. This is a normal practice for implementing the commutative pattern matching equational property for terms, which can be found in many literatures [20,23]. Second, for *Set* and *Map* terms, we merge identical elements and ensure a *Map* term being functional. For example, in Fig. 2, after a rewrite, the heap state may be $\langle (\text{x} \mapsto 1)(\text{x} \mapsto 1) \rangle_{\text{heap}}$, then the term is canonicalized to $\langle \text{x} \mapsto 1 \rangle_{\text{heap}}$ with one of the element $(\text{x} \mapsto 1)$ being removed. However, if the heap state is $\langle (\text{x} \mapsto 1)(\text{x} \mapsto 2) \rangle_{\text{heap}}$, the whole configuration results in a global error state because the map is not functional.

Semantics for Different Rules. We first define two kinds of configuration contexts. The first one is the configuration context $C[]_f^s$ as a *Bag* term with exactly one $\square$ subterm described in Sect. 3.1, whose sort s is defined as $s \in \textit{UsrSort} \cup \{\text{KItem}, \text{K}, \text{List}, \text{Map}, \text{Set}\}$. The configuration redex for the context is a term $c(kl)::s$, where a valid combination of the context and redex $(C[c(kl)::s]_f^s)$ is a *Bag* term C derived by replacing the $\square$ subterm with the redex $c(kl)::s$, and the sort for the $\square$ matches the sort s. The second kind of configuration context is a *BagItem* term, and the second context-redex pair is defined as $C[]_k$ and a $\mathcal{K}$ term t_k, such that $C[]_k$ has a unique $\square$ subterm (type *BagItem*) and $C[t_k]_k$ replaces the $\square$ subterm with the *BagItem* term ($\text{bConstr}(\text{k}, t_k)$) whose cell name (*CName*) is k and the $\mathcal{K}$ type subterm is t_k. The first context-redex pair represents the process of pulling out a function term from a subpart of a configuration for evaluation, while the second context-redex pair represents the process of pulling out the content of a k cell for evaluation.

Any **IsaK** evaluation ($\longrightarrow^\Theta$) can be viewed as an application of one of three different rules: function rule applications ($\longrightarrow_{\text{B},f}^\Theta$; (1) and (2) in Fig. 4), K rule applications ($\longrightarrow_k^\Theta$; (3) in Fig. 4), and configuration (*Bag*) rule applications ($\longrightarrow_\text{B}^\Theta$; (4) in Fig. 4). In these rules, right is a function to get the expression side of a rule, while cond is to get the condition expression of a rule. The term true is a built-in Boolean term in **IsaK** representing the true value. The Kleene star ($*$) in Fig. 4 represents applying the arrow-rule inside the parentheses multiple times until a final result (like true) shows up or there are no more such arrow-rules to apply. The basic evaluation strategy of these rule applications is to split the current configuration C into context-redex pairs mentioned above,

$$(1) \quad \frac{rl \in \Theta \quad m = \mathtt{match}(rl, c(kl)) \quad t = \mathtt{subs}(m, \mathtt{cond}(rl)) \quad t \, (\longrightarrow_f^\Theta)^* \, \mathtt{true}}{c(kl) \longrightarrow_f^\Theta \mathtt{subs}(m, \mathtt{right}(rl))}$$

$$(2) \quad \frac{C = C[c(kl){::}s]_f^s \quad c(kl) \, (\longrightarrow_f^\Theta)^+ \, t}{C \longrightarrow_{\mathtt{B},f}^\Theta \mathtt{norm}(C[t]_f^s)}$$

$$(3) \quad \frac{C = C[t_\mathbf{k}]_\mathbf{k} \quad rl \in \Theta \quad m = \mathtt{match}(rl, t_\mathbf{k}) \quad t = \mathtt{subs}(m, \mathtt{cond}(rl)) \quad t \, (\longrightarrow_f^\Theta)^* \, \mathtt{true}}{C \longrightarrow_\mathbf{k}^\Theta \mathtt{norm}(C[\mathtt{subs}(m, \mathtt{right}(rl))]_\mathbf{k})}$$

$$(4) \quad \frac{rl \in \Theta \quad m = \mathtt{match}(rl, C) \quad t = \mathtt{subs}(m, \mathtt{cond}(rl)) \quad t \, (\longrightarrow_f^\Theta)^* \, \mathtt{true}}{C \longrightarrow_\mathtt{B}^\Theta \mathtt{norm}(\mathtt{subs}(m, \mathtt{right}(rl)))}$$

$$(\mathtt{group}) \quad \Longrightarrow^\Theta \triangleq (\longrightarrow_{\mathtt{B},f}^\Theta)^* (\longrightarrow_\mathbf{k}^\Theta \mid \longrightarrow_\mathtt{B}^\Theta)$$

Fig. 4. IsaK semantics for different rules

apply a rule to rewrite the redex, and insert the new redex back into the context. The **(group)** definition in Fig. 4 represents a typical combination of rule applications in forming different $\mathbb{K}$ tools, mainly, the **krun** and **ksearch** tools. The **krun** tool is defined as $(\Longrightarrow^\Theta)^*$ or $(\Longrightarrow^\Theta)^n$ if users specify the number of trace steps n they want to see. The **ksearch** tool is defined by a set transition from a singleton set of a configuration to a set of configurations in the form $(\{C\} \Rightarrow^\Theta Cl)^*$, where the set configuration transition has the property:

$$Cl \Rightarrow^\Theta Cl' \triangleq (\forall C \in Cl.\ C \Longrightarrow^\Theta C' \Rightarrow C' \in Cl') \wedge (\forall C' \in Cl',\ \exists C \in Cl.\ C \Longrightarrow^\Theta C')$$

With the **IsaK** dynamic semantics and the **IsaK** sort system shown previously [28], we have the following type preservation property (proof sketch in [27] and formalization in Isabelle). Note that the **IsaK** type system does not satisfy the type progress property, since $\mathbb{K}$ allows users to define language semantics incrementally. It is fine in a $\mathbb{K}$ theory to define a language syntax without defining its semantics.

Theorem 1. For a type correct theory (Θ), for any type correct configuration C, if a sub-component e in C has type t, then the result of evaluating C has a type t' for the sub-component, where t' is a subtype of t.

4   TransK: Translation from $\mathbb{K}$ to Isabelle

Here, we introduce **TransK**, a translation from an **IsaK** theory to an Isabelle theory. The input of the translation is a deeply embedded **IsaK** specification (theory) (Sect. 3) in a functional system (Isabelle). A such specification contains a sort set (Ψ), subsort relation $(\sqsubseteq)$, symbol table (Υ), and a set of transition rules (Δ). The output translation of the specification by **TransK** is a shallowly embedded Isabelle theory containing a list of Isabelle datatypes, a list of quotient types with proofs, and a list of Isabelle rules translated from rules in the input **IsaK** specification.

4.1   Translating Datatypes

For a given **IsaK** theory $\Theta = (\Psi, \sqsubseteq, \Upsilon, \Delta)$, we first translate the tuple $(\Psi, \sqsubseteq, \Upsilon)$ to a pair of a finite quotient type set and a finite set of Isabelle proofs (Ω^q, Π) in the translated Isabelle theory (Ξ), such that all relations in $\sqsubseteq$ are removed in Ξ, but their functionalities are combined in Ω^q. The way to achieve this is to utilize Isabelle quotient types: we first translate the **IsaK** datatype tuples $(\Psi, \sqsubseteq, \Upsilon)$ to a finite Isabelle datatype set Ω by explicitly coercing every pair in $\sqsubseteq$; and then we translate Ω to a quotient type set Ω^q with a finite set of proofs (Π), one for each target sort in Ω^q, to show that each quotient type in Ω^q defines an equivalence relation over all of the syntax defined in Ω. We briefly describe the two processes with examples below. The detailed translation is found in [27].

Translation from $\mathbb{K}$ **Datatypes to Isabelle Datatypes.** The translation step from the tuple $(\Psi, \sqsubseteq, \Upsilon)$ to an Isabelle datatype set Ω has two parts: adding builtin datatypes (corresponding to terms in $\mathcal{B}uiltinSort$ in Fig. 3) and translating user defined datatypes (corresponding to terms in $\mathcal{U}srSort$ in Fig. 3). In [27], we show a complete datatype translation for a small language. The builtin datatypes that are additionally generated are in a one-to-one correspondence with the **IsaK** datatypes in Fig. 3, except for $\mathcal{K}Label/\mathcal{K}List$, which represent constructors and their arguments in $\mathbb{K}$ and which become implicit in Isabelle. We implement the builtin $\mathcal{K}$, $List$, Set, $\mathcal{M}ap$, and $\mathcal{B}ag$ datatypes as type synonyms for Isabelle builtin lists of corresponding singleton item datatypes, e.g. the $\mathcal{K}Item$ $list$ for $\mathcal{K}$. The reason is to capture the aspect that some builtin datatypes have implicit equational properties associated with them (listed in Fig. 3). By representing these datatypes as Isabelle list structures and representing a connection operation in **IsaK** (e.g. the set concatenation operation in $\mathbb{K}$) as an Isabelle list concatenation operation (@), we are able to capture the implicit associative and identitive equational properties on these datatypes without extra effort. This strategy can be generalized to deal with any datatypes with implicit associative and identitive equational properties. The other implicit equational properties are dealt with by quotient types. The translation of user-defined datatypes (from $\mathbb{K}$ to Isabelle) is to add explicit coercions for all subsort relation pairs in $\sqsubseteq$, e.g. the constructor `Var_Exp` coerces a term in sort Var to an Exp term (Fig. 2). This excludes all function constructs (e.g. `fresh` in Fig. 2), which are translated directly into inductive relations without having datatype definitions in Isabelle (Sect. 4.2). Additionally, we add an extra constructor (like `Exp_Hole`) for each sort that contains some syntactic definitions with [`strict`] attributes. The constructor represents the $\square$ term in **IsaK** (Sect. 3).

From Datatypes to Quotient Types. Here we translate the Isabelle datatype set Ω to the quotient type set Ω^q with a set of proofs Π. A quotient type is composed of a set of terms, with a fixed target sort, whose elements are equivalence classes that partition the whole term domain by a given set of equations. Some datatypes in Ω are only translated to "trivial" quotient types, meaning a quotient type with Isabelle's builtin = operation as its equivalence relation. For example, the translation of a sort Int term to a quotient type is a trivial one, and its translation and the quotient type proof in Isabelle are given as the one line statement (`quotient_type` *int*^{q} = "*int*" / "(=)" `by (rule identity_equivp)`).

For any datatype subset of Ω indexed by a specific target sort, there are four cases requiring non-trivial quotient type translations. The general strategy for translating non-trivial cases is to define inductive relations to capture the equivalence relations defined for the quotient types, and to prove that these really are such relations. Then, to ensure that the definitions are equivalence relations, we encode explicitly the reflexive (`rlx`), symmetry (`sym`), and, transitive (`trans`) rules for each possible relation of the four kinds of non-trivial translations. For example, for handling the communicative equational property (*comeq*) in *Bag* terms and the idempotent equational property (*idmeq*) in *Map* and *Set* terms (the first two cases), we have the following translation:

```
inductive comeq where
com: "comeq (x@y) (y@x)"
| recur: "comeq u v
    ⟹ comeq (x@u@y) (x@v@y)"
| rlx: "comeq x x"
| sym: "comeq x y
         ⟹ comeq y x"
| trans:"⟦comeq x y;comeq y z⟧
         ⟹ comeq x z"
```

```
inductive idmeq where
idem: "set x = set y
         ⟹ idmeq x y
| rlx: "idmeq x x"
| sym: "idmeq x y
         ⟹ idmeq y x"
| trans:"⟦idmeq x y;idmeq y z⟧
         ⟹ idmeq x z"
```

```
apply (simp add:
     equivp_reflp_symp_transp)
apply (rule conjI)
apply (simp add:reflp_def)
apply (simp add:rlx)
apply (rule conjI)
apply (simp add:
     symp_def,clarsimp)
apply (simp add:sym)
apply (simp add:
     transp_def,clarsimp)
apply (simp add:trans)
```

The above figure introduces two kinds (*comeq* and *idmeq*) of non-trivial quotient type translations. The Isabelle proof pattern listed in the right column is a general quotient type proof pattern for every quotient type translation in **TransK**. Obviously, the header signatures for different kinds of the quotient types are different. For example, the signature for introducing the quotient type *Bag*^{q} is: (`quotient_type` *Bag*^{q} = "*Bag*" / "*comeq*"), while the quotient type *Set*^{q} has the signature: (`quotient_type` *Set*^{q} = "*Set*" / "*idmeq*").

The other two kinds of non-trivial quotient type translations relate to the translation of subsorts in order-sorted algebras to explicit coercions in many-sorted algebras. In doing explicit coercions, when there is a chain of subsort relations for an **IsaK** term with the possibility of multiple paths from one end to the other, it is necessary to equalize all of the different paths. There are apparently only two kinds of explicit coercion patterns to take care.

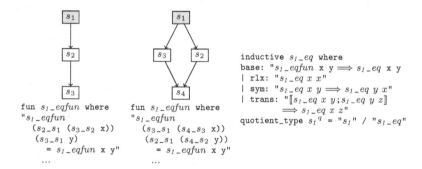

```
fun s1_eqfun where
"s1_eqfun
   (s2_s1 (s3_s2 x))
   (s3_s1 y)
     = s1_eqfun x y"
  ...
```

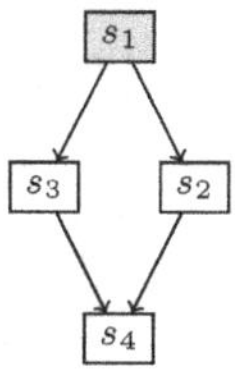


```
fun s1_eqfun where
"s1_eqfun
   (s3_s1 (s4_s3 x))
   (s2_s1 (s4_s2 y))
     = s1_eqfun x y"
  ...
```

```
inductive s1_eq where
base: "s1_eqfun x y ⟹ s1_eq x y
| rlx: "s1_eq x x"
| sym: "s1_eq x y ⟹ s1_eq y x"
| trans: "⟦s1_eq x y;s1_eq y z⟧
         ⟹ s1_eq x z"
quotient_type s1^q = "s1" / "s1_eq"
```

The first kind of pattern is listed in the left above. If there is a sort s_1, and it has a subsort s_2 that has a subsort s_3, we need to create a equivalence relation capturing that the consecutive coercions from s_3 to s_2 to s_1 is the same as the single coercion from s_3 to s_1. For example, in Fig. 2, the sorts KItem, Exp, and Int follow this pattern, and so we need to add the equivalence relation: `Int_Exp (Exp_KItem x) = Int_KItem x`. The second kind is listed in the middle column above. If there is a sort s_1, and two sorts s_2 and s_3 subsort to it, and then a fourth sort s_4 subsorts to both s_2 and s_3, then we need to capture the equivalence relation of the subsorts from s_4 to s_1 through two different paths – s_2 and s_3, respectively. In Isabelle, the relations generated for the two kinds of patterns are similar to the one listed in the right column above. They both add relations for the sort at the top (s_1) only. The only difference is their implementations of s_1_eqfun. For each s_1 sort that might have these two kinds of patterns, we need to generate one *eqfun*. For each function (sort s_1), we need to list all of the equivalence relations that captures the two kinds. In above, we list two different functions, each of which has one listed equivalence relation.

4.2   Translating $\mathbb{K}$ Terms and Rules

Here we discuss the translation of **IsaK** terms and rules. For an **IsaK** theory $(\Psi, \sqsubseteq, \Upsilon, \Delta)$, the translation algorithm for user defined terms simply walks down the ASTs of the terms by adding explicit coercions according to the syntactic translations described in Sect. 4.1. The translation algorithm is straightforward, following the symbol table Υ in determining the sort for every cell/construct in a configuration/term. In addition, the deeply embedded **IsaK** theory has the $\mathcal{KLabel}$ and $\mathcal{KList}$ terms, which are translated to constructors and argument lists in a term, respectively. The detailed translation is in [27].

A rule translation is to translate the rule set Δ to a new set of rules Δ^i, whose elements are all represented as inductive relations in Isabelle. The translated relations are all quantifier-free, with all meta-variables represented as universally quantified meta-variables in Isabelle. In Sect. 3, we introduced the **IsaK** rewriting system by dividing rules into three categories: function, K, and configuration rules. The rule translation deals with these groups separately.

Translating Function Rules. We first investigate the translation of function rules. Each rule translation is divided into two parts: a translated inductive relation in Isabelle that captures the meaning of the function rule, and a definition using the Hilbert's choice operator to produce the output of the relation. In $\mathbb{K}$, a function has a syntactic definition with several function rewrite rules, whose format is shown as the example in Sect. 3.1. Each function, with possibly many rules, is translated to a single inductive relation, with possibly many cases, as well as a definition created using Hilbert's choice operator. Given a subset (Υ_f) of the symbol table Υ containing only function constructs, and a subset (Δ_f) of Δ containing only function rules, we produce a set (Δ_f^i) of inductive relations in Isabelle that contains the translated results of Δ_f.

```
fresh(SetItem(n::Int) S, m)
  ⇒ fresh(S, n) when m <Int n
...
```
⟹
```
inductive fresh_ind where
  ⟦m < n; fresh_ind (S, n) x₁⟧
    ⟹ fresh_ind ([SConstr [Int_KItem n]@S, m) x₁
  ...
definition fresh where
  "fresh e = (SOME x . fresh_ind e x)"
```

In translating the **fresh** function in Fig. 2, we first look at all function rules in Δ_f whose top-most constructors of the rule patterns are **fresh**. The translation of each single rule for the function label **fresh** results in an inductive relation case in the relation **fresh_ind** (like the example rule translation above). The rule pattern ((SetItem(n:Int) S, m)) is translated to the first argument of **fresh_ind** with the correct coercions. The translation of the rule expression depends on if the expression contains recursion. In above example, since the expression contains a recursion step (**fresh**(S, n)), we then need to generate a variable (x_1) to represent the result of the recursion and put the recursion expression in the conditions of the inductive case. The rule condition is also translated to the conditions in the inductive case. After we construct all of the inductive cases for the function (or inductive relations for a set of mutually recursive functions), we create a definition with the Hilbert's choice operator SOME to force the inductive relation to output terms with the same type as the target sort of the **fresh** function defined in Fig. 2.

Translating $\mathbb{K}$ and Configuration Rules. The general strategies for translating a K rule or a configuration rule are very similar. We briefly introduce the K rule translation by an example. Further details are provided in [27].

```
v:Exp ⤳ □ / y ⤳ tl
  ⇒ v / y ⤳ tl when isKResult(v)
```
⟹
```
inductive k_rule where
  ...
  ⟦t = abs_K((Exp_KItem v)#((Div x Exp_Hole)#tl));
  isKResult((Exp_KItems v)); t' = abs_K((Div x v)#tl)⟧
    ⟹ k_rule t t'
  ...
```

All K rules in a theory are translated to cases in an inductive relation in Isabelle, while **Bag** rules are translated to cases in another inductive relation. The K rule translation is very similar to the translation of function rules, except that all translated terms of the former are quotient type terms, so we need to use a variable to suggest that an equivalent term to the quotient type term can also be applied by the rule. An example is the term t in the above figure. We use t to indicate that it is a quotient type term (by using **abs_K**) of the translation of the pattern term (v:Exp ⤳ □ / y ⤳ tl). Translating configuration rules is similar to translating K rules. The only difference is that the translated **Bag** inductive relation needs to contain transition cases for collecting all of the transitions that occur in K rule and function rule applications. Besides these rule translations, the final translated Isabelle theory also contains a top level transition relation capturing possible global error states, as mentioned in Sect. 3.2.

5   IsaK and TransK Bisimulations

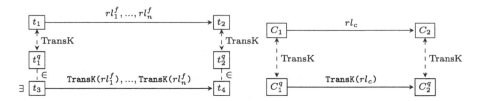

Fig. 5. Soundness and completeness of **IsaK** and **TransK**

Here we discuss the relationship between **IsaK** and **TransK**. Figure 5 describes the general relation diagrams between them (proof sketch in [27] and formalization in Isabelle). The **IsaK** deep embedding and **TransK** shallow embedding are implemented in Isabelle. We also implement a small Isabelle system (**Isab**) in Isabelle. **TransK** translates an **IsaK** theory to an Isabelle theory in **Isab**. the rewriting semantics of the Isabelle system (**Isab**) supporting necessary features for the translation proof is a simple typed λ-μ calculus with Hilbert's choice operator and quotient types. **Isab** is based on the λ-μ calculus developed by Matache et al. [32], and extended to support the rewriting theories of inductive relations and definitions using Hilbert's choice operator.

To prove soundness/completeness, we have to prove the soundness and completeness of the functions rules separately from the ones for K/configuration rules (Fig. 5). The problem is that the function rules are translated to a definition of inductive relations in the big-step format, and its execution can be infinite. The soundness and completeness proofs for function rules have to assume that every rewrite of the function rule application on the conditional expression terminates in a finite sequence whose length is n. Additionally, a function rule application deals with terms that are the translated datatypes not quotient types. Thus, a function rule is applied to a representative term in a given equivalence class, which is transitioned to another term as a representative in the resulting equivalence class, as described by the existential operation in the first diagram of Fig. 5. The term t_3 is a representative of the class t_1^q which is translated from the $\mathbb{K}$ term t_1. The function soundness/completeness theorems are listed below.

Theorem 2. (Soundness) In **IsaK**, assume that a sequence of function rules $rl_1^f, ..., rl_n^f$ applied to a term t_1 terminates in n steps and results in term t_2, and t_1^q and t_2^q are quotient type terms in **Isab** translated by **TransK**, there exists a term t_3 in t_1^q transitioning through sequence of corresponding rule applications $\mathtt{TransK}(rl_1^f), ..., \mathtt{TransK}(rl_n^f)$ to term t_4, such that t_4 is in the quotient type class t_2^q, which is a translation from t_2.

(Completeness) If there exist quotient type terms t_1^q and t_2^q, such that a representative t_3 of t_1^q is transitioned to t_4 in t_2^q through a sequence of function rule applications $rl_1^{f'}, ..., rl_n^{f'}$, and $t_1^q = \mathtt{TransK}(t_1)$, $t_2^q = \mathtt{TransK}(t_2)$, and $rl_1^{f'} = \mathtt{TransK}(rl_1^f), ..., rl_n^{f'} = \mathtt{TransK}(rl_n^f)$, then t_1 is transitioned to t_2 through the sequence of function rule applications $rl_1^f, ..., rl_n^f$.

The soundness and completeness for $\mathbb{K}$/configuration rule applications are described in the second diagram in Fig. 5 and below.

Theorem 3. (Soundness) In **IsaK**, assume that a configuration C_1 is transitioned to C_2 through a $\mathbb{K}$ (or configuration) rule rl_c, and C_1^q is a quotient type term translated from C_1, then C_2^q is translated from C_2 by rule $\mathtt{TransK}(rl_c)$.

(Completeness) If there exist quotient type configurations C_1^q and C_2^q, such that C_1^q transitions to C_2^q through a rule rl_c', $C_1^q = \mathtt{TransK}(C_1)$, and $rl_c' = \mathtt{TransK}(rl_c)$, then C_2 is transitioned from C_1 by rule rl_c and $C_2^q = \mathtt{TransK}(C_2)$.

6 Related Work

Order-sorted algebras were first introduced systematically by Goguen et al. [15]. Many people defined rewriting strategies, unifications and equational rules on top of order-sorted algebras and further extended the operational semantics of order-sorted algebras [1,6,16,22,35]. Based on order-sorted algebras, Meseguer et al. [31,33] developed rewriting logic. The biggest contribution of rewriting logic is to contain the operational semantics of order-sorted algebras and distinguish equations from rewriting rules – equations partition terms into equivalence classes while rewriting rules act like traditional transition rules in structural operational semantics. Maude [29] implemented the syntax and semantics of rewriting logic and provided several useful tools and applications [11,12,34]. Another implementation of an order-sorted algebra is PROTOS(L) [3], which has an operational semantics based on a polymorphic, order-sorted resolution. $\mathbb{K}$ [43,46], based on rewriting logic, is executable semantic framework in which programming languages, type systems and formal analysis tools can be defined using configurations, computations and rules. Matching Logic [47] is a logic system that is built on top of $\mathbb{K}$ for reasoning about structures. An invention recently developed from Matching Logic is Reachability Logic [9,10,45]. It is a seven rule proof system that is language independent. It generalizes transitions of operational language specifications defined by users and the Hoare triples of axiomatic semantics [19] to prove properties about programs in the specifications, so that users do not need to define the axiomatic semantics of a specification. In an ongoing project, Moore [38] is transferring the $\mathbb{K}$ specifications to Coq [7] and plans to prove properties of the programs of the specifications in Coq. At this time, Moore has managed to define a useful co-induction tool in Coq and prove some properties by defining small language specifications in Coq. Big language specifications have been defined in $\mathbb{K}$, including C [13], PHP [14], JavaScript [40], Java [5], and LLVM [26]. They are executable, have been validated by test banks, and, with the addition of some formal analysis tools produced by $\mathbb{K}$, have shown usefulness. On the other hand, the study of many sorted algebras has a long history. Their logic system was explored by Wang [48]. Many well-known programming languages such as C, Java, LLVM, and Python are based on them. One of the most prominent many-sorted programming language specifications is Standard ML by Milner, Tofte, Harper, and Macqueen [37], whose formal and executable specifications were given by Lee, Crary, and Harper [24], VanInwegen and Gunter [21], and Maharaj and Gunter [30]. The simple type systems of the two famous theorem provers Isabelle/HOL [41] and Coq [7] are also based on them. There have been a number of formal language specifications given in HOL and Coq. For example, A small step semantics of C in HOL was specified by Norrish [39], who proved substantial meta-properties, but the specification has not been tested for conformance with implementations. Blazy and Leroy [4] in the CompCert project verified an optimizing compiler based on CLight, including compilation steps and C-like modular systems. They used Coq to generate a compiled code behaving exactly as described by the specification of the language. Other projects based on CompCert include Appel's, which combined program verification with a verified compilation software tool chain [2]. Goguen et al. [15] introduced a way of translating solely initial free (algebras that have no equations or rules) order-sorted algebras to many-sorted ones. One recent attempt at translating order-sorted algebras into many-sorted ones was made by Meseguer and Skeirik [36]. Their translation still focused on initial free order-sorted algebras, and only provided a naive framework to translate order-sorted equations and rules to many-sorted ones by generating potentially exponentially many new copies of transition rules for each of the sorts subsorting to sorts in the original transition rules. In addition, Li and Gunter [25] provided a new translation method to translate order-sorted algebras into many-sorted ones, which is the theoretical foundation of our paper.

7   Conclusion and Future Work

In this paper, we proposed **IsaK**, a formal semantics of $\mathbb{K}$ in Isabelle. We mainly focused on the dynamic behavior that occurs when a $\mathbb{K}$ theory is executed on an input program. We also defined **TransK**, the shallow embedding of a $\mathbb{K}$ specification into an Isabelle theory, and showed that the execution of a program in the $\mathbb{K}$ specification is bisimilar to its Isabelle theory translated by **TransK**. For future work, we will endeavor to make the system solid enough to translate some real-world specifications from $\mathbb{K}$ into Isabelle, such as the LLVM semantics in $\mathbb{K}$ [26], so that we can prove theorems like semantic preservation properties of compiler optimizations based on the LLVM semantics translated in Isabelle. We can also link reachability logic [9,10,45], the new program logic being derived by the $\mathbb{K}$ team, with traditional program logics such as Hoare Logic [19] and Separation Logic [42].

References

1. Alpuente, M., Escobar, S., Espert, J., Meseguer, J.: A modular order-sorted equational generalization algorithm. Inf. Comput. **235**, 98–136 (2014)
2. Appel, A.W.: Verified software toolchain. In: Barthe, G. (ed.) ESOP 2011. LNCS, vol. 6602, pp. 1–17. Springer, Heidelberg (2011). https://doi.org/10.1007/978-3-642-19718-5_1 http://dl.acm.org/citation.cfm?id=1987211.1987212
3. Beierle, C., Meyer, G.: Run-time type computations in the Warren Abstract Machine. J. Log. Program. **18**(2), 123–148 (1994)
4. Blazy, S., Leroy, X.: Mechanized semantics for the Clight subset of the C language. J. Autom. Reason. **43**(3), 263–288 (2009)
5. Bogdănaş, D., Roşu, G.: K-Java: a complete semantics of Java. In: Proceedings of the 42nd Symposium on Principles of Programming Languages (POPL 2015), pp. 445–456. ACM, January 2015
6. Comon, H.: Equational formulas in order-sorted algebras. In: Paterson, M.S. (ed.) ICALP 1990. LNCS, vol. 443, pp. 674–688. Springer, Heidelberg (1990). https://doi.org/10.1007/BFb0032066
7. Corbineau, P.: A declarative language for the Coq proof assistant. In: Miculan, M., Scagnetto, I., Honsell, F. (eds.) TYPES 2007. LNCS, vol. 4941, pp. 69–84. Springer, Heidelberg (2008). https://doi.org/10.1007/978-3-540-68103-8_5
8. Şerbănuţă, T.F., Roşu, G.: K-Maude: a rewriting based tool for semantics of programming languages. In: Ölveczky, P.C. (ed.) WRLA 2010. LNCS, vol. 6381, pp. 104–122. Springer, Heidelberg (2010). https://doi.org/10.1007/978-3-642-16310-4_8
9. Ştefănescu, A., Ciobâcă, Ş, Mereuta, R., Moore, B.M., Şerbănută, T.F., Roşu, G.: All-path reachability logic. In: Dowek, G. (ed.) RTA 2014. LNCS, vol. 8560, pp. 425–440. Springer, Cham (2014). https://doi.org/10.1007/978-3-319-08918-8_29
10. Ştefănescu, A., Park, D., Yuwen, S., Li, Y., Roşu, G.: Semantics-based program verifiers for all languages. In: Proceedings of the 31th Conference on Object-Oriented Programming, Systems, Languages, and Applications (OOPSLA 2016), pp. 74–91. ACM, November 2016
11. Eker, S., Knapp, M., Laderoute, K., Lincoln, P., Talcott, C.: Pathway logic: executable models of biological networks. In: Fourth International Workshop on Rewriting Logic and Its Applications (WRLA 2002). Electronic Notes in Theoretical Computer Science, Pisa, Italy, 19–21 September 2002, vol. 71. Elsevier (2002). http://www.elsevier.nl/locate/entcs/volume71.html
12. Eker, S., Meseguer, J., Sridharanarayanan, A.: The Maude LTL model checker and its implementation. In: Ball, T., Rajamani, S.K. (eds.) SPIN 2003. LNCS, vol. 2648, pp. 230–234. Springer, Heidelberg (2003). https://doi.org/10.1007/3-540-44829-2_16 http://dl.acm.org/citation.cfm?id=1767111.1767127
13. Ellison, C., Rosu, G.: An executable formal semantics of C with applications. In: Proceedings of the 39th ACM SIGPLAN-SIGACT Symposium on Principles of Programming Languages (POPL 2012), pp. 533–544. ACM, January 2012
14. Filaretti, D., Maffeis, S.: An executable formal semantics of PHP. In: Jones, R. (ed.) ECOOP 2014. LNCS, vol. 8586, pp. 567–592. Springer, Heidelberg (2014). https://doi.org/10.1007/978-3-662-44202-9_23
15. Goguen, J.A., Jouannaud, J.-P., Meseguer, J.: Operational semantics for order-sorted algebra. In: Brauer, W. (ed.) ICALP 1985. LNCS, vol. 194, pp. 221–231. Springer, Heidelberg (1985). https://doi.org/10.1007/BFb0015747 http://dl.acm.org/citation.cfm?id=646239.683375

16. Goguen, J.A., Meseguer, J.: Order-sorted algebra I: equational deduction for multiple inheritance, overloading, exceptions and partial operations. Theor. Comput. Sci. **105**(2), 217–273 (1992)
17. Hathhorn, C., Ellison, C., Roşu, G.: Defining the undefinedness of C. In: Proceedings of the 36th ACM SIGPLAN Conference on Programming Language Design and Implementation (PLDI 2015), pp. 336–345. ACM, June 2015
18. Hills, M., Roşu, G.: Towards a module system for K. In: Corradini, A., Montanari, U. (eds.) WADT 2008. LNCS, vol. 5486, pp. 187–205. Springer, Heidelberg (2009). https://doi.org/10.1007/978-3-642-03429-9_13
19. Hoare, C.A.R.: An axiomatic basis for computer programming. Commun. ACM **12**(10), 576–580 (1969)
20. Hullot, J.M.: Associative commutative pattern matching. In: Proceedings of the 6th International Joint Conference on Artificial Intelligence, IJCAI 1979, vol. 1, pp. 406–412. Morgan Kaufmann Publishers Inc., San Francisco (1979)
21. Inwegen, M.V., Gunter, E.L.: HOL-ML. In: Proceedings of the 6th International Workshop on Higher Order Logic Theorem Proving and Its Applications, HUG 1993, Vancouver, BC, Canada, 11–13 August 1993, pp. 61–74 (1993)
22. Kirchner, C., Kirchner, H., Meseguer, J.: Operational semantics of OBJ-3. In: Lepistö, T., Salomaa, A. (eds.) ICALP 1988. LNCS, vol. 317, pp. 287–301. Springer, Heidelberg (1988). https://doi.org/10.1007/3-540-19488-6_123
23. Krebber, M.: Non-linear associative-commutative many-to-one pattern matching with sequence variables. ArXiv abs/1705.00907 (2017)
24. Lee, D.K., Crary, K., Harper, R.: Towards a mechanized metatheory of Standard ML. SIGPLAN Not. **42**(1), 173–184 (2007)
25. Li, L., Gunter, E.: A method to translate order-sorted algebras to many-sorted algebras. In: Proceedings of the Fourth International Workshop on Rewriting Techniques for Program Transformations and Evaluation, WPTE 2017. EPTCS (2017)
26. Li, L., Gunter, E.: K-LLVM: a relatively complete semantics of LLVM IR. In: Donaldson, A.F. (ed.) 34rd European Conference on Object-Oriented Programming, ECOOP 2020. LIPIcs, Berlin, Germany, 13–17 July 2020. Schloss Dagstuhl - Leibniz-Zentrum für Informatik (2020)
27. Li, L., Gunter, E.: Tech Report for a Complete Semantics of K and Its Translation to Isabelle (2021). https://github.com/liyili2/KtoIsabelle/blob/master/tech-report.pdf
28. Li, L., Gunter, E.L.: **IsaK-Static**: a complete static semantics of 𝕂. In: Bae, K., Ölveczky, P.C. (eds.) FACS 2018. LNCS, vol. 11222, pp. 196–215. Springer, Cham (2018). https://doi.org/10.1007/978-3-030-02146-7_10
29. Clavel, M., Eker, S., Lincoln, P., Meseguer, J.: Principles of maude. In: Meseguer, J. (ed.) Electronic Notes in Theoretical Computer Science, vol. 4. Elsevier Science Publishers (2000)
30. Maharaj, S., Gunter, E.: Studying the ML module system in HOL. In: Melham, T.F., Camilleri, J. (eds.) HUG 1994. LNCS, vol. 859, pp. 346–361. Springer, Heidelberg (1994). https://doi.org/10.1007/3-540-58450-1_53
31. Martí-Oliet, N., Meseguer, J.: Rewriting logic: roadmap and bibliography. Theor. Comput. Sci. **285**(2), 121–154 (2002). Rewriting Logic and Its Applications. http://www.sciencedirect.com/science/article/pii/S0304397501003577
32. Matache, C., Gomes, V.B.F., Mulligan, D.P.: The LambdaMu-calculus. Archive of Formal Proofs 2017 (2017). https://www.isa-afp.org/entries/LambdaMu.html
33. Meseguer, J.: Research directions in rewriting logic. In: Berger, U., Schwichtenberg, H. (eds.) Computational Logic. NATO ASI Series, vol. 165, pp. 347–398. Springer, Heidelberg (1999). https://doi.org/10.1007/978-3-642-58622-4_10

34. Meseguer, J.: Software specification and verification in rewriting logic. In: Nato Science Series Sub Series III Computer and Systems Sciences, vol. 191, pp. 133–194 (2003)
35. Meseguer, J., Goguen, J.A., Smolka, G.: Order-sorted unification. J. Symb. Comput. **8**(4), 383–413 (1989)
36. Meseguer, J., Skeirik, S.: Equational formulas and pattern operations in initial order-sorted algebras. Formal Aspects Comput. **29**(3), 423–452 (2017). https://doi.org/10.1007/s00165-017-0415-5
37. Milner, R., Tofte, M., Macqueen, D.: The Definition of Standard ML. MIT Press, Cambridge (1997)
38. Moore, B., Roşu, G.: Program verification by coinduction. Technical report, University of Illinois, February 2015. http://hdl.handle.net/2142/73177
39. Norrish, M.: C formalised in HOL. Technical report, Computer Laboratory, University of Cambridge (1998)
40. Park, D., Ştefănescu, A., Roşu, G.: KJS: a complete formal semantics of JavaScript. In: Proceedings of the 36th ACM SIGPLAN Conference on Programming Language Design and Implementation (PLDI 2015), pp. 346–356. ACM, June 2015
41. Paulson, L.C.: Isabelle: the next 700 theorem provers. In: Odifreddi, P. (ed.) Logic and Computer Science, pp. 361–386. Academic Press (1990)
42. Reynolds, J.C.: Separation logic: a logic for shared mutable data structures. In: Proceedings 17th Annual IEEE Symposium on Logic in Computer Science, pp. 55–74, July 2002
43. Roşu, G.: K: a rewriting-based framework for computations - preliminary version. Technical report, Department of Computer Science UIUCDCS-R-2007-2926 and College of Engineering UILU-ENG-2007-1827, University of Illinois at Urbana-Champaign (2007). Previous versions published as technical reports UIUCDCS-R-2006-2802 in December 2006, UIUCDCS-R-2005-2672 in 2005. K was first introduced in the context of Maude in Fall 2003 as part of a programming language design course (technical report UIUCDCS-R-2003-2897)
44. Roşu, G.: K Publications (2017). http://www.kframework.org/index.php/K_Publications
45. Roşu, G., Ştefănescu, A., Ciobâcă, C., Moore, B.M.: One-path reachability logic. In: Proceedings of the 28th Symposium on Logic in Computer Science (LICS 2013), pp. 358–367. IEEE, June 2013
46. Roşu, G., Şerbănuţă, T.F.: An overview of the K semantic framework. J. Log. Algebraic Program. **79**(6), 397–434 (2010)
47. Roşu, G., Ştefănescu, A.: Matching logic: a new program verification approach. In: Proceedings of the 2010 Workshop on Usable Verification (UV 2010). Microsoft Research (2010)
48. Wang, H.: Logic of many-sorted theories. J. Symb. Log. **17**(2), 105–116 (1952). https://doi.org/10.2307/2266241
49. Şerbănuţă, T.F., Arusoaie, A., Lazar, D., Ellison, C., Lucanu, D., Roşu, G.: The K primer (version 3.3). Electron. Notes Theor. Comput. Sci. **304**(Supplement C), 57–80 (2014). Proceedings of the Second International Workshop on the K Framework and Its Applications (K 2011). http://www.sciencedirect.com/science/article/pii/S1571066114000395

Quantum Computing

A New Connective in Natural Deduction, and Its Application to Quantum Computing

Alejandro Díaz-Caro[1,2]([✉]) and Gilles Dowek[3]

[1] DCyT, Universidad Nacional de Quilmes, Bernal, Argentina
[2] ICC, CONICET–Universidad de Buenos Aires, Buenos Aires, Argentina
adiazcaro@icc.fcen.uba.ar
[3] Inria, ENS Paris-Saclay, Gif-sur-Yvette, France
gilles.dowek@ens-paris-saclay.fr

Abstract. We investigate an unsuspected connection between non-harmonious logical connectives, such as Prior's *tonk*, and quantum computing. We argue that non-harmonious connectives model the information erasure, the non-reversibility, and the non-determinism that occur, among other places, in quantum measurement. We introduce a propositional logic with a non-harmonious connective *sup* and show that its proof language forms the core of a quantum programming language.

1 Introduction

We investigate an unsuspected connection between non-harmonious logical connectives, such as Prior's *tonk*, and quantum computing. We argue that non-harmonious connectives model the information erasure, the non-reversibility, and the non-determinism that occur, among other places, in quantum measurement.

More concretely, we introduce a propositional logic with a non-harmonious connective $\odot$ (read: "sup", for "superposition") and show that its proof language forms the core of a quantum programming language.

1.1 Insufficient, Harmonious, and Excessive Connectives

In natural deduction, to prove a proposition C, the elimination rule of a connective $\triangle$ requires a proof of $A \triangle B$ and a proof of C using, as extra hypotheses, exactly the premises needed to prove the proposition $A \triangle B$, with the introduction rules of the connective $\triangle$. This principle of inversion, or of harmony, has been introduced by Gentzen [10] and developed, among others, by Prawitz [16] and Dummett [8] in natural deduction, by Miller and Pimentel [12] in sequent calculus, and by Read [18–20] for the rules of equality.

Founded by STIC-AmSud 21STIC10, ECOS-Sud A17C03, and the IRP SINFIN.

A. Cerone and P. C. Ölveczky (Eds.): ICTAC 2021, LNCS 12819, pp. 175–193, 2021.
https://doi.org/10.1007/978-3-030-85315-0_11

For example, to prove the proposition $A \wedge B$, the introduction rule, in the usual additive style, of the conjunction requires proofs of A and B

$$\frac{\Gamma \vdash A \quad \Gamma \vdash B}{\Gamma \vdash A \wedge B} \; \wedge\text{-i}$$

Hence, to prove a proposition C, the generalized elimination rule of the conjunction [14,15,21] requires a proof of $A \wedge B$ and one of C, using, as extra hypotheses, the propositions A and B

$$\frac{\Gamma \vdash A \wedge B \quad \Gamma, A, B \vdash C}{\Gamma \vdash C} \; \wedge\text{-e}$$

Here we say that the extra hypotheses A and B are *provided* by the elimination rule, as they appear in the left-hand side of the premise. In the same way, the propositions A and B are *required* by the introduction rule, as they appear in the right-hand side of the premises.

This principle of inversion can thus be formulated as the fact that the propositions required by the introduction rule are the same as those provided by the elimination rule. It enables the definition of a reduction process where the proof

$$\frac{\dfrac{\dfrac{\pi_1}{\Gamma \vdash A} \quad \dfrac{\pi_2}{\Gamma \vdash B}}{\Gamma \vdash A \wedge B} \wedge\text{-i} \quad \dfrac{\pi_3}{\Gamma, A, B \vdash C}}{\Gamma \vdash C} \; \wedge\text{-e}$$

reduces to $(\pi_1/A, \pi_2/B)\pi_3$, that is the proof π_3 where the use of the axiom rule with the propositions A and B has been replaced with the proofs π_1 and π_2.

In the same way, to prove the proposition $A \vee B$, the introduction rules of the disjunction require a proof of A or a proof of B

$$\frac{\Gamma \vdash A}{\Gamma \vdash A \vee B} \; \vee\text{-i1} \qquad\qquad \frac{\Gamma \vdash B}{\Gamma \vdash A \vee B} \; \vee\text{-i2}$$

hence, to prove a proposition C, the elimination rule of the disjunction requires a proof of $A \vee B$ and two proofs of C, one using, as extra hypothesis, the proposition A and the other the proposition B

$$\frac{\Gamma \vdash A \vee B \quad \Gamma, A \vdash C \quad \Gamma, B \vdash C}{\Gamma \vdash C} \; \vee\text{-e}$$

and a proof reduction process can be defined in a similar way.

The property that the elimination rule provides exactly the propositions required by the introduction rules can be split in two properties that it provides no more and no less (called "harmony" and "reversed harmony" in [11]).

We can also imagine connectives that do not verify this inversion principle, either because the elimination rule provides propositions not required by the introduction rule, or because the introduction rule requires propositions not provided by the elimination rule, or both. When the propositions provided by the elimination rule are not all required by the introduction rule, we call the connective *insufficient*. When the propositions provided by the elimination rule are required by the introduction rule, but some propositions required by the introduction rule are not provided by the elimination rule we call it *excessive*.

An example of an *insufficient* connective is Prior's *tonk* [17] whose introduction rule requires the proposition A, but whose elimination rule provides the proposition B, which is not required by the introduction rule

$$\frac{\Gamma \vdash A}{\Gamma \vdash A \text{ tonk } B} \text{ tonk-i} \qquad \frac{\Gamma \vdash A \text{ tonk } B \quad \Gamma, B \vdash C}{\Gamma \vdash C} \text{ tonk-e}$$

Because of this insufficiency, the following proof cannot be reduced

$$\frac{\dfrac{\dfrac{\pi_1}{\Gamma \vdash A}}{\Gamma \vdash A \text{ tonk } B} \text{ tonk-i} \quad \dfrac{\pi_2}{\Gamma, B \vdash C}}{\Gamma \vdash C} \text{ tonk-e}$$

An example of an *excessive* connective is the connective • whose introduction rule requires the propositions A and B, but whose elimination rule provides the proposition A, but not B, although, both are required by the introduction rule

$$\frac{\Gamma \vdash A \quad \Gamma \vdash B}{\Gamma \vdash A \bullet B} \text{ •-i} \qquad \frac{\Gamma \vdash A \bullet B \quad \Gamma, A \vdash C}{\Gamma \vdash C} \text{ •-e}$$

This connective has the same introduction rule as conjunction, but a different elimination rule. Using the more common elimination rules of conjunction, it could be defined as having only one among its two elimination rules. For such connectives, a proof reduction process can be defined, for example the proof

$$\frac{\dfrac{\dfrac{\pi_1}{\Gamma \vdash A} \quad \dfrac{\pi_2}{\Gamma \vdash B}}{\Gamma \vdash A \bullet B} \text{ •-i} \quad \dfrac{\pi_3}{\Gamma, A \vdash C}}{\Gamma \vdash C} \text{ •-e}$$

can be reduced to $(\pi_1/A)\pi_3$.

Another example is the connective $\odot$ that has the introduction rule of the conjunction and the elimination rule of the disjunction

$$\frac{\Gamma \vdash A \quad \Gamma \vdash B}{\Gamma \vdash A \odot B} \text{ $\odot$-i} \qquad \frac{\Gamma \vdash A \odot B \quad \Gamma, A \vdash C \quad \Gamma, B \vdash C}{\Gamma \vdash C} \text{ $\odot$-e}$$

In this case also, proofs can be reduced. Moreover, several proof reduction processes can be defined, exploiting, in different ways, the excess of the connective. For example, the proof

$$\cfrac{\cfrac{\pi_1}{\Gamma \vdash A} \quad \cfrac{\pi_2}{\Gamma \vdash B}}{\Gamma \vdash A \odot B} \odot\text{-i} \quad \cfrac{\pi_3}{\Gamma, A \vdash C} \quad \cfrac{\pi_4}{\Gamma, B \vdash C}}{\Gamma \vdash C} \odot\text{-e}$$

can be reduced to $(\pi_1/A)\pi_3$, it can be reduced to $(\pi_2/B)\pi_4$, it also can be reduced, non-deterministically, either to $(\pi_1/A)\pi_3$ or to $(\pi_2/B)\pi_4$. Finally, to keep both proofs, we can add a rule "parallel"

$$\cfrac{\Gamma \vdash A \quad \Gamma \vdash A}{\Gamma \vdash A} \text{ par}$$

and reduce it to

$$\cfrac{\cfrac{(\pi_1/A)\pi_3}{\Gamma \vdash C} \quad \cfrac{(\pi_2/B)\pi_4}{\Gamma \vdash C}}{\Gamma \vdash C} \text{ par}$$

A final example is the quantifier $\forall\!\!\!\exists$, which has the introduction rule of the universal quantifier and the elimination rule of the existential quantifier

$$\cfrac{\Gamma \vdash A}{\Gamma \vdash \forall\!\!\!\exists x\, A} \;\forall\!\!\!\exists\text{-i } x \text{ not free in } \Gamma \qquad \cfrac{\Gamma \vdash \forall\!\!\!\exists x\, A \quad \Gamma, A \vdash C}{\Gamma \vdash C} \;\forall\!\!\!\exists\text{-e } x \text{ not free in } \Gamma, C$$

The quantifier ∇ [13], defined in sequent calculus rather than natural deduction, may also be considered as an excessive quantifier, as it has the right rule of the universal quantifier and the left rule of the existential one. But it involves a clever management of variable scoping, which we do not address here.

1.2 Information Loss

With harmonious connectives, when a proof is built with an introduction rule, the information contained in the proofs of the premises of this rule is preserved. For example, the information contained in the proof π_1 is *present* in the proof π

$$\cfrac{\cfrac{\pi_1}{\Gamma \vdash A} \quad \cfrac{\pi_2}{\Gamma \vdash B}}{\Gamma \vdash A \wedge B} \wedge\text{-i}$$

in the sense that π_1 is a subproof of π. But it is moreover accessible. We say that a subproof π' at tree-position p in π is *accessible*, if there exists a context

κ, such that for all proofs π'', putting the proof $\pi[\pi'']_p$ where π'' is grafted at tree-position p in π, in the context κ yields a proof $\kappa[\pi[\pi'']_p]$ that reduces to π''. Indeed, putting the proof

$$\dfrac{\dfrac{\pi_1}{\Gamma \vdash A} \quad \dfrac{\pi_2}{\Gamma \vdash B}}{\Gamma \vdash A \wedge B} \wedge\text{-i} \qquad \text{in the context} \qquad \dfrac{\dfrac{[\,]}{\Gamma \vdash A \wedge B} \quad \dfrac{}{\Gamma, A, B \vdash A} \text{ ax}}{\Gamma \vdash A} \wedge\text{-e}$$

yields the proof

$$\dfrac{\dfrac{\dfrac{\pi_1}{\Gamma \vdash A} \quad \dfrac{\pi_2}{\Gamma \vdash B}}{\Gamma \vdash A \wedge B} \wedge\text{-i} \quad \dfrac{}{\Gamma, A, B \vdash A} \text{ ax}}{\Gamma \vdash A} \wedge\text{-e}$$

that reduces to π_1. And the same holds for the proof π_2.

The situation is different with an excessive connective: the excess of information, required by the introduction rule, and not returned by the elimination rule in the form of an extra hypothesis in the required proof of C is lost. For example, the information contained in the proof π_2 is present in the proof π

$$\dfrac{\dfrac{\pi_1}{\Gamma \vdash A} \quad \dfrac{\pi_2}{\Gamma \vdash B}}{\Gamma \vdash A \bullet B} \bullet\text{-i}$$

but it is inaccessible as there is no context such that, for all π_2, putting the proof

$$\dfrac{\dfrac{\pi_1}{\Gamma \vdash A} \quad \dfrac{\pi_2}{\Gamma \vdash B}}{\Gamma \vdash A \bullet B} \bullet\text{-i}$$

in that context yields a proof that reduces to π_2.

The information contained in the proofs π_1 and π_2 is present in the proof

$$\dfrac{\dfrac{\pi_1}{\Gamma \vdash A} \quad \dfrac{\pi_2}{\Gamma \vdash B}}{\Gamma \vdash A \odot B} \odot\text{-i}$$

but its accessibility depends on the way we decide to reduce the proof

$$\dfrac{\dfrac{\dfrac{\pi_1}{\Gamma \vdash A} \quad \dfrac{\pi_2}{\Gamma \vdash B}}{\Gamma \vdash A \odot B} \odot\text{-i} \quad \dfrac{\pi_3}{\Gamma, A \vdash C} \quad \dfrac{\pi_4}{\Gamma, B \vdash C}}{\Gamma \vdash C} \odot\text{-e}$$

If we reduce it systematically to $(\pi_1/A)\pi_3$, then the information contained in π_1 is accessible, but that contained in π_2 is not. If we reduce it systematically to $(\pi_2/B)\pi_4$, then the information contained in π_2 is accessible, but not that contained in π_1. If we reduce it not deterministically to $(\pi_1/A)\pi_3$ or to $(\pi_2/B)\pi_4$, then the information contained in both π_1 and π_2 is accessible, but non-deterministically. If we reduce it to

$$\frac{(\pi_1/A)\pi_3 \qquad (\pi_2/B)\pi_4}{\dfrac{\Gamma \vdash C \qquad \Gamma \vdash C}{\Gamma \vdash C}} \ \text{par}$$

then the information contained in both π_1 and π_2 is inaccessible.

Indeed, the information contained in the proof π_1 is present in the proof

$$\frac{\dfrac{\pi_1}{\Gamma \vdash A} \quad \dfrac{\pi_2}{\Gamma \vdash A}}{\Gamma \vdash A} \ \text{par}$$

but it is inaccessible as there is no context such that for all π_1 putting the proof

$$\frac{\dfrac{\pi_1}{\Gamma \vdash A} \quad \dfrac{\pi_2}{\Gamma \vdash A}}{\Gamma \vdash A} \ \text{par}$$

in that context yields a proof that reduces to π_1. The same holds for π_2.

Note that, when the proof

$$\frac{\dfrac{\dfrac{\pi_1}{\Gamma \vdash A} \quad \dfrac{\pi_2}{\Gamma \vdash B}}{\Gamma \vdash A \odot B} \ \text{$\odot$-i} \qquad \dfrac{\pi_3}{\Gamma, A \vdash C} \qquad \dfrac{\pi_4}{\Gamma, B \vdash C}}{\Gamma \vdash C} \ \text{$\odot$-e}$$

is reduced, non-deterministically, to $(\pi_1/A)\pi_3$ or to $(\pi_1/A)\pi_3$, the information contained in π_1 or that contained in π_2 is erased. It is not even present in the reduct. When it is reduced to

$$\frac{(\pi_1/A)\pi_3 \qquad (\pi_2/B)\pi_4}{\dfrac{\Gamma \vdash C \qquad \Gamma \vdash C}{\Gamma \vdash C}} \ \text{par}$$

then the information is inaccessible, but it remains present in the proof.

So, while harmonious connectives model information preservation, reversibility, and determinism, these excessive connectives model information erasure, non-reversibility, and non-determinism. Such information erasure, non-reversibility, and non-determinism, occur, for example, in quantum physics, where the measurement of the superposition of two states does not yield both states back.

The introduction rules alone do not define the meaning of such non-harmonious connectives, and neither do the elimination rules alone. The discrepancy between the meaning conferred by the introduction rules and the elimination rules, and the information loss it implies, are part of the meaning of such connectives.

1.3 Quantum Physics and Quantum Languages

Several programming languages have been proposed to express quantum algorithms, for example [1–3,6,9,22,23]. The design of such quantum programming languages raises two main questions. The first is to take into account the linearity of unitary operators and for instance avoid cloning, and the second is to express the information erasure, non-reversibility, and non-determinism of measurement. The $\odot$ connective gives a new solution to this second problem. Qubits can be seen as proofs of the proposition $\top \odot \top$, in contrast with bits which are proofs of $\top \vee \top$, and measurement can be easily expressed with the elimination rule of $\odot$ (Sect. 4.4).

In previous work, we have attempted to formalize superposition in the λ-calculus. The calculus Lambda-$\mathcal{S}$ [9] contains a primitive constructor $+$ and a primitive measurement symbol π, together with a rule reducing $\pi(t + u)$ non-deterministically to t or to u. The superposition $t + u$ can be considered as the pair (t, u). Hence, it should have the type $A \wedge A$. In other words, it is a proof-term of the proposition $A \wedge A$. In System I [4], various type-isomorphisms have been introduced, in particular the commutativity isomorphism $A \wedge B \equiv B \wedge A$, hence $t + u \equiv u + t$. In such a system, where $A \wedge B$ and $B \wedge A$ are identical, it is not possible to define the two elimination rules as the two usual projections rules π_1 and π_2 of the λ-calculus. They were replaced with a single projection parametrized with a proposition A: π_A, such that if $t : A$ and $u : B$ then $\pi_A(t+u)$ reduces to t and $\pi_B(t + u)$ to u. When $A = B$, hence t and u both have type A, the proof-term $\pi_A(t + u)$ reduces, non-deterministically, to t or to u, like a measurement operator.

These works on Lambda-$\mathcal{S}$ and System I brought to light that the pair superposition/measurement, in a quantum programming language, behaves like a pair introduction/elimination, for some connective, in a proof language, as the succession of a superposition and a measurement yields a term that can be reduced. In System I, this connective was assumed to be a commutative conjunction, with a modified elimination rule, leading to a non-deterministic reduction.

But, as the measurement of the superposition of two states does not yield both states back, this connective should probably be excessive. Moreover, as, to prepare the superposition $a|0\rangle + b|1\rangle$, we need both $|0\rangle$ and $|1\rangle$ and the measurement, in the basis $|0\rangle, |1\rangle$, yields either $|0\rangle$ or $|1\rangle$, this connective should have the introduction rule of the conjunction, and the elimination rule of the disjunction. Hence, it should be the connective $\odot$.

$$\frac{A \in \Gamma}{\Gamma \vdash A} \; ax \qquad \frac{\Gamma \vdash A \quad \Gamma \vdash A}{\Gamma \vdash A} \; par \qquad \frac{}{\Gamma \vdash \top} \; \top\text{-i} \qquad \frac{\Gamma \vdash \bot}{\Gamma \vdash C} \; \bot\text{-e}$$

$$\frac{\Gamma, A \vdash B}{\Gamma \vdash A \Rightarrow B} \; \Rightarrow\text{-i} \qquad \frac{\Gamma \vdash A \Rightarrow B \quad \Gamma \vdash A}{\Gamma \vdash B} \; \Rightarrow\text{-e}$$

$$\frac{\Gamma \vdash A \quad \Gamma \vdash B}{\Gamma \vdash A \wedge B} \; \wedge\text{-i} \qquad \frac{\Gamma \vdash A \wedge B \quad \Gamma, A, B \vdash C}{\Gamma \vdash C} \; \wedge\text{-e}$$

$$\frac{\Gamma \vdash A}{\Gamma \vdash A \vee B} \; \vee\text{-i1} \qquad \frac{\Gamma \vdash B}{\Gamma \vdash A \vee B} \; \vee\text{-i2} \qquad \frac{\Gamma \vdash A \vee B \quad \Gamma, A \vdash C \quad \Gamma, B \vdash C}{\Gamma \vdash C} \; \vee\text{-e}$$

$$\frac{\Gamma \vdash A \quad \Gamma \vdash B}{\Gamma \vdash A \odot B} \; \odot\text{-i} \qquad \frac{\Gamma \vdash A \odot B \quad \Gamma, A \vdash C \quad \Gamma, B \vdash C}{\Gamma \vdash C} \; \odot\text{-e}$$

Fig. 1. The deduction rules of propositional logic with $\odot$

In this paper, we present a propositional logic with the connective $\odot$, a language of proof-terms, the $\odot$-calculus (read: "the sup-calculus"), for this logic, and we prove a proof normalization theorem (Sect. 2). We then extend this calculus, introducing scalars to quantify the propensity of a proof to reduce to another (Sect. 3) and show (Sect. 4) that its proof language forms the core of a quantum programming language. A vector $\binom{a}{b}$ will be expressed as the proof $a. * + b. *$ of $\top \odot \top$, where $*$ is the symbol corresponding to the introduction rule of $\top$, $+$ that of $\odot$, and a and b are scalars.

So, although propositional logic with $\odot$ is not a logic to reason about quantum programs, some of its propositions can be seen as types of quantum programs.

2   Propositional Logic with $\odot$

We consider a constructive propositional logic with the usual connectives $\top$, $\bot$, $\Rightarrow$, $\wedge$, and $\vee$, (as usual, negation is defined as $\neg A = (A \Rightarrow \bot)$), and the extra connective $\odot$. The syntax of this logic is

$$A = \top \mid \bot \mid A \Rightarrow A \mid A \wedge A \mid A \vee A \mid A \odot A$$

and its deduction rules are given in Fig. 1.

2.1   Proof Normalization

Reducible expressions (redexes) in this logic are the usual ones for the connectives $\Rightarrow$, $\wedge$, and $\vee$

$$\frac{\dfrac{\pi_1}{\dfrac{\Gamma, A \vdash B}{\Gamma \vdash A \Rightarrow B} \; \Rightarrow\text{-i} \quad \dfrac{\pi_2}{\Gamma \vdash A}}{\Gamma \vdash B} \; \Rightarrow\text{-e} \qquad \text{that reduces to} \qquad (\pi_2/A)\pi_1$$

$$\dfrac{\dfrac{\pi_1}{\Gamma \vdash A} \quad \dfrac{\pi_2}{\Gamma \vdash B}}{\dfrac{\Gamma \vdash A \wedge B}{\quad} \wedge\text{-i}} \quad \dfrac{\pi_3}{\Gamma, A, B \vdash C}}{\Gamma \vdash C} \wedge\text{-e} \qquad \text{that reduces to} \quad (\pi_1/A, \pi_2/B)\pi_3$$

$$\dfrac{\dfrac{\dfrac{\pi_1}{\Gamma \vdash A}}{\Gamma \vdash A \vee B} \vee\text{-i1} \quad \dfrac{\pi_2}{\Gamma, A \vdash C} \quad \dfrac{\pi_3}{\Gamma, B \vdash C}}{\Gamma \vdash C} \vee\text{-e} \qquad \text{that reduces to} \quad (\pi_1/A)\pi_2$$

and

$$\dfrac{\dfrac{\dfrac{\pi_1}{\Gamma \vdash B}}{\Gamma \vdash A \vee B} \vee\text{-i2} \quad \dfrac{\pi_2}{\Gamma, A \vdash C} \quad \dfrac{\pi_3}{\Gamma, B \vdash C}}{\Gamma \vdash C} \vee\text{-e} \qquad \text{that reduces to} \quad (\pi_1/B)\pi_3$$

and the redex for the connective $\odot$

$$\dfrac{\dfrac{\dfrac{\pi_1}{\Gamma \vdash A} \quad \dfrac{\pi_2}{\Gamma \vdash B}}{\Gamma \vdash A \odot B} \odot\text{-i} \quad \dfrac{\pi_3}{\Gamma, A \vdash C} \quad \dfrac{\pi_4}{\Gamma, B \vdash C}}{\Gamma \vdash C} \odot\text{-e}$$

that reduces, in some cases, non-deterministically, to $(\pi_1/A)\pi_3$ or to $(\pi_2/B)\pi_4$, erasing some information, and in others, preserving information, to

$$\dfrac{\dfrac{(\pi_1/A)\pi_3}{\Gamma \vdash C} \quad \dfrac{(\pi_2/B)\pi_4}{\Gamma \vdash C}}{\Gamma \vdash C} \text{par}$$

Adding rules, such as the parallel rule, permits to build proofs that cannot be reduced, because the introduction rule of some connectives and its elimination rule are separated by the parallel rule, for example

$$\dfrac{\dfrac{\dfrac{\pi_1}{\Gamma \vdash A} \quad \dfrac{\pi_2}{\Gamma \vdash B}}{\Gamma \vdash A \wedge B} \wedge\text{-i} \quad \dfrac{\dfrac{\pi_3}{\Gamma \vdash A} \quad \dfrac{\pi_4}{\Gamma \vdash B}}{\Gamma \vdash A \wedge B} \wedge\text{-i}}{\dfrac{\Gamma \vdash A \wedge B}{\quad} \text{par} \quad \dfrac{\pi_5}{\Gamma, A, B \vdash C}}{\Gamma \vdash C} \wedge\text{-e}$$

Reducing such a proof requires rules to commute the parallel rule either with the elimination rule below or with the introduction rules above.

As the commutation with the introduction rules above is not always possible, for example in the proof

$$
\cfrac{\cfrac{\pi_1}{\Gamma \vdash A}}{\Gamma \vdash A \vee B} \text{ V-i1} \quad \cfrac{\cfrac{\pi_2}{\Gamma \vdash B}}{\Gamma \vdash A \vee B} \text{ V-i2} \over \Gamma \vdash A \vee B} \text{ par}
$$

the commutation with the elimination rule below is often preferred. In this paper, we favor the commutation of the parallel rule with the introduction rules, rather than with the elimination rules, whenever it is possible, that is for all connectives except disjunction. For example the proof

$$
\cfrac{\cfrac{\pi_1}{\Gamma \vdash A} \quad \cfrac{\pi_2}{\Gamma \vdash B}}{\Gamma \vdash A \wedge B} \text{ ∧-i} \quad \cfrac{\cfrac{\pi_3}{\Gamma \vdash A} \quad \cfrac{\pi_4}{\Gamma \vdash B}}{\Gamma \vdash A \wedge B} \text{ ∧-i} \over \Gamma \vdash A \wedge B} \text{ par}
$$

reduces to

$$
\cfrac{\cfrac{\cfrac{\pi_1}{\Gamma \vdash A} \quad \cfrac{\pi_3}{\Gamma \vdash A}}{\Gamma \vdash A} \text{ par} \quad \cfrac{\cfrac{\pi_2}{\Gamma \vdash B} \quad \cfrac{\pi_4}{\Gamma \vdash B}}{\Gamma \vdash B} \text{ par}}{\Gamma \vdash A \wedge B} \text{ ∧-i}
$$

Such a commutation yields a stronger introduction property for the considered connective (Theorem 2.2).

2.2 Proof-Terms

We introduce a term language, the ⊙-calculus, for the proofs of this logic. Its syntax is

$$
\begin{aligned}
t = \ & x \mid t \parallel u \mid * \mid \delta_\perp(t) \\
& \mid \lambda x\ t \mid t\ u \mid (t, u) \mid \delta_\wedge(t, [x, y]u) \\
& \mid inl(t) \mid inr(t) \mid \delta_\vee(t, [x]u, [y]v) \\
& \mid t + u \mid \delta_\odot(t, [x]u, [y]v) \mid \delta_\odot^{\parallel}(t, [x]u, [y]v)
\end{aligned}
$$

The variables x express the proofs built with the axiom rule, the terms $t \parallel u$ those built with the parallel rule, the term $*$ that built with the ⊤-i rule, the terms $\delta_\perp(t)$ those built with the ⊥-e rule, the terms $\lambda x\ t$ those built with the ⇒-i rule, the terms $t\ u$ those built with the ⇒-e rule, the terms (t, u) those built with the ∧-i rule, the terms $\delta_\wedge(t, [x, y]u)$ those built with the ∧-e rule, the terms $inl(t)$ those built with the V-i1 rule, the terms $inr(t)$ those built with the V-i2 rule, the terms $\delta_\vee(t, [x]u, [y]v)$ those built with the V-e rule, the terms $t + u$ those

$$\dfrac{x : A \in \Gamma}{\Gamma \vdash x : A} \text{ ax} \qquad \dfrac{\Gamma \vdash t : A \quad \Gamma \vdash u : A}{\Gamma \vdash t \parallel u : A} \text{ par} \qquad \dfrac{}{\Gamma \vdash * : \top} \text{ $\top$-i} \qquad \dfrac{\Gamma \vdash t : \bot}{\Gamma \vdash \delta_\bot(t) : C} \text{ $\bot$-e}$$

$$\dfrac{\Gamma, x : A \vdash t : B}{\Gamma \vdash \lambda x\, t : A \Rightarrow B} \text{ $\Rightarrow$-i} \qquad \dfrac{\Gamma \vdash t : A \Rightarrow B \quad \Gamma \vdash u : A}{\Gamma \vdash t\, u : B} \text{ $\Rightarrow$-e}$$

$$\dfrac{\Gamma \vdash t : A \quad \Gamma \vdash u : B}{\Gamma \vdash (t, u) : A \wedge B} \text{ $\wedge$-i} \qquad \dfrac{\Gamma \vdash t : A \wedge B \quad \Gamma, x : A, y : B \vdash u : C}{\Gamma \vdash \delta_\wedge(t, [x, y]u) : C} \text{ $\wedge$-e}$$

$$\dfrac{\Gamma \vdash t : A}{\Gamma \vdash inl(t) : A \vee B} \text{ $\vee$-i1} \qquad \dfrac{\Gamma \vdash t : B}{\Gamma \vdash inr(t) : A \vee B} \text{ $\vee$-i2}$$

$$\dfrac{\Gamma \vdash t : A \vee B \quad \Gamma, x : A \vdash u : C \quad \Gamma, y : B \vdash v : C}{\Gamma \vdash \delta_\vee(t, [x]u, [y]v) : C} \text{ $\vee$-e}$$

$$\dfrac{\Gamma \vdash t : A \quad \Gamma \vdash u : B}{\Gamma \vdash t + u : A \odot B} \text{ $\odot$-i}$$

$$\dfrac{\Gamma \vdash t : A \odot B \quad \Gamma, x : A \vdash u : C \quad \Gamma, y : B \vdash v : C}{\Gamma \vdash \delta_\odot(t, [x]u, [y]v) : C} \text{ $\odot$-e}$$

$$\dfrac{\Gamma \vdash t : A \odot B \quad \Gamma, x : A \vdash u : C \quad \Gamma, y : B \vdash v : C}{\Gamma \vdash \delta_\odot^\parallel(t, [x]u, [y]v) : C} \text{ $\odot$-e}$$

Fig. 2. The typing rules of the $\odot$-calculus

built with the $\odot$-i rule, and the terms $\delta_\odot(t, [x]u, [y]v)$ and $\delta_\odot^\parallel(t, [x]u, [y]v)$ those built with the $\odot$-e rule.

The proofs of the form $*$, $\lambda x\, t$, (t, u), $inl(t)$, $inr(t)$, and $t + u$ are called *introductions*, and those of the form $\delta_\bot(t)$, $t\, u$, $\delta_\wedge(t, [x, y]u)$, $\delta_\vee(t, [x]u, [y]v)$, $\delta_\odot(t, [x]u, [y]v)$, or $\delta_\odot^\parallel(t, [x]u, [y]v)$ *eliminations*. Variables and terms of the form $t \parallel u$ are neither introductions nor eliminations. Free and bound variables are defined as usual. A proof-term is closed if it contains no free variables.

The typing rules of the $\odot$-calculus are given in Fig. 2 and its reduction rules in Fig. 3. The reduction relation is defined as usual as the smallest contextual relation that contains $\sigma l \longrightarrow \sigma r$, for all rules $l \longrightarrow r$ and substitutions σ.

The following two theorems are proved in the long version arXiv'ed at [5].

Theorem 2.1 (Termination). *If $\Gamma \vdash t : A$, then t strongly terminates.*

Theorem 2.2 (Introduction). *Let t be a closed irreducible proof of A.*

- *If A has the form $\top$, then t has the form $*$.*
- *The proposition A is not $\bot$.*
- *If A has the form $B \Rightarrow C$, then t has the form $\lambda x : B\, u$.*
- *If A has the form $B \wedge C$, then t has the form (u, v).*
- *If A has the form $B \vee C$, then t has the form $inl(u)$, $inr(u)$, or $u \parallel v$.*
- *If A has the form $B \odot C$, then t has the form $u + v$.*

$$(\lambda x\ t)\ u \longrightarrow (u/x)t$$
$$\delta_\wedge((t,u),[x,y]v) \longrightarrow (t/x,u/y)v$$
$$\delta_\vee(inl(t),[x]v,[y]w) \longrightarrow (t/x)v$$
$$\delta_\vee(inr(u),[x]v,[y]w) \longrightarrow (u/y)w$$
$$\delta_\odot(t+u,[x]v,[y]w) \longrightarrow (t/x)v$$
$$\delta_\odot(t+u,[x]v,[y]w) \longrightarrow (u/y)w$$
$$\delta_\odot^\parallel(t+u,[x]v,[y]w) \longrightarrow (t/x)v \parallel (u/y)w$$

$$(\lambda x\ t) \parallel (\lambda x\ u) \longrightarrow \lambda x\ (t \parallel u)$$
$$(t,u) \parallel (v,w) \longrightarrow (t \parallel v, u \parallel w)$$
$$\delta_\vee(t \parallel u,[x]v,[y]w) \longrightarrow \delta_\vee(t,[x]v,[y]w) \parallel \delta_\vee(u,[x]v,[y]w)$$
$$(t+u) \parallel (v+w) \longrightarrow (t \parallel v) + (u \parallel w)$$

$$t \parallel t \longrightarrow t$$

Fig. 3. The reduction rules of the $\odot$-calculus

3   Quantifying Non-determinism

When we have a non-deterministic reduction system, we often want to quantify the propensity of a proof to reduce to another. To do so, we enrich the term language with scalars, so that sums become linear combinations. Our set S of scalars can be any set containing an element 1 and equipped with addition and multiplication, such as $\mathbb{R}$ or $\mathbb{C}$.

We define the $\odot^S$-calculus (read: "the sup-S-calculus"), by extending the grammar of proofs, adding a category for weighted proofs

$$\phi = a.t$$

where a is a scalar and modifying the category of proofs as follows

$$
\begin{aligned}
t =\ & x \mid \phi \parallel \chi \mid * \mid \delta_\perp(t) \\
& \mid \lambda x\ t \mid t\ u \mid (t,u) \mid \delta_\wedge(t,[x,y]u) \\
& \mid inl(t) \mid inl(r) \mid \delta_\vee(t,[x]u,[y]v) \\
& \mid \phi + \chi \mid \delta_\odot(t,[x]u,[y]v) \mid \delta_\odot^\parallel(t,[x]u,[y]v)
\end{aligned}
$$

where the arguments of $\parallel$ and $+$ are weighted proofs. Note that even in the case where there is a scalar 0, we need a proof t of A to build the weighted proof $0.t$.

For example, the only irreducible proof of the proposition $\top \odot \top$ was $* + *$. Now, the irreducible proofs of this proposition will be all the proofs of the form $a.* + b.*$, for instance $\frac{1}{\sqrt{2}}.* + \frac{1}{\sqrt{2}}.*$, $1.* + 1.*$, $1.* + 0.*$, etc. For this, the typing rules are those of Fig. 2 extended with an extra rule for weighted proofs

$$\frac{\Gamma \vdash t : A}{\Gamma \vdash a.t : A}$$

$$(\lambda x\ t)\ u \longrightarrow (u/x)t$$
$$\delta_\wedge((t, u), [x, y]v) \longrightarrow (t/x, u/y)v$$
$$\delta_\vee(inl(t), [x]v, [y]w) \longrightarrow (t/x)v$$
$$\delta_\vee(inr(u), [x]v, [y]w) \longrightarrow (u/y)w$$
$$\delta_\odot(a.t + b.u, [x]v, [y]w) \longrightarrow (t/x)v$$
$$\delta_\odot(a.t + b.u, [x]v, [y]w) \longrightarrow (u/y)w$$
$$\delta_\odot^{\parallel}(a.t + b.u, [x]v, [y]w) \longrightarrow a.(t/x)v \parallel b.(u/y)w$$

$$a.(\lambda x\ t) \parallel b.(\lambda x\ u) \longrightarrow \lambda x\ (a.t \parallel b.u)$$
$$a.(t, u) \parallel b.(v, w) \longrightarrow (a.t \parallel b.v, a.u \parallel b.w)$$
$$\delta_\vee(a.t \parallel b.u, [x]v, [y]w) \longrightarrow a.\delta_\vee(t, [x]v, [y]w) \parallel b.\delta_\vee(u, [x]v, [y]w)$$
$$a.(c.t + d.u) \parallel b.(e.v + f.w) \longrightarrow 1.(ac.t \parallel be.v) + 1.(ad.u \parallel bf.w)$$

$$a.(b.t \parallel c.t) \longrightarrow (a(b + c)).t$$

Fig. 4. The reduction rules of the $\odot^S$-calculus

The reduction rules are those of Fig. 3 enriched with the scalars. They are given in Fig. 4. All these rules reduce proofs, except the last one that reduces weighted proofs. Note that the proof $a.t \parallel b.t$ is irreducible: only the weighted proof $1.(a.t \parallel b.t)$ reduces to $(a + b).t$.

The termination proof of the $\odot$-calculus extends directly to the $\odot^S$-calculus: it suffices to define a translation $^\circ$ from the $\odot^S$-calculus to the $\odot$-calculus, erasing the scalars, and check that if $t \longrightarrow u$ in the $\odot^S$-calculus, then $t^\circ \longrightarrow u^\circ$ in the $\odot$-calculus.

We can now use the scalars a and b to assign probabilities to the reductions

$$\delta_\odot(a.t + b.u, [x]v, [y]w) \longrightarrow (t/x)v \qquad\qquad \delta_\odot(a.t + b.u, [x]v, [y]w) \longrightarrow (u/y)w$$

For instance, if the scalars are complex numbers, we can assign the probabilities $|a|^2/(|a|^2 + |b|^2)$ and $|b|^2/(|a|^2 + |b|^2)$ to these two reductions. But other choices are possible, as we shall see in Sect. 4.

4   Application to Quantum Computing

We now show that the $\odot^{\mathbb{C}}$-calculus, with a reduction strategy allowing to reduce the proofs of the form $\delta_\odot(t, [x]u, [y]v)$ only when t is closed and irreducible, contains the core of a small quantum programming language. Requiring t to be closed and irreducible to reduce the proof $\delta_\odot(t, [x]u, [y]v)$ permits to assign probabilities to the reductions of this proof.

In the examples below, we focus on algorithms on one and two qubits. The generalization to algorithms on n qubits is straightforward. Note that the binary connective $\odot$ is always used with two identical propositions: $A \odot A$.

4.1   Bits

Definition 4.1 (Bit). *Let* $\mathcal{B} = \top \vee \top$. *The proofs* $\mathbf{0} = inl(*)$ *and* $\mathbf{1} = inr(*)$ *are closed irreducible proofs of* $\mathcal{B}$.

Remark 4.1. The proofs $inl(*)$ and $inr(*)$ are not the only closed irreducible proofs of $\mathcal{B}$, for example $1.inl(*) \parallel 1.inr(*)$ also is.

Definition 4.2 (Test). *We let* $If(t, u, v) = \delta_\vee(t, [x]u, [y]v)$ *where* x *and* y *are variables not occurring in* u *and* v. *We have* $If(\mathbf{0}, u, v) \longrightarrow u$ *and* $If(\mathbf{1}, u, v) \longrightarrow v$.

Boolean operators on $\mathcal{B}$ can be easily defined, for example, the exclusive or is the proof $\oplus = \lambda x \lambda y \ If(x, y, If(y, \mathbf{1}, \mathbf{0}))$ of $\mathcal{B} \Rightarrow \mathcal{B} \Rightarrow \mathcal{B}$.

Definition 4.3 (2-bit). *Let* $\mathcal{B}^2 = \mathcal{B} \wedge \mathcal{B}$. *The closed irreducible proofs of* $\mathcal{B}^2$, $(\mathbf{0}, \mathbf{0})$, $(\mathbf{0}, \mathbf{1})$, $(\mathbf{1}, \mathbf{0})$, *and* $(\mathbf{1}, \mathbf{1})$ *are written* $\mathbf{00}$, $\mathbf{01}$, $\mathbf{10}$, *and* $\mathbf{11}$.

4.2   Qubits

Definition 4.4 (Qubit). *Let* $\mathcal{Q} = \top \odot \top$. *A qubit* $a|0\rangle + b|1\rangle$ *is expressed as the proof* $a.* + b.*$ *of* $\mathcal{Q}$.

Remark 4.2. If the qubits $|\psi\rangle = a|0\rangle + b|1\rangle$ and $|\psi'\rangle = a'|0\rangle + b'|1\rangle$ are expressed as proofs of $\mathcal{Q}$, then the qubit $c|\psi\rangle + d|\psi'\rangle$, that is $(ca + da')|0\rangle + (cb + db')|1\rangle$, cannot be expressed in the $\odot^{\mathbb{C}}$-calculus with a linear combination $a.|\psi\rangle + b.|\psi'\rangle$, as the result would be a proof of $\mathcal{Q} \odot \mathcal{Q}$, and not of $\mathcal{Q}$. In contrast, the linear combination $c.|\psi\rangle \parallel d.|\psi'\rangle$ is a proof of $\mathcal{Q}$ and it reduces, in several steps, to $(ca + da'). * + (cb + db').*$.

Definition 4.5 (2-qubit). *Let* $\mathcal{Q}^{\otimes 2} = (\top \odot \top) \odot (\top \odot \top)$. *A 2-qubit* $a|00\rangle + b|01\rangle + c|10\rangle + d|11\rangle$ *is expressed as the proof* $1.(a. * + b.*) + 1.(c. * + d.*)$ *of* $\mathcal{Q}^{\otimes 2}$.

For instance the 2-qbit $|01\rangle$, that is $|0\rangle \otimes |1\rangle$, is expressed as the proof $1.(0. * + 1.*) + 1.(0. * + 0.*)$ and the entangled 2-qbit $\frac{1}{\sqrt{2}}|00\rangle + \frac{1}{\sqrt{2}}|11\rangle$ is expressed as the proof $1.(\frac{1}{\sqrt{2}}. * + 0.*) + 1.(0. * + \frac{1}{\sqrt{2}}.*)$.

4.3   Probabilities

If t is a closed irreducible proof of $\mathcal{Q}$ of the form $a. * + b.*$, where a and b are not both 0, then we assign the probability

$\frac{|a|^2}{|a|^2 + |b|^2}$ to the reduction $\delta_\odot(a. * + b.*, [x]v, [y]w) \longrightarrow (*/x)v$

and $\frac{|b|^2}{|a|^2 + |b|^2}$ to the reduction $\delta_\odot(a. * + b.*, [x]v, [y]w) \longrightarrow (*/y)w$.

If $a = b = 0$, we associate any probability, for example $\frac{1}{2}$, to both reductions.

If t is a closed irreducible proof of $\mathcal{Q}^{\otimes 2}$ of the form $1.(a. * + b.*) + 1.(c. * + d.*)$ where a, b, c, and d are not all 0, then we assign the probability

$$\pi(t) = \delta_\odot(t, [\_]\mathbf{0}, [\_]\mathbf{1})$$
$$\pi'(t) = \delta_\odot(t, [x]1.x + 0.*, [y]0. * +1.y)$$
$$\pi''(t) = \delta_\odot(t, [x](\mathbf{0}, 1.x + 0.*), [y](\mathbf{1}, 0. * +1.y))$$

$$\pi_2(t) = \delta_\odot(t, [\_]\mathbf{0}, [\_]\mathbf{1})$$
$$\pi_2'(t) = \delta_\odot(t, [x]1.x + 1.(0. * +0.*), [y]1.(0. * +0.*) + 1.y)$$
$$\pi_2''(t) = \delta_\odot(t, [x](\mathbf{0}, 1.x + 1.(0. * +0.*)), [y](\mathbf{1}, 1.(0. * +0.*) + 1.y))$$

Fig. 5. Measurement operators

$\frac{|a|^2 + |b|^2}{|a|^2 + |b|^2 + |c|^2 + |d|^2}$ to the reduction

$$\delta_\odot(1.(a. * +b.*) + 1.(c. * +d.*), [x]v, [y]w) \longrightarrow ((a. * +b.*)/x)v$$

and $\frac{|c|^2 + |d|^2}{|a|^2 + |b|^2 + |c|^2 + |d|^2}$ to the reduction

$$\delta_\odot(1.(a. * +b.*) + 1.(c. * +d.*), [x]v, [y]w) \longrightarrow ((c. * +d.*)/y)w$$

If a, b, c, and d are all 0, we associate any probability to these reductions.

4.4   Measure

The information erasing, non-reversible, and non-deterministic proof constructor $\delta_\odot$ permits to define several measurement operators in Fig. 5.

If t is an irreducible proof of $\mathcal{Q}$ of the form $a. * +b.*$, where a and b are not both 0, then the proof $\pi(a.*+b.*)$ of the proposition $\mathcal{B}$ reduces, with probabilities $\frac{|a|^2}{|a|^2 + |b|^2}$ and $\frac{|b|^2}{|a|^2 + |b|^2}$, to $\mathbf{0}$ and to $\mathbf{1}$. It is the result of the measurement. The proof $\pi'(a. * +b.*)$ of the proposition $\mathcal{Q}$ reduces, with the same probabilities as above, to $1. * +0.*$ and to $0. * +1.*$. It is the state after the measure. The proof $\pi''(a. * +b.*)$ of the proposition $\mathcal{B} \wedge \mathcal{Q}$ reduces, with the same probabilities as above, to $(\mathbf{0}, 1. * +0.*)$ and to $(\mathbf{1}, 0. * +1.*)$. It is the pair formed by the result of the measurement and the state after the measure.

If t is an irreducible proof of $\mathcal{Q}^{\otimes 2}$ of the form $1.(a. * +b.*) + 1.(c. * +d.*)$ where a, b, c, and d are not all 0, then the proof $\pi_2(t)$ of the proposition $\mathcal{B}$ reduces, with probabilities $\frac{|a|^2 + |b|^2}{|a|^2 + |b|^2 + |c|^2 + |d|^2}$ and $\frac{|c|^2 + |d|^2}{|a|^2 + |b|^2 + |c|^2 + |d|^2}$, to $\mathbf{0}$ and to $\mathbf{1}$. It is the result of the partial measurement of the first qubit. The proof $\pi_2'(t)$ of the proposition $\mathcal{Q}^{\otimes 2}$ reduces, with the same probabilities as above, to $1.(a. * +b.*) + 1.(0. * +0.*)$ and $1.(0. * +0.*) + 1.(c. * +d.*))$. It is the state after the partial measure of the first qubit. The proof $\pi_2''(t)$ of the proposition $\mathcal{B} \wedge \mathcal{Q}^{\otimes 2}$ reduces, with the same probabilities as above, to $(\mathbf{0}, 1.(a. * +b.*) + 1.(0. * +0.*))$ and to $(\mathbf{1}, 1.(0. * +0.*) + 1.(c. * +d.*)))$. It is the pair formed by the result of the measurement and the state after the partial measure of the first qubit.

Once we introduce the matrices, it will be possible to measure in a non-cannonical basis by changing basis, measuring, and changing basis again.

4.5 Matrices

The information erasing, non-reversible, and non-deterministic measurement operators are expressed with $\delta_\odot$. The information preserving, reversible, and deterministic unitary operators are expressed with $\delta_\odot^\|$.

Definition 4.6 (Matrix in $\mathcal{Q}$). *A matrix is a proof of $\mathcal{B} \Rightarrow \mathcal{Q}$, that is a function mapping bits to qubits. The matrix $M = \left(\begin{smallmatrix} m_{00} & m_{01} \\ m_{10} & m_{11} \end{smallmatrix}\right)$ mapping $\mathbf{0}$ to $M_0 = m_{00}.*+m_{10}.*$ and $\mathbf{1}$ to $M_1 = m_{01}.*+m_{11}.*$ is expressed as*

$$M = \lambda x \; If(x, M_0, M_1)$$

Note that $M\mathbf{0} \longrightarrow If(\mathbf{0}, M_0, M_1) \longrightarrow M_0$. Similarly, $M\mathbf{1} \longrightarrow^* M_1$.

In Lineal [2], a matrix $\lambda x \; t$, mapping canonical base vectors to arbitrary vectors, extends to an arbitrary vector $a.|0\rangle + b.|1\rangle$ as follows. When reducing the term $(\lambda x \; t) \; (a.|0\rangle + b.|1\rangle)$, the term $\lambda x \; t$ distributes over the linear combination $a.|0\rangle + b.|1\rangle$, yielding the term $a.(\lambda x \; t) \; |0\rangle + b.(\lambda x \; t) \; |1\rangle$ where, as the terms $|0\rangle$ and $|1\rangle$ are base vectors, the β-redexes $(\lambda x \; t) \; |0\rangle$ and $(\lambda x \; t) \; |1\rangle$ can be reduced. So the whole term reduces to $a.(|0\rangle/x)t + b.(|1\rangle/x)t$.

In the $\odot^C$-calculus, β-reduction is not restricted to base vectors, but the application of a matrix to a vector can be defined.

Definition 4.7 (Application of a matrix to a vector in $\mathcal{Q}$). *We let*

$$App = \lambda M \lambda t \; \delta_\odot^\|(t, [x]M \; \mathbf{0}, [y]M \; \mathbf{1})$$

If $M : \mathcal{B} \Rightarrow \mathcal{Q}$, then the proof $App \; M \; (a.*+b.*)$ reduces to $a.(M \; \mathbf{0}) \parallel b.(M \; \mathbf{1})$. Therefore if M is the expression of the matrix $\left(\begin{smallmatrix} m_{00} & m_{01} \\ m_{10} & m_{11} \end{smallmatrix}\right)$, as in Definition 4.6, we have $App \; M \; (a.*+b.*) \longrightarrow^* (am_{00} + bm_{01}).*+(am_{10} + bm_{11}).*$.

Definition 4.8 (Matrix in $\mathcal{Q}^{\otimes 2}$). *A matrix is a proof of $\mathcal{B}^2 \Rightarrow \mathcal{Q}^{\otimes 2}$, that is a function mapping 2-bits to 2-qubits. The matrix $M = (m_{ij})_{ij}$ is expressed as*

$$M = \lambda x \; \delta_\wedge\Big(x, [y, z]If(y, If(z, M_0, M_1), If(z, M_2, M_3))\Big)$$

where $M_i = 1.(m_{0i}.*+m_{1i}.*) + 1.(m_{2i}.*+m_{3i}.*)$ is the i-th column of M.
Note that $M\mathbf{00} \longrightarrow^* M_0$, $M\mathbf{01} \longrightarrow^* M_1$, $M\mathbf{10} \longrightarrow^* M_2$, and $M\mathbf{11} \longrightarrow^* M_3$.

Definition 4.9 *Taking $m_{ii} = 1$ and $m_{ij} = 0$ for $i \neq j$ yields the proof Qubits of $\mathcal{B}^2 \Rightarrow \mathcal{Q}^{\otimes 2}$ mapping each 2-bit to the corresponding 2-qubit. For example*

$$Qubits \; \mathbf{10} \rightarrow^* 1.(0.*+0.*) + 1.(1.*+0.*)$$

Definition 4.10 (Application of a matrix to a vector in $\mathcal{Q}^{\otimes 2}$). *We let*

$$App_2 = \lambda M \lambda t \; \delta_\odot^\|(t, [y]\delta_\odot^\|(y, [\_]M \; \mathbf{00}, [\_]M \; \mathbf{01}), [z]\delta_\odot^\|(z, [\_]M \; \mathbf{10}, [\_]M \; \mathbf{11}))$$

Hence, if $|\psi\rangle = 1.(a.*+b.*) + 1.(c.*+d.*)$ and $M : \mathcal{B}^2 \Rightarrow \mathcal{Q}^{\otimes 2}$, we have

$App_2 \; M \; |\psi\rangle$

$\longrightarrow^* 1.((am_{00} + bm_{01} + cm_{02} + dm_{03}).*+(am_{10} + bm_{11} + cm_{12} + dm_{13}).*)$

$\qquad + 1.((am_{20} + bm_{21} + cm_{22} + dm_{23}).*+(am_{30} + bm_{31} + cm_{32} + dm_{33}).*)$

4.6   An Example: Deutsch's Algorithm

Deutsch's algorithm allows to decide whether a 1-bit to 1-bit function f is constant or not, applying an oracle U_f, implementing f, only once. It is an algorithm operating on 2-qubits. It proceeds in four steps. (1) Prepare the initial state $|+-\rangle = \frac{1}{2}|00\rangle - \frac{1}{2}|01\rangle + \frac{1}{2}|10\rangle - \frac{1}{2}|11\rangle$. (2) Apply to it the unitary operator U_f, defined by $U_f|x,y\rangle = |x, y \oplus f(x)\rangle$ for $x, y \in \{0,1\}$, where $\oplus$ is the exclusive or. (3) Apply to it the unitary operator $H \otimes I = \frac{1}{\sqrt{2}}\begin{pmatrix} 1 & 0 & 1 & 0 \\ 0 & 1 & 0 & 1 \\ 1 & 0 & -1 & 0 \\ 0 & 1 & 0 & -1 \end{pmatrix}$. (4) Measure the first qubit. The output is $|0\rangle$, if f is constant and $|1\rangle$ if it is not.

In the $\odot^{\mathbb{C}}$-calculus, the initial state is $|+-\rangle = 1.(\frac{1}{2}.*+\frac{-1}{2}.*)+1.(\frac{1}{2}.*+\frac{-1}{2}).*$ the operator mapping f to U_f is expressed as in Definition 4.8

$$U = \lambda f \; \lambda x \; \delta_\wedge\Big(x, [y,z]If(y, If(z, M_0, M_1), If(z, M_2, M_3))\Big)$$

with $M_0 = Qubits\ (\mathbf{0}, \oplus \mathbf{0}\ (f\ \mathbf{0}))$ $M_2 = Qubits\ (\mathbf{1}, \oplus \mathbf{0}\ (f\ \mathbf{1}))$
    $M_1 = Qubits\ (\mathbf{0}, \oplus \mathbf{1}\ (f\ \mathbf{0}))$ $M_3 = Qubits\ (\mathbf{1}, \oplus \mathbf{1}\ (f\ \mathbf{1}))$

where $Qubits$ is defined in Definition 4.9 and the exclusive or $\oplus$ in Sect. 4.1. The operator $H \otimes I$ is expressed as in Definition 4.8 with $m_{00} = m_{20} = m_{11} = m_{31} = m_{02} = m_{13} = \frac{1}{\sqrt{2}}$, $m_{22} = m_{33} = -\frac{1}{\sqrt{2}}$, and all the other m_{ij} are 0.

Finally, Deutsch's algorithm is the proof of $(\mathcal{B} \Rightarrow \mathcal{B}) \Rightarrow \mathcal{B}$

$$Deutsch = \lambda f \; \pi_2(App_2\ (H \otimes I)\ (App_2\ (U\ f)\ |+-\rangle))$$

Given a constant function proof of $\mathcal{B} \Rightarrow \mathcal{B}$, we have $Deutsch\ f \to^* \mathbf{0}$, while if f if not constant, $Deutsch\ f \to^* \mathbf{1}$.

5   Conclusion

We have defined the notions of insufficient and excessive connectives in natural deduction, extended propositional logic with an excessive connective $\odot$, and investigated the properties of the proof language of the obtained logic. We leave open the question of the interpretation of this logic in a model, in particular a categorical one, besides the obvious Lindenbaum algebra.

These notions of insufficient and excessive connectives are not specific to natural deduction and similar notions could be defined, for instance, in sequent calculus. In sequent calculus however, harmony can be defined in a stronger sense, that includes, not only the possibility to normalize proofs, but also to reduce the use of the axiom rule on non-atomic propositions to smaller ones [12]: an analog of the η-expansion, but generalized to arbitrary connectives.

The $\odot^{\mathbb{C}}$-calculus, the proof language of this logic, can express all quantum circuits, as it can express matrices and measurement operators. However, it is not restricted to only quantum algorithms, since the $\odot$ connective addresses the question of the information erasure, non-reversibility, and non-determinism of measurement, but not that of linearity. We leave for future work the restriction of the calculus to linear operators, forbidding, for example, the non-linear proof of the proposition $Q \Rightarrow Q^{\otimes 2}$, that expresses cloning: $\lambda x \, \delta_\odot^\|(x, [\_]\delta_\odot^\|(x, [\_]|00\rangle, [\_]|01\rangle), [\_]\delta_\odot^\|(x, [\_]|10\rangle, [\_]|11\rangle)))$, where $|00\rangle$ is a notation for *Qubits* **00**, etc.

It is also possible to restrict to the fragment of the language where proofs of $Q \Rightarrow Q$ have the form $\lambda x \, (App \, M \, x)$, for some proof M of $B \Rightarrow Q$. Then, we can also enforce unitarity, following the methods of [1,6,7].

Acknowledgements. The authors want to thank Jean-Baptiste Joinet, Dale Miller, Alberto Naibo, and Alex Tsokurov for useful discussions.

References

1. Altenkirch, T., Grattage, J.: A functional quantum programming language. In: Proceedings of LICS 2005, pp. 249–258. IEEE (2005)
2. Arrighi, P., Dowek, G.: Lineal: a linear-algebraic lambda-calculus. Log. Methods Comput. Sci. **13**(1) (2017)
3. Coecke, B., Kissinger, A.: Picturing Quantum Processes: A First Course in Quantum Theory and Diagrammatic Reasoning. Cambridge University Press, Cambridge (2017)
4. Díaz-Caro, A., Dowek, G.: Proof normalisation in a logic identifying isomorphic propositions. In: Geuvers, H. (ed.) 4th International Conference on Formal Structures for Computation and Deduction (FSCD 2019). Leibniz International Proceedings in Informatics (LIPIcs), vol. 131, pp. 14:1–14:23. Schloss Dagstuhl-Leibniz-Zentrum fuer Informatik (2019)
5. Díaz-Caro, A., Dowek, G.: A new connective in natural deduction, and its application to quantum computing. arXiv:2012.08994 (2020)
6. Díaz-Caro, A., Guillermo, M., Miquel, A., Valiron, B.: Realizability in the unitary sphere. In: Proceedings of the 34th Annual ACM/IEEE Symposium on Logic in Computer Science (LICS 2019), pp. 1–13 (2019)
7. Díaz-Caro, A., Malherbe, O.: Quantum control in the unitary sphere: lambda-S_1 and its categorical model. arXiv:2012.05887 (2020)
8. Dummett, M.: The Logical Basis of Metaphysics. Duckworth (1991)
9. Díaz-Caro, A., Dowek, G., Rinaldi, J.P.: Two linearities for quantum computing in the lambda calculus. Biosystems **186**, 104012 (2019)
10. Gentzen, G.: Untersuchungen über das logische Schliessen. In: Szabo, M. (ed.) The Collected Papers of Gerhard Gentzen, North-Holland, pp. 68–131 (1969)
11. Jacinto, B., Read, S.: General-elimination stability. Stud. Log. **105**, 361–405 (2017)
12. Miller, D., Pimentel, E.: A formal framework for specifying sequent calculus proof systems. Theoret. Comput. Sci. **474**, 98–116 (2013)
13. Miller, D., Tiu, A.: A proof theory for generic judgments. ACM Trans. Comput. Log. **6**, 749–783 (2005)
14. Negri, S., von Plato, J.: Structural Proof Theory. Cambridge University Press, Cambridge (2008)
15. Parigot, M.: Free deduction: an analysis of "computations" in classical logic. In: Voronkov, A. (ed.) RCLP -1990. LNCS, vol. 592, pp. 361–380. Springer, Heidelberg (1992). https://doi.org/10.1007/3-540-55460-2_27
16. Prawitz, D.: Natural Deduction. A Proof-Theoretical Study. Almqvist & Wiksell (1965)

17. Prior, A.N.: The runabout inference-ticket. Analysis **21**(2), 38–39 (1960)
18. Read, S.: Identity and harmony. Analysis **64**, 113–119 (2004)
19. Read, S.: General-elimination harmony and the meaning of the logical constants. J. Philos. Log. **39**, 557–576 (2010)
20. Read, S.: Identity and harmony revisited (2014). https://www.st-andrews.ac.uk/~slr/identity_revisited.pdf
21. Schroeder-Heister, P.: A natural extension of natural deduction. J. Symb. Log. **49**(4), 1284–1300 (1984)
22. Selinger, P., Valiron, B.: A lambda calculus for quantum computation with classical control. Math. Struct. Comput. Sci. **16**(3), 527–552 (2006)
23. Zorzi, M.: On quantum lambda calculi: a foundational perspective. Math. Struct. Comput. Sci. **26**(7), 1107–1195 (2016)

Security and Privacy

An Incentive Mechanism for Trading Personal Data in Data Markets

Sayan Biswas[(✉)], Kangsoo Jung, and Catuscia Palamidessi

Inria and École Polytechnique, Palaiseau, France
{sayan.biswas,gangsoo.zeong}@inria.fr, catuscia@lix.polytechnique.fr

Abstract. With the proliferation of the digital data economy, digital data is considered as the crude oil in the twenty-first century, and its value is increasing. Keeping pace with this trend, the model of data market trading between data providers and data consumers, is starting to emerge as a process to obtain high-quality personal information in exchange for some compensation. However, the risk of privacy violations caused by personal data analysis hinders data providers' participation in the data market. Differential privacy, a de-facto standard for privacy protection, can solve this problem, but, on the other hand, it deteriorates the data utility. In this paper, we introduce a pricing mechanism that takes into account the trade-off between privacy and accuracy. We propose a method to induce the data provider to accurately report her privacy price and, we optimize it in order to maximize the data consumer's profit within budget constraints. We show formally that the proposed mechanism achieves these properties, and also, validate them experimentally.

Keywords: Data market · Differential privacy · Incentive mechanism · Game theory

1 Introduction

Nowadays, digital data is becoming an essential resource for the information society, and the value of personal data is increasing. In the past, data broker companies such as Acxiom collected personal data and sold them to companies that needed them. However, as the value of personal data is becoming clear to the data providers, and concern about their privacy is increasing among them, people are less and less willing to let their data to be collected for free. In this scenario, the model of *data market* is starting to emerge, as a process to obtain high-quality personal information in exchange of a compensation. Liveen [1] and Datacoup [2] are examples of prototypes of data market services, where the data providers can obtain additional revenue from selling their data, and the consumers can collect the desired personal data.

   The problem of privacy violation by personal data analysis is one of the major issues in such data markets. As the population becomes more and more aware of the negative consequences of privacy breaches, such as the Cambridge Analytica

© Springer Nature Switzerland AG 2021
A. Cerone and P. C. Ölveczky (Eds.): ICTAC 2021, LNCS 12819, pp. 197–213, 2021.
https://doi.org/10.1007/978-3-030-85315-0_12

scandal, people are reluctant to release their data, unless they are properly sanitised. In order to solve this problem, techniques like noise insertion [3], synthetic data [4], secure multi-party computation (SMC) [5], and homomorphic encryption [6] are being actively studied. Differential privacy [3], a de-facto standard for privacy protection, is one of the techniques to prevent privacy violations in the data market.

Differential privacy provides a privacy protection framework based on solid mathematical foundations, and enables quantified privacy protection according to the amount of noise insertion. However, like all privacy-protection methods, it deteriorates the data utility. If the data provider inserts too much noise because of privacy concern, the data consumer cannot proceed with the data analysis with the required performance. This trade-off between privacy and utility is a long-standing problem in differential privacy. The privacy protection and data utility depend on the amount of noise insertion while applying differential privacy, and the amount of noise insertion is determined by the noise parameter ϵ. Thus, determining the appropriate value of the parameter ϵ is a fundamental problem in differential privacy. It is difficult to establish the appropriate ϵ value because it depends on many factors that are difficult to quantify, like the attitude towards privacy of the data provider, which may be different from person to person.

We propose an incentive mechanism to encourage the data providers to join in the data market and motivate them to share more accurate data. The amount of noise insertion depends on the data providers' privacy preference and the incentives provided to them by data consumers, and the data consumers decide on incentives to pay to the data provider by considering the profit to be made from the collected data. By sharing some of the consumers' profit with the data provider as incentive, the data provider can get fair prices for providing her data. The proposed mechanism consists of the truthful price report mechanism and an optimization method within budget constraints. The truthful price report mechanism guarantees that the data provider takes the optimal profit when she reports her privacy price to the data consumer honestly. Based on a data provider's reported privacy price, a data consumer can maximize her profit within a potential budget constraint.

1.1   Contribution

The contributions of this paper are as follows:

(i) Truthful price report mechanism: We propose an incentive mechanism that guarantees that the data provider maximizes her benefit when she reports her privacy price honestly.

(ii) Optimized incentive mechanism within the budget constraints: We propose an optimization method to maximize the data consumer's profit and information gain in the setting where the data consumer has a fixed financial budget for data collection.

(iii) Optimized privacy budget splitting mechanism: We propose a method of splitting the privacy budget for the data providers, that allows them to maximize her utility-gain within a fixed privacy budget, in a multiple data consumer environment.

The properties of our methods are both proved formally and validated through experiments.

1.2   Structure of the Paper

The structure of this paper is as follows: we explain the related works and preliminaries in Sects. 2 and 3, respectively. We describe the proposed incentive mechanism in Sect. 4 and validate the proposed incentive mechanism through experiments in Sect. 5. Our conclusion and some potential directions of future work are discussed in Sect. 6.

2   Related Work

2.1   Methods for Choosing ϵ

In differential privacy concept, parameter ϵ is the knob to control the privacy-utility trade off. The smaller the ϵ, the higher is the privacy protection level and the more it deteriorates the data utility. Conversely, a larger ϵ decreases the privacy protection level and enhances the data utility. However, there is no gold standard to determine the appropriate value of ϵ. Apple has been promoting the use of differential privacy to protect user data since iOS 10 was released, but the analysis of [7] showed the ϵ value was set at approximately 10 without any particular reason. The work of [8] showed that the privacy protection level set by an arbitrary ϵ can be infringed by inference using previously disclosed information and proposed an ϵ setting method considering posterior probability. This matter is the main factor that undermines the claim that personal information is protected by differential privacy. Much research have been conducted to study and solve this problem [9–12]. Although a lot of research is being done in this area, the problem of determining a reasonable way of choosing an optimal value for ϵ still remains open, as there are many factors to consider in deciding the value of ϵ, and more studies are still needed. In this paper, we propose a technique to determine an appropriate value of ϵ by setting a price of the privacy of the data provider.

2.2   Pricing Mechanism

One of the solutions to find an appropriate value of ϵ is to price it according to the data accuracy [13–18]. In [13], strength of the privacy guarantee and the accuracy of the published results are considered to set the ϵ value, and a simple ϵ setting model that can satisfy data providers and consumers was suggested. In [14], the author proposed a compensation mechanism via auction in which data providers are rewarded based on data accuracy and data consumer's budget when they provide data with differential privacy. It is the most similar work to our study. The main differences between our paper and Ghosh and Roth's work are as follows:

(i) We define a truthful price report mechanism that a data provider get a best profit when she reports her privacy price honestly, and prove it.

(ii) We propose an optimized incentive mechanism to maximize the data consumer's profit with a fixed expense budget, and a privacy budget splitting method to maximize the data provider's utility-gain in a multi-data consumer environment.

In [17] the authors design a mechanism that can estimate statistics accurately without compromising the user's privacy. They propose a Bayesian incentive and privacy-preserving mechanism that guarantees privacy and data accuracy. The study of [18] proposes a Stackelberg game to maximize mobile users who provides their trajectory data.

Several techniques for pricing data assuming a data market environment have been studied in [19–26].

In [19] the authors suggested a data pricing mechanism to make the balance between privacy and price in data market environment. In [20], the authors propose the data market model in the IoT environment and show the proposed pricing model has a global optimal point. In [21] the authors proposed a theoretical framework for determining prices to noisy query answer in the differentially private data market. However, this research cannot flexibly reflect the requirements of the data market. In the study of [23], the author proposed an ϵ-choosing method based on Rubinstein bargaining and assumes a market manager that mediates a data provider and consumer in the data trading.

It is realistic to consider personal data as a digital asset, and reasonable to attempt to find a bridge between privacy protection level and price according to the value of ϵ in differential privacy, as has been done in this paper. Existing studies are attempting to find an equilibrium between data providers and consumers under the assumption that both are reasonable individuals. In this paper, we follow a research direction similar to existing studies, and focus on the incentive mechanism that motivates a data provider report her privacy price honestly. In particular, we consider that the value of differentially private data increases non-linearly with respect to the increase of the value of ϵ.

3   Preliminaries

In this section, we explain the basic concepts of differential privacy. Differential privacy is a mathematical model that guarantees the privacy protection at a specified level ϵ. For all datasets D_1 and D_2 differing exactly at a single element, it is defined to satisfy ϵ-differential privacy, if the probability distribution difference of the result of a specific query K on two databases is less than or equal to the threshold e^ϵ. The definition of the differential privacy is as follows:

Definition 1 (Differential privacy [3]). *A randomized function $\mathcal{K}$ provides ϵ-differential privacy if all datasets, D_1 and D_2, differing by one only element, and all subsets, $S \subseteq Range(\mathcal{K})$,*

$$\mathbb{P}[\mathcal{K}(D_1) \in S] \le e^\epsilon \mathbb{P}[\mathcal{K}(D_2) \in S]$$

The Laplace mechanism [3] is one of the most common methods for achieving the ϵ-differential privacy.

One of the important properties of differential privacy is the compositionality that allows query composing to facilitate modular design [3].

Sequential compositionality. For any database D, let we query on the randomization mechanism K_1 and K_2 which is independent for each query. The results of $K_1(D)$ and $K_2(D)$ whose guarantees are the ϵ_1 and ϵ_2-differential privacy, is $(\epsilon_1 + \epsilon_2)$-differentially private.

Parallel compositionality. Let A and B be the partition of any database $D(A \cup B = D, A \cap B = \phi)$. Then, the result of the query on the randomization mechanism $K_1(A)$ and $K_2(B)$, is the $\max(\epsilon_1, \epsilon_2)$-differentially private.

Recently, a variant of differential privacy called *local differential privacy* has been proposed [27–30]. In this model, data providers obfuscate their own data by themselves. Local differential privacy has an advantage that it does not need a trusted third party to satisfy the differential privacy. The properties of parallel and sequential compositionality hold for the local model as well.

In the rest of this paper, we consider the local model of differential privacy.

4 Incentive Mechanism for Data Markets

4.1 Overview of the Proposed Technique

The data market aims at collecting personal data legally with the consent of the provider. A data provider can sell her own data and get paid for it, and a data consumer can collect the personal data for analysis by paying a price, resulting in a win-win situation.

Naturally, the data consumer wants to collect personal data as accurately as possible at the lowest possible price, and the data provider wants to sell her data at a price as high as possible while protecting sensitive information. In general, every effective protection technique affects the utility of the data negatively. In the particular case of differential privacy, the levels of utility and privacy are determined by the parameter ϵ; thus, the data price is affected directly by the value of ϵ.

Determining the appropriate value of ϵ and the actual price of the data are critical to the success of the data market. However this is not an easy task, also because each data provider has different privacy needs [30].

We propose an incentive mechanism to find the price of the data and the value of ϵ that can satisfy both the data provider and the data consumer. The proposed method consists of two parts: an incentive mechanism encouraging the data provider to report her privacy price honestly to the data consumer, and an optimization scheme to maximize both the data consumer and provider's profit within a budget constraint.

We consider a scenario with n data providers, $u_1, \ldots, u_n$, and m data consumers, $D_1, \ldots, D_m$, and where each provider and consumer proceeds with the deal independently (we use the term "data provider" and "data producer" inter-changeably, in the same sense). The term "ϵ unit price" (e.g., 1$ per ϵ value 0.1) will be used to express the price, where ϵ is the parameter of differential privacy, which is a measure of the accuracy of information. We recall that, as ϵ increases, the data becomes less private and more information can be obtained from it, and vice versa. Thus, the price per unit ϵ represents the "value" of the provider's information[1]. The price of ϵ is expected to differ from one data provider to another, because each individual has a different privacy need. We denote the ϵ unit price reported by u_i as p_i and her true ϵ unit price as π_i.

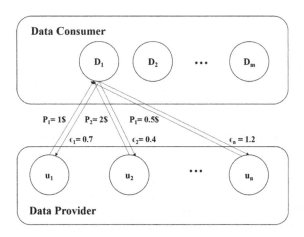

Fig. 1. An example of data trading process. In this figure, u_i means the ith data provider and D_j means the jth data consumer.

Figure 1 illustrates how the process works. At first, every data consumer broadcasts a function f to the data providers, which represents the amount of data (expresses in ϵ units) the consumer is willing to buy for a given ϵ unit price. Each consumer has her own such function, and it can differ from one consumer to another. We will call it ϵ-*allocating function*. We assume f to be monotonically decreasing, as the consumers naturally prefer to buy more data from those data producers who are willing to offer them for less. Note that the product $p_i f(p_i)$ represents the total amount that will be payed by the data producer to the consumer if they agree on the trade. The function f however has also a second purpose: as we shown in Sect. 4.2, it is designed to encourage providers to demand the price that they really consider the true price of their privacy, rather than asking for more.

Then, thanks to the truthful price report mechanism (cf. Sect. 4.2), the data providers report the prices of their data honestly to the data consumers in accordance with the published f. In the example in Fig. 1, u_1 reports her ϵ price per

---

[1] The ϵ unit price can be of any form, including a monetary one. The method we propose is independent from the nature of the price, so we do not need to specify it.

0.1 as 1\$ and u_2 reports her ϵ price per 0.1 as 2\$. Finally, the data consumer checks the price reported by the data provider and determines the total price and value of ϵ to be obtained from each provider using f. In this example, the data consumer D_1 determines ϵ_1 to be 0.7 and ϵ_2 to be 0.4.

Then, the data providers select the consumers to whom to sell their data in order to maximize their profits, and confirm with them the values of their ϵ and the total price they would receive. In the example in Fig. 1, D_1 pays 7\$ to u_1 and 8\$ to u_2. Finally, the data providers add noise to their data based on the determined ϵ and share the sanitized data with the respective consumers, and the consumers pay the corresponding prices to the providers. We assume that data providers and consumers keep the promise of the value of ϵ and compensation decided in the deal, once confirmed.

This process can be repeated until the data consumers exhaust all their budget or achieve the targeted amount of information. The task of allocating a suitable budget in each round and the how to determine the amount of needed information are also important topics, but they are out of the scope of this paper and are left for future work.

4.2   Truthful Price Report Mechanism

For the correct functioning of the data trading, the data provider should be honest and demand her true privacy price. However, she may be motivated to report a higher price, in the hope to persuade the data consumer that the information is "more valuable", and be willing to pay more. Note also that the true privacy price of each data provider is a personal information that only the provider herself knows and is not obliged to disclose.

To solve this problem, we propose a truthful price report mechanism to ensure that the data providers report their ϵ unit prices honestly. The purpose of the mechanism is to provide incentive so that the providers are guaranteed to get the greatest profit when they report their true price.

When the data provider reports her price p_i, the data consumer determines the amount of ϵ to purchase using $f(p_i)$, where f is the ϵ-allocating function introduced in Sect. 4.1. We recall that f is a monotonically decreasing function, chosen by the consumer. We assume that the domain of f, the ϵ price unit, is normalized to take values in the interval $[0, 1]$. The total price for the data estimated by the consumer is the product of the ϵ price unit and the amount to be purchased, namely, $p_i f(p_i)$. To this value, the consumer adds an *incentive* $\int_{p_i}^{\infty} f(z)\, dz$, the purpose of which is to make convenient for the data producer to report the true price (we assume that the data producer knows f and the strategy of the consumer in advance). The consumer should of course choose f so to be happy with the incentive. In particular, the incentive should be finite, so the contribution of $f(z)$ should vanish as z goes to ∞. An example of such a function is illustrated in Fig. 2.

Thus the data consumer sets the *offer* $\mu(p_i)$ to the provider u_i as follows:

Definition 2 (Payment offer). *The offer $\mu(p_i)$ is defined as:*

$$\mu(p_i) = p_i f(p_i) + \int_{p_i}^{\infty} f(z)\,dz$$

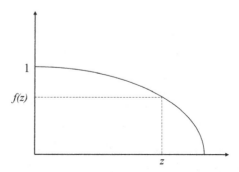

Fig. 2. An example of a monotonically decreasing function $f(z)$. Let c be a parameter representing the "reported value-to-admitted ϵ value" ratio. For $z \geq 0$, we set $f(z)$ as $f(z) = ln(e - cz)$ if $(e - cz) \leq 1$, and $f(x) = 0$ otherwise.

We now illustrate how this strategy achieves its purpose of convincing the consumer to report her true price. We start by defining the *utility* that the data provider obtains by selling her data as the difference between the offer and the true price of her data, represented by the product of the true ϵ unit price and the amount to be sold, namely $\pi_i f(p_i)$:

Definition 3 (Utility of the data provider). *The utility $\rho(p_i)$, of the provider u_i, for the reported price p_i, is defined as:*

$$\rho(p_i) = \mu(p_i) - \pi_i f(p_i)$$

We are now going to show that he proposed mechanism guarantees truthfulness. The basic reason is that each provider u_i achieves the best utility when reporting the true price. Namely, $\rho(\pi_i) \geq \rho(p_i)$ for any $p_i \in \mathbb{R}^+$, where we recall that π_i is the true price of the provider u_i. The only technical condition is that the function f is monotonically decreasing. Under this assumption, we have the following results (see also Fig. 3 to get the intuition of the proof):

Lemma 1. *If u_i reports a price greater than her true price, i.e., $p_i \geq \pi_i$, then her utility will be less than the utility for the true price, i.e., $\rho(p_i) \leq \rho(\pi_i)$.*

Proof. The proof can be found in the full version of this paper, available at [31].

Lemma 2. *If u_i reports a price smaller than her true price, i.e., $p_i \leq \pi_i$, then her utility will be less than the utility for the true price, i.e., $\rho(p_i) \leq \rho(\pi_i)$.*

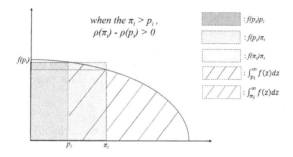

Fig. 3. Graphical illustration of Theorem 1. We prove that $\rho(\pi_i)$ (blue hatching area) is always larger than $\rho(p_i)$ (blue rectangle area+red hatching area−green rectangle area).

Proof. The proof can be found in the full version of this paper, available at [31].

Combining Lemma 1 and Lemma 2 gives the announced result. We assume of course that each data producer is a rational individual, i.e., capable of identifying the best strategy to maximize her utility.

Theorem 1. *If every data producer acts rationally, then the proposed incentive mechanism guarantees the truthfulness of the system.*

Proof. Immediate from Lemma 1 and Lemma 2.   □

4.3   Optimizing the Incentive Mechanism

In this section, we propose an optimization mechanism to identify an optimal function f for the data consumer with respect to the following two desiderata:

(i) *Maximum Information:* maximize the total information gain of the data consumer with a fixed budget.
(ii) *Maximum Profit:* maximize the total profit of the data consumer with a fixed budget.

By "budget" here we mean the budget of the data consumer to pay the data providers.

We start by introducing the notions of total information and profit for the consumer. Note that, *by the sequential compositionality of differential privacy*, the total information is the sum of the information obtained from each data provider.

Definition 4 (Total information). *The total information $\mathcal{I}(\boldsymbol{u})$ obtained by the data consumer by concluding trades with each of the data providers of the tuple $\boldsymbol{u} = (u_1, \ldots, u_n)$ is defined as*

$$\mathcal{I}(\boldsymbol{u}) = \sum_{i=1}^{n} f(p_i)$$

As for the profit, we can reasonably assume to be monotonically increasing with the amount of information obtained, and that the total profit is the sum of the profits obtained with each individual trading. The latter is naturally defined as the difference between the benefit (aka *payoff*) obtained by re-selling or processing the data, and the price payed to the data provider.

Definition 5 (Payoff and profit).

- *The payoff function for the data consumer, denoted by $\tau(\cdot)$, is the benefit that the data consumer receives by processing or selling the information gathered from the different data providers. The argument of $\tau(\cdot)$ is ϵ, the amount of the information received. We assume $\tau(\epsilon)$ to be monotonically increasing with ϵ.*
- *The total profit for the data consumer is given by $\sum_{i=1}^{n}(\tau(\epsilon_i) - \mu(\epsilon_i))$, where $\epsilon_i = f(p_i)$, i.e., the ϵ-value allocated to u_i.*

We will consider a family of functions $\mathcal{F}$ indexed by a parameter c, to which the ϵ-allocating function f belongs. The parameter c reflects the data consumer's will to collect the information and, for technical reasons, we assume f to be continuous, differentiable and concave with respect to it. For each data provider, different values of c will give different f, that, in turn, will give rise to a different incentive-curve as per equation (2), which the data consumer should adhere to for compensating for the information obtained from that data provider.

As described in previous sections, the ϵ-allocating functions should be monotonically decreasing with the ϵ unit price, as the consumer is motivated to buy more information from the consumers that offer it at a lower price. This property also ensures, by Theorem 1, that the prices reported by the data producers will be their true prices. Hence we impose the following constraint on $\mathcal{F}$:

$$\mathcal{F} \subseteq \{f(\cdot, \cdot) : c, p \in \mathbb{R}^+, f(c, p) \text{ is continuous, differentiable} \atop \text{and concave on } c, \text{and decreasing with } p\}. \tag{1}$$

Note that we have added the parameter c as an additional argument in f, so f has now two arguments.

Example 1. An example of such class $\mathcal{F}$ is that of Fig. 2:

$$\mathcal{F} = \{\ln(e - cp) : c \in \mathbb{R}^+\}.$$

Example 2. Another example is:

$$\mathcal{F} = \{1 - cp : c \in \mathbb{R}^+\}.$$

After the prices $p_1, \ldots, p_n$ have been reported by the data producers $u_1, \ldots, u_n$, the data consumer will try to choose an optimal c maximizing her profit. Figure 4 illustrates an example with two data provider's incentive graph and payoff for data consumer.

We will analyse the possibility to choose an optimal c, that, in turn, leads to an optimal $f(c, \cdot)$ addressing scenarios (i) and (ii).

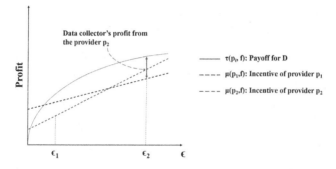

Fig. 4. Illustrating the payoff for c and the incentive-plots for the data consumer involving two data providers reporting p_1, p_2. The Y-intercept of μ_1 is $\int_{p_1}^{\infty} f(z)dz$ and that for μ_2 is $\int_{p_2}^{\infty} f(z)dz$.

In the context of differential privacy, we may assume that τ (the data consumer's payoff function) is additive, i.e.,

$$\textbf{Additivity} \quad \tau(a+b) = \tau(a) + \tau(b) \quad \text{for every } a, b \in \mathbb{R}^+. \tag{2}$$

This is a reasonable assumption that goes well along with the sequential compositionality property of differential privacy, at least for small values of ϵ^2.

We start by showing that the two desiderata (i) and (ii) are equivalent:

Theorem 2. *If $\tau(\cdot)$ is additive, then maximizing information and maximizing profit (desiderata (i) and (ii)) are equivalent, in the sense that a ϵ-allocating function $f(\cdot, \cdot)$ that maximizes the one, maximizes also the other.*

Proof. The proof can be found in the full version of this paper, available at [31].

Corollary 1. *If $\tau(\cdot)$ is additive, then the optimal choice of $f(\cdot, \cdot)$ w.r.t. the selected family of functions will maximize both the information gain and the profit for the data consumer.*

Proof. Immediate from Theorem 2. □

We now consider the complexity problem for finding the optimal $f(\cdot, \cdot)$. Due to the assumptions made in Eq. 1, and to the additivity of τ, we can apply the method of the Lagrangians to find such $f(\cdot, \cdot)$ (cf. Appendix A of the full version of this paper, available at [31]).

Theorem 3. *If τ is additive, then there exists a c that gives an optimal **profit-maximizing** function $f(c, \cdot) \in \mathcal{F}$, for a fixed budget, and we can derive such c via the method of the Lagrangians.*

---

2 From a technical point of view, the additive property holds also for large values of ϵ. However, from a practical point of view, for large values of ϵ, for instance 200 and 400, then the original information is almost entirely revealed in both cases, and would not make sense to pay twice the price of 200 ϵ units to achieve 400 ϵ units.

Proof. The proof can be found in the full version of this paper, available at [31]. □

Theorem 4. *There exists a c that gives an optimal* **information-maximizing** *function $f(c, \cdot) \in \mathcal{F}$, for a fixed budget, and we can derive such c via the method of the Lagrangians.*

Proof. The proof can be found in the full version of this paper, available at [31].

To demonstrate how the method works, we show how to compute the specific values of c on the two classes $\mathcal{F}$ of Examples 1 and 2. Such c gives the optimal ϵ-allocating function $f(c, \cdot)$, maximizing $\mathcal{I}(u)$ for a given budget. The derivations are described in detail in the full version of this paper, available at [31]. In each example, p_i is the reported ϵ unit price of u_i.

Example 3. Let $\mathcal{F} = \{\ln(e - cp) : c \in \mathbb{R}^+\}$. The optimal parameter c is the solution of the equation $\ln(\prod_{i=1}^n e^{p_i} (e - cp_i)^{\frac{e}{c}}) = B + \frac{n(e-1)}{c}$.

Example 4. Let $\mathcal{F} = \{1 - cp : c \in \mathbb{R}^+\}$. The optimal parameter c is the solution of the equation $c^2 \sum_{i=1}^n p_i^2 + 2Bc - n = 0$.

4.4   Discussion

In our model, for the scenario we have considered so far, the parameter c is determined by the number of providers and the budget. We observe that, in both Examples 3 and 4, if n increases than c increases, and vice versa. This seems natural, because in the families of both these example c the incentive that the consumer is going to propose decreases monotonically with c. This means that the larger is the offer, the smaller is the incentive that the consumer needs to be paying. In other words, the examples confirm the well known market law according to which the price decreases when the offer increases, and vice versa.

We note that we have been assuming that there is enough offer to satisfy the consumer's demand. If this hypothesis is not satisfied, i.e., if the offer is smaller than the demand, then the situation is quite different: now the data producer can choose to whom to sell hid data. In particular, the data consumer who sets a lower c will have a better chance to buy data because, naturally, the provider prefers to sell her data to the data consumers who give a higher incentive. In the next section we explore in more detail the process, from the perspective of the data provider, in the case in which the demand is higher than the offer.

4.5   Optimized Privacy Budget Splitting Mechanism for Data Providers

After optimizing an incentive mechanism for a given data consumer dealing with multiple data providers, we focus on the flip side of the setup. We assume a scenario in which a given data provider has to provide her data to multiple data consumers, and that there is enough demand so that she can sell all her data.

Let there be m data consumers, $D_1, \ldots, D_m$ seeking to obtain data from the user u. By truthful price report mechanism, as discussed in Sect. 4.2, u reports her true price to each D_i. As discussed in Sect. 4.3, D_i computes her optimal ϵ-allocating function f_i and requests data from u, differentially privatized with $\epsilon = f_i(\pi)$. After receiving $f_1, \ldots, f_m$, u would like to provide her data in such a way that maximizes her utility received after sharing her data.

Definition 6. *We say that the data provider has made a* deal *with the data consumer D_i if, upon reporting the true per-unit price of her information, π, she agrees to share her data privatized with privacy parameter $\epsilon = f_i(\pi)$.*

It is important to note here that u is not obliged to deal with any data consumer D_i, even after receiving f_i. Realistically, u has a privacy budget of ϵ_{total}, which she would not exceed at any price. Let $S = \{i_1, \ldots, i_k\}$ be an arbitrary subset $\{1, \ldots, m\}$. By the sequential composition property of differential privacy, the final privacy parameter achieved by u by sharing her data to an arbitrary set of data consumers $D_{i_1}, \ldots, D_{i_k}$ is $\epsilon_S = \sum_{j \in S} f_j(\pi)$. u's main intention is to share her data in such a way that ensures $\epsilon_S \leq \epsilon_{\text{total}}$ for all subset S of $\{1, \ldots, n\}$, while maximizing $\sum_{j \in S} \rho_i(\pi, f_j)$, i.e., the total utility received. Reducing it down to the $0/1$ knapsack problem, we propose that u should be dealing with $\{D_{i_1}, \ldots, D_{i_k}\}$ where $S^* = \{i_1, \ldots, i_k\} \subseteq \{1, \ldots, m\}$, chosen as

$$S^* = \arg\max_S \{ \sum_{j \in S} \rho(\pi, f_j) | S \subseteq \{1, \ldots, m\}, \sum_{j \in S} f_j(\pi) \leq \epsilon_{\text{total}} \} \quad (3)$$

We show the pseudocode for the ϵ allocation algorithm and the entire process in Algorithms 1 and 2.

Algorithm 1: Optimized privacy budget splitting algorithm

Input: $\{\epsilon_1, \ldots, \epsilon_n\}$ stored in array w, $\{p_1, \ldots, p_n\}$ stored in array v, ϵ_{total} ;
Output: List of data consumer $\{D_1 \ldots D_k\}$ that is selected to sell data;
initiate Two-dimension array m;
while $i \leq n$ **do**
    while $j \leq \epsilon_{total}$ **do**
        if $w[i] > \epsilon_{total}$ **then**
        | m[i, j] := m[i-1, j]
        else
        | m[i, j] := max(m[i-1, j], m[i-1, j-w[i]] + v[i])
        end
    end
end
backtrack using the final solution m and find the index of the data consumer ;
return List of selected data consumer ;

Algorithm 2: The proposed data trading process

Input: the data provider $\{u_1, \ldots, u_n\}$, the data consumer $\{D_1, \ldots, D_m\}$;
Output: List of the data provider and consumer pair that trade is completed;
while $i \leq m$ **do**

    D_i calculate the parameter c to optimize the $f_i(\cdot)$;
    D_i inform the $f_i(\cdot)$ to the data provider

while $j \leq n$ **do**

    u_j report price p_j to the data consumer

while $i \leq m$ **do**

    while $j \leq n$ **do**

       D_i calculate the ϵ_j based on p_j;
       D_i inform the ϵ_j to the u_j

while $j \leq n$ **do**

    u_j perform the **Optimized ϵ allocation algorithm** to maximize the utility

---

5   Experimental Results

In this section we perform some experiments to verify that the proposed optimization method can find the best profit for the data consumer. For the experiments, we consider the families $\mathcal{F}$ of Examples 3 and 4, namely $\mathcal{F} = \{\ln(e - cp) : c \in \mathbb{R}^+\}$ and $\mathcal{F} = \{1 - cp : c \in \mathbb{R}^+\}$. For these two families the optimal parameter c is also derived formally, as shown in Appendix B of the full version of this paper, available at [31].

The experimental variables are set as follows: we assume that there are 10 data consumers, and the total number of data providers n is set from 1000 to 2000 at an interval of 500. The data provider's ϵ unit price is distributed normally with mean 1 and standard deviation 1, i.e., $\mathcal{N}(1, 1)$, and convert ϵ unit price less than 0 or more than 2 to 0 and 2 respectively. We set the unit value ϵ to 0.1, and the maximum ϵ value of data provider to 3. We set the budgets as 60, 90, and 120 and the number of the data provider as $1,000, 1,500, 2,000$. We assumed that the data consumer earned a profit of 10 per 0.1 epsilon and set the parameter c to 1 and 10 for comparison.

The results are shown in Fig. 5. For instance, in the case of the log family $\ln(e - cp)$, the optimal parameter c is 5.36, and in the case of the linear family $1 - cp$, the optimal parameter c is 4.9. It is easy to verify that the optimal values of c correspond to those determined by solving Equations (8) and (13) in Appendix B of the full version of this paper, available at [31], of Examples 3 and 4, respectively.

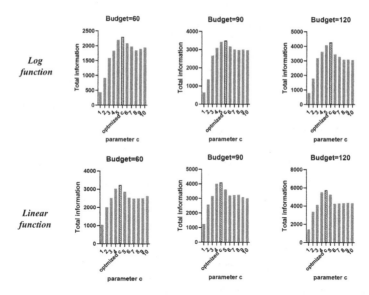

Fig. 5. Experimental result of profit under a fixed budget. Log function is the family $ln(e - cp)$ and Linear function is the family $1 - cp$. We let the parameter c range from 0 to 1. The red bin represents the optimal value of c, namely the c that gives maximum information.

6   Conclusion and Future Work

As machine learning and data mining are getting more and more deployed, individuals are becoming increasingly aware of the privacy issues and of the value of their data. This evolution of people's attitude towards privacy induces companies to develop new approaches to obtain personal data. We envision a scenario where data consumers can trade private data directly from the data provider by paying the price for the respective data, which has the potential to obtain personal information that could not be obtained in the traditional manner. In order to ensure a steady offer in the data market, it is imperative to provide the privacy protection that the data providers deem necessary. Differential privacy can be applied to meet this requirement. However, the lack of standards for setting an appropriate value for the differential privacy parameter ϵ, that determines the levels of data utility and privacy protection, makes it difficult to apply this framework in the data market.

In order to address this problem, we have developed a method, based on incentives and optimization, to find an appropriate value for ϵ in the process of data trading. The proposed incentive mechanism motivates every data provider to report her privacy price honestly in order to maximize her benefit, and the proposed optimization method maximizes the profit for the data consumer under a fixed financial budget. Additionally, in an environment involving multiple data consumers, our mechanism suggests an optimal way for the data providers to split the privacy budgets, maximizing their utility. Through experiments, we have verified that the proposed method provides the best profits to the provider and consumer.

Along the lines of what we have studied in this paper, there are many interesting research issues still open in this area. In future work, we plan to study the following issues:

1. Mechanism for a fair incentive share in an environment where the data providers make a federation for privacy protection
2. Maximization of the data consumers' profits by estimating privacy price distribution of the data providers in an environment where demand of the data providers may change dynamically.

References

1. Liveen. https://www.liveen.com/
2. Datacoup. https://datacoup.com/
3. Dwork, C., Roth, A.: The algorithmic foundations of differential privacy. Found. Trends Theor. Comput. Sci. **9**(3–4), 211–407 (2014)
4. Bowen, C., Snoke, J.: Comparative study of differentially private synthetic data algorithms from the NIST PSCR differential privacy synthetic data challenge, pp. 1–32. arXiv preprint arXiv:1911.12704 (2019)
5. Volgushev, N., et al.: Conclave: secure multi-party computation on big data. In: Proceedings of the 14th EuroSys Conference, pp. 1–18 (2019)
6. Acar, A., et al.: A survey on homomorphic encryption schemes: theory and implementation. ACM Comput. Surv. (CSUR) **51**(4), 1–35 (2018)
7. Tang, J., et al.: Privacy loss in Apple's implementation of differential privacy on macOS 10.12, pp. 1–12. arXiv preprint arXiv:1709.02753 (2017)
8. Lee, J., Clifton, C.: How much is enough? Choosing ε for differential privacy. In: Lai, X., Zhou, J., Li, H. (eds.) ISC 2011. LNCS, vol. 7001, pp. 325–340. Springer, Heidelberg (2011). https://doi.org/10.1007/978-3-642-24861-0_22
9. Chen, Y., et al.: Truthful mechanisms for agents that value privacy. ACM Trans. Econ. Comput. **4**(3), 1–30 (2016)
10. Ligett, K., Roth, A.: Take it or leave it: running a survey when privacy comes at a cost. In: Goldberg, P.W. (ed.) WINE 2012. LNCS, vol. 7695, pp. 378–391. Springer, Heidelberg (2012). https://doi.org/10.1007/978-3-642-35311-6_28
11. Xiao, D.: Is privacy compatible with truthfulness? In: Proceedings of the 4th Conference on Innovations in Theoretical Computer Science, pp. 67–86 (2013)
12. Nissim, K., Orlandi, C., Smorodinsky, R.: Privacy-aware mechanism design. In: Proceedings of the 13th ACM Conference on Electronic Commerce, pp. 774–789 (2012)
13. Hsu, J., et al.: Differential privacy: an economic method for choosing epsilon. In: Proceedings of the 27th IEEE Computer Security Foundations Symposium, pp. 1–29 (2014)
14. Ghosh, A., Roth, A.: Selling privacy at auction. Games Econ. Behav. **91**(1), 334–346 (2015)
15. Dandekar, P., Fawaz, N., Ioannidis, S.: Privacy auctions for recommender systems, pp. 1–23 (2012). https://arxiv.org/abs/1111.2885
16. Roth, A.: Buying private data at auction: the sensitive surveyor's problem. ACM SIGecom Exch. **11**(1), 1–8 (2012)

17. Fleischer, L.K., Lyu, Y.H.: Approximately optimal auctions for selling privacy when costs are correlated with data. In: Proceedings of the 13th ACM Conference on Electronic Commerce, pp. 568–585 (2012)
18. Li, W., Zhang, C., Liu, Z., Tanaka, Y.: Incentive mechanism design for crowdsourcing-based indoor localization. IEEE Access **6**, 54042–54051 (2018)
19. Nget, R., Cao, Y., Yoshikawa, M.: How to balance privacy and money through pricing mechanism in personal data market, pp. 1–10. arXiv preprint arXiv:1705.02982 (2018)
20. Oh, H., et al.: Personal data trading scheme for data brokers in IoT data marketplaces. IEEE Access **7**(2019), 40120–40132 (2019)
21. Li, C., Li, D.Y., Miklau, G., Suciu, D.: A theory of pricing private data. ACM Trans. Database Syst. **39**(4), 34–60 (2013)
22. Aperjis, C., Huberman, B.A.: A market for unbiased private data: paying individuals according to their privacy attitudes, pp. 1–17 (2012). SSRN: https://ssrn.com/abstract=2046861
23. Jung, K., Park, S.: Privacy bargaining with fairness: privacy-price negotiation system for applying differential privacy in data market environments. In: Proceedings of the International Conference on Big Data, pp. 1389–1394 (2019)
24. Krehbiel, S.: Choosing epsilon for privacy as a service. Proc. Priv. Enhanc. Technol. **2019**, 192–205 (2019)
25. Zhang, T., Zhu, Q.: On the differential private data market: endogenous evolution, dynamic pricing, and incentive compatibility, pp. 1–30. arXiv preprint arXiv:2101.04357 (2021)
26. Jorgensen, Z., Yu, T., Cormode, G.: Conservative or liberal? Personalized differential privacy. In: Proceedings of the 31St International Conference on Data Engineering, pp. 1023–1034. IEEE (2015)
27. Erlingsson, U., Pihur, V., Korolova, A.: Rappor randomized aggregatable privacy-preserving ordinal response. In: Proceedings of International Conference on Computer and Communications Security, pp. 1054–1067 (2014)
28. Cormode, G., et al.: Privacy at scale: local differential privacy in practice. In: Proceedings of the International Conference on Management of Data, pp. 1655–1658 (2018)
29. Thông, T.N., Xiaokui, X., Yin, Y., et al.: Collecting and analyzing data from smart device users with local differential privacy, pp. 1–11. https://arxiv.org/abs/1606.05053 (2016)
30. Kasiviswanathan, S.P., et al.: What can we learn privately. SIAM J. Comput. **40**(3), 7903–8826 (2011)
31. Biswas, S., Jung, K., Palamidessi, C.: An incentive mechanism for trading personal data in data markets, pp. 1–22. https://arxiv.org/abs/2106.14187 (2021)

Assessing Security of Cryptocurrencies with Attack-Defense Trees: Proof of Concept and Future Directions

Julia Eisentraut[1(✉)], Stephan Holzer[2], Katharina Klioba[3], Jan Křetínský[1], Lukas Pin[4], and Alexander Wagner[5]

[1] Technical University of Munich, Munich, Germany
julia.kraemer@in.tum.de
[2] Massachusetts Institute of Technology, Cambridge, USA
[3] Hamburg University of Technology, Hamburg, Germany
[4] Humboldt University of Berlin, Berlin, Germany
[5] University of Heidelberg, Heidelberg, Germany

Abstract. Cryptocurrencies such as Bitcoin have been one of the new major technologies of the last decade. In this paper, we assess the security of Bitcoin using attack-defense trees, an established formalism to evaluate the security of systems. In this paper, our main contributions are as follows: (1) We provide an extended attack-defense tree model for attacks on Bitcoin. (2) We demonstrate the general usability of existing analysis methods for attack-defense trees in this context. (3) We highlight further research directions necessary to extend attack-defense trees to a full-fledged overarching model for security assessment.

1 Introduction

During the last decade, cryptocurrencies like Bitcoin and other applications of *distributed ledger technologies* (DLT) attracted a lot of attention. However, investments in Bitcoin and other cryptocurrencies have repeatedly been lost due to malicious attacks. Hence, for investors, customers, and retailers to take well-justified business decisions, it is crucial to reliably assess their individual financial and reputational risks when investing in applications of DLT. For these investors, a mere technical analysis of the theoretical security of DLT protocols is by far not enough. Successful hacks on DLT – and thus loss of money – have ranged from attacks on exchanges[1] over stolen private keys[2] to user mistakes. A reliable individual threat modeling and risk assessment must thus holistically subsume these aspects.

In this paper, we model these risks by *attack(-defense) tree models*, e.g., see [22,27,39].

---

[1] https://money.cnn.com/2018/06/11/investing/coinrail-hack-bitcoin-exchange/index.html, 04/04/2020.

[2] https://www.wired.com/story/blockchain-bandit-ethereum-weak-private-keys/, 04/04/2020.

© Springer Nature Switzerland AG 2021
A. Cerone and P. C. Ölveczky (Eds.): ICTAC 2021, LNCS 12819, pp. 214–234, 2021.
https://doi.org/10.1007/978-3-030-85315-0_13

With the Bitcoin risk assessment as example, we demonstrate that DLT are exceptionally well-suited for *quantitative* model checking approaches, since probabilities and costs of events can be derived or estimated reliably from known real-world information with statistical methods such as *time series analysis*. While the analysis cannot be complete (we discuss reasons and the extent in Sect. 6), already the various aspects of risk we include demonstrate the holistic ability of attack-defense trees. Indeed, we argue that these models can play out their strengths as a meta-framework for a holistic risk assessment approach, combining results of various technical analyses. For that, we show how to estimate probabilities of successful attacks (see Subsect. 5.1) and how to obtain unknown courses of known attacks (Subsect. 5.2). Thus, we combine the analysis results of various attack vectors covering far more than mere technological aspects, ranging from exploiting software bugs to insider attacks and social engineering.

Finally, DLT turn out to be an especially valuable case study as it leads us to pointing out several directions of future research still necessary to turn attack-defense tree models into a full-fledged formalism for real-world risk analysis and threat modeling.

To summarize, our contributions are as follows:

- We provide an attack-defense tree model for attacks on Bitcoin and their risk assessment available for download at https://www.model.in.tum.de/~kraemerj/upload/. The general approach is discussed in Sect. 4.
- We demonstrate the general usability of existing analysis methods for attack-defense trees in this context. Deriving success probabilities is demonstrated in Subsect. 5.1 and the usage of strategy synthesis in Subsect. 5.2.
- We highlight further research directions necessary to extend attack-defense trees to a full-fledged overarching model for security assessment in Sect. 7.

2   Related Work

Information necessary to construct our models is taken from several surveys on security (and privacy) issues for Bitcoin [10,30], blockchain and DLT in general [25,32]. However, none of these surveys provide a comprehensive model overarching different analyses. Here we suggest that attack trees can serve as such an approach if currently open research questions are addressed.

Attack Trees and Their Extensions. *Attack Trees* were introduced two decades ago [39]. For an extensive overview, we refer the interested reader to [28] and [43]. An overview on graphical security models can be found in [23]. Recently, special focus has been put on providing extensions to attack trees and their semantics to deal with resources such as costs, probabilities and penalties [3], sequential behavior [2,24], defense mechanisms [6,29] and combinations thereof [22,35].

Case studies for attack trees so far comprise SCADA systems [34], online banking [12], ATMs [14], virtual reality learning environment applications [19] and connected vehicles [26], among many smaller examples. Bitcoin and other

DLT-techniques were not previously analyzed using attack-defense trees. Here, we propose them as another valuable source for realistic case studies.

DLT in Formal Methods. While attack trees and formal approaches to attack tree analysis have not been used to analyze DLT previously, verification of DLTs using formal methods in general has gained attention recently. For instance, numerous approaches mainly focusing on functional correctness of smart contracts are surveyed in [18]. In [9], smart contracts are analyzed by providing a simplified programming language for smart contracts, which can be automatically translated to a state-based game and then analyzed. Markov decision processes (MDP) have been used in [40] to explore conditions under which Bitcoin is resilient to selfish mining. MDP have also been used to deepen the understanding of double spending attacks in Bitcoin in [42]. In [8], ergodic mean-payoff games are used to study economic aspects of security violations.

3 Attack-Defense Trees

Intuitively, *attack trees* in their basic form are and-or trees, hierarchically decomposing a complex attack (in the root) into its simpler components. *Attack-defense trees* (ADT) as defined in [22] extend upon attack trees and other versions of attack-defense trees in various aspects, which turn out very helpful in modeling, as e.g., in Fig. 2.

Each node of the underlying tree structure is labeled with an *event*. The event at the root represents the overall *attack goal* (e.g., *transfer Bitcoin* in Fig. 2); all other events represent steps taken towards the attack goal; leaves of the tree are labeled by *basic events*, which represent atomic and unique happenings in the real world. In Fig. 2, we have, for instance, the basic events *outsider attack (10)* or *encrypt storage (5)*. These basic events are either governed by one of the players (Attacker or Defender) or driven by a counter (Time-driven).

In our setting, at any time, every event has a unique value – it has been either *not attempted yet* (uu) or *successfully* (tt) or *unsuccessfully* (ff) attempted. This three-valued logic approach allows us to capture the evolution of events over time. Initially, all basic events have not been attempted and thus receive value uu. They change their value if either a player tries to execute the event or if the counter has run out of time.

We call all remaining events *composed*. *Operators* specify how events contribute to a composed event being successfully attempted. The logic operators AND, OR and NOT have the standard logical meaning. In Fig. 2, most composed events are labeled by OR to represent various attack vectors. AND and OR are used to depict the defender's countermeasures. SAND and SOR, which stem from [22], are sequential variants of AND and OR: additionally, they require their subgoals to be attempted in a specific order. In graphical representations, the order is from left to right. Attack-defense trees also allow specifying costs of delaying or executing basic events. In the formalism we use, costs are accumulated in specific cost variables. The operator COST is equipped with a cost constraint over these variables and turns to tt if the valuation of the cost variables satisfy the cost constraint upon the subgoal turning true.

Additionally, we have two operators to modify the status of basic events, namely TR and RE. In general, we distinguish *triggerable* and *non-triggerable* basic events. A triggerable basic event causally depends on another event being successfully attempted, non-triggerable events do not. Thus, a player can attempt a triggerable basic event only if the event it depends on has previously been successfully attempted. We call this process *triggering*. Composed events labeled with TR propagate the values of their input. Whenever the input of an event e labeled by TR turns to true, the basic events which are triggered by event e become available for execution.

Furthermore, we distinguish *resettable* and *non-resettable* basic events. Non-resettable basic events can happen at most once, resettable basic events might happen several times or even periodically. They are set back to their initial value uu upon another event being successfully attempted, and we call this process *resetting*. Composed events labeled with RE propagate the values of their input. Whenever the input of an event e labeled by RE turns to true, the basic events which are resetted by event e are set back to their initial value.

Graphical Conventions. A small attack-defense tree using these graphical conventions can be found in Fig. 3. Triangular nodes represent basic events. Time-driven basic events (basic events (2), (5), (6) and (8) in Fig. 3) are gray and dotted, basic events of the Attacker are red and horizontally striped (basic events (1), (4), (7) and (9)), and basic events of the Defender are green and vertically striped (basic event (3)). Each basic event is of one of these three types, i.e., each basic event is either gray, red or green.

Composed events are boxes labeled by an operator. The goal event is the only composed event which is also red and horizontally striped (like IFN in Fig. 3). We have three different edge relations: plain arrows $\longrightarrow$ are (transitively) oriented from basic events to the root, i.e., the start vertex of the edge is the subgoal of the end vertex. Thus, basic event (9) is a subgoal of the subsequent composed event labeled with TR. Squiggled edges $\rightsquigarrow$ represent triggering, i.e., these edges point from a composed event labeled by TR to the triggered basic events (such as basic event (7)). Finally, dashed edges $\dashrightarrow$ represent resetting, i.e., these edges point from a composed event labeled by RE to the resetted basic events. While we do not use the operator RE in Fig. 3, an example can be found in Fig. 4. Here, RE has reset edges to all basic events, i.e., it resets all basic events upon turning true.

4   Overall Structure of the Model

We present an ADT model for Bitcoin exploits. While our model encompasses a broad range of attack vectors including their quantitative aspects, our intention here is not to provide a full-fledged risk assessment model for a specific stakeholder. We consider it rather a template for such modeling. For a comprehensive assessment, our model would have to be completed by the internal process details of the stakeholder who, by intention, remains abstract throughout the paper.

Our full model comprises three different attack vectors to exploit Bitcoin, previously reported in [10, 25, 30, 32]:

User attacks are discussed in Subsect. 5.1. With this submodel, we exemplify the derivation of success probabilities from real-world statistics.

Vendor attacks are discussed in Subsect. 5.2. In this submodel, our attention focuses on deriving new courses of known attacks.

Network attacks are part of the full model, but do not add a new technical aspect to the analysis.

Figure 1 provides a schematic overview.[3]

To construct our models, we mostly used descriptions of attacks on Bitcoin published in the last few years (and refer to these papers in the respective sections). Additionally, we take news reports into account, which document attacks on Bitcoin, and link to the respective news websites in footnotes.

We discuss the limits of our analysis in Sect. 6. In Sect. 7, we show open challenges preventing an analysis of the full model.

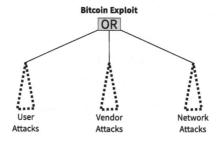

Fig. 1. Schematic model overview. User Attacks can be found in Fig. 2 and Vendor Attacks in Fig. 3. The third part of the model does not highlight any new analysis techniques. Thus, we omit it in this paper.

5 Modeling and Analysis of Attacks

5.1 User Attacks: Deriving Success Probabilities

Quantitative model checking can utilize quantitative knowledge such as probabilities, costs and time to compute how likely certain attacks are, how much cost/damage attacks may cause or how long attacks might take. First, we demonstrate how to derive success probabilities in the area of DLT using *time series*

---

[3] The full model is available for download at https://www.model.in.tum.de/~kraemerj/upload/.

analysis [20]. Second, we show how to compute *success probabilities for complex attacks* applying existing analysis methods to the model in Fig. 2.

Our main source for deriving success probabilities are various statistics, tracked and made publicly available for cryptocurrencies such as Bitcoin and Ethereum. We obtain, for instance, the following statistics for the Bitcoin blockchain:

- the total number of blocks is 18,702,068,[4]
- we have 7 m 43 s as average block time (see Footnote 4),
- one Bitcoin can be traded to $55,816.45 (see Footnote 4),
- the number of active exchanges (i.e. exchanges, where money has been traded in the last 24 h) is 69[5] and
- the number of reported hacks, for instance, on major exchanges, is at least 40 since the first launch of Bitcoin.[6]

With such information at hand, we can compute the probability that a specific attack vector is successful within a certain time frame, for instance, at the next Bitcoin block or within the next year. This paper focuses on predicting the success probability for the next year since most data is tracked yearly. Any more extended time frame in the future will lead to too unreliable results.

Remarkably, the discretized time model that ADT come with suits the DLT setting perfectly, as within Blockchain, time is naturally discretized by blocks. With this regard, the DLT use case stands out from many other use cases, where time discretization is an imposed abstraction from actual continuous time behavior. In our example model, we exemplarily demonstrate how to use this information to assess the probability that a successful attack on exchanges occurs within the year 2020. In this way, we can compare the number of attacks we predicted for 2020 and the number of attacks that actually occurred in 2020.

Figure 2 shows the submodel for *user attacks*, which subsumes attacks in which Bitcoin are stolen from the user. We refine the goal *maliciously transfer Bitcoin from a user's account* into three disjoint attack vectors (which correspond to the three vertices at level 2 of the tree) – attacks on the individual user's wallet, on Bitcoin exchanges and using fake services[7] or the Bitcoin protocol itself.[8] The model depicts many of the ways Bitcoin users have lost Bitcoin as reported in the user study presented in [30]. Additionally, we include various potential ways to steal Bitcoin discussed among Bitcoin practitioners on top of attacks reported in the research community and credit the respective discussions in footnotes.

---

[4] https://www.blockchain.com/en/stats and https://bitinfocharts.com/bitcoin/, last visited 07/05/2021.

[5] https://coin.market/exchanges, last visited 07/05/2021.

[6] https://coiniq.com/cryptocurrency-exchange-hacks/, https://selfkey.org/list-of-cryptocurrency-exchange-hacks/ and https://blog.idex.io/all-posts/a-complete-list-of-cryptocurrency-exchange-hacks-updated/#2020, last visited 13/12/2020.

[7] See https://bitcoin.org/en/scams, last visited 13/12/2020.

[8] See https://en.bitcoin.it/wiki/Common_Vulnerabilities_and_Exposures, last visited 13/12/2020.

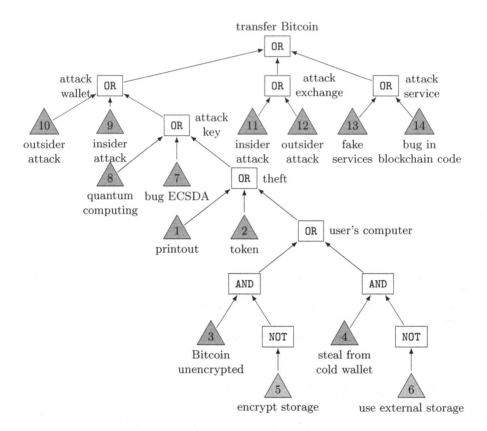

Fig. 2. A subtree representing attacks on the user side

Time Series Analysis. To reliably estimate the probabilities for successful attacks within the next year to come, we use *exponential smoothing* to compute the probabilities for basic events. Then, we compute the overall success probability in the ADT model using standard bottom-up approaches [24,27,33] for ADT. Exponential smoothing is a statistical method used in time series analysis that allows to predict the likelihood of future occurrences of an event at a specific point in time from the history of past occurrences. The further an occurrence lies in the past, the less influence it has on the forecast. In fact, its weight in the computation decays exponentially over time, so more recent occurrences have a much higher impact. For our model, this means that attacks only common in the early stage of Bitcoin have a significantly smaller success probability than currently popular attacks.

Since information on attacks has been only recorded annually and not at block level, we approximate the probability of occurrence of a basic event b per block within a given year k by

$$F_{b,k} := \frac{\#\text{attacks b in year } k}{\#\text{blocks in year } k} h$$

From the given information of the years 2010 to 2020, we predict the occurrence probabilities of events for all years until 2021. In the following, let $k \in \{1, 0, -1, \ldots, -10\}$, with $k = 1$ corresponding to the year 2021 (the predicted year) and 0 to -10 to the years 2020 to 2010, respectively.

Now, considering $F_{b,k}$ as a time series, we can compute an estimate of $F_{b,1}$, i.e. for the year 2021, using exponential smoothing.

Let $F_{b,k}^*$ denote the estimate of $F_{b,k}$. Then, we define for $k \in \{1, 0, \ldots, -9\}$, (following the standard definition of exponential smoothing),

$$F_{b,k}^* := \eta F_{b,k-1} + (1 - \eta) F_{b,k-1}^* = F_{b,k-1}^* + \eta (F_{b,k-1} - F_{b,k-1}^*) \tag{1}$$

with initial estimate $F_{b,-10}^* := F_{b,-10}$. Note that this equation can be seen as updating the estimate by adding a fraction of the estimation error in each time step.

Additionally, we need to choose a suitable smoothing parameter $\eta \in (0, 1)$. Overfitting can be avoided by choosing a smaller smoothing parameter, whereas choosing η closer to 1 gives more weight to recent data, thus avoiding underfitting. The optimal smoothing parameter can be chosen by minimizing the mean squared error (MSE) or the mean absolute error (MAE) of past predictions compared to the actual data. For the following data sets, we have used a grid search determining the optimal smoothing parameter η both with respect to the MSE and the MAE. To avoid over- or underfitting, the value closer to 0.5 is chosen as the final smoothing parameter.

Predicting Success Probabilities for Attacks on Exchanges. A typical event for which success probabilities can be predicted with this method are attacks on exchanges. From the statistics in Table 1 and the predictions derived using Eq. (1), we can satisfactorily forecast a success probability as follows. Assuming an average block time of 7 m 43 s, there are roughly $\frac{365 \cdot 24 \cdot 60}{7.7} \approx 68260$ blocks per year. Assuming the hacks occur independently, we arrive at the approximate success probability of $\frac{8.434}{68260 \cdot 69} \approx 1.79 \cdot 10^{-6}$ per block for a successful hack in 2021 (assuming all money is stored in only one of the 69 active exchanges). For the year 2021, we arrive at the success probability of $1 - (1 - (\frac{8.434}{68260 \cdot 69}))^{68260} \approx 0.115$ for a successful hack. As publicly available data does not allow to sufficiently distinguish between inside and outside attacks in this case, we predict the success probability for the composed event *attack exchanges*.

Predicting Success Probabilities for Bugs in Blockchain Code. Another attack vector of the model, where success probabilities can adequately be predicted from statistics with exponential smoothing, is using bugs in the Bitcoin blockchain implementations (basic event *bugs in blockchain code* (event (15) in Fig. 2). In fact, more than 40 bugs were found during the past nine years (detailed statistics can be found in Table 2). Using statistics on common vulnerabilities

Table 1. Number of hacks per year on major exchanges since the launch of Bitcoin and our (rounded) prediction using exponential smoothing with $\eta = 0.612$ minimizing the MSE (where the actual number of 2020 counts events until September)

	2010	2011	2012	2013	2014	2015	2016	2017	2018	2019	2020	2021
Prediction		0	1.224	3.535	3.820	7.602	6.010	4.780	4.915	8.639	10.696	8.434
Actual	0	2	5	4	10	5	4	5	11	12	7	

in Bitcoin[9] and exponential smoothing, we estimate the success probability per block for a bug to occur by $\frac{4.695}{68260} \approx 6.88 \cdot 10^{-5}$. Per year, the chance that a bug occurs is almost 1. However, none of the bugs so far have been exploited.

Table 2. Number of bugs per year in the bitcoin protocol since the launch of Bitcoin and our (rounded) prediction using exponential smoothing with $\eta = 0.423$ minimizing the MAE (where the actual number of 2020 counts events until December)

	2010	2011	2012	2013	2014	2015	2016	2017	2018	2019	2020	2021
Prediction		5	3.308	5.293	7.707	5.293	3.900	3.519	2.877	3.352	4.472	4.695
Actual	5	1	8	11	2	2	3	2	4	6	5	

Success Probability for Human Errors. Another category of basic events in Fig. 2 includes all those in which human inadvertencies or misconduct play a critical role. For instance, people may fall for fraud, *fake service* (event (14)), act unsafely (*printout* of keys or insecure storage of the security *token* (events (1) and (2))), or insider and outsider attacks are conducted. Here, on the one hand, we can rely on recent insight in the field of software psychology (for an overview, see [17]) for the modeling process. On the other hand, internal statistics or estimates of the client need to provide additional information. As our model is a proof-of-concept and not tailored towards a specific client, we set these probabilities to 0.

Success Probabilities for Remaining Events. To quantify the success probability of the remaining basic events (combination of events (9) and (10) to *attack wallet*) in this category, we mostly rely on a survey among 990 Bitcoin users conducted in 2016 by [30] (to the best of our knowledge, there is no more recent user experience study also assessing security issues). It reports that 22.5% of users have already experienced Bitcoin loss until 2016. Most Bitcoin losses are due to user faults such as a formatted hard drive or lost keys, followed by hardware and software failures, which we do not consider here. However, about 18% of

---

[9] https://en.bitcoin.it/wiki/Common_Vulnerabilities_and_Exposures,   visited 13/12/2020.

the users who have lost Bitcoin claim that their loss is the result of hacks or malware.

Additionally, in our example, an attacker might get access to the wallet by retrieving the private key used for signing transaction messages. With it, they can pretend to be the legitimate user, controlling their credit without them even knowing. Similarly, quantum computing can be used to attack the *Elliptic Curve Digital Signature Algorithm (ECDSA)* (event (8)), i.e., the algorithm that is used to sign transactions in Bitcoin.

Digital signatures in Bitcoin are very vulnerable to quantum attacks since their security relies on discrete logarithms. With Shor's algorithm [41] discrete logarithms can be solved in polynomial runtime on quantum computers, providing an exponential speed-up in comparison to classical computers. In general, the probability that such an attack actually happens within a specific time frame cannot be quantified reliably, as the technological development cannot be forecast precisely enough. In our example, we assume a probability of 0 that within one year practical quantum computing attacks on ECDSA happen.

Overall Analysis of Success Probabilities. While we computed the success probabilities of single basic events using time series analysis by hand, we use the bottom-up analysis of the ADTool 2.0 [15] to compute the overall success probability.[10] In this way, we have predicted the overall success probability that Bitcoin are stolen from a user within the next year. For 2021, we predict a chance of 0.07 to be a victim of a successful attack. Assuming the success probability to be 0.07 in every year since 2010, the success probability for an attack within these 10 years is even $1 - (1 - 0.07)^{10} \approx 0.52$. So even the comparatively small success probabilities for each basic event per block creation reduce the long-term security of an investment in Bitcoin drastically.

Quantitative Validation. The predicted 7% chance of being affected by an attack in 2021 thus translates to the probability of not being a victim of a successful attack within one year being $(1 - 0.07)^1 = 0.93$ and within three years $(1 - 0.07)^3 = 0.80$. As discussed above, the only survey querying users for never being a victim of a successful attack is [30] with most users using Bitcoin between one and three years in 2015, reporting 0.95. While this number indicates slightly higher security than the predicted interval $[0.8, 0.93]$, this is to be expected since the number of hacks was lower back in 2013–2015. Unfortunately, we cannot give our "prediction" for the 2015 setting (to faithfully compare to [30]) since our prediction heavily depends on the number of active exchanges, which is only available for the current moment but not (publicly) archived for past years. For a more reliable validation, either the old statistics or a new survey would be needed.

---

[10] To unify the representation of the attack-defense trees, we replaced countermeasure relations used in the ADTool with the operators AND and NOT.

Discussion. Various assumptions are underlying the findings in this section. Firstly, we assumed the input data (in this case the probabilities, but the same might hold true for costs) to be perfect. However, exponential smoothing and other statistical methods in general do not yield perfect estimates. The best we can hope for is to quantify the uncertainty. In Sect. 8, we discuss how bounding uncertainty on attack trees might work and what kind of future work remains open.

5.2 Vendor Attacks: Deriving Different Courses of Known Attacks

In security analyses, discovering new attacks plays a crucial role. A widespread criticism of model-based analyses is that models cannot be used to detect completely unknown bugs or attacks (since one can only analyze what has been thought of previously). We believe that attack trees still have their merits here because a lot of the recent infamous hacks were not carried out with new zero-day exploits but rather with known attacks applied in different contexts. Attack trees might help here to detect known vulnerabilities in new systems. Additionally, attack trees can also be used to derive different courses of known attacks.

Description of Double Spending Attack. So-called *Double Spending Attack* perfectly illustrates our point: In the course of two years, several variations of double spending attacks have been found and published independently of each other, while in fact they are – from a modeling perspective – the same attack. We think ADT modeling and analysis can make a contribution here in the future by speeding up the discovery of attacks significantly. Since ADT are a formalism that can also be used by domain experts who are not formal methods experts this insight is all the more important.

Double Spending Attacks are aimed towards vendors and have the goal to obtain goods without paying for them, i.e., tricking the vendor into accepting an illegal transaction. In general, they follow the course of actions which is represented in Fig. 3. First, the attacker issues a transaction t_1 (event (1)), for instance, to a vendor, and this transaction is then confirmed by some miners (event (2)). Since it is confirmed, the vendor provides its service to the attacker (event (3)). The attacker issues a second transaction t_2, in which the same Bitcoin as in t_1 are spent (event (9)). The transaction is added to a new block to the blockchain. This either happens by some other miners accepting t_2, who include the transaction in their next block (events (5) and (6)), or by the attacker himself proposing a new block (event (7)). It is important that the transaction t_2 is confirmed after the vendor provides its service. The whole attack can only succeed if no block containing t_1 is added to the blockchain (event (8)). The vertex labeled with IFN[11] represents the overall goal.

We omitted a trigger relation from the vertex labeled with TR* to event (8) for a clearer graphical representation. To construct the model, we only used

---

[11] Notational sugar for an event that turns out true if its first input turns true and the second one is either attempted unsuccessfully or not attempted at all.

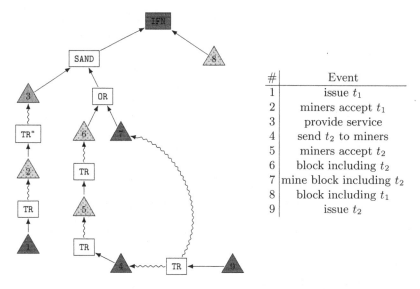

#	Event
1	issue t_1
2	miners accept t_1
3	provide service
4	send t_2 to miners
5	miners accept t_2
6	block including t_2
7	mine block including t_2
8	block including t_1
9	issue t_2

Fig. 3. A subtree representing double spending attacks, where the vendor corresponds to the defender and miners accepting transactions are purely time-driven.

the general description of how to perform a Double Spending Attacks from [10] and several variants on how to add blocks containing certain transactions to the blockchain.

In [10], several variants of double spending such as the *Finney Attack* and the *Brute-Force Attack* are discussed. The authors state that a (plain) Double Spending Attack occurs if two conflicting transactions (events (1) and first (9), then (4)) are issued in rapid succession, some miners accept t_1 and others accept t_2, but finally a block containing t_2 is added in the main blockchain. For the Finney attack, transaction t_1 is issued, but the attacker privately premines a block containing t_2, never plays event (4) and hopes to be able to issue it before a block containing t_1 is added to the blockchain. Finally, for a Brute-Force Attack the attacker privately mines on a larger blockchain fork, i.e., still issues transaction t_1 first, but would repetitively execute event (9) and (7) and does not play (4).

Qualitative Validation. In the model, the Double Spending Attack and the Finney attack are just different winning strategies (for the attacker), i.e., when using a timed approach like [4,13][12] to compute winning strategies, by modeling one of these attacks (together with basic Bitcoin functionality), we obtain the other attack by enumerating several winning strategies. Hence, strategy computation can be used to detect different variants of attacks.

---

[12] The approach in [4] is applicable to models containing TR since both operators rely on causal effects, a straight-forward restructuring is sufficient.

6   Current Limits of Modeling Economic Risks with ADT

To fully comprehend the economic risk when investing in Bitcoin, the analysis methodology needs to incorporate aspects which currently cannot be represented satisfactorily with ADT. In this section, we exemplarily discuss three such limitations. First, we discuss how satisfactorily detailed models cannot be sufficiently analyzed. Then, we show how real-world instabilities in exchange courses threaten the validity of our results. Finally, we present different interdependencies, which cannot be expressed in ADT so far.

Refinement of Events. Models can be made more precise by taking further information into account. For instance, the neutral events (2) and (5) in Fig. 3 can be replaced with a more detailed ADT considering how hardware acquisition and distribution of computing power influence the overall acceptance probability of new Bitcoin forks. For details and an example, see Appendix B. While more detailed models can be more accurate, they are also larger and, in particular, feature more basic events. Consequently, scalability issues may arise. In particular, the game-theoretic approach, which is needed to derive different winning strategies and thus different courses of attacks, currently does not scale well with the increasing number of basic events. As a cheaper alternative, the standard bottom-up analysis may be used to compute at least the sets of basic events leading to a successful attack, which might be sufficient in simpler contexts [24,27,33].

Financial Instability. A cryptocurrency-based monetary system is subject to the same forces of financial instability as the current fiat system. When analyzing the effects of the global financial crises on cryptocurrencies, one needs to differentiate between short-term and long-term effects. At the beginning of the financial crisis, people would try to sell their cryptocurrencies to, instead, buy as many tangible goods as possible. However, in the long term, the value of cryptocurrencies might increase due to the public's lost trust in both the banks and the government, and strive for decentralization; which is one of the very reasons why Bitcoin was invented [11].

Due to this instability, any approach to quantify the total loss in terms of any fiat currency (such as dollars) rather than Bitcoin (the number of Bitcoin lost due to an attack is dependent on the attack, but not the value of Bitcoin) needs to be repeatedly monitored. Additionally, changes in the exchange rate of Bitcoin might change the success probability of some attack steps such as bribing miners or bugs if their execution poses the threat of losing the block reward. Hence, the instability leads to a situation in which real-world events should (automatically) trigger a rerun of the analysis, which has not been studied so far to the best of our knowledge.

Malicious Network Providers. Having access to all technical parts of a network, the network provider can control the communication channels and thus deprive certain users from participating in the blockchain by excluding them from the communication with other users. Thus, the provider might effectively deny users access to necessary information. Such an intervention can facilitate 51%-attacks (see Appendix B) if honest nodes are excluded from the blockchain (since a lower number of malicious nodes is sufficient to form a majority).

To counter this attack, it is necessary to choose network providers wisely. However, the definition of a wise choice itself might be a complex economic decision (trade-off between costs for a suitable network provider vs. projected long-term loss through this attack). Hence, these two events have an *interdependency*, which attack trees are not capable of representing.

7   Future Challenges

In this section, we discuss what kind of future work remains open to build a complete methodology around attack trees and their extensions incorporating specific domain knowledge.

Overarching Notation for a Holistic Security Analysis. Model-based security analyses allow taking security into account right from the beginning and analysis results can be used to secure the structure of the system. For DLT, checking the design of new applications against all known vulnerabilities in this area can improve their security. To this end, an overarching notation like attack trees can facilitate analysis and verification of security-critical systems by providing a domain-independent, extensible model which can be used to verify the system design. In Sect. 4, we combined the results of papers, each addressing one specific security issue and text-based reviews giving an overview on the most recent developments into just a few models. For us, these models served as an overarching notation which allows to combine the results of these previous approaches into one overall result. However, we have identified the following points that need to be addressed first to make the notation really convenient. Manual construction of models can be tedious and error-prone, which is already stated in [16]. We believe that automated generation of attack trees needs to tackle *existing* sources such as *common vulnerability and exposure (CVE) databases, natural-language security guidelines* or *protocol specifications*. Any kind of learning some other sort of models – as suggested in [16] – just defers the workload for the construction of the model.

Compositional and Interdependent Analysis of Attack Trees. Compositional and incremental attack tree analyses need to be extended, allowing us, for instance, to carry forward results if models slightly change. This extends the idea of refinement-aware models of [16] to the analysis side (rather than to the generation side only). Compositional semantics are already quite frequent [1,2,22,31]. However, to the best of our knowledge, there is no work on incremental attack tree analysis taking the results of previous analyses on similar attack trees into account. Additionally, we identified event interdependencies beyond clear causal relations such as trigger and reset, which cannot be represented satisfactorily in most attack trees or their extensions. In more detail, these relations require to model that trade-off decisions at one vertex in the tree *influence* trade-off decision at another vertex and vise-versa. We discussed an example of these interdependencies in Sect. 6.

Building upon iterative and incremental attack tree analysis, there is also the need for automatic recomputations and changes to quantitative values triggered by outside events.

Bounding Uncertainty. In practice, there can be various sources of uncertainty in attack tree models. In quantitative approaches, quantitative inputs are often used to model one kind of uncertainty. While information on the cost, block time, exchange courses and attacks are closely tracked for Bitcoin and other cryptocurrencies, the success probabilities and costs we presented in Subsect. 5.1 are only estimates. Hence, there is a second kind of uncertainty. The best we can hope for is to quantify the uncertainty of the quantitative inputs. The authors of [16] mention that data validation is important in quantitative analysis. We see a need for more than just data validation and a need for bounding uncertainty in qualitative analyses. We can enhance quantitative analysis, for instance, by using probably approximately correct data or by using fuzzy numbers as in fault trees [38] to aggregate conflicting estimates of quantitative data. However, there are only a few approaches dealing with uncertainty [7,36,37] in attack trees. None of these methods can give formal guarantees on the degree of uncertainty and deal with uncertain inputs. To make attack trees and other risk analysis methods more amenable for practice, bounding uncertainty in attack tree analysis needs to be addressed further.

Even if there are no quantities, uncertainty may play a role, for instance, if the precise structure of the tree or the effect of successful attack steps are unknown. In fault trees, there has been work done on noisy gates [5] capturing these uncertainties. However, to the best of our knowledge, there is no comparable work for attack trees. If domain (but non-security) experts (for Bitcoin, for instance, traders) need to contribute to the attack tree to capture the complete security-critical system, noisy gates or trees might be important to systematically include expert knowledge from non-security experts.

Detailed Attack Statistics. To bound uncertainty, a clear tracking of potential attack steps and of successful attacks (at best, in a blockwise fashion) is necessary, too. Our derivations, for instance, of the success probability for attacks on exchanges in Subsect. 5.1 suffered from such a lack of well-documented attacks.

Human Comprehensibility. Human interactions with computer systems play a crucial role in security because insider attacks or human mistakes (like choosing weak passwords) always represent a security threat. To effectively communicate boundary conditions for the security of the system, attack trees might serve as one easily understandable human-readable notation. To verify this hypothesis, user studies are necessary. These studies might also reveal further ideas for improvements on readability. [16] discusses these aspects in detail. An additional challenge (not discussed in [16]) for any security methodology using attack trees is how to deal with assumptions, which need to be met for the analysis to be valid. It is not only unclear how assumptions can be systematically derived but also how to represent them understandably. The first issue arises since practitioners need to become aware of these assumptions in the first place. Hence, we also need user studies determining a good process to derive and examine understandable representations.

8   Conclusion

In this paper, we provided a proof-of-concept model for the security analysis of DLT using attack-(defense) trees. We demonstrated how realistic success probabilities for basic attacks can be derived from available statistics using time series analysis. Additionally, we demonstrated how to derive unknown courses of known attacks using strategy synthesis. While ADT represent attacks sufficiently in general, challenges arise for practical holistic security analyses: Firstly, automated generation of attack-defense trees from DLT protocols is necessary to facilitate the analysis of further DLT applications. Additionally, attack statistics need to be more detailed for reliable prediction. Secondly, user studies need to be conducted to find out how to make attack trees even more accessible for domain (but non-security) experts. Additionally, reliable surveys and user studies need to be done to obtain quantitative information on common user mistakes. These results will be applicable to other attack-defense tree models. Finally, more research on bounding the uncertainty in attack-defense tree analysis needs to be done.

Acknowledgments. This research was funded in part by the Studienstiftung des deutschen Volkes project "Formal methods for analysis of attack-defence diagrams", the Software Campus project "ProSec" and the German Research Foundation (DFG) project KR 4890/2-1 "Statistical Unbounded Verification".

A   Eclipse Attacks

Eclipse Attacks are a form of attack studied in [21]. A malicious party monopolizes all incoming and outgoing connections of a single node, which isolates the node from the rest of the network. Since the Bitcoin blockchain is saved in a decentralised way on many different nodes and needs exchange to become a valid Bitcoin view, the attacker can now let the victim believe in other Bitcoin forks, which are not generally agreed on or even use the victim's computing power for its own malicious behaviour. The authors of [21] estimate the likelihood of such an attack. *Sybil Attack* describes the process, in which an attacker creates fake identities who appear to be unique users to all other instances in the network, but in fact are controlled by a *single* malicious node with enough computing power. The malicious user can then influence democratic decisions within the network through additional voting power. This is *not* a problem for Bitcoin. However, these *fake* or *sybil nodes* may disconnect honest users from the network and thus, facilitate double spending attacks. *Routing Attacks* are another form of attacks performed on the network level. They are mainly based on an attacker intercepting with route advertisement on the network itself. Routing attacks also aim at isolating certain nodes from the network.

B   Detailed Description of 51% Attacks

In this section, we give a detailed ADT for the *51% Attack*, which refers to a scenario in which the attacker controls more than 50% of the network's overall hashing rate. This power can be used to delay confirmation of specific transactions on purpose and to facilitate double spending. In Fig. 4, we depict one possible way to model a 51% attack. We use event (1) due as a replacement for several events corresponding to bribing the biggest mining pools. To bribe a miner, the bribe must be higher than the expected block reward and transaction reward within the time frame.

Additionally, miners group up in pools to combine their hash power and thereby reduce the volatility of their income in exchange for a small fee paid to the pool manager. This behavior counteracts the concept of decentralization Bitcoin is founded on and increases its vulnerability to attacks such as DoS attacks and 51% attacks (event (3) in Fig. 4). About 80% of all blocks are mined by Chinese miner pools[13] and the biggest mining pool BTC.com accomplishes 15% of Bitcoin blocks[14]. This concentration of miners renders Bitcoin susceptible to Chinese regulation and energy policy. Power outages (event (4)) and the loss of the internet (event (5)) connection thus facilitate 51% attacks (if many miners are out of service, an attacker might suddenly possess more than 50% of the overall computing power across all active miners). Depending on the downtime, an attacker can more easily issue double-spending attacks by confirming his own malicious transactions. Since about 80% of the overall computing power is hold by Chinese miners, we have overestimated the increase in computing power by taking the computer power of the largest mining pools outside of China if all Chinese mining pools cannot contribute to the Bitcoin blockchain anymore. This is a clear overestimate since most of the mining pools have servers and contributors outside of China.

Chip Miners buy their chips based on two major criteria: *the Hashrate* and *power consumption* since the first determines how often miners might find a nonce while the other determines the money computing costs. Miners buy whatever is available on the market and based on the best performance regarding those two criteria. A possibility is that big chip companies, e.g. Asic, already are in possession of better chips than the chips they are currently selling. If companies held back inventions and use those for mining, they could control the network and issue a 51% attack (event (2)). However, companies are unlikely to conduct this procedure as they, likely, earn high revenues by selling their products.

---

[13] https://www.buyBitcoinworldwide.com/mining/pools/, visited 17/04/2019.

[14] https://www.blockchain.com/en/pools?timespan=4days, visited 17/04/2019.

We use two cost variables – one to accumulate the money an attacker needs to spend for a successful attack and one to accumulate the computing power he has acquired so far. Hence, we label basic events not only with costs, but also with a second cost resource corresponding to the percentage of computing power the attacker gains. Various defender's and random events may also influence this variable – such as power outages or failures on the internet connection of large mining pools, which we discuss further down. Advances in quantum computing change the likelihood of 51% attacks since the *Grover Algorithm* [44] provides a quadratic speed-up in comparison to classical computers in inverting cryptographic hash functions by performing a faster search through unsorted lists. Hence, nonces can be found more efficiently.

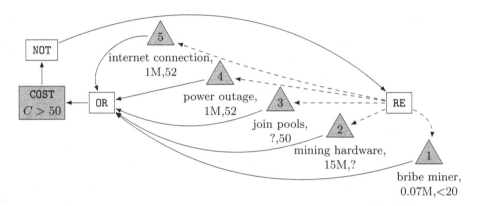

Fig. 4. A subtree depicting how to acquire more than 50% of the overall network computing power, where each vertex is labeled with its monetary cost as well as the fraction of computing power C acquired. We mark values that we cannot reliably estimate, with a question mark.

References

1. André, É., Lime, D., Ramparison, M., Stoelinga, M.: Parametric analyses of attack-fault trees. In: 2019 19th International Conference on Application of Concurrency to System Design (ACSD), pp. 33–42. IEEE (2019)
2. Arnold, F., Hermanns, H., Pulungan, R., Stoelinga, M.: Time-dependent analysis of attacks. In: Abadi, M., Kremer, S. (eds.) POST 2014. LNCS, vol. 8414, pp. 285–305. Springer, Heidelberg (2014). https://doi.org/10.1007/978-3-642-54792-8_16
3. Aslanyan, Z., Nielson, F.: Model checking exact cost for attack scenarios. In: Maffei, M., Ryan, M. (eds.) POST 2017. LNCS, vol. 10204, pp. 210–231. Springer, Heidelberg (2017). https://doi.org/10.1007/978-3-662-54455-6_10
4. Aslanyan, Z., Nielson, F., Parker, D.: Quantitative verification and synthesis of attack-defence scenarios. In: CSF, pp. 105–119 (2016). https://doi.org/10.1109/CSF.2016.15

5. Bobbio, A., Portinale, L., Minichino, M., Ciancamerla, E.: Improving the analysis of dependable systems by mapping fault trees into Bayesian networks. Reliab. Eng. Syst. Saf. **71**(3), 249–260 (2001)
6. Bossuat, A., Kordy, B.: Evil twins: handling repetitions in attack–defense trees. In: Liu, P., Mauw, S., Stølen, K. (eds.) GraMSec 2017. LNCS, vol. 10744, pp. 17–37. Springer, Cham (2018). https://doi.org/10.1007/978-3-319-74860-3_2
7. Buoni, A., Fedrizzi, M., Mezei, J.: A Delphi-based approach to fraud detection using attack trees and fuzzy numbers. In: Proceeding of the IASK International Conferences, pp. 21–28 (2010)
8. Chatterjee, K., Goharshady, A.K., Ibsen-Jensen, R., Velner, Y.: Ergodic mean-payoff games for the analysis of attacks in crypto-currencies. arXiv preprint arXiv:1806.03108 (2018)
9. Chatterjee, K., Goharshady, A.K., Velner, Y.: Quantitative analysis of smart contracts. In: Ahmed, A. (ed.) ESOP 2018. LNCS, vol. 10801, pp. 739–767. Springer, Cham (2018). https://doi.org/10.1007/978-3-319-89884-1_26
10. Conti, M., Kumar, E.S., Lal, C., Ruj, S.: A survey on security and privacy issues of bitcoin. Commun. Surv. Tutor. **20**(4), 3416–3452 (2018)
11. Danielsson, J.: Cryptocurrencies: policy, economics and fairness. Systemic Risk Centre Discussion Paper 86 (2018)
12. Edge, K.S., Raines, R.A., Grimaila, M.R., Baldwin, R.O., Bennington, R.W., Reuter, C.E.: The use of attack and protection trees to analyze security for an online banking system. In: Systems Science (HICSS), p. 144 (2007). https://doi.org/10.1109/HICSS.2007.558
13. Eisentraut, J., Křetínský, J.: Expected cost analysis of attack-defense trees. In: Parker, D., Wolf, V. (eds.) QEST 2019. LNCS, vol. 11785, pp. 203–221. Springer, Cham (2019). https://doi.org/10.1007/978-3-030-30281-8_12
14. Fraile, M., Ford, M., Gadyatskaya, O., Kumar, R., Stoelinga, M., Trujillo-Rasua, R.: Using attack-defense trees to analyze threats and countermeasures in an ATM: a case study. In: Horkoff, J., Jeusfeld, M.A., Persson, A. (eds.) PoEM 2016. LNBIP, vol. 267, pp. 326–334. Springer, Cham (2016). https://doi.org/10.1007/978-3-319-48393-1_24
15. Gadyatskaya, O., Jhawar, R., Kordy, P., Lounis, K., Mauw, S., Trujillo-Rasua, R.: Attack trees for practical security assessment: ranking of attack scenarios with ADTool 2.0. In: Agha, G., Van Houdt, B. (eds.) QEST 2016. LNCS, vol. 9826, pp. 159–162. Springer, Cham (2016). https://doi.org/10.1007/978-3-319-43425-4_10. http://dx.doi.org/10.1007/978-3-319-43425-4_10
16. Gadyatskaya, O., Trujillo-Rasua, R.: New directions in attack tree research: catching up with industrial needs. In: Liu, P., Mauw, S., Stølen, K. (eds.) GraMSec 2017. LNCS, vol. 10744, pp. 115–126. Springer, Cham (2018). https://doi.org/10.1007/978-3-319-74860-3_9
17. Gheyas, I.A., Abdallah, A.E.: Detection and prediction of insider threats to cyber security: a systematic literature review and meta-analysis. Big Data Anal. **1**(1), 6 (2016). https://doi.org/10.1186/s41044-016-0006-0
18. Grishchenko, I., Maffei, M., Schneidewind, C.: Foundations and tools for the static analysis of ethereum smart contracts. In: Chockler, H., Weissenbacher, G. (eds.) CAV 2018. LNCS, vol. 10981, pp. 51–78. Springer, Cham (2018). https://doi.org/10.1007/978-3-319-96145-3_4
19. Gulhane, A., et al.: Security, privacy and safety risk assessment for virtual reality learning environment applications. In: Consumer Communications Networking Conference (CCNC), pp. 1–9, January 2019. https://doi.org/10.1109/CCNC.2019.8651847

20. Hamilton, J.D.: Time Series Analysis, vol. 2. Princeton University Press, Princeton (1994)
21. Heilman, E., Kendler, A., Zohar, A., Goldberg, S.: Eclipse attacks on bitcoin's peer-to-peer network. In: 24th USENIX Security Symposium (USENIX Security 15), pp. 129–144 (2015)
22. Hermanns, H., Krämer, J., Krčál, J., Stoelinga, M.: The value of attack-defence diagrams. In: Piessens, F., Viganò, L. (eds.) POST 2016. LNCS, vol. 9635, pp. 163–185. Springer, Heidelberg (2016). https://doi.org/10.1007/978-3-662-49635-0_9. http://dx.doi.org/10.1007/978-3-662-49635-0_9
23. Hong, J.B., Kim, D.S., Chung, C.J., Huang, D.: A survey on the usability and practical applications of graphical security models. Comput. Sci. Rev. **26**, 1–16 (2017)
24. Jhawar, R., Kordy, B., Mauw, S., Radomirović, S., Trujillo-Rasua, R.: Attack trees with sequential conjunction. In: Federrath, H., Gollmann, D. (eds.) SEC 2015. IAICT, vol. 455, pp. 339–353. Springer, Cham (2015). https://doi.org/10.1007/978-3-319-18467-8_23
25. Joshi, A.P., Han, M., Wang, Y.: A survey on security and privacy issues of blockchain technology. Math. Found. Comput. **1**(2), 121–147 (2018)
26. Karray, K., Danger, J.-L., Guilley, S., Abdelaziz Elaabid, M.: Attack tree construction and its application to the connected vehicle. In: Koç, Ç.K. (ed.) Cyber-Physical Systems Security, pp. 175–190. Springer, Cham (2018). https://doi.org/10.1007/978-3-319-98935-8_9
27. Kordy, B., Mauw, S., Radomirović, S., Schweitzer, P.: Foundations of attack–defense trees. In: Degano, P., Etalle, S., Guttman, J. (eds.) FAST 2010. LNCS, vol. 6561, pp. 80–95. Springer, Heidelberg (2011). https://doi.org/10.1007/978-3-642-19751-2_6 http://dl.acm.org/citation.cfm?id=1964555.1964561
28. Kordy, B., Piètre-Cambacédès, L., Schweitzer, P.: Dag-based attack and defense modeling: don't miss the forest for the attack trees. CoRR abs/1303.7397 (2013). http://arxiv.org/abs/1303.7397
29. Kordy, B., Wideł, W.: On quantitative analysis of attack–defense trees with repeated labels. In: Bauer, L., Küsters, R. (eds.) POST 2018. LNCS, vol. 10804, pp. 325–346. Springer, Cham (2018). https://doi.org/10.1007/978-3-319-89722-6_14
30. Krombholz, K., Judmayer, A., Gusenbauer, M., Weippl, E.: The other side of the coin: user experiences with bitcoin security and privacy. In: Grossklags, J., Preneel, B. (eds.) FC 2016. LNCS, vol. 9603, pp. 555–580. Springer, Heidelberg (2017). https://doi.org/10.1007/978-3-662-54970-4_33
31. Kumar, R., Stoelinga, M.: Quantitative security and safety analysis with attack-fault trees. In: HASE, pp. 25–32 (2017). https://doi.org/10.1109/HASE.2017.12
32. Lin, I.C., Liao, T.C.: A survey of blockchain security issues and challenges. IJ Netw. Secur. **19**(5), 653–659 (2017)
33. Mauw, S., Oostdijk, M.: Foundations of attack trees. In: Won, D.H., Kim, S. (eds.) ICISC 2005. LNCS, vol. 3935, pp. 186–198. Springer, Heidelberg (2006). https://doi.org/10.1007/11734727_17. http://dx.doi.org/10.1007/11734727_17
34. McQueen, M.A., Boyer, W.F., Flynn, M.A., Beitel, G.A.: Quantitative cyber risk reduction estimation methodology for a small SCADA control system. In: Conference on System Sciences (HICSS), HICSS 2006, Washington, DC, USA, p. 226. IEEE Computer Society (2006). https://doi.org/10.1109/HICSS.2006.405. http://dx.doi.org/10.1109/HICSS.2006.405
35. Mediouni, B.L., Nouri, A., Bozga, M., Legay, A., Bensalem, S.: Mitigating security risks through attack strategies exploration. In: Margaria, T., Steffen, B. (eds.)

ISoLA 2018. LNCS, vol. 11245, pp. 392–413. Springer, Cham (2018). https://doi. org/10.1007/978-3-030-03421-4_25

36. Mezei, A.B., Mario Fedrizzi, J.: Combining attack trees and fuzzy numbers in a multi-agent approach to fraud detection. Int. J. Electron. Bus. **9**(3), 186–202 (2011)

37. Pekergin, N., Tan, S., Fourneau, J.-M.: Quantitative attack tree analysis: stochastic bounds and numerical analysis. In: Kordy, B., Ekstedt, M., Kim, D.S. (eds.) GraMSec 2016. LNCS, vol. 9987, pp. 119–133. Springer, Cham (2016). https://doi. org/10.1007/978-3-319-46263-9_8

38. Ruijters, E., Stoelinga, M.: Fault tree analysis: a survey of the state-of-the-art in modeling, analysis and tools. Comput. Sci. Rev. **15**, 29–62 (2015)

39. Salter, C., Saydjari, O.S., Schneier, B., Wallner, J.: Toward a secure system engineering methodology. In: New Security Paradigms (NSPW), New York, NY, USA, pp. 2–10. ACM (1998). https://doi.org/10.1145/310889.310900. http://doi.acm. org/10.1145/310889.310900

40. Sapirshtein, A., Sompolinsky, Y., Zohar, A.: Optimal selfish mining strategies in bitcoin. In: Grossklags, J., Preneel, B. (eds.) FC 2016. LNCS, vol. 9603, pp. 515–532. Springer, Heidelberg (2017). https://doi.org/10.1007/978-3-662-54970-4_30

41. Shor, P.W.: Polynomial-time algorithms for prime factorization and discrete logarithms on a quantum computer. SIAM Rev. **41**(2), 303–332 (1999)

42. Sompolinsky, Y., Zohar, A.: Bitcoin's security model revisited. arXiv preprint arXiv:1605.09193 (2016)

43. Wideł, W., Audinot, M., Fila, B., Pinchinat, S.: Beyond 2014: formal methods for attack tree-based security modeling. ACM Comput. Surv. **2**(4), 75:1–75:36 (2019). https://doi.org/10.1145/3331524. http://doi.acm.org/10.1145/3331524

44. Zalka, C.: Grover's quantum searching algorithm is optimal. Phys. Rev. A **60**, 2746–2751 (1999). https://doi.org/10.1103/PhysRevA.60.2746. https://link.aps.org/doi/ 10.1103/PhysRevA.60.2746

Compositional Analysis of Protocol Equivalence in the Applied π-Calculus Using Quasi-open Bisimilarity

Ross Horne⬛, Sjouke Mauw⬛, and Semen Yurkov⁽⊠⁾⬛

Department of Computer Science, University of Luxembourg,
Esch-sur-Alzette, Luxembourg
semen.yurkov@uni.lu

Abstract. This paper shows that quasi-open bisimilarity is the *coarsest bisimilarity congruence* for the applied π-calculus. Furthermore, we show that this equivalence is suited to security and privacy problems expressed as an equivalence problem in the following senses: (1) being a bisimilarity is a safe choice since it does not miss attacks based on rich strategies; (2) being a congruence it enables a compositional approach to proving certain equivalence problems such as unlinkability; and (3) being the coarsest such bisimilarity congruence it can establish proofs of some privacy properties where finer equivalences fail to do so.

Keywords: Cryptographic calculi · Bisimilarity · Security · Privacy · Compositionality

1 Introduction

The applied π-calculus [2,5] is a generalisation and extension of the π-calculus [37] useful for verifying security and privacy properties of cryptographic protocols. Some security and privacy properties may be expressed as an equivalence problem, for instance by comparing the actual protocol to an idealised specification that trivially satisfies the desired property [8,23,24,28,33]. This paper employs good-practice principles for designing process equivalences for cryptographic calculi. We define two equivalences: one based on testing and another based on labelled transitions. The two equivalences are proven to coincide; thereby establishing that observables represented by the labels on transitions capture all relevant information about all testing contexts. This paradigm is suited to cryptographic calculi, where the testing environment contains attackers that can be inserted into a network without direct access to key material and other secrets, yet may violate security and privacy requirements of a protocol. By using an equivalence based on labelled transitions for cryptographic calculi we learn that we do not need to know all details of such malicious agents, and that to characterise such attackers it is sufficient to look only at the input and output actions of honest agents

---

S. Yurkov is supported by the Luxembourg National Research Fund through grant PRIDE15/10621687/SPsquared.

A. Cerone and P. C. Ölveczky (Eds.): ICTAC 2021, LNCS 12819, pp. 235–255, 2021.
https://doi.org/10.1007/978-3-030-85315-0_14

modelled in the specification of the protocol. Considering only the inputs and outputs of honest agents makes the formulation of process equivalence problems in terms of labelled transitions easier to check, compared to checking all malicious agents in full.

Amongst the most powerful testing equivalences proposed over the years is *open barbed bisimilarity* [41], and its equivalent mild simplification *saturated bisimilarity* [13], which were inspired by *dynamic bisimilarity* [38]. These testing equivalences consider all contexts at every execution step, hence, by definition, we obtain a congruence – an equivalence relation preserved in all contexts. Considering all contexts at every execution step reflects that new knowledge about the environment may be discovered during execution. Such testing equivalences have been used to inform the design of labelled transition systems and their corresponding notions of labelled equivalence for a range of process calculi including the π-calculus, which led to the emergence of *quasi-open bisimilarity* [29,41] – the notion of labelled bisimilarity that coincides with open barbed bisimilarity for the π-calculus.

In this work, we make use of the testing regime offered by open barbed bisimilarity to design a labelled transition system and notion of quasi-open bisimilarity for the applied π-calculus. We argue here that employing a bisimilarity that coincides with the testing regime offered by open barbed bisimilarity, is a win-win choice for the applied π-calculus: not only is such an equivalence well-designed according to good-practice process-design principles; but also it is useful for verifying security and privacy properties. We should always be inclined to select an equivalence that is a congruence over one that is not a congruence without a compelling reason not to; and, in the setting of the applied π-calculus, having a congruence relation opens up new proof techniques, such as the ability to reason about equivalence problems compositionally.

It is possible to design other congruence relations for the applied π-calculus, such as the more famous open bisimilarity [28,40]. What we found to be fascinating about quasi-open bisimilarity is that, although, in order to be both a congruence relation and a bisimilarity relation, it is necessary that we obtain a finer equivalence compared to the more common early bisimilarity [5] that is not a congruence, the notion of equivalence is not too fine for security and privacy problems. Moving from early bisimilarity to quasi-open bisimilarity for security and privacy problems that can be formulated as equivalence problems, such as unlinkability, strong secrecy (non-interference), voter privacy, anonymity, does not appear to invalidate established properties. While it is impossible to check and anticipate all possible security and privacy problems that can be formulated as an equivalence problem in the applied π-calculus, there is the following compelling reason why we are confident in making this claim. Despite being finer than early bisimilarity, quasi-open bisimilarity still treats classically the important content of security and privacy problems, which is the treatment of private information such as nonces and keys. In contrast, this is not the case for the finer open bisimilarity, since we, in this paper, will demonstrate a representative example of a scenario in which open bisimilarity discovers a spurious attack, whereas quasi-open bisimilarity discovers the expected proof. Indeed, we are yet to encounter a disadvantage of using open barbed bisimilarity rather than observational equivalence for privacy problems.

Outline of Paper. Section 2 provides motivation and explains minimal examples illustrating why quasi-open bisimilarity is an objective choice of bisimilarity congruence.

The rest of the paper develops a theory of quasi-open bisimilarity for the applied π-calculus. Section 3 introduces *open barbed bisimilarity*, which is, by definition, the greatest bisimilarity congruence (we focus on the strong variant). Section 4 introduces an open variant of labelled bisimilarity called *quasi-open bisimilarity* and proves that it coincides with open barbed bisimilarity. A technical report provides further details [27].

2 Motivating Quasi-open Bisimilarity for the Applied π-Calculus

In the paper, we target properties expressed as a process equivalence. Whether a system satisfies such properties depends not only on the system but also on the choice of equivalence relation, and this choice in fact contributes to the attacker model [28]. In this motivating section, we present the advantages of employing the coarsest bisimilarity congruence and present motivating examples to justify our proposal.

2.1 A Finer Equivalence Discovers Spurious Attacks

Below we provide an example of a property expressed as an equivalence and show that a finer relation can fail to reflect a real attack on the system. Our running example is a cut-down variant of a classic private server example [3,22]. We express the privacy property as an equivalence between the "real" and the "ideal" behaviours.

Consider a server *Server A* that responds with an encrypted message only when it receives a particular public key. Otherwise, it responds with a nonce, indistinguishable from a ciphertext. We assume an attacker knows public key $\mathrm{pk}(k)$ but does not know private key k or nonce r.

Server A can be modelled formally in the applied π-calculus as follows.

$$Server\,A:\quad \nu k.\overline{s}\langle\mathrm{pk}(k)\rangle.!\,\nu a.\overline{c}\langle a\rangle.a(x).\nu r.$$
$$\mathrm{if}\,x = \mathrm{pk}(k)\,\mathrm{then}\,\overline{a}\langle\mathrm{aenc}(\langle m,r\rangle,\mathrm{pk}(k))\rangle\,\mathrm{else}\,\overline{a}\langle r\rangle$$

In *Server A*, the prefix $\nu k.\overline{s}\langle\mathrm{pk}(k)\rangle$ stands for announcing a public key. The prefix $!\,\nu a.\overline{c}\langle a\rangle.a(x).\nu r$ represents the start of an unbounded number of sessions on a fresh channel a where, in each session, an input is received and a nonce r is freshly generated. In each session, one of the following decisions is made, based on the input received. If an input is a public key output previously, *Server A* responds with a message-nonce pair encrypted with the public key $\overline{a}\langle\mathrm{aenc}(\langle m,r\rangle,\mathrm{pk}(k))\rangle$. Otherwise, *Server A* sends a dummy random message r indistinguishable from a random cyphertext.

Note that in this minimal formulation of the problem, we refrain from modelling the clients (possibly knowing key k). Of course, the fact that clients transmit their public keys in plaintext may introduce further privacy concerns, which we do not model in this minimal illustration.

We approach the problem of proving that the privacy of the owner of secret key k is preserved by providing a reference specification. The reference specification models how the private server should ideally behave from the perspective of an attacker. The specification, defined as *Server B* below, differs from *Server A* in that it transmits a nonce regardless of the message received.

$$Server\,B:\quad \nu k.\overline{s}\langle\mathrm{pk}(k)\rangle.!\,\nu a.\overline{c}\langle a\rangle.a(x).\nu r.\overline{a}\langle r\rangle$$

Server A and *Server B* are indistinguishable to an external observer – the attacker. An attacker cannot learn that *Server A* responds in a special way to input $\mathrm{pk}(k)$. The idea is that an attacker without private key k cannot learn that *Server A* serves some data m to the owner of k. Thus the privacy of the intended recipient of the data is preserved.

We can verify this privacy property by showing *Server A* and *Server B* are bisimilar. The point is that there is a warning: we must take care about which bisimilarity we employ. If we employ the famous *open bisimilarity* (which also is a congruence), the processes are **not** equivalent.

Using a suitable labelled transition system [28], *Server A* can reach the following state, at which point open bisimilarity still allows x (a free variable representing an input) to be instantiated with the message bound to u (i.e., $\mathrm{pk}(k)$), representing a previously output message.

$$\nu k, a_1, r_1.\left(\ \left\{{}^{\mathrm{pk}(k),a_1}/_{u,v}\right\}\ |\ \text{if } x = \mathrm{pk}(k) \text{ then } \overline{a_1}\langle\mathrm{aenc}(\langle m, r_1\rangle, \mathrm{pk}(k))\rangle \text{ else } \overline{a_1}\langle r_1\rangle\right.$$
$$|\ !\nu a.\overline{a}\langle a\rangle.a(x).\nu r.$$
$$\left.\text{if } x = \mathrm{pk}(k) \text{ then } \overline{a}\langle\mathrm{aenc}(\langle m, r\rangle, \mathrm{pk}(k))\rangle \text{ else } \overline{a}\langle r\rangle\ \right)$$

Thus, we have not yet committed to $x = \mathrm{pk}(k)$ or $x \neq \mathrm{pk}(k)$, and hence we cannot proceed until we provide more information about x. Therefore the guard in the *if-then-else* statement above **cannot yet** be resolved; but *Server B* cannot reach an equivalent state, since it can only reach a state which is **immediately ready** to perform an action regardless of whether $x = \mathrm{pk}(k)$ or $x \neq \mathrm{pk}(k)$. Note we do not assume $x = \mathrm{pk}(k) \vee x \neq \mathrm{pk}(k)$ holds, which would be an instance of the law of excluded middle; hence we are in an intuitionistic setting [6,7]. The presented distinguishing strategy, does not correspond to a real attack on the privacy of *Server A*; hence open bisimilarity **is not sufficiently coarse** to verify this privacy property.

Fortunately, we will see in this paper that *quasi-open bisimilarity* addresses the above limitation of open bisimilarity. Quasi-open bisimilarity is also intuitionistic [29]. It handles open terms (with free variables) intuitionistically; but handles private messages that an attacker cannot interfere with more subtly. Private information, such as $\mathrm{pk}(k)$ (bound to u in the above state), can only be received eagerly by an input action; the effect being that messages such as $\mathrm{pk}(k)$ in the above example are treated classically. Thereby, after receiving the input either $x = \mathrm{pk}(k)$ or $x \neq \mathrm{pk}(k)$ holds; from which we establish that *Server A* and *Server B* are indeed *quasi-open bisimilar*.

The example above, elaborated on in the body of the paper, is selected as a minimal explanation for why quasi-open bisimilarity defines an appropriate attacker model.

A Still More Sophisticated Argument. Those that are not yet satisfied with the above illustration, may question whether the limitation of open bisimilarity is due to a particular lifting of open bisimilarity to the applied π-calculus. This is not the case. There are several possible definitions of open bisimilarity for the applied π-calculus that are, firstly, conservative with respect to the original definition of open bisimilarity for the π-calculus [40] and, secondly, also a congruence relation. However, none of them would be able to prove the privacy property illustrated above. The problem lies with mismatch (the else branches in the above example), which is exactly the problem isolated and explored in related work [29].

We illustrate the argument, by drawing attention to two possible ways of conservatively extending open bisimilarity to the applied π-calculus (which features mismatch or else branches). One approach is to extend the histories in the past (see Sect. 5 [29]); while another is to add explicit inequality constraints [28]. Each of these approaches provide different expressive power, as illustrated by the following pair of processes.

$$Server\ C \triangleq \nu k.\nu l.\overline{s}\langle\mathrm{pk}(k)\rangle.\overline{s}\langle\mathrm{pk}(l)\rangle.P(k) \quad v.s. \quad Server\ D \triangleq \nu k.\nu l.\overline{s}\langle\mathrm{pk}(k)\rangle.\overline{s}\langle\mathrm{pk}(l)\rangle.P(l)$$

where $P(t) \triangleq \nu a.\overline{a}\langle a\rangle.a(x).\nu r.\mathtt{if}\ x = \mathrm{pk}(t)\ \mathtt{then}\ \overline{a}\langle\mathtt{aenc}(\langle m, r\rangle, \mathrm{pk}(t))\rangle\ \mathtt{else}\ \overline{a}\langle r\rangle$

When we specify that $Server\ C$ and $Server\ D$ should be equivalent, we specify that two servers that respond to different keys (the first or second output) should be indistinguishable. This differs from our previous private server example, where, recall, the specification is stipulated in terms of another private server, $Server\ B$, that has no information to leak. Surprisingly, the above processes are equivalent under the notion of open bisimilarity obtained by extending histories [29], yet are not equivalent under the notion of open bisimilarity with inequality constraints [28]. Furthermore, processes $Server\ A$ and $Server\ B$ from the previous sections are not equivalent under either of the notions of open bisimilarity described, and hence neither extension of open bisimilarity is sufficiently coarse to verify that privacy property.

The fundamental insight is that open bisimilarity is heavily tied to the way it symbolically represents constraints, which gives rise to equivalences that differ for technical reasons which have little to do with the semantics of protocols. Quasi-open bisimilarity however is canonical, as we prove in this work via a completeness result that is independent of any internal constraint system. Finally, quasi-open bisimilarity supports proofs of privacy properties that we expect to hold, as illustrated by the equivalence of $Server\ A$ and $Server\ B$ (Sect. 4.2), making it a robust choice that enables compositional reasoning without introducing spurious attacks.

2.2 Too Coarse an Equivalence Misses Real Attacks

Above we have seen an example when a finer property leads to a spurious attack. The situation is mirrored, however, if we attempt to formulate a property using too coarse equivalence: real attacks may be missed. Recent work [26, 28], comprehensively explains an attack on ePassports that allows unauthorised observers to track movements of the holder. This attack was overlooked by trace equivalence, which is strictly coarser than bisimilarity. Thus, taking into consideration both ends of the spectrum, we find that quasi-open bisimilarity is neither too coarse, since it is a bisimilarity, nor too fine, since it does not introduce spurious attacks.

2.3 A Congruence Enables Compositional Reasoning

To illustrate the importance of the presented equivalence being a congruence we briefly introduce a discussion on unlinkability, that is the incapability of determining relationships between two observed protocol sessions. The state-of-the-art approach to unlinkability developed in [28] is as follows. If the process *System*, reflecting the actual behaviour of the protocol, is equivalent to the process *Spec*, which specifies the ideal behaviour (from the attacker's perspective), we say that such a protocol is unlinkable.

Consider an abstract authentication protocol with two roles: C and T. The agent playing role C holds credentials signed by the secret key s of the certification authority CA and wants to be able to assume the same identity multiple times without the risk of being reidentified. The goal of the agent playing T is to verify these credentials using the public key $\text{pk}(s)$ of the CA and authenticate C. The real-world behaviour of the system can be modelled as follows.

$$System \triangleq \nu s.\Big(\,!\nu a.!\nu ch_c.\overline{c_C}\langle ch_c\rangle.C(s, ch_c, a) \mid \overline{out}\langle\text{pk}(s)\rangle.!\nu ch_t.\overline{c_T}\langle ch_t\rangle.T(\text{pk}(s), ch_t) \,\Big)$$

Initially, the CA's secret key s is created. The first parallel component above defines agents with identity a that can participate in an **arbitrary number of sessions** of the protocol. Each session begins with advertising a fresh session channel ch_c on the public channel c_C, modelling a new connection to a new session. The leftmost replication models that any number of agents can exist in the system, while the subsequent replication is what allow an agent to appear with the same identity across multiple sessions. The second parallel component above makes the public key $\text{pk}(s)$ of the CA available to the environment via the output on the public channel out. After that, the role T is specified which tries to authenticate a genuine agent in role C making use of $\text{pk}(s)$. Such sessions in role T also begin by advertising a fresh session channel on public channel c_T. The processes $C(s, ch_t)$ and $T(\text{pk}(s), ch_t)$ can be instantiated to model various protocols.

On the other hand, the ideal system is obtained from *System* by removing the second replication, which means that the agent with the identity a can participate in **one protocol run** only.

$$Spec \triangleq \nu s.\Big(\,!\nu a.\nu ch_c.\overline{c_C}\langle ch_c\rangle.C(s, ch_c, a) \mid \overline{out}\langle\text{pk}(s)\rangle.!\nu ch_t.\overline{c_T}\langle ch_t\rangle.T(\text{pk}(s), ch_t) \,\Big)$$

The definition of unlinkability is as follows.

Definition 1 (*unlinkability*). *The system satisfies unlinkability if System $\approx$ Spec holds, where $\approx$ is weak early bisimilarity.*

The fact that quasi-open bisimilarity is a congruence allows us to verify an equivalence property for a smaller system and extend the proof to a larger system. Consider a smaller system comprising only agents playing the role C.

$$Small\_System \triangleq \nu s.\overline{out}\langle\text{pk}(s)\rangle.!\nu a.!\nu ch_c.\overline{c_C}\langle ch_c\rangle.C(s, ch_c, a)$$

The corresponding, smaller version of the idealised specification where there is one session per identity is as follows.

$$Small\_Spec \triangleq \nu s.\overline{out}\langle\text{pk}(s)\rangle.!\nu a.\nu ch_c.\overline{c_C}\langle ch_c\rangle.C(s, ch_c, a)$$

We are ready now to prove that if we prove properties using the smaller specification with one role then they hold in the more traditional specification with two roles.

Theorem 1. *If $Small\_System \sim Small\_Spec$, where $\sim$ is quasi-open bisimilarity, then $System \approx Spec$.*

Proof. Consider the following context, where out' is a fresh variable.

$$\mathcal{C}\{\cdot\} \triangleq \nu out.\Big(\{\cdot\} \mid out(pks).\overline{out'}\langle pks\rangle.!\nu ch_t.\overline{c_T}\langle ch_t\rangle.T(\mathrm{pk}(s), ch_t)\Big)$$

Firstly,
$\mathcal{C}\{Small\_System\}\{{}^{out}/_{out'}\} \sim \tau.System$ and $\mathcal{C}\{Small\_Spec\}\{{}^{out}/_{out'}\} \sim \tau.Spec$
hold. Furthermore, by the assumption, $Small\_System \sim Small\_Spec$ and the fact that since quasi-open bisimilarity is a congruence (Theorem 2), the following holds.

$$\mathcal{C}\{Small\_System\} \sim \mathcal{C}\{Small\_Spec\}$$

Furthermore, since quasi-open bisimilarity is closed under substitutions involving free variables (by definition) we have that the following holds.

$$\mathcal{C}\{Small\_System\}\{{}^{out}/_{out'}\} \sim \mathcal{C}\{Small\_Spec\}\{{}^{out}/_{out'}\}$$

Hence, since quasi-open bisimilarity is an equivalence relation, we have the following.

$$\tau.Spec \sim \tau.System$$

Thus there exists a quasi-open bisimulation $\mathcal{R}$ such that $\tau.Spec\ \mathcal{R}\ \tau.System$. Hence, since $\tau.Spec \xrightarrow{\tau} Spec$ it must be the case that $\tau.System \xrightarrow{\tau} System$ and $Spec\ \mathcal{R}$ $System$. Therefore $Spec \sim System$. Finally, since $\sim\,\subseteq\,\approx$ we have $Spec \approx System$. $\square$

The key difficulty is, of course, to prove that $Small\_System \sim Small\_Spec$, but studying a smaller system significantly reduces the amount of work. This approach to verifying unlinkability for a subsystem was taken in [30], where authors study key agreement for contactless payments and employ only honest cards in their model of unlinkability.

3   The Coarsest Bisimilarity Congruence

This section concerns the coarsest (strong) bisimilarity congruence – open barbed bisimilarity. Open barbed bisimilarity is a natural choice of bisimilarity, being, by definition, the greatest bisimilarity congruence. Since open barbed bisimilarity has an objective language-independent definition, there are no design decisions – there is only one reasonable definition as explored in this section.

3.1   An Example Message Term Language and Equational Theory

In the applied π-calculus messages can be defined with respect to any message language subject to any equational theory ($=_E$). The example equational theory we provide in Fig. 1 is for the purpose of providing meaningful examples. Further theories can

$$M, N, K ::= x \qquad\qquad\qquad\qquad \text{variable}$$

$$\mid \text{pk}(M) \qquad\qquad\qquad \text{public key}$$
$$\mid \text{h}(M) \qquad\qquad\qquad\qquad \text{hash}$$
$$\mid \langle M, N \rangle \qquad\qquad\qquad\qquad \text{tuple}$$
$$\mid \text{aenc}(M, N) \quad \text{asymmetric encryption}$$
$$\mid \text{adec}(M, N) \quad \text{asymmetric decryption}$$
$$\mid \text{fst}(M) \qquad\qquad\qquad\qquad \text{left}$$
$$\mid \text{snd}(M) \qquad\qquad\qquad\quad \text{right}$$

$$\text{fst}(\langle M, N \rangle) =_E M$$

$$\text{snd}(\langle M, N \rangle) =_E N$$

$$\text{adec}(\text{aenc}(M, \text{pk}(K)), K) =_E M$$

$$\text{aenc}(\text{adec}(M, K), \text{pk}(K)) =_E M$$

Fig. 1. The applied π-calculus can be instantiated with **any** message language and equational theory for messages. This example message theory is provided *only* to provide meaningful examples.

also be devised not limited to: sub-term convergent theories [1]; blind signatures and homomorphic encryption [20]; and locally stable theories with inverses [9].

The example theory provided in Fig. 1 covers asymmetric encryption. A message encrypted with public key $\text{pk}(k)$ can only be decrypted using private key k. The theory includes a collision-resistant hash function, with no equations. This theory assumes we have the power to detect whether a message is a pair, but cannot distinguish a failed decryption from a random number.

3.2   Active Substitutions and Labelled Transitions

We define a syntax for the applied π-calculus. The syntax is similar to the π-calculus, except messages and channels can be any term rather than just variables. There is no separate syntactic class of terms for names – names are variables bound by new name binders. In addition to processes, *extended processes* are defined, which allow *active substitutions*, denoted σ, to float alongside processes and in the scope of new name binders, defined in Fig. 2.

Extended processes in normal form $\nu x.(\sigma \mid P)$ are subject to the restriction that the variables in $\text{dom}(\sigma)$ are fresh for x, $\text{fv}(P)$ and $\text{fv}(y\sigma)$, for all variables y (i.e., σ is idempotent, and substitutions are fully applied to P). We follow the convention that operational rules are defined directly on extended processes in normal form up to α-conversion. This avoids numerous complications caused by the structural congruence in the original definition of bisimilarity for the applied π-calculus. The set of free variables and α-conversion are as standard, where $\nu x.P$ and $M(x).P$ bind x in P.

Intuitionistic mismatch. Mismatch requires special attention. Mismatch models the else branch of an if-then-else statement with an equality guard. Hence we can encode a conditional branching statement if $M = N$ then P else Q using process $[M = N]P + [M \neq N]Q$.

As uncovered in related work [29], the trick for handling mismatch such that we obtain a congruence is to treat mismatch intuitionistically. Intuitionistic negation enjoys the property that it is preserved under substitutions; a property that fails for classical negation in general. E.g., there are substitutions under which $[x \neq \text{h}(y)]a(z)$ can perform an input transition and others where it cannot, hence neither $x = \text{h}(y)$ nor $x \neq \text{h}(y)$ holds in the intuitionistic setting until more information is provided about the

SYNTAX OF EXTENDED PROCESSES AND LABELS

$P, Q ::= 0$ deadlock

      $| \; \overline{M}\langle N\rangle.P$ send

      $| \; M(y).P$ receive

      $| \; [M = N]P$ match

      $| \; [M \neq N]P$ mismatch

      $| \; vx.P$ new

      $| \; P \mid Q$ parallel

      $| \; P + Q$ choice

      $| \; !P$ replication

Extended processes:

$A, B ::= \sigma \mid P$ active substitution and process

      $| \; vx.A$ new

actions on labels:

$\pi ::= \tau$ internal action

     $| \; \overline{M}(z)$ bound output

     $| \; M\,N$ free input

LABELLED TRANSITION SYSTEM

$$\frac{M\sigma =_E K}{z: \sigma \mid K(x).P \xrightarrow{M\,N} \sigma \mid P\{N\sigma/x\}} \text{ INP} \qquad \frac{x \,\#\, M, N, P, \sigma, z \quad M\sigma =_E K}{z: \sigma \mid \overline{K}\langle N\rangle.P \xrightarrow{\overline{M}(x)} \{N/x\} \circ \sigma \mid P} \text{ OUT}$$

$$\frac{z: \sigma \mid P \xrightarrow{\pi} A}{z: \sigma \mid P + Q \xrightarrow{\pi} A} \text{ SUM-L} \qquad \frac{z: \sigma \mid Q \xrightarrow{\pi} A}{z: \sigma \mid P + Q \xrightarrow{\pi} A} \text{ SUM-R}$$

$$\frac{z: \sigma \mid P \xrightarrow{\pi} A \quad M =_E N}{z: \sigma \mid [M = N]P \xrightarrow{\pi} A} \text{ MAT} \qquad \frac{z: \sigma \mid P \xrightarrow{\pi} A \quad z \models M \neq N}{z: \sigma \mid [M \neq N]P \xrightarrow{\pi} A} \text{ MISMATCH}$$

$$\frac{z, x: \sigma \mid P \xrightarrow{\pi} B \quad x \,\#\, z, \sigma, \mathrm{n}(\pi)}{z: \sigma \mid vx.P \xrightarrow{\pi} vx.B} \text{ EXTRUDE} \qquad \frac{z, x: A \xrightarrow{\pi} B \quad x \,\#\, z, \mathrm{n}(\pi)}{z: vx.A \xrightarrow{\pi} vx.B} \text{ RES}$$

$$\frac{z: \sigma \mid P \xrightarrow{\pi} vx.(\sigma \mid R) \quad x \cup \mathrm{bn}(\pi) \,\#\, Q}{z: \sigma \mid P \mid Q \xrightarrow{\pi} vx.(\sigma \mid R \mid Q)} \text{ PAR-L} \qquad \frac{z: \sigma \mid Q \xrightarrow{\pi} vx.(\sigma \mid R) \quad x \cup \mathrm{bn}(\pi) \,\#\, P}{z: \sigma \mid P \mid Q \xrightarrow{\pi} vx.(\sigma \mid P \mid R)} \text{ PAR-R}$$

$$\mathrm{n}(\pi) = \begin{cases} \mathrm{fv}(M) \cup \{x\} & \text{if } \pi = \overline{M}(x) \\ \mathrm{fv}(M) \cup \mathrm{fv}(N) & \text{if } \pi = M\,N \\ \emptyset & \text{otherwise} \end{cases} \qquad \mathrm{bn}(\pi) = \begin{cases} \{x\} & \text{if } \pi = \overline{M}(x) \\ \emptyset & \text{otherwise} \end{cases}$$

$$\frac{z: \sigma \mid P \xrightarrow{\overline{M}(x)} vy.(\{N/x\} \circ \sigma \mid P') \quad z: \sigma \mid Q \xrightarrow{M\,N} vw.(\sigma \mid Q') \quad \{x\} \cup y \,\#\, Q \quad w \,\#\, P, y}{z: \sigma \mid P \mid Q \xrightarrow{\tau} vy, w.(\sigma \mid P' \mid Q')} \text{ CLOSE-L}$$

$$\frac{z: \sigma \mid P \xrightarrow{M\,N} vy.(\sigma \mid P') \quad z: \sigma \mid Q \xrightarrow{\overline{M}(x)} vw.(\{N/x\} \circ \sigma \mid Q') \quad \{x\} \cup w \,\#\, P \quad y \,\#\, Q, w}{z: \sigma \mid P \mid Q \xrightarrow{\tau} vy, w.(\sigma \mid P' \mid Q')} \text{ CLOSE-R}$$

$$\frac{z: \sigma \mid P \xrightarrow{\pi} vx.(\sigma \mid Q) \quad x \cup \mathrm{bn}(\pi) \,\#\, P}{z: \sigma \mid !P \xrightarrow{\pi} vx.(\sigma \mid Q \mid !P)} \text{ REP-ACT}$$

$$\frac{z: \sigma \mid P \xrightarrow{\overline{M}(x)} vy.(\{N/x\} \circ \sigma \mid Q) \quad z: \sigma \mid P \xrightarrow{M\,N} vw.(\sigma \mid R) \quad y \,\#\, P, w \quad w \,\#\, P}{z: \sigma \mid !P \xrightarrow{\tau} vy, w.(\sigma \mid Q \mid R \mid !P)} \text{ REP-CLOSE}$$

Fig. 2. Syntax of extended processes and an *open early* labelled transition system.

environment. In order to define intuitionistic negation, we require the notion of a fresh substitution.

Definition 2 (fresh). *Consider a set of variables z. We say z is fresh for set of variables y, whenever $z \cap y = \emptyset$. Given a term, say P, we say z is fresh for P, whenever z is fresh for the free variables of P. Given a substitution σ, we say z is fresh for σ whenever z is fresh for $\mathrm{dom}(\sigma)$, and, for all $y \notin z$, we have z is fresh for $y\sigma$. Freshness extends point-wise to lists of entities and is denoted $u, v, \ldots \mathbin{\#} M, N, \sigma, \ldots$.*

We say entailment $z \models M \neq N$ holds whenever there is no σ such that $z \mathbin{\#} \sigma$ and $M\sigma =_E N\sigma$.

Consider the following examples that hold or fail to hold for different reasons. Entailment $\emptyset \models x \neq h(x)$ holds, since there exists no unifier, witnessed by a simple occurs check. In contrast, $\emptyset \models x \neq h(y)$ does not hold, since there exists substitution $\left\{ {}^{h(y)}\!/_x \right\}$ unifying messages x and $h(y)$, so it is still possible the messages could be equal; thus, there is insufficient information to decide whether the messages are equal or not. By extending the environment such that y is a private name, entailment $y \models x \neq h(y)$ holds, since y is not fresh for the most general unifier $\left\{ {}^{h(y)}\!/_x \right\}$ – an observer who can influence x, cannot make x equal to $h(y)$ without access to y.

To define open barbed bisimilarity, we require the labelled transition system for the applied π-calculus in Fig. 2. It is an *early* labelled transition system due to the way inputs are treated, and open early, since it does not assume that free variables are ground names, unless stated so explicitly in the name environment to the left of the transition relation. There are three types of label: τ representing internal progress due to communication; bound output $\overline{M}(x)$ representing that something bound to x is sent on channel M; and free input $M\,N$ representing that we receive N on channel M.

The MISMATCH and RES Rules. The MISMATCH rule is defined in terms of entailment in Definition 2. The RES rule can also influence mismatches by introducing fresh names. For example, the following derivation shows an input is enabled.

$$
\cfrac{\cfrac{\cfrac{\quad}{y\colon z(w) \xrightarrow{z\,w} 0}\ \text{INP} \qquad y \models x \neq h(y)}{y\colon [x \neq h(y)]z(w) \xrightarrow{z\,w} 0}\ \text{MISMATCH} \qquad y \mathbin{\#} z\,w}{\emptyset\colon \nu y.[x \neq h(y)]z(w) \xrightarrow{z\,w} \nu y.0}\ \text{RES}
$$

Notice, the bound variable y is added to the set of names, enabling $y \models x \neq h(y)$.

Active Substitutions and Labels. For a non-trivial example where the active substitution affects the label, observe that the following transition is derivable.

$$
\cfrac{\cfrac{\mathtt{fst}(\langle m, n\rangle) =_E m}{m\colon \left\{ {}^{\langle m,n\rangle}\!/_w \right\} \mid m(x) \xrightarrow{\mathtt{fst}(w)\,x} \left\{ {}^{\langle m,n\rangle}\!/_w \right\} \mid 0}\ \text{INP} \qquad m \mathbin{\#} \mathtt{fst}(w)\,x}{\emptyset\colon \nu m.\left(\left\{ {}^{\langle m,n\rangle}\!/_w \right\} \mid m(x) \right) \xrightarrow{\mathtt{fst}(w)\,x} \nu m.\left(\left\{ {}^{\langle m,n\rangle}\!/_w \right\} \mid 0 \right)}\ \text{RES}
$$

The conditions on the RES rule ensure bound name m cannot appear in the terms on the label. Fortunately, the INP rule allows m to be expressed in terms of extruded variable

w. Since we have $m =_E \mathtt{fst}(\langle m, n\rangle)$ and the equational theory can be applied in rule INP, the above input action is enabled, where message $\mathtt{fst}(w)$ indirectly refers to channel m.

The OUT Rule. The OUT rule for the applied π-calculus does not record the message sent on the label; instead, the message is recorded in an active substitution. The domain of the active substitution is chosen to be a fresh variable appearing as the bound variable in the output action on the label.

In the following example a message is sent using the OUT rule, then the RES rule is applied such that the private name n in the active substitution remains bound after the transition.

$$\frac{n, k \colon \overline{a}\langle \mathtt{aenc}(n, \mathtt{pk}(k))\rangle.n(x) \xrightarrow{\overline{a}(w)} \left\{ {}^{\mathtt{aenc}(n,\mathtt{pk}(k))}\!/_w \right\} \mid n(x)}{k \colon \nu n.\overline{a}\langle \mathtt{aenc}(n, \mathtt{pk}(k))\rangle.n(x) \xrightarrow{\overline{a}(w)} \nu n.\left(\left\{ {}^{\mathtt{aenc}(n,\mathtt{pk}(k))}\!/_w \right\} \mid n(x) \right)}$$

Observe, by rule INP, the following input action is enabled.

$$k \colon a(w).\overline{\mathtt{adec}(w, k)}\langle a\rangle \xrightarrow{a\ \mathtt{aenc}(n,\mathtt{pk}(k))} \overline{\mathtt{adec}(\mathtt{aenc}(n, \mathtt{pk}(k)), k)}\langle a\rangle$$

Hence, by CLOSE-L and the above input and output transitions, the following interaction is enabled; and RES is used to bind the key k.

$$\frac{k \colon \nu n.\overline{a}\langle \mathtt{aenc}(n, \mathtt{pk}(k))\rangle.n(x) \mid a(w).\overline{\mathtt{adec}(w, k)}\langle a\rangle \xrightarrow{\tau} \nu n.(n(x) \mid \overline{n}\langle a\rangle)}{\emptyset \colon \nu k.\left(\nu n.\overline{a}\langle \mathtt{aenc}(n, \mathtt{pk}(k))\rangle.n(x) \mid a(w).\overline{\mathtt{adec}(w, k)}\langle a\rangle \right) \xrightarrow{\tau} \nu k.\nu n.(n(x) \mid \overline{n}\langle a\rangle)} \text{ RES}$$

Note this labelled approach to interaction follows closely how interaction traditionally works in the π-calculus. Thus this formulation of labelled transitions facilitates the lifting of results from the π-calculus to the applied π-calculus. An advantage of our labelled transition system is *strong*, *weak*, and other variants of bisimilarity can be studied. In contrast, the original system proposed for the applied π-calculus [2] used a hybrid labelled/reduction system that can only be used to formalise weak equivalences. Furthermore, avoiding a structural congruence avoids having to consider all transitions up to an associative-commutative theory (which can make proofs cumbersome). Also, the use of REP-ACT and REP-CLOSE for defining replication, respects image-finiteness (up to α-conversion) [39].

Note, trying to obtain strong bisimilarity by naïvely restricting the original definition of labelled bisimilarity [2] such that every τ-transition is matched by exactly one τ-transition results in an ill-formulated notion of strong bisimilarity. Doing so, would allow processes, such as *Server A* and *Server B* from Sect. 2, to be wrongly distinguished by counting the number of τ-transitions induced by branching statements. The rule SUM-L and its counterpart SUM-R avoid this problem.

3.3 A Testing Regime Defining a Bisimilarity Congruence

A barb represents the ability to observe an input or output action on a channel. Barbs are typically used to define *barbed equivalence*, or *observational equivalence* [36]. However, barbed equivalence is a congruence but not a bisimilarity; while observational equivalence is a bisimilarity but not a congruence. For this reason, we prefer *open barbed bisimilarity* [41], which is, by definition, both a bisimilarity and a congruence. We adopt the convention of writing $A \xrightarrow{\pi} B$ whenever $\emptyset : A \xrightarrow{\pi} B$. We say process P has barb M, written $P \downarrow M$, whenever, for some A, $P \xrightarrow{\overline{M}(z)} A$, or $P \xrightarrow{M\,N} A$.

Definition 3 (open barbed bisimilarity). *An open barbed bisimulation $\mathcal{R}$ is a symmetric relation over processes such that whenever $P \,\mathcal{R}\, Q$ holds the following hold:*

- *For all contexts $\mathcal{C}\{\,\cdot\,\}$, $\mathcal{C}\{P\}\,\mathcal{R}\,\mathcal{C}\{Q\}$.*
- *If $P \downarrow M$ then $Q \downarrow M$.*
- *If $P \xrightarrow{\tau} P'$, there exists Q' such that $Q \xrightarrow{\tau} Q'$ and $P' \,\mathcal{R}\, Q'$ holds.*

Open barbed bisimilarity $\simeq$ is the greatest open barbed bisimulation. More specifically, processes P and Q are open barbed bisimilar, written $P \simeq Q$, whenever there exists an open barbed bisimulation $\mathcal{R}$ such that $P \,\mathcal{R}\, Q$.

The power of open barbed bisimilarity comes from closing by all contexts at every step, not only at the beginning of an execution. Closing by all contexts at every step ensures the robustness of open barbed bisimilarity even if the environment is extended at runtime; i.e., we stay within a congruence relation at every step of the bisimulation game.

Recall that a congruence is an equivalence relation preserved in all contexts. Symmetry and context closure of open barbed bisimilarity are immediate from the definition. Reflexivity is trivial since the identity relation is an open barbed bisimulation. Transitivity is only slightly more involved, proven by checking that the composition of two open barbed bisimulation relations is an open barbed bisimulation.

Open barbed bisimilarity is concise – the definition requires only the open labelled transition system in Fig. 2 and the three clauses in Definition 3. Furthermore, it is the coarsest bisimilarity congruence, in the objective sense that it is defined to be a congruence and defined independently of the content of the messages sent and received. Notice, due to the independence of the information on the labels, open barbed bisimilarity applies to any language; indeed open barbed bisimilarity is a generalisation of dynamic observational equivalence [38], that, historically, was used to objectively identify the greatest bisimulation congruence for CCS. Related work also uses the term saturated bisimilarity for such a reference bisimilarity congruence [13,14], which shows that a single barb, say *ok* suffices.

For the above reasons, open barbed bisimilarity is an ideal reference definition. However, it is unwieldy due to closure of the definition under all contexts. This leads us to the notion of quasi-open bisimilarity, defined in the next section.

4   Quasi-open Bisimilarity for the Applied π-Calculus

As highlighted in the previous section, open barbed bisimilarity has a concise and objective definition but is difficult to check, due to the quantification over all contexts. An open variant of labelled bisimilarity, called *quasi-open bisimilarity*, avoids quantifying over all contexts; and furthermore, coincides with open barbed bisimilarity. In this section, we define quasi-open bisimilarity for the applied π-calculus, generalising established results for the π-calculus [29,41].

4.1   Introducing Quasi-open Bisimilarity for the Applied π-Calculus

To extend quasi-open bisimilarity to the applied π-calculus the notion of static equivalence is required. Static equivalence is defined over the static information in an extended process – the active substitutions and name restrictions.

Definition 4 (static equivalence). *Two extended processes $\nu x.(\sigma \mid P)$ and $\nu y.(\theta \mid Q)$ are statically equivalent whenever for all messages M and N such that $x, y \mathrel{\#} M, N$, we have $M\sigma =_E N\sigma$ if and only if $M\theta =_E N\theta$.*

In the above definition, messages M and N represent two different "recipes" for producing messages. Two extended processes are distinguished by static equivalence only when the two recipes produce equivalent messages under one substitution, but distinct messages under the other substitution. The concept of static equivalence is no different from original work on the applied π-calculus [5].

Static Equivalence Example. For example, the following extended processes are not statically equivalent.

$$\nu k.\left(\left\{ {}^{\mathsf{aenc}(x,\mathsf{pk}(k)),\,\mathsf{aenc}(x,\mathsf{pk}(k))}\big/_{v,\,w} \right\} \mid 0\right) \text{ is distinct from } \nu k.\left(\left\{ {}^{\mathsf{aenc}(x,\mathsf{pk}(k)),\,\mathsf{aenc}(z,\mathsf{pk}(k))}\big/_{v,\,w} \right\} \mid 0\right)$$

The above are distinguished by messages v and w. Notice $v\left\{ {}^{\mathsf{aenc}(x,\mathsf{pk}(k)),\,\mathsf{aenc}(x,\mathsf{pk}(k))}\big/_{v,\,w} \right\}$ and $w\left\{ {}^{\mathsf{aenc}(x,\mathsf{pk}(k)),\,\mathsf{aenc}(x,\mathsf{pk}(k))}\big/_{v,\,w} \right\}$ are both equal to $\mathsf{aenc}(x, \mathsf{pk}(k))$; but the following messages are distinct: $v\left\{ {}^{\mathsf{aenc}(x,\mathsf{pk}(k)),\,\mathsf{aenc}(z,\mathsf{pk}(k))}\big/_{v,\,w} \right\}$ vs. $w\left\{ {}^{\mathsf{aenc}(x,\mathsf{pk}(k)),\,\mathsf{aenc}(z,\mathsf{pk}(k))}\big/_{v,\,w} \right\}$.

In order to define quasi-open bisimilarity, we require the notion of an *open relation* between extended processes. An open relation is preserved under substitutions (respecting bound names, including the domain of active substitution) and extensions of the active substitutions and names in environment. In the following, $\theta\!\restriction_D$ is the restriction of a substitution to a set D.

Definition 5 (open). *A relation over extended processes $\mathcal{R}$ is open whenever we have that if $\nu x.(\theta_1 \mid P) \; \mathcal{R} \; \nu y.(\theta_2 \mid Q)$ and there exist idempotent substitutions σ, ρ and variables z such that: $x, y \mathrel{\#} \sigma, \rho$ and $z \mathrel{\#} \mathrm{dom}(\rho)$, x, y and $\mathrm{dom}(\theta_i) \mathrel{\#} \sigma, \rho, z$ for $i \in \{1, 2\}$, we have the following:*

$$\nu z, x.\big((\theta_1 \circ \sigma)\!\restriction_{\mathrm{dom}(\theta_1)} \circ\, \rho \mid P\sigma\big) \; \mathcal{R} \; \nu z, y.\big((\theta_2 \circ \sigma)\!\restriction_{\mathrm{dom}(\theta_2)} \circ\, \rho \mid Q\sigma\big)$$

Given the definition of an open relation, static equivalence, and the labelled transition system, we can provide the following concise definition of quasi-open bisimilarity for the applied π-calculus.

Definition 6 (quasi-open bisimilarity). *An **open** symmetric relation between extended processes $\mathcal{R}$ is a quasi-open bisimulation whenever, if $A \mathrel{\mathcal{R}} B$ then the following hold:*

- *A and B are statically equivalent.*
- *If $A \xrightarrow{\pi} A'$ there exists B' such that $B \xrightarrow{\pi} B'$ and $A' \mathrel{\mathcal{R}} B'$.*

Processes P and Q are quasi-open bisimilar, written $P \sim Q$, whenever $P \mathrel{\mathcal{R}} Q$ for some quasi-open bisimulation $\mathcal{R}$.

The keyword in the definition above is "open" in the sense of Definition 5. Without ensuring that properties are preserved under reachability, the above definition would simply be a strong version of the classical *labelled bisimilarity* for the applied π-calculus [5]. We illustrate the impact of insisting on an open relation and allowing messages as channels in the following examples.

Remark 1. The definition of quasi-open bisimilarity above is arguably simpler than in the setting of the π-calculus [41]. In contrast to the original definition, since private names are recorded in extended processes, all types of action are handled by one clause. The π-calculus definition maintains an additional index of extruded private names.

Mobility Example. This work builds on a recent evolution of the applied π-calculus [5], which allows processes such as $\nu z.\overline{x}\langle z, y\rangle.z(w)$ and $\nu z.\overline{x}\langle z, y\rangle$ to be evaluated. These processes should not be equivalent, since they are polyadic π-calculus processes [35] (the π-calculus with tuples), and the applied π-calculus should be conservative with respect to the polyadic π-calculus, which was not the case for older definitions of bisimilarity for the applied π-calculus [2]. The trick to allow processes such as the above to be evaluated is simple: allow channels to be messages. This way, a message, such as $\mathtt{fst}(u)$, can be used to indirectly refer to channels. To see why we can distinguish these processes, firstly, consider the following two transitions with matching actions.

$$\nu z.\overline{x}\langle z, y\rangle.z(w) \xrightarrow{\overline{x}(v)} \nu z.\left(\left\{\langle z,y\rangle/v\right\} \mid z(w)\right) \qquad \nu z.\overline{x}\langle z, y\rangle \xrightarrow{\overline{x}(v)} \nu z.\left(\left\{\langle z,y\rangle/v\right\} \mid 0\right)$$

The labelled transition $\nu z.\left(\left\{\langle z,y\rangle/v\right\} \mid z(w)\right) \xrightarrow{\mathtt{fst}(v)\,x} \nu z.\left(\left\{\langle z,y\rangle/v\right\} \mid 0\right)$ is enabled for the process on the left. The process on the right above $\nu z.\left(\left\{\langle z,y\rangle/v\right\} \mid 0\right)$ is dead-locked, so cannot match this transition. Notice the use of message $\mathtt{fst}(v)$ on the input label to refer to the private channel output at the first step.

Example Showing Impact of an Open Relation on Static Equivalence. By insisting that a quasi-open bisimulation is an open relation (Definition 5), static equivalence must also be preserved by all fresh substitutions. This has an impact on examples such as the following.

Processes $\nu x.\overline{a}\langle \mathtt{aenc}(x, z)\rangle$ and $\nu x.\overline{a}\langle \mathtt{aenc}(\langle x, y\rangle, z)\rangle$ are labelled bisimilar but not quasi-open bisimilar. To see why, observe both processes can perform a $\overline{a}(v)$-transition to the respective extended processes $\nu x.\left(\left\{\mathtt{aenc}(x,z)/v\right\} \mid 0\right)$ and $\nu x.\left(\left\{\mathtt{aenc}(\langle x,y\rangle,z)/v\right\} \mid 0\right)$. These extended process are **statically** equivalent (recall z cannot be used to decrypt these cyphertexts in asymmetric cryptography). How-ever, since a quasi-open bisimulation must be preserved under fresh substitutions and $v \;\#\{\mathtt{pk}(w)/z\}$, we check static equivalence for $\nu x.\left(\left\{\mathtt{aenc}(x,z)/v\right\} \mid 0\right)\{\mathtt{pk}(w)/z\}$ and $\nu x.\left(\left\{\mathtt{aenc}(\langle x,y\rangle,z)/v\right\} \mid 0\right)\{\mathtt{pk}(w)/z\}$. After applying the substitution, the extended processes are no longer statically equivalent, witnessed by distinguishing recipes $\mathtt{snd}(\mathtt{adec}(v, w))$ and y. Thus the processes are not quasi-open bisimilar.

Note that the fact that the attack succeeds above suggests the attacker has the power to influence the message bound to z, in order to stage an attack. In the above example the message chosen is a public key $\mathtt{pk}(w)$ for which the attacker knows the

$$vk.\overline{s}\langle pk(k)\rangle.va.\overline{c}\langle a\rangle.a(x).vr.\overline{a}\langle r\rangle \; \mathcal{S} \quad \begin{array}{l} vk.\overline{s}\langle pk(k)\rangle. \; va.\overline{c}\langle a\rangle.a(x). \\ \quad vr. \, \mathtt{if} \, x = pk(k) \\ \qquad \mathtt{then}\,\overline{a}\langle aenc(\langle m,r\rangle, pk(k))\rangle\,\mathtt{else}\,\overline{a}\langle r\rangle \end{array}$$

$$vk.\left(\left\{^{pk(k)}/_u\right\} \mid va.\overline{c}\langle a\rangle.a(x).vr.\overline{a}\langle r\rangle\right) \mathcal{S} \quad \begin{array}{l} vk.\left(\left\{^{pk(k)}/_u\right\} \mid va.\overline{c}\langle a\rangle.a(x). \\ \quad vr. \, \mathtt{if} \, x = pk(k) \\ \qquad \mathtt{then}\,\overline{a}\langle aenc(\langle m,r\rangle, pk(k))\rangle\,\mathtt{else}\,\overline{a}\langle r\rangle\right) \end{array}$$

$$vk, a.\left(\left\{^{pk(k),a}/_{u,v}\right\} \mid a(x).vr.\overline{a}\langle r\rangle\right) \mathcal{S} \quad \begin{array}{l} vk, a.\left(\left\{^{pk(k),a}/_{u,v}\right\} \mid a(x). \\ \quad vr. \, \mathtt{if} \, x = pk(k) \\ \qquad \mathtt{then}\,\overline{a}\langle aenc(\langle m,r\rangle, pk(k))\rangle\,\mathtt{else}\,\overline{a}\langle r\rangle\right) \end{array}$$

$$vk, a, r.\left(\left\{^{pk(k),a}/_{u,v}\right\} \mid \overline{a}\langle r\rangle\right) \mathcal{S} \quad \begin{array}{l} vk, a, r.\left(\left\{^{pk(k),a}/_{u,v}\right\} \mid \mathtt{if}\,n^{\{pk(k),a}/_{u,v\}} = pk(k) \\ \qquad \mathtt{then}\,\overline{a}\langle aenc(\langle m,r\rangle, pk(k))\rangle\,\mathtt{else}\,\overline{a}\langle r\rangle\right) \end{array}$$

$$vk, a, r.\left(\left\{^{pk(k),a,r}/_{u,v,w}\right\} \mid 0\right) \mathcal{S}\, vk, a, r.\left(\left\{^{pk(k),a,aenc(\langle m,r\rangle,pk(k))}/_{u,v,w}\right\} \mid 0\right)$$

$$vk, a, r.\left(\left\{^{pk(k),a,r}/_{u,v,w}\right\} \mid 0\right) \mathcal{S}\, vk, a, r.\left(\left\{^{pk(k),a,r}/_{u,v,w}\right\} \mid 0\right)$$

where s, c, m and n are messages and u, v and w are variables such that $s, c, m, n \# k, a, r$, and $u \# s, c, m, k, a, r$, and $v \# s, c, m, k, a, r, u$, and $w \# s, c, m, n, k, a, r, u, v$.

Fig. 3. Relation $\mathcal{S}$ defining a quasi-open bisimulation verifying the anonymity of *Server A* in the case for a single session, without replication.

secret key w. For another such example, $vk.\overline{a}\langle aenc(x, pk(k))\rangle.\overline{a}\langle aenc(y, pk(k))\rangle$ and $vk.\overline{a}\langle aenc(x, pk(k))\rangle.\overline{a}\langle aenc(z, pk(k))\rangle$ are labelled bisimilar (which assumes x, y, z are distinct names), but not quasi-open bisimilar (which instead assumes x, y, z are variables). To see why, observe the above processes can reach the extended processes $vk.\left(\left\{^{aenc(x,pk(k)),aenc(y,pk(k))}/_{v,w}\right\} \mid 0\right)$ and $vk.\left(\left\{^{aenc(x,pk(k)),aenc(z,pk(k))}/_{v,w}\right\} \mid 0\right)$, at which point the attacker has the power to set $x = y$, thereby reaching a scenario explained after Definition 4, where the attacker can observe the same message is output twice for the process on the left but not for the process on the right. This feature of quasi-open bisimilarity is related to the security property of *strong secrecy* [11], where the open nature of secrets represents that the attacker may interfere with messages at runtime.

4.2 Running Example of a Privacy Property

We now have the mechanisms to verify the minimal privacy example from Sect. 2. For greater clarity, firstly consider the case of a single session, i.e., with replication removed. The equivalence of running examples *Server A* and *Server B* for the single session case (without replication) can be established by taking the least *symmetric open* relation satisfying the constraints in Fig. 3. The critical observation is that message n in Fig. 3 ranges over all permitted inputs. Since $n = u$ is permitted, we have the following pair in relation $\mathcal{S}$.

$$vk, a, r.\left(\left\{^{pk(k),a}/_{u,v}\right\} \mid \overline{a}\langle r\rangle\right) \; \mathcal{S} \; vk.a, r.\left(\left\{^{pk(k),a}/_{u,v}\right\} \mid \begin{array}{l}\mathtt{if}\,pk(k) = pk(k) \,\mathtt{then} \\ \qquad \overline{a}\langle aenc(\langle m,r\rangle, pk(k))\rangle\,\mathtt{else}\,\overline{a}\langle r\rangle\right) \end{array}$$

In the above, observe the branch sending an encrypted message is enabled. In contrast to the above, if n is any message term not equivalent to u then we have $k, a, r \models n\{^{\text{pk}(k),a}/_{u,v}\} \neq \text{pk}(k)$ since if n were a message term such that $k, a, r \# n$ such that $n\{^{\text{pk}(k),a}/_{u,v}\} = \text{pk}(k)$, then n must be equivalent to u. Thus in all other cases the $\texttt{else}$ branch is enabled.

Notice $\nu k, a, r.\left(\{^{\text{pk}(k),a,\text{aenc}(\langle m,r\rangle,\text{pk}(k))}/_{u,v,w}\}|0\right)$ and $\nu k, a, r.\left(\{^{\text{pk}(k),a,r}/_{u,v,w}\}|0\right)$ are statically equivalent, reachable when $n =_E u$. To see why, observe that an attacker neither has the key k to decrypt $\texttt{aenc}(\langle m,r\rangle, \text{pk}(k))$, nor can an attacker reconstruct the message $\langle m, r\rangle$, without knowing r.

For the unbounded case, consider the least symmetric open relation $\mathcal{T}$ satisfying the constraints in Fig. 4. This generalises the finite case by defining all scenarios where there are l parallel sessions that are either in the state of having just announced the communication channel a, having just received a message, or have responded already. This definition is closed under all transitions and reachability, as required to establish that $\mathcal{T}$ is a quasi-open bisimulation. Indeed $\mathcal{T}$ is a quasi-open bisimulation such that *Server A* $\mathcal{T}$ *Server B*. Hence the desired privacy property of *Server A*, first mentioned in Sect. 2, is verified.

$$Responder \triangleq va.\overline{c}\langle a\rangle.a(x).vr.\texttt{if } x = \text{pk}(k) \texttt{ then } \overline{a}\langle\texttt{aenc}(\langle m,r\rangle,\text{pk}(k))\rangle \texttt{ else } \overline{a}\langle r\rangle$$

$$vk.\overline{s}\langle\text{pk}(k)\rangle.!va.\overline{c}\langle a\rangle.a(x).vr.\overline{a}\langle r\rangle \quad \mathcal{T} \quad vk.\overline{s}\langle\text{pk}(k)\rangle.!Responder$$

$$vk, a_1, \ldots, a_l, r_1, \ldots r_l.\Big(\sigma \mid P_1 \mid \ldots P_l \atop \mid !va.\overline{c}\langle a\rangle.a(x).vr.\overline{a}\langle r\rangle \Big) \quad \mathcal{T} \quad vk, a_1, \ldots, a_l, r_1, \ldots r_l.\Big(\theta \mid Q_1 \mid \ldots Q_l \atop \mid !Responder \Big)$$

for any I, J, I', J' partitioning $\{1, \ldots l\}$ such that the following hold

$$
\begin{array}{ll}
u\sigma = \text{pk}(k) & u\theta = \text{pk}(k) \\
v_i\sigma = a_i \quad \text{if } i \in \{1, \ldots l\} & v_i\theta = a_i \quad\quad\quad\quad\quad\quad\quad \text{if } l \in \{1, \ldots l\} \\
w_i\sigma = r_i \quad \text{if } i \in I' \cup J' & w_i\theta = \texttt{aenc}(\langle m, r_i\rangle, \text{pk}(k)) \text{ if } l \in I' \\
& w_i\theta = r_i \quad\quad\quad\quad\quad\quad\quad\quad \text{if } l \in J'
\end{array}
$$

$$P_i \triangleq \begin{cases} a_i(x).vr.\overline{a}_i\langle r\rangle & \text{if } i \in I \\ \overline{a}_i\langle r_i\rangle & \text{if } i \in J \\ 0 & \text{if } l \in I' \cup J' \end{cases}$$

$$Q_i \triangleq \begin{cases} a_i(x).vr.\texttt{if } x\theta = \text{pk}(k) \texttt{ then } \overline{a}_i\langle\texttt{aenc}(\langle m,r\rangle,\text{pk}(k))\rangle \texttt{ else } \overline{a}_i\langle r\rangle & \text{if } i \in I \\ \texttt{if } n_i\theta = \text{pk}(k) \texttt{ then } \overline{a}_i\langle\texttt{aenc}(\langle m,r_i\rangle,\text{pk}(k))\rangle \texttt{ else } \overline{a}_i\langle r_i\rangle & \text{if } i \in J \\ 0 & \text{if } l \in I' \cup J' \end{cases}$$

s, c, m, n_i are messages such that $s, c, m, n_i \# k, a_1, \ldots a_l, r_1, \ldots r_l$ and $u, v_1, \ldots, v_l, w_1, \ldots w_l$ are distinct variables such that $u, v_1, \ldots v_l, w_1 \ldots w_l \# s, c, m, a_1, \ldots a_l, k, r_1, \ldots r_l$

Fig. 4. Relation $\mathcal{T}$ verifying *Server B* $\sim$ *Server A* in the unbounded case.

A subtlety is that $\mathcal{T}$ is not the least quasi-open bisimulation witnessing *Server A* $\sim$ *Server B*, since we *over approximated* by allowing inputs to possibly use outputs from the future. This over approximation is correct, since we can always have additional redundant terms in a bisimulation set, as long as they are also closed under the relevant conditions. Indeed, this illustrates a practical benefit of bisimilarity – we can find abstractions that reduce the amount of verification work.

4.3 Quasi-open Bisimilarity is Sound and Complete

As illustrated in the previous sub-section, a core guarantee offered by quasi-open bisimilarity is that it is a congruence relation. We prove quasi-open bisimilarity is preserved by all contexts, notably under input prefixes; and, furthermore, coincides exactly with open barbed bisimilarity, which is the coarsest (strong) bisimilarity congruence.

Theorem 2 (contexts). *If $P \sim Q$ then for all contexts $C\{ \cdot \}$, we have $C\{P\} \sim C\{Q\}$.*

The most involved cases of Theorem 2 are those showing quasi-open bisimilarity is preserved under parallel composition and replication; while the most novel case is for mismatch, which relies on the notion of an open relation given in Definition 5. Given Theorem 2, the soundness of quasi-open bisimilarity with respect to open barbed bisimilarity follows immediately.

Corollary 1 (soundness). *If $P \sim Q$ then $P \simeq Q$.*

Completeness, expressed in Theorem 3, supports our claim that quasi-open bisimilarity in Definition 6 is a correct and canonical (strong) bisimilarity congruence for the applied π-calculus. This theorem is the fundamental property of quasi-open bisimilarity that does not hold for open bisimilarity.

Theorem 3 (completeness). *Quasi-open bisimilarity coincides with open barbed bisimilarity.*

It is interesting to compare the proof of Theorem 3 to the corresponding proof for the π-calculus [41]. In the corresponding proof for the π-calculus checks are built into bound output transitions to ensure extruded private names are fresh. In the proof of Theorem 3 no such checks are required for output transitions; such checks are subsumed by checking static equivalence.

Strong v.s. Weak Bisimilarity. Observe Theorem 3 is for a strong formulation of quasi-open bisimilarity. The weak/strong dimension [44] (as with other dimensions such as interleaving v.s. true concurrency [45], for instance) is a perpendicular issue to the focus of this paper. Quasi-open variants of various equivalences and preorders can also be defined, so this scientific discussion on attacker models should not be limited to strong bisimilarity. Sometimes weak equivalences can be avoided. For example, for privacy properties, such as unlinkability of ePassports, the traditional formulation in terms of a weak bisimilarity problem [8] has been shown to be reducible to an equivalent strong bisimilarity problem that is easier to check, since we have image finiteness [28], i.e., for any label π each process has finitely many π-labelled transitions.

5 Comparison to Related Work on Observational Equivalence

Most notions of bisimilarity previously introduced for cryptographic calculi (e.g., hedged bisimilarity, labelled bisimilarity, early bisimilarity) coincide with observational equivalence [2,4,5,10,15–17,31,32,34]. Observational equivalence is a restriction of open barbed bisimilarity (Definition 3), considering only contexts of the form $\{ \cdot \} \mid P$

that add a new process in parallel at every step of the bisimulation game. This makes the equivalence strictly coarser than open barbed bisimilarity, however observational equivalence is not a congruence relation. Intermediate results on symbolic bisimulations [18,25] also closely approximate observational equivalence.

The gap between observational equivalences and open barbed bisimilarity is thoroughly explored in the context of the π-calculus [7,29,40,41]. Open barbed bisimilarity is finer than observational equivalence since, $\pi.P + \pi.Q$ is observationally equivalent to $\pi.P + \pi.Q + \pi.\text{if } x = y \text{ then } P \text{ else } Q$, but these processes are not open barbed bisimilar in general. Yet these processes are equivalent if we take barbed equivalence [36], which is the largest congruence contained within observational equivalence, lying strictly between open barbed bisimilarity and observational equivalence. In Sect. 4.1, we did mention there are examples of noninterference properties that can be formulated using a congruence. However, it remains an open question whether there exists a realistic privacy property, as opposed to the toy equation immediately above, that cannot be verified using open barbed bisimilarity but can be analysed using barbed equivalence.

If one does insist that a property is defined in terms of observational equivalence, we may still use quasi-open bisimilarity as an under-approximation. If an attack is discovered, we can check whether an attack is also valid classically (possibly making use of modal logic intuitionistic $\mathcal{FM}$ described in the extended technical report [29]). If the attack is also classically valid it is also a counterexample for observational equivalence. This methodology was used to resolve the problem of whether there is an attack on the BAC protocol for ePassports [26,28], as originally stated in terms of observational equivalence [8].

6   Conclusion

This paper justifies the bisimilarity congruence quasi-open bisimilarity as a method for reasoning about protocols expressed using the applied π-calculus. The equivalence we converge on, *quasi-open bisimilarity*, can be seen as an enhancement of existing methods, balancing between the strengths of *labelled bisimilarity* [4,10,15–17,31,32, 34] and *open bisimilarity*.

The bisimilarity congruence, *open bisimilarity*, has previously been introduced for the spi-calculus [19,42,43]. However, the spi-calculus could not verify privacy properties demanding mismatch, and is less abstract, being hard-wired with a fixed message theory; which were problems addressed in recent work that lifts open bisimilarity to the more general setting of the applied π-calculus [28]. By moving to the coarser equivalence *quasi-open bisimilarity* we are able to verify more privacy properties, such as the typical privacy-preserving protocol in Sect. 2, involving *if-then-else* with a guard depending on private information. Some equivalences, such as differential equivalence [12,21], which compares two structurally identical processes that differ only in the terms they exchange, are incomplete and hence may report attacks that trivially do not exist. Hence when differential equivalence reports an attack, it may not exist for trivial reasons – a problem minimised by the fact that quasi-open bisimilarity adheres to a completeness criterion for observational congruences (Theorem 3).

Equivalences coarser than quasi-open bisimilarity are either not congruences or are not bisimilarities, meaning that some corresponding proof techniques cannot be applied.

The gap between quasi-open bisimilarity and classical *labelled bisimilarity* is small—we insist on an open relation (Definition 2). However, the gap is significant, since we obtain a complete congruence. In an extended version of this paper in a technical report [27], we go further by demonstrating that we are able to logically characterise quasi-open bisimilarity, using an intuitionistic modal logic useful for describing attacks.

References

1. Abadi, M., Cortier, V.: Deciding knowledge in security protocols under equational theories. Theor. Comput. Sci. **367**(1–2), 2–32 (2006). https://doi.org/10.1016/j.tcs.2006.08.032
2. Abadi, M., Fournet, C.: Mobile values, new names, and secure communication. In: POPL, pp. 104–115 (2001). https://doi.org/10.1145/360204.360213
3. Abadi, M., Fournet, C.: Private authentication. Theor. Comput. Sci. **322**(3), 427–476 (2004). https://doi.org/10.1016/j.tcs.2003.12.023
4. Abadi, M., Gordon, A.D.: A bisimulation method for cryptographic protocols. Nord. J. Comput. **5**(4), 267–303 (1998)
5. Abadi, M., Blanchet, B., Fournet, C.: The applied pi calculus: mobile values, new names, and secure communication. J. ACM **65**(1), 1–41 (2017). https://doi.org/10.1145/3127586
6. Ahn, K.Y., Horne, R., Tiu, A.: A characterisation of open bisimilarity using an intuitionistic modal logic. In: Meyer, R., Nestmann, U. (eds.) 28th International Conference on Concurrency Theory, CONCUR 2017, 5–8 September 2017, Berlin, Germany, vol. 85 of LIPIcs, pp. 7:1–7:17 (2017). https://doi.org/10.4230/LIPIcs.CONCUR.2017.7
7. Ahn, K.Y., Horne, R., Tiu, A.: A characterisation of open bisimilarity using an intuitionistic modal logic. Log. Meth. Comp. Sci. (2021). https://arxiv.org/abs/1701.05324. In press
8. Arapinis, M., Chothia, T., Ritter, E., Ryan, M.: Analysing unlinkability and anonymity using the applied pi calculus. In 23rd IEEE Computer Security Foundations Symposium, pp. 107–121 (2010). https://doi.org/10.1109/CSF.2010.15
9. Ayala-Rincón, M., Fernández, M., Nantes-Sobrinho, D.: Intruder deduction problem for locally stable theories with normal forms and inverses. Theor. Comput. Sci. **672**, 64–100 (2017). https://doi.org/10.1016/j.tcs.2017.01.027
10. Bengtson, J., Johansson, M., Parrow, J., Victor, B.: Psi-calculi: a framework for mobile processes with nominal data and logic. Log. Meth. Comp. Sci. **7**(1) (2011). https://doi.org/10.2168/LMCS-7(1:11)2011
11. Blanchet, B.: Automatic proof of strong secrecy for security protocols. In: 2004 Proceedings of IEEE Symposium on Security and Privacy, pp. 86–100. IEEE (2004). https://doi.org/10.1109/SECPRI.2004.1301317
12. Blanchet, B., Abadi, M., Fournet, C.: Automated verification of selected equivalences for security protocols. J. Log. Algebr. Program. **75**(1), 3–51 (2008). https://doi.org/10.1016/j.jlap.2007.06.002
13. Bonchi, F., König, B., Montanari, U.: Saturated semantics for reactive systems. In: 21th IEEE Symposium on Logic in Computer Science (LICS 2006), 12–15 August 2006, Seattle, WA, USA, Proceedings, pp. 69–80. IEEE Computer Society (2006). https://doi.org/10.1109/LICS.2006.46
14. Bonchi, F., Gadducci, F., Monreale, G.V.: A general theory of barbs, contexts, and labels. ACM Trans. Comput. Log. **15**(4), 35:1-35:27 (2014). https://doi.org/10.1145/2631916

15. Boreale, M., De Nicola, R., Pugliese, R.: Proof techniques for cryptographic processes. SIAM J. Comput. **31**(3), 947–986 (2001). https://doi.org/10.1137/S0097539700377864
16. Borgström, J.: A complete symbolic bisimilarity for an extended Spi calculus. Electron. Notes Theor. Comput. Sci. **242**(3), 3–20 (2009). https://doi.org/10.1016/j.entcs.2009.07.078
17. Borgström, J., Nestmann, U.: On bisimulations for the Spi calculus. Math. Struct. Comput. Sci. **15**(3), 487–552 (2005). https://doi.org/10.1017/S0960129505004706
18. Borgström, J., Briais, S., Nestmann, U.: Symbolic bisimulation in the Spi calculus. In: Gardner, P., Yoshida, N. (eds.) CONCUR 2004. LNCS, vol. 3170, pp. 161–176. Springer, Heidelberg (2004). https://doi.org/10.1007/978-3-540-28644-8_11
19. Briais, S., Nestmann, U.: Open bisimulation, revisited. Theor. Comput. Sci. **386**(3), 236–271 (2007). https://doi.org/10.1016/j.tcs.2007.07.010
20. Bursuc, S., Comon-Lundh, H., Delaune, S.: Deducibility constraints and blind signatures. Inf. Comput. **238**, 106–127 (2014). https://doi.org/10.1016/j.ic.2014.07.006
21. Cheval, V., Blanchet, B.: Proving more observational equivalences with ProVerif. In: Basin, D., Mitchell, J.C. (eds.) POST 2013. LNCS, vol. 7796, pp. 226–246. Springer, Heidelberg (2013). https://doi.org/10.1007/978-3-642-36830-1_12
22. Cheval, V., Comon-Lundh, H., Delaune, S.: A procedure for deciding symbolic equivalence between sets of constraint systems. Inf. Comput. **255**(Part 1), 94–125 (2017). https://doi.org/10.1016/j.ic.2017.05.004
23. Cortier, V., Smyth, B.: Attacking and fixing Helios: an analysis of ballot secrecy. In: 2011 IEEE 24th Computer Security Foundations Symposium, pp. 297–311, June 2011. https://doi.org/10.1109/CSF.2011.27
24. Delaune, S.: Analysing privacy-type properties in cryptographic protocols. In: Kirchner, H. (ed.) 3rd International Conference on Formal Structures for Computation and Deduction (FSCD 2018), volume 108 of LIPIcs, Dagstuhl, Germany, pp. 1:1–1:21. Schloss Dagstuhl-Leibniz-Zentrum fuer Informatik (2018). https://doi.org/10.4230/LIPIcs.FSCD.2018.1
25. Delaune, S., Kremer, S., Ryan, M.D.: Symbolic bisimulation for the applied pi calculus. J. Comput. Secur. **18**(2), 317–377 (2010). https://doi.org/10.3233/JCS-2010-0363
26. Filimonov, I., Horne, R., Mauw, S., Smith, Z.: Breaking unlinkability of the ICAO 9303 standard for e-passports using bisimilarity. In: Sako, K., Schneider, S., Ryan, P.Y.A. (eds.) ESORICS 2019. LNCS, vol. 11735, pp. 577–594. Springer, Cham (2019). https://doi.org/10.1007/978-3-030-29959-0_28
27. Horne, R.: A bisimilarity congruence for the applied pi-calculus sufficiently coarse to verify privacy properties. Arxiv, arXiv:1811.02536, pp. 1–31 (2018.). https://arxiv.org/abs/1811.02536
28. Horne, R., Mauw, S.: Discovering ePassport vulnerabilities using bisimilarity. Logical Methods in Computer Science **17**(2), 24:1-24:52 (2021). https://doi.org/10.23638/LMCS-17(2:24)2021
29. Horne, R., Ahn, K.Y., Lin, S., Tiu, A.: Quasi-open bisimilarity with mismatch is intuitionistic. In: Dawar, A., Grädel, E. (eds.) Proceedings of LICS 2018: 33rd Annual ACM/IEEE Symposium on Logic in Computer Science (LICS 2018), Oxford, United Kingdom, 9–12 July 2018, p. 10 (2018). https://doi.org/10.1145/3209108.3209125
30. Horne, R., Mauw, S., Yurkov, S.: Breaking and fixing unlinkability of the key agreement protocol for 2nd gen EMV payments (2021). https://arxiv.org/abs/2105.02029
31. Johansson, M., Bengtson, J., Victor, B., Parrow, J.: Weak equivalences in psi-calculi. In: 2010 25th Annual IEEE Symposium on Logic in Computer Science, pp. 322–331, July 2010. https://doi.org/10.1109/LICS.2010.30
32. Johansson, M., Victor, B., Parrow, J.: Computing strong and weak bisimulations for psi-calculi. J. Logic Algebraic Program. **81**(3), 162–180 (2012). https://doi.org/10.1016/j.jlap.2012.01.001

33. Kremer, S., Ryan, M.: Analysis of an electronic voting protocol in the applied pi calculus. In: Sagiv, M. (ed.) ESOP 2005. LNCS, vol. 3444, pp. 186–200. Springer, Heidelberg (2005). https://doi.org/10.1007/978-3-540-31987-0_14

34. Liu, J., Lin, H.: A complete symbolic bisimulation for full applied pi calculus. Theor. Comput. Sci. **458**, 76–112 (2012). https://doi.org/10.1016/j.tcs.2012.07.034

35. Milner, R.: The polyadic π-calculus: a tutorial. In: Bauer, F.L., Brauer, W., Schwichtenberg, H. (eds.) Logic and Algebra of Specification. NATO ASI Series, vol. 94, pp. 203–246 (1993). https://doi.org/10.1007/978-3-642-58041-3_6

36. Milner, R., Sangiorgi, D.: Barbed bisimulation, pp. 685–695 (1992). https://doi.org/10.1007/3-540-55719-9_114

37. Milner, R., Parrow, J., Walker, D.: A calculus of mobile processes, Part I and II. Inf. Comput. **100**(1), 1–100 (1992). https://doi.org/10.1016/0890-5401(92)90008-4

38. Montanari, U., Sassone, V.: Dynamic congruence vs. progressing bisimulation for CCS. Fundam. Inf. **16**(2), 171–199 (1992)

39. Sangiorgi, D.: On the proof method for bisimulation. In: Wiedermann, J., Hájek, P. (eds.) MFCS 1995. LNCS, vol. 969, pp. 479–488. Springer, Heidelberg (1995). https://doi.org/10.1007/3-540-60246-1_153

40. Sangiorgi, D.: A theory of bisimulation for the π-calculus. Acta Inf. **33**(1), 69–97 (1996). https://doi.org/10.1007/s002360050036

41. Sangiorgi, D., Walker, D.: On barbed equivalences in π-calculus. In: Larsen, K.G., Nielsen, M. (eds.) CONCUR 2001. LNCS, vol. 2154, pp. 292–304. Springer, Heidelberg (2001). https://doi.org/10.1007/3-540-44685-0_20

42. Tiu, A.: A trace based bisimulation for the Spi calculus: an extended abstract. In: Shao, Z. (ed.) APLAS 2007. LNCS, vol. 4807, pp. 367–382. Springer, Heidelberg (2007). https://doi.org/10.1007/978-3-540-76637-7_25

43. Tiu, A., Nguyen, N., Horne, R.: SPEC: an equivalence checker for security protocols. In: Igarashi, A. (ed.) APLAS 2016. LNCS, vol. 10017, pp. 87–95. Springer, Cham (2016). https://doi.org/10.1007/978-3-319-47958-3_5

44. Glabbeek, R.J.: The linear time—branching time spectrum II. In: Best, E. (ed.) CONCUR 1993. LNCS, vol. 715, pp. 66–81. Springer, Heidelberg (1993). https://doi.org/10.1007/3-540-57208-2_6. ISBN 3-540-57208-2

45. van Glabbeek, R.J., Goltz, U.: Refinement of actions and equivalence notions for concurrent systems. Acta Inf. **37**(4/5), 229–327 (2001). https://doi.org/10.1007/s002360000041

Card-Based Cryptographic Protocols with a Standard Deck of Cards Using Private Operations

Yoshifumi Manabe$^{(\boxtimes)}$ and Hibiki Ono

Kogakuin University, Shinjuku, Tokyo 163–8677, Japan
manabe@cc.kogakuin.ac.jp

Abstract. This paper shows new kinds of card-based cryptographic protocols with a standard deck of cards using private operations. They are multi-party secure computations executed by multiple players without computers. Most card-based cryptographic protocols use a special deck of cards that consists of many cards with two kinds of marks. Though these protocols are simple and efficient, the users need to prepare such special cards. Few protocols were shown that use a standard deck of playing cards. Though the protocols with a standard deck of cards can be easily executed in our daily life, the numbers of cards used by these protocols are larger than the ones that use the special deck of cards. This paper shows logical AND, logical XOR, and copy protocols for a standard deck of cards that use the minimum number of cards. Any Boolean functions can be calculated with a combination of the above protocols. The new protocols use private operations that are executed by a player where the other players cannot see. The results show the effectiveness of private operations in card-based cryptographic protocols.

Keywords: Multi-party secure computation · Card-based cryptographic protocols · Private operations · Logical computations · Copy · Playing cards

1 Introduction

Card-based cryptographic protocols [13,34,36] were proposed in which physical cards are used instead of computers to securely calculate values. They can be used when computers cannot be used or users cannot trust the software on the computer. Also, the protocols are easy to understand, thus the protocols can be used to teach the basics of cryptography [4,28]. den Boer [2] first showed a five-card protocol to securely calculate logical AND of two inputs. Since then, many protocols have been proposed to realize primitives to calculate any Boolean functions [7,12,17,37,48,57] and specific computations such as a class of Boolean functions [1,23,24,29,33,42,43,45,50,51,55,62,64], millionaires' problem [25,39,46], realizing Turing machines [6,15], voting [31,40,44,63], random permutation [8,10,11,38], grouping [9], ranking [60], lottery [58], proof

© Springer Nature Switzerland AG 2021
A. Cerone and P. C. Ölveczky (Eds.): ICTAC 2021, LNCS 12819, pp. 256–274, 2021.
https://doi.org/10.1007/978-3-030-85315-0_15

of knowledge of a puzzle solution [3,5,21,26,27,49,52–54], and so on. This paper considers calculations of logical AND and logical XOR functions and copy operation since any Boolean function can be realized with a combination of these calculations.

Most of the above works are based on a two-color card model. In the two-color card model, there are two kinds of cards, ♣ and ♡. Cards of the same marks cannot be distinguished. In addition, the back of both types of cards is ?. It is impossible to determine the mark in the back of a given card of ?. Though the model is simple, such special cards are not available in our daily life. When the players make the special cards using white cards and a printer, the person who prints the marks to cards might add tiny marks on the cards for the person to distinguish the cards and obtain secret data. Thus, hand-made cards are not so easy to realize.

To solve the problem, card-based cryptographic protocols using a standard deck of playing cards were shown [14,18,19,30,41,56]. Playing cards are available at many houses and easy to buy. Niemi and Renvall first showed protocols that use a standard deck of playing cards [41]. They showed logical XOR, logical AND, and copy protocols since any Boolean functions can be realized by a combination of these protocols. Their protocols are 'Las Vegas' type protocols, that is, the execution times of the protocols are not limited. The protocols are expected to terminate within a finite time, but if the sequence of the random numbers is bad, the protocols do not terminate forever. Mizuki showed fixed time logical XOR, logical AND, and copy protocols [30]. Though the number of cards used by the XOR protocol is the minimum, the ones used by the logical AND and copy protocols are not the minimum. Koch et al. showed a four-card 'Las Vegas' type AND protocol and it is impossible to obtain four-card finite time protocol with the model without private operations [14]. Koyama et al. showed a three-input 'Las Vegas' type AND protocol with the minimum number of cards [18]. Koyama et al. showed an efficient 'Las Vegas' type copy protocol [19]. Shinagawa and Mizuki showed protocols to calculate any n-variable function using a standard deck of playing cards and a deck of UNO[1] cards [56].

Randomization or a private operation is the most important primitive in these card-based protocols. If every primitive executed in a card-based protocol is deterministic and public, the relationship between the private input values and output values is known to the players. When the output value is disclosed, the private input value can be known to the players from the relationship. Thus, all protocols need some random or private operation.

First, public randomization primitives have been discussed and then recently, private operations are considered. Many protocols use random bisection cuts [37], which randomly execute swapping two decks of cards or not swapping. If the random value used in the randomization is disclosed, the secret input value is known to the players. If some player privately brings a high-speed camera, the random value selected by the randomization might be known by analyzing the image. Though the size of a high-speed camera is very large, the size might

---

[1] https://www.letsplayuno.com.

become very small shortly. To prepare for the situation, we need to consider using private operations.

Operations that a player executes in a place where the other players cannot see are called private operations. These operations are considered to be executed under the table or in the back. Private operations are shown to be the most powerful primitives in card-based cryptographic protocols. They were first introduced to solve millionaires' problem [39]. Using three private operations shown later, committed-input and committed-output logical AND, logical XOR, and copy protocols can be achieved with the minimum number of cards on the two-color card model [48]. Another class of private operations is private input operations that are used when a player inputs a private value [20,46,59,63]. These operations are not discussed in this paper since the protocols need the players to know the input values. The protocols without private input operations can be used when the players do not know private input values.

So the research question is whether we can achieve the minimum number of cards for a standard deck of cards if we use private operations. We show positive results to the question. This paper shows new logical AND and copy protocols with a standard deck of playing cards that achieves the minimum number of cards by using private operations. The results show that the private operations are also effective for a standard deck of cards.

Note that in this paper, all players are assumed to be semi-honest. Few works are done for the case when some players are malicious or make mistakes [16,22,32,35,61].

In Sect. 2, basic notations and the private operations introduced in [48] are shown. Section 3 shows logical AND, copy, and logical XOR protocols. Then, protocols to calculate any n-variable Boolean function are shown. Section 4 concludes the paper.

2 Preliminaries

2.1 Basic Notations

This section gives the notations and basic definitions of card-based protocols with a standard deck of cards. A deck of playing cards consists of 52 distinct mark cards, which are named as 1 to 52. The number of each card (for example, 1 is the ace of spade and 52 is the king of club) is common knowledge among the players. The back of all cards is the same $\boxed{?}$. It is impossible to determine the mark in the back of a given card of $\boxed{?}$.

One bit data is represented by two cards as follows: $\boxed{i}\boxed{j} = 0$ and $\boxed{j}\boxed{i} = 1$ if $i < j$.

One pair of cards that represents one bit $x \in \{0,1\}$, whose face is down, is called a commitment of x, and denoted as $commit(x)$. It is written as $\underbrace{\boxed{?}\boxed{?}}_{x}$.

The base of a commitment is the pair of cards used for the commitment. If card i and $j(i < j)$ are used to set $commit(x)$ (That is, set $\boxed{i}\boxed{j}$ if $x = 0$ and set

| j | i |

if $x = 1$), the commitment is written as $commit(x)^{\{i,j\}}$ and written as

| ? | ? |

. When the base information is obvious or unnecessary, it is not written.

$x^{\{i,j\}}$

Note that when these two cards are swapped, $commit(\bar{x})^{\{i,j\}}$ can be obtained. Thus, logical negation can be calculated without private operations.

A set of cards placed in a row is called a sequence of cards. A sequence of cards S whose length is n is denoted as $S = s_1, s_2, \ldots, s_n$, where s_i is i-th card of the sequence. $S = $ | ? | | ? | | ? | $\ldots$ | ? | . A sequence whose length is even is

$\underbrace{}_{s_1}$ $\underbrace{}_{s_2}$ $\underbrace{}_{s_3}$ $\underbrace{}_{s_n}$

called an even sequence. $S_1 \| S_2$ is a concatenation of sequence S_1 and S_2.

All protocols are executed by two players, Alice and Bob. The players are semi-honest, that is, they obey the rule of the protocols but try to obtain secret values. There is no collusion between Alice and Bob, otherwise private input data can be easily revealed. The inputs of the protocols are given in a committed format, that is, the players do not know the input values. The output of the protocol must be given in a committed format so that the result can be used as an input to further calculation.

A protocol is secure when the following two conditions are satisfied: (1) If the output cards are not opened, each player obtains no information about the private input values from the view of the protocol for the player (the sequence of the cards opened to the player). (2) When the output cards are opened, each player obtains no additional information about the private input values other than the information by the output of the protocol. For example, if the output cards of an AND protocol for input x and y are opened and the value is 1, the players can know that $x = 1$ and $y = 1$. If the output value is 0, the players must not know whether the input (x, y) is $(0, 0)$, $(0, 1)$, or $(1, 0)$.

The following protocols use random numbers. Random numbers can be generated without computers using coin-flipping or some similar methods. During the protocol executions, cards are sent and received between the players. The communication is executed by handing the cards between the players to avoid information leakage during the communication. If the players are not in the same place during the protocol execution, a trusted third party (for example, post office) is necessary to send and receive cards between players.

2.2   Private Operations

We show three private operations introduced in [48]: private random bisection cuts, private reverse cuts, and private reveals.

Primitive 1 *(Private random bisection cut)*
A private random bisection cut is the following operation on an even sequence $S_0 = s_1, s_2, \ldots, s_{2m}$. A player selects a random bit $b \in \{0, 1\}$ and outputs

$$S_1 = \begin{cases} S_0 & \text{if } b = 0 \\ s_{m+1}, s_{m+2}, \ldots, s_{2m}, s_1, s_2, \ldots, s_m & \text{if } b = 1 \end{cases}$$

The player executes this operation in a place where the other players cannot see. The player must not disclose the bit b.

Note that if the private random cut is executed when $m = 1$ and $S_0 = commit(x)$, given $S_0 = \boxed{?}\boxed{?}$, The player's output $S_1 = \boxed{?}\boxed{?}$, which is $\boxed{?}\boxed{?}$

$\qquad\qquad\qquad\qquad\qquad\qquad\quad \underbrace{}_{x} \qquad\qquad\qquad\qquad \underbrace{}_{x \oplus b} \qquad\quad \underbrace{}_{x}$

or $\boxed{?}\boxed{?}$.

$\quad \underbrace{}_{\overline{x}}$

Note that a private random bisection cut is the same as the random bisection cut [37], but the operation is executed in a hidden place.

Primitive 2 *(Private reverse cut, Private reverse selection)*
  A private reverse cut is the following operation on an even sequence $S_2 = s_1, s_2, \ldots, s_{2m}$ and a bit $b \in \{0, 1\}$. A player outputs

$$S_3 = \begin{cases} S_2 & \text{if } b = 0 \\ s_{m+1}, s_{m+2}, \ldots, s_{2m}, s_1, s_2, \ldots, s_m & \text{if } b = 1 \end{cases}$$

The player executes this operation in a place where the other players cannot see. The player must not disclose b.

Note that the bit b is not newly selected by the player. This is the difference between the primitive in Primitive 1, where a random bit must be newly selected by the player.
  Note that in some protocols below, selecting left m cards is executed after a private reverse cut. The sequence of these two operations is called a private reverse selection. A private reverse selection is the following procedure on an even sequence $S_2 = s_1, s_2, \ldots, s_{2m}$ and a bit $b \in \{0, 1\}$. A player outputs

$$S_3 = \begin{cases} s_1, s_2, \ldots, s_m & \text{if } b = 0 \\ s_{m+1}, s_{m+2}, \ldots, s_{2m} & \text{if } b = 1 \end{cases}$$

Primitive 3 *(Private reveal).* *A player privately opens a given committed bit. The player must not disclose the obtained value.*

Using the obtained value, the player privately sets a sequence of cards.
  Consider the case when Alice executes a private random bisection cut on $commit(x)$ and Bob executes a private reveal on the bit. Since the committed bit is randomized by the bit b selected by Alice, the opened bit is $x \oplus b$. Even if Bob privately opens the cards, Bob obtains no information about x if b is randomly selected and not disclosed by Alice. Bob must not disclose the obtained value. If Bob discloses the obtained value to Alice, Alice knows the value of the committed bit.

2.3 Opaque Commitment Pair

An opaque commitment pair is defined as a useful situation to design a secure protocol using a standard deck of cards [30]. It is a pair of commitments whose bases are unknown to a player. Let us consider the following two commitments using cards i, j, i' and j'. The left(right) commitment has value x (y), respectively, but it is unknown that (1) the left (right) commitment is made using i and j (i' and j'), respectively, or (2) the left (right) commitment is made using i' and j' (i and j), respectively. Such pair of commitment is called an opaque commitment pair and written as $commit(x)^{\{i,j\},\{i',j'\}}||commit(y)^{\{i,j\},\{i',j'\}}$. Note that there is a case when Alice thinks a pair is an opaque commitment pair but Bob knows the base, especially when Bob privately makes the pair of commitments with the knowledge of x and y. For example, Bob randomly selects a bit $b \in \{0,1\}$ and

$$S = \begin{cases} commit(x)^{\{i,j\}}||commit(y)^{\{i',j'\}} & \text{if } b = 0 \\ commit(x)^{\{i',j'\}}||commit(y)^{\{i,j\}} & \text{if } b = 1 \end{cases}$$

then $S = commit(x)^{\{i,j\},\{i',j'\}}||commit(y)^{\{i,j\},\{i',j'\}}$ for Alice.

2.4   Space and Time Complexities

The space complexity of card-based protocols is evaluated by the number of cards. Minimizing the number of cards is discussed in many works.

The number of rounds was proposed as a criterion to evaluate the time complexity of card-based protocols using private operations [47]. The first round begins from the initial state. The first round is (possibly parallel) local executions by each player using the cards initially given to each player. It ends at the instant when no further local execution is possible without receiving cards from another player. The local executions in each round include sending cards to some other players but do not include receiving cards. The result of every private execution is known to the player. For example, shuffling whose result is unknown to the player himself is not executed. Since the private operations are executed in a place where the other players cannot see, it is hard to force the player to execute such operations whose result is unknown to the player. The $i(> 1)$-th round begins with receiving all the cards sent during the $(i - 1)$-th round. Each player executes local executions using the received cards and the cards left to the player at the end of the $(i - 1)$-th round. Each player executes local executions until no further local execution is possible without receiving cards from another player. The number of rounds of a protocol is the maximum number of rounds necessary to output the result among all possible inputs and random values.

Let us show an example of a protocol execution, its space complexity, and time complexity with the conventional two-color card model. In the two-color card model, there are two kinds of marks, ♣ and ♡. One bit data is represented by two cards as follows: ♣♡ = 0 and ♡♣ = 1.

Protocol 1 *(AND protocol in [48])*
Input: commit(x) and commit(y).
Output: commit(x ∧ y).

1. *Alice executes a private random bisection cut on commit(x). Let the output be commit(x'). Alice sends commit(x') and commit(y) to Bob.*
2. *Bob executes a private reveal on commit(x'). Bob privately sets*

$$S_2 = \begin{cases} commit(y)||commit(0) & if\ x' = 1 \\ commit(0)||commit(y) & if\ x' = 0 \end{cases}$$

and sends S_2 to Alice.
3. *Alice executes a private reverse selection on S_2 using the bit b generated in the private random bisection cut. Let the obtained sequence be S_3. Alice outputs S_3.*

The AND protocol realizes the following equation.

$$x \wedge y = \begin{cases} y & if\ x = 1 \\ 0 & if\ x = 0 \end{cases}$$

The correctness of the protocol is shown in [48]. The number of cards is four, since the cards of $commit(x')$ are re-used to set $commit(0)$.

Let us consider the time complexity of the protocol. The first round ends at the instant when Alice sends $commit(x')$ and $commit(y)$ to Bob. The second round begins at receiving the cards by Bob. The second round ends at the instant when Bob sends S_2 to Alice. The third round begins at receiving the cards by Alice. The number of rounds of this protocol is three.

Since each operation is relatively simple, the dominating time to execute protocols with private operations is the time to sending cards between players and setting up so that the cards are not seen by the other players. Thus the number of rounds is the criterion to evaluate the time complexity of card-based protocols with private operations.

2.5   Problems with a Standard Deck of Cards

The above AND protocol cannot be executed as it is with a standard deck of cards.

The protocol uses the property that all $\boxed{\heartsuit}$ cards ($\boxed{\clubsuit}$ cards) are indistinguishable. Even if the final cards are opened to see the result, it is impossible to know that the opened cards are the cards of $commit(y)$ or $commit(0)$. If it is possible to detect the above information, the value of x is known to the players.

First, let us consider a simple encoding using a standard deck of a playing card that heart and diamond cards mean $\boxed{\heartsuit}$ and all club and spade cards mean $\boxed{\clubsuit}$. With this simple encoding, let us consider the case when the aces of diamond and spade are used to set $commit(x)$ and the aces of heart and club are used to set $commit(y)$.

Suppose that $x = 1$ and $y = 0$. In this case, the result is $commit(y)$, thus the result is correct since $y = 0$. At step 2 of the protocol, aces of diamond and spade are re-used to set $commit(0)$. Since $x = 1$, the result is $commit(y)$. When the cards are opened to see the result, the cards are the aces of heart and club.

The players can know that y is selected as the output, thus x must be 1. The execution reveals the information of inputs from the cards used to set the input commitments.

Next, consider the case when the encoding rule $\boxed{i}\,\boxed{j} = 0$, $\boxed{j}\,\boxed{i} = 1$ if $i < j$ is used to the standard deck of playing cards. Suppose again that $x = 1$ and $y = 0$. When two inputs are given as $commit(x)^{\{1,2\}}$ and $commit(y)^{\{3,4\}}$, $commit(0)$ and $commit(y)$ are set as $commit(0)^{\{1,2\}}$ and $commit(y)^{\{3,4\}}$, respectively at Step 2. Since $x = 1$, the result is $commit(y)^{\{3,4\}}$. When the cards are opened to see the result, the cards are 3 and 4. The players can know that y is selected as the output, thus x must be 1. This execution also reveals the information of inputs from the base of the commitments.

When we design a protocol with a standard deck of cards, we must consider the information leakage from the base of the commitment.

3   AND, XOR, and Copy with a Standard Deck of Cards

This section shows our new protocols for AND, and copy with the minimum number of cards using private operations. We also show XOR protocol using private operations to show the minimum number of cards can also be achieved using private operations. Before we show the protocols, we show subroutines to change the base of a given commitment.

3.1   Base Change Protocols

A base change protocol changes the base of a commitment without changing the value of the commitment. A base change protocol is also shown in [30], but the protocol uses a public shuffle, thus we show a new protocol that uses private operations.

Protocol 2 *(Base change protocol (1))*
   Input: $commit(x)^{\{1,2\}}$ and two new card 3 and 4.
   Output: $commit(x)^{\{3,4\}}$.

1. *Bob executes a private random bisection cut on $commit(x)^{\{1,2\}}$. Let $b \in \{0,1\}$ be the bit Bob selected. The result is $S_1 = commit(x \oplus b)^{\{1,2\}}$. Bob sends S_1 to Alice.*
2. *Alice executes a private reveal on S_1. Alice sees $x \oplus b$. Alice makes $S_2 = commit(x \oplus b)^{\{3,4\}}$ and sends S_2 to Bob.*
3. *Bob executes a private reverse cut using b on S_2. The result is $commit(x)^{\{3,4\}}$.*

The protocol is three rounds. The security of the protocol is as follows. When Alice sees the cards at Step 2, the value is $x \oplus b$. Since b is a random value unknown to Alice, Alice has no information about x by the reveal. Bob sees no open cards, thus Bob has no information about x. Note again that Bob must not disclose b to Alice.

Another base change protocol from an opaque commitment pair can be considered. In the following protocol, the second input value $\perp$ is random and meaningless to Alice.

Protocol 3 *(Base change protocol (2))*
    Input: $commit(x)^{\{1,2\},\{3,4\}}||commit(\perp)^{\{1,2\},\{3,4\}}$.
    Output: $commit(x)^{\{1,2\}}$.

1. *Bob executes a private random bisection cut on the left pair, $commit(x)^{\{1,2\},\{3,4\}}$. Let $b \in \{0,1\}$ be the bit Bob selected. The result $S_1 = commit(x \oplus b)^{\{1,2\},\{3,4\}}||commit(\perp)^{\{1,2\},\{3,4\}}$. Bob sends S_1 to Alice.*
2. *Alice executes a private reveal on S_1. Alice sees $x \oplus b$. If the base of the left pair is $\{1,2\}$, Alice just faces down the left pair and the cards, S_2, be the result. Otherwise, the base of the right pair is $\{1,2\}$. Alice makes $S_2 = commit(x \oplus b)^{\{1,2\}}$ using the right cards. Alice sends S_2 to Bob.*
3. *Bob executes a private reverse cut using b on S_2. The result is $commit(x)^{\{1,2\}}$.*

In this protocol, Alice knows the bases of the input commitments. The protocol can be used only when this information leakage does not cause a security problem, for example, the bases are randomly set by Bob. The security of the input value x is just the same as the first base change protocol.

3.2 And Protocol

In the following AND, copy, and XOR protocols, the bases of the output commitments are fixed to avoid information leakage from the bases when the outputs are opened.

Protocol 4 *(AND protocol)*
    Input: $commit(x)^{\{1,2\}}$ and $commit(y)^{\{3,4\}}$.
    Output: $commit(x \wedge y)^{\{1,2\}}$.

1. *Alice executes a private random bisection cut on $commit(x)^{\{1,2\}}$ and $commit(y)^{\{3,4\}}$ using two different bits b_1 and b_2. Alice sends the results, $S_1 = commit(x \oplus b_1)^{\{1,2\}}$ and $S_2 = commit(y \oplus b_2)^{\{3,4\}}$, to Bob.*
2. *Bob executes private reveals on S_1 and S_2. Bob sees $x \oplus b_1$ and $y \oplus b_2$. Bob randomly selects bit $b_3 \in \{0,1\}$. Bob privately sets*

$$S_{3,0} = \begin{cases} commit(x \oplus b_1)^{\{1,2\}} & if\ b_3 = 0 \\ commit(x \oplus b_1)^{\{3,4\}} & if\ b_3 = 1 \end{cases}$$

and

$$S_{3,1} = \begin{cases} commit(y \oplus b_2)^{\{3,4\}} & if\ b_3 = 0 \\ commit(y \oplus b_2)^{\{1,2\}} & if\ b_3 = 1 \end{cases}$$

$S_{3,0} = commit(x \oplus b_1)^{\{1,2\},\{3,4\}}$ and $S_{3,1} = commit(y \oplus b_2)^{\{1,2\},\{3,4\}}$ for Alice. Bob sends $S_{3,1}$ to Alice.
3. *Alice executes a private reverse cut using b_2 on $S_{3,1}$. The result $S'_{3,1} = commit(y)^{\{1,2\},\{3,4\}}$. Alice sends $S'_{3,1}$ to Bob.*

4. *Bob executes a private reveal on $S_{3,0}$ and sees $x \oplus b_1$. Bob privately sets cards*

$$S_4 = \begin{cases} commit(0)^{\{1,2\},\{3,4\}} || S'_{3,1} & \text{if } x \oplus b_1 = 0 \\ S'_{3,1} || commit(0)^{\{1,2\},\{3,4\}} & \text{if } x \oplus b_1 = 1 \end{cases}$$

Note that the cards used for $S_{3,0}$ are reused to set $commit(0)$. Since $S_{3,0} = commit(\cdot)^{\{1,2\},\{3,4\}}$, the result is $commit(0)^{\{1,2\},\{3,4\}}$ for Alice. Bob sends S_4 to Alice.

5. *Alice executes a private reverse selection on S_4 using b_1. Let S_5 be the result and the remaining two cards be S_6. The result $S_5 = commit(y)^{\{1,2\},\{3,4\}}$ if ($b_1 = 0$ and $x \oplus b_1 = 1$) or ($b_1 = 1$ and $x \oplus b_1 = 0$). The condition equals to $x = 1$.*
$S_5 = commit(0)^{\{1,2\},\{3,4\}}$ if ($b_1 = 0$ and $x \oplus b_1 = 0$) or ($b_1 = 1$ and $x \oplus b_1 = 1$). The condition equals to $x = 0$. Thus,

$$S_5 = \begin{cases} commit(y)^{\{1,2\},\{3,4\}} & \text{if } x = 1 \\ commit(0)^{\{1,2\},\{3,4\}} & \text{if } x = 0 \end{cases}$$

$$= commit(x \wedge y)^{\{1,2\},\{3,4\}}$$

Alice sends S_5 and S_6 to Bob.

6. *Bob executes a private random bisection cut on S_6 to erase the value to Alice. Let b' be the random bit selected by Bob and S'_6 be the result.*
Bob and Alice execute Protocol 3 (Base change protocol (2)) to $S_5 || S'_6$. Then they obtain $commit(x \wedge y)^{\{1,2\}}$.

The protocol is eight rounds since the first round of the base change protocol can be executed in the sixth round of AND protocol by Bob. The number of cards is four. Since four cards are necessary to input x and y, the number of cards is the minimum. The correctness of the output value is shown in the protocol, thus we show the security.

Theorem 1. *The AND protocol is secure.*

Proof. First, we show the security for Bob. Though Bob sees cards at Step 2 and 4, the cards, $S_1 = commit(x \oplus b_1)^{\{1,2\}}$ and $S_2 = commit(y \oplus b_2)^{\{3,4\}}$, are randomized by b_1 and b_2. Thus Bob obtains no information about the input values.

Alice sees cards at the second step of the base change protocol. At Step 3 after the private reverse selection by Alice,

$$S'_{3,1} = \begin{cases} commit(y)^{\{3,4\}} & \text{if } b_3 = 0 \\ commit(y)^{\{1,2\}} & \text{if } b_3 = 1 \end{cases}$$

and $commit(y)$ $(commit(0))$ is finally selected as S_5 if $x = 1$ $(x = 0)$, respectively. The value is then randomized using b as $commit(y \oplus b)$ $(commit(b))$ at Step 1 of the base change protocol (2).

$$S_6 = \begin{cases} commit(0)^{\{1,2\},\{3,4\}} & \text{if } x = 1 \\ commit(y)^{\{1,2\},\{3,4\}} & \text{if } x = 0 \end{cases}$$

S_6 is also randomized at Step 6 using b'.

Thus at Step 2 of the base change protocol (2), Alice sees the randomized cards of $S_5||S_6$, which are

$$\begin{cases} commit(b)^{\{1,2\}}||commit(y \oplus b')^{\{3,4\}} & \text{if } b_3 = 0 \text{ and } x = 0 \\ commit(y \oplus b)^{\{3,4\}}||commit(b')^{\{1,2\}} & \text{if } b_3 = 0 \text{ and } x = 1 \\ commit(b)^{\{3,4\}}||commit(y \oplus b')^{\{1,2\}} & \text{if } b_3 = 1 \text{ and } x = 0 \\ commit(y \oplus b)^{\{1,2\}}||commit(b')^{\{3,4\}} & \text{if } b_3 = 1 \text{ and } x = 1 \end{cases}$$

Therefore, Alice sees

$$\begin{cases} commit(0)^{\{1,2\}}||commit(0)^{\{3,4\}} \\ \quad \text{if } (b_3 = 0 \wedge x = 0 \wedge b = 0 \wedge y \oplus b' = 0) \vee (b_3 = 1 \wedge x = 1 \wedge y \oplus b = 0 \wedge b' = 0) \\ commit(0)^{\{1,2\}}||commit(1)^{\{3,4\}} \\ \quad \text{if } (b_3 = 0 \wedge x = 0 \wedge b = 0 \wedge y \oplus b' = 1) \vee (b_3 = 1 \wedge x = 1 \wedge y \oplus b = 0 \wedge b' = 1) \\ commit(1)^{\{1,2\}}||commit(0)^{\{3,4\}} \\ \quad \text{if } (b_3 = 0 \wedge x = 0 \wedge b = 1 \wedge y \oplus b' = 0) \vee (b_3 = 1 \wedge x = 1 \wedge y \oplus b = 1 \wedge b' = 0) \\ commit(1)^{\{1,2\}}||commit(1)^{\{3,4\}} \\ \quad \text{if } (b_3 = 0 \wedge x = 0 \wedge b = 1 \wedge y \oplus b' = 1) \vee (b_3 = 1 \wedge x = 1 \wedge y \oplus b = 1 \wedge b' = 1) \\ commit(0)^{\{3,4\}}||commit(0)^{\{1,2\}} \\ \quad \text{if } (b_3 = 0 \wedge x = 1 \wedge y \oplus b = 0 \wedge b' = 0) \vee (b_3 = 1 \wedge x = 0 \wedge b = 0 \wedge y \oplus b' = 0) \\ commit(0)^{\{3,4\}}||commit(1)^{\{1,2\}} \\ \quad \text{if } (b_3 = 0 \wedge x = 1 \wedge y \oplus b = 0 \wedge b' = 1) \vee (b_3 = 1 \wedge x = 0 \wedge b = 0 \wedge y \oplus b' = 1) \\ commit(1)^{\{3,4\}}||commit(0)^{\{1,2\}} \\ \quad \text{if } (b_3 = 0 \wedge x = 1 \wedge y \oplus b = 1 \wedge b' = 0) \vee (b_3 = 1 \wedge x = 0 \wedge b = 1 \wedge y \oplus b' = 0) \\ commit(1)^{\{3,4\}}||commit(1)^{\{1,2\}} \\ \quad \text{if } (b_3 = 0 \wedge x = 1 \wedge y \oplus b = 1 \wedge b' = 1) \vee (b_3 = 1 \wedge x = 0 \wedge b = 1 \wedge y \oplus b' = 1) \end{cases}$$

Let $P_{ij}(i \in \{0,1\}, j \in \{0,1\})$ be the probability when $x = i$ and $y = j$. The probabilities $P(b = 0), P(b = 1), P(b' = 0), P(b_3 = 0)$, and $P(b_3 = 1)$ are $1/2$, thus the probabilities when Alice sees $commit(v)^{\{i,i+1\}}||commit(w)^{\{4-i,5-i\}}(v, w \in \{0,1\}, i \in \{1,3\})$ are the same value $(P_{00}+P_{01}+P_{10}+P_{11})/8$. Thus, Alice obtains no information from the cards she sees.   □

The comparison of AND protocols is shown in Table 1.

3.3   Copy Protocol

Next, we show a new copy protocol. Note that the protocol is essentially the same as the one in [48] for the two-color card model. The number of cards is the minimum.

Table 1. Comparison of AND protocols with a standard deck of cards.

Article	# of cards	Note
Niemi et al. [41]	5	Las Vegas algorithm
Koch et al. [14]	4	Las Vegas algorithm
Mizuki [30]	8	Fixed time algorithm
This paper	4	Fixed time algorithm

Table 2. Comparison of copy protocols with a standard deck of cards

Article	# of cards	Note
Niemi et al. [41]	6	Las Vegas algorithm
Koyama et al. [19]	6	Las Vegas algorithm
Mizuki [30]	6	Fixed time algorithm
This paper	4	Fixed time algorithm

Protocol 5 *(Copy protocol)*
  Input: $commit(x)^{\{1,2\}}$ and two new cards 3 and 4.
  Output: $commit(x)^{\{1,2\}}$ and $commit(x)^{\{3,4\}}$

1. *Alice executes a private random bisection cut on $commit(x)^{\{1,2\}}$. Let b the random bit Alice selects. Alice sends the result, $commit(x \oplus b)^{\{1,2\}}$, to Bob.*
2. *Bob executes a private reveal on $commit(x \oplus b)^{\{1,2\}}$ and sees $x \oplus b$. Bob privately makes $commit(x \oplus b)^{\{3,4\}}$. Bob sends $commit(x \oplus b)^{\{1,2\}}$ and $commit(x \oplus b)^{\{3,4\}}$ to Alice.*
3. *Alice executes a private reverse cut on each of the pairs using b. The result is $commit(x)^{\{1,2\}}$ and $commit(x)^{\{3,4\}}$.*

The protocol is three rounds.

Theorem 2. *The copy protocol is secure.*

Proof. Since Alice sees no open cards, Alice obtains no information about the input value. Though Bob sees $x \oplus b$, input x is randomized by b and Bob obtains no information about x. □

The comparison of copy protocols are shown in Table 2.
The number of rounds can be decreased to two if we use six cards using the protocol in [47] for the two-color card model.

3.4 XOR Protocol

Though the minimum number of cards is already achieved in [30], the protocol uses public shuffles. We show a new protocol that uses private operations. The protocol is essentially the same as the one in [47] for the two-color card model.

Table 3. Comparison of XOR protocols with a standard deck of cards.

Article	# of cards	Note
Niemi et al. [41]	4	Las Vegas algorithm
Mizuki [30]	4	Fixed time algorithm
This paper	4	Fixed time algorithm

Protocol 6 *(XOR protocol)*
   Input: $commit(x)^{\{1,2\}}$ and $commit(y)^{\{3,4\}}$.
   Output: $commit(x \oplus y)^{\{1,2\}}$.

1. *Alice executes a private random bisection cut on $commit(x)^{\{1,2\}}$ and $commit(y)^{\{3,4\}}$ using the same random bit $b \in \{0,1\}$. The result is $commit(x \oplus b)^{\{1,2\}}$ and $commit(y \oplus b)^{\{3,4\}}$. Alice sends these cards to Bob.*
2. *Bob executes a private reveal on $commit(y \oplus b)^{\{3,4\}}$. Bob sees $y \oplus b$. Bob executes a private reverse cut on $commit(x \oplus b)^{\{1,2\}}$ using $y \oplus b$. The result is $commit((x \oplus b) \oplus (y \oplus b))^{\{1,2\}} = commit(x \oplus y)^{\{1,2\}}$.*

The protocol is two rounds. The protocol uses four cards. Since any protocol needs four cards to input x and y, the number of cards is the minimum.

Note that if Bob sends $commit(y \oplus b)^{\{3,4\}}$ to Alice and Alice executes a private reverse cut using b, an input $commit(y)^{\{3,4\}}$ can be obtained without additional cards. This protocol is called an input preserving XOR and it is used in Sect. 3.5.

Theorem 3. *The XOR protocol is secure.*

Proof. Since Alice sees no open cards, Alice obtains no information about the input values. Though Bob sees $y \oplus b$, input y is randomized by b and Bob obtains no information about y. □

The comparison of XOR protocols is shown in Table 3.

3.5 Any Boolean Function

We show two kinds of protocols to calculate any n-variable Boolean function. The first one uses many cards but the number of rounds is constant. The second one uses fewer cards but needs many rounds. Let $f(x_1, x_2, \ldots, x_n)$ be an n-variable Boolean function.

Protocol 7 *(Protocol for any n-variable Boolean function (1))*
   Input: $commit(x_i)^{\{2i-1,2i\}} (i = 1, 2, \ldots, n)$.
   Output: $commit(f(x_1, x_2, \ldots, x_n))^{\{1,2\}}$.

1. *Alice executes a private random bisection cut on $commit(x_i)^{\{2i-1,2i\}} (i = 1, 2, \ldots, n)$. Let the output be $commit(x_i')^{\{2i-1,2i\}} (i = 1, 2, \ldots, n)$. Note that one random bit b_i is selected for each $x_i (i = 1, 2, \ldots, n)$. $x_i' = x_i \oplus b_i (i = 1, 2, \ldots, n)$. Alice sends $commit(x_i')^{\{2i-1,2i\}} (i = 1, 2, \ldots, n)$ to Bob.*

2. Bob executes a private reveal on $commit(x_i')^{\{2i-1,2i\}}(i = 1, 2, \ldots, n)$. Bob selects a random bit $b \in \{0, 1\}$. Bob privately makes 2^n commitments $S_{a_1,a_2,\ldots,a_n}$ $(a_i \in \{0, 1\}, i = 1, 2, \ldots, n)$ as $S_{a_1,a_2,\ldots,a_n} = commit(f(a_1 \oplus x_1', a_2 \oplus x_2', \ldots, a_n \oplus x_n') \oplus b)$ using card $3, 4, \ldots, 2^{n+1} + 1, 2^{n+1} + 2$. Note that the cards used to set each commitment are randomly selected by Bob. Bob executes a private random bisection cut on $commit(\cdot)^{\{1,2\}}$ to erase the value. Bob sends these commitments to Alice.

3. Alice privately reveals $S_{b_1,b_2,\ldots,b_n}$. Alice sees $f(b_1 \oplus x_1', b_2 \oplus x_2', \ldots, b_n \oplus x_n') \oplus b = f(x_1, x_2, \ldots, x_n) \oplus b$, since $x_i' = x_i \oplus b_i(i = 1, 2, \ldots, n)$. Alice privately makes $S = commit(f(x_1, x_2, \ldots, x_n) \oplus b)^{\{1,2\}}$ and sends S to Bob.

4. Bob executes a private reverse cut using b on S. The result is $commit(f(x_1, x_2, \ldots, x_n))^{\{1,2\}}$. Bob outputs the result.

Note that Bob can re-use cards of $3, 4, \ldots, 2n-1$, and $2n$ to set $S_{a_1,a_2,\ldots,a_n}$. The protocol uses $2^{n+1} + 2$ cards. The number of rounds is four.

Theorem 4. *The Protocol 7 is secure.*

Proof. Bob sees $x_i' = x_i \oplus b_i$, but the input x_i is randomized by b_i and Bob obtains no information about x_i. Alice sees $f(x_1, x_2, \ldots, x_n) \oplus b$, but the value is randomized by b and Alice obtains no information about $f(x_1, x_2, \ldots, x_n)$. Alice obtains no information from the base of the commitment since the base is randomly selected by Bob. □

The main idea of the other protocol is the same as the one in [48] for the two-color card model, which uses an input preserving AND protocol. After the AND protocol, the unused pair of cards has $g = \bar{x} \wedge y$ [48]. Let $h = x \wedge y$. The last step of AND protocol (the first step of the base change protocol) is changed so that Alice sets $commit(h \oplus b)^{\{1,2\}}$ and $commit(g \oplus b')^{\{3,4\}}$. By the private reverse cut by Bob, Bob obtains $commit(h)^{\{1,2\}}$ and $commit(g)^{\{3,4\}}$. Execute the input preserving XOR protocol to g and h so that h is preserved. The output $g \oplus h = x \wedge y \oplus \bar{x} \wedge y = y$, thus we can obtain $commit(x \wedge y)^{\{1,2\}}$ and $commit(y)^{\{3,4\}}$. Therefore, one input can be preserved without additional cards by the AND protocol.

Any Boolean function $f(x_1, x_2, \ldots, x_n)$ can be represented as follows:
$$f(x_1, x_2, \ldots, x_n) = \bar{x}_1 \wedge \bar{x}_2 \wedge \cdots \bar{x}_n \wedge f(0, 0, \ldots, 0) \oplus x_1 \wedge \bar{x}_2 \wedge \cdots \bar{x}_n \wedge f(1, 0, \ldots, 0) \oplus$$
$$\bar{x}_1 \wedge x_2 \wedge \cdots \bar{x}_n \wedge f(0, 1, \ldots, 0) \oplus \cdots \oplus x_1 \wedge x_2 \wedge \cdots x_n \wedge f(1, 1, \ldots, 1).$$

Since the terms with $f(i_1, i_2, \ldots, i_n) = 0$ can be removed, this function f can be written as $f = \bigoplus_{i=1}^{k} v_1^i \wedge v_2^i \wedge \cdots \wedge v_n^i$, where $v_j^i = x_j$ or $\bar{x}_j$. Let us write $T_i = v_1^i \wedge v_2^i \wedge \cdots \wedge v_n^i$. The number of terms $k(< 2^n)$ depends on f.

Protocol 8 *(Protocol for any n-variable Boolean function (2))*
    Input: $commit(x_i)^{\{2i+3,2i+4\}}(i = 1, 2, \ldots, n)$.
    Output: $commit(f(x_1, x_2, \ldots, x_n))^{\{1,2\}}$.
    The additional four cards (two pairs of cards) 1,2,3, and 4 are used as follows.
    1 and 2 store the intermediate value to calculate f.
    3 and 4 store the intermediate value to calculate T_i.

Table 4. Comparison of protocols to calculate any n-variable Boolean function with a standard deck of cards.

Article	# of cards	Note
Shinagawa et al. [56]	$2n + 8$	Fixed time algorithm
This paper's Protocol 7	$2^{n+1} + 2$	Fixed time algorithm
This paper's Protocol 8	$2n + 4$	Fixed time algorithm

Execute the following steps for $i = 1, 2, \ldots, k$.

1. *Copy v_1^i from the input $commit(x_1)$ as $commit(v_1^i)^{\{3,4\}}$. (Note that if v_1^i is $\bar{x}_1$, NOT is taken after the copy).*
2. *For $j = 2, \ldots, n$, execute the following procedure: Execute the input preserving AND protocol to $commit(\cdot)^{\{3,4\}}$ and $commit(v_j^i)$ so that input $commit(v_j^i)$ is preserved. The result is stored as $commit(\cdot)^{\{3,4\}}$. (Note that if v_j^i is $\bar{x}_j$, NOT is taken before the AND protocol and NOT is taken again for the preserved input.)*
   At the end of this step, T_i is obtained as $commit(v_1^i \wedge v_2^i \wedge \cdots \wedge v_n^i)^{\{3,4\}}$.
3. *If $i = 1$, copy $commit(\cdot)^{\{3,4\}}$ to $commit(\cdot)^{\{1,2\}}$. If $i > 1$, apply the XOR protocol between $commit(\cdot)^{\{3,4\}}$ and $commit(\cdot)^{\{1,2\}}$. The result is stored as $commit(\cdot)^{\{1,2\}}$.*

At the end of the protocol, $commit(f(x_1, x_2, \ldots x_n))^{\{1,2\}}$ is obtained.

The comparison of protocols to calculate any n-variable Boolean function is shown in Table 4.

The number of additional cards in [56] with a standard deck of cards is 8. Thus the number of additional cards is reduced using private operations.

4 Conclusion

This paper showed AND, XOR, and copy protocols that use a standard deck of cards. The numbers of cards used by the protocols are the minimum. The results show the effectiveness of private operations. One of the remaining problems is obtaining protocols when a player is malicious.

Acknowledgements. The authors would like to thank anonymous referees for their careful reading of our manuscript and their many insightful comments and suggestions.

References

1. Abe, Y., Hayashi, Y.I., Mizuki, T., Sone, H.: Five-card and computations in committed format using only uniform cyclic shuffles. New Gener. Comput. 1–18 (2021)

2. den Boer, B.: More efficient match-making and satisfiability *The Five Card Trick*. In: Quisquater, J.-J., Vandewalle, J. (eds.) EUROCRYPT 1989. LNCS, vol. 434, pp. 208–217. Springer, Heidelberg (1990). https://doi.org/10.1007/3-540-46885-4_23

3. Bultel, X., et al.: Physical zero-knowledge proof for Makaro. In: Izumi, T., Kuznetsov, P. (eds.) SSS 2018. LNCS, vol. 11201, pp. 111–125. Springer, Cham (2018). https://doi.org/10.1007/978-3-030-03232-6_8

4. Cheung, E., Hawthorne, C., Lee, P.: CS 758 project: secure computation with playing cards (2013). http://cdchawthorne.com/writings/secure_playing_cards.pdf

5. Dumas, J.-G., Lafourcade, P., Miyahara, D., Mizuki, T., Sasaki, T., Sone, H.: Interactive physical zero-knowledge proof for Norinori. In: Du, D.-Z., Duan, Z., Tian, C. (eds.) COCOON 2019. LNCS, vol. 11653, pp. 166–177. Springer, Cham (2019). https://doi.org/10.1007/978-3-030-26176-4_14

6. Dvořák, P., Koucký, M.: Barrington plays cards: the complexity of card-based protocols. arXiv preprint arXiv:2010.08445 (2020)

7. Francis, D., Aljunid, S.R., Nishida, T., Hayashi, Y., Mizuki, T., Sone, H.: Necessary and sufficient numbers of cards for securely computing two-bit output functions. In: Phan, R.C.-W., Yung, M. (eds.) Mycrypt 2016. LNCS, vol. 10311, pp. 193–211. Springer, Cham (2017). https://doi.org/10.1007/978-3-319-61273-7_10

8. Hashimoto, Y., Nuida, K., Shinagawa, K., Inamura, M., Hanaoka, G.: Toward finite-runtime card-based protocol for generating hidden random permutation without fixed points. IEICE Trans. Fundam. Electron. Commun. Comput. Sci. **101-A**(9), 1503–1511 (2018)

9. Hashimoto, Y., Shinagawa, K., Nuida, K., Inamura, M., Hanaoka, G.: Secure grouping protocol using a deck of cards. IEICE Trans. Fundam. Electron. Commun. Comput. Sci. **101**(9), 1512–1524 (2018)

10. Ibaraki, T., Manabe, Y.: A more efficient card-based protocol for generating a random permutation without fixed points. In: Proceedings of 3rd International Conference on Mathematics and Computers in Sciences and in Industry (MCSI 2016), pp. 252–257 (2016)

11. Ishikawa, R., Chida, E., Mizuki, T.: Efficient card-based protocols for generating a hidden random permutation without fixed points. In: Calude, C.S., Dinneen, M.J. (eds.) UCNC 2015. LNCS, vol. 9252, pp. 215–226. Springer, Cham (2015). https://doi.org/10.1007/978-3-319-21819-9_16

12. Kastner, J., et al.: The minimum number of cards in practical card-based protocols. In: Takagi, T., Peyrin, T. (eds.) ASIACRYPT 2017. LNCS, vol. 10626, pp. 126–155. Springer, Cham (2017). https://doi.org/10.1007/978-3-319-70700-6_5

13. Koch, A.: The landscape of optimal card-based protocols. IACR Cryptology ePrint Archive, Report 2018/951 (2018)

14. Koch, A., Schrempp, M., Kirsten, M.: Card-based cryptography meets formal verification. N. Gener. Comput. **39**(1), 115–158 (2021)

15. Koch, A., Walzer, S.: Private function evaluation with cards. Cryptology ePrint Archive, Report 2018/1113 (2018). https://eprint.iacr.org/2018/1113

16. Koch, A., Walzer, S.: Foundations for actively secure card-based cryptography. In: Proceedings of 10th International Conference on Fun with Algorithms (FUN 2020). Schloss Dagstuhl-Leibniz-Zentrum für Informatik (2020)

17. Koch, A., Walzer, S., Härtel, K.: Card-based cryptographic protocols using a minimal number of cards. In: Iwata, T., Cheon, J.H. (eds.) ASIACRYPT 2015. LNCS, vol. 9452, pp. 783–807. Springer, Heidelberg (2015). https://doi.org/10.1007/978-3-662-48797-6_32

18. Koyama, H., Miyahara, D., Mizuki, T., Sone, H.: A secure three-input AND protocol with a standard deck of minimal cards. In: Santhanam, R., Musatov, D. (eds.) CSR 2021. LNCS, vol. 12730, pp. 242–256. Springer, Cham (2021). https://doi.org/10.1007/978-3-030-79416-3_14

19. Koyama, H., Toyoda, K., Miyahara, D., Mizuki, T.: New card-based copy protocols using only random cuts. In: Proceedings of the 8th ACM on ASIA Public-Key Cryptography Workshop, APKC 2021, pp. 13–22. Association for Computing Machinery, New York (2021). https://doi.org/10.1145/3457338.3458297

20. Kurosawa, K., Shinozaki, T.: Compact card protocol. In: Proceedings of 2017 Symposium on Cryptography and Information Security (SCIS 2017), pp. 1A2-6 (2017). (in Japanese)

21. Lafourcade, P., Miyahara, D., Mizuki, T., Sasaki, T., Sone, H.: A physical ZKP for Slitherlink: how to perform physical topology-preserving computation. In: Heng, S.-H., Lopez, J. (eds.) ISPEC 2019. LNCS, vol. 11879, pp. 135–151. Springer, Cham (2019). https://doi.org/10.1007/978-3-030-34339-2_8

22. Manabe, Y., Ono, H.: Secure card-based cryptographic protocols using private operations against malicious players. In: Maimut, D., Oprina, A.-G., Sauveron, D. (eds.) SecITC 2020. LNCS, vol. 12596, pp. 55–70. Springer, Cham (2021). https://doi.org/10.1007/978-3-030-69255-1_5

23. Manabe, Y., Ono, H.: Card-based cryptographic protocols for three-input functions using private operations. In: Flocchini, P., Moura, L. (eds.) IWOCA 2021. LNCS, vol. 12757, pp. 469–484. Springer, Cham (2021). https://doi.org/10.1007/978-3-030-79987-8_33

24. Marcedone, A., Wen, Z., Shi, E.: Secure dating with four or fewer cards. IACR Cryptology ePrint Archive, Report 2015/1031 (2015)

25. Miyahara, D., Hayashi, Y.I., Mizuki, T., Sone, H.: Practical card-based implementations of Yao's millionaire protocol. Theor. Comput. Sci. **803**, 207–221 (2020)

26. Miyahara, D., et al.: Card-based ZKP protocols for Takuzu and Juosan. In: Proceedings of 10th International Conference on Fun with Algorithms (FUN 2020). Schloss Dagstuhl-Leibniz-Zentrum für Informatik (2020)

27. Miyahara, D., Sasaki, T., Mizuki, T., Sone, H.: Card-based physical zero-knowledge proof for kakuro. IEICE Trans. Fundam. Electron. Commun. Comput. Sci. **102**(9), 1072–1078 (2019)

28. Mizuki, T.: Applications of card-based cryptography to education. In: IEICE Technical Report ISEC2016-53, pp. 13–17 (2016). (in Japanese)

29. Mizuki, T.: Card-based protocols for securely computing the conjunction of multiple variables. Theor. Comput. Sci. **622**, 34–44 (2016)

30. Mizuki, T.: Efficient and secure multiparty computations using a standard deck of playing cards. In: Foresti, S., Persiano, G. (eds.) CANS 2016. LNCS, vol. 10052, pp. 484–499. Springer, Cham (2016). https://doi.org/10.1007/978-3-319-48965-0_29

31. Mizuki, T., Asiedu, I.K., Sone, H.: Voting with a logarithmic number of cards. In: Mauri, G., Dennunzio, A., Manzoni, L., Porreca, A.E. (eds.) UCNC 2013. LNCS, vol. 7956, pp. 162–173. Springer, Heidelberg (2013). https://doi.org/10.1007/978-3-642-39074-6_16

32. Mizuki, T., Komano, Y.: Analysis of information leakage due to operative errors in card-based protocols. In: Iliopoulos, C., Leong, H.W., Sung, W.-K. (eds.) IWOCA 2018. LNCS, vol. 10979, pp. 250–262. Springer, Cham (2018). https://doi.org/10.1007/978-3-319-94667-2_21

33. Mizuki, T., Kumamoto, M., Sone, H.: The five-card trick can be done with four cards. In: Wang, X., Sako, K. (eds.) ASIACRYPT 2012. LNCS, vol. 7658, pp. 598–606. Springer, Heidelberg (2012). https://doi.org/10.1007/978-3-642-34961-4_36

34. Mizuki, T., Shizuya, H.: A formalization of card-based cryptographic protocols via abstract machine. Int. J. Inf. Secur. **13**(1), 15–23 (2014)
35. Mizuki, T., Shizuya, H.: Practical card-based cryptography. In: Ferro, A., Luccio, F., Widmayer, P. (eds.) FUN 2014. LNCS, vol. 8496, pp. 313–324. Springer, Cham (2014). https://doi.org/10.1007/978-3-319-07890-8_27
36. Mizuki, T., Shizuya, H.: Computational model of card-based cryptographic protocols and its applications. IEICE Trans. Fundam. Electron. Commun. Comput. Sci. **100**(1), 3–11 (2017)
37. Mizuki, T., Sone, H.: Six-card secure AND and four-card secure XOR. In: Deng, X., Hopcroft, J.E., Xue, J. (eds.) FAW 2009. LNCS, vol. 5598, pp. 358–369. Springer, Heidelberg (2009). https://doi.org/10.1007/978-3-642-02270-8_36
38. Murata, S., Miyahara, D., Mizuki, T., Sone, H.: Efficient generation of a card-based uniformly distributed random derangement. In: Uehara, R., Hong, S.-H., Nandy, S.C. (eds.) WALCOM 2021. LNCS, vol. 12635, pp. 78–89. Springer, Cham (2021). https://doi.org/10.1007/978-3-030-68211-8_7
39. Nakai, T., Misawa, Y., Tokushige, Y., Iwamoto, M., Ohta, K.: How to solve millionaires' problem with two kinds of cards. N. Gener. Comput. **39**(1), 73–96 (2021)
40. Nakai, T., Shirouchi, S., Iwamoto, M., Ohta, K.: Four cards are sufficient for a card-based three-input voting protocol utilizing private permutations. In: Shikata, J. (ed.) ICITS 2017. LNCS, vol. 10681, pp. 153–165. Springer, Cham (2017). https://doi.org/10.1007/978-3-319-72089-0_9
41. Niemi, V., Renvall, A.: Solitaire zero-knowledge. Fundamenta Informaticae **38**(1, 2), 181–188 (1999)
42. Nishida, T., Hayashi, Y., Mizuki, T., Sone, H.: Card-based protocols for any Boolean function. In: Jain, R., Jain, S., Stephan, F. (eds.) TAMC 2015. LNCS, vol. 9076, pp. 110–121. Springer, Cham (2015). https://doi.org/10.1007/978-3-319-17142-5_11
43. Nishida, T., Hayashi, Y., Mizuki, T., Sone, H.: Securely computing three-input functions with eight cards. IEICE Trans. Fundam. Electron. Commun. Comput. Sci. **98**(6), 1145–1152 (2015)
44. Nishida, T., Mizuki, T., Sone, H.: Securely computing the three-input majority function with eight cards. In: Dediu, A.-H., Martín-Vide, C., Truthe, B., Vega-Rodríguez, M.A. (eds.) TPNC 2013. LNCS, vol. 8273, pp. 193–204. Springer, Heidelberg (2013). https://doi.org/10.1007/978-3-642-45008-2_16
45. Nishimura, A., Nishida, T., Hayashi, Y., Mizuki, T., Sone, H.: Card-based protocols using unequal division shuffles. Soft. Comput. **22**(2), 361–371 (2018)
46. Ono, H., Manabe, Y.: Efficient card-based cryptographic protocols for the millionaires' problem using private input operations. In: Proceedings of 13th Asia Joint Conference on Information Security (AsiaJCIS 2018), pp. 23–28 (2018)
47. Ono, H., Manabe, Y.: Card-based cryptographic protocols with the minimum number of rounds using private operations. In: Pérez-Solà, C., Navarro-Arribas, G., Biryukov, A., Garcia-Alfaro, J. (eds.) DPM/CBT -2019. LNCS, vol. 11737, pp. 156–173. Springer, Cham (2019). https://doi.org/10.1007/978-3-030-31500-9_10
48. Ono, H., Manabe, Y.: Card-based cryptographic logical computations using private operations. N. Gener. Comput. **39**(1), 19–40 (2021)
49. Robert, L., Miyahara, D., Lafourcade, P., Mizuki, T.: Interactive physical ZKP for connectivity: applications to Nurikabe and Hitori. In: De Mol, L., Weiermann, A., Manea, F., Fernández-Duque, D. (eds.) CiE 2021. LNCS, vol. 12813, pp. 373–384. Springer, Cham (2021). https://doi.org/10.1007/978-3-030-80049-9_37

50. Ruangwises, S., Itoh, T.: AND protocols using only uniform shuffles. In: van Bevern, R., Kucherov, G. (eds.) CSR 2019. LNCS, vol. 11532, pp. 349–358. Springer, Cham (2019). https://doi.org/10.1007/978-3-030-19955-5_30
51. Ruangwises, S., Itoh, T.: Securely computing the n-variable equality function with $2n$ cards. In: Chen, J., Feng, Q., Xu, J. (eds.) TAMC 2020. LNCS, vol. 12337, pp. 25–36. Springer, Cham (2020). https://doi.org/10.1007/978-3-030-59267-7_3
52. Ruangwises, S., Itoh, T.: Physical zero-knowledge proof for numberlink puzzle and k vertex-disjoint paths problem. N. Gener. Comput. **39**(1), 3–17 (2021)
53. Ruangwises, S., Itoh, T.: Physical zero-knowledge proof for ripple effect. In: Uehara, R., Hong, S.-H., Nandy, S.C. (eds.) WALCOM 2021. LNCS, vol. 12635, pp. 296–307. Springer, Cham (2021). https://doi.org/10.1007/978-3-030-68211-8_24
54. Sasaki, T., Miyahara, D., Mizuki, T., Sone, H.: Efficient card-based zero-knowledge proof for sudoku. Theor. Comput. Sci. **839**, 135–142 (2020)
55. Shinagawa, K., Mizuki, T.: The six-card trick: secure computation of three-input equality. In: Lee, K. (ed.) ICISC 2018. LNCS, vol. 11396, pp. 123–131. Springer, Cham (2019). https://doi.org/10.1007/978-3-030-12146-4_8
56. Shinagawa, K., Mizuki, T.: Secure computation of any Boolean function based on any deck of cards. In: Chen, Y., Deng, X., Lu, M. (eds.) FAW 2019. LNCS, vol. 11458, pp. 63–75. Springer, Cham (2019). https://doi.org/10.1007/978-3-030-18126-0_6
57. Shinagawa, K., Nuida, K.: A single shuffle is enough for secure card-based computation of any Boolean circuit. Discret. Appl. Math. **289**, 248–261 (2021)
58. Shinoda, Y., Miyahara, D., Shinagawa, K., Mizuki, T., Sone, H.: Card-based covert lottery. In: Maimut, D., Oprina, A.-G., Sauveron, D. (eds.) SecITC 2020. LNCS, vol. 12596, pp. 257–270. Springer, Cham (2021). https://doi.org/10.1007/978-3-030-69255-1_17
59. Shirouchi, S., Nakai, T., Iwamoto, M., Ohta, K.: Efficient card-based cryptographic protocols for logic gates utilizing private permutations. In: Proceedings of 2017 Symposium on Cryptography and Information Security(SCIS 2017), p. 1A2-2 (2017). (in Japanese)
60. Takashima, K., et al.: Card-based protocols for secure ranking computations. Theor. Comput. Sci. **845**, 122–135 (2020)
61. Takashima, K., Miyahara, D., Mizuki, T., Sone, H.: Actively revealing card attack on card-based protocols. Natural Comput. 1–14 (2021)
62. Toyoda, K., Miyahara, D., Mizuki, T., Sone, H.: Six-card finite-runtime XOR protocol with only random cut. In: Proceedings of the 7th ACM Workshop on ASIA Public-Key Cryptography, pp. 2–8 (2020)
63. Watanabe, Y., Kuroki, Y., Suzuki, S., Koga, Y., Iwamoto, M., Ohta, K.: Card-based majority voting protocols with three inputs using three cards. In: Proceedings of 2018 International Symposium on Information Theory and Its Applications (ISITA), pp. 218–222. IEEE (2018)
64. Yasunaga, K.: Practical card-based protocol for three-input majority. IEICE Trans. Fundam. Electron. Commun. Comput. Scie. **E103.A**(11), 1296–1298 (2020). https://doi.org/10.1587/transfun.2020EAL2025

Normalising Lustre Preserves Security

Sanjiva Prasad[(✉)] and R. Madhukar Yerraguntla

Indian Institute of Technology Delhi, New Delhi, India
{sanjiva,madhukar.yr}@cse.iitd.ac.in

Abstract. The synchronous reactive data flow language LUSTRE is an expressive language, equipped with a suite of tools for modelling, simulating and model-checking a wide variety of safety-critical systems. A critical intermediate step in the formally certified compilation of LUSTRE involves translation to a well-behaved sub-language called "Normalised LUSTRE" (NLUSTRE). Recently, we proposed a simple Denning-style lattice-based secure information flow type system for NLUSTRE, and proved its soundness by establishing that security-typed programs are non-interfering with respect to the co-inductive stream semantics.

In this paper, we propose a similar security type system for unrestricted LUSTRE, and show that Bourke *et al.*'s semantics-preserving normalisation transformations from LUSTRE to NLUSTRE are security-preserving as well. A novelty is the use of refinement security types for node calls. The main result is the preservation of security types by the normalisation transformations. The soundness of our security typing rules is shown by establishing that well-security-typed programs are non-interfering, via a reduction to type-preservation (here), semantics-preservation (Bourke *et al.*) and our previous result of non-interference for NLUSTRE.

Keywords: Synchronous reactive data flow · LUSTRE · Compiler transformation · Security type system · Non-interference · Security preservation

1 Introduction

The synchronous reactive data flow language LUSTRE [6,11] is an expressive language with an elegant formal semantics. Its underlying deterministic, clocked model makes it a versatile programming paradigm, with diverse applications such as distributed embedded controllers, numerical computations, and complex Scade 6 [7] safety-critical systems. It is also equipped with a suite of tools, comprising: (a) a certified compilation framework from the high-level model into lower-level imperative languages [2,3]; (b) model-checkers [13,18] (c) simulation tools [12] for program development.

The development of a formally certified compiler from LUSTRE to an imperative language is the subject of active research [2,3]. A critical intermediate step involves the translation from LUSTRE to a well-behaved sub-language called

© Springer Nature Switzerland AG 2021
A. Cerone and P. C. Ölveczky (Eds.): ICTAC 2021, LNCS 12819, pp. 275–292, 2021.
https://doi.org/10.1007/978-3-030-85315-0_16

"Normalised LUSTRE" (NLUSTRE), presented in [3]. A recent paper (in French, graciously shared by the authors) defines the normalisation transformations from LUSTRE to NLUSTRE, and establishes formally that they are semantics-preserving with respect to the stream semantics [4] (see Theorems 2 and 3).

Recently we proposed a Denning-style lattice-based secure information flow (SIF) type system for NLUSTRE, and proved its soundness by establishing that securely-typed programs are *non-interfering* with respect to the co-inductive stream semantics [17]. The main ideas underlying the security type system are (i) that each stream is assigned (w.r.t. assumptions on variables) a *symbolic* security type, (ii) equations induce *constraints* on security types of the defined variables and of the defining expressions, and (iii) the output streams from a node have security levels at least as high as those of the input streams on which they depend. The symbolic constraint-based formulations allows us to *infer* constraints that suffice to ensure security. The rules are simple, intuitive and amenable to being incorporated into the mechanised certified compilation [15] already developed for LUSTRE [5]. In this paper, we propose a similar secure-information-flow type system for unrestricted LUSTRE (Sect. 3). The main innovation is formulating symbolic constraint-based *refinement* (sub)types. These are necessitated by the presence in LUSTRE of nested node calls (in NLUSTRE, direct nesting is disallowed).

The security type system is shown by reduction to be *sound* with respect to LUSTRE's *co-inductive* stream semantics. While it is possible to do so directly by establishing that well-security-typed programs exhibit non-interference [10] using exactly the approach in [17], here we do so via a sound *compiler transformation*: We show that the semantics-preserving normalisation transformations (de-nesting and distribution, and explicit initialisation of fby) from LUSTRE to NLUSTRE proposed in [4] *preserve security types* as well (Theorem 1 in Sect. 4). In particular, there is a strong correspondence at the level of *node definitions*. The preservation of *security signatures* of node definitions is established via Lemma 3 in Sect. 3. The main idea is to remove local variable types via a substitution procedure simplify (Fig. 9), showing that this maintains satisfiability of type constraints. Since these transformations preserve operational behaviour *as well as security types of nodes*, and since we have already established non-interference for the target language NLUSTRE [17, Theorem 5], non-interference holds for well-security-typed LUSTRE programs as well (Theorem 5 in Sect. 5).

Although this paper is intimately dependent on results of earlier work, we have endeavoured to keep it self-contained. The reader interested in the complete stream semantics of LUSTRE, as well as other auxiliary definitions and examples, may refer to the appendices of a fuller version of this paper [16].

Related Work. We mention only the immediately relevant work here; a fuller discussion on related work can be found in [17]. The formalisation of LUSTRE semantics and its certified compilation are discussed in detail in [1–3]. The normalisation transformations examined here are proposed in [4]. Our lattice-based SIF framework harks back to Denning's seminal work [9]. The idea of type systems for SIF can be found in *e.g.*, [20]. That work also expressed soundness of a SIF type system in terms of the notion of non-interference [10]. Our previous work [17] adapted that framework to a declarative data flow setting, showing that it is possible to *infer* minimal *partial-ordering constraints* between *symbolic types*. The idea of type-preservation under the rewriting of programs is commonplace in logic and proof systems (where it is called "subject reduction").

2   LUSTRE and NLUSTRE

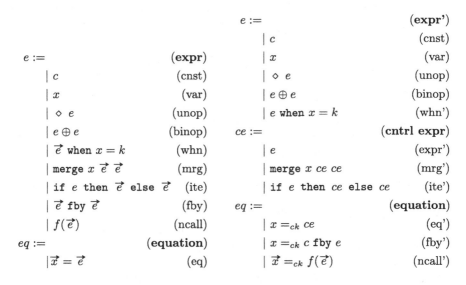

$$e := \qquad\qquad\qquad\qquad \textbf{(expr)}$$
$$\mid c \qquad\qquad\qquad\qquad \text{(cnst)}$$
$$\mid x \qquad\qquad\qquad\qquad \text{(var)}$$
$$\mid \diamond\, e \qquad\qquad\qquad\qquad \text{(unop)}$$
$$\mid e \oplus e \qquad\qquad\qquad \text{(binop)}$$
$$\mid \vec{e} \text{ when } x = k \qquad\qquad \text{(whn)}$$
$$\mid \textbf{merge } x \; \vec{e} \; \vec{e} \qquad\qquad \text{(mrg)}$$
$$\mid \textbf{if } e \textbf{ then } \vec{e} \textbf{ else } \vec{e} \quad \text{(ite)}$$
$$\mid \vec{e} \textbf{ fby } \vec{e} \qquad\qquad\qquad \text{(fby)}$$
$$\mid f(\vec{e}) \qquad\qquad\qquad\qquad \text{(ncall)}$$
$$eq := \qquad\qquad\qquad\qquad \textbf{(equation)}$$
$$\mid \vec{x} = \vec{e} \qquad\qquad\qquad\qquad \text{(eq)}$$

Fig. 1. LUSTRE syntax

$$e := \qquad\qquad\qquad\qquad \textbf{(expr')}$$
$$\mid c \qquad\qquad\qquad\qquad \text{(cnst)}$$
$$\mid x \qquad\qquad\qquad\qquad \text{(var)}$$
$$\mid \diamond\, e \qquad\qquad\qquad\qquad \text{(unop)}$$
$$\mid e \oplus e \qquad\qquad\qquad \text{(binop)}$$
$$\mid e \text{ when } x = k \qquad\qquad \text{(whn')}$$
$$ce := \qquad\qquad\qquad\qquad \textbf{(cntrl expr)}$$
$$\mid e \qquad\qquad\qquad\qquad \text{(expr')}$$
$$\mid \textbf{merge } x \; ce \; ce \qquad\qquad \text{(mrg')}$$
$$\mid \textbf{if } e \textbf{ then } ce \textbf{ else } ce \qquad \text{(ite')}$$
$$eq := \qquad\qquad\qquad\qquad \textbf{(equation)}$$
$$\mid x =_{ck} ce \qquad\qquad\qquad \text{(eq')}$$
$$\mid x =_{ck} c \textbf{ fby } e \qquad\qquad \text{(fby')}$$
$$\mid \vec{x} =_{ck} f(\vec{e}) \qquad\qquad \text{(ncall')}$$

Fig. 2. NLUSTRE syntax

$$ck := \qquad\qquad\qquad \textbf{(clock)}$$
$$\mid \textbf{base} \qquad\qquad \text{(base)}$$
$$\mid ck \textbf{ on } (x = k) \qquad \text{(on)}$$

$$d := \qquad\qquad\qquad\qquad\qquad \textbf{(node declr)}$$
$$\mid \textbf{node } f(\overrightarrow{x^{ck}}) \textbf{ returns } \overrightarrow{y^{ck}}$$
$$\qquad \textbf{var } \vec{z} \textbf{ let } \overrightarrow{eq} \textbf{ tel}$$
$$G := \vec{d} \qquad\qquad\qquad \textbf{(program)}$$

Fig. 3. Common syntax of nodes and clocks

A LUSTRE program describes a synchronous network with *clocked* streams of data flowing between operators and *nodes*. A program consists of a set of *node definitions*, each parameterised by clocked input and output flows. A clock is a boolean stream – either a **base** clock or one *derived* from another clock when a variable takes a specific (boolean) value (**on** $x = k$, where $k \in \{\text{T}, \text{F}\}$).

Each node comprises a set of (possibly mutually recursive) *equations*, which define local variables and output flows in terms of flow *expressions*. Such definitions are unique, and may appear in any order. LUSTRE satisfies the *definition* and *substitution* principles, namely that the context does not determine the meaning of an expression and that referential transparency holds. Nodes do not have free variables. Nodes cannot make recursive calls; therefore, the dependency order on nodes forms a DAG. All expressions and equations can be *annotated* with a clock, following a static analysis to determine clock dependencies.

Figures 1, 2 and 3 present the syntax of LUSTRE and NLUSTRE.

LUSTRE expressions (Fig. 1) include flows described by constants, variables, unary and binary operations on flows, as well as the flows obtained by sampling when a variable takes a particular boolean value (when), interpolation based on a boolean variable flow (merge), and conditional combinations of flows (if_then_else). Of particular interest are flows involving guarded delays (fby) and those involving *node calls*.

NLUSTRE is a sub-language into which LUSTRE can be translated, from which subsequent compilation is easier. The main differences between LUSTRE and NLUSTRE are (i) the former supports *lists* of flows (written $\vec{e}$) for conciseness, whereas in the latter all flows are single streams; (ii) NLUSTRE requires that conditional and merge "control" expressions are not nested below unary and binary operators or sampling; (iii) node call and delayed flows (fby) are treated as first-class expressions, whereas in NLUSTRE, they can appear only in the context of equations; (iv) LUSTRE permits nested node calls, whereas nesting in disallowed in NLUSTRE; (v) finally, the first argument of fby expressions in NLUSTRE must be a *constant*, to enable a well-defined initialisation that can be easily implemented.

The *translation* from LUSTRE to NLUSTRE [4] involves *distributing* constructs over the individual components of lists of expressions, and *de-nesting* expressions by introducing fresh local variables (See Sect. 4). The reader can see an example, adapted from [4], of a LUSTRE program and its translation into NLUSTRE in Fig. 12 (ignoring for the moment the security type annotations therein).

2.1   Stream Semantics

The semantics of LUSTRE and NLUSTRE programs are *synchronous*: Each variable and expression defines a data stream which pulses with respect to a *clock*. A clock is a stream of booleans (CompCert/Coq's [8,15] true and false in Vélus). A flow takes its nth value on the nth clock tick, *i.e.*, some value, written ⟨v⟩, is present at instants when the clock value is true, and none (written ⟨⟩) when it is false. The *temporal operators* when, merge and fby are used to express the complex clock-changing and clock-dependent behaviours of sampling, interpolation and delay respectively.

Formally the stream semantics is defined using predicates over the program graph G, a (co-inductive) stream *history* ($H_* : Ident \rightarrow value\ Stream$) that associates value streams to variables, and a clock bs [3,4,17]. Semantic operations on (lists of) streams are written in blue sans serif typeface. Streams are written in red, with lists of streams usually written in **bold face**. All these stream operators, defined co-inductively, enforce the clocking regime, ensuring the presence of a value when the clock is true, and absence when false.

The predicate $G, H_*, bs \vdash e \Downarrow_e \mathbf{es}$ relates an *expression* e to a *list* of streams, written $\mathbf{es}$. A list consisting of only a single stream es is explicitly denoted as $[es]$. The semantics of *equations* are expressed using the predicate $G, H_*, bs \vdash \overrightarrow{eq_i}$, which requires *consistency* between the assumed and defined stream histories in H_* for the program variables, induced by the equations $\overrightarrow{eq_i}$. Finally, the semantics of a *node* named f in program G is given via a predicate $G \vdash \widehat{f}(\mathbf{xs}) \searrow \mathbf{ys}$, which defines a stream history transformer $\widehat{f}$ that maps the list of streams $\mathbf{xs}$ to the list of streams $\mathbf{ys}$.

We discuss here only some constructs which relate to the normalisation transformations (see [16] for a complete account).

$$\frac{H_*(x) = xs}{G, H_*, bs \vdash x \Downarrow_e [xs]} \ (\text{LSvar})$$

Rule (LSvar) associates a variable x to the stream given by $H_*(x)$.

$$\frac{\forall i: \ G, H_*, bs \vdash e0_i \Downarrow_e \mathbf{e0s}_i \quad \forall j: \ G, H_*, bs \vdash e_j \Downarrow_e \mathbf{es}_j \quad \widehat{\text{fby}_L} \ (\flat(\overrightarrow{\mathbf{e0s}_i})) \ (\flat(\overrightarrow{\mathbf{es}_j})) = \mathbf{os}}{G, H_*, bs \vdash \overrightarrow{e0_i} \ \text{fby} \ \overrightarrow{e_j} \Downarrow_e \mathbf{os}} \ (\text{LSfby})$$

A delay operation is implemented by $e0 \ \text{fby} \ e$. The rule (LSfby) is to be read as follows. Let each expression $e0_i$ denote a list of streams $\mathbf{e0s}_i$, and each expression e_j denote a list of streams $\mathbf{es}_j$. The predicate $\widehat{\text{fby}_L}$ *maps* the predicate fby_L to act on the corresponding components of *lists* of streams, *i.e.*,

$$\widehat{\text{fby}_L} \ \mathbf{xs} \ \mathbf{ys} = \mathbf{zs} \ \text{abbreviates} \ \bigwedge_{i \in [1,m]} \text{fby}_L \ xs_i \ ys_i = zs_i$$

(Similarly for the predicates $\widehat{\text{when}}$, $\widehat{\text{merge}}$, and $\widehat{\text{ite}}$.) The operation $\flat(\_)$ flattens a list of lists (of possibly different lengths) into a single list. Flattening is required since expression e_i may in general denote a *list* of streams $\mathbf{es}_i$. The output list of streams $\mathbf{os}$ consists of streams whose first elements are taken from each stream in $\flat(\overrightarrow{\mathbf{e0s}_i})$ with the rest taken from the corresponding component of $\flat(\overrightarrow{\mathbf{es}_j})$.

$$\frac{\forall i \in [1,..,k] \ G, H_*, bs \vdash e_i \Downarrow_e \mathbf{es}_i \quad [H_*(x_1), \ldots, H_*(x_n)] = \flat(\overrightarrow{\mathbf{es}_i})}{G, H_*, bs \vdash \overrightarrow{x_j} = \overrightarrow{e_i}} \ (\text{LSeq})$$

The rule (LSeq) for equations checks the consistency between the assumed meanings for the defined variables x_j according to the history H_* with the corresponding components of the tuple of streams $\flat(\overrightarrow{\mathbf{es}_i})$ to which a tuple of right-hand side expressions evaluates.

$$\frac{\left\{ \begin{matrix} \mathsf{name} = \ \mathtt{f}; \ \mathsf{in} = \ \overrightarrow{x}; \ \mathsf{var} = \ \overrightarrow{z}; \\ \mathsf{out} = \ \overrightarrow{y}; \ \mathsf{eqs} = \ \overrightarrow{eq} \end{matrix} \right\} \in G \quad H_*(f.\mathbf{in}) = \mathbf{xs}}{} $$

$$\frac{H_*(f.\mathbf{out}) = \mathbf{ys} \quad \text{base-of} \ \mathbf{xs} = bs \quad \forall eq \in \overrightarrow{eq}: \ G, H_*, bs \vdash eq}{G \vdash \widehat{f}(\mathbf{xs}) \searrow \mathbf{ys}} \ (\text{LSndef})$$

The rule (LSndef) presents the meaning given to the definition of a node $f \in G$ as a stream list transformer. If history H_* assigns lists of streams to the input and output variables for a node in a manner such that the semantics of the equations $\vec{eq}$ in the node are satisfied, then the semantic function $\widehat{f}$ transforms input stream list **xs** to output stream list **ys**. The operation base-of finds an appropriate base clock with respect to which a given list of value streams pulse.

$$\frac{G, H_*, bs \vdash \vec{e_i} \Downarrow_{\mathbf{e}} \mathbf{es} \quad G \vdash_{\mathbf{s}} \widehat{f}(\mathbf{es}) \searrow \mathbf{os}}{G, H_*, bs \vdash f(\vec{e_i}) \Downarrow_{\mathbf{e}} \mathbf{os}} \quad \text{(LSncall)}$$

The rule (LSncall) applies the stream transformer semantic function $\widehat{f}$ defined in rule (LSndef) to the stream list **es** corresponding to the tuple of arguments $\vec{e_i}$, and returns the stream list **os**.

Stream Semantics for NLUSTRE. The semantic relations for NLUSTRE are either identical to (as in constants, variables, unary and binary operations) or else the singleton cases of the rules for LUSTRE (as in merge, ite, when). The main differences lie in the occurrences of fby (now in a restricted form) and node call, which can only be in the context of (clock-annotated) equations (Fig. 4).

$$\frac{H_*, bs \vdash e :: ck \Downarrow_{\mathbf{e}} [vs] \quad \mathsf{fby}_{NL} \ c \ vs = H_*(x)}{G, H_*, bs \vdash x =_{ck} c \ \mathsf{fby} \ e} \quad \text{(NSfby')}$$

$$\frac{\left\{ \begin{array}{l} \mathsf{name} = \ \mathtt{f}; \ \mathsf{in} = \ \vec{x}; \ \mathsf{var} = \ \vec{z}; \\ \mathsf{out} = \ \vec{y}; \ \mathsf{eqs} = \ \vec{eq} \end{array} \right\} \in G \quad H_*(f.\mathsf{in}) = \mathbf{xs} \quad \mathsf{base\text{-}of}\,\mathbf{xs} = bs}{G \vdash_{\mathbf{s}} \widehat{f}(\mathbf{xs}) \searrow \mathbf{ys}} \\ \underline{\mathsf{respects\text{-}clock}\,H_* \ bs \quad H_*(f.\mathsf{out}) = \mathbf{ys} \quad \forall eq \in \vec{eq}: \ G, H_*, bs \vdash eq} \quad \text{(NSndef')}$$

$$\frac{H_*, bs \vdash \vec{e} \Downarrow_{\mathbf{e}} \mathbf{es} \quad H_*, bs \vdash ck \Downarrow_{ck} \mathsf{base\text{-}of}\,\mathbf{es} \quad G \vdash_{\mathbf{s}} \widehat{f}(\mathbf{es}) \searrow \overrightarrow{H_*(x_i)}}{G, H_*, bs \vdash \vec{x} =_{ck} f(\vec{e})} \quad \text{(NSncall')}$$

Fig. 4. Stream semantics of NLUSTRE nodes and equations

The (NSfby') rule for fby in an equational context uses the semantic operation fby_{NL}, which differs from fby_L in that it requires its first argument to be a constant rather than a stream. The (NSndef') rule only differs from (LSndef) in that after clock alignment during *transcription*, we have an additional requirement of H_* being in accordance with the base clock bs, enforced by respects-clock. Finally, the rule rule (NSncall') for node call, now in an equational context, is similar to (LSncall) combined with (LSeq), with the condition that base clock of the input flows annotates the equation.

3   A Security Type System for LUSTRE

We define a secure information flow type system, where under security-level type assumptions for program variables, LUSTRE expressions are given a *symbolic security type*, and LUSTRE equations induce a set of *ordering constraints* over security types.

Syntax. Security type expressions ($\alpha, \beta \in ST$) for LUSTRE are either (i) *type variables* (written δ) drawn from a set STV, or (ii) of the form $\alpha \sqcup \beta$ where $\sqcup$ is interpreted as an associative, commutative and idempotent operation. (iii) The identity element of $\sqcup$ is $\bot$. While this idempotent abelian monoid structure suffices for NLUSTRE, node calls in LUSTRE require (iv) *refinement types* $\alpha\{\!|\rho|\!\}$, where type expression α is subject to a symbolic constraint ρ. Constraints on security types, typically ρ, are (conjunctions of) relations of the form $\alpha \sqsubseteq \beta$. The comparison $\sqsubseteq$ is defined in terms of the equational theory: $\alpha \sqsubseteq \beta$ exactly when $\alpha \sqcup \beta = \beta$. Our proposed security types and their equational theory are presented in Fig. 5. The security types for NLUSTRE and their equational theory [17] are highlighted in grey within the diagram. This congruence on NLUSTRE types (henceforth $\equiv_{NL}$), which is given in the highlighted second line of Fig. 5, is significantly simpler since it does not involve refinement types!

Types: $\alpha, \beta, \gamma, \theta ::= \bot \mid \delta \in STV \mid \alpha \sqcup \beta \mid \alpha\{\!|\rho|\!\}$ Constraints: $\rho ::= (\theta \sqsubseteq \alpha)^*$

$(\alpha \sqcup \beta) \sqcup \theta = \alpha \sqcup (\beta \sqcup \theta), \quad \alpha \sqcup \alpha = \alpha, \quad \alpha \sqcup \beta = \beta \sqcup \alpha, \quad \alpha \sqcup \bot = \alpha = \bot \sqcup \alpha,$

$\alpha\{\!|\,|\!\} = \alpha, \quad \alpha_1\{\!|\rho_1|\!\} \sqcup \alpha_2\{\!|\rho_2|\!\} = (\alpha_1 \sqcup \alpha_2)\{\!|\rho_1 \cup \rho_2|\!\}, \quad \alpha\{\!|\rho_1|\!\}\{\!|\rho_2|\!\} = \alpha\{\!|\rho_1 \cup \rho_2|\!\},$

$\overrightarrow{\alpha_i}\{\!|\rho|\!\} = \overrightarrow{\alpha_i\{\!|\rho|\!\}}, \quad \{\!\{\alpha\{\!|\rho_1|\!\} \sqsubseteq \beta\{\!|\rho_2|\!\}\} = \{\alpha \sqsubseteq \beta\} \cup \rho_1 \cup \rho_2, \quad \overrightarrow{\alpha_j}[\theta_i/\delta_i] = \overrightarrow{\alpha_j[\theta_i/\delta_i]},$

$\alpha\{\!|\rho|\!\}[\theta_i/\delta_i] = \alpha[\theta_i/\delta_i]\{\!|\rho[\theta_i/\delta_i]|\!\}, \qquad\qquad (\alpha \sqsubseteq \beta)[\theta_i/\delta_i] = \alpha[\theta_i/\delta_i] \sqsubseteq \beta[\theta_i/\delta_i].$

Fig. 5. Security types, constraints and their properties

We write $\alpha[\theta_i/\delta_i]$ for $i = 1, \ldots, k$ to denote the (simultaneous) substitution of security types θ_i for security type variables δ_i in security type α. The notation extends to substitutions on tuples $(\overrightarrow{\alpha}[\theta_i/\delta_i])$ and constraints $((\alpha \sqsubseteq \beta)[\theta_i/\delta_i])$.

Semantics. Security types are interpreted with respect to a complete lattice $\langle SC, \sqsubseteq, \sqcup, \bot \rangle$ of security levels [9]. Given a ground instantiation $s : STV \to SC$, security type expressions and tuples are interpreted according to its homomorphic extension: $s(\bot) = \bot$, $s(\alpha \sqcup \beta) = s(\alpha) \sqcup s(\beta)$, $s(\overrightarrow{\alpha}) = \overrightarrow{s(\alpha_i)}$, and constraints are interpreted according to the lattice ordering: $s(\alpha \sqsubseteq \beta) = s(\alpha) \sqsubseteq s(\beta)$. The "refinement types" are interpreted as: $s(\alpha\{\!|\rho|\!\}) = s(\alpha)$ if $s(\rho)$ holds wrt SC, *i.e.*, if "s satisfies ρ", else is undefined.

Lemma 1 (Soundness). *The equational theory induced by the equalities in Fig. 5 is sound with respect to any ground instantiation s, i.e., (i) $\alpha = \beta$ implies $s(\alpha) = s(\beta)$, and (ii) $\rho_1 = \rho_2$ implies $s(\rho_1)$ is satisfied iff $s(\rho_2)$ is.*

The following facts are useful since we often want to reason about equality of security types or about constraints independently of any given security lattice.

Lemma 2 (Confluence). *All equations other than those of associativity and commutativity (AC) can be oriented (left-to-right) into rewriting rules. The rewriting system is confluent modulo AC. Equal types (respectively, equal constraints) can be rewritten to a common form modulo AC.*

PROOF SKETCH. The equational theory $\equiv_{NL}$ trivially yields a convergent rewriting system modulo AC. The rules in lines 3 and 4 of Fig. 5 can all be oriented left to right. We use Knuth-Bendix-completion [14] to introduce rules $\alpha_1\{\!|\rho_1|\!\} \sqcup \alpha_2 \longrightarrow (\alpha_1 \sqcup \alpha_2)\{\!|\rho_1|\!\}$, when α_2 is not a refinement type. Type equality and constraints are efficiently decided using the theory of strongly coherent rewriting modulo AC [19]. □

3.1 Security Typing Rules

Assume typing environment $\Gamma : Ident \rightharpoonup ST$, a partial function associating a security type to each free variable x in a LUSTRE program phrase. Expressions and clocks are type-checked using the predicates: $\Gamma \overset{e}{\vdash} e : \vec{\alpha}$ and $\Gamma \overset{ck}{\vdash} ck : \alpha$ respectively. These are read as "under the context Γ mapping variables to security types, e and ck have security types $\vec{\alpha}$ and α". The types for tupled expressions are (flattened) tuples of the types of the component expressions. For equations, we use the predicate: $\Gamma \overset{eqn}{\vdash} eq :\!\!> \rho$, which states that under the context Γ, equation eq when type-elaborated generates constraints ρ. Elementary constraints for equations are of the form $\alpha \sqsubseteq \beta$, where β is the security type of the defined variable, and α the security type obtained from that of the defining expression joined with the clock's security type. Since every flow in LUSTRE is defined *exactly once*, by the Definition Principle, no further security constraints apply.

The security typing rules for LUSTRE are presented in Figs. 6, 7 and 8, plus the rules for node definition and node call. These rules generalise those in [17] to handle expressions representing lists of flows, and nested node calls. The rules for NLUSTRE expressions other than node call and fby are just the singleton cases. Node call and fby are handled by the rule for equations.

$$\frac{\Gamma(\mathsf{base}) = \gamma}{\Gamma \overset{ck}{\vdash} \mathsf{base} : \gamma} \text{(LTbase)} \qquad \frac{\Gamma(x) = \gamma_1 \quad \Gamma \overset{ck}{\vdash} ck : \gamma_2}{\Gamma \overset{ck}{\vdash} ck \text{ on } x = k : \gamma_1 \sqcup \gamma_2} \text{(LTon)}$$

Fig. 6. LUSTRE security typing rules for clocks

$$\frac{\Gamma(x) = \alpha}{\Gamma \overset{e}{\vdash} x : \alpha} \; \text{(LTvar)} \qquad \frac{\Gamma \overset{e}{\vdash} e : \alpha}{\Gamma \overset{e}{\vdash} \diamond \, e : \alpha} \; \text{(LTunop)} \qquad \frac{\Gamma \overset{e}{\vdash} e_1 : \alpha_1 \quad \Gamma \overset{e}{\vdash} e_2 : \alpha_2}{\Gamma \overset{e}{\vdash} e_1 \oplus e_2 : \alpha_1 \sqcup \alpha_2} \; \text{(LTbinop)}$$

$$\frac{\theta = \Gamma(x) \quad \Gamma \overset{e}{\vdash} \vec{e_t} : \vec{\alpha} \quad \Gamma \overset{e}{\vdash} \vec{e_f} : \vec{\beta}}{\Gamma \overset{e}{\vdash} \text{merge } x \; \vec{e_t} \; \vec{e_f} : \overrightarrow{(\theta \sqcup \alpha_i \sqcup \beta_i)_i}} \; \text{(LTmrg)} \qquad \frac{}{\Gamma \overset{e}{\vdash} c : \bot} \; \text{(LTcnst)}$$

$$\frac{\Gamma \overset{e}{\vdash} e : \theta \quad \Gamma \overset{e}{\vdash} \vec{e_t} : \vec{\alpha} \quad \Gamma \overset{e}{\vdash} \vec{e_f} : \vec{\beta}}{\Gamma \overset{ce}{\vdash} \text{if } e \text{ then } \vec{e_t} \text{ else } \vec{e_f} : \overrightarrow{(\theta \sqcup \alpha_i \sqcup \beta_i)_i}} \; \text{(LTite)}$$

$$\frac{\Gamma \overset{e}{\vdash} \vec{e_0} : \vec{\alpha} \quad \Gamma \overset{e}{\vdash} \vec{e} : \vec{\beta}}{\Gamma \overset{e}{\vdash} \vec{e_0} \text{ fby}_l \; \vec{e} : \overrightarrow{(\alpha_i \sqcup \beta_i)_i}} \; \text{(LTfby)} \qquad \frac{\Gamma \overset{e}{\vdash} e_1 : \alpha_1 \dots \Gamma \overset{e}{\vdash} e_n : \alpha_n \quad \Gamma(x) = \gamma}{\Gamma \overset{e}{\vdash} \vec{e} \text{ when } x = k : \overrightarrow{(\alpha_i \sqcup \gamma)_i}} \; \text{(LTwh)}$$

Fig. 7. LUSTRE security typing rules for expressions

$$\frac{\vec{\beta} = \Gamma(\vec{x}) \quad \Gamma \overset{e}{\vdash} \vec{e} : \vec{\alpha} \quad \Gamma \overset{ck}{\vdash} ck : \gamma}{\Gamma \overset{eqn}{\vdash} \vec{x}^{ck} = \vec{e} \; :> \{(\gamma \sqcup \alpha_i \sqsubseteq \beta_i)_i\}} \; \text{(LTeq)} \qquad \frac{\Gamma \overset{eqn}{\vdash} eq \; :> \rho \quad \Gamma \overset{eqn}{\vdash} eqs \; :> \rho'}{\Gamma \overset{eqn}{\vdash} eq; eqs \; :> \rho \cup \rho'} \; \text{(LTeqs)}$$

Fig. 8. LUSTRE security typing rules for equations

In (LTbase), we assume Γ maps the base clock `base` to some security variable (γ by convention). In (LTon), the security type of the derived clock is the join of the security types of the clock ck and that of the variable x.

Constants have security type $\bot$, irrespective of the context (rule (LTcnst)). For variables, in rule (LTvar), we look up their security type in the context Γ. Unary operations preserve the type of their arguments (rule (LTunop)). Binary ($\oplus$, `when` and `fby`) and ternary (`if-then-else` and `merge`) operations on flows generate a flow with a security type that is the join of the types of the operand flows (rules (LTbinop), (LTwhn), (LTmrg), (LTite), and (LTfby)). In operations on *lists of flows*, the security types are computed component-wise. There is an implicit dependency on the security level of the common clock of the operand flows for these operators. This dependence on the security level of the clock is made explicit in the rule for equations. In general, the security type for any constructed expression is the join of those of its components (and of the clock).

Node Call. Node calls assume that we have a security signature for the node definition (described below). We can then securely type node calls by instantiating the security signature with the types of the actual arguments (and that of the base clock). Note that the rule (LTncall) creates refinement types consisting of the output types β_i constrained by ρ', *i.e.*, the instantiated set of constraints ρ taken from the node signature:

$$\frac{\overset{Node}{\vdash} \text{Node f } (\vec{\alpha})^\gamma \overset{\rho}{\to} \vec{\beta} \quad \Gamma \overset{e}{\vdash} \vec{e} : \vec{\alpha'} \quad \Gamma(\text{base}) = \gamma' \quad \rho' = \rho[\gamma'/\gamma][\overrightarrow{\alpha'}/\vec{\alpha}]}{\Gamma \overset{e}{\vdash} f(\vec{e}) : \vec{\beta}\{|\rho'|\}} \; \text{(LTncall)}$$

Node Definition. A node definition is given a signature $\overset{Node}{\vdash}$ Node f $(\vec{\alpha})^\gamma \overset{\rho}{\to} \vec{\beta}$, which is to be read as saying that the node named f relates the security types $\vec{\alpha}$ of the input variables (and γ, that of the base clock) to the types of the output variables $\vec{\beta}$, via the constraints ρ.

Let $\alpha_1, \ldots, \alpha_n, \delta_1, \ldots \delta_k, \beta_1, \ldots \beta_m, \gamma$ be distinct *fresh type variables.* Assume these to be the types of the input, local and output variables, and that of the base clock. We compute the constraints over these variables induced by the node's equations. Finally, we eliminate, via substitution using procedure simplify, the type variables δ_i given to the local program variables, since these should not appear in the node's interface. The security signature of a node definition is thus given as:

$$G(f) = n : \{\texttt{in} = \vec{x}, \texttt{out} = \vec{y}, \texttt{var} = \vec{z}, \texttt{eqn} = \vec{eq}\}$$

$$\Gamma_F := \{\vec{x} \mapsto \vec{\alpha}, \vec{y} \mapsto \vec{\beta}, \texttt{base} \mapsto \gamma\} \quad \Gamma_L := \{\vec{z} \mapsto \vec{\delta}\}$$

$$\frac{\Gamma_F \cup \Gamma_L \overset{eqn}{\vdash} \vec{eq} :> \rho' \quad (\_, \rho) = \mathsf{simplify}\ (\_, \rho')\ \vec{\delta}}{\overset{Node}{\vdash} \texttt{Node f } (\vec{\alpha})^\gamma \overset{\rho}{\to} \vec{\beta}} \text{(LTndef)}$$

The node signature (and call) rules can be formulated in this step-wise and modular manner since LUSTRE does not allow recursive node calls and cyclic dependencies. Further, all variables in a node definition are explicitly accounted for as input and output parameters or local variables, so no extra contextual information is required.

$$\frac{}{(\vec{\alpha}, \rho) = \mathsf{simplify}\ (\vec{\alpha}, \rho)\ [\,]}$$

$$\frac{(\vec{\alpha'}, \rho') = \mathsf{simplify}\ (\vec{\alpha}[\nu/\delta], \rho[\nu/\delta])\ \vec{\delta}}{(\vec{\alpha'}, \rho') = \mathsf{simplify}\ (\vec{\alpha}, \rho \cup \{\nu \sqsubseteq \delta\})\ (\delta :: \vec{\delta})} \ \delta \text{ not in } \nu$$

$$\frac{(\vec{\alpha'}, \rho') = \mathsf{simplify}\ (\vec{\alpha}[\nu/\delta], \rho[\nu/\delta])\ \vec{\delta}}{(\vec{\alpha'}, \rho') = \mathsf{simplify}\ (\vec{\alpha}, \rho \cup \{\nu \sqcup \delta \sqsubseteq \delta\})\ (\delta :: \vec{\delta})} \ \delta \text{ not in } \nu$$

Fig. 9. Eliminating local variables' security type constraints

Observe that in the (LTndef) rule, δ_i are fresh security type variables assigned to the local variables. Since there will be exactly one defining equation for any local variable z_i, note that in constraints ρ', there will be exactly one constraint in which δ_i is on the right, and this is of the form $\nu_i \sqsubseteq \delta_i$. Procedure simplify (Fig. 9) serially (in some arbitrary but fixed order for the δ_i) eliminates such type variables via substitution in the types and type constraints. Our definition of simplify here generalises that given for the types of NLUSTRE in [17].

Lemma 3 (Correctness of simplify $(\vec{\alpha}, \rho)\vec{\delta}$). *Let ρ be a set of constraints such that for a security type variable δ, there is at most one constraint of the form $\mu \sqsubseteq \delta$. Let s be a ground instantiation of security type variables wrt a security class lattice SC such that ρ is satisfied by s.*

1. If $\rho = \rho_1 \cup \{\nu \sqsubseteq \delta\}$, where variable δ is not in ν, then $\rho_1[\nu/\delta]$ is satisfied by s. (Assume disjoint union).
2. If $\rho = \rho_1 \cup \{\nu \sqcup \delta \sqsubseteq \delta\}$, where variable δ is not in ν, then $\rho_1[\nu/\delta]$ is satisfied by s. (Assume disjoint union).

Lemma 3 is central to establishing that the type signature of a node does not change in the normalisation transformations of Sect. 4, which introduce equations involving fresh local program variables.

Revisiting Fig. 12, the reader can see the type system at work, with the security types and constraints annotated. Also shown is the simplification of constraints using simplify.

4   Normalisation

We now present Bourke et al.'s "normalisation transformations" , which de-nest and distribute operators over lists (tuples) of expressions, and finally transform fby expressions to a form where the first argument is a constant.

Normalising an n-tuple of LUSTRE expressions yields an m-tuple of LUSTRE expressions without tupling and nesting, and a set of equations, defining fresh local variables (Fig. 10). We denote the transformation as

$$([e'_1, \ldots, e'_m]^{\alpha_1, \ldots, \alpha_m}, eqs^{\rho}) \leftarrow \lfloor e_1, \ldots, e_n \rfloor$$

where we have additionally decorated the transformations of [4] with security types for each member of the tuple of expressions, and with a set of type constraints for the generated equations. We show that the normalisation transformations are indeed *typed transformations*. Our type annotations indicate why security types and constraints of well-security-typed LUSTRE programs are preserved (modulo satisfaction), as in Theorem 1.

The rules *(Xcnst)-(Xbinop)* for constants, variables, unary and binary operators are obvious, generating no new equations. In rule *(Xwhn)*, where the sampling condition is distributed over the members of the tuple, the security type for each expression is obtained by taking a join of the security type α_i of the expression e'_i with γ, i.e., that of the variable x.

Of primary interest are the rules *(Xfby)* for fby and *(Xncall)* for *node call*, where fresh variables x_i and their defining equations are introduced. In these cases, we introduce *fresh* security type variables δ_i for the x_i, and add appropriate constraints. The rules *(Xite)* and *(Xmrg)* resemble *(Xfby)* in most respects. In rule *(Xncall)*, the constraints are obtained from the node signature via substitution.

The rules *(Xbase)* and *(Xon)* for clocks also introduce no equations. The rules *(Xtup)* for tuples (lists) of expressions and *(Xeqs)* for equations regroup the resulting expressions appropriately. The translation of node definitions involves translating the equations, and adding the fresh local variables.

$$\lfloor c \rfloor = ([c^\perp], [\,]^\emptyset) \qquad\qquad\qquad\qquad\qquad Xcnst$$
$$\lfloor x^\alpha \rfloor = ([x]^\alpha, [\,]^\emptyset) \qquad\qquad\qquad\qquad\qquad Xvar$$

$$\lfloor \diamond\, e \rfloor = \text{let } ([e']^\alpha, eqs^\rho) \leftarrow \lfloor e \rfloor \qquad\qquad\qquad Xunop$$
$$\text{in } ([\diamond\, e']^\alpha, eqs^\rho)$$

$$\lfloor e_1 \oplus e_2 \rfloor = \text{let } ([e_1']^{\alpha_1}, eqs_1^{\rho_1}) \leftarrow \lfloor e_1 \rfloor \text{ and } ([e_2']^{\alpha_2}, eqs_2^{\rho_2}) \leftarrow \lfloor e_2 \rfloor \quad Xbinop$$
$$\text{in } ([e_1' \oplus e_2']^{\alpha_1 \sqcup \alpha_2}, (eqs_1 \cup eqs_2)^{\rho_1 \cup \rho_2})$$

$$\lfloor \vec{e} \text{ when } x^\gamma = k \rfloor = \text{let } ([e_1'{}^{\alpha_1}, \ldots, e_m'{}^{\alpha_m}], eqs^\rho) \leftarrow \lfloor \vec{e} \rfloor \qquad\qquad Xwhn$$
$$\text{in } ([e_1' \text{ when } x = k^{\alpha_1 \sqcup \gamma}, \ldots, e_m' \text{ when } x = k^{\alpha_m \sqcup \gamma}], eqs^\rho)$$

$$\lfloor \vec{e_0} \text{ fby } \vec{e_1} \rfloor = \text{let } (\vec{e_0'}^{\vec{\alpha}}, eqs_0^{\rho_0}) \leftarrow \lfloor \vec{e_0} \rfloor \text{ and } (\vec{e_1'}^{\vec{\beta}}, eqs_1^{\rho_1}) \leftarrow \lfloor \vec{e_1} \rfloor \qquad Xfby$$
$$\text{in } (\vec{x}^{\vec{\delta}}, (\{(x_i = e_{0i}' \text{ fby } e_{1i}')_{i=1}^k\} \cup eqs_0 \cup eqs_1)^\rho)$$
$$\text{where } \rho = \{(\alpha_i \sqcup \beta_i \sqsubseteq \delta_i)_{i=1}^k\} \cup \rho_0 \cup \rho_1$$

$$\lfloor \text{merge } x^\gamma\ \vec{e_1}\ \vec{e_2} \rfloor = \text{let } (\vec{e_1'}^{\vec{\alpha}}, eqs_1^{\rho_1}) \leftarrow \lfloor \vec{e_1} \rfloor \text{ and } (\vec{e_2'}^{\vec{\beta}}, eqs_2^{\rho_2}) \leftarrow \lfloor \vec{e_2} \rfloor \qquad Xmrg$$
$$\text{in } (\vec{x}^{\vec{\delta}}, (\{(x_i = \text{merge } x\ e_{1i}'\ e_{2i}')_{i=1}^k\} \cup eqs_1 \cup eqs_2)^\rho)$$
$$\text{where } \rho = \{(\gamma \sqcup \alpha_i \sqcup \beta_i \sqsubseteq \delta_i)_{i=1}^k\} \cup \rho_1 \cup \rho_2$$

$$\lfloor \text{if } e \text{ then } \vec{e_t}$$
$$\text{else } \vec{e_f} \rfloor = \text{let } (e'^\kappa, eqs_c^{\rho_c}) \leftarrow \lfloor e \rfloor \text{ and } (\vec{e_t'}^{\vec{\alpha}}, eqs_t^{\rho_t}) \leftarrow \lfloor \vec{e_t} \rfloor \qquad Xite$$
$$\text{and } (\vec{e_f'}^{\vec{\beta}}, eqs_f^{\rho_f}) \leftarrow \lfloor \vec{e_f} \rfloor \text{ in}$$
$$(\vec{x}^{\vec{\delta}}, (\{(x_i = \text{if } e' \text{ then } e_{ti}' \text{ else } e_{fi}')_{i=1}^k\} \cup eqs)^\rho)$$
$$\text{where } eqs = eqs_c \cup eqs_t \cup eqs_f$$
$$\rho = (\kappa \sqcup \alpha_i \sqcup \beta_i \sqsubseteq \delta_i)_{i=1}^k \cup \rho_c \cup \rho_t \cup \rho_f$$

$$\lfloor f(e_1, ..., e_n) \rfloor = \text{let } ([e_1', ..., e_m']^{\vec{\alpha'}}, eqs^{\rho_1}) \leftarrow \lfloor e_1, ..., e_n \rfloor \qquad Xncall$$
$$\text{in } ([x_1^{\delta_1}, ..., x_k^{\delta_k}],$$
$$(\{(x_1, ..., x_k) = f(e_1', ..., e_m')\} \cup eqs)^{\rho_2})$$
$$\text{where } \rho_2 = \rho[\vec{\alpha'}/\vec{\alpha}][\vec{\delta}/\vec{\beta}][\gamma'/\gamma] \cup \rho_1$$
$$\text{given } \overset{Node}{\vdash} \text{ Node f } (\vec{\alpha})^\gamma \overset{\rho}{\to} \vec{\beta} \text{ and } \gamma' = \Gamma(\text{base})$$

$$\lfloor [e_1, \ldots, e_k] \rfloor = \text{let for } i \in \{1, \ldots, k\} : \qquad\qquad\qquad Xtup$$
$$([e_{i1}'{}^{\alpha_{i1}}, \ldots, e_{im_i}'{}^{\alpha_{im_i}}], eqs_i^{\rho_i}) \leftarrow \lfloor e_i \rfloor$$
$$\text{in } ([e_{11}'{}^{\alpha_{11}}, \ldots, e_{1m_1}'{}^{\alpha_{1m_1}}, \ldots, e_{k1}'{}^{\alpha_{k1}} \ldots, e_{km_k}'{}^{\alpha_{km_k}}],$$
$$(\bigcup_{i=1..k} eqs_i)^{\cup_i \rho_i})$$

$$\lfloor \text{base} \rfloor = \text{base} \qquad\qquad\qquad\qquad\qquad Xbase$$
$$\lfloor ck \text{ on } x = k \rfloor = \lfloor ck \rfloor \text{ on } x = k \qquad\qquad\qquad Xon$$

$$\lfloor \vec{x}^{\vec{\beta}} =_{ck\gamma} \vec{e} \rfloor = \text{let } (\vec{e'}^{\vec{\alpha}}, eqs^\rho) \leftarrow \lfloor \vec{e} \rfloor \qquad\qquad\qquad Xeqs$$
$$\text{in } (\{(\vec{x}_j =_{ck} e_j')_{j=1}^m\} \cup eqs)^{\{(\gamma \sqcup \alpha_i \sqsubseteq \beta_i)_{i=1}^k\} \cup \rho}$$

Fig. 10. LUSTRE to NLUSTRE normalisation

$$\lfloor x^\theta =_{ck^\gamma} e_0^\alpha \ \mathtt{fby}_l \ e^\beta \rfloor_{fby} = \begin{cases} xinit^{\delta_1} =_{ck^\gamma} \mathtt{true}^\perp \ \mathtt{fby}_{nl} \ \mathtt{false}^\perp & \perp \sqcup \gamma \sqsubseteq \delta_1 \\ px^{\delta_2} =_{ck^\gamma} c^\perp \ \mathtt{fby}_{nl} \ e^\beta & \gamma \sqcup \beta \sqsubseteq \delta_2 \\ x^\theta =_{ck^\gamma} \mathtt{if} \ xinit^{\delta_1} \mathtt{then} \ e_0^\alpha & \gamma \sqcup \delta_1 \sqcup \alpha \sqcup \delta_2 \sqsubseteq \theta \\ \qquad \mathtt{else} \ px^{\delta_2} \end{cases}$$

Fig. 11. Explicit $\mathtt{fby}$ initialisation

Theorem 1 (Preservation of security types). *Let $f \in G$ be a node in* LUSTRE *program G. If the node signature for f in G is $\overset{Node}{\vdash} \ \textit{Node} \ f \ (\vec{\alpha})^\gamma \xrightarrow{\rho} \vec{\beta}$, correspondingly in $\lfloor G \rfloor$ it is $\overset{Node}{\vdash} \ \textit{Node} \ f \ (\vec{\alpha})^\gamma \xrightarrow{\rho'} \vec{\beta}$, and for any ground instantiation s, $s(\rho)$ implies $s(\rho')$.*

The proof is on the DAG structure of G. Here we rely on the modularity of nodes, and the correctness of simplify (Lemma 3). The proof employs induction on the structure of expressions. For the further explicit initialisation of $\mathtt{fby}$ (Fig. 11), the preservation of security via simplify is easy to see.

Semantics Preservation. We recall the important results from [4], which establish the preservation of stream semantics by the transformations.

Theorem 2 (Preservation of semantics. Theorem 2 of [4]). *De-nesting and distribution preserve the semantics of* LUSTRE *programs. (La passe de désimbrication et distributivité préserve la sémantique des programmes.)*

$$\forall G \ f \ \mathbf{xs} \ \mathbf{ys}: \quad G \vDash \widehat{f}(\mathbf{xs}) \searrow \mathbf{ys} \implies \lfloor G \rfloor \vDash \widehat{f}(\mathbf{xs}) \searrow \mathbf{ys}$$

Theorem 3 (Preservation of semantics. Theorem 3 of [4]). *The explicit initialisations of $\mathtt{fby}$ preserve the semantics of the programs. (L'explicitation des initialisations préserve la sémantique des programmes.)*

$$\forall G \ f \ \mathbf{xs} \ \mathbf{ys}: \quad G \vDash \widehat{f}(\mathbf{xs}) \searrow \mathbf{ys} \implies \lfloor G \rfloor_{fby} \vDash \widehat{f}(\mathbf{xs}) \searrow \mathbf{ys}$$

4.1 Example

We adapt an example from [4] to illustrate the translation and security-type preservation. The $\mathtt{re\_trig}$ node in Fig. 12 uses the $\mathtt{cnt\_dn}$ node (see Fig. 21 in [16] for details) to implement a count-down timer that is explicitly triggered whenever there is a rising edge (represented by $\mathtt{edge}$) on i. If the count v expires to 0 before a T on i, the counter isn't allowed restart the count. Output o represents an active count in progress.

We annotate the program with security types (superscripts) and constraints for each equation (as comments), according to the typing rules. $\mathtt{cnt\_dn}$ is assumed to have security signature $\overset{Node}{\vdash} \ \textit{Node} \ \mathtt{cnt\_dn} \ (\alpha_1, \alpha_2)^\gamma \xrightarrow{\{\gamma \sqcup \alpha_1 \sqcup \alpha_2 \sqsubseteq \beta\}} \beta$.

Using simplify to eliminate the security types $\delta'_1, \delta'_2, \delta'_3$, and δ'_6, of the local variables edge, ck, v and nested call to cnt_dn respectively from the constraints (in lines 8, 11, 16–17, 19 on the left), we get the constraint $\{\gamma' \sqcup \alpha'_1 \sqcup \alpha'_2 \sqsubseteq \beta'\}$.

Normalisation introduces local variables (v21, v22, v24) with security types $\delta'_4, \delta'_5, \delta'_6$ (see lines 7, 12, 16 on the right). (Identical names have been used to show the correspondence.) The δ'_i are eliminated by simplify, and the refinement type $\delta'_6\{|\rho'|\}$ for the node call in the LUSTRE version becomes an explicit constraint ρ_5 (line 19) in NLUSTRE. Observe that due to simplify, the security signature remains the same across the translation.

```
 1  node re_trig(iᵅ¹:bool; nᵅ²:int)       node re_trig(iᵅ¹:bool; nᵅ²:int)   1
 2    returns (oᵝ  : bool)                   returns (oᵝ  : bool)             2
 3    var edgeᵟ¹, ckᵟ²:bool,                 var edgeᵟ¹, ckᵟ²:bool, vᵟ³:int,  3
 4      vᵟ³:int;                             v22ᵟ⁴:bool, v21ᵟ⁵:bool,         4
 5  let                                      v24ᵟ⁶:int when ck;              5
 6    (edgeᵇᵃˢᵉ)ᵟ¹ᵞ' = iᵅ¹ and            let                               6
 7      (falseᵗ fby (not iᵅ¹));             v22ᵟ⁴ =ᵧ' falseᵗ fby            7
 8  -- ρ1L = {γ' ⊔ α'1 ⊔ ⊥ ⊔ α'1 ⊑ δ'1}      (not iᵅ¹);                    8
 9    (ckᵇᵃˢᵉ)ᵟ²ᵞ' = edgeᵟ¹ or          -- ρ1 = {γ' ⊔ ⊥ ⊔ α'1 ⊑ δ'4}     9
10      (falseᵗ fby oᵝ');                    edgeᵟ¹ =ᵧ' iᵅ¹ and v22ᵟ⁴;   10
11  -- ρ2L = {γ' ⊔ δ'1 ⊔ ⊥ ⊔ β' ⊑ δ'2}    -- ρ2 = {γ' ⊔ α'1 ⊔ δ'4 ⊑ δ'1}  11
12    (vᵇᵃˢᵉ)ᵟ³ᵞ' = merge ckᵟ²             v21ᵟ⁵ =ᵧ' falseᵗ fby oᵝ';     12
13      (cnt_dn((edgeᵟ¹, nᵅ²)             -- ρ3 = {γ' ⊔ ⊥ ⊔ β' ⊑ δ'5}     13
14      when ckᵟ²))ᵟ⁶{|ρ'|}ᵟ²              ckᵟ² =ᵧ' edgeᵟ¹ or v21ᵟ⁵;     14
15    (0 when not ckᵟ²);                   -- ρ4 = {γ' ⊔ δ'1 ⊔ δ'5 ⊑ δ'2}  15
16  -- ρ' = {δ'2 ⊔ (δ'1 ⊔ δ'2) ⊔ (α'2 ⊔ δ'2) ⊑ δ'6}  v24ᵟ⁶ =ᵟ² cnt_dn(    16
17  -- ρ3L = {γ' ⊔ δ'2 ⊔ δ'6 ⊔ ⊥ ⊔ δ'2 ⊑ δ'3} ∪ ρ'   edgeᵟ¹ when ckᵟ²,   17
18    (oᵇᵃˢᵉ)ᵝᵞ' = vᵟ³ > 0ᵗ;               nᵅ² when ckᵟ²);               18
19  -- ρ4L = {γ' ⊔ δ'3 ⊔ ⊥ ⊑ β'}         -- ρ5 = {δ'2 ⊔ (δ'1 ⊔ δ'2) ⊔ (α'2 ⊔ δ'2) ⊑ δ'6}  19
20  tel                                     vᵟ³ =ᵧ' merge ckᵟ² v24ᵟ⁶     20
                                            (0ᵗ when not ckᵟ²);           21
                                          -- ρ6 = {γ' ⊔ δ'2 ⊔ δ'6 ⊔ ⊥ ⊔ δ'2 ⊑ δ'3}  22
                                            oᵝ =ᵧ' vᵟ³>0ᵗ;               23
                                          -- ρ7 = {γ' ⊔ δ'3 ⊔ ⊥ ⊑ β'}     24
                                          tel                             25
```

$$\text{simplify}_L \ (\beta', \{\rho_{1L} \cup \rho_{2L} \cup \rho_{3L} \cup \rho_{4L}\}) \ \{\delta'_1, \delta'_2, \delta'_3, \delta'_6\} = (\beta', \{\gamma' \sqcup \alpha'_1 \sqcup \alpha'_2 \sqsubseteq \beta'\})$$

$$\text{simplify}_{NL} \ (\beta', \{\rho_1 \cup \rho_2 \cup \rho_3 \cup \rho_4 \cup \rho_5 \cup \rho_6 \cup \rho_7\}) \ \{\delta'_1, \delta'_2, \delta'_3, \delta'_4, \delta'_5, \delta'_6\}$$
$$= (\beta', \{\gamma' \sqcup \alpha'_1 \sqcup \alpha'_2 \sqsubseteq \beta'\})$$

Fig. 12. Example: Security analysis and normalisation. when ck and when not ck abbreviate when ck = T and when ck = F.

5   Security and Non-Interference

We first recall and adapt concepts from our previous work [17].

Lemma 4 (Security of Node Calls; *cf.* Lemma 3 in [17]). *Assume the following, for a call to a node with the given security signature*

$$\overset{Node}{\vdash} \textbf{Node } f\,(\overrightarrow{\alpha})^{\gamma} \xrightarrow{\rho} \overrightarrow{\beta} \qquad \Gamma\overset{e}{\vdash}\overrightarrow{e} : \overrightarrow{\alpha'} \qquad \Gamma\overset{e}{\vdash}f(\overrightarrow{e}) : \overrightarrow{\beta'} \qquad \Gamma\overset{ck}{\vdash}ck : \gamma$$

where ck is the base clock underlying the argument streams $\overrightarrow{e}$. Let s be a ground instantiation of type variables such that for some security classes $\overrightarrow{t}, w \in SC$: $s(\overrightarrow{\alpha'}) = \overrightarrow{t}$ and $s(\gamma) = w$.
Now, if ρ is satisfied by the ground instantiation $\{\overrightarrow{\alpha} \mapsto \overrightarrow{t}, \overrightarrow{\beta} \mapsto \overrightarrow{u}, \gamma \mapsto w\}$, then the $s(\overrightarrow{\beta'})$ are defined, and $s(\overrightarrow{\beta'}) \sqsubseteq s(\overrightarrow{\beta}\{\!|\rho|\!\})$.

Lemma 4 relates the satisfaction of constraints on security types generated during a node call to satisfaction in a security lattice via a ground instantiation. Again we rely on the modularity of nodes—that no recursive calls are permitted, and nodes do not have free variables.

Definition 1 (Node Security; Definition III.1 in [17]). *Let f be a node in the program graph G with security signature $\overset{Node}{\vdash} \textbf{Node } f\,(\overrightarrow{\alpha})^{\gamma} \xrightarrow{\rho} \overrightarrow{\beta}$. Let s be a ground instantiation that maps the security type variables in the set $\{(\alpha_1, \ldots \alpha_n)\} \cup \{(\beta_1, \ldots \beta_m)\} \cup \{\gamma\}$ to security classes in lattice SC.*
Node f is secure with respect to s if (i) ρ is satisfied by s; (ii) For each node g' on which f is directly dependent, g' is secure with respect to the appropriate ground instantiations for each call to g' in f as given by Lemma 4.

This definition captures the intuition of node security in that all the constraints generated for the equations within the node must be satisfied, and that each internal node call should also be secure.

The notion of non-interference requires limiting observation to streams whose security level is at most a given security level t.

Definition 2 (($\sqsubseteq t$)-projected Stream; Definition IV.1 in [17]). *Suppose $t \in SC$ is a security class. Let X be a set of program variables, Γ be security type assumptions for variables in X, and s be a ground instantiation, i.e., $\Gamma \circ s$ maps variables in X to security classes in SC. Let us define $X_{\sqsubseteq t} = \{x \in X \mid (\Gamma \circ s)(x) \sqsubseteq t\}$. Let H_* be a Stream history such that $X \subseteq dom(H_*)$. Define $H_*|_{X_{\sqsubseteq t}}$ as the projection of H_* to $X_{\sqsubseteq t}$, i.e., restricted to those variables that are at security level t or lower:*

$$H_*|_{X_{\sqsubseteq t}}(x) = H_*(x) \quad for\ x \in X_{\sqsubseteq t}.$$

Theorem 4 (Non-interference for NLUSTRE; Theorem 5 in [17]). *Let $f \in G$ be a node with security signature*

$$\overset{Node}{\vdash} \textbf{Node } f\,\overrightarrow{\alpha}^{\gamma} \xrightarrow{\rho} \overrightarrow{\beta}$$

which is secure with respect to ground instantiation s of the type variables. Let eqs be the set of equations in f. Let $X = fv(eqs) - dv(eqs)$, i.e., the input *variables in eqs.*

Let $V = fv(eqs) \cup dv(eqs)$, *i.e., the input, output and local variables.*

Let Γ *(and s) be such that* $\Gamma \overset{eqn}{\vdash} eqs :> \rho$ *and* ρ *is satisfied by s. Let* $t \in SC$ *be any security level. Let bs be a given (base) clock stream.*

Let H_* *and* H'_* *be such that*

1. *for all* $eq \in eqs$: $G, H_*, bs \vdash eq$ *and* $G, H'_*, bs \vdash eq$, *i.e., both* H_* *and* H'_* *are consistent Stream histories on each of the equations.*
2. $H_*|_{X_{\sqsubseteq t}} = H'_*|_{X_{\sqsubseteq t}}$, *i.e.,* H_* *and* H'_* *agree on the input variables which are at a security level t or below.*

Then $H_*|_{V_{\sqsubseteq t}} = H'_*|_{V_{\sqsubseteq t}}$, *i.e.,* H_* *and* H'_* *agree on all variables of the node f that are given a security level t or below.*

Theorem 5 (Non-interference for LUSTRE**).** *If program G is well-security-typed in* LUSTRE, *then it exhibits non-interference with respect to* LUSTRE*'s stream semantics.*

PROOF SKETCH. Let G be well-security-typed in LUSTRE. This means that each node $f \in G$ is well-security-typed. By induction on the DAG structure of G, using Theorem 1, $\lfloor G \rfloor$ is well-security-typed. By Theorem 4, $\lfloor G \rfloor$ exhibits non-interference. By Theorems 2 and 3, $\lfloor G \rfloor$ and G have the same *extensional* semantics for each node. Therefore, G exhibits non-interference.

6   Conclusions

We have presented a novel security type system for LUSTRE using the notion of constraint-based refinement (sub)types, generalising the type system of [17]. Using security-type preservation and earlier results, we have shown its semantic soundness, expressed in terms of non-interference, with respect to the language's stream semantics. We are developing mechanised proofs of these results, which can be integrated into the Velús verified compiler framework [5].

While LUSTRE's value type system is quite jejune, this security type system is not. It is therefore satisfying to see that it satisfies a subject reduction property[1]. A difficult aspect encountered during the transcription phase [4] concerns alignment of clocks in the presence of complex clock dependencies. We clarify that our type system, being static, only considers security levels of clocks, not actual clock behaviour, and therefore is free from such complications. Further, the clocks induce no timing side-channels since the typing rules enforce, *a fortiori*, that the security type of any (clocked) expression is at least as high as that of its clock.

Acknowledgements. This work was initiated under an Indo-Japanese project DST/INT/JST/P-30/2016(G) *Security in the IoT Space*, DST, Govt of India.

---

[1]   At SYNCHRON 2020, De Simone asked Jeanmaire and Pesin whether the terminology "normalisation" used in their work [4] was related in any way to notions of normalisation seen in, *e.g.*, the λ-calculus. We've shown it is!.

References

1. Auger, C.: Certified compilation of SCADE/LUSTRE. Theses, Université Paris Sud - Paris XI (2013)
2. Bourke, T., Brun, L., Dagand, P.-E., Leroy, X., Pouzet, M., Rieg, L.: A formally verified compiler for Lustre. In: Proceedings of the 38th ACM SIGPLAN Conference on Programming Language Design and Implementation, PLDI 2017, pp. 586–601. Association for Computing Machinery, New York (2017)
3. Bourke, T., Brun, L., Pouzet, M.: Mechanized semantics and verified compilation for a dataflow synchronous language with reset. Proc. ACM Program. Lang. 4(POPL), 1–29 (2019)
4. Bourke, T., Jeanmaire, P., Pesin, B., Pouzet, M.: Normalisation vérifiée du langage Lustre. In: Regis-Gianas, Y., Keller, C. (eds.) $32^{\text{ièmes}}$ Journées Francophones des Langages Applicatifs (JFLA 2021) (2021)
5. Brun, L., Bourke, T., Pouzet, M.: Vélus compiler repository (2020). https://github.com/INRIA/velus. Accessed 20 Jan 2020
6. Caspi, P., Pilaud, D., Halbwachs, N., Plaice, J.A.: LUSTRE: a declarative language for programming synchronous systems. In: Proceedings of 14th Symposium on Principles of Programming Languages (POPL 1987). ACM (1987)
7. Colaço, J., Pagano, B., Pouzet, M.: SCADE 6: A formal language for embedded critical software development (invited paper). In 2017 International Symposium on Theoretical Aspects of Software Engineering (TASE), pp. 1–11, September 2017
8. Coq Development Team. The Coq proof assistant reference manual (2020). https://coq.inria.fr/distrib/V8.9.1/refman/. Accessed 20 June 2021
9. Denning, D.E.: A lattice model of secure information flow. Commun. ACM 19(5), 236–243 (1976)
10. Goguen, J.A., Meseguer, J.: Security policies and security models. In: 1982 IEEE Symposium on Security and Privacy, Oakland, CA, USA, 26–28 April 1982, pp. 11–20. IEEE Computer Society (1982)
11. Halbwachs, N., Caspi, P., Raymond, P., Pilaud, D.: The synchronous data flow programming language LUSTRE. Proc. IEEE 79(9), 1305–1320 (1991)
12. Jahier, E.: The Lurette V2 user guide, V2 ed. Verimag, October 2015. http://www-verimag.imag.fr/DIST-TOOLS/SYNCHRONE/lurette/doc/lurette-man.pdf
13. Kind 2 group. Kind 2 User Documentation, version 1.2.0 ed. Department of Computer Science, The University of Iowa, April 2020. https://kind.cs.uiowa.edu/kind2_user_doc/doc.pdf
14. Knuth, D.E., Bendix, P.B.: Simple word problems in universal algebras. In: Leech, J. (ed.) Computational Problems in Abstract Algebra, pp. 263–297. Pergamon (1970)
15. Leroy, X.: Formal verification of a realistic compiler. Commun. ACM 52(7), 107–115 (2009)
16. Prasad, S., Yerraguntla, R.M.: Normalising Lustre preserves security. CoRR abs/2105.10687 (2021)
17. Prasad, S., Yerraguntla, R.M., Sharma, S.: Security types for synchronous data flow systems. In: 2020 18th ACM-IEEE International Conference on Formal Methods and Models for System Design (MEMOCODE), pp. 1–12 (2020)
18. Raymond, P.: Synchronous program verification with Lustre/Lesar. In: Modeling and Verification of Real-Time Systems: Formalisms and Software Tools, pp. 171–206. Wiley (2010)

19. Viry, P.: Equational rules for rewriting logic. Theoret. Comput. Sci. **285**(2), 487–517 (2002)
20. Volpano, D., Irvine, C., Smith, G.: A sound type system for secure flow analysis. J. Comput. Secur. **4**(2–3), 167–187 (1996)

Synthesis and Learning

Learning Probabilistic Automata Using Residuals

Wenjing Chu[1]($\boxtimes$), Shuo Chen[2], and Marcello Bonsangue[1]

[1] Leiden Institute of Advanced Computer Science, Leiden University,
Leiden, The Netherlands
`chuw@liacs.leidenuniv.nl`
[2] Informatics Institute, University of Amsterdam, Amsterdam, The Netherlands
`s.chen3@uva.nl`

Abstract. A probabilistic automaton is a non-deterministic finite automaton with probabilities assigned to transitions and states that define a distribution on the set of all strings. In general, there are distributions generated by automata with a non-deterministic structure that cannot be generated by a deterministic one. There exist several methods in machine learning that can be used to approximate the probabilities of an automaton given its structure and a finite number of strings independently drawn with respect to an unknown distribution. In this paper, we efficiently construct a probabilistic automaton from a sample by first learning its non-deterministic structure using residual languages and then assigning appropriate probabilities to the transitions and states. We show that our method learns the structure of the automaton precisely for a class of probabilistic automata strictly including deterministic one and give some experimental results to compare the learned distribution with respect to other methods. To this end, we present a novel algorithm to compute the Euclidean distance between two weighted graphs effectively.

Keywords: Probabilistic automata · Residual finite state automata · Learning automata · L_2 distance between discrete distributions

1 Introduction

Probabilistic models like hidden Markov models and probabilistic finite automaton (PFA) are widely used in the field of machine learning, for example, in computational biology [2], speech recognition [1,14,15], and information extraction [20]. It has become increasingly clear that learning probabilistic models is essential to support these downstream tasks.

Passively learning a probabilistic automaton aims at constructing an approximation of a finite representation of an unknown distribution D through a finite number of strings independently drawn with respect to D. Many passive learning algorithms for probabilistic automata have been proposed. Still, most of them concentrate only on the restricted class of deterministic probabilistic finite

© Springer Nature Switzerland AG 2021
A. Cerone and P. C. Ölveczky (Eds.): ICTAC 2021, LNCS 12819, pp. 295–313, 2021.
https://doi.org/10.1007/978-3-030-85315-0_17

automata (DPFA). The most famous algorithm is ALERGIA [4] based on state merging and folding given a positive sample. ALERGIA has been extended to deal with deterministic probabilistic automata [8,23], and at the limit, it characterizes the original distribution. However, because of the underlying determinism, the resulting automata are often very large (exponential on the size of the sample), so that it may easily become impractical.

In this paper, we propose a more efficient representation using non-determinism. We first learn from a finite sample the non-deterministic structure of the support of the distribution using residual languages and then add probabilities to the transitions solving non-determinism by a fair distribution of the probabilities. As such, the algorithm also approximates distributions generated by probabilistic automata that cannot be generated by deterministic ones [12].

There are not so many algorithms for learning general probabilistic automata. The most well known is the Baum-Welch algorithm [3] that constructs a fully connected graph on the estimated number of states needed and is therefore not very practical. Our work is based on the learning algorithm for residual automata introduced in [10]. The residual (also called derivative) of a language L with respect to a word u is the set of words v such that uv is in L. Residual automata are non-deterministic automata that can be used to learn efficiently any regular language. In the probabilistic setting, a learning algorithm using probabilistic residual distributions has been proposed in [13]. The starting point of their work is very similar to ours, but the resulting algorithm assumes, differently from ours, precise probabilities for each word in the sample.

To compare the goodness of our algorithm, we adapted the algorithm for computing the L_2 distance between two distributions presented in [18] in the context of weighted automata, i.e. automata transitions and states labeled with weights from a field (or more generally semirings) instead of probabilities. The novelty is in the computation of the shortest distance algorithm for weighted graphs using a weaker condition than the original one. This step was necessary in order to be able to apply it to classical probabilistic automata. The L_2 distance is used in few experiments to compare our algorithm with ALERGIA and with learning through k-testable languages [5]. The latter are language that can be accepted by an automaton that can see at most k many symbols. We also use other metrics in this comparison, such as accuracy, precision and sensitivity weighted with a confidence factor to recognize the probabilistic nature of the experiments.

2   Preliminaries

Let Σ be a finite alphabet and Σ^* be the set of all finite strings over Σ, with ε denoting the empty string. A language L is a subset of Σ^*. For any string u and any language L, we define $Pref(u) = \{v \in \Sigma^* | \exists w \in \Sigma^*, vw = u\}$ to be the set of prefixes of u and $Pref(L) = \bigcup_{u \in L} Pref(u)$ to be the prefix closure of L.

Definition 1. Non-deterministic finite automaton. *A non-deterministic finite automaton (NFA) is a 5-tuple $A = \langle \Sigma, Q, I, F, \delta \rangle$, where*

- Σ is a finite alphabet,
- Q is a finite set of states,
- $I : Q \rightarrow 2$ is characterizing the set of initial states,
- $F : Q \rightarrow 2$ is characterizing the set of final states,
- $\delta : Q \times \Sigma \rightarrow 2^Q$ is the transition function.

The transition function δ can be naturally extended from symbol in Σ to arbitrary strings by defining the extended transition function $\delta^* : Q \times \Sigma^* \rightarrow 2^Q$ inductively as follows:

- For every $q \in Q$, $\delta^*(q, \varepsilon) = q$,
- For every $q \in Q$, $x \in \Sigma^*$, and $a \in \Sigma$, $\delta^*(q, xa) = \bigcup\{\delta(p, a) | p \in \delta^*(q, x)\}$.

A string $x \in \Sigma^*$ is accepted by a NFA A from a state $q \in Q$ if $\delta^*(q, x) \cap F \neq \emptyset$. We denote by $L(A, q)$ the set of all those strings. The language $L(A)$ accepted by A is the set of all strings accepted by A from some $q_0 \in I$. A language L is called regular if there is a NFA A that accepts exactly the language L [17].

For a NFA A, an accepting path π for a string $x = a_1 \ldots a_n$ is a sequence of states $q_0 \ldots q_n$ such that $q_{i+1} \in \delta(q_i, a_{i+1})$ for all $0 \leq i \leq n-1$, starting from an initial state, i.e. $I(q_0) = 1$, and ending in a final state, i.e. $F(q_n) = 1$. We denote by $Paths(x)$ the set of all accepting paths for a given string x. Note that the set $Paths(x)$ is finite. An accepting path contains a cycle if there is a repeating state. That is, there exists different i and j such that $q_i = q_j$.

For any language L and for any string $u \in \Sigma^*$, the residual language of L associated with u is defined by the u-derivative $L_u = \{x \in \Sigma^* | ux \in L\}$, and we call u a characterizing word for L_u. A language $L' \subseteq \Sigma^*$ is a residual language of L if there exists a string $u \in \Sigma^*$ such that $L' = L_u$. The number of residual languages of a language L is finite if and only if L is regular [11]. This implies that there exists a finite set of strings $\mathcal{B}(L)$ such that $x \in \mathcal{B}(L)$ if L_x is a residual language of a regular language L. The set $\mathcal{B}(L)$ can be constructed depending on the representation of the language L. For example, if L is the language accepted by a trimmed NFA A (i.e., minimal and with all states reachable from an initial state), then $\mathcal{B}(L)$ can be constructed as a finite set of minimal length strings reaching all states of A from some initial state.

Definition 2. Residual finite state automaton [7]. *A residual finite state automaton (RFSA) is a NFA $A = \langle \Sigma, Q, Q_0, F, \delta \rangle$ such that, for each state $q \in Q$, $L(A, q)$ is a residual language of $L(A)$.*

In other words, a RFSA A is a non-deterministic automaton whose states correspond exactly to the residual languages of the language recognized by A.

Non-deterministic automata can be generalized to frequency and probabilistic automata. Frequency finite automata associate a positive rational number to each transition, initial states and final ones representing the 'number of occurrences' of a transition or state.

Definition 3. Frequency finite automaton. *A frequency finite automaton (FFA) is a 5-tuple $A = \langle \Sigma, Q, I_f, F_f, \delta_f \rangle$, where:*

- $\varSigma$ is a finite alphabet,
- Q is a finite set of states,
- $I_f : Q \to \mathbb{Q}^+$,
- $F_f : Q \to \mathbb{Q}^+$,
- $\delta_f : Q \times \varSigma \to \mathbb{Q}^{+Q}$

such that for every state $q \in Q$ the weight of the incoming transitions is equal to the weight of the outgoing transitions:

$$I_f(q) + \sum_{q' \in Q, a \in \varSigma} \delta_f(q', a)(q) = F_f(q) + \sum_{q' \in Q, a \in \varSigma} \delta_f(q, a)(q').$$

Intuitively, the above condition says that frequency is preserved by passing through states. Note that we allowed weights to be positive rational numbers instead of positive integers. This is for technical convenience, but has no effect on the definition. Frequency automata are strictly related to probabilistic automata. Recall that a probabilistic language over $\varSigma^*$ is a function $D : \varSigma^* \to [0,1]$ that is also a discrete distribution, that is:

$$\sum_{x \in \varSigma^*} D(x) = 1.$$

An interesting class of probabilistic languages can be described by a generalization of non-deterministic automata with probabilities as weight on states and transitions.

Definition 4. Probabilistic finite automaton. *A probabilistic finite automaton (PFA) is a 5-tuple $A = \langle \varSigma, Q, I_p, F_p, \delta_p \rangle$, where:*

- $\varSigma$ is a finite alphabet,
- Q is a finite set of states,
- $I_p : Q \to (\mathbb{Q} \cap [0,1])$ is the initial probability such that $\sum_{q \in Q} I_p(q) = 1$,
- $F_p : Q \to (\mathbb{Q} \cap [0,1])$,
- $\delta_p : Q \times \varSigma \to (\mathbb{Q} \cap [0,1])^Q$ is the transition function such that $\forall q \in Q$,

$$F_p(q) + \sum_{a \in \varSigma, q' \in Q} \delta_p(q, a)(q') = 1.$$

We define the support of a PFA $A = \langle \varSigma, Q, I_p, F_p, \delta_p \rangle$ is the NFA $supp(A) = \langle \varSigma, Q, I, F, \delta \rangle$, where $I = \{q \mid I_p(q) > 0\}$, $F = \{q \mid F_p(q) > 0\}$, and $\delta(q, x)(q') = 1$ iff $\delta_p(q, x)(q') > 0$.

Given a string $x = a_1 \cdots a_n \in \varSigma^*$ of length n, an accepting (or valid) path π for x is a sequence of states $q_0 \cdots q_n$ such that:

- $I_p(q_0) > 0$,
- $\delta_p(q_i, a_{i+1})(q_{i+1}) > 0$ for all $0 \le i < n$, and
- $F_p(q_n) > 0$.

We denote by $Paths_p(x)$ the set of all accepting paths for a string x. Note that this set is necessarily finite. A probabilistic automaton is said to be unambiguous if for any string $x \in \varSigma^*$ there is at most one path for x. Examples of unambiguous probabilistic automata are the deterministic ones, restricting the initial probability and the transition function to have a support of at most one state:

Definition 5. *Deterministic probabilistic finite automaton.* *A PFA* $A = \langle \Sigma, Q, I_p, F_p, \delta_p \rangle$ *is called deterministic probabilistic finite automaton (DPFA) if*

- $|\{q \mid I_p(q) > 0\}| \le 1$ *(at most one single initial state),*
- $\forall q \in Q, \forall a \in \Sigma, |\{q' \mid \delta_p(q,a)(q') > 0\}| \le 1$ *((at most one next state).*

Basically, a DPFA is deterministic if its support is a DFA. All deterministic probabilistic automata are unambiguous, but not all unambiguous automata are deterministic because they can have more that one next state leading to a non-accepting path.

Given a path $\pi = q_0 \cdots q_n$ for a string $x = a_1 \cdots a_n$, we denote by $i_p(\pi)$ the probability $I_p(q_0)$ of its initial state q_0, by $e_p(\pi)$ the probability $F_p(q_n)$ of the last state q_n of π, and by $\delta_p(\pi)$ the product of all probabilities along the transitions in the path, that is $\delta_p(\pi) = 1$ if x is the empty string and otherwise

$$\delta_p(\pi) = \Pi_{i=0}^{n-1} \delta_p(q_i, a_{i+1})(q_{i+1}).$$

Note that $i_p(\pi)$, $e_p(\pi)$ and $\delta_p(\pi)$ are always strictly positive for an accepting path π. Given a probabilistic automaton A, the probability of a path $\pi \in Paths_p(x)$ is given by $i_p(\pi) \cdot \delta_p(\pi) \cdot e_p(\pi)$, while the probability of a string $x \in \Sigma^*$ is defined by:

$$\llbracket A \rrbracket(x) = \sum_{\pi \in Paths_p(x)} i_p(\pi) \cdot \delta_p(\pi) \cdot e_p(\pi). \tag{1}$$

A PFA is said to be consistent if all its states appear into at least one accepting path. If a PFA A is consistent then it is easy to show [12] that $\llbracket A \rrbracket$ gives a distribution on Σ^*, that is $\sum_{x \in \Sigma^*} \llbracket A \rrbracket(x) = 1$. A distribution D is called regular if it is generated by a PFA A, that is $D = \llbracket A \rrbracket$.

The language $L(A)$ accepted by a probabilistic automaton A is the support of its distribution and is given by all strings x with a strictly positive probability $\llbracket A \rrbracket(x)$. In other words, $L(A)$ is the language of the support of A. A language is regular if and only if it is accepted by a (deterministic) probabilistic finite automaton. However, differently, than for ordinary automata, the class of distributions characterized by DPFAs is a proper subclass of the regular ones, characterized by PFAs [12].

The following lemma will be useful later stating that if an accepting path contains a cycle then we can pump that cycle to obtain infinitely many other accepting paths.

Lemma 1. *For a probabilistic automaton A, the probability of an accepting path π with a cycle is strictly smaller than 1.*

A useful tool for proving that a regular distribution generated by a PFA A cannot be expressed by a DPFA, is given by the function $\rho_A : \Sigma^* \to [0,1]$ defined by

$$\rho_A(x) = \begin{cases} \frac{\llbracket A \rrbracket(x)}{\overline{\llbracket A \rrbracket}(x)} & if\ \overline{\llbracket A \rrbracket}(x) > 0 \\ 0 & otherwise. \end{cases}$$

where $\overline{[\![A]\!]}(x)$ is the probability of generating in the automaton A a (possibly infinite) string with finite prefix $x \in \Sigma^*$:

$$\overline{[\![A]\!]}(x) = \sum_{\pi \in Paths_p(x)} i_p(\pi) \cdot \delta_p(\pi)$$

Note that the above definition does not make use of the final probability F of the automaton A, and as such can be considered as a generator of prefixes of finite and infinite strings. Important here is that if A is a DPFA, the set $\{\rho(x)|x \in \Sigma^*\}$ is necessarily finite and bound by the number of states q with $F_p(q) > 0$ [12].

3   Learning Probabilistic Languages Using Residuals

A *sample* (S, f) consists of a finite set of strings $S \subseteq \Sigma^*$ together with a frequency function $f : S \rightarrow \mathbb{N}$ assigning the number of occurrences of each string in the sample. The frequency function f partitions the strings in S into positive samples and negative ones. We denote by $S_+ = \{x \mid f(x) > 0\}$ the set of positive samples and by $S_- = \{x \mid f(x) = 0\}$ the set of negative samples. A *simple sample* is a sample (S, f) such that $f(x) \leq 1$ for every $x \in S$. In other words, a simple sample consists only of a set of strings that must be accepted together with a set of strings that should not be accepted.

A NFA $A = \langle \Sigma, Q, I, F, \delta \rangle$ is *consistent* with respect to a sample (S, f), if every positive sample is accepted by A and every negative sample is not, i.e. $S_+ \subseteq L(A)$ and $S_- \cap L(A) = \emptyset$.

A sample (S, f) is *complete* with respect to a regular language L if there exists a finite characteristic set $\mathcal{B}(L) \in \Sigma^*$ such that

- the positive samples cover the language, that is, both x and xa are in $Pref(S_+)$ for every $x \in \mathcal{B}(L)$ and $a \in \Sigma$,
- the positive samples contain enough strings of L, that is, $Pref(S_+) \cap L \subseteq S_+$,
- distinguishable strings in the language are distinguishable in the sample too, that is, for every $u, v \in Pref(S_+)$, if $L_u \not\subseteq L_v$ then there exists $x \in \Sigma^*$ such that $ux \in S_+$ but $vx \in S_-$.

The first condition guarantees that prefixes of strings in S_+ are enough to reach all residual languages of L and to cover all possible transitions from it. The second condition is about requiring all characteristic strings of the residual languages to be in S_+. And the third condition ensures that S_- is large enough to distinguish different residual languages.

Learning a regular language L from a simple sample (S, f) means building a non-deterministic finite automaton A consistent with the sample and such that if the sample is complete with respect to L, then $L(A) = L$. Of course, one should consider time and space complexity bounded on the two steps above, which are typically required to be polynomial on the number of strings in the sample and of the model representing the language L [7].

Learning a regular distribution D from a sample (S, f) of finite strings independently drawn with a frequency f according to the distribution D means building a probabilistic finite automaton A with a support learning the language of the support of D and with a distribution associated with A that gets arbitrarily closer to D when the size of the sample (S, f) increases. In general, we cannot realistically expect to get exact information on the learned distribution with respect to the target one.

Next, we present our algorithm to learn an unknown regular distribution D from a sample (S, f). The idea is to first learn the non-deterministic structure of the automaton underlying D using residual languages, and then labelling the transitions consistently with the frequency of the sample using a fair distribution when needed.

In our first step, we use Algorithm 1 below to build a RFSA from a simple sample (S, f). The algorithm is similar to that presented in [9] but approximates the inclusion relation between residual languages by calculating on the fly the transitivity and right-invariant (with respect to concatenation) closure $\prec^{tr}$ of the following relation. For $u, v \in Pref(S_+)$, we define:

- $u \prec v$ if there is no string x such that $ux \in S_+$ and $vx \in S_-$,
- $u \simeq v$ if $u \prec v$ and $v \prec u$.

The idea is to characterize all distinguishable states (seen as prefixes of the positive samples). Intuitively, $u \prec^{tr} v$ is an estimate for the inclusion between the residuals $L_u \subseteq L_v$, and if the sample is complete with respect to the unknown language L, this is indeed the case.

Initially, the set of states Q of the automaton is empty. All prefixes of S_+ are explored, and only those which are distinguishable are added to the Q. States below ε with respect to $\prec$ are set to be initial states, while states that belong to S_+ are final ones. Finally, a transition $\delta(u, a) = v$ is added when $v \prec ua$, where $a \in \Sigma$. The algorithm ends either when u is the last string in $Pref$ or when the learned automaton is consistent with the sample.

Example 1. Given a sample (S, f) with $f(\epsilon) = 3, f(aa) = f(ba) = 2, f(bb) = f(abb) = f(bab) = 1$ and $f(a) = f(b) = f(ab) = f(abb) = 0$ we have $S_+ = \{\varepsilon, aa, ba, bb, abb, bab\}$ and $S_- = \{a, b, ab, aab\}$. The Algorithm 1 terminates in three iterations:

- First, the state ε is added. Since $\varepsilon \prec^{tr} \varepsilon$, the state ε is an initial state, and it is also an accepting state because $\varepsilon \in S_+$. No transitions will be added yet, since a and b are not in S_- and thus distinguishable from ε
- In the next iteration, a is added to the states as $a \not\prec^{tr} \varepsilon$. Clearly, a is neither an initial state nor an accepting one. However, $a \prec \varepsilon a$, $\varepsilon \prec aa$, so two transitions $\delta(\varepsilon, a) = a$ and $\delta(a, a) = \varepsilon$ are added. As the automaton is not consistent with the sample, another iteration is needed.
- Finally, the state b is added because $b \not\prec^{tr} \varepsilon$ and $b \not\prec^{tr} a$. Also, b is neither initial nor final state because $b \in S_-$. Six transitions are added to the automaton, as $a \prec \varepsilon b$, $b \prec \varepsilon b$, $\varepsilon \prec ba$, $\varepsilon \prec bb$, $b \prec ab$ and $b \prec ba$. These transitions are $\delta(\varepsilon, b) = a$, $\delta(\varepsilon, b) = b$, $\delta(b, a) = \varepsilon$, $\delta(b, b) = \varepsilon$, $\delta(a, b) = b$ and $\delta(b, a) = b$. Since the automaton constructed so far is consistent with the sample, the algorithm terminates.

Algorithm 1: Building a RFSA from a simple sample

Input: A simple sample (S, f)
Output: A RFSA $\langle \Sigma, Q, I, F, \delta \rangle$
1: Pref := $Pref(S_+)$ ordered by length-lexicographic order
2: $Q := I := F := \delta := \emptyset$
3: $u := \varepsilon$
4: **loop**
5:     **if** $\exists u' \in Q$ such that $u \simeq^{tr} u'$ **then**
6:         Pref := Pref $\setminus u\Sigma^*$
7:     **else**
8:         $Q := Q \cup \{u\}$
9:         **if** $u \prec^{tr} \varepsilon$ **then**
10:             $I := I \cup \{u\}$
11:         **if** $u \in S_+$ **then**
12:             $F := F \cup \{u\}$
13:         **for** $u' \in Q$ and $a \in \Sigma$ **do**
14:             **if** $u'a \in$ Pref and $u \prec^{tr} u'a$ **then**
15:                 $\delta := \delta \cup \{\delta(u', a) = u\}$
16:             **if** $ua \in$ Pref and $u' \prec^{tr} ua$ **then**
17:                 $\delta := \delta \cup \{\delta(u, a) = u')\}$
18:     **if** u is the last string of Pref or $\langle \Sigma, Q, I, F, \delta \rangle$ is consistent with S **then**
19:         exit loop
20:     **else**
21:         $u :=$ next string in Pref
22: **return** $\langle \Sigma, Q, I, F, \delta \rangle$

The resulting automaton is shown in Fig. 1a.

Once we have learned the structure of a RFSA from a sample (S, f), the next step is adding frequencies to get a FFA based on the frequency information of the sample. This step will not change the structure of the automaton, so Σ and Q are the same as the ones resulting from Algorithm 1. Frequency is distributed fairly by dividing it among non-deterministic transitions.

Algorithm 2: Building a FFA from a RFSA

Input: A RFSA $\langle \Sigma, Q, I, F, \delta \rangle$ consistent with a sample (S, f)
Output: A FFA $\langle \Sigma, Q, I_f, F_f, \delta_f \rangle$
1: $I_f(q) := 0$ for all $q \in Q$
2: $F_f(q) := 0$ for all $q \in Q$
3: $\delta_f(q, a) := 0$ for all $q \in Q$ and $a \in \Sigma$.
4: **for** $a_1 \cdots a_n \in S_+$ **do**
5:     compute $Paths(x)$
6:     **for** every $\pi := q_0 \ldots q_n \in Paths(x)$ **do**
7:         $I_f(q_0) := I_f(q_0) + \frac{f(x)}{|Paths(x)|}$
8:         $F_f(q_n) := F_f(q_n) + \frac{f(x)}{|Paths(x)|}$
9:         **for** $i := 0, i := i + 1, i \leq n - 1$ **do**
10:            $\delta_f(q_i, a_{i+1})(q_{i+1}) := \delta_f(q_i, a_{i+1})(q_{i+1}) + \frac{f(x)}{|Paths(x)|}$
11: **return** $\langle \Sigma, Q, I_f, F_f, \delta_f \rangle$

It is not hard to prove that the resulting automaton is indeed a FFA, satisfying the frequency preservation condition when passing through states.

Example 2. Continuing from the previous example, let us consider the case of $ba \in S_+$. Two paths are accepting this string, namely $\varepsilon\, a\, \varepsilon$ and $\varepsilon\, b\, \varepsilon$. As they both start from and end to the same state, $I_f(\varepsilon)$ and $F_f(\varepsilon)$ are incremented by 2, respectively. However, the frequency $f(ba) = 2$ is divided equally between the two b-transitions from state ε, incrementing each of them by 1. After all strings in S_+ are treated, we get the FFA shown in Fig. 1b.

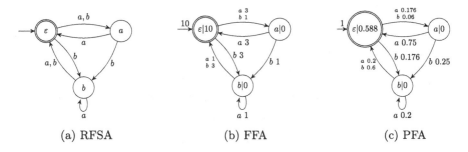

(a) RFSA   (b) FFA   (c) PFA

Fig. 1. Three automata learned from the sample (S, f), with $f(\varepsilon) = 3, f(aa) = f(ba) = 2, f(bb) = f(abb) = 1 = f(bab) = 1$, and $f(a) = f(b) = f(ab) = f(abb) = 0$.

The last step is the standard for building a PFA from a given FFA. Again, the structure is not modified, but frequencies labelling the transitions and the states are used to calculate the probabilities. In the algorithm below, $FREQ(q)$ denotes the number both of strings either passing through a state q or ending in it, and SUM_I denotes the number of strings entering all initial states. For every state q in Q, the probability of being initial state is $\frac{I_f(q)}{SUM_I}$ and of being final state is $\frac{F_f(q)}{FREQ(q)}$, while the probability associated to each transition from q to q' with input a is $\frac{\delta_f(q,a)(q')}{FREQ(q)}$.

Algorithm 3: Building a PFA from a FFA

Input: A FFA $\langle \Sigma, Q, I_f, F_f, \delta_f \rangle$
Output: A PFA $\langle \Sigma, Q, I_p, F_p, \delta_p \rangle$
1: **for** $q \in Q$ **do**
2:     $FREQ(q) := F_f(q) + \sum_{a \in \Sigma, q' \in Q} \delta_f(q, a)(q')$
3:     $F_p(q) := \frac{F_f(q)}{FREQ(q)}$
4:     **for** $a \in \Sigma_1, q' \in Q$ **do**
5:         $\delta_p(q, a)(q') := \frac{\delta_f(q,a)(q')}{FREQ(q)}$
6: $SUM_I := \sum_{q \in Q} I_f(q)$
7: **for** $q \in Q$ **do**
8:     $I_p(q) := \frac{I_f(q)}{SUM_I}$
9: **return** $\langle \Sigma, Q, I_p, F_p, \delta_p \rangle$

When the input is a FFA, the above algorithm returns a probabilistic automaton.

Example 3. The probabilistic automaton A resulting from the FFA in Fig. 1b is shown in Fig. 1c. The support automaton is consistent with the sample (S, f).

4 Metrics for Probabilistic Automata

In the previous section, we have presented an algorithm to learn a distribution presented via a PFA. The support of the learned automaton learns the support language of the original distribution. Precise learning of the distribution itself is not realistic, so next, we consider the problem of computing how close the resulting distribution is to the original one. We consider two methods: one when the original distribution is presented via a PFA itself and another to compute easily understandable metrics such as accuracy, precision, or recall when comparing the learned automaton against a sample.

4.1 The L_2 Distance Between Probabilistic Automata

There are many standard distances that can be used to compare regular distributions by means of their representations as probabilistic automata. Here we will concentrate on L_p metrics using a variation of the algorithm presented in [6] for stochastic weighted automata. The L_p distance between two distributions D_1 and D_2 on Σ^* is defined as

$$L_p(D_1, D_2) = \left(\sum_{x \in \Sigma^*} |D_1(x) - D_2(x)|^p \right)^{\frac{1}{p}}.$$

Examples include the Euclidean distance L_2 and the 'Manhattan' distance L_1. Another useful distance is the L_∞, adapted from the L_1 by substituting the sum with the supremum. In general, the problem of computing L_{2p+1} and L_∞ given two probabilistic automata is shown to be NP-hard [6,16], even for automata without cycles.

In this paper we restrict to L_2 using an adaptation of the algorithm to compute it for probabilistic automata by [6]. The basic idea is that

$$\begin{aligned}
(L_2(A_1, A_2)) &= \left(\sum_{x \in \Sigma^*} |[\![A_1]\!](x) - [\![A_2]\!](x)|^2 \right)^{\frac{1}{2}} \\
&= \left(\sum_{x \in \Sigma^*} ([\![A_1]\!](x) - [\![A_2]\!](x))^2 \right)^{\frac{1}{2}} \\
&= \left(\sum_{x \in \Sigma^*} [\![A_1]\!](x)^2 - 2[\![A_1]\!](x)[\![A_2]\!](x) + [\![A_2]\!](x))^2 \right)^{\frac{1}{2}} \\
&= \left(\sum_{x \in \Sigma^*} [\![A_1]\!](x)^2 - 2 \sum_{x \in \Sigma^*} [\![A_1]\!](x)[\![A_2]\!](x) + \sum_{x \in \Sigma^*} [\![A_2]\!](x)^2 \right)^{\frac{1}{2}}.
\end{aligned} \tag{2}$$

In the second equality, the absolute values can be removed since they are squared. The last three summations can be computed separately via a shortest distance algorithm for weighted graphs (see below). In general, we consider three different situations.

First, when A_1 and A_2 are acyclic, those summations are finite and can be computed directly.

Second, when A_1, A_2 are deterministic probabilistic automata, we compute their intersection automaton A using the product construction. To avoid computing three intersections, we can keep the label of each transition

$$\delta_p((q_1, q_2), a)(q_1', q_2')$$

as a pair $(\delta_{p1}(q_1, a)(q_1'), \delta_{p2}(q_2, a)(q_2'))$, where δ_{p1} is the transition function of A_1 and δ_{p2} is the one of A_2. When calculating $[\![A_i]\!](x)^2$, we only need to square the i-th component of the pair, while we will multiply the two components to calculate $[\![A_1]\!](x)[\![A_2]\!](x)$. This is possible because, for any string $x \in \Sigma^*$, there is at most one accepting path in A_1 and A_2. In the end, we use the shortest distance algorithm over the intersection automaton with weight modified as described above to compute $\sum_{x \in \Sigma^*}([\![A_1]\!](x))^i([\![A_2]\!](x))^{2-i}$ for $i = 0, 1$ and 2.

Third, when A_1 and A_2 are arbitrary automata, there may be multiple paths with the same label, which means we cannot avoid performing three different intersection automata: one of A_1 with itself, another of A_1 with A_2, and the last of A_2 with itself. As before, we use the shortest distance algorithm over the intersection automaton to compute $\sum_{x \in \Sigma^*}([\![A_1]\!](x))^i([\![A_2]\!](x))^{2-i}$ for $i = 0, 1$ and 2.

A Shortest Distance Algorithm for Weighted Graphs. Classical shortest paths problems compute the shortest paths from one set of source vertices to all other vertices in a weighted graph. The classical shortest paths problem has been generalized to the weighted graph [18]: The shortest distance from a set of vertices I to a vertex F is the sum of the weights of all paths from nodes in I to nodes in F [18] presented a generic algorithm to compute single-source shortest distances for a directed graph with weight in a semiring. Termination of the algorithm depends on the graph being k-closed, a condition that unfortunately is not satisfied by our probabilistic automata (or their intersection). Therefore we have to adapt the algorithm so as to work with a weaker condition, boundness.

A weighted graph $\langle \Sigma, Q, I, F, \delta \rangle$ consists of a finite alphabet Σ, a finite set of states, an initial weight $I : Q \to \mathbb{Q}$, a final weight $F : Q \to \mathbb{Q}$, and a transition function $\delta : Q \times \Sigma \to \mathbb{Q}^Q$. It is similar to a probabilistic automaton, but it does not need to satisfy its restriction. In fact every probabilistic automaton is a weighted graph, and also the intersection of two probabilistic automata as defined in the previous section is a weighted graph (but, in general, not a probabilistic automaton).

Definition 6. *A weighted graph $\langle \Sigma, Q, I, F, \delta \rangle$ is bounded, if for any cycle π there exists a $k \in \mathbb{Q}$ such that:*

$$\sum_{n=1}^{\infty} \delta(\pi)^n = k$$

For example, every probabilistic automaton $\langle \Sigma, Q, I_p, F_p, \delta_p \rangle$ is bounded because the probability of a path with a cycle is always strictly less than 1. It follows that $\sum_{n=1}^{\infty} \delta_p(\pi) = \frac{r}{1-r}$, where $\delta_p(\pi) = r < 1$. Also, the intersection of two probabilistic automata is a bounded weighted graph, but not necessarily a probabilistic automaton because weights need to normalized.

Next, we provide a shortest distances algorithm for bounded weighted graphs. The pseudo-code is given in Algorithm 4.

Algorithm 4: A shortest distance algorithm for weighted graphs

---

Input: A bounded weighted graph $\langle \Sigma, Q, I, F, \delta \rangle$
Output: A rational number d, the shortest distance between I and F
1: Let S and M be an empty set
2: **for** $q \in Q$ **do**
3:     **if** $I_p(q) \neq 0$ **then**
4:         $d[q] := I_p(q)$
5:         $r[q] := I_p(q)$
6:         $M[q] := \{q\}$
7:         add state q to S
8:     **else**
9:         $d[q] := 0$
10:        $r[q] := 0$
11: **while** $S \neq \emptyset$ **do**
12:     $q := S[0]$
13:     remove q from S
14:     add q to P
15:     $r' := r[q]$
16:     $r[q] := 0$
17:     **for all** $a \in \Sigma, q' \in Q$ **do**
18:         **if** $\delta_p(q, a)(q') \neq 0$ **then**
19:             **if** q' is not in $M[q]$ **then**
20:                 $M[q'] := M[q] + aq'$
21:                 $d[q'] := d[q'] + (r' \times \delta_p(q, a)(q'))$
22:                 $r[q'] := r[q'] + (r' \times \delta_p(q, a)(q'))$
23:                 **if** $q' \notin S$ **then**
24:                     add q' to S
25:             **else**
26:                 find cyclic subsequence $q'xq'$ in M[q] and store it Re
27:                 remove alphabet symbols from $q'xq'$ and store the resulting path in π
28:                 **if** $Re \notin M[q']$ **then**
29:                     $l := \delta_p(\pi)$
30:                     $k := \frac{l}{1-l}$
31:                     $d[q'] := d[q'] + (r' \times k)$
32:                     $r[q'] := r[q'] + (r' \times k)$
33: **for** $q \in Q$ **do**
34:     $d[q] := d[q] \times F_p[q]$
35: **return** d

The algorithm uses a set S to maintain the set of next states after transitions and M to store the sequence of transitions visited. S is initialized as a set of initial states. $d[q]$ is the total weight from an initial state to the current state q, $r[q]$ is the weight of the current transition from an initial state to state q.

In the while loop from line 11 to 31, each time we extract a state q from set S, then store the value of $r[q]$ in r' and set $r[q]$ to 0. Lines 17–31 is calculating distances. First, for all transitions starting from state q, if next state q' does not exist in $M[q]$, update $M[q']$ and the value of $d[q']$ and $r[q']$. If next state q' is not in S, add q' into S. If next state q' exists in $M[q]$, find path π of repetition part, then update $d[q]$. When q is the last state in set S, and there are no more transitions, the while loop ends. In the end, for each state q, $d[q]$ is multiplied by the final weight of the state.

4.2   Metrics Using the Sample

In practice, we usually don't know the target distribution of its PFA representation. So we often metric such as Accuracy, Precision, or Sensitivity when testing a PFA against a sample. To measure the similarity or dissimilarity of strings from the sample and ones from the learned automaton, the learned strings are categorized in terms of a confusion matrix [21], as shown in Table 1.

Table 1. Confusion matrix

Classification by sample	Classification by learned automaton	
	$\omega \in L(A)$	$\omega \notin L(A)$
$\omega \in S_+$	True Positive (TP)	False Negative (FN)
$\omega \in S_-$	False Positive (FP)	True Negative (TN)

Since the confusion matrix only takes into account the support of a probabilistic language, we propose a generalization of true positive and false negative weighted by a confidence measure, based on the L_1 distance between the sample and the distribution of the learned automaton. This leads to a new definition of precision, sensitivity and accuracy for probabilistic automata:

$$Precision = \frac{cTP}{|TP| + cFP}, \qquad Sensitivity = \frac{cTP}{|TP| + cFN},$$

$$Accuracy = \frac{|TP| + |TN|}{|TP| + |TN| + |FP| + |FN|}.$$

where $cTP = \sum_{x \in TP} 1 - |P_s(x) - [\![A]\!](x)|$, and $cFN = \sum_{x \in FN} P_s(x)$. Here $P_s(x) = \frac{f(x)}{\sum_{y \in S} f(y)}$, is the probability of the string x given the sample S. Similarly, we could define the confidence false positive $cFP = \sum_{x \in FP} [\![A]\!](x)$. We do not weight TN with a confidence value, as the probability of not belonging to the sample and to the language of A is both 0, and therefore have 0 distance. Also, note the asymmetry between $|TP|$ and cFP in the denominator of Precision and Sensitivity (TP does not use the confidence extensions). This is because $|TP|$ simply refers to the total number of samples and is needed to average cTP.

When the distribution of the learned automaton coincides with that of the sample, $cTP = |TP| = |S_+|$, $|TN| = |S_-|$, and $|FP| = |FN| = 0$. In this case, precision, sensitivity and accuracy will be all 1. On the other opposite, when there are no true positive but only false positive and false negative, then $cTP = |TP| = |TN| = 0$, $|FP| = |S_-|$, $|FN| = |S_+|$ and $cFP = cFN = 1$ meaning that the precision, sensitivity and accuracy will be 0.

5 Experimental Results

We used the metrics introduced above to study the performance of our algorithm for learning probabilistic languages. We used different sizes of samples independently draw according to a distribution presented by four different probabilistic automata depicted in Fig. 2: one DPFA, one PFA, one RFSA and one PFA that cannot be expressed by a DPFA. First, we generate a set S of size n of strings from the alphabet by length-lexicographic order and assign the probability of each strings according to the target automaton. Given a fixed number of total occurrences m, we then calculate the frequency of each string in the sample based on its assigned probability. Note that samples generated in this way need not to be complete. All target automata we consider have 3 to 5 states, for which we generate a sample set of size $n < 50$ and total number of occurrences m varying between 10 to 200.

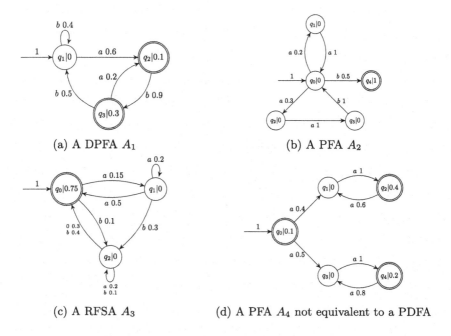

(a) A DPFA A_1

(b) A PFA A_2

(c) A RFSA A_3

(d) A PFA A_4 not equivalent to a PDFA

Fig. 2. The four target automata for our experiments

We compare our algorithm to ALERGIA [4] and k-testable algorithms [5]. Contrary to our algorithm presented here, the performance of these other algorithms may be impacted by a parameter setup. For ALERGIA we choose two different parameters $\alpha = 0.9$ and $\alpha = 0.1$. For k-testable algorithms, we set k to be $2, 3, 4$ and 5.

For the case of the DPFA A_1, the distribution found by all algorithms converges with respect to the L_2 distance rather quickly towards the original one. The 5-testable algorithm has the highest precision and sensitivity and the smallest L_2 distance, but it needs 19 states to learn an automaton of 3. Our algorithm has the best accuracy and is the only one learning the same structure as the original automata (Fig. 3).

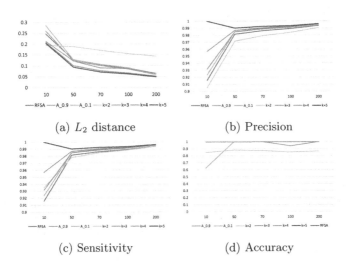

(a) L_2 distance

(b) Precision

(c) Sensitivity

(d) Accuracy

Fig. 3. Results of learning A_1

A similar situation happens when learning the RFSA A_3. In this case, our algorithm learns a distribution that cannot be described by any DPFA (see appendix for proof that the distribution generated by A_3 cannot be generated by any DFPA). We omit the tables here because of a lack of space.

When considering the PFA A_2, our algorithm, ALERGIA and 5-testable algorithm outperform all the others, see Fig. 4. Only our algorithm can learn the same number of states but with few more transitions. Accuracy is 1 again. Some errors are introduced because of the fair distribution among non-deterministic transitions.

Finally, we considered the PFA A_4 that cannot be expressed by any DPFA, and that does not have an equivalent RFSA as support, either. All algorithms cannot learn the same structure as the target automaton. Nevertheless, our algorithm achieves the best performance. The L_2 distance is smallest, precision is highest, sensitivity is second highest, and accuracy is always 1 (something not true for all other algorithms). Even if we perform better because the RFSA we learn has the same structure as the support of target distribution, our algorithms will never be able to identify it. We omit the tables here because of a lack of space.

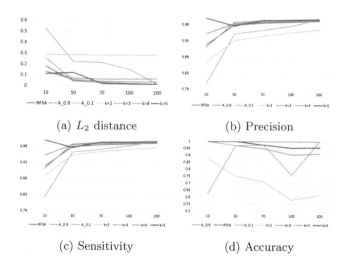

(a) L_2 distance

(b) Precision

(c) Sensitivity

(d) Accuracy

Fig. 4. Results of learning A_2

6 Conclusion

We proposed a new algorithm to learn regular distributions using residual language and adapted existing metrics to evaluate its performance. Our experimental results show that our algorithm can learn the structure of the target automaton efficiently, but distributing probabilities fairly among non-deterministic transitions can cause problems in learning the target distribution at the limit. Other techniques could be used to alleviate this problem and finding a better approximating solution. For example, we will investigate the use of evolutionary computing, and machine learning to better distribute probabilities among non-deterministic transition. Alternatively, we will investigate the use of iterative methods for polynomial constraint solving. Contrary to most existing algorithms, we have shown that our method can learn some PFA with a RFSA support that does not generate a deterministic regular distribution. Furthermore, it would be interesting in having larger samples so to experiment, for example, the impact of passive learning of probabilistic automata in model checking [19,22]. It would also be interesting to have a deeper analysis of the distance algorithm and the new metrics we introduced. We leave both these points for future work.

A   Appendix

In this appendix we prove that the probabilistic language described automaton A_3 cannot generated by any deterministic automata.

Proof. For A_3, we have

$$
\begin{aligned}
\rho_A(a^{2n}) &= \frac{[\![A]\!](a^{2n})}{\overline{[\![A]\!]}(a^{2n})} \\
&= \frac{\sum_{\pi \in Path_p(a^{2n})} \delta_p(\pi) \cdot e_p(\pi)}{\sum_{\pi \in Path_p(a^{2n})} \delta_p(\pi)} \\
&= \frac{\sum_{\pi_0 \in Path_p(a^{2n})} \delta_p(\pi_0) 0.5 + \sum_{\pi_1 \in Path_p(a^{2n})} \delta_p(\pi_1) 0}{\sum_{\pi_0 \in Path_p(a^{2n})} \delta_p(\pi_0) + \sum_{\pi_0 \in Path_p(a^{2n})} \delta_p(\pi_1)} \\
&= \frac{\sum_{\pi_0 \in Path_p(a^{2n})} \delta_p(\pi_0)}{2[\sum_{\pi_0 \in Path_p(a^{2n})} \delta_p(\pi_0) + \sum_{\pi_0 \in Path_p(a^{2n})} \delta_p(\pi_1)]}
\end{aligned}
\tag{3}
$$

where π_0 is the path for the string x ending at state q_0, and π_1 is a path for the string string x ending at state q_1. Let r_{2n} denote $\sum_{\pi_0 \in Path_p(a^{2n})} \delta_p(\pi_0)$, and s_{2n} denote $\sum_{\pi_0 \in Path_p(a^{2n})} \delta_p(\pi_1)$. Then $\frac{[\![A]\!](a^{2n})}{\overline{[\![A]\!]}(a^{2n})} = \frac{3r_{2n}}{4(r_{2n}+s_{2n})}$. Suppose $\frac{[\![A]\!](a^{2n})}{\overline{[\![A]\!]}(a^{2n})} = \frac{[\![A]\!](a^{2(n+1)})}{\overline{[\![A]\!]}(a^{2(n+1)})}$, we can get:

$$
\begin{aligned}
\frac{[\![A]\!](a^{2n})}{\overline{[\![A]\!]}(a^{2n})} &= \frac{[\![A]\!](a^{2(n+1)})}{\overline{[\![A]\!]}(a^{2(n+1)})} \\
\frac{3r_{2n}}{4(r_{2n}+s_{2n})} &= \frac{3}{4} \frac{r_{2n} \cdot 0.15 \cdot 0.5 + s_{2n} \cdot 0.5 \cdot 0.2}{r_{2n}(0.15 \cdot 0.5 + 0.15 \cdot 0.2) + s_{2n}(0.2 \cdot 0.5 + 0.2 \cdot 0.2 + 0.5 \cdot 0.15)} \\
\frac{r_{2n}}{r_{2n}+s_{2n}} &= \frac{0.075r_{2n} + 0.1s_{2n}}{0.105r_{2n} + 0.215s_{2n}} \\
\frac{\frac{r_{2n}}{s_{2n}}}{\frac{r_{2n}}{s_{2n}} + 1} &= \frac{0.075\frac{r_{2n}}{s_{2n}} + 0.1}{0.105\frac{r_{2n}}{s_{2n}} + 0.215}
\end{aligned}
\tag{4}
$$

Since $\frac{r_{2n}}{s_{2n}}$ is greater than 0, we get $\frac{r_{2n}}{s_{2n}} = 29.6125$.

$$
\frac{r_{2n}}{s_{2n}} = \frac{0.075r_{2(n-1)} + 0.1s_{2(n-1)}}{0.03r_{2(n-1)} + 0.04s_{2(n-1)}}
\tag{5}
$$

It is easy to find that $\frac{r_{2(n-1)}}{s_{2(n-1)}}$ is strictly smaller than 29.6125, so the set $\{\rho(a^{2n}) \mid n > 0\}$ cannot be finite. Therefore, the automaton show as Fig. 2c cannot be expressed as deterministic probabilistic automaton.

$\square$

References

1. Bahl, L.R., Brown, P.F., de Souza, P.V., Mercer, R.L.: Estimating hidden Markov model parameters so as to maximize speech recognition accuracy. IEEE Trans. Speech Audio Process. **1**(1), 77–83 (1993)
2. Baldi, P., Brunak, S., Bach, F.: Bioinformatics: The Machine Learning Approach. MIT Press, Cambridge (2001)

3. Baum, L.E., Petrie, T., Soules, G., Weiss, N.: A maximization technique occurring in the statistical analysis of probabilistic functions of Markov chains. Ann. Math. Stat. **41**(1), 164–171 (1970)
4. Carrasco, R.C., Oncina, J.: Learning stochastic regular grammars by means of a state merging method. In: Carrasco, R.C., Oncina, J. (eds.) ICGI 1994. LNCS, vol. 862, pp. 139–152. Springer, Heidelberg (1994). https://doi.org/10.1007/3-540-58473-0_144
5. Chu, W., Bonsangue, M.: Learning probabilistic languages by k-testable machines. In: 2020 International Symposium on Theoretical Aspects of Software Engineering (TASE), pp. 129–136. IEEE (2020)
6. Cortes, C., Mohri, M., Rastogi, A.: LP distance and equivalence of probabilistic automata. Int. J. Found. Comput. Sci. **18**(04), 761–779 (2007)
7. De La Higuera, C.: Characteristic sets for polynomial grammatical inference. Mach. Learn. **27**(2), 125–138 (1997)
8. De La Higuera, C., Oncina, J.: Identification with probability one of stochastic deterministic linear languages. In: Gavaldá, R., Jantke, K.P., Takimoto, E. (eds.) ALT 2003. LNCS (LNAI), vol. 2842, pp. 247–258. Springer, Heidelberg (2003). https://doi.org/10.1007/978-3-540-39624-6_20
9. Denis, F., Lemay, A., Terlutte, A.: Learning regular languages using RFSA. In: Abe, N., Khardon, R., Zeugmann, T. (eds.) ALT 2001. LNCS, vol. 2225, pp. 348–363. Springer, Heidelberg (2001). https://doi.org/10.1007/3-540-45583-3_26
10. Denis, F., Lemay, A., Terlutte, A.: Residual finite state automata. Fund. Inform. **51**(4), 339–368 (2002)
11. Denis, F., Lemay, A., Terlutte, A.: Some classes of regular languages identifiable in the limit from positive data. In: Adriaans, P., Fernau, H., van Zaanen, M. (eds.) ICGI 2002. LNCS (LNAI), vol. 2484, pp. 63–76. Springer, Heidelberg (2002). https://doi.org/10.1007/3-540-45790-9_6
12. Dupont, P., Denis, F., Esposito, Y.: Links between probabilistic automata and hidden Markov models: probability distributions, learning models and induction algorithms. Pattern Recogn. **38**(9), 1349–1371 (2005)
13. Esposito, Y., Lemay, A., Denis, F., Dupont, P.: Learning probabilistic residual finite state automata. In: Adriaans, P., Fernau, H., van Zaanen, M. (eds.) ICGI 2002. LNCS (LNAI), vol. 2484, pp. 77–91. Springer, Heidelberg (2002). https://doi.org/10.1007/3-540-45790-9_7
14. Jelinek, F.: Statistical Methods for Speech Recognition. MIT Press, Cambridge (1997)
15. Lee, K.F.: Large-vocabulary speaker-independent continuous speech recognition: the SPHINX system. Carnegie Mellon University (1988)
16. Lyngsø, R.B., Pedersen, C.N.: The consensus string problem and the complexity of comparing hidden Markov models. J. Comput. Syst. Sci. **65**(3), 545–569 (2002)
17. Martin, J.C.: Introduction to Languages and the Theory of Computation, vol. 4. McGraw-Hill, New York (1991)
18. Mohri, M.: Semiring frameworks and algorithms for shortest-distance problems. J. Autom. Lang. Comb. **7**(3), 321–350 (2002)
19. Nouri, A., Raman, B., Bozga, M., Legay, A., Bensalem, S.: Faster statistical model checking by means of abstraction and learning. In: Bonakdarpour, B., Smolka, S.A. (eds.) RV 2014. LNCS, vol. 8734, pp. 340–355. Springer, Cham (2014). https://doi.org/10.1007/978-3-319-11164-3_28
20. Seymore, K., McCallum, A., Rosenfeld, R., et al.: Learning hidden Markov model structure for information extraction. In: AAAI-99 Workshop on Machine Learning for Information Extraction, pp. 37–42 (1999)

21. Sokolova, M., Lapalme, G.: A systematic analysis of performance measures for classification tasks. Inf. Process. Manage. **45**(4), 427–437 (2009)
22. Tappler, M., Aichernig, B.K., Bacci, G., Eichlseder, M., Larsen, K.G.: L*-based learning of Markov decision processes (extended version). arXiv preprint arXiv:1906.12239 (2019)
23. Thollard, F., Dupont, P., De La Higuera, C., et al.: Probabilistic DFA inference using Kullback-Leibler divergence and minimality. In: ICML, pp. 975–982 (2000)

AlCons: Deductive Synthesis of Sorting Algorithms in *Theorema*

Isabela Drămnesc[1](✉)📷 and Tudor Jebelean[2]📷

[1] Department of Computer Science, West University, Timişoara, Romania
Isabela.Dramnesc@e-uvt.ro
[2] RISC, Johannes Kepler University, Linz, Austria
Tudor.Jebelean@jku.at
https://staff.fmi.uvt.ro/~isabela.dramnesc
https://risc.jku.at/m/tudor-jebelean

Abstract. We describe the principles and the implementation of *AlCons* (*Algorithm Constructor*), a system for the automatic proof–based synthesis of sorting algorithms on lists and on binary trees, in the frame of the *Theorema* system. The core of the system is a dedicated prover based on specific inference rules and strategies for constructive proofs over the domains of lists and of binary trees, aimed at the automatic synthesis of sorting algorithms and their auxiliary functions from logical specifications. The specific distinctive feature of our approach is the use of multisets for expressing the fact that two lists (trees) have the same elements. This allows a more natural expression of the properties related to sorting, compared to the classical approach using the permutation relation (a list is a permutation of another). Moreover, the use of multisets leads to special inference rules and strategies which make the proofs more efficient, as for instance: expand/compress multiset terms and solve meta-variables using multiset equalities. Additionally we use a Noetherian induction strategy based on the relation induced by the strict inclusion of multisets, which facilitates the synthesis of arbitrary recursion structures, without having to indicate the recursion schemes in advance. The necessary auxiliary algorithms (like, e.g., for insertion and merging) are generated by the same principles from the synthesis conjectures that are automatically produced during the main proof, using a "cascading" method, which in fact contributes to the automation of theory exploration. The prover is implemented in the frame of the *Theorema* system and works in natural style, while the generated algorithms can be immediately tested in the same system.

Keywords: Deductive synthesis · Sorting · Lists · Binary trees · Multisets · Noetherian induction

1 Introduction

Automatic synthesis of algorithms is an interesting and challenging problem in automated reasoning, because algorithm invention appears to be difficult even

© Springer Nature Switzerland AG 2021
A. Cerone and P. C. Ölveczky (Eds.): ICTAC 2021, LNCS 12819, pp. 314–333, 2021.
https://doi.org/10.1007/978-3-030-85315-0_18

for the human intellect. Synthesis of sorting algorithms is especially challenging because the content and structure of the specification appears to be completely different from the expression of the algorithms. Thus case studies and automation attempts for synthesis of sorting algorithms have the potential of increasing our knowledge about possible general methods for algorithm synthesis.

We address the automated synthesis of algorithms which satisfy certain given specifications[1]. The specification is transformed into a synthesis conjecture from whose constructive proof a main algorithm is extracted. Usually this main algorithm needs some auxiliary algorithms, whose synthesis conjectures are produced during the main proof and then additional synthesis proofs are performed – the process may repeat as by "cascading" [4]. Our focus is on automating proofs for such conjectures, on the mechanical generation of the synthesis conjectures for the necessary auxiliary algorithms, and on the automatic extraction of the algorithms from the proofs. Cascading also constitutes a contribution to the automation of *theory exploration*[2] [3].

The implementation of the synthesis methods constitutes the automated proof–based synthesizer *AlCons* for sorting algorithms on lists and on binary trees using multisets, built as a prover in the *Theorema* system [7,36] (based on *Mathematica*[3]). In order to illustrate the principles of the prover we present in this paper a summary of our experiments on binary trees. (Experiments on lists are presented in [16]).

The prover uses *general* inference rules and strategies for predicate logic, as well as *domain-specific* rules and strategies, which make the proof search more efficient.

1.1   Main Contribution

The novelty of this work consists of: the use of *multisets* and the proof techniques related to them on binary trees, *nested use of cover sets*, the use of *cover sets on meta-variables*, the systematic principle for generating synthesis conjectures for the auxiliary functions (*cascading*), and the first description of the technical *implementation* in the current version of *Theorema*.

Multisets allow a very natural expression of the fact that two lists (trees) have the same objects[4]. More importantly, the use of multisets triggers some new proof techniques which make the proof search more efficient. Crucially for our current approach, we can use the Noetherian ordering on the domains of lists and of trees induced by the strict inclusion of the corresponding multisets, which is conveniently reflected at object level by the strict inclusion of multisets

---

[1] This ensures the correctness of algorithms and it is dual to algorithm verification, where the algorithms are first created and then checked.

[2] Theory exploration is the generation of interesting statements following from a certain set of axioms and/or for the purpose of developing certain proofs or algorithms.

[3] https://www.wolfram.com/mathematica.

[4] In other approaches one uses the *permutation* notion, which must be expressed by specific algorithmic definitions, and whose properties are more difficult to infer.

of constants and variables occurring in the list/tree terms, and this allows a dynamic creation of concrete induction hypotheses according to the needs of the proof. Both lists and binary trees are addressed by **AlCons** with the same proof techniques[5], which demonstrates the possibility of generalization of such techniques to new domains, and also allows future work on algorithms combining lists and trees.

Cover Sets and Dynamic Induction. Induction is implicitly realized using *cover sets*. A cover set [34] for a certain domain is a set of possibly non-ground terms whose set of ground instances covers the whole domain. From the algorithmic point of view the cover set represents a recipe for decomposing the input in order to be processed (technically it is applied to a certain Skolem constant), thus the synthesis will produce an equality (rewrite rule) for every cover set term – therefore we use mutually exclusive[6] terms. Every term from the cover set is used to generate an *induction conclusion* over a certain ground term (the *target object*). During the proof of this induction conclusion, the necessary *induction hypotheses* are generated dynamically by instantiating the induction conclusion with terms representing domain objects which are smaller in the Noetherian ordering than the current target object. Nested use of cover sets is novel w. r. t. the simple use of cover sets for realizing induction: while this technique allows to discover concrete induction principles by generating appropriate induction hypotheses during the proof, nested use of cover sets allows the discovery of nested recursions, which is rarely present in synthesized algorithms.

We extend the use of cover sets to meta–variables[7] in a similar way. Cover sets on meta–variables implement the algorithmic idea of combining intermediate results according to a certain "recipe" (because meta–variables represent the output of the computation). This is complementary to the use of cover–sets for Skolem constants, which implement the algorithmic idea of decomposing the input in a certain way (because the Skolem constants represent the input). In this way algorithmic ideas can be represented by proof techniques.

Cascading. Using specific heuristics, the prover decides when the current goal should be used for the creation of a conjecture for the synthesis of one or more auxiliary algorithms. This is proven separately and leads to the synthesis of one or more algorithms in the general context of the theory of lists/trees, thus it discovers some possibly interesting functions (therefore it contributes to the automation of theory exploration). The process can repeat in the new proofs, leading to more new functions. The synthesis conjectures for the auxiliary algorithms are generated by a novel strategy which: detects the need of an auxiliary function, produces the conjecture itself using the current proof situation, adds the appropriate property which allows new auxiliary function to be used later

---

[5] However some fine tuning of the implementation has been necessary, since trees have a more complex structure.

[6] Every element of the inductive domain is a ground instance of exactly one term from the cover set.

[7] Meta–variables designate terms (witnesses for existential goals) which are unknown at the current stage of the proof.

in the proof, and changes the current goal by inserting the new function calls at the appropriate places.

Implementation. The prover is implemented in the frame of the *Theorema* system, which offers a flexible and intuitive user interface, construction of theories and development of proofs in natural style, as well as direct execution of the synthesized algorithms, as they are produced in form of a set of (conditional) equalities. The implementation principles in the frame of *Theorema* 2.0 are in many respects different from the implementation in the previous version of *Theorema* and in the same time more powerful both from the point of view of interface as well as performance and readability. The prover is appropriate for the synthesis of sorting algorithms both for lists as well as for binary trees, however in this paper we describe only experiments on binary trees. An extensive presentation of experiments on lists is presented in [16].

1.2   Related Work and Originality

The problem of algorithms synthesis, including the synthesis of sorting algorithms is well-studied in the literature, but full automation of synthesis constitutes still a challenge. An overview of the most common approaches used to tackle the synthesis problem is given in [33]. Most approaches are based on special techniques for transformation of expressions (for program instance program transformation, Hoare-like or tableaux-like calculae). In contrast our approach emphasizes proving in natural style, and intuitive inference rules. Most synthesis methods use certain algorithm templates, or explicit induction schemas, while we use cover sets and dynamic induction instead. No other approaches use multisets, and only few address a systematic method for generating auxiliary algorithms.

Significant work has been done in the synthesis of sorting algorithms[8]. Six versions of sorting algorithms are derived in [10] by applying transformation rules. An extension of this work is in [1], see also [21]. Some specific transformation techniques which complement the ones in [10] are used by [19]. [26] classifies sorting algorithms.

[27] introduces deductive techniques for constructing recursive algorithms. [35] applies manually the techniques in [27] and derives several sorting algorithms in the theories of integers and strings. Later implementations using some of these principles are in [24,32]. We follow some of the principles from [27,35].

Systematic methods for generating auxiliary algorithms are also presented in [27,29]. We use a different cascading strategy which transforms the failing goal together with the current assumptions into a new conjecture. [25] applies deductive tableau techniques [27], uses some heuristics and rippling [8] for the automated synthesis of several functions in Lisp in the theory of integers and lists. [25] shows how to prepare induction hypotheses to be used in the rippling proofs by using deductive rules.

[30] implemented the tool Synquid which is able to automatically synthesize several recursive algorithms operating on lists (including sorting algorithms)

---

[8] We presented a more detailed survey of the synthesis methods in [11].

and operations on trees (but not sorting), except the automatic synthesis of auxiliary functions. This work was extended by [20], using a technique based on some given templates in order to synthesize algorithms on lists and binary trees (e.g., converting a binary tree to a list, or a list to a binary search tree) together with some auxiliary functions. In [22] the authors describe an approach that combines deductive synthesis with cyclic proofs for automatically synthesizing recursive algorithms with recursive auxiliary functions and mutual recursion. They implement the tool Cypress and they synthesize algorithms operating on lists (including some sorting algorithms), and on trees (e.g., flattening a tree into a list, insertion, deletion, etc.). Their approach complements the one in [20] by considering a proof-driven approach instead of template-driven approach for synthesizing auxiliary functions. However, the synthesis of sorting algorithms on trees is not approached.

A valuable formalization, in a previous version of *Theorema* [6], of the synthesis of sorting algorithms is in [5], where an algorithm scheme is given together with the specification of the desired function. In contrast, **AlCons** uses cover–set decomposition and no algorithm scheme.

The theory of *multisets* (also called *bags*) is well studied in the literature, including computational formalizations, see e.g. [28]. The theory of multisets and a detailed survey of the literature related to multisets and their usage is presented in [2] and some interesting practical developments are in [31].

A systematic formalization of the theory of lists using multisets the correctness proofs of various sorting algorithms is mechanized in Isabelle/HOL[9], but it does not address algorithm synthesis. The use of multisets and of the special techniques related to them, as well as the systematic approach to the generation of synthesis conjectures for the auxiliary algorithms and the use of cover set induction constitute also significant improvements w. r. t. our previous work on this problem [11,17].

Most related to this paper are our recent case studies on sorting algorithms for lists [13–16], and some of the auxiliary algorithms on binary trees [12,18]. The current paper presents the main principles and techniques resulting from these case studies, integrating all methods and improving them in order to realize a comprehensive tool, which works for both lists and binary trees. Also [12,18] complement the current presentation with illustrative fragments of synthesis proofs of the auxiliary algorithms on binary trees. [12] applies explicit induction in order to derive some auxiliary algorithms, [18] extends [12] by applying cover sets and dynamic induction instead of explicit induction, and some different proof techniques for deriving several more auxiliary algorithms on binary trees. Complementary, the current paper presents the synthesis of several versions of sorting algorithms on binary trees and the synthesis of two more auxiliary algorithms (*SmallerEq, Bigger*), including *Insert* by using cover sets instead of explicit induction, and refines the proof techniques.

A prover for algorithm synthesis on lists [11] and another one for binary trees [17] was implemented in a previous version of *Theorema* [6]. There we

---

[9] https://isabelle.in.tum.de/library/HOL/HOL-Library/Sorting_Algorithms.html.

use different synthesis methods and we do not use multisets. The novel system *AlCons* works both on lists and on binary trees.

Except for the previous work using the *Theorema* system, a distinctive feature of our approach is the use of natural style proving, and except for our own previous work, there is no approach in the literature to the direct sorting of binary trees.

2 Algorithm Synthesis

2.1 Context and Notation

Terms and Formulae. Brackets are used for function and predicate application (like $f[x]$, $P[a]$). Quantifiers are denoted like $\forall_X$ and $\exists_Y$. Metavariables are starred (e.g., T^*, T_1^*, Z^*) and Skolem constants have integer indices (e.g., X_0, X_1, a_0).

Objects and Theories. We consider three types: simple objects (*elements*) and composite objects (finite *binary trees* and finite *multisets*). Both in this presentation and in the prover typing is implicit, based on the notation conventions specified below.

Elements (denoted by a, b, c) are objects from a total ordered domain. The ordering on elements (notation $\leq$ and $<$) is extended to orderings between an element and a composite object and between composite objects, by requiring that all elements of the composite object observe the ordering relation[10].

Binary trees (denoted by L, R, S, T) are objects from an inductive domain: either ε (empty) or a triplet $\langle L, a, R \rangle$, where L and R are the left and right subtrees, and a is the root element.

Multisets (denoted by A, B, C) are objects whose elements can occur repeatedly. $\emptyset$ is the empty multiset, $\{\{a\}\}$ denotes the multiset containing the element a with multiplicity 1, and $\mathcal{M}[T]$ denotes the multiset of elements of a binary tree T. The union of multisets is additive $\uplus$ like in [23]. Some inference rules use implicitly the properties of union (commutativity, associativity, and unit $\emptyset$).

Knowledge. This contains the main properties of union of multisets, the definition of multisets of a tree, etc. For illustration the definition of sorted trees is:

$$\forall_{a,L,R} \left(\begin{array}{c} IsSorted[\varepsilon] \\ IsSorted[\langle L, a, R \rangle] \iff (IsSorted[L] \wedge IsSorted[R] \wedge L \leq a \leq R) \end{array} \right)$$

2.2 Approach

The **specification** consists in an input condition $I[X, X', \ldots]$ applied to the inputs and an output condition $O[Y, X, X', \ldots]$ applied to the output Y and the same inputs. For the sorting problem the input condition is *True* (thus it

---

[10] Note that this introduces certain exceptions to antisymmetry and transitivity when the empty composite object is involved.

is missing), but it may be present in the specification of some auxiliary algorithms. The output condition for sorting is: $\mathcal{M}[Y] = \mathcal{M}[X] \wedge \textit{IsSorted}[Y]$, and for the auxiliary functions is similar, but it typically contains some additional requirements. The **conjecture** corresponding to the specification is

$$\underset{X,X',\ldots}{\forall} \ (I[X, X', \ldots] \implies \underset{Y}{\exists} O[Y, X, X', \ldots]).$$

In some experiments we use a conjecture of the form:

$$\underset{X,X',\ldots}{\forall} \ (I[X, X', \ldots] \implies O[F[X, X', \ldots], X, X', \ldots]),$$

where F is the name of the function to be synthesized.

The **proof** is developed by applying the techniques (inference rules and strategies) described in the sequel, and it generates one or more algorithms and possibly some conjectures for further synthesis (cascading).

The **algorithm** for a function $F[X, X', \ldots]$ is presented as a set of conditional equalities of the form:

$$Q[Y, Y', \ldots] \Rightarrow F[P[Y, Y', \ldots], P'[Y, Y', \ldots], \ldots] = T[Y, Y', \ldots],$$

where $P[Y, Y', \ldots], P'[Y, Y', \ldots], \ldots$ are patterns[11], Q is a formula, and T is a term. These conditional equalities can be applied as rewrite rules in order to compute F.

The theoretical basis and the correctness of this proof based synthesis scheme is well–known, see [9,27] and was used in some recent publications by [11,17], see also [12,13,16].

3 Proof Techniques

By proof techniques we understand *inference rules*, which describe one step of the proof, and *strategies*, which describe how to group several inference rules.

AlCons uses some of the common natural style inference rules, which are already implemented in *Theorema*: split assumed conjunction, Skolemization of the universal goal (but not of the existential assumptions), meta–variable for the existential goal (but not of the universal assumptions), rewriting by equality, matching and instantiation for forward and backward inferences, etc.

Some of the inference rules and strategies were first introduced in [12,13,16], and there we illustrate them on concrete examples on sorting and auxiliary algorithms on lists and on auxiliary algorithms on binary trees, however here they are first comprehensively integrated in one system and applied to synthesize sorting algorithms on binary trees.

We describe in the sequel only those techniques which are specific to *AlCons* and are very important for synthesis on binary trees.

---

[11] In our context, a pattern is a term possibly containing variables, whose ground instantiations define an injective function into the domain.

3.1   Inference Rules

IR-1: *Reduce Composite Argument.* Transform an atom of a goal (which is typically a conjunction of atoms) or an assumption (when it is an atom) into simpler atoms whose arguments do not contain function symbols. For the goal generate possibly few atoms, for the assumptions possibly many, because then some of the assumed atoms will match and cancel some of the goal atoms.
Example 1: $a \leq Concat[L_0, R_0]$ becomes $a \leq L_0 \wedge a \leq R_0$.
Example 2: $IsSorted[\langle T_1, a, T_2\rangle]$ becomes $IsSorted[T_1] \wedge T_1 \leq a \wedge a \leq T_2 \wedge IsSorted[T_2]$.

IR-2: *Simple Goal as Condition.* When the target metavariable already has a solution and the goal (after all possible reductions) is ground and contains only constant time functions and predicates[12], then this goal is taken as a condition and with the current solution to the metavariable it becomes a clause of the synthesized algorithm (see the partial proof in Fig. 2).

IR-3: *Use Equivalence.* The equivalence relation between composite objects induced by the equality of the corresponding multisets is used to rewrite parts of the goal (or of the assumptions) by replacing composite objects with equivalent ones, when they occur in equality atoms or in ordering atoms.
Example 1: The goal $\mathcal{M}[\langle Sort[T_1^*], a^*, Sort[T_2^*]\rangle] = \mathcal{M}[T^*] \wedge Sort[T_1^*] \leq a^* \wedge a^* \leq Sort[T_2^*]$ becomes $\mathcal{M}[\langle T_1^*, a^*, T_2^*\rangle] = \mathcal{M}[T^*] \wedge T_1^* \leq a^* \wedge a^* \leq T_2^*$.
Example 2: The goal is $b \leq S_1$ is transformed into $b \leq L_0 \wedge b \leq a \wedge b \leq R_0$ using the assumption: $\mathcal{M}[S_1] = \mathcal{M}[L_0] \uplus \{\{a\}\} \uplus \mathcal{M}[R_0]$.

IR-4: *Expand Multiset.* This rule expands a multiset term in the goal into several multiset terms. This is useful because then different groupings can be performed.
Example: The goal $\mathcal{M}[T^*] = \mathcal{M}[\langle L_0, a, R_0\rangle] \uplus \mathcal{M}[S_0]$, becomes $\mathcal{M}[T^*] = \mathcal{M}[L_0] \uplus \{\{a\}\} \uplus \mathcal{M}[R_0] \uplus \mathcal{M}[S_0]$.

IR-5: *Compress Multiset.* This rule is the dual of the previous one, and it typically applies when the arguments contain terms which correspond to the recursive calls of the desired function. Example: if a part of the goal is $\mathcal{M}[T^*] = \mathcal{M}[T_1] \uplus \{\{a\}\} \uplus \mathcal{M}[T_2] \uplus \ldots$, then on one alternative branch[13] this part becomes $\mathcal{M}[T^*] = \mathcal{M}[\langle T_1, a, T_2\rangle] \uplus \ldots$. By repeated application this rule one reaches the situation of **IR-6**, as described in **ST-4**.

IR-6: *Solve Metavariable.* When a part of the goal is $\mathcal{M}[X^*] = \mathcal{M}[T]$ for a ground term T, obtain the substitution $\{X^* \rightarrow T\}$ and continue the proof with the remaining goal. In order to ensure the soundness, the prover keeps track of the order in which Skolem constants and metavariables have been introduced, and allows the use in a solution for a metavariable only the Skolem constants which have been generated before that metavariable.

---

[12] This is just a matter of efficiency, the goal could contain anything as long as the currently synthesized function is not involved.

[13] The rule generates proof alternatives for different groupings of the multiset terms.

IR-7: *Forward Inference.* This rule is applied in order to produce new assumptions. If a ground atomic assumption matches a part of another (typically universal) assumption, instantiate the later and replace in it the resulting copy of the ground assumption by the constant *True*, then simplify truth constants to produce a new assumption.

IR-8: *Backward Inference.* Transform the goal using some assumption or a specific logical principle. If a ground atomic assumption matches a part of a ground or existential goal, instantiate the goal and replace in it the resulting copy of the ground assumption by the constant *True*, then simplify truth constants to produce a new goal.

3.2   Strategies

ST-1: *Cover Set.* This strategy organizes the structure of each synthesis conjecture proof and the extraction of the synthesized algorithm, as in fact implements the Noetherian induction based on the ordering between objects induced by strict inclusion of multisets.

Each conjecture for the synthesis of a *target function* is a quantified statement over some *main universal variable.* A *cover set* is a set of universal terms[14] which represent the domain of the main universal variable, as described in [17].

We project this concept on Skolem constants: first the main universal variable is Skolemized ("arbitrary but fixed")—we call this the *target constant*, and we call the corresponding Skolemized goal the *target goal* – and then the corresponding cover–set terms are also grounded by Skolemization, we call these the *cover-set terms* and the corresponding constants the *cover-set constants.* The proof starts with a certain cover set (typically the one suggested by the recursive definition of the domain), and starts a proof branch for each ground term ("proof by cases"). On each proof branch the input conditions of the function are assumed, and then the existential variable corresponding to the output value of the function is transformed into a metavariable whose value (the "witness") will be found on the respective branch of the proof. Finally the algorithm will be generated as a set of [conditional] equalities: the terms of the cover set become arguments ("patterns") on the LHS of the equalities, and the corresponding witnesses become the RHS of these, after replacing back the Skolem constants by variables. The strategy can be applied in a *nested* way, by choosing a new target constant among the Skolem constants of the goal. Using this nesting scheme one can synthesize algorithms with nested recursion (see, e.g., Algorithm 9) as well as with recursion on several arguments, as for instance in the case of merging of lists in the merge-sort algorithm for lists (see [16], Algorithm 15).

Furthermore we use cover sets in a novel way also on meta–variables: this generates a certain structure for the synthesized algorithm by imposing on the

---

[14] Terms containing universally quantified variables, such that for every element of the domain there exists exactly one term in the set which instantiates to that element.

result the structure of the corresponding term of the cover set (see for instance Algorithm 5 for sorting).

ST-2: *Dynamic Induction.* (described in more detail in [13]) is used to dynamically generate induction hypotheses during the proof. When a ground term t represents an object which is smaller than the target constant X_0 of the target goal $P[X_0]$, then $P[t]$ is added as a new assumption, but modified by inserting the corresponding call of the target function instead of the existential variable.

This strategy is applied in a similar manner to metavariables, when they occur in the goal. When a metavariable Y^* represents an object which is smaller than the target constant X_0, then $P[Y^*]$ may be added as new assumption.

ST-3: *Cascading.* This strategy consists in proving separately a conjecture for synthesizing the algorithm for some auxiliary functions needed in the current proof. The Skolem constants from the current goal become universal variables $x, x', \ldots$, the metavariables from the current goal become existential variables $y, y', \ldots$, and the conjecture has the structure[15]:

$$\forall_x \forall_{x'} \ldots (P[x, x', \ldots] \implies \exists_y \exists_{y'} \ldots Q[x, x', \ldots, y, y', \ldots]) \tag{1}$$

$P[x, x', \ldots]$ is composed from the assumptions which contain *only* the Skolem constants present in the goal, and $Q[x, x', \ldots, y, y', \ldots]$ is composed from the goal. A successful proof of the conjecture generates the functions $f[x, x', \ldots]$, $f'[x, x', \ldots], \ldots$, which have the property:

$$\forall_x \forall_{x'} \ldots (P[x, x', \ldots] \implies Q[x, x', \ldots, f[x, x', \ldots], f'[x, x', \ldots], \ldots]) \tag{2}$$

The current proof continues after adding this property to the assumptions[16], thus if some of the generated functions are necessary later in the proof, they can be used without a new cascading step. The new assumption will trigger the simplification of the current goal by inserting the auxiliary function.

ST-4: *Group Multisets.* This strategy uses **IR-5** and applies when the goal contains an equality of the form: $\mathcal{M}[Y^*] = \mathcal{M}[t_1] \uplus \mathcal{M}[t_2] \uplus \ldots$, where Y^* is the metavariable we need to solve, and $t_1, t_2, \ldots$ are ground terms. The flow of the proof consists in transforming the union on the RHS of the equality into a single $\mathcal{M}[t]$, because this gives the solution $Y^* \to t$. The prover groups pairs or triplets of operands of $\uplus$ together (no matter whether they are contingent or not, because commutativity) and creates an alternative for each group. On each alternative the multiset term which equals the union of the group is constructed by application of the appropriate function in one of the following ways:

1. the auxiliary function is already known, the proof works by predicate logic;
2. induction can be applied (if the target function has the same structure);
3. a separate synthesis proof of the function is necessary by **ST-3** (cascading).

---

[15] By local convention, here x, x', y, y' represent any kind of objects.

[16] Note that these kind of new assumptions are *global*: they can be used on any branch of the current proof.

3.3 Implementation

In the *Theorema* system, the proof develops as a tree of *proof situations*, each consisting of a set of assumptions and a goal, and also other various information which may be prover specific. Every proof situation is transformed into one or more proof situations by applying an *inference rule*, which creates or modifies the goal and/or one or more assumptions, and thus extends the proof tree. When several proof situations are created, there are two types of proof tree nodes: the AND nodes (all subproofs must succeed), and the OR nodes (at least one subproof must succeed – these are "proof alternatives"). Many inference rules produce alternatives (e.g. *compress multiset, backward chaining*), from which some may be unsuccessful. Each successful alternative has typically several AND branches, each of them corresponding to a clause in the definition of the synthesized algorithm. Since the cover set strategy is applied in a nested way, the proof tree is theoretically infinite, and may produce an arbitrary number of algorithms. The concrete proofs are however finite because we limit the depth of the proof tree.

As it is usual in the *Theorema* system, our prover consists of a collection of rewrite rules which correspond to the intended inferences. Each rule rewrites the *proof situation* into new one, and produces additionally a *proof information* (a list of elements necessary for the presentation of the proof). The proof information is language independent and is aggregated in a tree which represents finally the whole proof: the *proof object*. Using a set of language-dependent rewrite rules corresponding to the proof steps, the proof object is finally transformed in a *Mathematica* notebook explaining the proof.

In our case the proof object also contains the information relevant for the synthesized algorithm, which is extracted automatically at the end of the proof.

Contextual Information. Besides the current goal and the list of the current assumptions, which are the core elements of the proof situation, the prover uses certain contextual information for guiding the realization of the inference rules and strategies. The contextual information is split into *global* and *local.*

The **global context** consists of constants which are available to the prover on all branches of the proof. This contains among other: the table with the names of the variables assigned to the different types, the table with the cover sets corresponding to lists and to trees, and the list of rewrite rules for the simplification of truth constants.

The **local context** consists of information which is specific to every branch of the proof, and it is dynamically updated. This contains: the type table, which indicates the type of each item; the target goal, the target Skolem constant and the target meta-variable used for the realization of the strategy **ST-1** (cover set); the table of the Noetherian relation between Skolem constants, used for induction; and the table of rewrite rules corresponding to the current assumptions (see below), etc.

In order to ease the use of the current assumptions, they are reflected in certain rewrite rules in a special table of the local context. When new goals [assumptions] are produced, the prover tries to simplify them using these rules, depending on the situation in the proof.

The tables composing the local context are implemented as associative memory structures: each element or group of elements is associated with a textual keyword. This makes it easy to access an element by using the rewrite mechanism provided by *Mathematica*, and also to write inference rules based on pattern matching.

Both the global and the local contexts are implemented in a generic way, both the structures and the manipulating functions are type independent, thus any relevant information (like, e.g., cover set information) can be added to the context and maintained by the functions provided, without having to change the implementation.

The *Theorema* system[17] and an example of the prover usage[18] are available online.

4   Experiments on Binary Trees

In order to illustrate the proof techniques of **AlCons** we summarize in this section our experiments on binary trees. (The experiments on lists are detailed in [16].) The synthesized algorithms relevant to binary trees are:

(i) sorting algorithms (not yet presented in our papers): Algorithm 1 (which uses *Insert, Concat*), Algorithm 2, Algorithm 3, Algorithm 4 (which use *Insert, Merge*), Algorithm 5 (which uses *Concat, SmallerEq, Bigger*), Algorithm 6 (which uses *Merge, SmallerEq, Bigger*), as well as some similar versions of them;

(ii) auxiliary algorithms: *Insert* (Algorithm 7) [12], derived here by different techniques; numerous versions of *Concat*: the synthesis of Algorithm 8 and first three similar versions of it are presented in [12], and other twenty versions in [18]; four versions of *Merge*: the synthesis of the first two (Algorithm 9, Algorithm 10) is presented in [12], and the other two in [18]; novel: *SmallerEq* (Algorithm 11) and *Bigger* (Algorithm 12).

The algorithms presented also in [12] are generated using explicit induction (thus the user has to anticipate the structure of the algorithm), and the algorithms 1 to 4 can also be derived in this way. In contrast, by using cover sets and dynamic induction, all algorithms mentioned above are synthesized without any prior anticipation of the algorithm structure. Moreover, algorithms 5 and 6 (and their similar versions), as well as the selection auxiliary functions *SmallerEq* and *Bigger* are consequent to the use of the novel paradigm of applying cover sets to meta-variables.

The following subsections illustrate the process of synthesis by describing some parts of the proofs.

---

[17] https://www.risc.jku.at/research/theorema/software/.

[18] https://www.risc.jku.at/people/tjebelea/AlCons.html.

4.1   Sorting Algorithms

The synthesis conjecture is:

Conjecture 1. $\underset{XT}{\forall\exists}(\mathcal{M}[T] = \mathcal{M}[X] \wedge \mathit{IsSorted}[T])$.

The goal after Skolemization and introduction of the meta–variable is:

$$\mathcal{M}[T^*] = \mathcal{M}[X_0] \wedge \mathit{IsSorted}[T^*]. \tag{3}$$

Strategy **ST-1** (cover set) starts two branches: on the Skolem constant and on the meta-variable.

Branch 1. Strategy **ST-1** applies to X_0 using the cover set $\{\varepsilon, \langle L_0, a_0, R_0 \rangle\}$ and generates two cases:

Case 1.1: $X_0 = \varepsilon$ is trivial and the solution is $\{T^* \to \varepsilon\}$.

Case 1.2: $X_0 = \langle L_0, a_0, R_0 \rangle$. The goal becomes:

$$\mathcal{M}[T^*] = \mathcal{M}[\langle L_0, a_0, R_0 \rangle] \wedge \mathit{IsSorted}[T^*]. \tag{4}$$

This is expanded by **IR-4** (expand multiset) into:

$$\mathcal{M}[T^*] = \mathcal{M}[L_0] \uplus \{\{a_0\}\} \uplus \mathcal{M}[R_0] \wedge \mathit{IsSorted}[T^*]. \tag{5}$$

Strategy **ST-4** (pair multisets) applies on goal (5) and then strategy **ST-3** (cascading) generates the conjectures corresponding to the synthesis of *Concat*, and *Merge* (see details in [12]) on two different cases, adds the assumptions expressing the properties of these auxiliary functions, and rewrites the goal in each case by using *Concat* and *Merge*, respectively.

Case 1.2.1. Goal (5) becomes:

$$\mathcal{M}[T^*] = \{\{a_0\}\} \uplus \mathcal{M}[\mathit{Concat}[L_0, R_0]] \wedge \mathit{IsSorted}[T^*]. \tag{6}$$

Strategy **ST-2** (induction) uses $\mathit{Concat}[L_0, R_0]$, which is smaller in the Noetherian ordering than $\langle L_0, a_0, R_0 \rangle$, to produce the assumption:

$$\begin{aligned}\mathcal{M}[\mathit{Sort}[\mathit{Concat}[L_0, R_0]]] = \mathcal{M}[\mathit{Concat}[L_0, R_0]] \wedge \\ \mathit{IsSorted}[\mathit{Sort}[\mathit{Concat}[L_0, R_0]]].\end{aligned} \tag{7}$$

Goal (5) is rewritten using (7) into:

$$\mathcal{M}[T^*] = \{\{a_0\}\} \uplus \mathcal{M}[\mathit{Sort}[\mathit{Concat}[L_0, R_0]]] \wedge \mathit{IsSorted}[T^*]. \tag{8}$$

ST-4 applied to $\{\{a_0\}\}$ and $\mathcal{M}[\mathit{Sort}[\mathit{Concat}[L_0, R_0]]]$ uses **ST-3** to produce *Conjecture 2* for the synthesis of *Insert*. By s **ST-3** the generated assumption is:

$$\begin{aligned}\underset{X}{\forall}\Big(\mathit{IsSorted}[X] \Longrightarrow \\ \underset{a}{\forall}\big(\mathcal{M}[\mathit{Insert}[a, X]] = \{\{a\}\} \uplus \mathcal{M}[X] \wedge \mathit{IsSorted}[\mathit{Insert}[a, X]]\big)\Big). \end{aligned} \tag{9}$$

and goal (5) becomes

$$\mathcal{M}[T^*] = \mathcal{M}[Insert[a_0, Sort[Concat[L_0, R_0]]]] \wedge IsSorted[T^*]. \qquad (10)$$

The solution for T^* is $Insert[a_0, Sort[Concat[L_0, R_0]]]$. The proof succeeds on this branch and the extracted algorithm is:

Algorithm 1. Sorting trees, version 1.

$$\underset{a,L,R}{\forall} \left(\begin{array}{c} Sort[\varepsilon] = \varepsilon \\ Sort[\langle L, a, R \rangle] = Insert[a, Sort[Concat[L, R]]] \end{array} \right)$$

Case 1.2.2. Goal (5) becomes:

$$\mathcal{M}[T^*] = \{\{a_0\}\} \uplus \mathcal{M}[Merge[L_0, R_0]] \wedge IsSorted[T^*]. \qquad (11)$$

Strategy **ST-2** uses $Merge[L_0, R_0]$ (which is smaller than $\langle L_0, a_0, R_0 \rangle$) to produce the assumption:

$$\mathcal{M}[Merge[Sort[L_0], Sort[R_0]]] = \mathcal{M}[Merge[L_0, R_0]] \wedge \\ IsSorted[Merge[Sort[L_0], Sort[R_0]]]. \qquad (12)$$

Goal (5) is rewritten using (12) into:

$$\mathcal{M}[T^*] = \{\{a_0\}\} \uplus \mathcal{M}[Merge[Sort[L_0], Sort[R_0]]] \wedge IsSorted[T^*]. \qquad (13)$$

Strategy **ST-4** applied to $\{\{a_0\}\}$ and $\mathcal{M}[Merge[Sort[L_0], Sort[R_0]]]$ uses now the already known function *Insert* to update the goal into:

$$\mathcal{M}[T^*] = Insert[a_0, Merge[Sort[L_0], Sort[R_0]]] \wedge IsSorted[T^*]. \qquad (14)$$

This gives a solution for T^* and the algorithm:

Algorithm 2. Sorting trees, version 2. $Insert[a, Merge[Sort[L], Sort[R]]]$

$$\underset{a,L,R}{\forall} \left(\begin{array}{c} Sort[\varepsilon] = \varepsilon \\ Sort[\langle L, a, R \rangle] = Insert[a, Merge[Sort[L], Sort[R]]] \end{array} \right)$$

Remark: Since for all sorting algorithms the base case is the same, as well as the LHS of the recursive equality, we to state only its RHS for the other algorithms.

The proof is similar for two other cases produced by **ST-4** from goal (5) by grouping first the unit multiset with another, and generates:

Algorithm 3. Sorting trees, version 3. $Merge[Sort[L], Insert[a, Sort[R]]]$

Algorithm 4. Sorting trees, version 4. $Merge[Insert[a, Sort[L]], Sort[R]]$

Branch 2. **ST-1** applies to T^* using the cover set $\{\varepsilon, \langle L^*, a^*, R^* \rangle\}$ and two cases are generated:

Case 2.1: $T^* = \varepsilon$ is trivial.

Case 2.2: $T^* = \langle L^*, a^*, R^* \rangle$. The goal becomes:

$$\mathcal{M}[\langle L^*, a^*, R^* \rangle] = \mathcal{M}[\langle L_0, a_0, R_0 \rangle] \wedge \mathit{IsSorted}[T^*]. \tag{15}$$

This is transformed by **IR-4** (expand multiset) and **IR-1** (reduce composite argument on *IsSorted*) into:

$$\mathcal{M}[L^*] \uplus \{\{a^*\}\} \uplus \mathcal{M}[R^*] = \mathcal{M}[L_0] \uplus \{\{a_0\}\} \uplus \mathcal{M}[R_0] \wedge \\ \mathit{IsSorted}[L^*] \wedge \mathit{IsSorted}[R^*] \wedge L^* \le a^* < R^*. \tag{16}$$

Using the equality the prover computes the partial solution $a^* = a_0$ and reduces the goal correspondingly, and then **ST-4** starts two alternatives:

Case 2.2.1. By pairing $\mathcal{M}[L_0], \mathcal{M}[R_0]$ using *Concat* the goal becomes:

$$\mathcal{M}[L^*] \uplus \mathcal{M}[R^*] = \mathcal{M}[\mathit{Concat}[L_0, R_0]] \wedge \\ \mathit{IsSorted}[L^*] \wedge \mathit{IsSorted}[R^*] \wedge L^* \le a_0 < R^*. \tag{17}$$

By **ST-2** (dynamic induction) $\mathit{Concat}[L_0, R_0]$ is replaced by $\mathit{Sort}[\mathit{Concat}[L_0, R_0]]$, and then **ST-3** generates *Conjecture 6* for the synthesis of *SmallerEq* and *Bigger*, adds the corresponding properties of them to the global assumptions, and updates the goal to:

$$\mathcal{M}[L^*] \uplus \mathcal{M}[R^*] = \\ \mathcal{M}[\mathit{SmallerEq}[a_0, \mathit{Sort}[\mathit{Concat}[L_0, R_0]]]] \uplus \mathcal{M}[\mathit{Bigger}[a_0, \mathit{Sort}[\mathit{Concat}[L_0, R_0]]]] \wedge \\ \mathit{IsSorted}[L^*] \wedge \mathit{IsSorted}[R^*] \wedge L^* \le a_0 < R^*. \tag{18}$$

This gives the obvious solutions to L^*, R^* and the algorithm:

Algorithm 5. Sorting trees, version 5.

$$\mathop{\forall}_{a,L,R} \left(\begin{array}{c} \mathit{Sort}[\langle L, a, R \rangle] = \\ \langle \mathit{SmallerEq}[a, \mathit{Sort}[\mathit{Concat}[L, R]]], a, \mathit{Bigger}[a, \mathit{Sort}[\mathit{Concat}[L, R]]] \rangle \end{array} \right)$$

(In an efficient implementation $\mathit{Sort}[\mathit{Concat}[L, R]]$ must be computed only once.)

Case 2.2.1. In a similar way but with different pairing of multiset terms, and using the already known selection functions, one obtains the algorithm:

Algorithm 6. Sorting trees, version 6.

$$\mathop{\forall}_{a,L,R} \left(\begin{array}{c} \mathit{Sort}[\langle L, a, R \rangle] = \\ \langle \mathit{Merge}[\mathit{SmallerEq}[a, \mathit{Sort}[L]], \mathit{SmallerEq}[a, \mathit{Sort}[R]]], \\ a, \\ \mathit{Merge}[\mathit{Bigger}[a, \mathit{Sort}[L]], \mathit{Bigger}[a, \mathit{Sort}[R]]] \rangle \end{array} \right)$$

Several similar versions of the latest two algorithms are generated by ST-4 permuting the multiset terms corresponding to L and R.

4.2 Auxiliary Algorithms

Insert. Inserts an element in a sorted tree such that the result remains sorted.

Conjecture 2. $\underset{a}{\forall}\underset{X}{\forall}\Big(IsSorted[X] \Longrightarrow \underset{S}{\exists}\big(\mathcal{M}[S] = \{\{a\}\} \uplus \mathcal{M}[X] \wedge IsSorted[S]\big)\Big)$

is used in the practical experiment as:

Conjecture 3.
$\underset{X}{\forall}\Big(IsSorted[X] \Longrightarrow \underset{a}{\forall}\big(\mathcal{M}[Insert[a, X]] = \{\{a\}\} \uplus \mathcal{M}[X] \wedge IsSorted[Insert[a, X]]\big)\Big)$

Figure 1 shows the formalization of the conjecture in *Theorema* and the graphical user interface of the prover.

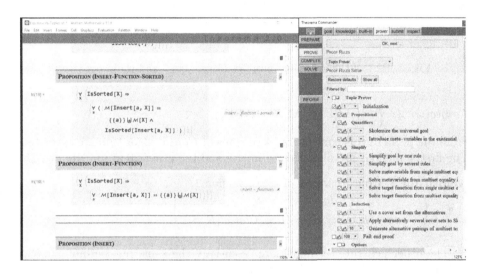

Fig. 1. Setup for proving *Conjecture 3*.

The proof uses the cover set $\{\varepsilon, \langle L_0, b_0, R_0\rangle\}$ for the Skolem constant X_0 and generates the algorithm:

Algorithm 7. Insertion in a sorted tree.
$$\underset{a,b,L,R}{\forall}\left(\begin{array}{c} Insert[a, \varepsilon] = \langle \varepsilon, a, \varepsilon\rangle \\ Insert[a, \langle L, b, R\rangle] = \left\{ \begin{array}{l} \langle Insert[a, L], b, R\rangle, \text{ if } a \leq b \\ \langle L, b, Insert[a, R]\rangle, \text{ if } b < a \end{array}\right.\end{array}\right)$$

Figure 2 shows a part of the proof of the conjecture, with the successful generation of the first clause of the algorithm.

This algorithm was derived with different methods in [17] and by explicit induction in [12] instead of using cover sets.

Concat. Combine two [unsorted] trees into an [unsorted] tree.

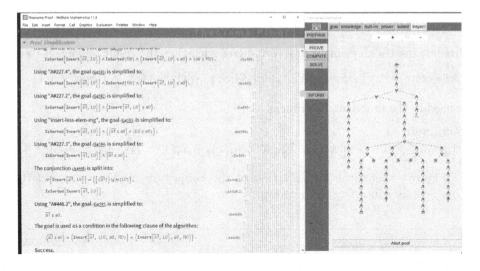

Fig. 2. Part of the generated proof of *Conjecture* 3 and the proof tree.

Conjecture 4. $\underset{XYZ}{\forall\forall\exists}\left(\mathcal{M}[Z] = \mathcal{M}[X] \uplus \mathcal{M}[Y]\right)$

From the proof of this conjecture 24 versions of *Concat* algorithm are extracted. The first 4 versions are also derived in [12] and the other 20 are in [18].

Algorithm 8. Concatenation of trees, version 1.
$$\underset{a,L,R,S}{\forall}\left(\begin{array}{c} Concat[\varepsilon, S] = S \\ Concat[\langle L, a, R\rangle, S] = \langle L, a, Concat[R, S]\rangle \end{array}\right)$$

The other generated versions are essentially the same but permute L, R, S and the two main branches of the resulting tree.

Merge. Combine two sorted trees into a sorted tree.

Conjecture 5.
$$\underset{XY}{\forall\forall}\left((IsSorted[X] \wedge IsSorted[Y]) \Longrightarrow \underset{Z}{\exists}\left(\mathcal{M}[Z] = \mathcal{M}[X] \uplus \mathcal{M}[Y] \wedge IsSorted[Z]\right)\right)$$

From the proof of this the following two versions of *Merge* are extracted [12]:

Algorithm 9. Merge sorted trees, version 1.
$$\underset{a,L,R,S}{\forall}\left(\begin{array}{c} Merge[\varepsilon, S] = S \\ Merge[\langle L, a, R\rangle, S] = Merge[L, Merge[R, Insert[a, S]]] \end{array}\right)$$

Algorithm 10. Merge sorted trees, version 2 (the inductive step).
$$\underset{a,L,R,S}{\forall}\left(Merge[\langle L, a, R\rangle, S] = Merge[Concat[L, R], Insert[a, S]]]\right)$$

as well as (by applying cover sets to meta-variables), the following two versions described in [18], which have in the second equality:

$\langle SmallerEq[a, Merge[L, S]], a, Bigger[a, Merge[R, S]]\rangle,$
$\langle Merge[L, SmallerEq[a, S]], a, Merge[R, Bigger[a, S]]\rangle.$

SmallerEq and **Bigger**. Select from a sorted tree the elements that are smaller, respectively bigger than a given element.

Conjecture 6. $\underset{X}{\forall} \Big(IsSorted[X] \implies \underset{a}{\forall} \underset{T_1}{\exists} \underset{T_2}{\exists} \Big(\mathcal{M}[X] = \mathcal{M}[T_1] \uplus \mathcal{M}[T_2] \quad \wedge$

$\qquad T_1 \leq a \ \wedge a < T_2 \wedge \ IsSorted[T_1] \wedge IsSorted[T_2] \Big) \Big).$

Algorithm 11

$$\underset{a,b,L,R}{\forall} \left(\begin{array}{l} SmallerEq[a, \varepsilon] = \varepsilon \\[4pt] SmallerEq[a, \langle L, b, R\rangle] = \begin{cases} \langle SmallerEq[a, L], a, SmallerEq[a, R]\rangle & \text{if } a = b \\ SmallerEq[a, L], & \text{if } a < b \\ \langle L, b, SmallerEq[a, R]\rangle, & \text{if } b < a \end{cases} \end{array} \right)$$

Algorithm 12

$$\underset{a,b,L,R}{\forall} \left(\begin{array}{l} Bigger[a, \varepsilon] = \varepsilon \\[4pt] Bigger[a, \langle L, b, R\rangle] = \begin{cases} \langle Bigger[a, L], b, R\rangle, & \text{if } a < b \\ Bigger[a, R], & \text{if } b \leq a \end{cases} \end{array} \right)$$

5 Conclusions and Further Work

This paper gives the description of **AlCons**, a powerful system for proof–based algorithm synthesis on lists and binary trees using multisets. The proofs generated by **AlCons** are easy to understand (similar to human proofs) and they are generated in a few seconds.

The most important proof strategies are: use cover sets together with multiset based Noetherian induction, pairing of multisets, and cascading. By using cover sets, no algorithm scheme and no concrete induction principles are needed in advance, as they are dynamically produced during the proof, and even nested induction algorithms can be generated automatically.

As future work one can extend **AlCons** to generate algorithms which combine operations on both lists and trees (e.g., algorithms for transforming a tree in a sorted list, transforming a non–sorted list into a balanced binary search tree), as well as more complex algorithms for sorting and searching – for instance on balanced trees. Moreover one can extend the prover with capabilities for automatic analysis of time and space complexity of the synthesized algorithms.

References

1. Barstow, D.R.: Remarks on "A synthesis of several sorting algorithms" by John Darlington. Acta Inf. **13**, 225–227 (1980)
2. Blizard, W.D.: Multiset theory. Notre Dame J. Formal Log. **30**(1), 36–66 (1989). https://doi.org/10.1305/ndjfl/1093634995

3. Buchberger, B.: Theory exploration with Theorema. Analele Univ. Din Timisoara Ser. Mat.-Inf. **XXXVIII**(2), 9–32 (2000)
4. Buchberger, B.: Algorithm invention and verification by lazy thinking. Analele Univ. din Timisoara Ser. Mat. - Inf. **XLI**, 41–70 (2003)
5. Buchberger, B., Craciun, A.: Algorithm synthesis by lazy thinking: Using problem schemes. In: Proceedings of SYNASC 2004, pp. 90–106 (2004)
6. Buchberger, B., et al.: The Theorema project: A progress report. In: Calculemus 2000, pp. 98–113. A.K. Peters, Natick (2000)
7. Buchberger, B., Jebelean, T., Kutsia, T., Maletzky, A., Windsteiger, W.: Theorema 2.0: Computer-assisted natural-style mathematics. J. Formal. Reason. **9**(1), 149–185 (2016). https://doi.org/10.6092/issn.1972-5787/4568
8. Bundy, A., Basin, D., Hutter, D., Ireland, A.: Rippling: Meta-level Guidance for Mathematical Reasoning. Cambridge University Press, Cambridge (2005)
9. Bundy, A., Dixon, L., Gow, J., Fleuriot, J.: Constructing induction rules for deductive synthesis proofs. Electron. Notes Theor. Comput. Sci. **153**, 3–21 (2006). https://doi.org/10.1016/j.entcs.2005.08.003
10. Darlington, J.: A synthesis of several sorting algorithms. Acta Inf. **11**, 1–30 (1978)
11. Dramnesc, I., Jebelean, T.: Synthesis of list algorithms by mechanical proving. J. Symb. Comput. **68**, 61–92 (2015). https://doi.org/10.1016/j.jsc.2014.09.030
12. Drămnesc, I., Jebelean, T.: Automatic synthesis of merging and inserting algorithms on binary trees using multisets in Theorema. In: Slamanig, D., Tsigaridas, E., Zafeirakopoulos, Z. (eds.) MACIS 2019. LNCS, vol. 11989, pp. 153–168. Springer, Cham (2020). https://doi.org/10.1007/978-3-030-43120-4_13
13. Dramnesc, I., Jebelean, T.: Proof-based synthesis of sorting algorithms using multisets in Theorema. In: FROM 2019, pp. 76–91. EPTCS 303 (2019). https://doi.org/10.4204/EPTCS.303.6
14. Dramnesc, I., Jebelean, T.: Deductive synthesis of bubble-sort using multisets. In: SAMI 2020, pp. 165–172. IEEE (2020). https://doi.org/10.1109/SAMI48414.2020.9108725
15. Dramnesc, I., Jebelean, T.: Deductive synthesis of min-max-sort using multisets. In: SACI 2020, pp. 165–172. IEEE (2020). https://doi.org/10.1109/SACI49304.2020.9118814
16. Dramnesc, I., Jebelean, T.: Synthesis of sorting algorithms using multisets in Theorema. J. Log. Algebraic Methods Programm. **119**(100635) (2020). https://doi.org/10.1016/j.jlamp.2020.100635
17. Dramnesc, I., Jebelean, T., Stratulat, S.: Mechanical synthesis of sorting algorithms for binary trees by logic and combinatorial techniques. J. Symb. Comput. **90**, 3–41 (2019). https://doi.org/10.1016/j.jsc.2018.04.002
18. Dramnesc, I., Jebelean, T.: Synthesis of merging algorithms on binary trees using multisets in Theorema. In: SACI 2021, pp. 497–502. IEEE (2021). https://doi.org/10.1109/SACI51354.2021.9465619
19. Dromey, R.G.: Derivation of sorting algorithms from a specification. Comput. J. **30**(6), 512–518 (1987)
20. Eguchi, S., Kobayashi, N., Tsukada, T.: Automated synthesis of functional programs with auxiliary functions. In: Ryu, S. (ed.) APLAS 2018. LNCS, vol. 11275, pp. 223–241. Springer, Cham (2018). https://doi.org/10.1007/978-3-030-02768-1_13
21. Howard, B.T.: Another iteration on "A synthesis of several sorting algorithms" Technical report KSU CIS 94–8. Kansas State University, Department of Computing and Information Sciences (1994)

22. Itzhaky, S., Peleg, H., Polikarpova, N., Rowe, R.N.S., Sergey, I.: Cyclic program synthesis. In: PLDI 2021, pp. 944–959. ACM (2021). https://doi.org/10.1145/3453483.3454087

23. Knuth, D.E.: The Art of Computer Programming, Volume 2: Seminumerical Algorithms. 3 edn. Addison-Wesley (1998). https://doi.org/10.1137/1012065

24. Korukhova, Y.: Automatic deductive synthesis of lisp programs in the system ALISA. In: Fisher, M., van der Hoek, W., Konev, B., Lisitsa, A. (eds.) JELIA 2006. LNCS (LNAI), vol. 4160, pp. 242–252. Springer, Heidelberg (2006). https://doi.org/10.1007/11853886_21

25. Korukhova, Y.: An approach to automatic deductive synthesis of functional programs. Ann. Math. Artif. Intell. **50**(3–4), 255–271 (2007). https://doi.org/10.1007/s10472-007-9079-9

26. Lau, K.K.: Top-down synthesis of sorting algorithms. Comput. J. **35**, A001–A007 (1992)

27. Manna, Z., Waldinger, R.: A deductive approach to program synthesis. ACM Trans. Programm. Lang. Syst. **2**(1), 90–121 (1980). https://doi.org/10.1145/357084.357090

28. Manna, Z., Waldinger, R.: The Logical Basis for Computer Programming, vol. 1: Deductive Reasoning. Addison-Wesley (1985). https://doi.org/10.2307/2275898

29. Manna, Z., Waldinger, R.: Fundamentals of deductive program synthesis. IEEE Trans. Softw. Eng. **18**(8), 674–704 (1992). https://doi.org/10.1109/32.153379

30. Polikarpova, N., Kuraj, I., Solar-Lezama, A.: Program synthesis from polymorphic refinement types. In: PLDI 2016, pp. 522–538 (2016). https://doi.org/10.1145/2908080.2908093

31. Radoaca, A.: Properties of multisets compared to sets. In: SYNASC 2015, pp. 187–188 (2015). https://doi.org/10.1109/SYNASC.2015.37

32. Smith, D.R.: KIDS: a semiautomatic program development system. IEEE Trans. Softw. Eng. **16**(9), 1024–1043 (1990). https://doi.org/10.1109/32.578788

33. Srivastava, S., Gulwani, S., Foster, J.S.: From program verification to program synthesis. SIGPLAN Not. **45**(1), 313–326 (2010). https://doi.org/10.1145/1707801.1706337

34. Stratulat, S.: A general framework to build contextual cover set induction provers. J. Symb. Comput. **32**, 403–445 (2001)

35. Traugott, J.: Deductive synthesis of sorting programs. J. Symb. Comput. **7**(6), 533–572 (1989). https://doi.org/10.1016/S0747-7171(89)80040-9

36. Windsteiger, W.: Theorema 2.0: A system for mathematical theory exploration. In: Hong, H., Yap, C. (eds.) ICMS 2014. LNCS, vol. 8592, pp. 49–52. Springer, Heidelberg (2014). https://doi.org/10.1007/978-3-662-44199-2_9

Reactive Synthesis from Visibly Register Pushdown Automata

Ryoma Senda[1(✉)], Yoshiaki Takata[2], and Hiroyuki Seki[1]

[1] Graduate School of Informatics, Nagoya University,
Furo-cho, Chikusa, Nagoya 464-8601, Japan
ryoma.private@sqlab.jp, seki@i.nagoya-u.ac.jp
[2] Graduate School of Engineering, Kochi University of Technology, Tosayamada,
Kami City, Kochi 782-8502, Japan
takata.yoshiaki@kochi-tech.ac.jp

Abstract. The realizability problem for a given specification $\mathcal{S}$ is to decide whether there exists an implementation satisfying $\mathcal{S}$. Although the problem is important in the field of reactive synthesis of recursive programs, the problem has not been studied yet when specification and implementation are given by pushdown computational models. This paper investigates the realizability problem for the cases that a specification and an implementation are given by a pushdown automaton (PDA) and a pushdown transducer (PDT), and a register pushdown automata (RPDA) and a register pushdown transducer (RPDT).

1 Introduction

Reactive synthesis is a method of synthesizing a system that satisfies a given specification representing the input-output relation of the system. A specification is formally a subset of an infinite alternate sequences of input and output symbols. When an environment or a user gives inputs $i_0, i_1, \ldots$ in this order to a system, the latter is required to emit a sequence of outputs $o_0, o_1, \ldots$ such that $(i_0, o_0)(i_1, o_1) \cdots \in S$. The realizability problem is to decide whether for a given specification S, there exists a reactive system satisfying S, and if exists, to generate such a system (called an implementation of S).

Studies on reactive synthesis have their origin in 1960s and have been one of central topics in formal methods [11]. Among them, Büchi and Landweber [8] showed EXPTIME-completeness of the problem when a specification is given by a finite ω-automaton (a finite automaton on infinite words). Pnueli and Rosner [28] showed 2EXPTIME-completeness of the problem when a specification is given by an LTL formula. We can find an excellent tutorial and survey of the previous studies on the synthesis problem in [2]. The standard approach to the problem is as follows. Assume that, for example, a specification is given as a deterministic ω-automaton $\mathcal{A}$. We convert $\mathcal{A}$ to a tree automaton (or equivalently, a parity game) $\mathcal{B}$ by separating the input and output streams. Then, we test whether $L(\mathcal{B}) \neq \emptyset$ (or equivalently, there is a winning strategy for player I

© Springer Nature Switzerland AG 2021
A. Cerone and P. C. Ölveczky (Eds.): ICTAC 2021, LNCS 12819, pp. 334–353, 2021.
https://doi.org/10.1007/978-3-030-85315-0_19

in $\mathcal{B}$). The answer to the problem is affirmative if and only if $L(\mathcal{B}) \neq \emptyset$, and any $t \in L(\mathcal{B})$ (or any winning strategy for $\mathcal{B}$) is an implementation of the specification.

Classical models such as a finite automaton cannot deal with objects from an infinite set (called data values). However, when we add an ability of manipulating data values to such a classical model, the model easily becomes Turing-complete and basic problems become undecidable. Register automaton (RA) is an extension of finite automaton by adding limited ability of manipulating data values [7, 21, 27, 30]. An RA has a finite number of registers for storing data values taken from an input word and it can compare the contents of its registers with the current input data value to determine the next transition. RA inherits some good properties from finite automaton such as the closure under some language operations. The membership and emptiness are decidable for RA while the universality is undecidable. With the increase of interest in RA, the realizability problem for register models has been investigated recently [16, 19, 22, 23]. A specification is given by an RA and an implementation is represented by a register transducer (abbreviated as RT).

Pushdown automaton (PDA) is a simple model for recursive programs. Model checking algorithms for pushdown systems (PDA without input) has been extensively studied [6, 17, 18, 20, 36]. Extensions by adding registers are also done for PDA [12, 26, 33], called register pushdown automaton (RPDA). Since many real-world programs are recursive and also manipulate data values, it is important to investigate the realizability problem for PDA/RPDA.

This paper first extends the realizability problem to PDA and pushdown transducer. A pushdown transducer (PDT) is a deterministic PDA with output. PDT serves as a model of a recursive program that emits outputs according to the inputs given from its environment. The main difficulties to solve the realizability problem in this setting come from the facts that the class of languages recognized by nondeterministic PDA (NPDA) (i.e., context-free languages) does not have the closure properties under some set operations and some relevant decision problems such as the universality are undecidable for PDA. To avoid these difficulties, this paper mainly considers deterministic PDA (DPDA). (Note that, PDT is deterministic by definition.) In Sect. 4, we show that the realizability problem for DPDA is decidable while the problem is undecidable for NPDA. The former is proved by using the well-known property that the (two-players zero-sum parity) pushdown game is decidable and a winning strategy of the game can be constructed as a PDT [36].

Then, the paper moves to the realizability problem for RPDA and register PDT. In Sect. 5, we introduce RPDA and register PDT (RPDT). Both RPDA and RPDT read a data word, which is an infinite sequence of a pair (a, d) of a symbol a from a finite alphabet and a data value d from an infinite set. We show that the projection of the language recognized by a nondeterministic RPDA onto the finite alphabet can be recognized by a nondeterministic PDA, when we assume the freshness of input data values [35] for RPDA.

In Sect. 6, we discuss the realizability problem for deterministic RPDA (DRPDA) and RPDT. Our approach is to reduce the problem for DRPDA to the problem for DPDA. In this reduction, we want to convert a given DRPDA to a DPDA that recognizes the projection onto the finite alphabet of the former language by using the method in Sect. 5. For this purpose, we further assume that a given DPDA has the visibility on the guard condition inherited from the DRPDA as well as the visibility of stack operation (see [1] for the visibility of stack operation). Finally, we show that the realizability problem is decidable for visibly DRPDA and RPDT.

Related Work. RA is frequently used as computation models for querying structured data such as XML documents and graph databases [24,25]. LTL with the freeze quantifier (LTL↓) [14,15] is an extension of LTL by adding the ability of memorizing and comparing data values. LTL↓ has the strong relationship with two-way alternate extension of RA. Two-variable first-order logic on data words [3] is another famous logic for data values, whose expressive power is incomparable with LTL↓. Other extensions of RA are found in [4,5,9,13]. Nominal automaton [4] is an extension of finite automaton by using nominal sets, which are infinite sets having finite orbits of group actions and equivariant functions among them.

When considering the realizability for RA, the difficulty is to identify the number of registers needed for implementing the specification, i.e., the number of registers of RT. If the upperbound of the registers of RT is not given as an input, the realizability problem is undecidable for both of nondeterministic and universal RA [19]. If the upperbound of the registers is *a priori* known, the problem (called the bounded realizability problem) is shown to be decidable in EXPTIME for universal RA [22]. In [19], it is shown that the bounded realizability problem remains undecidable for nondeterministic RA (NRA) and becomes decidable in 2EXPTIME for a subclass called test-free NRA.

Extensions by adding registers are also done for PDA [12,26,33] and context-free grammar [10,31,32], called register pushdown automaton (RPDA) and register context-free grammar (RCFG), respectively. The expressive powers of RPDA and RCFG are the same. RPDA is a natural model for recursive programs with data values while RCFG has an advantage such that explicit representation of pushdown stack is not needed. For other extensions of PDA and verification of them, see [29,34,37].

2   Preliminaries

Let $\mathbb{N} = \{1, 2, \ldots\}$, $\mathbb{N}_0 = \{0\} \cup \mathbb{N}$ and $[n] = \{1, \cdots, n\}$ for $n \in \mathbb{N}$. For a set A, let $\mathscr{P}(A)$ be the power set of A, let A^* and A^ω be the sets of finite and infinite words over A, respectively. We denote $A^+ = A^* \setminus \{\varepsilon\}$ and $A^\infty = A^* \cup A^\omega$. For a word $\alpha \in A^\infty$ over a set A, let $\alpha(i) \in A$ be the i-th element of α ($i \geq 0$), $\alpha(i : j) = \alpha(i)\alpha(i + 1) \cdots \alpha(j - 1)\alpha(j)$ for $i \leq j$ and $\alpha(i :) = \alpha(i) \cdots$ for $i \geq 0$. Let $\langle u, w \rangle = u(0)w(0)u(1)w(1) \cdots \in A^\infty$ for words $u, w \in A^\infty$ and $\langle B, C \rangle = \{\langle u, w \rangle \mid u \in B, w \in C\}$ for sets $B, C \subseteq A^\infty$. By $|\beta|$, we mean the cardinality of β if β is a set and the length of β if β is a finite sequence. For a function $f : A \to B$ from a set A to a set B, let $f(w) = f(w(0))f(w(1))\ldots$ for a word $w \in A^\infty$ and let $f(L) = \{f(w) \mid w \in L\}$ for a set $L \subseteq A^\infty$ of words. Let fst and snd be the functions such that $fst((a, b)) = a$ and $snd((a, b)) = b$ for any pair (a, b). Let id be the identity function; i.e., $id(a) = a$ for any a.

2.1 Transition Systems

Definition 1. *A transition system (TS) is* $\mathcal{S} = (S, s_0, A, E, \to_\mathcal{S}, c)$ *where*

- S *is a (finite or infinite) set of states,*
- $s_0 \in S$ *is the initial state,*
- A, E *are (finite or infinite) alphabets such that* $A \cap E = \emptyset$,
- $\to_\mathcal{S} \subseteq S \times (A \cup E) \times S$ *is a transition relation, written as* $s \to^a s'$ *if* $(s, a, s') \in \to_\mathcal{S}$ *and*
- $c : S \to [n]$ *is a coloring function where* $n \in \mathbb{N}$.

An element of A is an observable label and an element of E is an internal label. A *run* of TS $\mathcal{S} = (S, s_0, A, E, \to_\mathcal{S}, c)$ is a pair $(\rho, w) \in S^\omega \times (A \cup E)^\omega$ that satisfies $\rho(0) = s_0$ and $\rho(i) \to^{w(i)} \rho(i+1)$ for $i \geq 0$. Let $\min_{\inf} : S^\omega \to [n]$ be the minimal coloring function such that $\min_{\inf}(\rho) = \min\{m \mid$ there exist an infinite number of $i \geq 0$ such that $c(\rho(i)) = m\}$. We call $\mathcal{S}$ deterministic if $s \to^a s_1$ and $s \to^a s_2$ implies $s_1 = s_2$ for all $s, s_1, s_2 \in S$ and $a \in A \cup E$.

For $w \in (A \cup E)^\omega$, let $ef(w) = a_0 a_1 \cdots \in A^\infty$ be the sequence obtained from w by removing all symbols belonging to E. Note that $ef(w)$ is not always an infinite sequence even if w is an infinite sequence. We define the *language* of $\mathcal{S}$ as $L(\mathcal{S}) = \{ef(w) \in A^\omega \mid$ there exists a run (ρ, w) such that $\min_{\inf}(\rho)$ is even$\}$. For $m \in \mathbb{N}_0$, we call $\mathcal{S}$ an m-TS if for every run (ρ, w) of $\mathcal{S}$, w contains no contiguous subsequence $w' \in E^*$ such that $|w'| > m$.

Consider two TSs $\mathcal{S}_1 = (S_1, s_{01}, A_1, E_1, \to_{\mathcal{S}_1}, c_1)$ and $\mathcal{S}_2 = (S_2, s_{02}, A_2, E_2, \to_{\mathcal{S}_2}, c_2)$ and a function $\sigma : (A_1 \cup E_1) \to (A_2 \cup E_2)$. We call $R \subseteq S_1 \times S_2$ a σ-*bisimulation relation* from $\mathcal{S}_1$ to $\mathcal{S}_2$ if R satisfies the followings:

(1) $(s_{01}, s_{02}) \in R$.
(2) For any $s_1, s_1' \in S_1$, $s_2 \in S_2$, and $a_1 \in A_1 \cup E_1$, if $s_1 \to^{a_1}_{\mathcal{S}_1} s_1'$ and $(s_1, s_2) \in R$, then $\exists s_2' \in S_2 : s_2 \to^{\sigma(a_1)}_{\mathcal{S}_2} s_2'$ and $(s_1', s_2') \in R$.
(3) For any $s_1 \in S_1$, $s_2, s_2' \in S_2$, and $a_2 \in A_2 \cup E_2$, if $s_2 \to^{a_2}_{\mathcal{S}_2} s_2'$ and $(s_1, s_2) \in R$, then $\exists s_1' \in S_1, \exists a_1 \in A_1 \cup E_1 : \sigma(a_1) = a_2$ and $s_1 \to^{a_1}_{\mathcal{S}_1} s_1'$ and $(s_1', s_2') \in R$.
(4) If $(s_1, s_2) \in R$, then $c_1(s_1) = c_2(s_2)$.

We say $\mathcal{S}_1$ is σ-*bisimilar* to $\mathcal{S}_2$ if there exists a σ-bisimulation relation from $\mathcal{S}_1$ to $\mathcal{S}_2$. We call R a bisimulation relation if R is an id-bisimulation relation. We say $\mathcal{S}_1$ and $\mathcal{S}_2$ are bisimilar if $\mathcal{S}_1$ is id-bisimilar to $\mathcal{S}_2$.

The following lemma can be proved by definition.

Lemma 2. *If* $\mathcal{S}_1 = (S_1, s_{01}, A_1, E_1, \to_{\mathcal{S}_1}, c_1)$ *is* σ-*bisimilar to* $\mathcal{S}_2 = (S_2, s_{02}, A_2, E_2, \to_{\mathcal{S}_2}, c_2)$ *for a function* $\sigma : (A_1 \cup E_1) \to (A_2 \cup E_2)$ *that satisfies* $a \in A_1 \Leftrightarrow \sigma(a) \in A_2$ *for any* $a \in A_1 \cup E_1$, *then* $\sigma(L(\mathcal{S}_1)) = L(\mathcal{S}_2)$.

3   Pushdown Transducers, Automata and Games

In this section, we review definitions of pushdown automaton (PDA), pushdown transducer (PDT) and pushdown game (PDG), together with a well-known property of PDG. The next section discusses the realizability problem for PDA as specifications and PDT as implementations. As described in the introduction, the approach to solve the realizability problem is as follows. We first convert a given specification (PDA) to a PDG $\mathcal{B}$ by separating the input and output streams. The answer to the realizability problem is affirmative if and only if there is a winning strategy for player I in $\mathcal{B}$. An implementation of the specification is easily obtained as a PDT from any winning strategy for $\mathcal{B}$.

We assume that disjoint sets $\Sigma_{\mathbb{i}}$, $\Sigma_{\mathbb{o}}$ and Γ are given as a (finite) input alphabet, an output alphabet and a stack alphabet, respectively, and $\Sigma = \Sigma_{\mathbb{i}} \cup \Sigma_{\mathbb{o}}$. Let $\text{Com}(\Gamma) = \{\text{pop}, \text{skip}\} \cup \{\text{push}(z) \mid z \in \Gamma\}$ be the set of stack commands over Γ.

3.1   Pushdown Transducers

Definition 3. *A pushdown transducer (PDT) over* $\Sigma_{\mathbb{i}}$, $\Sigma_{\mathbb{o}}$ *and* Γ *is* $\mathcal{T} = (P, p_0, z_0, \Delta)$ *where* P *is a finite set of states,* $p_0 \in P$ *is the initial state,* $z_0 \in \Gamma$ *is the initial stack symbol and* $\Delta : P \times \Sigma_{\mathbb{i}} \times \Gamma \to P \times \Sigma_{\mathbb{o}} \times \text{Com}(\Gamma)$ *is a finite set of deterministic transition rules having one of the following forms:*

- $(p, a, z) \to (q, b, \text{pop})$ *(pop rule)*
- $(p, a, z) \to (q, b, \text{skip})$ *(skip rule)*
- $(p, a, z) \to (q, b, \text{push}(z))$ *(push rule)*

where $p, q \in P$, $a \in \Sigma_{\mathbb{i}}$, $b \in \Sigma_{\mathbb{o}}$ *and* $z \in \Gamma$.

For a state $p \in P$ and a finite sequence representing stack contents $u \in \Gamma^*$, (p, u) is called a *configuration* or *instantaneous description (abbreviated as ID)* of PDT $\mathcal{T}$. Let $ID_{\mathcal{T}}$ denote the set of all IDs of $\mathcal{T}$. For $u \in \Gamma^+$ and $\text{com} \in \text{Com}(\Gamma)$, let us define $\text{upds}(u, \text{com})$ as $\text{upds}(u, \text{pop}) = u(1 :)$, $\text{upds}(u, \text{skip}) = u$ and $\text{upds}(u, \text{push}(z')) = z'u$.

For two IDs $(p, u), (q, u') \in ID_{\mathcal{T}}$, $a \in \Sigma_{\mathbb{i}}$ and $b \in \Sigma_{\mathbb{o}}$, $((p, u), ab, (q, u')) \in \Rightarrow_{\mathcal{T}}$, written as $(p, u) \Rightarrow_{\mathcal{T}}^{ab} (q, u')$, if there exist a rule $(p, a, z) \to (q, b, \text{com}) \in \Delta$ such that $z = u(0)$ and $u' = \text{upds}(u, \text{com})$. If $\mathcal{T}$ is clear from the context, we abbreviate $\Rightarrow_{\mathcal{T}}^{ab}$ as $\Rightarrow^{ab}$. We will use similar abbreviations for the other models defined later. Note that there is no transition from an ID with empty stack. We define a run and the language $L(\mathcal{T}) \subseteq (\Sigma_{\mathbb{i}} \cdot \Sigma_{\mathbb{o}})^{\omega}$ of PDT $\mathcal{T}$ as those of deterministic 0-TS $(ID_{\mathcal{T}}, (q_0, z_0), \Sigma_{\mathbb{i}} \cdot \Sigma_{\mathbb{o}}, \emptyset, \Rightarrow_{\mathcal{T}}, c)$ where $c(s) = 2$ for all $s \in ID_{\mathcal{T}}$. In this paper, we assume that no run of PDT reaches an ID whose stack is empty. We can realize this assumption by specifying a unique stack bottom symbol $z_{\perp}$ and forcing that every rule $(q, a, z_{\perp}) \to (q', \text{com}) \in \delta$ satisfies $\text{com} \neq \text{pop}$. Let **PDT** be the class consisting of all PDT.

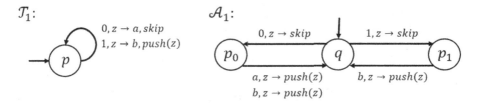

Fig. 1. States and transitions of $\mathcal{T}_1$ (left) and $\mathcal{A}_1$ (right). Labels $a, b \rightarrow c, d$ and $a, b \rightarrow c$ from q to q' mean $(q, a, b) \rightarrow (q', c, d) \in \Delta$ and $(q, a, b) \rightarrow (q', c) \in \delta$, respectively.

Example 4. Let us consider a PDT $\mathcal{T}_1 = (\{p\}, p, z, \Delta)$ over $\{0, 1\}, \{a, b\}$ and $\{z\}$ where $\Delta = \{(p, 0, z) \rightarrow (p, a, \mathtt{skip}), (p, 1, z) \rightarrow (p, b, \mathtt{push}(z))\}$. (See Fig. 1, left.) We can see a pair of sequences (ρ, w) where $\rho = (p, z)(p, z)$ $(p, zz)(p, zz)(p, zzz)(p, zzz) \cdots$ and $w = (0a1b)^\omega$ is a run of $\mathcal{T}_1$. Also, $L(\mathcal{T}_1) = (\{0a\} \cup \{1b\})^\omega$.

3.2 Pushdown Automata

Definition 5. *A nondeterministic pushdown automata (NPDA) over $\Sigma_\mathtt{i}$, $\Sigma_\mathtt{o}$ and Γ is $\mathcal{A} = (Q, Q_\mathtt{i}, Q_\mathtt{o}, q_0, z_0, \delta, c)$ where $Q, Q_\mathtt{i}, Q_\mathtt{o}$ are finite sets of states such that $Q = Q_\mathtt{i} \cup Q_\mathtt{o}$ and $Q_\mathtt{i} \cap Q_\mathtt{o} = \emptyset$, $q_0 \in Q_\mathtt{i}$ is the initial state, $z_0 \in \Gamma$ is the initial stack symbol, $c : Q \rightarrow [n]$ is the coloring function where $n \in \mathbb{N}$ is the number of priorities and $\delta : Q \times (\Sigma \cup \{\tau\}) \times \Gamma \rightarrow \mathscr{P}(Q \times \mathrm{Com}(\Gamma))$ is a finite set of transition rules having one of the following forms:*

- $(q_\mathtt{x}, a_\mathtt{x}, z) \rightarrow (q_{\overline{\mathtt{x}}}, \mathtt{com})$ *(input/output rules)*
- $(q_\mathtt{x}, \tau, z) \rightarrow (q'_\mathtt{x}, \mathtt{com})$ *(τ rules, where $\tau \notin \Sigma$)*

where $(\mathtt{x}, \overline{\mathtt{x}}) \in \{(\mathtt{i}, \mathtt{o}), (\mathtt{o}, \mathtt{i})\}$, $q_\mathtt{x}, q'_\mathtt{x} \in Q_\mathtt{x}, q_{\overline{\mathtt{x}}} \in Q_{\overline{\mathtt{x}}}, a_\mathtt{x} \in \Sigma_\mathtt{x}$, $z \in \Gamma$ and $\mathtt{com} \in \mathrm{Com}(\Gamma)$.

We define $ID_\mathcal{A} = Q \times \Gamma^*$ and the transition relation $\vdash_\mathcal{A} \subseteq ID_\mathcal{A} \times (\Sigma \cup \{\tau\}) \times ID_\mathcal{A}$ as $((q, u), a, (q', u')) \in \vdash_\mathcal{A}$ iff there exist a rule $(q, a, z) \rightarrow (q', \mathtt{com}) \in \delta$ and a sequence $u \in \Gamma^*$ such that $z = u(0)$ and $u' = \mathtt{upds}(u, \mathtt{com})$. We write $(q, u) \vdash_\mathcal{A}^a$ (q', u') iff $((q, u), a, (q', u')) \in \vdash_\mathcal{A}$. We define a run and the language $L(\mathcal{A})$ of $\mathcal{A}$ as those of TS $\mathcal{S}_\mathcal{A} = (ID_\mathcal{A}, (q_0, z_0), \Sigma, \{\tau\}, \vdash_\mathcal{A}, c')$ where $c'((q, u)) = c(q)$ for every $(q, u) \in ID_\mathcal{A}$. We call a PDA $\mathcal{A}$ deterministic if $\mathcal{S}_\mathcal{A}$ is deterministic. We call $\mathcal{A}$ an m-NPDA (or m-DPDA when $\mathcal{A}$ is deterministic) if $\mathcal{S}_\mathcal{A}$ is an m-TS. We abbreviate 0-NPDA (0-DPDA) as NPDA (DPDA). Let **DPDA** and **NPDA** be the classes of DPDA and NPDA, respectively.

Example 6. Let us consider a DPDA $\mathcal{A}_1 = (\{q, p_0, p_1\}, \{q\}, \{p_0, p_1\}, q, z, \delta, c)$ over $\{0, 1\}, \{a, b\}$ and $\{z\}$ where $c(q) = c(p_0) = c(p_1) = 2$ and $\delta = \{(q, 0, z) \rightarrow (p_0, \mathtt{skip}), (q, 1, z) \rightarrow (p_1, \mathtt{skip}), (p_0, a, z) \rightarrow (q, \mathtt{push}(z)), (p_0, b, z) \rightarrow (q, \mathtt{push}(z)), (p_1, b, z) \rightarrow (q, \mathtt{push}(z))\}$. (See Fig. 1, right.) We can see a pair of sequences (ρ, w) where $\rho = (q, z)(p_0, z)(q, zz)(p_1, zz) \cdots$ and $w = (0a1b)^\omega$ is a run of $\mathcal{A}_1$. Also, $L(\mathcal{A}_1) = (\{0a\} \cup \{0b\} \cup \{1b\})^\omega$.

The following lemma states that the class of languages recognized by m-DPDA and 0-DPDA are the same for a fixed m.

Lemma 7. *For a given m-DPDA $\mathcal{A}$, we can construct a 0-DPDA $\mathcal{A}'$ such that $L(\mathcal{A}) = L(\mathcal{A}')$*

Proof Sketch. We define the stack alphabet Γ' of $\mathcal{A}'$ as $\Gamma' = \Gamma^m$. We can simulate m-steps with consecutive push rules (or pop rules) of $\mathcal{A}$ by a single step with a push (or pop) rule of $\mathcal{A}'$.

3.3   Pushdown Games

Definition 8. *A pushdown game of DPDA $\mathcal{A} = (Q, Q_{\text{II}}, Q_{\text{I}}, q_0, z_0, \delta, c)$ over $\Sigma_{\text{II}}, \Sigma_{\text{I}}$ and Γ is $\mathcal{G}_{\mathcal{A}} = (V, V_{\text{II}}, V_{\text{I}}, E, C)$ where $V = Q \times \Gamma^*$ is the set of vertices with $V_{\text{II}} = Q_{\text{II}} \times \Gamma^*, V_{\text{I}} = Q_{\text{I}} \times \Gamma^*, E \subseteq V \times V$ is the set of edges defined as $E = \{(v, v') \mid v \vdash^a v' \text{ for some } a \in \Sigma_{\text{II}} \cup \Sigma_{\text{I}}\}$ and $C : V \to [n]$ is the coloring function such that $C((q, u)) = c(q)$ for all $(q, u) \in V$.*

The game starts with $(q_0, z_0) \in V_{\text{II}}$. When the current vertex is $v \in V_{\text{II}}$, Player II chooses a successor $v' \in V_{\text{I}}$ of v as the next vertex. When the current vertex is $v \in V_{\text{I}}$, Player I chooses a successor $v' \in V_{\text{II}}$ of v. Formally, a finite or infinite sequence $\rho \in V^\infty$ is *valid* if $\rho(0) = (q_0, z_0)$ and $(\rho(i-1), \rho(i)) \in E$ for every $i \geq 1$. A *play* of $\mathcal{G}_{\mathcal{A}}$ is an infinite and valid sequence $\rho \in V^\omega$. Let PL be the set of plays. A play $\rho \in PL$ is *winning* for Player I iff $\min\{m \in [n] \mid \text{there exists an infinite number of } i \geq 0 \text{ such that } c(\rho(i)) = m\}$ is even. Note that by definition, a play ρ is winning for Player I iff (ρ, w) is an accepting run of $\mathcal{A}$ for some w.

Since $\mathcal{A}$ is deterministic, the following lemma holds.

Lemma 9. *Let $f_1 : PL \to (Q \times \text{Com}(\Gamma))^\omega$ and $f_2 : (\Sigma_{\text{II}} \cdot \Sigma_{\text{I}})^\omega \to PL$ be the functions defined as follows:*

- *$f_1(\rho) = (q_0, \text{com}_0)(q_1, \text{com}_1) \cdots \in (Q \times \text{Com})^\omega$ where $\rho = (q_0, u_0)(q_1, u_1) \cdots \in PL$ and $u_{i+1} = \text{upds}(u_i, \text{com}_i)$ for all $i \geq 0$ and*
- *$f_2(w) = \rho$ where $\rho = (q_0, u_0)(q_1, u_1) \cdots \in PL$ and $\rho(i) \vdash^{w(i)} \rho(i+1)$ for all $i \geq 0$.*

Then, f_1 and f_2 are well-defined, f_1 is an injection and $f_2(L(\mathcal{A}))$ is the set of all the winning plays of Player I.

Theorem 10 [36]. *If player I has a winning strategy of $\mathcal{G}_{\mathcal{A}}$, we can construct a PDT $\mathcal{T}$ over $Q_{\text{II}} \times \text{Com}(\Gamma), Q_{\text{I}} \times \text{Com}(\Gamma)$ and a stack alphabet Γ' that gives a winning strategy of $\mathcal{G}_{\mathcal{A}}$. That is, $\rho \in PL$ is winning for Player I if $f_1(\rho) \in L(\mathcal{T})$.*

By Lemma 9, a winning strategy can be also given as a subset of sequences $w \in (\Sigma_{\text{II}} \cdot \Sigma_{\text{I}})^\omega$ such that the play $f_2(w)$ is winning for Player I. Thus, we can obtain the following lemma in a similar way to Theorem 10.

Corollary 11. *If player I has a winning strategy of $\mathcal{G}_{\mathcal{A}}$, we can construct a PDT $\mathcal{T}$ over $\Sigma_{\text{II}}, \Sigma_{\text{I}}$ and a stack alphabet Γ' that gives a winning strategy of $\mathcal{G}_{\mathcal{A}}$. That is, $f_2(w) \in PL$ is winning for Player I if $w \in L(\mathcal{T})$.*

4   Realizability Problems for PDA and PDT

For a specification S and an implementation I, we write $I \models S$ if $L(I) \subseteq L(S)$.

Definition 12. *Realizability problem* REAL$(S, \mathcal{I})$ *for a class of specifications* S *and of implementations* $\mathcal{I}$: *For a specification* $S \in S$, *is there an implementation* $I \in \mathcal{I}$ *such that* $I \models S$?

Example 13. By Examples 4 and 6, $L(\mathcal{T}_1) \subseteq L(\mathcal{A}_1)$ holds for PDT $\mathcal{T}_1$ and DPDA $\mathcal{A}_1$ defined in the examples. Thus, $\mathcal{T}_1 \models \mathcal{A}_1$ holds.

Theorem 14. REAL(**DPDA**, **PDT**) *is in EXPTIME.*

Proof.   Let $\mathcal{A}$ be a given DPDA. By definitions, $w \in L(\mathcal{A})$ iff $f_2(w)$ is a winning play for Player I of $\mathcal{G}_\mathcal{A}$. By Corollary 11, if Player I has a winning strategy, we can construct a PDT $\mathcal{T}$ such that $f_2(w)$ is a winning play of $\mathcal{G}_\mathcal{A}$ if $w \in L(\mathcal{T})$. Hence, $\mathcal{T} \models \mathcal{A}$ holds. If Player I does not have a winning strategy, there is no $\mathcal{T}$ such that $\mathcal{T} \models \mathcal{A}$. Because there is an EXPTIME algorithm for constructing $\mathcal{T}$ (if exists) in [36], REAL(**DPDA**, **PDT**) is in EXPTIME.

Theorem 15. REAL(**NPDA**, **PDT**) *is undecidable.*

Proof.   We prove the theorem by a reduction from the universality problem of NPDA, which is undecidable. For a given NPDA $\mathcal{A} = (Q, Q_\$, Q_\circ, q_0, z_0, \delta, c)$ over $\Sigma_\$, \Sigma_\circ$ and Γ, we can construct an NPDA $\mathcal{A}' = (Q \times [2], Q \times \{1\}, Q \times \{2\}, q_0, z_0, \delta', c')$ over $\Sigma_\$', \Sigma_\circ'$ and Γ where $\Sigma_\$' = \Sigma_\$ \cup \Sigma_\circ$, $\Sigma_\circ'$ is an arbitrary (nonempty) alphabet, $c'((q, 1)) = c'((q, 2)) = c(q)$ for all $q \in Q$ and $((q, 1), a, z) \to ((q', 2), \mathsf{com}) \in \delta'$ iff $(q, a, z) \to (q', \mathsf{com}) \in \delta$, and $((q', 2), b, z) \to ((q', 1), \mathsf{skip}) \in \delta'$ for all $b \in \Sigma_\circ'$ and $z \in \Gamma$.
    We show $L(\mathcal{A}) = (\Sigma_\$')^\omega$ iff there exists $\mathcal{T}$ such that $\mathcal{T} \models \mathcal{A}$. By the construction of $\mathcal{A}'$, $L(\mathcal{A}') = \langle L(\mathcal{A}), (\Sigma_\circ')^\omega \rangle$ holds. If $L(\mathcal{A}) = (\Sigma_\$')^\omega$, then $L(\mathcal{A}') = \langle (\Sigma_\$')^\omega, (\Sigma_\circ')^\omega \rangle$ and thus $\mathcal{T} \models \mathcal{A}$ holds for every $\mathcal{T}$. Assume that $L(\mathcal{A}) \neq (\Sigma_\$')^\omega$. Then, there exists a word $w \in (\Sigma_\$')^\omega$ such that $w \notin L(\mathcal{A})$. For any PDT $\mathcal{T}$ and any $u \in (\Sigma_\$')^\omega$, there is $v \in (\Sigma_\circ')^\omega$ such that $\langle u, v \rangle \in L(\mathcal{A}')$. On the other hand, $\langle w, v \rangle \notin L(\mathcal{A}')$ holds for any $v \in (\Sigma_\circ')^\omega$. Hence, $\mathcal{T} \not\models \mathcal{A}'$ holds for any PDT $\mathcal{T}$. This completes the reduction and the realizability problem for NPDA and PDT is undecidable.

5   Register Pushdown Transducers and Automata

5.1   Data Words and Registers

We assume a countable set D of *data values*. For finite alphabets $\Sigma_\$, \Sigma_\circ$, an infinite sequence $(a_1^\$, d_1)(a^\circ, d_1') \cdots \in ((\Sigma_\$ \times D) \cdot (\Sigma_\circ \times D))^\omega$ is called a *data word*. We let $\mathrm{DW}(\Sigma_\$, \Sigma_\circ, D) = ((\Sigma_\$ \times D) \cdot (\Sigma_\circ \times D))^\omega$. We define the projection $\mathrm{Lab} : \Sigma \times D \to \Sigma$ as $\mathrm{Lab}((a, d)) = a$ for $(a, d) \in \Sigma \times D$. For $k \in \mathbb{N}_0$, a mapping $\theta : [k] \to D$ is called an *assignment* (of data values to k registers). Let Θ_k denote the collection of assignments to k registers. We assume $\perp \in D$ as the initial data value and let $\theta_\perp^k \in \Theta_k$ be the initial assignment such that $\theta_\perp^k(i) = \perp$ for all $i \in [k]$.

We denote $\mathtt{Tst}_k = \mathscr{P}([k] \cup \{\mathtt{top}\})$ and $\mathtt{Asgn}_k = \mathscr{P}([k])$ where $\mathtt{top} \notin \mathbb{N}$ is a unique symbol that represents a stack top value. $\mathtt{Tst}_k$ is the set of guard conditions. For $\mathtt{tst} \in \mathtt{Tst}_k$, $\theta \in \Theta_k$ and $d, e \in D$, we denote $(\theta, d, e) \models \mathtt{tst}$ if $(\theta(i) = d \Leftrightarrow i \in \mathtt{tst})$ and $(e = d \Leftrightarrow \mathtt{top} \in \mathtt{tst})$ hold. In the definitions of register pushdown transducer and automaton in the next section, the data values d and e correspond to an input data value and a stack top data value, respectively. $\mathtt{Asgn}_k$ is the set of assignment conditions. For $\mathtt{asgn} \in \mathtt{Asgn}_k$, $\theta \in \Theta_k$ and $d \in D$, let $\theta[\mathtt{asgn} \leftarrow d]$ be the assignment $\theta' \in \Theta_k$ such that $\theta'(i) = d$ for $i \in \mathtt{asgn}$ and $\theta'(i) = \theta(i)$ for $i \notin \mathtt{asgn}$.

5.2   Register Pushdown Transducers

Definition 16. *A register pushdown transducer with k registers (k-RPDT) over finite alphabets $\Sigma_{\mathfrak{i}}, \Sigma_{\mathfrak{o}}$ and Γ is $\mathcal{T} = (P, p_0, z_0, \Delta)$ where P is a finite set of states, $p_0 \in P$ is the initial state, $z_0 \in \Gamma$ is the initial stack symbol and $\Delta : P \times \Sigma_{\mathfrak{i}} \times \mathtt{Tst}_k \times \Gamma \to P \times \Sigma_{\mathfrak{o}} \times \mathtt{Asgn}_k \times [k] \times \mathtt{Com}(\Gamma \times [k])$ is a finite set of deterministic transition rules.*

For $u \in (\Gamma \times D)^+$, $\theta' \in \Theta_k$ and $\mathtt{com} \in \mathtt{Com}(\Gamma \times [k])$, let us define $\mathtt{upds}(u, \theta', \mathtt{com})$ as $\mathtt{upds}(u, \theta', \mathtt{pop}) = u(1 :)$, $\mathtt{upds}(u, \theta', \mathtt{skip}) = u$ and $\mathtt{upds}(u, \theta', \mathtt{push}((z, j'))) = (z, \theta'(j'))u$. Let $ID_\mathcal{T} = P \times \Theta_k \times (\Gamma \times D)^*$ and $\Rightarrow_\mathcal{T} \subseteq ID_\mathcal{T} \times ((\Sigma_{\mathfrak{i}} \times D) \cdot (\Sigma_{\mathfrak{o}} \times D)) \times ID_\mathcal{T}$ be the transition relation of $\mathcal{T}$ such that $((p, \theta, u), (a, d^{\mathfrak{i}})(b, d^{\mathfrak{o}}), (q, \theta', u')) \in \Rightarrow_\mathcal{T}$ iff there exists a rule $(p, a, \mathtt{tst}, z) \to (q, b, \mathtt{asgn}, j, \mathtt{com}) \in \Delta$ that satisfies the following conditions: $(\theta, d^{\mathfrak{i}}, snd(u(0))) \models \mathtt{tst}$, $\theta' = \theta[\mathtt{asgn} \leftarrow d^{\mathfrak{i}}]$, $\theta'(j) = d^{\mathfrak{o}}$, $z = fst(u(0))$ and $u' = \mathtt{upds}(u, \theta', \mathtt{com})$, and we write $(p, \theta, u) \Rightarrow_\mathcal{T}^{(a, d^{\mathfrak{i}})(b, d^{\mathfrak{o}})} (q, \theta', u')$.

A run and the language $L(\mathcal{T})$ of $\mathcal{T}$ are those of deterministic 0-TS $(ID_\mathcal{T}, (q_0, \theta_\perp^k, (z_0, \perp)), (\Sigma_{\mathfrak{i}} \times D) \cdot (\Sigma_{\mathfrak{o}} \times D), \emptyset, \Rightarrow_\mathcal{T}, c)$ where $c(s) = 2$ for all $s \in ID_\mathcal{T}$. In this paper, we assume that no run of RPDT reaches an ID whose stack is empty. Let $\mathbf{RPDT}[k]$ be the class of k-RPDT and $\mathbf{RPDT} = \bigcup_{k \in \mathbb{N}_0} \mathbf{RPDT}[k]$.

5.3   Register Pushdown Automata

Definition 17. *A nondeterministic register pushdown automaton with k registers (k-NRPDA) over $\Sigma_{\mathfrak{i}}, \Sigma_{\mathfrak{o}}$ and Γ is $\mathcal{A} = (Q, Q_{\mathfrak{i}}, Q_{\mathfrak{o}}, q_0, z_0, \delta, c)$, where Q is a finite set of states, $Q_{\mathfrak{i}} \cup Q_{\mathfrak{o}} = Q$, $Q_{\mathfrak{i}} \cap Q_{\mathfrak{o}} = \emptyset$, $q_0 \in Q$ is the initial state, $z_0 \in \Gamma$ is the initial stack symbol, $c : Q \to [n]$ where $n \in \mathbb{N}$ is the number of priorities and $\delta : Q \times (\Sigma \cup \{\tau\}) \times \mathtt{Tst}_k \times \Gamma \to \mathscr{P}(Q \times \mathtt{Asgn}_k \times \mathtt{Com}(\Gamma \times [k]))$ is a transition function having one of the forms:*

- *$(q_{\mathfrak{x}}, a_{\mathfrak{x}}, \mathtt{tst}, z) \to (q_{\overline{\mathfrak{x}}}, \mathtt{asgn}, \mathtt{com})$ (input/output rule)*
- *$(q_{\mathfrak{x}}, \tau, \mathtt{tst}, z) \to (q'_{\mathfrak{x}}, \mathtt{asgn}, \mathtt{com})$ (τ rules, where $\tau \notin \Sigma$)*

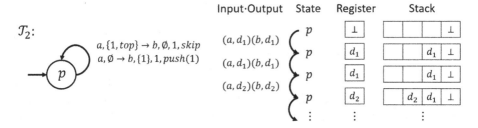

Fig. 2. A figure of $\mathcal{T}_2$ (left) and the run (ρ, w) of $\mathcal{T}_2$ (right). A label $a, \mathtt{tst} \rightarrow b, \mathtt{asgn}, 1, \mathtt{com}$ means $(p, a, \mathtt{tst}) \rightarrow (p, b, \mathtt{asgn}, 1, \mathtt{com}) \in \Delta$

where $(\varkappa, \bar{\varkappa}) \in \{(\mathfrak{i}, \mathtt{o}), (\mathtt{o}, \mathfrak{i})\}$, $q_\varkappa, q'_\varkappa \in Q_\varkappa, q_{\bar{\varkappa}} \in Q_{\bar{\varkappa}}, a_\varkappa \in \Sigma_\varkappa$, $\mathtt{tst} \in \mathrm{Tst}_k$, $z \in \Gamma$, $\mathtt{asgn} \in \mathrm{Asgn}_k$ and $\mathtt{com} \in \mathrm{Com}(\Gamma \times [k])$.

Let $ID_\mathcal{A} = Q \times \Theta_k \times (\Gamma \times D)^*$. We define the transition relation $\vdash_\mathcal{A} \subseteq ID_\mathcal{A} \times ((\Sigma \cup \{\tau\}) \times D) \times ID_\mathcal{A}$ as $((q, \theta, u), (a, d), (q', \theta', u')) \in \vdash_\mathcal{A}$, written as $(q, \theta, u) \vdash_\mathcal{A}^{(a,d)} (q', \theta', u')$, iff there exists a rule $(p, a, \mathtt{tst}, z) \rightarrow (q, \mathtt{asgn}, \mathtt{com}) \in \delta$ such that $(\theta, d, snd(u(0))) \models \mathtt{tst}$, $\theta' = \theta[\mathtt{asgn} \leftarrow d]$, $z = fst(u(0))$ and $u' = \mathtt{upds}(u, \theta', \mathtt{com})$. For $s, s' \in ID_\mathcal{A}$ and $w \in ((\Sigma_{\mathfrak{i}} \times D) \cdot (\Sigma_{\mathtt{o}} \times D))^m$, we write $s \vdash^w s'$ if there exists $\rho \in ID_\mathcal{A}^{m+1}$ such that $\rho(0) = s, \rho(m) = s'$, and $\rho(0) \vdash^{w(0)} \cdots \vdash^{w(m-1)} \rho(m)$.

A run and the language $L(\mathcal{A})$ of k-DRPDA $\mathcal{A}$ are those of TS $\mathcal{S}_\mathcal{A} = (ID_\mathcal{A}, (q_0, \theta_\perp^k, (z_0, \perp)), \Sigma \times D, \{\tau\} \times D, \vdash_\mathcal{A}, c')$ where $c'((q, \theta, u)) = c(q)$ for all $(q, \theta, u) \in ID_\mathcal{A}$. We call $\mathcal{A}$ deterministic, or k-DRPDA, if $\mathcal{S}_\mathcal{A}$ is deterministic. We call $\mathcal{A}$ an (m, k)-NRPDA (or an (m, k)-DRPDA when $\mathcal{A}$ is deterministic) if $\mathcal{S}_\mathcal{A}$ is an m-TS. We abbreviate $(0, k)$-NRPDA $((0, k)$-DPDA) as k-NRPDA $(k$-DRPDA). Let **DRPDA** and **NRPDA** be the unions of k-DRPDA and k-NRPDA for all $k \in \mathbb{N}_0$, respectively.

For simplicity, we assume that the set of stack alphabet Γ is the singleton $\{z\}$. We abbreviate k-RPDT $\mathcal{T} = (P, p_0, z_0, \Delta)$ as $\mathcal{T} = (P, p_0, \Delta)$, the set of all IDs of k-RPDT $P \times \Theta_k \times (\Gamma \times D)^+$ as $P \times \Theta_k \times D^+$, the stack command $\mathrm{Com}(\Gamma \times [k])$ as $\mathrm{Com}([k])$, every rule $(p, a, \mathtt{tst}, z) \rightarrow (q, b, \mathtt{asgn}, j, \mathtt{com})$ of $\mathcal{T}$ as $(p, a, \mathtt{tst}) \rightarrow (q, b, \mathtt{asgn}, j, \mathtt{com}')$ where $\mathtt{com} \in \mathrm{Com}(\Gamma \times [k])$ and $\mathtt{com}' \in \mathrm{Com}([k])$ such that $\mathtt{com}' = \mathtt{com}$ if $\mathtt{com} = \mathtt{pop}$ or $\mathtt{skip}$ and $\mathtt{com}' = \mathtt{push}(j')$ if $\mathtt{com} = \mathtt{push}(z, j')$ for some $j' \in [k]$. except in the proof of Theorem 24. We apply a similar abbreviation to those of RPDA.

Example 18. Let us consider a 1-RPDT $\mathcal{T}_2 = (\{p\}, p, \Delta)$ over $\{a\}, \{b\}$ and $\{z\}$ where $\Delta = \{(p, a, \{1, \mathtt{top}\}) \rightarrow (p, b, \emptyset, 1, \mathtt{skip}), (p, a, \emptyset) \rightarrow (p, b, \{1\}, 1, \mathtt{push}(1))\}$. (See Fig. 2.) Let $\rho = (p, [\perp], \perp)(p, [d_1], d_1 \perp)(p, [d_1], d_1 \perp)(p, [d_2], d_2 d_1 \perp) \cdots$ where $[d] \in \Theta_1$ is the assignment such that $[d](1) = d$, and $w = (a, d_1)(b, d_1)(a, d_1)(b, d_1)(a, d_2)(b, d_2) \cdots$. Then (ρ, w) is a run of $\mathcal{T}_2$.

5.4   Visibly RPDA

Let $\mathrm{Com}_v = \{\mathrm{pop}, \mathrm{skip}, \mathrm{push}\}$ and $v : \mathrm{Com}([k]) \to \mathrm{Com}_v$ be the function such that $v(\mathrm{push}(j)) = \mathrm{push}$ for $j \in [k]$ and $v(\mathrm{com}) = \mathrm{com}$ otherwise. We say that a k-DRPDA $\mathcal{A}$ over $\Sigma_{\!\S}, \Sigma_{\!\circ}$ and Γ visibly manipulates its stack (or a *stack-visibly* RPDA) if there exists a function $\mathrm{vis} : \Sigma \to \mathrm{Com}_v$ such that every rule $(q, a, \mathrm{tst}) \to (q', \mathrm{asgn}, \mathrm{com})$ of $\mathcal{A}$ satisfies $\mathrm{vis}(a) = v(\mathrm{com})$. We also define a stack-visibly PDA in a similar way. Stack-visibility of RPDA will be used in the proof of Lemma 22 in order to take the intersection of the two DRPDA.

Also, we say that $\mathcal{A}$ is a *test-visibly* DRPDA if there exists a function $\mathrm{vis}_t : \Sigma \to \mathrm{Tst}_k$ such that every rule $(q, a, \mathrm{tst}) \to (q', \mathrm{asgn}, \mathrm{com})$ of $\mathcal{A}$ satisfies $\mathrm{vis}_t(a) = \mathrm{tst}$. In the next subsection, we prove that the projection of the language recognized by an NRPDA $\mathcal{A}$ onto the finite alphabets can be recognized by an NPDA $\mathcal{A}'$, and if $\mathcal{A}$ is a test-visibly DRPDA, $\mathcal{A}'$ is deterministic.

If $\mathcal{A}$ is a stack-visibly and test-visibly DRPDA, we call $\mathcal{A}$ a visibly DRPDA. Let **DRPDAv** be the union of visibly k-DRPDA for all $k \in \mathbb{N}_0$, respectively.

5.5   PDA Simulating RPDA

In this subsection, we show that we can construct an NPDA $\mathcal{A}'$ from a given k-NRPDA $\mathcal{A}$ over $\Sigma_{\!\S}$, $\Sigma_{\!\circ}$, Γ such that $\mathrm{Lab}(L(\mathcal{A})) = L(\mathcal{A}')$.

Let Φ_k be the set of *equivalence relations* over the set of $2k + 1$ symbols $X_k = \{\mathbf{x}_1, \mathbf{x}_2, \ldots, \mathbf{x}_k, \mathbf{x}'_1, \mathbf{x}'_2, \ldots, \mathbf{x}'_k, \mathbf{x}_{\mathrm{top}}\}$. We write $a \equiv_\phi b$ and $a \not\equiv_\phi b$ to mean $(a, b) \in \phi$ and $(a, b) \notin \phi$, respectively, for $a, b \in X_k$ and $\phi \in \Phi_k$. Intuitively, each $\phi \in \Phi_k$ represents the equality and inequality among the data values in the registers and the stack top, as well as the transfer of the values in the registers between two assignments. Two assignments θ, θ' and a value d at the stack top satisfy ϕ, denoted as $\theta, d, \theta' \models \phi$, if and only if for $i, j \in [k]$,

$$\mathbf{x}_i \equiv_\phi \mathbf{x}_j \Leftrightarrow \theta(i) = \theta(j), \qquad \mathbf{x}_i \equiv_\phi \mathbf{x}_{\mathrm{top}} \Leftrightarrow \theta(i) = d,$$
$$\mathbf{x}_i \equiv_\phi \mathbf{x}'_j \Leftrightarrow \theta(i) = \theta'(j), \qquad \mathbf{x}'_j \equiv_\phi \mathbf{x}_{\mathrm{top}} \Leftrightarrow \theta'(j) = d,$$
$$\mathbf{x}'_i \equiv_\phi \mathbf{x}'_j \Leftrightarrow \theta'(i) = \theta'(j).$$

Let $\phi_\perp \in \Phi_k$ be the equivalence relation satisfying $a \equiv_{\phi_\perp} b$ for any $a, b \in X_k$.

For $\mathrm{tst} \subseteq [k] \cup \{\mathrm{top}\}$ and $\mathrm{asgn} \subseteq [k]$, define a subset $\Phi_k^{\mathrm{tst}, \mathrm{asgn}}$ of Φ_k as:

$$\Phi_k^{\mathrm{tst}, \mathrm{asgn}} = \{\phi \in \Phi_k \mid (\forall i \in \mathrm{tst} : \forall j \in [k] \cup \{\mathrm{top}\} : j \in \mathrm{tst} \Leftrightarrow \mathbf{x}_i \equiv_\phi \mathbf{x}_j),$$
$$(\forall i \in \mathrm{asgn} : \forall j \in [k] \cup \{\mathrm{top}\} : j \in \mathrm{tst} \Leftrightarrow \mathbf{x}_j \equiv_\phi \mathbf{x}'_i),$$
$$(\forall i, j \in \mathrm{asgn} : \mathbf{x}'_i \equiv_\phi \mathbf{x}'_j), \ (\forall i \in [k] \setminus \mathrm{asgn} : \mathbf{x}_i \equiv_\phi \mathbf{x}'_i)\}.$$

For $j \in [k]$, define $\Phi_k^{=, j} = \{\phi \in \Phi_k \mid \mathbf{x}_{\mathrm{top}} \equiv_\phi \mathbf{x}_j, \forall i \in [k] : \mathbf{x}_i \equiv_\phi \mathbf{x}'_i\}$. By definition, $\theta, e, \theta' \models \phi$ for $\phi \in \Phi_k^{\mathrm{tst}, \mathrm{asgn}}$ iff $(\theta, d, e) \models \mathrm{tst}$ and $\theta' = \theta[\mathrm{asgn} \leftarrow d]$ for some $d \in D$. Similarly, $\theta, e, \theta' \models \phi$ for $\phi \in \Phi_k^{=, j}$ iff $\theta' = \theta$ and $\theta(j) = e$.

Let $\odot$ and $\odot_{\mathrm{T}}$ be binary predicates over Φ_k defined as:

$$\phi_1 \odot \phi_2 :\Leftrightarrow \left(\mathbf{x}'_i \equiv_{\phi_1} \mathbf{x}'_j \Leftrightarrow \mathbf{x}_i \equiv_{\phi_2} \mathbf{x}_j \text{ for } i, j \in [k]\right).$$
$$\phi_1 \odot_{\mathrm{T}} \phi_2 :\Leftrightarrow \left(\phi_1 \odot \phi_2 \text{ and } (\mathbf{x}'_i \equiv_{\phi_1} \mathbf{x}_{\mathrm{top}} \Leftrightarrow \mathbf{x}_i \equiv_{\phi_2} \mathbf{x}_{\mathrm{top}} \text{ for } i \in [k])\right).$$

Below we will define the *composition* of two equivalence relations, and $\phi_1 \odot \phi_2$ means that ϕ_1 and ϕ_2 are composable. For $\phi \in \Phi_k$ and $\Phi' \subseteq \Phi_k$, let $\phi \odot \Phi' = \{\phi' \in \Phi' \mid \phi \odot \phi'\}$ and $\phi \odot_{\mathsf{T}} \Phi' = \{\phi' \in \Phi' \mid \phi \odot_{\mathsf{T}} \phi'\}$. By definition, $\phi \odot_{\mathsf{T}} \Phi_k^{\mathsf{tst,asgn}}$ consists of at most one equivalence relation for any $\phi \in \Phi_k$, $\mathsf{tst} \subseteq [k] \cup \{\mathsf{top}\}$, and $\mathsf{asgn} \subseteq [k]$. Similarly, $\phi \odot \Phi_k^{=,j}$ consists of exactly one equivalence relation for any $\phi \in \Phi_k$ and $j \in [k]$.

For $\phi_1, \phi_2 \in \Phi_k$ with $\phi_1 \odot \phi_2$, the *composition* $\phi_1 \circ \phi_2$ of them is the equivalence relation in Φ_k that satisfies the followings:

$$\mathsf{x}_i \equiv_{\phi_1} \mathsf{x}_j \Leftrightarrow \mathsf{x}_i \equiv_{\phi_1 \circ \phi_2} \mathsf{x}_j \text{ for } i,j \in [k] \cup \{\mathsf{top}\},$$
$$\mathsf{x}'_i \equiv_{\phi_2} \mathsf{x}'_j \Leftrightarrow \mathsf{x}'_i \equiv_{\phi_1 \circ \phi_2} \mathsf{x}'_j \text{ for } i,j \in [k],$$
$$(\exists l \in [k] : \mathsf{x}_i \equiv_{\phi_1} \mathsf{x}'_l \wedge \mathsf{x}_l \equiv_{\phi_2} \mathsf{x}'_j) \Leftrightarrow \mathsf{x}_i \equiv_{\phi_1 \circ \phi_2} \mathsf{x}'_j \text{ for } i \in [k] \cup \{\mathsf{top}\},\ j \in [k].$$

By definition, $\circ$ is associative. We say that $\theta_1, d_1, \theta_2, \theta_3$ satisfy the *freshness* property if for every $i, j \in [k]$, $(\theta_1(i) \neq \theta_2(l) \text{ for all } l \in [k] \text{ implies } \theta_1(i) \neq \theta_3(j))$ and $(d_1 \neq \theta_2(l) \text{ for all } l \in [k] \text{ implies } d_1 \neq \theta_3(j))$. By definition, if $\theta_1, d_1, \theta_2 \models \phi_1$ and $\theta_2, d_2, \theta_3 \models \phi_2$ and $\theta_1, d_1, \theta_2, \theta_3$ satisfy the freshness property, then $\theta_1\, d_1, \theta_3 \models \phi_1 \circ \phi_2$. We extend the freshness property to a sequence $\theta_0, d_0, \theta_1, d_1, \ldots, d_{n-1}, \theta_n$. This sequence satisfies the freshness property if $\theta_i, d_i, \theta_l, \theta_j$ satisfy the property for every i, l, j such that $0 \leq i < l < j \leq n$.

Similarly, we define $\phi_1 \circ_{\mathsf{T}} \phi_2$ for $\phi_1, \phi_2 \in \Phi_k$ with $\phi_1 \odot_{\mathsf{T}} \phi_2$ as follows:

$$\mathsf{x}_i \equiv_{\phi_1} \mathsf{x}_j \Leftrightarrow \mathsf{x}_i \equiv_{\phi_1 \circ_{\mathsf{T}} \phi_2} \mathsf{x}_j \text{ for } i,j \in [k] \cup \{\mathsf{top}\},$$
$$\mathsf{x}'_i \equiv_{\phi_2} \mathsf{x}'_j \Leftrightarrow \mathsf{x}'_i \equiv_{\phi_1 \circ_{\mathsf{T}} \phi_2} \mathsf{x}'_j \text{ for } i,j \in [k],$$
$$\left((\exists l \in [k] : \mathsf{x}_i \equiv_{\phi_1} \mathsf{x}'_l \wedge \mathsf{x}_l \equiv_{\phi_2} \mathsf{x}'_j)\right.$$
$$\left. \vee (\mathsf{x}_i \equiv_{\phi_1} \mathsf{x}_{\mathsf{top}} \wedge \mathsf{x}_{\mathsf{top}} \equiv_{\phi_2} \mathsf{x}'_j)\right) \Leftrightarrow \mathsf{x}_i \equiv_{\phi_1 \circ_{\mathsf{T}} \phi_2} \mathsf{x}'_j \text{ for } i \in [k] \cup \{\mathsf{top}\},\ j \in [k].$$

2 By definition, $\circ_{\mathsf{T}}$ is associative.

Let $\mathcal{A} = (Q, Q_{\mathbb{i}}, Q_{\mathsf{o}}, q_0, \delta, c)$ be a k-NRPDA over $\Sigma_{\mathbb{i}}$, Σ_{o}, and Γ. As mentioned in Sect. 5.3, we assume that Γ is a singleton and use the simplified definition of δ for readability. Note that we can extend the following results to arbitrary Γ by replacing Φ_k used as the stack alphabet of the constructed PDA with $\Gamma \times \Phi_k$. From $\mathcal{A}$, we construct a PDA $\mathcal{A}' = (Q', Q'_{\mathbb{i}}, Q'_{\mathsf{o}}, q'_0, \phi_\perp, \delta', c')$ over $\Sigma_{\mathbb{i}}$, Σ_{o}, and Φ_k, where $Q' = Q \times \Phi_k$, $Q'_{\mathbb{i}} = Q_{\mathbb{i}} \times \Phi_k$, $Q'_{\mathsf{o}} = Q_{\mathsf{o}} \times \Phi_k$, $q'_0 = (q_0, \phi_\perp)$, $c'((q, \phi)) = c(q)$ for any $q \in Q$ and $\phi \in \Phi_k$, and for any $(q, \phi_2) \in Q'$, $a \in \Sigma \cup \{\tau\}$, and $\phi_1 \in \Phi_k$, $\delta'((q, \phi_2), a, \phi_1)$ is the smallest set satisfying the following inference rules:

$$\frac{\delta(q, a, \mathsf{tst}) \ni (q', \mathsf{asgn}, \mathsf{skip}),\ \phi_1 \odot \phi_2,\ \phi_3 \in \phi_2 \odot_{\mathsf{T}} \Phi_k^{\mathsf{tst,asgn}}}{\delta'((q, \phi_2), a, \phi_1) \ni ((q', \phi_2 \circ_{\mathsf{T}} \phi_3), \mathsf{skip})} \tag{1}$$

$$\frac{\delta(q, a, \mathsf{tst}) \ni (q', \mathsf{asgn}, \mathsf{pop}),\ \phi_1 \odot \phi_2,\ \phi_3 \in \phi_2 \odot_{\mathsf{T}} \Phi_k^{\mathsf{tst,asgn}}}{\delta'((q, \phi_2), a, \phi_1) \ni ((q', \phi_1 \circ (\phi_2 \circ_{\mathsf{T}} \phi_3)), \mathsf{pop})} \tag{2}$$

$$\frac{\delta(q, a, \mathsf{tst}) \ni (q', \mathsf{asgn}, \mathsf{push}(j)),\ \phi_1 \odot \phi_2,\ \phi_3 \in \phi_2 \odot_{\mathsf{T}} \Phi_k^{\mathsf{tst,asgn}},\ \phi_4 \in \phi_3 \odot \Phi_k^{=,j}}{\delta'((q, \phi_2), a, \phi_1) \ni ((q', \phi_4), \mathsf{push}(\phi_2 \circ_{\mathsf{T}} \phi_3))} \tag{3}$$

Note that if $\mathcal{A}$ is a test-visibly DRPDA, $\mathcal{A}'$ is deterministic. The number of equivalence relations in Φ_k equals the $(2k+1)$th Bell number and is $2^{O(k \log k)}$. When constructing δ', we choose arbitrary ϕ_1 and ϕ_2 for each transition rule of $\mathcal{A}$ in general, and thus the size of $\mathcal{A}'$ is exponential to the one of $\mathcal{A}$.

The main idea of this construction is as follows: $\mathcal{A}'$ simulates $\mathcal{A}$ without keeping data values in the stack. When pop is performed, $\mathcal{A}'$ must know whether or not the data value in the new stack top of $\mathcal{A}$ equals the *current* value of each register. For this purpose, $\mathcal{A}'$ keeps an abstract "history" of the register assignments in the stack, which tells whether each of the data values in the stack of $\mathcal{A}$ equals the current value of each register. The precise meanings of the stack of $\mathcal{A}'$ will become clear by considering the Lab-bisimulation relation shown in the proof of Lemma 19 below.

Let $\mathcal{S}_{\mathcal{A}'} = (ID_{\mathcal{A}'}, (q'_0, \phi_\perp), \Sigma, \{\tau\}, \vdash_{\mathcal{A}'}, c_{\mathcal{A}'})$ be the TS that represents the semantics of $\mathcal{A}'$. We define a TS $\mathcal{S}_{\mathcal{A}}^{\mathrm{aug}} = (ID_{\mathcal{A}}^{\mathrm{aug}}, (q_0, \theta_\perp, (\perp, \theta_\perp)), \Sigma \times D, \{\tau\} \times D, \vdash_{\mathcal{A}^{\mathrm{aug}}}, c_{\mathcal{A}})$ where $ID_{\mathcal{A}}^{\mathrm{aug}} = Q \times \Theta_k \times (D \times \Theta_k)^*$, $c_{\mathcal{A}}((q, \theta, u)) = c(q)$ for any $(q, \theta, u) \in ID_{\mathcal{A}}^{\mathrm{aug}}$, and $\vdash_{\mathcal{A}^{\mathrm{aug}}}$ is defined as follows: $(q, \theta, u) \vdash_{\mathcal{A}^{\mathrm{aug}}}^{(a,d)} (q', \theta', u')$ iff $\delta(q, a, \mathtt{tst}) \ni (q', \mathtt{asgn}, \mathtt{com})$, $(\theta, d, \mathit{fst}(u(0))) \models \mathtt{tst}$, $\theta' = \theta[\mathtt{asgn} \leftarrow d]$, and $u' = u(1:)$, u, or $(\theta'(j'), \theta')u$ if $\mathtt{com} = \mathtt{pop}$, $\mathtt{skip}$, or $\mathtt{push}(j')$, respectively. $\mathcal{S}_{\mathcal{A}}^{\mathrm{aug}}$ is essentially the same as the TS $\mathcal{S}_{\mathcal{A}}$ for $\mathcal{A}$, but $\mathcal{S}_{\mathcal{A}}^{\mathrm{aug}}$ "saves" the current register assignment in the stack when performing push. The saved assignments do not take part in transitions and thus the behavior of $\mathcal{S}_{\mathcal{A}}^{\mathrm{aug}}$ is the same as $\mathcal{S}_{\mathcal{A}}$. Additionally, we define the freshness property of $\mathcal{S}_{\mathcal{A}}^{\mathrm{aug}}$ as follows: A transition $(q, \theta, u) \vdash_{\mathcal{A}^{\mathrm{aug}}}^{(a,d)} (q', \theta', u')$ of $\mathcal{S}_{\mathcal{A}}^{\mathrm{aug}}$ by a rule $\delta(q, a, \mathtt{tst}) \ni (q', \mathtt{asgn}, \mathtt{com})$ with $\mathtt{tst} = \emptyset$ and $\mathtt{asgn} \neq \emptyset$ is allowed only when d does not appear in any saved assignment in u. Intuitively, this property means that when tst designates a data value not in the registers or the stack top, the RPDA chooses a *fresh* data value that has never been used before. We assume that $\mathcal{S}_{\mathcal{A}}^{\mathrm{aug}}$ satisfies the freshness property. This assumption guarantees that for every $(q, \theta_n, (d_{n-1}, \theta_{n-1}) \ldots (d_1, \theta_1)(d_0, \theta_0)) \in ID_{\mathcal{A}}^{\mathrm{aug}}$ reachable from the initial state of $\mathcal{S}_{\mathcal{A}}^{\mathrm{aug}}$, (i) the sequence $\theta_0, d_0, \theta_1, d_1, \ldots, d_{n-1}, \theta_n$ satisfies the freshness property; (ii) for $\theta' = \theta_n[\mathtt{asgn} \leftarrow d]$ where d is a data value chosen by the RPDA to satisfy $\theta_n, d, d_{n-1} \models \mathtt{tst}$, $\theta_{n-1}, d_{n-1}, \theta_n \models \phi_1$ and $\theta_n, d_{n-1}, \theta' \models \phi_2$ imply $\theta_{n-1}, d_{n-1}, \theta' \models \phi_1 \circ_\mathrm{T} \phi_2$.

Each equivalence relation in the stack of $\mathcal{A}'$ represents the relation among each data value in the stack and two adjacent saved assignments of $\mathcal{S}_{\mathcal{A}}^{\mathrm{aug}}$, which yields Lab-bisimilarity from $\mathcal{S}_{\mathcal{A}}^{\mathrm{aug}}$ to $\mathcal{S}_{\mathcal{A}'}$, as shown in the following lemma.

Lemma 19. *If $\mathcal{S}_{\mathcal{A}}^{\mathrm{aug}}$ satisfies the freshness property, then $\mathcal{S}_{\mathcal{A}}^{\mathrm{aug}}$ is Lab-bisimilar to $\mathcal{S}_{\mathcal{A}'}$.*

Proof sketch. Let $R \subseteq ID_{\mathcal{A}}^{\mathrm{aug}} \times ID_{\mathcal{A}'}$ be the relation that satisfies for every $q \in Q$, $u = (d_{n-1}, \theta_{n-1}) \ldots (d_1, \theta_1)(d_0, \theta_0) \in (D \times \Theta_k)^*$, and $v = \phi_{n-1} \ldots \phi_1 \phi_0 \in \Phi_k^*$, $((q, \theta_n, u), ((q, \phi_n), v)) \in R$ iff (q, θ_n, u) is reachable from the initial state of $\mathcal{S}_{\mathcal{A}}^{\mathrm{aug}}$, $\forall i \in [n] : \theta_{i-1}, d_{i-1}, \theta_i \models \phi_i$ and $\theta_\perp, \perp, \theta_0 \models \phi_0$. If $((q, \theta_n, u), ((q, \phi_n), v)) \in R$ and $(q, \theta_n, u) \vdash_{\mathcal{A}^{\mathrm{aug}}}^{(a,d)} (q', \theta', u')$, then by the definition of δ', $((q, \phi_n), v) \vdash_{\mathcal{A}'}^{a} ((q', \phi'), v')$ such that $((q', \theta', u'), ((q', \phi'), v')) \in R$. Conversely, if $((q, \theta_n, u),$

$((q, \phi_n), v)) \in R$ and $((q, \phi_n), v) \vdash^a_{\mathcal{A}'} ((q', \phi'), v')$, then by the definition of δ', there must be a transition of $\mathcal{A}$ that enables $(q, \theta_n, u) \vdash^{(a,d)}_{\mathcal{A}^{aug}} (q', \theta', u')$ such that $((q', \theta', u'), ((q', \phi'), v')) \in R$. Therefore, R is a Lab-bisimulation relation from $\mathcal{S}^{aug}_{\mathcal{A}}$ to $\mathcal{S}_{\mathcal{A}'}$.

By Lemmas 2 and 19, we obtain the following theorem.

Theorem 20. *For a given (m, k)-NRPDA (resp. test-visibly (m, k)-DRPDA) $\mathcal{A}$, we can construct an m-NPDA (resp. m-DPDA) $\mathcal{A}'$ such that $\mathtt{Lab}(L(\mathcal{A})) = L(\mathcal{A}')$, if we assume the freshness property on the semantics of $\mathcal{A}$.*

6 Realizability Problems for RPDA and RPDT

6.1 Finite Actions

In [19], the abstraction of the behavior of k-register transducer (k-RT), called finite actions, was introduced to reduce the realizability problem for register automata (RA) and RT to the problem on finite alphabets. We extend the idea of [19] and define the finite actions of k-RPDT.

For $k \in \mathbb{N}_0$, we define the set of finite input actions as $A^{\S}_k = \Sigma_{\S} \times \mathtt{Tst}_k$ and the set of finite output actions as $A^{\circ}_k = \Sigma_{\circ} \times \mathtt{Asgn}_k \times [k] \times \mathtt{Com}([k])$. Note that $\mathtt{Com}([k])$ appearing in the definition of A°_k is not the abbreviation of $\mathtt{Com}(\Gamma \times [k])$. Finite actions have no information on finite stack alphabet Γ even if Γ is not a singleton. A sequence $w = (a^{\S}_0, d^{\S}_0)(a^{\circ}_0, d^{\circ}_0) \cdots \in \mathtt{DW}(\Sigma_{\S}, \Sigma_{\circ}, D)$ is *compatible* with a sequence $\overline{a} = (a^{\S}_0, \mathtt{tst}_0)(a^{\circ}_0, \mathtt{asgn}_0, j_0, \mathtt{com}_0) \cdots \in (A^{\S}_k \cdot A^{\circ}_k)^{\omega}$ iff there exists a sequence $(\theta_0, u_0)(\theta_1, u_1) \cdots \in (\Theta_k \times D^*)^{\omega}$, called a *witness*, such that $\theta_0 = \theta^k_{\perp}$, $u_0 = \perp$, $(\theta_i, d^{\S}_i, u_i(0)) \models \mathtt{tst}_i$, $\theta_{i+1} = \theta_i[\mathtt{asgn}_i \leftarrow d^{\S}_i]$, $\theta_{i+1}(j_i) = d^{\circ}_i$ and $u_{i+1} = \mathtt{upds}(u_i, \theta_{i+1}, \mathtt{com}_i)$. Let $\mathtt{Comp}(\overline{a}) = \{w \in \mathtt{DW}(\Sigma_{\S}, \Sigma_{\circ}, D) \mid w$ is compatible with $\overline{a}\}$. For a specification $S \subseteq \mathtt{DW}(\Sigma_{\S}, \Sigma_{\circ}, D)$, we define $W_{S,k} = \{\overline{a} \mid \mathtt{Comp}(\overline{a}) \subseteq S\}$.

For a data word $w \in \mathtt{DW}(\Sigma_{\S}, \Sigma_{\circ}, D)$ and a sequence $\overline{a} \in (A^{\S}_k \cdot A^{\circ}_k)^{\omega}$ such that for each $i \geq 0$, there exists $a \in \Sigma$ and we can write $w(i) = (a, d)$ and $\overline{a}(i) = (a, \mathtt{tst})$ if i is even and $\overline{a}(i) = (a, \mathtt{asgn}, j, \mathtt{com})$ if i is odd, we define $w \otimes \overline{a} \in \mathtt{DW}(A^{\S}_k, A^{\circ}_k, D)$ as $w \otimes \overline{a}(i) = (\overline{a}(i), d)$ where $w(i) = (a, d)$.

6.2 Decidability and Undecidability of Realizability Problems

Lemma 21. $L_k = \{w \otimes \overline{a} \mid w \in \mathtt{Comp}(\overline{a})\}$ *is definable as the language of a* $(2, k + 2)$-DRPDA.

Proof sketch. Let $(2, k+2)$-DRPDA $\mathcal{A}_1 = (Q_1, Q^{\S}_1, Q^{\circ}_1, p, \delta_1, c_1)$ over $A^{\S}_k, A^{\circ}_k$ and Γ where $Q_1 = \{p, q\} \cup (\mathtt{Asgn}_k \times [k] \times \mathtt{Com}([k])) \cup [k]$, $Q^{\S}_1 = \{p\}$, $Q^{\circ}_1 = Q_1 \setminus Q^{\S}_1$, $c_1(s) = 2$ for every $s \in Q$ and δ_1 consists of all the rules of the form

$$(p, (a_{\S}, \mathtt{tst}), \mathtt{tst} \cup \mathtt{tst}') \rightarrow (q, \{k+1\}, \mathtt{skip}) \tag{4}$$

$$(q, (a_{\circ}, \mathtt{asgn}, j, \mathtt{com}), \mathtt{tst}'') \rightarrow ((\mathtt{asgn}, j, \mathtt{com}), \{k+2\}, \mathtt{skip}) \tag{5}$$

$$((\mathtt{asgn}, j, \mathtt{com}), \tau, \{k+1\} \cup \mathtt{tst}'') \rightarrow (j, \mathtt{asgn}, \mathtt{com}) \tag{6}$$

$$(j, \tau, \{j, k+2\} \cup \mathtt{tst}'') \rightarrow (p, \emptyset, \mathtt{skip}) \tag{7}$$

for $(a_\S, \mathtt{tst}) \in A_k^\S$, $(a_\circ, \mathtt{asgn}, j, \mathtt{com}) \in A_k^\circ$, $\mathtt{tst}' \subseteq \{k+1, k+2\}$ and $\mathtt{tst}'' \in \mathtt{Tst}_{k+2}$. As in Fig. 3, $\mathcal{A}_1$ checks whether an input sequence satisfies the conditions of compatibility by nondeterministically generating a candidate of a witness of the compatibility step by step.

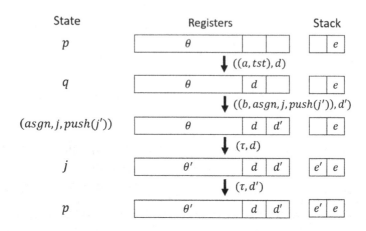

Fig. 3. An example of transitions of $\mathcal{A}_k$.

Lemma 22. *For a specification S defined by some visibly k'-DRPDA, $L_{\overline{S},k} = \{w \otimes \overline{a} \mid w \in \mathtt{Comp}(\overline{a}) \cap \overline{S}\}$ is definable as the language of a $(4, k+k'+4)$-DRPDA.*

Proof sketch. Let $L_{\overline{S}} = \{w \otimes \overline{a} \mid w \in \overline{S}, \overline{a} \in (A_k^\S \cdot A_k^\circ)^\omega\}$. Because the class of languages defined by visibly DRPDA is closed under the complement, we can construct a visibly k'-DRPDA $\mathcal{A}_2 = (Q_2, Q_2^\S, Q_2^\circ, q_2^0, \delta_2, c_2)$ over $A_k^\S, A_k^\circ$ and Γ such that $L(\mathcal{A}_2) = L_{\overline{S}}$. Let $\mathcal{A}_1$ be the $(2, k+2)$-DRPDA such that $L(\mathcal{A}_1) = L_k$, which is given in Lemma 21. Because $L_{\overline{S},k} = L_{\overline{S}} \cap L_k$, we will construct a $(4, k+k'+4)$-DRPDA $\mathcal{A}$ over $A_k^\S, A_k^\circ$ and Γ such that $L(\mathcal{A}) = L(\mathcal{A}_1) \cap L(\mathcal{A}_2)$. We use the properties of $\mathcal{A}_1$ that $c_1(q)$ is even for every $q \in Q_1$ and δ_1 consists of several groups of three consecutive rules having the following forms:

$$(q_1, a, \mathtt{tst}_1) \to (q_2, \mathtt{asgn}_1, \mathtt{skip}) \tag{5'}$$

$$(q_2, \tau, \mathtt{tst}_2) \to (q_3, \mathtt{asgn}_2, \mathtt{com}_1) \tag{6'}$$

$$(q_3, \tau, \mathtt{tst}_3) \to (q_4, \mathtt{asgn}_3, \mathtt{skip}). \tag{7'}$$

Note that $\mathtt{vis}(a) = v(\mathtt{com}_1)$ always holds for such three consecutive rules. (5'), (6') and (7') correspond to (5), (6) and (7), respectively, and (4) is also converted to three consecutive rules like (5')–(7') by adding dummy τ rules.

We let $k_1 = k+2$ and $k_2 = k'$. We construct $(4, k_1 + k_2 + 2)$-DRPDA $\mathcal{A} = (Q_\S \cup Q_\circ \cup \{q_0\}, Q_\S \cup \{q_0\}, Q_\circ, q_0, \delta, c)$ where $Q_\S = Q_1^\S \times Q_2^\S \times [5]$, $Q_\circ = Q_1^\circ \times Q_2^\circ \times [5]$. c is defined as $c(q_0) = 1$ and $c((q_1, q_2, i)) = c_2(q_2)$ for all $(q_1, q_2, i) \in Q$. δ has a τ rule $(q_0, \tau, [k] \cup \{\mathtt{top}\}) \to ((p, q_0^2, 1), \mathtt{push}(1))$. For all rules (5'), (6'), (7') in δ_1

and $(q, a, \mathtt{tst}) \rightarrow (q', \mathtt{asgn}, \mathtt{com}) \in \delta_2$ (8) such that $v(\mathtt{com}_1) = v(\mathtt{com}) (= \mathtt{vis}(a))$ for $a \in A_k^{\mathtt{i}} \cup A_k^{\mathtt{o}}$, we construct the rules in δ that can do the transitions as in Fig. 4. The figure illustrates an example of transitions of $\mathcal{A}$ from $(q_1, q, 1)$ to $(q_4, q', 1)$ with updating contents of its registers and stack. The first to k_1-th registers simulate the registers of $\mathcal{A}_1$, (k_1+1)-th to (k_1+k_2)-th registers simulate the registers of $\mathcal{A}_2$ and $(k_1 + k_2 + 1)$-th and $(k_1 + k_2 + 2)$-th registers are for keeping the first and second stack top contents, respectively. The stack contents of $\mathcal{A}$ simulates those of $\mathcal{A}_1$ and $\mathcal{A}_2$ by restoring the contents of stacks of $\mathcal{A}_1$ and $\mathcal{A}_2$ alternately. The transition rules from $(q_1, q, 1)$ to $(q_1, q, 3)$ are for moving the two data values at the stack top to $(k_1 + k_2 + 1)$-th and $(k_1 + k_2 + 2)$-th registers. The transition rule from $(q_1, q, 3)$ to $(q_2, q', 4)$ is for updating states, registers and stacks by simulating the rules (5') and (8) The transition rules from $(q_2, q', 4)$ to $(q_4, q', 1)$ simulate the rules (6') and (7'), respectively. We can show $L(\mathcal{A}) = L(\mathcal{A}_1) \cap L(\mathcal{A}_2)$ by checking the simulation in Fig. 4 is correct.

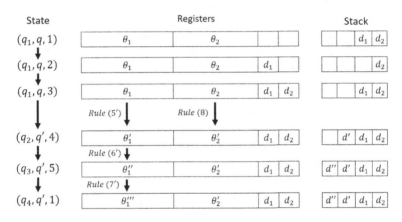

Fig. 4. An example of transitions of $\mathcal{A}$ with $\mathtt{vis}(a) = \mathtt{push}$.

Lemma 23. $W_{S,k} = \overline{\mathrm{Lab}(L_{\overline{S},k})}$.

Proof. For every $\bar{a} \in (A_k^{\mathtt{i}} A_k^{\mathtt{o}})^{\omega}$, $\bar{a} \notin W_{S,k} \Leftrightarrow \mathrm{Comp}(\bar{a}) \not\subseteq S \Leftrightarrow \exists w.w \in \mathrm{Comp}(\bar{a}) \cap \overline{S} \Leftrightarrow \exists w.w \otimes \bar{a} \in L_{\overline{S},k} \Leftrightarrow \bar{a} \in \mathrm{Lab}(L_{\overline{S},k})$. Thus, $W_{S,k} = \overline{\mathrm{Lab}(L_{\overline{S},k})}$ holds.

Theorem 24. For all $k \geq 0$, REAL(**DRPDAv**, **RPDT**$[k]$) is in 2EXPTIME.

Proof. By Lemma 22 and Theorem 20, $W_{S,k}$ is definable by a 4-DPDA $\mathcal{A}_f$. By Lemma 7, we can construct a 0-DPDA $\mathcal{A}'_f$ where $L(\mathcal{A}'_f) = L(\mathcal{A}_f)$. By the construction of $\mathcal{A}$ in Lemma 22, the stack height of the current ID increases by two during the transitions from $(q_1, q, 1)$ to $(q_4, q', 1)$ in Fig. 4 if $\mathtt{vis}(a) = \mathtt{push}$, does not change if $\mathtt{vis}(a) = \mathtt{skip}$ and decreases by two if $\mathtt{vis}(a) = \mathtt{pop}$. Thus, $\mathcal{A}'_f$ is a stack-visibly DPDA, that is, every transition rule $(p, a, z) \rightarrow (q, \mathtt{com})$ of $\mathcal{A}'_f$ satisfies $\mathtt{vis}(a) = v(\mathtt{com})$. We show the following two conditions are equivalent.

- There exists a k-RPDT $\mathcal{T}$ such that $L(\mathcal{T}) \subseteq S$.
- There exists a PDT $\mathcal{T}'$ such that $L(\mathcal{T}') \subseteq W_{S,k}$.

Assume that a k-RPDT $\mathcal{T}$ over $\Sigma_{\S}, \Sigma_{\odot}$ and Γ satisfies $L(\mathcal{T}) \subseteq S$. Then, consider the PDT $\mathcal{T}'$ over $A_k^{\S}, A_k^{\odot}$ and Γ such that $(q, (a, \mathtt{tst}), z) \to (q', (b, \mathtt{asgn}, j, \mathtt{com}), \mathtt{com}')$ is a rule of $\mathcal{T}'$ iff $(q, a, \mathtt{tst}, z) \to (q', b, \mathtt{asgn}, j, \mathtt{com})$ is a rule of $\mathcal{T}$ where $\mathtt{com}' = \mathtt{com}$ if $v(\mathtt{com}) = \mathtt{pop}$ or $\mathtt{skip}$ and $\mathtt{com}' = \mathtt{push}(z')$ if $\mathtt{com} = \mathtt{push}(z', j')$ for some $j' \in [k]$. For $\overline{a} \in L(\mathcal{T}')$, every $w \in \mathrm{Comp}(\overline{a})$ has a witness (see Sect. 6.1) and thus $w \in L(\mathcal{T})$ holds. By the assumption $L(\mathcal{T}) \subseteq S$, $\mathrm{Comp}(\overline{a}) \subseteq S$ holds and thus $\overline{a} \in W_{S,k}$. Hence, we obtain $L(\mathcal{T}') \subseteq W_{S,k}$.

Conversely, assume there exists a PDT $\mathcal{T}'$ over $A_k^{\S}, A_k^{\odot}$ and Γ that satisfies $L(\mathcal{T}') \subseteq W_{S,k}$. We can in particular construct a PDT $\mathcal{T}''$ such that $L(\mathcal{T}'') \subseteq W_{S,k}$ and every rule $(q, (a, \mathtt{tst}), z) \to (q', (b, \mathtt{asgn}, j, \mathtt{com}), \mathtt{com}')$ satisfies $\mathtt{vis}(b) = v(\mathtt{com}')$ (note that $\mathtt{vis}(a) = \mathtt{skip}$ always holds) by the construction algorithm in [36]. In the rule, $v(\mathtt{com}) = v(\mathtt{com}')$ holds because $\mathcal{A}_f'$ is a stack-visibly PDA and thus $\mathtt{vis}(b) = v(\mathtt{com})$ holds. Consider the k-RPDT $\mathcal{T}$ over $\Sigma_{\S}, \Sigma_{\odot}$ and Γ such that $(q, a, \mathtt{tst}, z) \to (q', b, \mathtt{asgn}, j, \mathtt{com}'')$ is a rule of $\mathcal{T}$ iff $(q, (a, \mathtt{tst}), z) \to (q', (b, \mathtt{asgn}, j, \mathtt{com}), \mathtt{com}')$ is a rule of $\mathcal{T}''$ where $\mathtt{com}'' = \mathtt{com}'$ if $\mathtt{com}' = \mathtt{pop}$ or $\mathtt{skip}$ and $\mathtt{com}'' = \mathtt{push}(z', j')$ if $\mathtt{com}' = \mathtt{push}(z')$ and $\mathtt{com} = \mathtt{push}(j')$. Further, assume $w \in L(\mathcal{T})$, and let $\overline{a} \in (A_k^{\S} \cdot A_k^{\odot})^\omega$ be the sequence with which w is compatible. Then, by the definition of $\mathcal{T}$, $\overline{a} \in L(\mathcal{T}'')$. By the assumption $L(\mathcal{T}'') \subseteq W_{S,k}$, every $\overline{a} \in L(\mathcal{T}'')$ satisfies $\mathrm{Comp}(\overline{a}) \subseteq S$, and thus $w \in S$ holds. Hence, we obtain $L(\mathcal{T}) \subseteq S$.

By the equivalence, we can check REAL(**DPDA**, **PDT**) for $\mathcal{A}_f'$, which is shown to be EXPTIME in Theorem 14, instead of checking REAL(**DRPDAv**, **RPDT**[k]). Because the size of $\mathcal{A}_f'$ is exponential to $k + k'$, REAL(**DRPDAv**, **RPDT**[k]) is in 2EXPTIME.

Theorem 25. *For all $k \geq 0$, REAL(**NRPDA**, **RPDT**[k]) is undecidable.*

Proof. We can easily reduce the REAL(**NPDA**, **PDT**), whose undecidability is proved in Theorem 15, to this problem.

7   Conclusion

We have discussed the realizability problem whose specification and implementation are DPDA (NPDA) and PDT in Sect. 4. By using the result in [36], we show REAL(**DPDA,PDT**) is in EXPTIME. We also show the undecidability of REAL(**NPDA,PDT**) by a reduction from the universality problem of NPDA. In Sect. 5, we have defined RPDT, RPDA and shown a way to recognize the label of the language of RPDA by PDA. We have introduced the notions of stack-visibly [1] and test-visibly to discuss the decidability of realizability for RPDA and RPDT. We show that the behavior of registers and stack of RPDT can be simulated by the finite alphabets defined as finite actions, and prove that REAL(**DRPDAv,RPDT**[k]) can be reduced to REAL(**DPDA,PDT**) and is in 2EXPTIME.

It is still unknown whether the realizability problem is decidable in several cases such as a specification is given by a universal PDA, DRPDA has no restriction on visibility and the number of registers of RPDT is not given. Investigating these cases are future work.

References

1. Alur, R., Madhusudan, P.: Visibly pushdown languages. In: 36th ACM Symposium Theory of Computing (STOC 2004) (2004)
2. Bloem, R., Chatterjee, K., Jobstmann, B.: Graph games and reactive synthesis. In: Clarke, E., Henzinger, T., Veith, H., Bloem, R. (eds.) Handbook of Model Checking, pp. 921–962. Springer, Cham (2018). https://doi.org/10.1007/978-3-319-10575-8_27
3. Bojańczyk, M., David, C., Muscholl, A., Schwentick, T., Segoufin, L.: Two-variable logic on data words. ACM Trans. Comput. Logic **12**(4) (2011)
4. Bojańczyk, M., Klin, B., Lasota, S.: Automata theory in nominal sets. Logical Methods Comput. Sci. **10**(3:4), 1–44 (2014)
5. Bollig, B., Cyriac, A., Gastin, P., Narayan Kumar, K.: Model checking languages of data words. In: Birkedal, L. (ed.) FoSSaCS 2012. LNCS, vol. 7213, pp. 391–405. Springer, Heidelberg (2012). https://doi.org/10.1007/978-3-642-28729-9_26
6. Bouajjani, A., Esparza, J., Maler, O.: Reachability analysis of pushdown automata: application to model-checking. In: Mazurkiewicz, A., Winkowski, J. (eds.) CONCUR 1997. LNCS, vol. 1243, pp. 135–150. Springer, Heidelberg (1997). https://doi.org/10.1007/3-540-63141-0_10
7. Bouyer, P.: A logical characterization of data languages. Inform. Process. Lett. **84**(2), 75–85 (2002)
8. Büchi, J.R., Landweber, L.H.: Solving sequential conditions by finite-state strategies. Trans. Am. Math. Soc. **138**, 295–311 (1969)
9. Chen, Y.-F., Lengál, O., Tan, T., Wu, Z.: Register automata with linear arithmetic. In: 32nd Annual ACM/IEEE Symposium on Logic in Computer Science (LICS 2017) (2017)
10. Cheng, E.Y.C., Kaminski, M.: Context-free languages over infinite alphabets. Acta Informatica **35**, 245–267 (1998)
11. Clarke, E.M., Grumberg, O., Peled, D.A.: Model Checking. MIT Press, Cambridge (2001)
12. Clemente, L., Lasota, S.: Reachability analysis of first-order definable pushdown systems. In: 24th EACSL Annual Conference on Computer Science Logic (CSL 2015), pp. 244–259 (2015)
13. D'Antoni, L., Ferreira, T., Sammartino, M., Silva, A.: Symbolic register automata. In: Dillig, I., Tasiran, S. (eds.) CAV 2019. LNCS, vol. 11561, pp. 3–21. Springer, Cham (2019). https://doi.org/10.1007/978-3-030-25540-4_1
14. Demri, S., Lazić, R.: LTL with freeze quantifier and register automata. ACM Trans. Comput. Logic **10**(3) (2009)
15. Demri, S., Lazić, R., Nowak, D.: On the freeze quantifier in constraint LTL: decidability and complexity. Inform. Comput. **205**(1), 2–24 (2007)
16. Ehlers, R., Seshia, S.A., Kress-Gazit, H.: Synthesis with identifiers. In: McMillan, K.L., Rival, X. (eds.) VMCAI 2014. LNCS, vol. 8318, pp. 415–433. Springer, Heidelberg (2014). https://doi.org/10.1007/978-3-642-54013-4_23

17. Esparza, J., Hansel, D., Rossmanith, P., Schwoon, S.: Efficient algorithms for model checking pushdown systems. In: Emerson, E.A., Sistla, A.P. (eds.) CAV 2000. LNCS, vol. 1855, pp. 232–247. Springer, Heidelberg (2000). https://doi.org/10.1007/10722167_20

18. Esparza, J., Kučera, A., Schwoon, S.: Model checking LTL with regular valuations for pushdown systems. Inform. Comput. **186**(2), 355–376 (2003)

19. Exibard, L., Filiot, E., Reynier, P.-A.: Synthesis of data word transducers. In: 30th International Conference on Concurrency Theory (CONCUR 2019) (2019)

20. Greibach, S.A.: A note on pushdown store automata and regular systems. Proc. Am. Math. Soc. **18**, 263–268 (1967)

21. Kaminski, M., Francez, N.: Finite-memory automata. Theor. Comput. Sci. **134**, 322–363 (1994)

22. Khalimov, A., Kupferman, O.: Register-bounded synthesis. In: 30th International Conference on Concurrency Theory (CONCUR 2019) (2019)

23. Khalimov, A., Maderbacher, B., Bloem, R.: Bounded synthesis of register transducers. In: Lahiri, S.K., Wang, C. (eds.) ATVA 2018. LNCS, vol. 11138, pp. 494–510. Springer, Cham (2018). https://doi.org/10.1007/978-3-030-01090-4_29

24. Libkin, L., Tan, T., Vrgoč, D.: Regular expressions for data words. J. Comput. Syst. Sci. **81**(7), 1278–1297 (2015)

25. Libkin, L., Vrgoč, D.: Regular path queries on graphs with data. In: 15th International Conference on Database Theory (ICDT 2012), pp. 74–85 (2012)

26. Murawski, A.S., Ramsay, S.J., Tzevelekos, N.: Reachability in pushdown register automata. J. Comput. Syst. Sci. **87**, 58–83 (2017)

27. Neven, F., Schwentick, T., Vianu, V.: Finite state machines for strings over infinite alphabets. ACM Trans. Comput. Logic **5**(3), 403–435 (2004)

28. Pnueli, A., Rosner, R.: On the synthesis of a reactive module. In: 16th ACM Symposium on Principles of Programming Languages (POPL 1989), pp. 179–190 (1989)

29. Rot, J., de Boer, F., Bonsangue, M.: Pushdown system representation for unbounded object creation, Technical report KIT-13, Karlsruhe Institute of Technology, pp. 38–52 (2010)

30. Segoufin, L.: Automata and logics for words and trees over an infinite alphabet. In: Ésik, Z. (ed.) CSL 2006. LNCS, vol. 4207, pp. 41–57. Springer, Heidelberg (2006). https://doi.org/10.1007/11874683_3

31. Senda, R., Takata, Y., Seki, H.: Complexity results on register context-free grammars and register tree automata. In: Fischer, B., Uustalu, T. (eds.) ICTAC 2018. LNCS, vol. 11187, pp. 415–434. Springer, Cham (2018). https://doi.org/10.1007/978-3-030-02508-3_22

32. Senda, R., Takata, Y., Seki, H.: Generalized register context-free grammars. In: 13th International Conference on Language and Automata Theory and Applications (LATA 2019), pp. 259–271 (2019). Revised version: IEICE Trans. Inf. Syst. **E103-D**(3), 540–548 (2020)

33. Senda, R., Takata, Y., Seki, H.: Forward regularity preservation property of register pushdown systems. IEICE Trans. Inf. Syst. **E104-D**(3), 370–380 (2021)

34. Song, F., Touili, T.: Pushdown model checking for malware detection. TACAS 2012. Extended version. Int. J. Softw. Tools. Tehchnol. Transfer **16**, 147–173 (2014)

35. Tzevelekos, N.: Fresh-register automata. In: 36th ACM Annual Symposium on Principles of Programming Languages (POPL 2009), pp. 295–306 (2009)

36. Walukiewicz, I.: Pushdown processes: games and model-checking. In: 8th International Conference on Computer Aided Verification (CAV 1996), pp. 62–74 (1996). Revised version: Inform. Comput. **164**, 234–263 (2001)

37. Cai, X., Ogawa, M.: Well-structured pushdown systems. In: D'Argenio, P.R., Melgratti, H. (eds.) CONCUR 2013. LNCS, vol. 8052, pp. 121–136. Springer, Heidelberg (2013). https://doi.org/10.1007/978-3-642-40184-8_10

Systems Calculi and Analysis

COMPLEXITYPARSER: An Automatic Tool for Certifying Poly-Time Complexity of Java Programs

Emmanuel Hainry[(✉)], Emmanuel Jeandel, Romain Péchoux, and Olivier Zeyen

Project Mocqua, CNRS, Inria, LORIA, Université de Lorraine, Nancy, France
`Emmanuel.Hainry@loria.fr`

Abstract. COMPLEXITYPARSER is a static complexity analyzer for Java programs providing the first implementation of a tier-based typing discipline. The input is a file containing Java classes. If the main method can be typed and, provided the program terminates, then the program is guaranteed to do so in polynomial time and hence also to have heap and stack sizes polynomially bounded. The application uses ANTLR to generate a parse tree on which it performs an efficient type inference: linear in the input size, provided that the method arity is bounded by some constant.

1 Introduction

Motivations. The use of tiering techniques to certify program complexity was kick-started by the seminal works of Bellantoni-Cook [4] and Leivant-Marion [22], that provide sound and complete characterizations of the class of functions computable in polynomial time FP. Tiering was later adapted to several other complexity classes such as FPSPACE [23], NC [8,21,28], or L [28].

Despite these numerous theoretical results, tiering, until now, had no practical application in automatic complexity analysis because of a lack of expressive power. Indeed, the tiering discipline severely constrains the way first order functional programs can be written. This problem has been solved by the cornerstone work of [25] that has exhibited and studied the relations between tiering and non-interference on imperative programs. It has been extended to fork processes [13], object-oriented programs [14,15,24], and type-2 polynomial time [12], hence showing its portability and paving the way for practical implementations.

The core idea is the design of a type discipline ensuring polynomial time termination. The type system, inspired by non-interference, splits program variables, expressions, and statements in two disjoint *tiers*, denoted **0** and **1**, and enforces constraints on the data flow, the control flow and sizes:

- *Data flow.* Data flows from tier **0** to tier **1** are prohibited, *e.g.* if x is of tier **0** and y is of tier **1** then the statement y = x; cannot be typed, and data flows from tier **1** to tier **0** are prevented for non-primitive data. It forbids tier **1** data from increasing by side effects.

A. Cerone and P. C. Ölveczky (Eds.): ICTAC 2021, LNCS 12819, pp. 357–365, 2021.
https://doi.org/10.1007/978-3-030-85315-0_20

- *Control flow.* Loop control flows depending on tier **0** data are forbidden. *I.e.* in a while(e){c} statement, the expression e is enforced to be of tier **1**. This implies that all the variables of e are of tier **1**.
- *Size control.* Tier **1** data cannot make the memory size increase, *e.g.* if x is of tier **1** then x = x-1; is typable but x = x+1; and x = new C(x); are not typable.

Theorem 1 ([15]). *If a program is typable and terminates on input d then its runtime, heap space, and stack space are polynomially bounded in the size of d.*

Contribution. This paper describes the architecture of COMPLEXITYPARSER, a tier-based automatic cost analyzer for Java programs implementing the type system of [14,15] in Java, built using Maven, and whose source code is fully available at https://gitlab.inria.fr/hainry/complexityparser. The application receives as input a text file program and infers a type (called tier) as output. If the type inference succeeds and the analyzed program terminates then: the program is certified to have a worst case execution time bounded polynomially, by Theorem 1. Even in case the full program cannot be typed, the success of typing some methods will be indicated, giving a complexity certificate for those methods provided they terminate.

COMPLEXITYPARSER is, to our knowledge, the first implementation of a tier-based technique to a realistic programming language: the analysis can deal with an expressive fragment of Java programs with while loops, recursive methods, exception handlers, and inheritance (including overriding methods) and allowing the programmer to define inductive and cyclic data (List and Ring for example). This application is, with RAJA [18,19] and RaML [17], one of the first practical type-based approaches for certifying program complexity. It provides the first implementation of a complete technique with respect to polynomial time. Its code is open source (Apache 2.0 license), and its performance is good: the type analysis is linear in the size of the input program in practice. Moreover, it is fully automatic as types (tiers) are inferred and do not need to be explicitly provided by the programmer.

The implemented analyses [14,15,25] are complete for the class of polynomial time computable functions, *i.e.* capture all functions. However they can yield false negatives, *i.e.* programs running in polynomial time that cannot pass the type inference, which cannot be avoided as the problem of knowing if a program computes a polytime function is not decidable [16].

Related Works. We know of few alternative tools studying the complexity of Object Oriented programs.

- APROVE [9], initially a termination tool, was expanded to treat complexity by translating constraints into integer constraints, then using an external integer programming solver. APROVE works on Java bytecode and supports most features of the language except recursion. It outputs $O(n^k)$ bounds.

- COSTA [1,2] infers symbolic costs upper bounds on Java bytecode by generating recurrence equations relatively to a chosen cost measure and then by finding an upper bound on a solution to these equations. The upper bounds it computes are combinations of polynomials and logarithms.
- RAJA [19] automatically computes linear bounds on the heap space used by a Featherweight Java program. It translates the memory constraints into graphs and solves linear cases. Exceptions, overloading and variable shadowing are also not treated. Note that this tool captures LinSpace.
- SPEED [10,11] infers symbolic complexity bounds on the number of statements executed by a C++ program. It relies on integer counters inserted in the program by the programmer. As such, it is not fully automatic and does not treat objects as first class citizens.
- TcT [3,27] is a generic complexity tool which, for what interests us analyzes Jinja bytecode. It translates code into term rewriting systems for which it uses integer programming techniques. Jinja bytecode does not support recursion and cyclic data but otherwise has all language features we checked.

A summary of the above tools' features is presented in the following table. For each tool, we check language features support (recursion, exceptions, inheritance, cyclic data), whether it gives explicit bounds, whether it works on a High-Level language (HLL) or on bytecode, and last if it is fully automatic.

Tool	Recursion	Exceptions	Inheritance	Cyclic	Bounds	HLL	Auto
COMPLEXITYPARSER	Yes	Yes	Yes	Yes	No	Yes	Yes
AProVE	No	Yes	Yes	Yes	Yes	No	Yes
COSTA	Yes	Yes	Yes	No	Yes	No	Yes
RAJA	Yes	No	Partial	Yes	Yes	Yes	Yes
SPEED	Yes	No	No	No	Yes	Yes	No
TcT	No	Yes	Yes	No	Yes	No	Yes

2   COMPLEXITYPARSER **Overview**

COMPLEXITYPARSER concretizes the principles presented in Sect. 1. It is implemented in Java with around 5000 lines. To illustrate the analyzed language, a reduced example is given in Fig. 1. More examples are available in the repository[1].

Example 1. Figure 1 implements a BList class (representing binary numbers as lists of booleans). It is annotated with the tiers inferred by the type system. For methods, the tier is of the form $\alpha_0 \times \cdots \times \alpha_n \rightarrow \alpha$ to denote that the current object is of tier α_0, the n arguments have tiers α_i, for $i \geq 1$, and the output has tier α.

---

[1] https://gitlab.inria.fr/hainry/complexityparser/-/tree/master/examples.

```
 1   class BList {
 2       boolean value;
 3       BList tail;
 4
 5       BList(boolean v, BList q) { value = v; tail = q; }
 6
 7       boolean getValue() { return value; }     // 0→0 or 1→1
 8       void setTail(BList t) { tail = t; }       // 0×0→0
 9       BList getTail() { return tail; }          // 0→0 or 1→1
10       void concat(BList other) { /* ... */ }    // 1×0→1
11       int length() { /* recursive method */ } // 1→0
12       boolean isEqual(BList other) { /* simple while loop */}
13       // isEqual: 1×1→1
14       boolean lessOrEqual(BList other) { /* while loop */ }
15       // lessOrEqual: 1×1→1
16   }
17
18   class Exe {
19       void main(String[] args) {
20           #init
21               BList b1 = new BList(true, null);
22               b1 = new BList(false, b1);
23               b1 = new BList(true, b1);
24               BList b2 = new BList(true, null);
25               b2 = new BList(false, b2);
26               // b1: 1; b2: 1
27           #init
28
29           BList tail1 = b1.clone();          // tail1: 0
30           tail1 = tail1.getTail();           // tail1: 0
31           boolean res = b1.lessOrEqual(b2); // res: 1
32           res = b1.isEqual(b2);              // res: 1
33           b1.concat(b2.clone());             // OK
34           res = tail1.isEqual(b1);
35           // Fails as isEqual needs tail1 to be of tier 1
36       }
37   }
```

Fig. 1. Binary numbers as lists (extract from `example11.txt`)

- Getters have two possible tier signatures: $0 \to 0$ or $1 \to 1$, illustrating the fact that if the current object is of tier α, its fields are of tier α;
- `setTail` modifies a field, hence current object and argument must have the same tier. Since it can make the current object grow, this tier must be **0**;
- `length` is recursive hence input tiers must be **1**;
- `isEqual` iterates on the current object and on `other` they must be of tier **1**.
- Variables `b1`, `b2` created inside the `#init` block automatically get tier **1**;
- The next lines of method `main` check, except the last one (line 35) which tries to apply `isEqual` on an object of tier **0** instead of tier **1**.

COMPLEXITYPARSER's behavior is described by the state diagram of Fig. 2. We will describe this behaviour in detail in the rest of this section.

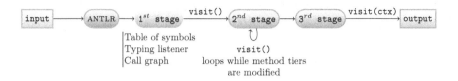

Fig. 2. Program state diagram

Input and Parse Tree Generation. The **input** is a string encoding of a text file containing a collection of Java classes. As illustrated in Fig. 1, some statements in the **main** method can be encompassed between **#init** tags to be treated as the input data of the complexity analysis. No tier-based complexity analysis is performed on these statements and, consequently, they are not subject to the typing constraints described in Sect. 1. While this block is necessarily fixed in our textual examples, it should be understood as a modifiable block: it is the way for the user to build the input on which the program should run. We chose this somewhat clunky way of representing input instead of simply passing them as arguments of the **main** method because Java only allows **String** arrays as arguments and translating such inputs would blur the point. The program uses ANTLR[2], a lexer/parser generator, and creates a new parser instance based on the full Java grammar described in [29] extended with an input tag **#init**, a declassification tag **#declass**, and variable tier declarations (e.g. **int<0> x;**).

Stages of Type Inference. Tiers and typing judgments of [15] are implemented in an object hierarchy. The class **Tier** contains the constants T0, T1 and None for representing the tiers **0**, **1**, and "undefined", plus some useful static methods on tiers. A method can have several types that will depend on its caller context (encoded in an environment tier field **env**). When typing a method, the tiers of the **this** object and of input arguments should be mapped to the tier of the output.

Type inference is performed in 3 stages (see Fig. 2) to compute the admissible method tiers and finally visiting the parse tree to check if the whole program types. The methods' admissible tier list, which is initialized as all the combinatorial possible tiers for each input and output in the 1st stage, is progressively reduced to encompass only the set of admissible tiers in the 2nd stage. The 3rd stage checks for admissible constructor tiers.

The typing discipline is performed using visitors that are specialized for each node type of the parse tree. For example, the code of the **while** statement visitor is provided in Fig. 3. It implements the following rule (rephrased rule

---

[2] www.antlr.org.

```
1     public Object visitStatement_while (... ctx) {
2         visitChildren (ctx);
3         Tier t = getTier(ctx.expression ());
4         Tier env = getEnvironmentTier (ctx.expression ());
5         incrementWhileCount ();
6         Tier res;
7         if (getRecursiveCallsCount() != 0) {
8             res = Tier.None;
9             env = Tier.None;
10        }
11        if (t == Tier.T1 && env != Tier.None){
12            Tier st = getTier(ctx.statement ());
13            if (st == Tier.None || st == null) {
14                res = Tier.None;
15            } else { res = Tier.T1;}
16        } else { res = Tier.None;}
17        putTier(ctx, res, Tier.T1);
18        return res;
19    }
```

Fig. 3. Visitor method for while statements in BaseStatementVisitor

(Wh) from [15]) enforcing any while statement to be controlled by a tier T1 expression:

$$\frac{\Gamma \vdash_{env} \texttt{ctx.expression()} : \texttt{T1} \quad \Gamma \vdash \texttt{ctx.statement()} : \texttt{st} \quad \texttt{env, st} \in \{\texttt{T0, T1}\}}{\Gamma \vdash \texttt{while(ctx.expression())\{ctx.statement()\}} : \texttt{T1}}$$

Output. The output consists in the GUI displaying the "Final result", the tier of main method body. 0 and 1 represent *success* and entail, by Theorem 1, that if the program terminates then its runtime is polynomial. The final result can also be None, indicating a failure to type. This latter case does not imply that the main method complexity is not polynomial as there are false negatives. However some other method declarations in the program may have typed, which guarantees their complexity to be polytime under the termination assumption.

Complexity. Type inference for tier-based typing disciplines was shown to be linear in the size of the input program using a reduction to 2-SAT [13,15]. However COMPLEXITYPARSER's inference algorithm is based on a brute force implementation that remains linear in practice but is exponential in theory.

Let $|p|$ be the size (*i.e.* number of symbols) of the Java program given as input and $ar(p)$ be the maximal number of parameters of a method in the program p.

The first part of our algorithm builds the parse tree of the considered program using the ANTLR $ALL(*)$ algorithm that is in $O(|p|^4)$ in theory [30] and produces a parse tree of size linear in the size of the input program.

Then, the 3 stages of Fig. 2 visit the parse tree nodes linearly often. In the 1st stage, when visiting a method declaration node, all admissible tier combinations are added to the typing environment, costing $O(2^n)$, for a method with n

parameters. Searching fixpoints in the 2nd stage has a WCET in $O(2^{ar(p)}|p|)$: at each step, either the list of possible tier combinations is decremented or the environment is unchanged and the program jumps to the 3rd stage. Typing recursive methods relies on computing the strongly connected components of a graph using the standard Kosaraju DFS algorithm [32] which also has linear complexity. The 3rd stage performs in $O(|p|)$ as it simply type-checks constructor bodies.

Putting all together, the complexity of the analysis is in $O(2^{ar(p)}|p| + |p|^4)$. We argue that $ar(p)$ should be a small constant independent of the program. Indeed, following [7], it is a good practice to *"avoid long parameter lists. As a rule, three parameters should be viewed as a maximum, and fewer is better."* The $O(|p|^4)$ part is due to ANTLR's complexity which, according to its authors, *"performs linearly on grammars used in practice"*, such as the Java grammar. Finally, we claim that the whole analysis also has linear complexity in practice, as highlighted by our tests on sample programs.

3 Conclusion

COMPLEXITYPARSER is an efficient and automatic high level complexity analyzer for Java programs. The analysis can deal with most well-known Java constructs. There are still some syntactic restrictions on the expressive power of the analysis such as not treating `for` loops. Plans for future work include the treatment of threads as in [26], and symbolic computation of the polynomial bounds as in [15] on execution time, heap space, and stack space. Unfortunately, due to object data controlling the flow, tight bounds are difficult to infer. Our approach requires a termination certificate (see Theorem 1). This issue can be overcome by combining our tool with existing termination techniques, *e.g.* [20,31] or loop invariant generation techniques, *e.g.* [5,6,33]. We also consider interfacing with existing termination analyzers working on Java such as Julia [34], or other complexity analyzers that prove termination like AProVE or COSTA.

References

1. Albert, E., Arenas, P., Genaim, S., Puebla, G., Zanardini, D.: Cost analysis of Java bytecode. In: De Nicola, R. (ed.) ESOP 2007. LNCS, vol. 4421, pp. 157–172. Springer, Heidelberg (2007). https://doi.org/10.1007/978-3-540-71316-6_12
2. Albert, E., Arenas, P., Genaim, S., Puebla, G., Zanardini, D.: Cost analysis of object-oriented bytecode programs. Theoret. Comput. Sci. **413**(1), 142–159 (2012)
3. Avanzini, M., Moser, G., Schaper, M.: TcT: tyrolean complexity tool. In: Chechik, M., Raskin, J.-F. (eds.) TACAS 2016. LNCS, vol. 9636, pp. 407–423. Springer, Heidelberg (2016). https://doi.org/10.1007/978-3-662-49674-9_24
4. Bellantoni, S., Cook, S.A.: A new recursion-theoretic characterization of the polytime functions. Comput. Complex. **2**, 97–110 (1992)
5. Ben-Amram, A.M., Genaim, S.: On the linear ranking problem for integer linear-constraint loops. In: 2013 Principles of Programming Languages (POPL), pp. 51–62 (2013)

6. Ben-Amram, A.M., Hamilton, G.W.: Tight worst-case bounds for polynomial loop programs. In: 2019 Foundations of Software Science and Computation Structure (FoSSaCS), pp. 80–97 (2019)
7. Bloch, J.J.: Effective Java. The Java Series ... from the Source, 2nd edn. Addison-Wesley, Boston (2008)
8. Bonfante, G., Kahle, R., Marion, J.Y., Oitavem, I.: Two function algebras defining functions in NC^k boolean circuits. Inf. Comput. **248**, 82–103 (2016)
9. Frohn, F., Giesl, J.: Complexity analysis for Java with AProVE. In: Polikarpova, N., Schneider, S. (eds.) IFM 2017. LNCS, vol. 10510, pp. 85–101. Springer, Cham (2017). https://doi.org/10.1007/978-3-319-66845-1_6
10. Gulwani, S.: SPEED: symbolic complexity bound analysis. In: Bouajjani, A., Maler, O. (eds.) CAV 2009. LNCS, vol. 5643, pp. 51–62. Springer, Heidelberg (2009). https://doi.org/10.1007/978-3-642-02658-4_7
11. Gulwani, S., Mehra, K.K., Chilimbi, T.M.: SPEED: precise and efficient static estimation of program computational complexity. In: 2009 Principles of Programming Languages (POPL), pp. 127–139 (2009)
12. Hainry, E., Kapron, B.M., Marion, J.Y., Péchoux, R.: A tier-based typed programming language characterizing feasible functionals. In: 2020 Logic in Computer Science (LICS), pp. 535–549 (2020)
13. Hainry, E., Marion, J.-Y., Péchoux, R.: Type-based complexity analysis for fork processes. In: Pfenning, F. (ed.) FoSSaCS 2013. LNCS, vol. 7794, pp. 305–320. Springer, Heidelberg (2013). https://doi.org/10.1007/978-3-642-37075-5_20
14. Hainry, E., Péchoux, R.: Objects in polynomial time. In: Feng, X., Park, S. (eds.) APLAS 2015. LNCS, vol. 9458, pp. 387–404. Springer, Cham (2015). https://doi.org/10.1007/978-3-319-26529-2_21
15. Hainry, E., Péchoux, R.: A type-based complexity analysis of object oriented programs. Inf. Comput. **261**, 78–115 (2018)
16. Hájek, P.: Arithmetical hierarchy and complexity of computation. Theoret. Comput. Sci. **8**, 227–237 (1979)
17. Hoffmann, J., Aehlig, K., Hofmann, M.: Resource aware ML. In: Madhusudan, P., Seshia, S.A. (eds.) CAV 2012. LNCS, vol. 7358, pp. 781–786. Springer, Heidelberg (2012). https://doi.org/10.1007/978-3-642-31424-7_64
18. Hofmann, M., Rodriguez, D.: Efficient type-checking for amortised heap-space analysis. In: Grädel, E., Kahle, R. (eds.) CSL 2009. LNCS, vol. 5771, pp. 317–331. Springer, Heidelberg (2009). https://doi.org/10.1007/978-3-642-04027-6_24
19. Hofmann, M., Rodriguez, D.: Automatic type inference for amortised heap-space analysis. In: Felleisen, M., Gardner, P. (eds.) ESOP 2013. LNCS, vol. 7792, pp. 593–613. Springer, Heidelberg (2013). https://doi.org/10.1007/978-3-642-37036-6_32
20. Lee, C.S., Jones, N.D., Ben-Amram, A.M.: The size-change principle for program termination. In: 2001 Principles of Programming Languages (POPL), pp. 81–92 (2001)
21. Leivant, D.: A characterization of NC by tree recurrence. In: Foundations of Computer Science 1998, pp. 716–724. IEEE (1998)
22. Leivant, D., Marion, J.-Y.: Lambda calculus characterizations of poly-time. In: Bezem, M., Groote, J.F. (eds.) TLCA 1993. LNCS, vol. 664, pp. 274–288. Springer, Heidelberg (1993). https://doi.org/10.1007/BFb0037112
23. Leivant, D., Marion, J.-Y.: Ramified recurrence and computational complexity II: substitution and poly-space. In: Pacholski, L., Tiuryn, J. (eds.) CSL 1994. LNCS, vol. 933, pp. 486–500. Springer, Heidelberg (1995). https://doi.org/10.1007/BFb0022277

24. Leivant, D., Marion, J.-Y.: Evolving graph-structures and their implicit computational complexity. In: Fomin, F.V., Freivalds, R., Kwiatkowska, M., Peleg, D. (eds.) ICALP 2013, Part II. LNCS, vol. 7966, pp. 349–360. Springer, Heidelberg (2013). https://doi.org/10.1007/978-3-642-39212-2_32

25. Marion, J.Y.: A type system for complexity flow analysis. In: 2011 Logic in Computer Science (LICS), pp. 123–132. IEEE (2011)

26. Marion, J.-Y., Péchoux, R.: Complexity information flow in a multi-threaded imperative language. In: Gopal, T.V., Agrawal, M., Li, A., Cooper, S.B. (eds.) TAMC 2014. LNCS, vol. 8402, pp. 124–140. Springer, Cham (2014). https://doi.org/10.1007/978-3-319-06089-7_9

27. Moser, G., Schaper, M.: From Jinja bytecode to term rewriting: a complexity reflecting transformation. Inf. Comput. **261**, 116–143 (2018)

28. de Naurois, P.J.: Pointers in recursion: exploring the tropics. In: 2019 Formal Structures for Computation and Deduction (FSCD), pp. 29:1–29:18 (2019)

29. Parr, T.: The definitive ANTLR 4 reference. Pragmatic Bookshelf (2013)

30. Parr, T., Harwell, S., Fisher, K.: Adaptive LL(*) parsing: the power of dynamic analysis. In: 2014 Object-Oriented Programming Systems, Languages, and Applications (OOPSLA), pp. 579–598 (2014)

31. Podelski, A., Rybalchenko, A.: Transition predicate abstraction and fair termination. ACM Trans. Program. Lang. Syst. **29**(3), 15 (2007)

32. Sharir, M.: A strong-connectivity algorithm and its applications in data flow analysis. Comput. Math. Appl. **7**(1), 67–72 (1981)

33. Shkaravska, O., Kersten, R., van Eekelen, M.C.J.D.: Test-based inference of polynomial loop-bound functions. In: 2010 Principles and Practice of Programming in Java (PPPJ), pp. 99–108 (2010)

34. Spoto, F., Mesnard, F., Payet, É.: A termination analyzer for java bytecode based on path-length. ACM Trans. Program. Lang. Syst. **32**(3), 1–70 (2010)

A Calculus for Attribute-Based Memory Updates

Marino Miculan and Michele Pasqua$^{(\boxtimes)}$

Department of Mathematics, Computer Science and Physics,
University of Udine, Udine, Italy
{marino.miculan,michele.pasqua}@uniud.it

Abstract. In this paper, we present AbU a new ECA-inspired calculus
with *attribute-based communication*, an interaction model recently introduced for coordinating large numbers of nodes. Attribute-based communication is similar to broadcast, but the actual receivers are selected "on
the fly" by means of predicates over nodes' attributes.

After having defined syntax and formal semantics of AbU, with some
examples, we give sufficient conditions on AbU systems to guarantee termination of internal steps. Then we show how to encode into AbU components written in AbC, the archetypal calculus with attribute-based
communication, and we prove the correctness of such encoding.

Keywords: ECA rules · Attribute-based communication · Distributed
systems · Formal methods · Autonomic computing

1 Introduction

Event Condition Action (ECA) languages are an intuitive and powerful paradigm
for programming reactive systems. The fundamental construct of ECA languages are rules of the form "**on** *Event* **if** *Condition* **do** *Action*" which means:
when *Event* occurs, if *Condition* is verified then execute *Action*. ECA systems
receive inputs (as events) from the external environment and react by performing
internal actions, updating the node's local memory, or *external* actions, which
influence the environment itself. Due to their reactive nature, ECA languages
are well-suited for programming smart systems, in particular in IoT scenarios [11,17]. Indeed, this paradigm can be found in various commercial frameworks like IFTTT, Samsung SmartThings, Microsoft Power Automate, Zapier,
etc.

In most cases, the rules are stored and executed by a central computing
node, possibly in the cloud: the components of the adaptive system do not communicate directly, and the coordination is demanded to the central node/cloud
service. Although simple, such a centralized architecture does not scale well to

Work supported by the Italian MIUR project PRIN 2017FTXR7S *IT MATTERS*
(Methods and Tools for Trustworthy Smart Systems).

A. Cerone and P. C. Ölveczky (Eds.): ICTAC 2021, LNCS 12819, pp. 366–385, 2021.
https://doi.org/10.1007/978-3-030-85315-0_21

large systems, and the central node/cloud service is a Single Point Of Failure, hindering availability. Thus, in these situations we may prefer to move computation closer to the edge of the network, akin *fog computing*: the ECA rules should be stored and executed directly in the nodes, in a truly distributed setting. This approach reduces data transfers between the edge and the center of the network—in fact, there can be no center at all, thus increasing scalability and resilience—but, on the other hand, it requires a distributed coordination and communication of these components.

In order to model these issues, in this paper we introduce AbU (for "Attribute-based Updates"), a new calculus aiming at merging the simplicity of ECA programming with distributed coordination mechanisms in the spirit of *attribute-based communication*. Attribute-based communication is a time-coupled, space-uncoupled interaction model recently introduced for coordinating large numbers of components and subsuming several interaction paradigms used in "smart systems", such as channels, agents, pub/sub, broadcast and multicast [2,4,5]. The key aspect of attribute-based communication is that the actual receivers are selected "on the fly" by means of *predicates*. Using a syntax similar to AbC [5] (the archetypal calculus for attribute-based communication), $\langle e @ \Pi \rangle.P$ means "send (the value of) e to all nodes satisfying Π, then continue as P"; dually, $(x \,|\, \Pi).P$ means "when receiving a message x such that Π holds, continue as P".

Integrating attribute-based communication in the ECA paradigm is not obvious. One could try to add some primitives similar to AbC's, but this would yield a disharmonious *patchwork* of different paradigms, i.e., message-passing vs. memory-based events. Instead, in AbU we choose a different path: communications are reduced to events of the same kind ECA programs already deal with, that is, memory updates. For instance, a AbU rule like the following:

$$accessT \; @(\overline{role} = \texttt{logger}) : \overline{log} \leftarrow \overline{log} + accessT$$

means "when (my local) variable $accessT$ changes, add its value to the variable log of all nodes whose variable $role$ has value $\texttt{logger}$". Clearly, the update of log may trigger other rules on these (remote) nodes, and so on. We call this mechanism *attribute-based memory updates*, since it can be seen as the memory-based counterpart of attribute-based (message-passing) communication.

This smooth integration of communication within the ECA paradigm makes easier to extend to the distributed setting known results and techniques. As an example, we will provide a simple syntactic check to guarantee *stabilization*, i.e., that a chain of rule executions triggered by an external event will eventually terminate. Furthermore, we will discuss how implementations can leverage well-known optimization strategies for ECA rules, like the RETE algorithm [12].

Synopsis. After a summary of related work in Sect. 2, in Sect. 3 we introduce AbU, the new ECA-inspired calculus with attribute-based memory updates. After its syntax and operational semantics, we give a simple termination criterion based on a syntactic condition. Then, in Sect. 4 we show how to encode AbC components in AbU, providing encoding correctness and examples. In Sect. 5 we discuss some issues concerning the distributed implementation of AbU. Conclusions and directions for future work are in Sect. 6. Full proofs of the results can be found in the companion technical report [29].

2   Related Work

To the best of our knowledge, no work in literature aims at merging the two programming paradigms taken into consideration in the present paper. An approach close in spirit to ours is that based on associative memories, that is *tuple spaces*, as in the Linda language [18] and the KLAIM calculus [20]. In fact, also tuple spaces have events (insertion or deletion of tuples) that can be notified to nodes. Furthermore, tuple spaces can be inspected via pattern matching, which can be seen as a restricted form of attribute-based lookup. Despite these analogies, tuple spaces and AbU differ on many aspects: the latter is based on ECA rules, attribute-based communication is implemented by means of remote memory updates (and hence transparent to the nodes involved in the distributed system) and the logic for predicating over attributes is more expressive than simple pattern matching.

Concerning ECA programming, [14,19] introduce IRON, a language based on ECA rules for the IoT domain. Following other work about ECA languages, [30,31] present verification mechanisms to check properties on IRON programs, such as termination, confluence, redundant or contradicting rules. Other work proposes approaches to verify ECA programs by using Petri Nets [27] and BDD [13]. In [16,17], the authors present a tool-supported method for verifying and controlling the correct interactions of ECA rules. All these works do not deal with distributed systems, hence communication is not taken into account.

AbC has been introduced and studied in [2,4,5] as a core calculus for SCEL [22], a language à la KLAIM with collective communication primitives. Focusing on the attribute-based communication model, AbC is well-suited to model Collective Adaptive Systems (CAS) [10] from a process standpoint (as opposed to Multi-Agents Systems (MAS) that follow a logical approach [32]; we refer to [4] for more details). Various extensions of AbC has been proposed [3,6], as well as correct implementations in Erlang [21] and Golang [1,24]. AbC, and its parent languages, adopt a message-passing communication mechanism and a sequential, process-like, execution flow, which are orthogonal with respect to the ECA rules setting. Since the goal of the present work is to extend the ECA programming style with attributed-based communication mechanisms, we will focus on the most fundamental primitives of AbC, omitting features not strictly necessary.

Some work combining message-passing primitives and shared-memory mechanisms have been recently proposed [8,9]. In particular, the *m&m model* of [8] allows processes to both pass messages and share memory. This approach is increasingly used in practice (e.g., in data centers), as it seems to have great impact on the performance of distributed systems. An example application is given by *Remote Direct Memory Access* (RDMA) [9], that provides processes primitives both for send/receive communication, and for direct remote memory access. This mixed approach has been recently applied also in the MAS context [7], where the local behavior of agents is based on shared variables and the global behavior is based on message-passing. These results could be very helpful for the implementation of AbU, since a message-passing with shared-memory approach perfectly fits the attribute-based memory updates setting.

3   The AbU Calculus

We present here AbU, a calculus following the Event Condition Action (ECA) paradigm, augmented with attribute-based communication. This solution embodies the programming simplicity prerogative of ECA rules, but it is expressive enough to model complex coordination scenarios, typical of distributed systems.

3.1   Syntax

A AbU *system* S is either a *node*, of the form $R\langle \Sigma, \Theta \rangle$, or a parallel composition $S_1 \parallel S_2$ of systems. A *state* $\Sigma \in \mathbb{X} \to \mathbb{V}$, is a map from resource (names) in $\mathbb{X}$ to values in $\mathbb{V}$, while an *execution pool* $\Theta \subseteq \bigcup_{n \in \mathbb{N}} \mathbb{U}^n$ is a set of *updates*. An update upd is a finite list of pairs $(x, v) \in \mathbb{U}$, meaning that the resource x will take the value v after the execution of the update. Each node is equipped with a non-empty finite list R of *ECA rules*, generated by the following grammar.

rule ::= evt $\gg$ act, task	cnd ::= $\varphi \mid @\varphi$
evt ::= $x \mid$ evt evt	φ ::= $\bot \mid \top \mid \neg\varphi \mid \varphi \wedge \varphi \mid \varphi \vee \varphi \mid \varepsilon \bowtie \varepsilon$
act ::= $\epsilon \mid x \leftarrow \varepsilon$ act $\mid \overline{x} \leftarrow \varepsilon$ act	ε ::= $v \mid x \mid \overline{x} \mid \varepsilon \otimes \varepsilon$
task ::= cnd : act	$x \in \mathbb{X} \quad v \in \mathbb{V}$

A ECA rule evt $\gg$ act, task is guarded by an *event* evt, which is a non-empty finite list of resources. When one of these resources is modified, the rule is *fired*: the *default* action act and the task are *evaluated*. Evaluation does not change the resource states immediately; instead, it yields update operations which are added to the execution pools, and applied later on.

An action is a finite (possibly empty) list of assignments of value expressions to *local* x or *remote* $\overline{x}$ resources. The default action can access and update only local resources. On the other hand, a task consists in a condition cnd and an action act. A *condition* is a boolean expression, optionally prefixed with the modifier @. If @ is not present, the task is *local*: all resources in the condition and in the action refer to the local node (thus variables of the form $\overline{x}$ cannot occur). So, the condition is evaluated locally; if it holds, the action is evaluated. Otherwise, if @ is present, then the task is *remote*: the task $@\varphi$: act reads as "for *all* external nodes where φ holds, do act". On every node where the condition holds, the action is evaluated yielding an update to be added to that node's pool. So, in remote tasks each assignment in act is on remote resources only, but still they can use values from the local node. As an example, the task $@\top : \overline{x} \leftarrow \overline{x} + x$ means "add the value of this node's x to the x of every other node".

In the syntax for boolean expressions φ and value expressions ε we let implicit comparison operators, e.g., $\bowtie \in \{<, \leq, >, \geq, =, \neq\}$, and binary operations, e.g., $\otimes \in \{+, -, *, /\}$. In expressions we can have both local and remote instance of resources, although the latter can occur only inside remote tasks.

When we have a rule of the form $\mathsf{evt} \gg \epsilon, \mathsf{task}$, namely when we have rules with empty default action, we write more concisely $\mathsf{evt}\ \mathsf{task}$ in place of $\mathsf{evt} \gg \epsilon, \mathsf{task}$.

3.2 Semantics

Given a list R of rules and a set X of resources that have been modified, we define the set of *active* rules as $\mathsf{Active}(R, X) \triangleq \{\mathsf{evt} \gg \mathsf{act}, \mathsf{task} \in R \mid \mathsf{evt} \cap X \neq \varnothing\}$, namely the rules in R that listen on resources in X and, hence, that may be fired. Given an action act, its evaluation $[\![\mathsf{act}]\!]$ in the state Σ returns an update. Formally: $[\![x_1 \leftarrow \varepsilon_1 \ldots x_n \leftarrow \varepsilon_n]\!]\Sigma \triangleq (x_1, [\![\varepsilon_1]\!]\Sigma) \ldots (x_n, [\![\varepsilon_n]\!]\Sigma)$. The evaluation semantics for value expressions ε is standard. As we will see in a moment, the semantic function $[\![\cdot]\!]$ is applied only to local actions, that do not contain instances of external resources $\overline{x}$.

The *default updates* are the updates originated from the default actions of active rules in R, namely:

$$\mathsf{DefUpds}(R, X, \Sigma) \triangleq \{[\![\mathsf{act}]\!]\Sigma \mid \exists \mathsf{evt} \gg \mathsf{act}, \mathsf{task} \in \mathsf{Active}(R, X)\}$$

The *local updates* are the updates originated from the tasks of the active rules in R that act only locally ($@$ is not present in the tasks' condition) and that satisfy the task's condition, namely:

$$\mathsf{LocalUpds}(R, X, \Sigma) \triangleq \{[\![\mathsf{act}_2]\!]\Sigma \mid \exists \mathsf{evt} \gg \mathsf{act}_1, \varphi : \mathsf{act}_2 \in \mathsf{Active}(R, X) . \Sigma \models \varphi\}$$

The satisfiability relation is defined as: $\Sigma \models \varphi \triangleq [\![\varphi]\!]\Sigma = \mathsf{tt}$ (the evaluation semantics for boolean expressions φ is standard as well).

When we have a task containing the modifier $@$, an external node is needed to evaluate the task's condition. In our semantics, when a node needs to evaluate a task involving external nodes, it partially evaluates the task (with its own state) and then it sends the partially evaluated task to all other nodes. The latter, receive the task and complete the evaluation, potentially adding updates to their pool. In particular, the partial evaluation of tasks works as follows. With $\{\!|\mathsf{task}|\!\}\Sigma$ we denote the task obtained from task with each occurrence of x in the task's condition and the right-hand sides of the assignments in task's action replaced with the value $\Sigma(x)$. After that, each instance of $\overline{x}$ in the task's action is replaced with x and each instance of x in the task's action is replaced with $\overline{x}$ (this happens, in case, only on the left-hand sides of the assignments of the task's action). For instance, $\{\!|@(x \leq \overline{x}) : \overline{y} \leftarrow x + \overline{y}|\!\}[x \mapsto 1\ y \mapsto 0] = @(1 \leq x) : y \leftarrow 1 + y$. Note that, once the task is partially evaluated and sent to other nodes, then it becomes "syntactically local" for the receiving nodes[1]. Finally, we define the *external tasks*

---

[1] This means that we can evaluate the task's action with the semantic function $[\![\cdot]\!]$.

$$\text{(Exec)}\ \frac{\begin{array}{c}\text{upd} \in \Theta \quad \text{upd} = (x_1, v_1) \ldots (x_k, v_k) \quad \Sigma' = \Sigma[v_1/x_1 \ldots v_k/x_k] \\ \Theta'' = \Theta \setminus \{\text{upd}\} \quad X = \{x_i \mid i \in [1..k] \wedge \Sigma(x_i) \neq \Sigma'(x)\} \\ \Theta' = \Theta'' \cup \mathsf{DefUpds}(R, X, \Sigma) \cup \mathsf{LocalUpds}(R, X, \Sigma) \quad T = \mathsf{ExtTasks}(R, X, \Sigma)\end{array}}{R\langle \Sigma, \Theta \rangle \xrightarrow{\rhd T} R\langle \Sigma', \Theta' \rangle}$$

$$\text{(Input)}\ \frac{\begin{array}{c}v_1, \ldots, v_k \in \mathbb{V} \quad \Sigma' = \Sigma[v_1/x_1 \ldots v_k/x_k] \quad X = \{x_1, \ldots, x_k\} \\ \Theta' = \Theta \cup \mathsf{DefUpds}(R, X, \Sigma) \cup \mathsf{LocalUpds}(R, X, \Sigma) \quad T = \mathsf{ExtTasks}(R, X, \Sigma)\end{array}}{R\langle \Sigma, \Theta \rangle \xrightarrow{\blacktriangleright T} R\langle \Sigma', \Theta' \rangle}$$

$$\text{(Disc)}\ \frac{\Theta'' = \{[\![\text{act}]\!]\Sigma \mid \exists i \in [1..n] . \mathsf{task}_i = @\varphi : \text{act} \wedge \Sigma \models \varphi\} \quad \Theta' = \Theta \cup \Theta''}{R\langle \Sigma, \Theta \rangle \xrightarrow{\mathsf{task}_1 \ldots \mathsf{task}_n} R\langle \Sigma, \Theta' \rangle}$$

$$\text{(Step)}\ \frac{\mathsf{S}_1 \xrightarrow{\alpha} \mathsf{S}_1' \quad \mathsf{S}_2 \xrightarrow{T} \mathsf{S}_2'}{\mathsf{S}_1 \parallel \mathsf{S}_2 \xrightarrow{\alpha} \mathsf{S}_1' \parallel \mathsf{S}_2'}\ \alpha \in \{\rhd T, \blacktriangleright T\}$$

Fig. 1. AbU semantics for nodes and systems.

as $\mathsf{ExtTasks}(R, X, \Sigma) \triangleq \{\!|\mathsf{task}_1\!|\}\Sigma \ldots \{\!|\mathsf{task}_n\!|\}\Sigma$ such that for each $i \in [1..n]$ there exists a rule $\text{evt} \gg \text{act}, \mathsf{task}_i \in \mathsf{Active}(R, X)$ such that $\mathsf{task}_i = @\varphi : \text{act}$, namely the tasks of active rules in R whose condition contains @ (i.e., tasks that require an external node to be evaluated).

The (small-step) semantics of a AbU system is modeled as a labeled transition system $\mathsf{S}_1 \xrightarrow{\alpha} \mathsf{S}_2$ whose labels are given by $\alpha ::= T \mid \rhd T \mid \blacktriangleright T$ where T is a finite list of tasks. A transition can modify the state and the execution pool of the nodes. The semantics is *distributed*, in the sense that each node's semantics does not have a global knowledge about the system. The rules are in Fig. 1. A rule (Exec) executes an update picked from the pool; while a rule (Input) models an external modification of some resources. The execution of an update, or the change of resources, may trigger some rules of the nodes. Hence, after updating a node's state, the semantics of a node launches a *discovery phase*, with the goal of finding new updates to add to the local pool (or some pools of remote nodes), given by the activation of some rules. The discovery phase is composed by two parts, the local and the external one. A node $R\langle \Sigma, \Theta \rangle$ performs a local discovery by means of the functions $\mathsf{DefUpds}$ and $\mathsf{LocalUpds}$, that add to the local pool Θ all updates originated by the activation of some rules in R. Then, by means of the function $\mathsf{ExtTasks}$, the node computes a list of tasks that may update external nodes and sends it to all nodes in the system. This is modeled with the labels $\rhd T$, produced by the rule (Exec), and $\blacktriangleright T$, produced by the rule (Input). On the other side, when a node receives a list of tasks (executing the rule (Disc) with a label T) it evaluates them and adds to its pool the actions generated by the tasks whose condition is satisfied.

Finally, the rule (Step) completes (on all nodes in the system) a discovery phase launched by a given node. Note that, not necessarily all nodes have to modify their pool (indeed, a task's condition may not hold in an external node).

At the same time, the rule synchronizes the whole discovery phase, originated by a change in the state of a node in the system. When a node executes an action originating only local updates, the rule (STEP) is applied with $S'_2 = S_2$, producing the label $\triangleright \varepsilon$ or the label $\blacktriangleright \varepsilon$ (i.e., with an empty tasks' list). The parallel composition of systems $\|$ is associative and commutative.

Note that, in order to start the computation for a system of nodes, an input (i.e., an external modification of the environment) is needed since, at the beginning, all pools of all nodes in the system are empty.

Wave Semantics. A AbU system $S = R_1\langle \Sigma_1, \Theta_1 \rangle \| \ldots \| R_n\langle \Sigma_n, \Theta_n \rangle$ is *stable* when no more execution steps can be performed, namely when all execution pools Θ_i, for $i \in [1..n]$, are empty. We will use $R\langle \Sigma \rangle$ as a shorthand for $R\langle \Sigma, \varnothing \rangle$. So, a system is stable when it is of the form $R_1\langle \Sigma_1 \rangle \| \ldots \| R_n\langle \Sigma_n \rangle$. In the case of a stable system, only the rule (INPUT) can be applied, i.e., an external environment change is needed to (re)start the computation.

We can define a big-step semantics $S \rightsquigarrow S'$ between stable systems, dubbed *wave semantics*, in terms of the small-step semantics. Let $\rightarrow^*$ be the transitive closure of $\rightarrow$, without occurrences of labels of the form $\blacktriangleright T$, namely $\rightarrow^*$ denotes a finite sequence of internal execution steps (with the corresponding discovery phases), without interleaving input steps. The wave semantics for a system S is:

$$(\text{WAVE})\frac{S = R_1\langle \Sigma_1 \rangle \| \ldots \| R_n\langle \Sigma_n \rangle \quad S \xrightarrow{\blacktriangleright T} S'' \rightarrow^* S' \quad S' = R_1\langle \Sigma'_1 \rangle \| \ldots \| R_n\langle \Sigma'_n \rangle}{S \rightsquigarrow S'}$$

The idea is that a (stable) system reacts to an external stimulus by executing a series of tasks (a "wave"), until it becomes stable again, waiting for the next stimulus. Note that, in the wave semantics inputs do not interleave with internal steps: this leaves the system the time to reach stability before the next input. If we allow arbitrary input steps during the computation, possibly a system may never reach stability since the execution pools could be never emptied. This assumption has a practical interpretation: in the IoT context, usually, external changes (in sensors) take much more time than internal computation steps [15].

3.3   A Working Example

Let us consider the scenario sketched in the Introduction, where an "access" node aims at sending its local access time to all "logger" nodes in the system. In other words, this node is activated when *accessT* changes, namely when a new user performs access. Suppose now that the node, together with the time-stamp, aims at sending the IP address of the user and the name of the accessed resource. On the other side, the logger nodes record the access time, the IP address and the resource's name. Furthermore, suppose that these nodes contain a black-list of IP addresses. This list can be updated at run-time, by external entities communicating with logger nodes, so it may be the case that different logger nodes have different black-lists. A logger node that notices an access from a black-listed IP is in charge of notifying an intrusion detection system (IDS).

The system is formalized in AbU as follows. We suppose to have two access nodes and two logger nodes. We also suppose that log is a structured type, i.e., a list of records of the form $|IP; accessT; res|$. An append to the list log is given by append log $|IP; accessT; res|$, with $|IP; accessT; res|.IP$ we denote the access of the field IP, and $\text{tail}[log]$ returns the last record inserted in the list log.

$$\mathsf{S}_1 \triangleq R_a\langle \Sigma_1, \varnothing \rangle = R_a\langle [IP \mapsto \varepsilon \ accessT \mapsto 00{:}00{:}00 \ res \mapsto \mathtt{camera}], \varnothing \rangle$$

$$\mathsf{S}_2 \triangleq R_a\langle \Sigma_2, \varnothing \rangle = R_a\langle [IP \mapsto \varepsilon \ accessT \mapsto 00{:}00{:}00 \ res \mapsto \mathtt{lock}], \varnothing \rangle$$

$$\mathsf{S}_3 \triangleq R_l\langle \Sigma_3, \varnothing \rangle = R_l\langle [role \mapsto \mathtt{logger} \ log \mapsto \varepsilon \ Blist \mapsto \varepsilon \ IDS \mapsto \varepsilon], \varnothing \rangle$$

$$\mathsf{S}_4 \triangleq R_l\langle \Sigma_4, \varnothing \rangle = R_l\langle [role \mapsto \mathtt{logger} \ log \mapsto \varepsilon \ Blist \mapsto 167.123.23.2; \ IDS \mapsto \varepsilon], \varnothing \rangle$$

$$R_a \triangleq accessT \ @(\overline{role} = \mathtt{logger}) : \overline{log} \leftarrow \text{append } \overline{log} \ |IP; accessT; res|$$

$$R_l \triangleq log \ (\text{tail}[log].IP \in Blist) : IDS \leftarrow \text{tail}[log]$$

At the beginning, the AbU system $\mathsf{S}_1 \parallel \mathsf{S}_2 \parallel \mathsf{S}_3 \parallel \mathsf{S}_4$ is stable, since all pools are empty. At some point, an access is made on the resource $\mathtt{camera}$, so the rule (INPUT) is applied on S_1, namely $R_a\langle \Sigma_1, \varnothing \rangle \xrightarrow{\blacktriangleright T} R_a\langle \Sigma_1', \varnothing \rangle$, where $\Sigma_1' = [accessT \mapsto 15{:}07{:}00 \ res \mapsto \mathtt{camera} \ IP \mapsto 167.123.23.2]$ and

$$T = @(role = \mathtt{logger}) : log \leftarrow \text{append } log \ |167.123.23.2; 15{:}07{:}00; \mathtt{camera}|$$

Now, a discovery phase is performed on all other nodes. In particular, we have: $R_a\langle \Sigma_2, \varnothing \rangle \xrightarrow{T} R_a\langle \Sigma_2, \varnothing \rangle$, $R_l\langle \Sigma_3, \varnothing \rangle \xrightarrow{T} R_l\langle \Sigma_3, \Theta \rangle$, and $R_l\langle \Sigma_4, \varnothing \rangle \xrightarrow{T} R_l\langle \Sigma_4, \Theta \rangle$. Here, the pool Θ is the set $\{(log, |167.123.23.2; 15 : 07 : 00; \mathtt{camera}|)\}$. Now, let $\mathsf{S}_1' = R_a\langle \Sigma_1', \varnothing \rangle$, $\mathsf{S}_3' = R_l\langle \Sigma_3', \Theta \rangle$ and $\mathsf{S}_4' = R_l\langle \Sigma_4', \Theta \rangle$. The derivation tree for the resulting system $\mathsf{S}_1' \parallel \mathsf{S}_2 \parallel \mathsf{S}_3' \parallel \mathsf{S}_4'$ is depicted in Fig. 2[top]. For space reasons, we abbreviate rules' names and we omit the premises of leaf rules.

Now, the third and the fourth nodes can apply an execution step, since their pools are not empty. Suppose the third node is chosen, namely we have $R_l\langle \Sigma_3, \Theta \rangle \xrightarrow{\rhd \varepsilon} R_l\langle \Sigma_3', \varnothing \rangle$, by applying the rule (EXEC), and $\Sigma_3' = [role \mapsto \mathtt{logger} \ log \mapsto |167.123.23.2; 15 : 07 : 00; \mathtt{camera}| \ Blist \mapsto \varnothing \ IDS \mapsto \varepsilon]$. Note that, in this case, no rule is triggered by the executed update. Since there is nothing to discover, all the other nodes do not have to update their pool and the derivation tree for the resulting system $\mathsf{S}_1' \parallel \mathsf{S}_2 \parallel \mathsf{S}_3'' \parallel \mathsf{S}_4'$, where $\mathsf{S}_3'' = R_l\langle \Sigma_3', \varnothing \rangle$, is given in Fig. 2[bottom]. Finally, the fourth node can execute, namely we have that $R_l\langle \Sigma_4, \Theta \rangle \xrightarrow{\rhd \varepsilon} R_l\langle \Sigma_4', \Theta' \rangle$, by applying the rule (EXEC). Here, $\Sigma_4' = [role \mapsto \mathtt{logger} \ log \mapsto |167.123.23.2; 15{:}07{:}00; \mathtt{camera}| \ Blist \mapsto 167.123.23.2; \ IDS \mapsto \varepsilon]$ and $\Theta' = \{(IDS, |167.123.23.2; 15 : 07 : 00; \mathtt{camera}|)\}$. In this case, the execution of the update triggers a rule of the node but the rule is local so, also in this case, the discovery phase does not have effect. The derivation tree for this step is analogous to the derivation tree for the previous one. Finally, with a further execution on the fourth node, we obtain the system $\mathsf{S}_1' \parallel \mathsf{S}_2 \parallel \mathsf{S}_3'' \parallel \mathsf{S}_4''$, where $\mathsf{S}_4'' = R_l\langle \Sigma_4'', \varnothing \rangle$ and $\Sigma_4'' = [role \mapsto \mathtt{logger} \ log \mapsto |167.123.23.2; 15 : 07 : 00; \mathtt{camera}| \ Blist \mapsto 167.123.23.2; \ IDS \mapsto |167.123.23.2; 15 : 07 : 00; \mathtt{camera}|]$. Since all pools are empty, the resulting system is stable. This means that we can perform a wave semantics step:

$$(\text{WAVE})\frac{S_1 \parallel S_2 \parallel S_3 \parallel S_4 \xrightarrow{\blacktriangleright T} S_1' \parallel S_2 \parallel S_3' \parallel S_4' \qquad S_1' \parallel S_2 \parallel S_3' \parallel S_4' \xrightarrow{\rhd \varepsilon} S_1' \parallel S_2 \parallel S_3'' \parallel S_4' \xrightarrow{\rhd \varepsilon} \dots \xrightarrow{\rhd \varepsilon} S_1' \parallel S_2 \parallel S_3'' \parallel S_4''}{S_1 \parallel S_2 \parallel S_3 \parallel S_4 \rightsquigarrow S_1' \parallel S_2 \parallel S_3'' \parallel S_4''}$$

$$(\text{S})\cfrac{(\text{I})\cfrac{\dots}{R_a\langle \Sigma_1, \varnothing\rangle \xrightarrow{\blacktriangleright T} R_a\langle \Sigma_1', \varnothing\rangle} \quad (\text{D})\cfrac{\dots}{R_a\langle \Sigma_2, \varnothing\rangle \xrightarrow{T} R_a\langle \Sigma_2, \varnothing\rangle}}{(\text{S})\cfrac{S_1 \parallel S_2 \xrightarrow{\blacktriangleright T} S_1' \parallel S_2 \quad (\text{D})\cfrac{\dots}{R_l\langle \Sigma_3, \varnothing\rangle \xrightarrow{T} R_l\langle \Sigma_3, \Theta\rangle}}{(\text{S})\cfrac{S_1 \parallel S_2 \parallel S_3 \xrightarrow{\blacktriangleright T} S_1' \parallel S_2 \parallel S_3' \quad (\text{D})\cfrac{\dots}{R_l\langle \Sigma_4, \varnothing\rangle \xrightarrow{T} R_l\langle \Sigma_4, \Theta\rangle}}{S_1 \parallel S_2 \parallel S_3 \parallel S_4 \xrightarrow{\blacktriangleright T} S_1' \parallel S_2 \parallel S_3' \parallel S_4'}}}$$

$$(\text{S})\cfrac{(\text{E})\cfrac{\dots}{R_l\langle \Sigma_3, \Theta\rangle \xrightarrow{\rhd \varepsilon} R_l\langle \Sigma_3', \varnothing\rangle} \quad (\text{D})\cfrac{\dots}{R_a\langle \Sigma_1', \varnothing\rangle \xrightarrow{\varepsilon} R_a\langle \Sigma_1', \varnothing\rangle}}{(\text{S})\cfrac{S_3' \parallel S_1' \xrightarrow{\rhd \varepsilon} S_3'' \parallel S_1' \quad (\text{D})\cfrac{\dots}{R_a\langle \Sigma_2, \varnothing\rangle \xrightarrow{\varepsilon} R_a\langle \Sigma_2, \varnothing\rangle}}{(\text{S})\cfrac{S_3' \parallel S_1' \parallel S_2 \xrightarrow{\rhd \varepsilon} S_3'' \parallel S_1' \parallel S_2 \quad (\text{D})\cfrac{\dots}{R_l\langle \Sigma_4, \Theta\rangle \xrightarrow{\varepsilon} R_l\langle \Sigma_4, \Theta\rangle}}{S_3' \parallel S_1' \parallel S_2 \parallel S_4' \xrightarrow{\rhd \varepsilon} S_3'' \parallel S_1' \parallel S_2 \parallel S_4'}}}$$

Fig. 2. Derivation trees for AbU semantic steps: (INPUT) [top] and (EXEC) [bottom].

3.4   Termination Guarantee

The wave semantics (and, hence, a AbU system) may exhibit *internal divergence*: once an input step starts the computation, the subsequent execution steps may not reach a stable system, even if intermediate inputs are not performed.

Consider the case of the book "The Making of a fly", that reached the stellar selling price of \$23,698,655.93 on Amazon, in 2001[2]. Two Amazon retailers, *profnath* and *bordeebook*, used Amazon's automatic pricing primitives to set the price of their book's copy, depending the competitor's book price. The strategy of *profnath* was to automatically set the price 0.99 times the *bordeebook*'s price; conversely, the strategy of *bordeebook* was to set the price 1.27 times the *profnath*'s price. Each retailer was not aware of the competitor's strategy. This scenario can be modeled with the following ECA rules:

when *bordeebook-price* changes, set *profnath-price* to *bordeebook-price* ∗ 0.99

when *profnath-price* changes, set *bordeebook-price* to *profnath-price* ∗ 1.27

It is easy to see that these rules generate a loop, leading to an uncontrolled raise of the book's price (as it happened). In order to prevent these situations, we define a simple syntactic condition on the rules that guarantees (internal) termination. In other words, each system satisfying the condition eventually becomes stable, after an initial input and without further interleaving inputs. This condition can be checked before the rules are deployed in the system.

The *output resources* of a AbU rule, namely the resources involved in the actions performed by the rule, are given by the resources assigned in the default

---

[2] https://www.michaeleisen.org/blog/?p=358.

action and in the rule's task. The output resources of an action act are the set $\mathsf{Out}(\mathsf{act}) \triangleq \{x \mid \exists i \in \mathbb{N}.\,\mathsf{act}[i] = x \leftarrow \varepsilon \vee \mathsf{act}[i] = \overline{x} \leftarrow \varepsilon\}$. So, the output resources of a rule are $\mathsf{Out}(\mathsf{evt} \rhd \mathsf{act}_1, \mathsf{cnd} : \mathsf{act}_2) \triangleq \mathsf{Out}(\mathsf{act}_1) \cup \mathsf{Out}(\mathsf{act}_2)$.

The *input resources* of a AbU rule are the resources that the rule listen on, namely the set $\mathsf{In}(\mathsf{evt} \rhd \mathsf{act}, \mathsf{task}) \triangleq \{x \mid \exists i \in \mathbb{N}.\,\mathsf{evt}[i] = x\}$. Given a list R of AbU rules, its output resources $\mathsf{Out}(R)$ are the union of the output resources of all rules in the list. Analogously, its input resources $\mathsf{In}(R)$ are the union of the input resources of all rules in the list.

Definition 1 (ECA dependency graph). *Given a AbU system* S *such that* $\mathsf{S} = R_1\langle \Sigma_1, \Theta_1\rangle \parallel \ldots \parallel R_n\langle \Sigma_n, \Theta_n \rangle$, *the ECA dependency graph of* S *is a directed graph* (N, E) *where the nodes* N *and the edges* E *are:*

$$N \triangleq \bigcup_{i \in [1..n]} \mathsf{In}(R_i) \cup \mathsf{Out}(R_i) \quad E \triangleq \left\{ (x_1, x_2) \left| \begin{array}{l} \exists i \in [1..n]\,\exists j \in [1..k]\,.\,R_i = \mathsf{rule}_1 \ldots \mathsf{rule}_k \\ \wedge\, x_1 \in \mathsf{In}(\mathsf{rule}_j) \wedge x_2 \in \mathsf{Out}(\mathsf{rule}_j) \end{array} \right. \right\}$$

The sufficient syntactic condition for the termination of the wave semantics (i.e., stabilization) consists in the acyclicity of the ECA dependency graph.

Proposition 1 (Termination of the wave semantics). *Given a AbU system* S, *if the ECA dependency graph of* S *is acyclic, then there exists a system* S' *such that* $\mathsf{S} \rightsquigarrow \mathsf{S}'$.

Therefore, a naive termination enforcing mechanism consists in computing the transitive closure E^+ of E and to check if it contains reflexive pairs, i.e., elements of the form (x, x), for a resource identifier x. If there are no reflexive elements then the graph is acyclic and the condition is fulfilled.

4   Encoding Attribute-Based Communication

To showcase the generality of our calculus, in this section we encode the archetypal calculus AbC [5] in AbU. Our aim is not to prove that AbU subsumes AbC: the two calculi adopt different programming paradigms, with different peculiarities, that fit different application scenarios. Our goal here is to show that we can model within the ECA programming style the attribute-based communication.

4.1   The AbC Calculus

We focus on a minimal version of AbC [5], for which we define an operational semantics, on the line of [4]. As already pointed out, we do not aim at a full-fledged version of AbC, since the aim of this section is to encode in AbU the essence of the attribute-based communication, comprehensively expressed by the core version of AbC that we will present in the following paragraphs.

A AbC component C may be a process paired with an attribute environment, written $\Gamma : P$, or the parallel composition of two components, written $C_1 \parallel C_2$. An attribute environment Γ is a map from attribute identifiers $a \in \mathcal{A}$ to values $v \in \mathcal{V}$. Our syntax of AbC processes is as follows.

$$P ::= 0 \mid (x \mid \Pi).P \mid \langle e @ \Pi \rangle.P \mid [a := e]P \mid [\Pi]P \mid P_a + P_b \mid K$$
$$\Pi ::= \text{ff} \mid \text{tt} \mid \Pi_1 \vee \Pi_2 \mid \Pi_1 \wedge \Pi_2 \mid \neg \Pi \mid e \bowtie e \quad \text{with } \bowtie \in \{<, \leq, >, \geq, =, \neq\}$$
$$e ::= v \mid a \mid x \mid \text{this}.a \mid e \otimes e \quad \text{with } \otimes \in \{+, -, *, /\}$$

In particular, the *input* $(x \mid \Pi)$ receives a message from components that satisfy the predicate Π, saving the message in the variable x. The *output* $\langle e @ \Pi \rangle$ sends (the evaluation of) the expression e to all components that satisfy the predicate Π. The awareness process $[\Pi]P$ waits until Π is satisfied and then continues the execution as P. The other constructors are as in [5] (the inactive process 0, non-deterministic choice between $P_a + P_b$ and process calls K). Predicates Π and expressions e are standard. The reader can refer to [5] for more details.

We now briefly explain the semantics for AbC. $\llbracket e \rrbracket (\Gamma)$ evaluates an expression e in the environment Γ and yields a value, while $\llbracket \Pi \rrbracket (\Gamma)$ evaluates a predicate Π in Γ and yields tt or ff. Their formal definition is straightforward, the only interesting cases are: $\llbracket a \rrbracket (\Gamma) = \llbracket \text{this}.a \rrbracket (\Gamma) = \Gamma(a)$. When $\llbracket \Pi \rrbracket (\Gamma)$ is tt we say that Γ satisfies Π, written $\Gamma \models \Pi$. We assume that processes do not have free variables, i.e., x is always under the scope of an input $(x \mid \Pi)$. Finally, in $\{\!\{\Pi\}\!\}(\Gamma)$ we substitute expressions of the form $\text{this}.a$ with $\Gamma(a)$. The semantics for processes (Fig. 3[top]) and for components (Fig. 3[bottom]) is given by a labeled transition system, where a process label δ is of the form $\overline{\Pi}\langle v \rangle$ (output) or $\Pi(v)$ (input) and a component label λ can be either a process label δ or a silent action τ (i.e., a communication to a false predicate). Transitions rules in Fig. 3 are self-explanatory (symmetric rules are omitted). The parallel composition of components $\parallel$ is associative and commutative. The inactive process semantics is modeled as a communication on false, i.e., $\Gamma : 0 \xrightarrow{\overline{\text{ff}}\langle 0 \rangle} \Gamma : 0$.

Note that, if the rule (COMM) is applicable then Π cannot be false, since the rule (RCV) cannot be applied with false predicates. When Π is false, (INT) is applied, representing an internal execution step of C_1. This rule applies also when C_2 is not ready (or it does not want) to communicate, allowing C_1 to progress.

4.2   Encoding AbC in AbU

Given a AbC component $\Gamma_1 : P_1 \parallel \ldots \parallel \Gamma_n : P_n$, we define a AbU system $R_1\langle \Sigma_1 \rangle \parallel \ldots \parallel R_n\langle \Sigma_n \rangle$ composed by n nodes, where the state Σ_i of the ith node is given by the ith attribute environment Γ_i (with some modifications). All nodes' pools are initially empty. In order to simulate process communication, we add to each node a special resource msg. If a node wants to communicate a message, it has to update the msg resource of all the selected communication partners. The execution of each AbC component is inherently sequential while AbU nodes follow an event-driven architecture. In order to simulate AbC's causality, we associate each generated AbU rule with a special resource, a *rule flag*, whose purpose is to enable and disable the rule. The sequential execution flow of an AbC component is reconstructed modifying the *active* flag of the rules: this simulates a "token" that rules have to hold in order to be executed. Formally,

$$(\text{Brd})\frac{\{\Pi'\}(\Gamma) = \Pi \quad \llbracket e \rrbracket(\Gamma) = v}{\Gamma : \langle e \,@\, \Pi' \rangle.P \xrightarrow{\overline{\Pi}\langle v \rangle} \Gamma : P}$$

$$(\text{Aware})\frac{\Gamma \models \Pi \quad \Gamma : P \xrightarrow{\delta} \Gamma' : P'}{\Gamma : [\Pi]P \xrightarrow{\delta} \Gamma' : P'}$$

$$(\text{Rcv})\frac{\Gamma \models \Pi \quad \Gamma \models \Pi'[v/x]}{\Gamma : (x \mid \Pi').P \xrightarrow{\Pi(v)} \Gamma : P[v/x]}$$

$$(\text{Sum})\frac{\Gamma : P_a \xrightarrow{\delta} \Gamma' : P_1'}{\Gamma : P_a + P_b \xrightarrow{\delta} \Gamma' : P_1'}$$

$$(\text{Upd})\frac{\llbracket e \rrbracket(\Gamma) = v \quad \Gamma[v/a] : P \xrightarrow{\delta} \Gamma[v/a]' : P'}{\Gamma : [a := e]P \xrightarrow{\delta} \Gamma[v/a]' : P'}$$

$$(\text{Rec})\frac{K \triangleq P \quad \Gamma : P \xrightarrow{\delta} \Gamma' : P'}{\Gamma : K \xrightarrow{\delta} \Gamma' : P'}$$

$$(\text{Comp})\frac{\Gamma : P \xrightarrow{\delta} \Gamma' : P'}{\Gamma : P \xrightarrow{\delta} \Gamma' : P'}$$

$$(\text{Sync})\frac{C_1 \xrightarrow{\Pi(v)} C_1' \quad C_2 \xrightarrow{\Pi(v)} C_2'}{C_1 \parallel C_2 \xrightarrow{\Pi(v)} C_1' \parallel C_2'}$$

$$(\text{Comm})\frac{C_1 \xrightarrow{\overline{\Pi}\langle v \rangle} C_1' \quad C_2 \xrightarrow{\Pi(v)} C_2'}{C_1 \parallel C_2 \xrightarrow{\overline{\Pi}\langle v \rangle} C_1' \parallel C_2'}$$

$$(\text{Int})\frac{C_1 \xrightarrow{\overline{\Pi}\langle v \rangle} C_1' \quad C_2 \xrightarrow{\Pi(v)}\!\!\!\!\!/}{C_1 \parallel C_2 \xrightarrow{\tau} C_1' \parallel C_2}$$

Fig. 3. AbC semantics for processes [top] and components [bottom].

the state of the ith nodes is augmented as follows:

$$\Sigma_i = \Gamma_i \cup \{(msg, 0)\} \cup \bigcup_{j \in [1..n]} \mathcal{R}^j(P_j)$$

A rule is generated for each process instance present in the AbC component to be encoded. To this end, each node is augmented with all rule flags, of all rules, given by the translation of all processes of the AbC component. Rule flags are resource of the form $P_h r_i$, with $h \in [1..n]$ and $i \geq 0$, representing the ith rule generated from the component h. The function $\mathcal{R}^h$, given a process of the component h, with $h \in [1..n]$, computes the resources to add to the nodes[3].

$\mathcal{R}^h$ returns $\varnothing$ for the inactive process and for process calls, i.e., $\mathcal{R}^h(0) \triangleq \mathcal{R}^h(K) \triangleq \varnothing$, and nothing is added. For the other processes, it returns $\mathcal{R}^h(P) \triangleq \{(P_h r_0, \text{ff})\} \cup \mathcal{R}^h(P, 0)$. The flag $P_h r_0$ is the starting point of the computation, indeed it does not represent any actual rule, and it is set to tt in order to start the computation. The function $\mathcal{R}^h(P, i)$, for $i \geq 0$, is defined inductively on the structure of P. In the base cases $P = 0$ and $P = K$, it returns $\varnothing$ (i.e., nothing is added), otherwise it is defined as follows, where the auxiliary function Next generates a fresh index for the next rule to add.

If the process is an input $P = (x \mid \Pi).P'$, we add the flag for the current rule and another resource for the variable x: $\{(x, 0), (P_h r_j, \text{ff})\} \cup \mathcal{R}^h(P', j)$, given $\text{Next}(i) = j$. If the process is a non-deterministic choice, i.e., $P = P_a + P_b$, we add two flags, one for each branch, that will originate two different rules: $\{(P_h r_j, \text{ff}), (P_h r_k, \text{ff})\} \cup \mathcal{R}^h(P_a, j) \cup \mathcal{R}^h(P_b, k)$, given $\text{Next}(i) = j, \text{Next}(j) = k$. In

---

[3] $\mathcal{R}^h$ is parametric in h, since rules are binded to the component generating them.

all other cases, i.e., $P = [\Pi]P'$, $P = [a := e]P'$ or $P = \langle e \otimes \Pi \rangle.P'$, we add the flag for the current rule: $\{(P_h r_j, \text{ff}) \cup \mathcal{R}^h(P', j)$, given $\text{Next}(i) = j$.

Concerning AbU rules, we adopt the following mechanism. The ith generated rule, of the component h, listens on the rule flag $P_h r_i$: when the latter becomes tt, the rule can execute. Its execution disables $P_h r_i$ (it is set to ff) and enables the next rule, setting the flag $P_h r_j$, with $j = \text{Next}(i)$, to tt. In this way, the execution token can be exchanged between rules. The function $\mathcal{T}^h$, given a process of the component h, with $h \in [1..n]$, generates the rules to add to the translation. It relies on Next, that outputs a fresh index for the next rule to generate. We assume that Next in $\mathcal{T}^h$ is consistent with Next in $\mathcal{R}^h$, i.e., they have to produce the same sequence of indexes given a specific process. The function $\mathcal{T}^h(P, i)$, for $i \geq 0$, is defined inductively on the structure of P. In the base case $P = 0$, it returns ϵ (i.e., nothing is added), otherwise it is defined as follows.

If the process is a call to K, a new *call* rule is added. This rule enables the first flag (the dummy rule r_0) of the called process, defined by K.

$P = \text{K}$	$\text{K} \triangleq P_k$
$P_h r_i \ (P_h r_i = \top) : P_h r_i \leftarrow \bot \ P_k r_0 \leftarrow \top$	

If the process is an input x on the predicate Π, a new *receive* rule is added. The rule checks the condition given by the translation of the predicate Π. Here, Repl replaces, in a given AbU boolean expression, every instance of a specific service (x in this case) with msg. As an example, the predicate $\Pi = x < n$ is translated to $\text{Repl}(\mathcal{T}(\Pi), x) = msg < n$. When the condition is satisfied, the rule saves the value msg received from the sender (in the resource x), ends the communication and enables the next rule.

$P = (x \mid \Pi).P'$	$\text{Next}(i) = j$
$P_h r_i \ (P_h r_i = \top \wedge \text{Repl}(\mathcal{T}(\Pi), x)) : x \leftarrow msg \ P_h r_i \leftarrow \bot \ P_h r_i \leftarrow \top \ \mathcal{T}^h(P', i)$	

If the process is a non-deterministic choice between P_a and P_b, two new *choice* rules are added. Both rules listen to the same flag, so the scheduler can choose non-deterministically the one to execute. The action of the first choice rule enables the next rule given by the translation of P_a, while the action of the second choice rule enables the next rule given by the translation of P_b.

$P = P_a + P_b$	$\text{Next}(i) = j, \ \text{Next}(j) = k$
$P_h r_i \ (P_h r_i = \top) : P_h r_i \leftarrow \bot \ P_h r_j \leftarrow \top \ \mathcal{T}^h(P_a, j)$	
$P_h r_i \ (P_h r_i = \top) : P_h r_i \leftarrow \bot \ P_h r_k \leftarrow \top \ \mathcal{T}^h(P_b, j)$	

If the process is waiting on the predicate Π (awareness), a new *awareness* rule is added, that listens on the resources contained in Π. The latter are retrieved by the function Vars that inspects the predicate Π and returns a list of resource identifiers. In particular, variables x are left untouched, while AbC expressions a and $\text{this}.a$ are both translated to the resource a. The condition in the rule's task is the translation of Π. When it is satisfied, the next rule is enabled.

$P = [\Pi]P'$	$\text{Next}(i) = j$
$P_h r_i \ \text{Vars}(\Pi) \ (P_h r_i = \top \wedge \mathcal{T}(\Pi)) : P_h r_i \leftarrow \bot \ P_h r_i \leftarrow \top \ \mathcal{T}^h(P', i)$	

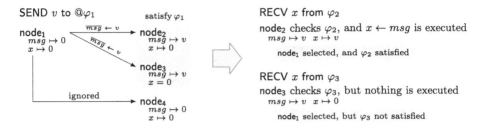

Fig. 4. Communication: a receive phase (right) after a send phase (left).

If the process updates the attribute a with the expression e, an *update* rule is added, assigning the translation of e to a and enabling the next rule.

$$\frac{P = [a := e]P' \qquad\qquad\qquad\qquad\qquad\qquad\qquad \mathsf{Next}(i) = j}{P_h r_i \ (P_h r_i = \top) : a \leftarrow \mathcal{T}(e) \ P_h r_i \leftarrow \bot \ P_h r_i \leftarrow \top \ \ \mathcal{T}^h(P', j)}$$

If the process is an output of the expression e on the predicate Π, a new *send* rule is added. The rule checks the condition given by the translation of the predicate Π. Note that, in the AbC semantics, the predicate is partially evaluated before the send, namely expressions of the form this.a are substituted with $\Gamma(a)$. To simulate this mechanism in AbU we use an auxiliary transformation Ext that takes a AbC predicate Π and returns its translation $\mathcal{T}(\Pi)$ where each instance (in Π) of an attribute a not prefixed by this. is translated to $\bar{a}$. As an example, the predicate $\Pi = \text{this}.n < n$ is translated to $\mathsf{Ext}(\Pi) = n < \bar{n}$. For each external node satisfying the predicate Π, the rule writes the translation of e to the external node resource msg (with $\overline{msg} \leftarrow \mathcal{T}(e)$). Outputs are non-blocking, so the rule has a default code, executed without caring about the satisfaction of the condition. It disables the current rule and enables the next one.

$$\frac{P = \langle e @ \Pi \rangle.P' \qquad\qquad\qquad\qquad\qquad\qquad \mathsf{Next}(i) = j}{P_h r_i > P_h r_i \leftarrow \bot \ P_h r_i \leftarrow \top, @(P_h r_i = \top \wedge \mathsf{Ext}(\Pi)) : \overline{msg} \leftarrow \mathcal{T}(e) \ \ \mathcal{T}^h(P', j)}$$

Finally, the translation of predicates $\mathcal{T}(\Pi)$ and expressions $\mathcal{T}(e)$ is recursively defined on Π and e, respectively. Its definition is straightforward, the only interesting cases are: $\mathcal{T}(\text{this}.a) \triangleq \mathcal{T}(a) \triangleq a$. To start the execution of the translated system, an (INPUT) is needed, enabling all rule flags $P_h r_0$, of all nodes.

In Fig. 4 we graphically explain how an attribute-based communication is performed in AbU, by means of attribute-based memory updates. The node node_1 aims to send the value v to nodes node_2 and node_3, since they satisfy $\varphi_1 = \mathsf{Ext}(\Pi_1)$. So, it updates with v the resource msg on the remote nodes node_2 and node_3. On the other side, node_2 and node_3 check if some node aims to communicate and node_1 is indeed selected. Since node_1 satisfies $\varphi_2 = \mathsf{Repl}(\mathcal{T}(\Pi_2), x)$ and does not satisfy $\varphi_3 = \mathsf{Repl}(\mathcal{T}(\Pi_3), x)$, only node_2 accepts the value v, saving it in the resource x, while node_3 ignores the communication.

In the following, we denote with $\mathcal{T}(C)$ the AbU encoding of C, where node states are defined as explained above, node pools are empty and nodes' ECA rules are generated by $\mathcal{T}$ (given a process of C).

Encoding Example. Given N agents, each associated with an integer in $[1..N]$, we wish to find one holding the maximum value. This problem can be modeled in AbC by using one component type P with two attributes: s, initially set to 1, indicating that the current component is the max; and n, that stores the component's value. Formally, the process P (with Max $\triangleq P$) is:

$$P = [s = 1]\,(\,\langle n @ n \leq \texttt{this.}n\rangle\,.\,\text{Max} + (x \mid x \geq \texttt{this.}n)\,.\,[s := 0]0\,)$$

P waits until s becomes 1 and then either: it sends its own value n to all other components with smaller n; or it receives (on x) a value from another component with a greater n and sets s to 0. Supposing $N = 3$, the problem is modeled in AbC with the component $C_{\max} = [s \mapsto 1\ n \mapsto 1] : P \parallel [s \mapsto 1\ n \mapsto 2] : P \parallel [s \mapsto 1\ n \mapsto 3] : P$. This AbC component translates to AbU as follows.

$$R\langle[msg \mapsto 0\ n \mapsto 1\ x \mapsto 0\ s \mapsto 0\ P_1 r_0 \mapsto \texttt{ff} \ldots P_1 r_6 \mapsto \texttt{ff}]\rangle$$
$$R\langle[msg \mapsto 0\ n \mapsto 2\ x \mapsto 0\ s \mapsto 0\ P_1 r_0 \mapsto \texttt{ff} \ldots P_1 r_6 \mapsto \texttt{ff}]\rangle$$
$$R\langle[msg \mapsto 0\ n \mapsto 3\ x \mapsto 0\ s \mapsto 0\ P_1 r_0 \mapsto \texttt{ff} \ldots P_1 r_6 \mapsto \texttt{ff}]\rangle$$

$R = P_1 r_0\ (P_1 r_0 = \top \land s = 1) : P_1 r_0 \leftarrow \bot\ P_1 r_1 \leftarrow \top$	aware rule
$\quad P_1 r_1\ (P_1 r_1 = \top) : P_1 r_1 \leftarrow \bot\ P_1 r_2 \leftarrow \top$	choice$_1$ rule
$\quad P_1 r_1\ (P_1 r_1 = \top) : P_1 r_1 \leftarrow \bot\ P_1 r_3 \leftarrow \top$	choice$_2$ rule
$\quad P_1 r_2 \rhd P_1 r_2 \leftarrow \bot\ P_1 r_4 \leftarrow \top, @(P_1 r_2 = \top \land \overline{n} \leq n) : \overline{msg} \leftarrow n$	send rule
$\quad P_1 r_4\ (P_1 r_4 = \top) : P_1 r_4 \leftarrow \bot\ P_1 r_0 \leftarrow \top$	call rule
$\quad P_1 r_3\ (P_1 r_3 = \top \land msg \geq n) : x \leftarrow msg\ P_1 r_3 \leftarrow \bot\ P_1 r_5 \leftarrow \top$	receive rule
$\quad P_1 r_5\ (P_1 r_5 = \top) : s \leftarrow 0\ P_1 r_5 \leftarrow \bot\ P_1 r_6 \leftarrow \top$	update rule

4.3   Correctness of the Encoding

Since a AbU node contains auxiliary resources, in addition to those corresponding to AbC attributes, we have to establish a notion of compatibility between AbU node states and AbC attribute environments. Given a AbU node state Σ and a AbC attribute environment Γ, we say that Σ is *compatible* with Γ, written $\Sigma \succeq \Gamma$, when for each $(a, v) \in \Gamma$ there exists $(a, v) \in \Sigma$ (i.e., $\Gamma \subseteq \Sigma$). This basically means that Σ agrees, at least, on all attributes of Γ. This notion can be extended to systems and components. Given a AbC component $C = \Gamma_1 : P_1 \parallel \ldots \parallel \Gamma_n : P_n$ and a AbU system $\mathsf{S} = R_1\langle\Sigma_1, \Theta_1\rangle \parallel \ldots \parallel R_n\langle\Sigma_n, \Theta_n\rangle$, we say that S is *compatible* with C, written $\mathsf{S} \succeq C$, when $\Sigma_i \succeq \Gamma_i$, for each $i \in [1..n]$.

Recall that, the AbU translation $\mathcal{T}(C)$ of C yields n (one for each process) initial rule flags $P_1 r_0, \ldots, P_n r_0$, initially set to ff. In order to start the computation of $\mathcal{T}(C)$, the latter have to be initialized (i.e., set to tt). In this regards, we assume an initial *input phase*, comprising n AbU (INPUT) steps, enabling all initial rule flags (without interleaving execution steps). Let $\rightarrow^*$ be the transitive closure of $\rightarrow$ without occurrences of labels of the form $\rhd\ T$. In other words,

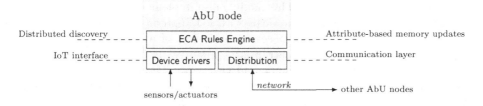

Fig. 5. High-level view of a AbU node implementation.

$\rightarrow^*$ denotes a finite sequence of internal input steps (with the corresponding discovery phases), without interleaving execution steps.

Now we are ready to state the correctness of the AbC encoding. The following Theorem 1 says that if a AbC component performs some computation steps, producing a residual component C', then the AbU translation of C, after an initial input phase, is able to perform an arbitrary number of computation steps, yielding a residual system attribute compatible with C'. This basically means that $\mathcal{T}(C)$ is able to "simulate" each possible execution of C.

Theorem 1 (AbC to AbU correctness). *Consider a AbC component C and its corresponding AbU encoding $S = \mathcal{T}(C)$. Then, for all C' such that $C \rightarrow^* C'$ there exists S' such that $S \rightarrow^* \twoheadrightarrow^* S'$ and $S' \succeq C'$.*

5 Towards a Distributed Implementation

In impementing AbU, we can basically follow two approaches. We can implement the calculus from scratch, dealing with all the problems related to a distributed infrastructure; or we can extend an existing distributed language with an abstraction layer to support ECA rules and their event-driven behavior. The latter approach can be less efficient, but more suitable for fast prototyping.

In any case, we have to deal with the intrinsic issues of distributed systems. In particular, by the CAP theorem [23] we cannot have, at the same time, consistency, availability and partition-tolerance. Hence, some compromises have to be taken, depending on the application context. For instance, in a scenario with low network traffic we can aim for correctness, implementing a robust, but slow, communication protocol. Vice versa, when nodes exchange data at a high rate (or when the network is not stable), communication should take very short time, hence we may prefer to renounce to consistency in favour of eventual consistency.

For these reasons, a flexible and modular implementation is mandatory, where modules can be implemented in different ways, depending on the application context. Hence, we present a modular architecture suitable to implement AbU nodes (see Fig. 5). A AbU node consists in a state (mapping resources to values), an execution pool (a set of updates to execute) and a list of ECA rules (modeling the node's behavior). A *ECA rules engine module* is in charge of executing the updates in the pool and to discover new rules to trigger, potentially on external nodes (distributed discovery). This module also implements the attribute-based memory updates mechanism and deals with IoT inputs (from sensors) and outputs (to actuators), which are accessed by means of a dedicated interface. A separate *Device drivers module* translates low-level IoT devices primitives to high-level signals for the rule engine and vice versa. The *Distribution module* is in charge of joining a cluster of AbU nodes and exchanging messages with them. It embodies all distributed infrastructure-related aspects, that can be tuned to meet the desired context-related requirements. Moreover, it provides the communication APIs needed by the rule engine to implement the (distributed) discovery phase (and, in turn, attributed-based memory updates). For instance, the labels ▶ T and ▷ T of the AbU semantics generate a broadcast communication.

In some respects, AbU is quite close to AbC, so we can borrow from one of its implementation the mechanisms that can be easily adapted to AbU. In particular, we can exploit the GoAt [1,24] library, in order to implement the Distribution module. GoAt is written in Golang, so we can delegate the communication layer to a Go routine, encapsulating the send and receive primitives of AbC and the cluster infrastructure, both provided by GoAt. Finally, the Device drivers module can be built on top of GOBOT [25], a mature Go library for the IoT ecosystem, with a great availability of IoT device drivers. In Fig. 5, we show a diagram describing the structure of a AbU node (here, the Device drivers and the Distribution modules can exploit GOBOT and GoAt, respectively). At the time of writing, we are developing a prototype implementation for the AbU calculus, written in Golang and following the modular architecture sketched above. The Distribution module is now based on HashiCorp's Memberlist [26], a popular Go library for cluster membership and failures detection that uses a gossip-based protocol. We plan to integrate the module with GoAt in the near future.

6   Conclusion

In this paper we have introduced AbU, a new calculus merging the simplicity of ECA programming with *attribute-based memory updates*. This new time-coupled, space-uncoupled interaction mechanism can be seen as the memory-based counterpart of attribute-based communication hinged on message-passing, and fits neatly within the ECA programming paradigm. We have shown how AbC components can be encoded in AbU systems; this result is not meant to prove that AbU subsumes AbC, but to highlight that it is possible to encode attribute-based communication within the ECA rules programming paradigm. Furthermore, we have provided a syntactic termination criterion for AbU systems, in order to assure that a AbU system does not exhibit divergent behaviors due to some cyclic interactions between nodes rules. Finally, we have discussed how the proposed calculus can be implemented, in a fully-distributed and IoT-ready setting.

Future Work. The present work is the basis for several research directions. First, we plan to encode in AbU a real-world ECA language like IRON (in particular, its core version presented in [15]), similarly to what we have done for AbC.

Then, we are interested in porting to AbU the verification techniques developed for IRON and other ECA languages [27,30,31]. Efficient distributed implementations of AbU could be obtained by extending the RETE algorithm [12] with the attribute-based memory updates mechanism. The latter can be implemented using RPCs or message-passing, taking inspiration from the implementations of AbC [1,21,24], as discussed in Sect. 5. Another interesting issue is *distributed runtime verification and monitoring*, in order to detect violations at runtime of given correctness properties, e.g., expressed in temporal logics like the μ-calculus [28]. These would be useful, for instance, to extend (and refine) the termination criterion presented in Sect. 3. Similarly, we can define syntactic criteria and corresponding verification mechanisms to guarantee *confluence*. Indeed, in some practical IoT scenarios, it is important to ensure that execution order does not impact the overall behavior (which is, basically, a sort of rule determinism). Finally, we can think of defining suitable behavioural equivalences for AbU systems, e.g., based on bisimulations, to compare systems with their specifications.

References

1. Abd Alrahman, Y., De Nicola, R., Garbi, G.: GoAt: Attribute-based interaction in Google Go. In: Margaria, T., Steffen, B. (eds.) ISoLA 2018, Part III. LNCS, vol. 11246, pp. 288–303. Springer, Cham (2018). https://doi.org/10.1007/978-3-030-03424-5_19

2. Abd Alrahman, Y., De Nicola, R., Loreti, M.: On the power of attribute-based communication. In: Albert, E., Lanese, I. (eds.) FORTE 2016. LNCS, vol. 9688, pp. 1–18. Springer, Cham (2016). https://doi.org/10.1007/978-3-319-39570-8_1

3. Abd Alrahman, Y., De Nicola, R., Loreti, M.: A calculus for collective-adaptive systems and its behavioural theory. Inf. Comput. **268**, 104457 (2019). https://www.sciencedirect.com/science/article/pii/S0890540119300732

4. Abd Alrahman, Y., De Nicola, R., Loreti, M.: Programming interactions in collective adaptive systems by relying on attribute-based communication. Sci. Comput. Program. **192**, 102428 (2020). https://doi.org/10.1016/j.scico.2020.102428

5. Abd Alrahman, Y., De Nicola, R., Loreti, M., Tiezzi, F., Vigo, R.: A calculus for attribute-based communication. In: Proceedings of the 30th Annual ACM Symposium on Applied Computing, pp. 1840–1845. ACM, New York (2015). https://doi.org/10.1145/2695664.2695668

6. Abd Alrahman, Y., Garbi, G.: A distributed API for coordinating AbC programs. Int. J. Softw. Tools Technol. Transf. (2020). https://doi.org/10.1007/s10009-020-00553-4

7. Abd Alrahman, Y., Perelli, G., Piterman, N.: Reconfigurable interaction for MAS modelling. In: Proceedings of the 19th International Conference on Autonomous Agents and MultiAgent Systems, AAMAS 2020, pp. 7–15. International Foundation for Autonomous Agents and Multiagent Systems, Richland (2020)

8. Aguilera, M.K., Ben-David, N., Calciu, I., Guerraoui, R., Petrank, E., Toueg, S.: Passing messages while sharing memory. In: Proceedings of the 2018 ACM Symposium on Principles of Distributed Computing, PODC 2018, pp. 51–60. ACM, New York (2018). https://doi.org/10.1145/3212734.3212741

9. Aguilera, M.K., Ben-David, N., Guerraoui, R., Marathe, V., Zablotchi, I.: The impact of RDMA on agreement. In: Proceedings of the 2019 ACM Symposium on

Principles of Distributed Computing, PODC 2019, pp. 409–418. ACM, New York (2019). https://doi.org/10.1145/3293611.3331601

10. Anderson, S., Bredeche, N., Eiben, A., Kampis, G., van Steen, M.: Adaptive collective systems: herding black sheep (2013)

11. Balliu, M., Merro, M., Pasqua, M., Shcherbakov, M.: Friendly fire: Cross-app interactions in IoT platforms. ACM Trans. Priv. Secur. **24**(3) (2021). https://doi.org/10.1145/3444963

12. Berstel, B.: Extending the RETE algorithm for event management. In: Proceedings of 9th International Symposium on Temporal Representation and Reasoning, pp. 49–51. IEEE (2002)

13. Beyer, D., Stahlbauer, A.: BDD-based software verification. Int. J. Softw. Tools Tech. Transf. **16**(5), 507–518 (2014). https://doi.org/10.1007/s10009-014-0334-1

14. Cacciagrano, D.R., Culmone, R.: Formal semantics of an IoT-specific language. In: 32nd International Conference on Advanced Information Networking and Applications Workshops (WAINA), pp. 579–584 (2018). https://doi.org/10.1109/WAINA.2018.00148

15. Cacciagrano, D.R., Culmone, R.: IRON: Reliable domain specific language for programming IoT devices. Internet Things **9**, 100020 (2020). https://doi.org/10.1016/j.iot.2018.09.006

16. Cano, J., Delaval, G., Rutten, E.: Coordination of ECA rules by verification and control. In: Kühn, E., Pugliese, R. (eds.) COORDINATION 2014. LNCS, vol. 8459, pp. 33–48. Springer, Heidelberg (2014). https://doi.org/10.1007/978-3-662-43376-8_3

17. Cano, J., Rutten, E., Delaval, G., Benazzouz, Y., Gurgen, L.: ECA rules for IoT environment: A case study in safe design. In: Proceedings of the 8th Int. Conf. on Self-Adaptive and Self-Organizing Systems Workshops (SASOW), pp. 116–121. IEEE Computer Society, USA (2014). https://doi.org/10.1109/SASOW.2014.32

18. Carriero, N., Gelernter, D.: The S/Net's Linda kernel (extended abstract). In: Proceedings of the 10th ACM Symposium on Operating Systems Principles, SOSP 1985, p. 160. ACM, New York (1985). https://doi.org/10.1145/323647.323643

19. Corradini, F., Culmone, R., Mostarda, L., Tesei, L., Raimondi, F.: A constrained ECA language supporting formal verification of WSNs. In: 2015 IEEE 29th International Conference on Advanced Information Networking and Applications Workshops, pp. 187–192 (2015). https://doi.org/10.1109/WAINA.2015.109

20. De Nicola, R., Ferrari, G., Pugliese, R.: KLAIM: a kernel language for agents interaction and mobility. IEEE Trans. Softw. Eng. **24**(5), 315–330 (1998). https://doi.org/10.1109/32.685256

21. De Nicola, R., Duong, T., Loreti, M.: Provably correct implementation of the AbC calculus. Sci. Comput. Programm. **202**, 102567 (2021). http://www.sciencedirect.com/science/article/pii/S0167642320301751

22. De Nicola, R., et al.: The SCEL language: Design, implementation, verification. In: Wirsing, M., Hölzl, M., Koch, N., Mayer, P. (eds.) Software Engineering for Collective Autonomic Systems. LNCS, vol. 8998, pp. 3–71. Springer, Cham (2015). https://doi.org/10.1007/978-3-319-16310-9_1

23. Gilbert, S., Lynch, N.: Brewer's conjecture and the feasibility of consistent, available, partition-tolerant web services. ACM SIGACT News **33**(2), 51–59 (2002). https://doi.org/10.1145/564585.564601

24. giulio-garbi.github.io: GoAt. https://giulio-garbi.github.io/goat/

25. gobot.io: GOBOT. https://gobot.io/

26. hashicorp.com: Memberlist. https://github.com/hashicorp/memberlist/

27. Jin, X., Lembachar, Y., Ciardo, G.: Symbolic verification of ECA rules. In: Moldt, D. (ed.) Proceedings of the International Workshop on Petri Nets and Software Engineering (PNSE 2013), Milano, Italy, 24–25 June 2013, vol. 989, pp. 41–59. CEUR-WS.org (2013). http://ceur-ws.org/Vol-989/paper17.pdf

28. Miculan, M.: On the formalization of the modal μ-calculus in the calculus of inductive constructions. Inf. Comput. **164**(1), 199–231 (2001). https://doi.org/10.1006/inco.2000.2902

29. Miculan, M., Pasqua, M.: A Calculus for Attribute-based Memory Updates (supplementary material), July 2021. https://doi.org/10.5281/zenodo.5057165

30. Vannucchi, C., et al.: vIRONy: A tool for analysis and verification of ECA rules in intelligent environments. In: 2017 International Conference on Intelligent Environments, IE 2017, Seoul, Korea (South), 21–25 August 2017, pp. 92–99. IEEE (2017). https://doi.org/10.1109/IE.2017.32

31. Vannucchi, C., et al.: Symbolic verification of event-condition-action rules in intelligent environments. J. Reliab. Intell. Environ. **3**(2), 117–130 (2017). https://doi.org/10.1007/s40860-017-0036-z

32. Wooldridge, M.: Reasoning About Rational Agents. Intelligent Robotics and Autonomous Agents. The MIT Press, Cambridge/London (2000)

A Proof Method for Local Sufficient Completeness of Term Rewriting Systems

Tomoki Shiraishi[1], Kentaro Kikuchi[2(✉)], and Takahito Aoto[1]

[1] Niigata University, Niigata, Japan
shiraishi@nue.ie.niigata-u.ac.jp, aoto@ie.niigata-u.ac.jp
[2] Tohoku University, Sendai, Japan
kentaro.kikuchi@riec.tohoku.ac.jp

Abstract. A term rewriting system (TRS) is said to be sufficiently complete when each function yields some value for any input. In this paper, we present a proof method for local sufficient completeness of TRSs, which is a generalised notion of sufficient completeness and is useful for proving inductive theorems of non-terminating TRSs. The proof method is based on a sufficient condition for local sufficient completeness of TRSs that consist of functions on natural numbers and (possibly infinite) lists of natural numbers. We also make a comparison between the proof abilities of the methods by the sufficient condition and by a derivation system introduced in previous work.

1 Introduction

Term rewriting is a computational model based on equational logic. A term rewriting system (TRS) is said to be sufficiently complete when each function yields as a result of computation some value for any input, where a value means a term consisting only of constructors. Sufficient completeness has an important role in automated inductive theorem proving of TRSs. One of the sufficient conditions of sufficient completeness of a TRS is that it is terminating (strongly normalising) and quasi-reducible. For terminating TRSs, various decision procedures of sufficient completeness have been proposed [2,9,11].

On the other hand, little is known about automated proof methods for sufficient completeness of non-terminating TRSs. Besides, in the case of non-terminating TRSs, it is appropriate to consider not all ground terms as the starting points of computations, but only terms of specific form, specific sort, etc. The property with such modifications has been introduced in [10], called *local sufficient completeness*. In fact, a framework for proving inductive theorems based on local sufficient completeness has been proposed in [10].

In this paper, we present a proof method for local sufficient completeness that is applicable to non-terminating TRSs. Specifically, we give a sufficient condition for local sufficient completeness of TRSs that consist of functions on natural numbers and (possibly infinite) lists of natural numbers. Using this sufficient condition, we can prove local sufficient completeness for various functions including

© Springer Nature Switzerland AG 2021
A. Cerone and P. C. Ölveczky (Eds.): ICTAC 2021, LNCS 12819, pp. 386–404, 2021.
https://doi.org/10.1007/978-3-030-85315-0_22

ones for which the property is difficult to show by means of the derivation system introduced in [10].

One of the difficulties in proving local sufficient completeness comes from the fact that the property is not closed under the subterm relation, in contrast to the cases of termination and usual sufficient completeness on all ground terms. As a consequence, the measure for a proof by induction is not necessarily compatible with the subterm relation. To cope with this difficulty, our sufficient condition uses a partition of function symbols into several kinds: ones for which the property holds, ones for which it does not hold, and ones for which it holds by a hypothesis. Other ingredients of our proof of the correctness of the sufficient condition include novel notions of ω-sufficient completeness and ω-quasi-reducibility; the latter plays such a role as quasi-reducibility does in the case of terminating TRSs.

In this paper, we restrict our attention to TRSs that are defined on natural numbers and lists of natural numbers. They are representative examples of data types defined inductively and coinductively, and in this setting we analyse how to prove local sufficient completeness of non-terminating TRSs.

Related Work. The notion of sufficient completeness was originally introduced in [6,7]. Since then, numerous works have treated the property in the fields of algebraic specification and term rewriting. In the literature, sufficient completeness has often been defined not w.r.t. reduction but w.r.t. conversion. Sufficient completeness w.r.t. reduction, as in the present paper, was introduced in [11]. In most cases, efforts have been devoted to TRSs consisting of those functions for which computations are always terminating.

In [15], Toyama studied sufficient completeness w.r.t. reduction in the light of a more general notion of 'reachability'. He also gave a proof method for reachability, and applied it to some examples of left-linear non-terminating TRSs. The method was applied not to local sufficient completeness in general, but to special cases of ground terms in which function symbols are restricted. Some of the conditions for applying the method are not suitable to automation.

In [4,5], Gnaedig and Kirchner studied sufficient completeness w.r.t. reduction (called $\mathcal{C}$-reducibility) of possibly non-terminating TRSs. However, they studied only usual sufficient completeness, and did not address any kind of local sufficient completeness. Accordingly, their proof method is essentially different from the case of local sufficient completeness (as remarked above).

In [13], Nakamura et al. studied related notions of sort reducible operation symbols and correctness on a set of sorts in the frame work of context-sensitive rewriting [12]. However, they did not introduce a corresponding notion of local sufficient completeness and did not relate it to inductive theorem proving.

Organisation of the Paper. The paper is organised as follows. In Sect. 2, we explain basic notions and notations of term rewriting. In Sect. 3, we present a sufficient condition for local sufficient completeness. In Sect. 4, we prove the correctness of the sufficient condition. In Sect. 5, we give some examples of applying the sufficient condition and discuss applicability of the condition. In Sect. 6, we compare our method to previous work, and conclude in Sect. 7.

2   Preliminaries

In this section, we introduce some notations and notions from the field of term rewriting. For detailed information about term rewriting, see, e.g. [1,14].

A *many-sorted signature* is given by a non-empty set $\mathcal{S}$ of *sorts* and a set $\mathcal{F}$ of *function symbols*; each $f \in \mathcal{F}$ is equipped with its *sort declaration* $f : \alpha_1 \times \cdots \times \alpha_n \to \alpha_0$ where $\alpha_0, \ldots, \alpha_n \in \mathcal{S}$ $(n \geq 0)$. We also use $f : \alpha_1 \times \cdots \times \alpha_n \to \alpha_0$ to mean that f is equipped with the sort declaration, or to denote such a function symbol f itself. We use $\mathcal{V}$ to denote the set of *variables* where $\mathcal{F} \cap \mathcal{V} = \emptyset$ and each $x \in \mathcal{V}$ has a unique sort $\alpha \in \mathcal{S}$. The set of variables with sort α is denoted by $\mathcal{V}^\alpha$. Then the set $T^\alpha(\mathcal{F}, \mathcal{V})$ of *terms of sort* α is defined inductively as follows:

1. If $x \in \mathcal{V}^\alpha$ then $x \in T^\alpha(\mathcal{F}, \mathcal{V})$.
2. If $f \in \mathcal{F}$, $f : \alpha_1 \times \cdots \times \alpha_n \to \alpha$ and $t_i \in T^{\alpha_i}(\mathcal{F}, \mathcal{V})$ for each i $(1 \leq i \leq n)$ then $f(t_1, \ldots, t_n) \in T^\alpha(\mathcal{F}, \mathcal{V})$.

We define $T(\mathcal{F}, \mathcal{V}) = \bigcup_{\alpha \in \mathcal{S}} T^\alpha(\mathcal{F}, \mathcal{V})$, and $sort(t) = \alpha$ for each $t \in T^\alpha(\mathcal{F}, \mathcal{V})$.

For a term $t = f(t_1, \ldots, t_n)$, its *root symbol* f is denoted by $root(t)$. The sets of function symbols and variables in a term t are denoted by $\mathcal{F}(t)$ and $\mathcal{V}(t)$, respectively. A term t is *ground* if $\mathcal{V}(t) = \emptyset$; the set of ground terms is denoted by $T(\mathcal{F})$. A term t is *linear* if each variable occurs at most once in t.

Positions are finite sequences of positive integers. The empty sequence is denoted by ε. The set of positions in a term t, denoted by $Pos(t)$, is defined as follows: $Pos(x) = \{\varepsilon\}$; $Pos(f(t_1, \ldots, t_n)) = \bigcup_i \{ip \mid p \in Pos(t_i)\} \cup \{\varepsilon\}$. The subterm of t at a position $p \in Pos(t)$ is written as $t|_p$. We use $s \trianglelefteq t$ to mean that s is a subterm of t. The *depth* of a position p is the length of p, denoted by $|p|$. The *height* of t, denoted by $height(t)$, is defined as $max\{|p| \mid p \in Pos(t)\}$.

A *context* is a term $C \in T(\mathcal{F} \cup \{\Box^\alpha \mid \alpha \in \mathcal{S}\}, \mathcal{V})$ where $\mathcal{F} \cap \{\Box^\alpha \mid \alpha \in \mathcal{S}\} = \emptyset$ and the special symbol $\Box^\alpha$, called a *hole*, is a term of sort α. We write $\Box$ for $\Box^\alpha$ when the sort is understood, and also write $\{\Box\}$ for the set $\{\Box^\alpha \mid \alpha \in \mathcal{S}\}$. For a context C, the holes are assumed not to be included in $\mathcal{F}(C)$. A context C with only one hole is denoted by $C[\ ]$, and $C[t]$ denotes the term obtained by filling the hole with a term t of the same sort.

A *substitution* is a mapping $\theta : \mathcal{V} \to T(\mathcal{F}, \mathcal{V})$ such that $sort(x) = sort(\theta(x))$ for every $x \in \mathcal{V}$, and $dom(\theta) = \{x \in \mathcal{V} \mid \theta(x) \neq x\}$ is finite. A substitution θ is *ground* if $\theta(x) \in T(\mathcal{F})$ for every $x \in dom(\theta)$. The term obtained by applying a substitution θ to a term t is written as $t\theta$. If θ_g is a ground substitution and $\mathcal{V}(t) \subseteq dom(\theta_g)$, the ground term $t\theta_g$ is called a *ground instance* of t.

A *rewrite rule*, written as $l \to r$, is an ordered pair of terms l and r such that $l \notin \mathcal{V}$, $\mathcal{V}(r) \subseteq \mathcal{V}(l)$ and $sort(l) = sort(r)$. A *term rewriting system* (*TRS*, for short) is a finite set of rewrite rules. Let $\mathcal{R}$ be a TRS . The binary relation $\to_\mathcal{R}$ on $T(\mathcal{F}, \mathcal{V})$ is defined by $s \to_\mathcal{R} t$ iff $s = C[l\theta]$ and $t = C[r\theta]$ for some $l \to r \in \mathcal{R}$, some context $C[\ ]$ and some substitution θ. The reflexive transitive closure of $\to_\mathcal{R}$ is denoted by $\overset{*}{\to}_\mathcal{R}$. A term s is in *normal form* if $s \to_\mathcal{R} t$ for no term t. The set of terms in normal form is denoted by $NF(\mathcal{R})$.

A TRS $\mathcal{R}$ is *terminating* if there exists no infinite sequence $t_0 \to_\mathcal{R} t_1 \to_\mathcal{R} \cdots$. Let $\mathcal{R}_1$ and $\mathcal{R}_2$ be TRSs. The binary relation $\to_{\mathcal{R}_1/\mathcal{R}_2}$ on $T(\mathcal{F}, \mathcal{V})$ is defined by

$\rightarrow_{\mathcal{R}_1/\mathcal{R}_2} = \stackrel{*}{\rightarrow}_{\mathcal{R}_2} \circ \rightarrow_{\mathcal{R}_1} \circ \stackrel{*}{\rightarrow}_{\mathcal{R}_2}$. We say that $\mathcal{R}_1$ is *relatively terminating* over $\mathcal{R}_2$ if there exists no infinite sequence $t_0 \rightarrow_{\mathcal{R}_1/\mathcal{R}_2} t_1 \rightarrow_{\mathcal{R}_1/\mathcal{R}_2} \cdots$. Note that it disallows infinite applications of $\rightarrow_{\mathcal{R}_1}$. We use $SN(\mathcal{R}_1/\mathcal{R}_2)$ to denote that $\mathcal{R}_1$ is relatively terminating over $\mathcal{R}_2$. The set of terms s such that $s \rightarrow_{\mathcal{R}_1/\mathcal{R}_2} t$ for no term t is denoted by $NF(\mathcal{R}_1/\mathcal{R}_2)$.

Let $\mathcal{R}$ be a TRS. The set $\mathcal{D}$ of *defined symbols* is given by $\mathcal{D} = \{root(l) \mid l \rightarrow r \in \mathcal{R}\}$, and the set $\mathcal{C}$ of *constructors* is given by $\mathcal{C} = \mathcal{F}\backslash\mathcal{D}$. Terms in $T(\mathcal{C}, \mathcal{V})$ are called *constructor terms*, and terms in $T(\mathcal{C})$ are called *ground constructor terms*. For $\mathcal{R}' \subseteq \mathcal{R}$, we define $\mathcal{D}_{\mathcal{R}'} = \{root(l) \mid l \rightarrow r \in \mathcal{R}'\}$.

Next we define the notion of sufficient completeness w.r.t. reduction.

Definition 1 (Sufficient completeness). A TRS $\mathcal{R}$ is *(globally) sufficiently complete* if for every ground term $t_g \in T(\mathcal{F})$, there exists a ground constructor term $s_g \in T(\mathcal{C})$ such that $t_g \stackrel{*}{\rightarrow}_{\mathcal{R}} s_g$.

A TRS $\mathcal{R}$ is said to be *quasi-reducible* if $f(t_1, \ldots, t_n) \notin NF(\mathcal{R})$ for every $f(t_1, \ldots, t_n) \in T(\mathcal{F})$ with $f \in \mathcal{D}$ and $t_1, \ldots, t_n \in T(\mathcal{C})$. The next proposition provides a criterion of sufficient completeness of $\mathcal{R}$. (For its proof, see, e.g. Proposition 2.4 of [10]).

Proposition 1. *Let $\mathcal{R}$ be a terminating TRS. Then, $\mathcal{R}$ is sufficiently complete if and only if $\mathcal{R}$ is quasi-reducible.*

3 A Sufficient Condition for Local Sufficient Completeness

In this section, we propose a sufficient condition under which a given TRS is locally sufficiently complete. The proposed condition consists of conditions on the signature (Definition 3) and on the rewrite rules (Definition 9).

First, we give a definition of local sufficient completeness [10].

Definition 2 (Local sufficient completeness). Let $\mathcal{R}$ be a TRS, and let $T \subseteq T(\mathcal{F})$ and $t \in T(\mathcal{F}, \mathcal{V})$. Then $LSC(T, t)$ denotes that for every ground instance $t\theta_g$ of t with $\theta_g : \mathcal{V} \rightarrow T$, there exists a ground constructor term $s_g \in T(\mathcal{C})$ such that $t\theta_g \stackrel{*}{\rightarrow}_{\mathcal{R}} s_g$. We say that $\mathcal{R}$ is *locally sufficiently complete* for t if $LSC(T(\mathcal{F}), t)$, and that $\mathcal{R}$ is *locally sufficiently complete* for $f \in \mathcal{F}$ if $LSC(T(\mathcal{F}), f(x_1, \ldots, x_n))$ where $x_1, \ldots, x_n$ are distinct variables.

The next example illustrates how different the notions of global and local sufficient completeness are.

Example 1. Consider a signature with $\mathcal{S} = \{N, L\}$ and

$$\mathcal{F} = \left\{ \begin{array}{ll} \mathsf{sum} : N \times L \rightarrow N, & + : N \times N \rightarrow N, \\ \mathsf{nat} : L, & \mathsf{inc} : L \rightarrow L, \\ 0 : N, & [] : L, \\ \mathsf{s} : N \rightarrow N, & :: : N \times L \rightarrow L \end{array} \right\}.$$

Let $\mathcal{R}$ be the following TRS where $\mathsf{sum}(n, ts)$ computes the summation of the first n elements of a (possibly infinite) list ts of natural numbers:

$$\mathcal{R} = \left\{ \begin{array}{ll} \mathsf{sum}(0, xs) & \to 0 \\ \mathsf{sum}(\mathsf{s}(x), []) & \to 0 \\ \mathsf{sum}(\mathsf{s}(x), y :: ys) & \to +(y, \mathsf{sum}(x, ys)) \\ \mathsf{nat} & \to 0 :: \mathsf{inc}(\mathsf{nat}) \\ \mathsf{inc}([]) & \to [] \\ \mathsf{inc}(x :: xs) & \to \mathsf{s}(x) :: \mathsf{inc}(xs) \\ +(0, y) & \to y \\ +(\mathsf{s}(x), y) & \to \mathsf{s}(+(x, y)) \end{array} \right\}.$$

$\mathcal{R}$ is not terminating since $\mathsf{nat} \to_{\mathcal{R}} 0 :: \mathsf{inc}(\mathsf{nat}) \xrightarrow{*}_{\mathcal{R}} 0 :: \mathsf{s}(0) ::$ $\mathsf{inc}(\mathsf{inc}(\mathsf{nat})) \xrightarrow{*}_{\mathcal{R}} \cdots$. $\mathcal{R}$ is not globally sufficiently complete either since $u \notin T(\mathcal{C})$ for any u with $\mathsf{nat} \xrightarrow{*}_{\mathcal{R}} u$. However, it can be shown that $\mathcal{R}$ is locally sufficiently complete for sum (cf. Examples 4 and 5).   □

Henceforth, we fix a TRS $\mathcal{R}$ to discuss its local sufficient completeness. We also fix a function symbol for which local sufficient completeness is expected to be proved, like sum of Example 1, and denote it by f_{tar} (representing the *target* function symbol).

Definition 3 (Conditions on the signature). We assume the following conditions S1–S4 on the signature of $\mathcal{R}$.

S1. $\mathcal{S} = \{N, L\}$, where N denotes the sort of natural numbers, and L denotes the sort of lists of natural numbers. The sets $\mathcal{N}$ and $\mathcal{L}$ of function symbols are defined by $\mathcal{N} = \{f \in \mathcal{F} \mid f : \alpha_1 \times \cdots \times \alpha_n \to N, \alpha_1, \ldots, \alpha_n \in \mathcal{S}, n \geq 0\}$ and $\mathcal{L} = \{f \in \mathcal{F} \mid f : \alpha_1 \times \cdots \times \alpha_n \to L, \alpha_1, \ldots, \alpha_n \in \mathcal{S}, n \geq 0\}$. The sets of defined symbols in $\mathcal{N}$ and $\mathcal{L}$ (i.e. the sets $\mathcal{N} \cap \mathcal{D}$ and $\mathcal{L} \cap \mathcal{D}$) are denoted by $\mathcal{N}_{\mathcal{D}}$ and $\mathcal{L}_{\mathcal{D}}$, respectively.

S2. The set $\mathcal{C} = \mathcal{F} \backslash \mathcal{D}$ of constructors is given by

$$\mathcal{C} = \left\{ \begin{array}{ll} 0 : N, & [] : L, \\ \mathsf{s} : N \to N, & :: \; : N \times L \to L \end{array} \right\}.$$

S3. (a) The sets $\mathcal{N}_{\mathcal{D}}$ and $\mathcal{L}_{\mathcal{D}}$ are partitioned as follows: $\mathcal{N}_{\mathcal{D}} = \mathcal{N}_{\mathcal{G}} \uplus \mathcal{N}_{\mathcal{H}}$ and $\mathcal{L}_{\mathcal{D}} = \mathcal{L}_{\mathcal{G}} \uplus \mathcal{L}_{\mathcal{H}} \uplus \mathcal{L}_{\mathcal{B}}$. (We use $\uplus$ for the disjoint union).
   (b) The set $\mathcal{G}$ of function symbols is defined by $\mathcal{G} = \mathcal{N}_{\mathcal{G}} \cup \mathcal{L}_{\mathcal{G}} \cup \mathcal{C}$.
   (c) The set $\mathcal{H}$ of defined symbols is defined by $\mathcal{H} = \mathcal{N}_{\mathcal{H}} \cup \mathcal{L}_{\mathcal{H}}$, and it satisfies $f_{tar} \in \mathcal{H}$.
S4. For every $g \in \mathcal{N}_{\mathcal{G}}$, if $g : \alpha_1 \times \cdots \times \alpha_n \to N$ then $\alpha_1 = \cdots = \alpha_n = N$.

$\mathcal{N}_{\mathcal{G}}$ and $\mathcal{L}_{\mathcal{G}}$ denote sets of defined symbols for which local sufficient completeness (on $T(\mathcal{C})$) hold, like $+$ and inc of Example 1, while $\mathcal{L}_{\mathcal{B}}$ denotes a set of defined symbols for which local sufficient completeness does not hold, like nat of Example 1. The set $\mathcal{H}$ contains f_{tar} and other defined symbols for which local sufficient completeness is supposed to hold when applying the sufficient condition recursively.

To prove local sufficient completeness for f_{tar}, which can have an arbitrary sort declaration with N and L, we basically assume that computation on N is always possible. The condition S4 of Definition 3, which might seem to be strict, requires that every function symbol in $\mathcal{N}_{\mathcal{D}}$ whose argument has sort L must be in $\mathcal{N}_{\mathcal{H}}$. For more discussions on this restriction, see Sect. 5.

Next we introduce some key notions for proving the correctness of the sufficient condition. The notion of ω-sufficient completeness is a very weak form of sufficient completeness which only requires reachability to ground terms whose root symbols are constructors.

Definition 4 (ω-sufficient completeness). Let $\mathcal{R}' \subseteq \mathcal{R}$ and $T \subseteq T(\mathcal{F})$. Then $\mathcal{R}'$ is ω-sufficiently complete on T, denoted by $SC^\omega(T, \mathcal{R}')$, if for every ground term $t_g \in T$, there exists a ground term $s_g \in T$ such that $t_g \twoheadrightarrow_{\mathcal{R}'} s_g$ and $root(s_g) \in \mathcal{C}$.

To define the notion of ω-quasi-reducibility, we give two auxiliary definitions.

Definition 5 (Covered with constructors to depth n). Let $t \in T(\mathcal{F}, \mathcal{V})$. We say that t is *covered with constructors to depth n* if for every position $p \in Pos(t)$ with $|p| \leq n$, $root(t|_p) \in \mathcal{C}$.

We define a function that gives the maximum height of the arguments of rewrite rules.

Definition 6 (h_c). Let $\mathcal{R}' \subseteq \mathcal{R}$. We define $h_c(\mathcal{R}')$ by $h_c(\mathcal{R}') = max\{height(l_i) \mid l \to r \in \mathcal{R}', l = f(l_1, \ldots, l_n)\}$.

Intuitively, ω-quasi-reducibility expresses that each function application is reducible if the arguments are covered with constructors to some depth.

Definition 7 (ω-quasi-reducibility). Let $\mathcal{R}' \subseteq \mathcal{R}$. We say that $\mathcal{R}'$ is ω-quasi-reducible, denoted by $QR^\omega(\mathcal{R}')$, if the following holds:

For every $f(t_1, \ldots, t_n) \in T(\mathcal{F}, \mathcal{V})$ with $f \in \mathcal{D}_{\mathcal{R}'}$, if either $h_c(\mathcal{R}') = 0$ or each t_i $(1 \leq i \leq n)$ is covered with constructors to depth $h_c(\mathcal{R}') - 1$, then $f(t_1, \ldots, t_n) \notin NF(\mathcal{R}')$.

Example 2. Consider the following TRS $\mathcal{R}_{\mathsf{sum}}$ which is a subset of the TRS $\mathcal{R}$ of Example 1:

$$\mathcal{R}_{\mathsf{sum}} = \left\{ \begin{array}{ll} \mathsf{sum}(0, xs) & \to 0 \\ \mathsf{sum}(\mathsf{s}(x), []) & \to 0 \\ \mathsf{sum}(\mathsf{s}(x), y :: ys) & \to +(y, \mathsf{sum}(x, ys)) \end{array} \right\}.$$

It can be seen that $\mathcal{R}_{\mathsf{sum}}$ is ω-quasi-reducible. Indeed, $h_c(\mathcal{R}_{\mathsf{sum}}) = 1$, and for each t_1, t_2 covered with constructors to depth $h_c(\mathcal{R}_{\mathsf{sum}}) - 1 = 0$, we have $\mathsf{sum}(t_1, t_2) \notin NF(\mathcal{R}_{\mathsf{sum}})$ because none of $\mathsf{sum}(0, [])$, $\mathsf{sum}(\mathsf{s}(x), [])$, $\mathsf{sum}(0, y :: ys)$ and $\mathsf{sum}(\mathsf{s}(x), y :: ys)$ is in normal form. □

Next we introduce a special kind of contexts, which are used in the conditions on the rewrite rules. The idea is that, assuming local sufficient completeness for the defined symbols in $\mathcal{H}$, the problem turns into how the reducibility to a ground constructor term is affected by the remaining part that consists of variables (which may be instantiated by arbitrary ground terms) and function symbols except those in $\mathcal{H}$. Based on this observation, we introduce the function $Con_{\bar{\mathcal{H}}}$ which assigns a special context to each term.

Definition 8 ($Con_{\bar{\mathcal{H}}}$). For each $t \in T(\mathcal{F}, \mathcal{V})$, we define $Con_{\bar{\mathcal{H}}}(t)$ as follows:

$$Con_{\bar{\mathcal{H}}}(t) = \begin{cases} x & \text{if } t = x \in \mathcal{V}, \\ f(Con_{\bar{\mathcal{H}}}(t_1), \ldots, Con_{\bar{\mathcal{H}}}(t_n)) & \text{if } t = f(t_1, \ldots, t_n) \text{ and } f \notin \mathcal{H}, \\ \Box & \text{if } t = f(t_1, \ldots, t_n) \text{ and } f \in \mathcal{H}. \end{cases}$$

Example 3. Let $+(y, \times(\mathsf{s}(0), x)) \in T(\mathcal{F}, \mathcal{V})$ and $\mathcal{H} = \{\times\}$. Then we have

$$\begin{aligned} Con_{\{\bar{\times}\}}(+(y, \times(\mathsf{s}(0), x))) &= +(Con_{\{\bar{\times}\}}(y), Con_{\{\bar{\times}\}}(\times(\mathsf{s}(0), x))) \\ &= +(y, \Box). \end{aligned}$$

$\Box$

We show some lemmas on $Con_{\bar{\mathcal{H}}}$.

Lemma 1. *For every* $t \in T(\mathcal{F}, \mathcal{V})$, $\mathcal{H} \cap \mathcal{F}(Con_{\bar{\mathcal{H}}}(t)) = \emptyset$.

Proof. By induction on the structure of t. $\Box$

Lemma 2. *If* $\mathcal{H} \cap \mathcal{F}(t) = \emptyset$ *then* $Con_{\bar{\mathcal{H}}}(t) = t$.

Proof. By induction on the structure of t. $\Box$

Lemma 3. *Let* θ *be a substitution. Suppose that* θ_c *is a substitution defined by* $\theta_c(x) = Con_{\bar{\mathcal{H}}}(x\theta)$. *Then, for every* $t \in T(\mathcal{F}, \mathcal{V})$, $Con_{\bar{\mathcal{H}}}(t\theta) = Con_{\bar{\mathcal{H}}}(t)\theta_c$.

Proof. By induction on the structure of t.

1. $t = x \in \mathcal{V}$. Then by the definition of $Con_{\bar{\mathcal{H}}}$, we have $Con_{\bar{\mathcal{H}}}(x) = x$. On the other hand, by the definition of θ_c, we have $x\theta_c = Con_{\bar{\mathcal{H}}}(x\theta)$. Hence we have $Con_{\bar{\mathcal{H}}}(x\theta) = Con_{\bar{\mathcal{H}}}(x)\theta_c$.
2. $t = f(t_1, \ldots, t_n)$ and $f \notin \mathcal{H}$. Then we have

$$\begin{aligned} Con_{\bar{\mathcal{H}}}(f(t_1, \ldots, t_n)\theta) &= Con_{\bar{\mathcal{H}}}(f(t_1\theta, \ldots, t_n\theta)) \\ &= f(Con_{\bar{\mathcal{H}}}(t_1\theta), \ldots, Con_{\bar{\mathcal{H}}}(t_n\theta)) \quad \text{(by def. of } Con_{\bar{\mathcal{H}}}) \\ &= f(Con_{\bar{\mathcal{H}}}(t_1)\theta_c, \ldots, Con_{\bar{\mathcal{H}}}(t_n)\theta_c) \text{ (by ind. hyp.)} \\ &= f(Con_{\bar{\mathcal{H}}}(t_1), \ldots, Con_{\bar{\mathcal{H}}}(t_n))\theta_c \\ &= Con_{\bar{\mathcal{H}}}(f(t_1, \ldots, t_n))\theta_c. \quad \text{(by def. of } Con_{\bar{\mathcal{H}}}) \end{aligned}$$

3. $t = f(t_1, \ldots, t_n)$ and $f \in \mathcal{H}$. Then by the definition of $Con_{\bar{\mathcal{H}}}$, we have $Con_{\bar{\mathcal{H}}}(t\theta) = \Box = \Box\theta_c = Con_{\bar{\mathcal{H}}}(t)\theta_c$. $\Box$

Now we give the conditions on the rewrite rules. The necessity of these conditions as well as the conditions of Definition 3 are discussed in Sect. 5.

Definition 9 (Conditions on the rewrite rules). Let $\mathcal{R}$ be partitioned into the following three sets $\mathcal{R}_{f_{tar}}$, $\mathcal{R}_N$ and $\mathcal{R}_L$ of rewrite rules:

$$\mathcal{R}_{f_{tar}} = \{\, l \to r \in \mathcal{R} \mid root(l) = f_{tar} \,\},$$

$$\mathcal{R}_N = \{\, l \to r \in \mathcal{R} \mid sort(l) = N,\ root(l) \neq f_{tar} \,\},$$

$$\mathcal{R}_L = \{\, l \to r \in \mathcal{R} \mid sort(l) = L,\ root(l) \neq f_{tar} \,\}.$$

In what follows, we denote the set $\mathcal{R}_N \cup \mathcal{R}_L$ by $\mathcal{R}_{N,L}$. We assume the following conditions R1–R6 on the rewrite rules of $\mathcal{R}$.

R1. $SN(\mathcal{R}_{f_{tar}}/\mathcal{R}_{N,L})$.
R2. $SC^\omega(T(\mathcal{F} \setminus \{f_{tar}\}), \mathcal{R}_{N,L})$.
R3. $QR^\omega(\mathcal{R}_{f_{tar}})$.
R4. For every $g \in \mathcal{G}$, $LSC(T(\mathcal{C}), g(x_1, \ldots, x_n))$.
R5. For every $f \in \mathcal{H} \setminus \{f_{tar}\}$, $LSC(T(\mathcal{F} \setminus \{f_{tar}\}), f(x_1, \ldots, x_n))$.
R6. For every $l \to r \in \mathcal{R}$, the following hold.
  (a) If $l \to r \in \mathcal{R}_{f_{tar}}$ then $\mathcal{F}(Con_{\widetilde{\mathcal{H}}}(r)) \subseteq \mathcal{G}$ and $\mathcal{V}(Con_{\widetilde{\mathcal{H}}}(r)) \subseteq \mathcal{V}^N$.
  (b) If $l \to r \in \mathcal{R}_{N,L}$ and $root(l) \in \mathcal{G} \cup \mathcal{H}$ then
    $\mathcal{F}(Con_{\widetilde{\mathcal{H}}}(r)) \subseteq \mathcal{G}$ and $\mathcal{V}(Con_{\widetilde{\mathcal{H}}}(r)) \cap \mathcal{V}^L \subseteq \mathcal{V}(Con_{\widetilde{\mathcal{H}}}(l))$.

Now the correctness of our sufficient condition for local sufficient completeness is stated as follows.

Theorem 1. *Suppose that $\mathcal{R}$ satisfies the conditions on the signature (Definition 3) and the conditions on the rewrite rules (Definition 9). Then, $\mathcal{R}$ is locally sufficiently complete for f_{tar}.*

A proof of this theorem is given in the next section.

Example 4. The TRS $\mathcal{R}$ of Example 1 can be partitioned into the following three sets of rewrite rules:

$$\mathcal{R}_{\mathsf{sum}} = \left\{ \begin{array}{ll} \mathsf{sum}(0, xs) & \to 0 \\ \mathsf{sum}(\mathsf{s}(x), [\,]) & \to 0 \\ \mathsf{sum}(\mathsf{s}(x), y :: ys) & \to +(y, \mathsf{sum}(x, ys)) \end{array} \right\},$$

$$\mathcal{R}_N = \left\{ \begin{array}{l} +(0, y) \to y \\ +(\mathsf{s}(x), y) \to \mathsf{s}(+(x, y)) \end{array} \right\},$$

$$\mathcal{R}_L = \left\{ \begin{array}{ll} \mathsf{nat} & \to 0 :: \mathsf{inc}(\mathsf{nat}) \\ \mathsf{inc}([\,]) & \to [\,] \\ \mathsf{inc}(x :: xs) \to \mathsf{s}(x) :: \mathsf{inc}(xs) \end{array} \right\}.$$

We check that the conditions R1–R6 of Definition 9 are satisfied. Let $f_{tar} = \mathsf{sum}$, $\mathcal{H} = \{\mathsf{sum}\}$ and $\mathcal{G} = \{+, \mathsf{inc}\} \cup \mathcal{C}$ where $\mathcal{C} = \{0, \mathsf{s}, [\,], :: \}$. The condition R1 can be shown by a proof method for relative termination [3] (cf. Lemma 5 of [8]). The condition R2 can be proved by induction on the ground terms in $T(\mathcal{F} \setminus \{\mathsf{sum}\})$. The condition R3 was seen in Example 2. The condition R4 holds by termination and quasi-reducibility of the rewrite rules for $+$ and inc. The condition R5 holds since $\mathcal{H} \setminus \{\mathsf{sum}\} = \emptyset$. The condition R6 can be checked according to the forms of the rewrite rules. □

4   Correctness of the Sufficient Condition

In this section, we give a proof of Theorem 1. Throughout this section, we suppose that the TRS $\mathcal{R}$ satisfies the conditions on the signature (Definition 3) and the conditions on the rewrite rules (Definition 9).

A brief outline of the proof is as follows. First we aim to find, for each ground term $f_{tar}(t_1, \ldots, t_n)$, a ground term s_k such that $f_{tar}(t_1, \ldots, t_n) = s_0 \overset{*}{\to}_\mathcal{R} s_k$ and $f_{tar} \notin \mathcal{F}(s_k)$. This is achieved by the conditions R1–R3. Then we show that the property $Con_{\bar{\mathcal{H}}}(s_i) \in T(\mathcal{G} \cup \{\Box\})$ is preserved during the reduction steps $s_0 \overset{*}{\to}_\mathcal{R} s_k$. Finally we show $s_k \overset{*}{\to}_\mathcal{R} u_g$ for some ground constructor term u_g.

In the following, we show a series of lemmas. The first two lemmas are consequences of ω-sufficient completeness and ω-quasi-reducibility.

Lemma 4. *Let n be an arbitrary natural number. Then, for every ground term $t_g \in T(\mathcal{F})$ with $f_{tar} \notin \mathcal{F}(t_g)$, there exists a ground term $s_g \in T(\mathcal{F})$ such that $t_g \overset{*}{\to}_{\mathcal{R}_{N,L}} s_g$ and s_g is covered with constructors to depth n.*

Proof. By induction on n.

- $n = 0$. Then it suffices to show that there exists a ground term $s_g \in T(\mathcal{F})$ such that $t_g \overset{*}{\to}_{\mathcal{R}_{N,L}} s_g$ and $root(s_g) \in \mathcal{C}$. This holds since we have $SC^\omega(T(\mathcal{F} \setminus \{f_{tar}\}), \mathcal{R}_{N,L})$ by the condition R2 of Definition 9.
- Suppose that the claim holds for $n-1$. From $SC^\omega(T(\mathcal{F} \setminus \{f_{tar}\}), \mathcal{R}_{N,L})$, there exist $f \in \mathcal{C}$ and $u_1, \ldots, u_m \in T(\mathcal{F} \setminus \{f_{tar}\})$ such that $t_g \overset{*}{\to}_{\mathcal{R}_{N,L}} f(u_1, \ldots, u_m)$. By the induction hypothesis, for each i $(1 \leq i \leq m)$, there exists $\hat{u}_i \in T(\mathcal{F})$ such that $u_i \overset{*}{\to}_{\mathcal{R}_{N,L}} \hat{u}_i$ and $\hat{u}_i$ is covered with constructors to depth $n-1$. Hence we have $t_g \overset{*}{\to}_{\mathcal{R}_{N,L}} f(u_1, \ldots, u_m) \overset{*}{\to}_{\mathcal{R}_{N,L}} f(\hat{u}_1, \ldots, \hat{u}_m) \in T(\mathcal{F})$ and $f(\hat{u}_1, \ldots, \hat{u}_m)$ is covered with constructors to depth n. □

Lemma 5. *Let $t_g \in T(\mathcal{F})$ with $t_g \in NF(\mathcal{R}_{f_{tar}}/\mathcal{R}_{N,L})$. Then, for every $u \trianglelefteq t_g$, $root(u) \neq f_{tar}$.*

Proof. Suppose that there exists u such that $u \trianglelefteq t_g$ and $root(u) = f_{tar}$, and take a minimal such $u = f_{tar}(u_1, \ldots, u_n)$. Then by the minimality, $f_{tar} \notin \bigcup_{1 \leq i \leq n} \mathcal{F}(u_i)$. By Lemma 4, for each i $(1 \leq i \leq n)$, there exists $\hat{u}_i$ such that $u_i \overset{*}{\to}_{\mathcal{R}_{N,L}} \hat{u}_i$ and $\hat{u}_i$ is covered with constructors to depth $h_c(\mathcal{R}_{f_{tar}}) - 1$ (or we set $\hat{u}_i = u_i$ when $h_c(\mathcal{R}_{f_{tar}}) = 0$). Hence $f_{tar}(u_1, \ldots, u_n) \overset{*}{\to}_{\mathcal{R}_{N,L}} f_{tar}(\hat{u}_1, \ldots, \hat{u}_n) \notin NF(\mathcal{R}_{f_{tar}})$, since $QR^\omega(\mathcal{R}_{f_{tar}})$ by the condition R3 of Definition 9. Thus for the context $C[\ ]$ with $t_g = C[u]$, we have $t_g = C[f_{tar}(u_1, \ldots, u_n)] \overset{*}{\to}_{\mathcal{R}_{N,L}} C[f_{tar}(\hat{u}_1, \ldots, \hat{u}_n)] \to_{\mathcal{R}_{f_{tar}}} s$ for some s. This contradicts $t_g \in NF(\mathcal{R}_{f_{tar}}/\mathcal{R}_{N,L})$. □

Next we show some properties on $Con_{\bar{\mathcal{H}}}(t)$. The following is about the case where the sort of t is N.

Lemma 6. *Let* $t_g \in T(\mathcal{F})$ *with* $sort(t_g) = N$. *Then,* $Con_{\bar{\mathcal{H}}}(t_g) \in T(\mathcal{G} \cup \{\Box\})$.

Proof. By induction on the structure of t_g.

1. $t_g = x \in \mathcal{V}$. This case is impossible since $t_g \in T(\mathcal{F})$.
2. $t_g = f(t_1, \ldots, t_n)$.
   (a) $f \in \mathcal{C}(\subseteq \mathcal{G})$. If $f = 0$, i.e. $t_g = 0$, then $Con_{\bar{\mathcal{H}}}(t_g) = 0 \in T(\mathcal{G} \cup \{\Box\})$. Let us consider the case $f = \mathsf{s}$. Let $t_g = \mathsf{s}(t_1)$. Then $sort(t_1) = N$ and $t_1 \in T(\mathcal{F})$ since $t_g \in T(\mathcal{F})$. So by the induction hypothesis, $Con_{\bar{\mathcal{H}}}(t_1) \in T(\mathcal{G} \cup \{\Box\})$. Hence we have $Con_{\bar{\mathcal{H}}}(t_g) = Con_{\bar{\mathcal{H}}}(\mathsf{s}(t_1)) = \mathsf{s}(Con_{\bar{\mathcal{H}}}(t_1)) \in T(\mathcal{G} \cup \{\Box\})$.
   (b) $f \in \mathcal{N}_{\mathcal{G}}(\subseteq \mathcal{G})$. By the condition S4 of Definition 3, we have $sort(t_i) = N$ for each i $(1 \leq i \leq n)$. Also, we have $t_i \in T(\mathcal{F})$ since $t_g \in T(\mathcal{F})$. So by the induction hypothesis, $Con_{\bar{\mathcal{H}}}(t_i) \in T(\mathcal{G} \cup \{\Box\})$. Hence we have $Con_{\bar{\mathcal{H}}}(t_g) = Con_{\bar{\mathcal{H}}}(f(t_1, \ldots, t_n)) = f(Con_{\bar{\mathcal{H}}}(t_1), \ldots, Con_{\bar{\mathcal{H}}}(t_n)) \in T(\mathcal{G} \cup \{\Box\})$.
   (c) $f \in \mathcal{N}_{\mathcal{H}}(\subseteq \mathcal{H})$. Then we have $Con_{\bar{\mathcal{H}}}(f(t_1, \ldots, t_n)) = \Box \in T(\mathcal{G} \cup \{\Box\})$. □

A key lemma for proving the theorem is Lemma 9, which states that the property $Con_{\bar{\mathcal{H}}}(t_g) \in T(\mathcal{G} \cup \{\Box\})$ is preserved under reduction. Before proving the lemma, we show two auxiliary lemmas.

Lemma 7. *Let* $r \in T(\mathcal{F}, \mathcal{V})$ *with* $\mathcal{F}(Con_{\bar{\mathcal{H}}}(r)) \subseteq \mathcal{G}$ *and* $\mathcal{V}(Con_{\bar{\mathcal{H}}}(r)) \subseteq \mathcal{V}^N$. *Then, for every ground instance* $r\theta_g$, $Con_{\bar{\mathcal{H}}}(r\theta_g) \in T(\mathcal{G} \cup \{\Box\})$.

Proof. By induction on the structure of r.

1. $r = x \in \mathcal{V}$. By assumption, $\mathcal{V}(Con_{\bar{\mathcal{H}}}(r)) \subseteq \mathcal{V}^N$, so $sort(x) = N$. Then for every ground instance $x\theta_g$, $sort(x\theta_g) = N$. Hence by Lemma 6, $Con_{\bar{\mathcal{H}}}(x\theta_g) \in T(\mathcal{G} \cup \{\Box\})$.
2. $r = f(r_1, \ldots, r_n)$ and $f \notin \mathcal{H}$. Then $Con_{\bar{\mathcal{H}}}(r) = f(Con_{\bar{\mathcal{H}}}(r_1), \ldots, Con_{\bar{\mathcal{H}}}(r_n))$. Since $\mathcal{F}(Con_{\bar{\mathcal{H}}}(r)) \subseteq \mathcal{G}$, we have $f \in \mathcal{G}$ and $\mathcal{F}(Con_{\bar{\mathcal{H}}}(r_i)) \subseteq \mathcal{G}$ for each i $(1 \leq i \leq n)$. Also, since $\mathcal{V}(Con_{\bar{\mathcal{H}}}(r)) \subseteq \mathcal{V}^N$, we have $\mathcal{V}(Con_{\bar{\mathcal{H}}}(r_i)) \subseteq \mathcal{V}^N$ for each i $(1 \leq i \leq n)$. Hence by the induction hypothesis, for every ground instance $r_i\theta_g$, we have $Con_{\bar{\mathcal{H}}}(r_i\theta_g) \in T(\mathcal{G} \cup \{\Box\})$. Thus for every ground instance $r\theta_g$, $Con_{\bar{\mathcal{H}}}(r\theta_g) = Con_{\bar{\mathcal{H}}}(f(r_1\theta_g, \ldots, r_n\theta_g)) = f(Con_{\bar{\mathcal{H}}}(r_1\theta_g), \ldots, Con_{\bar{\mathcal{H}}}(r_n\theta_g)) \in T(\mathcal{G} \cup \{\Box\})$.
3. $r = f(r_1, \ldots, r_n)$ and $f \in \mathcal{H}$. Then $Con_{\bar{\mathcal{H}}}(r\theta_g) = Con_{\bar{\mathcal{H}}}(f(r_1\theta_g, \ldots, r_n\theta_g)) = \Box \in T(\mathcal{G} \cup \{\Box\})$. □

Lemma 8. *Let* $l \to r \in \mathcal{R}_{N,L}$. *Then, for every ground instances* $l\theta_g$ *and* $r\theta_g$, *if* $Con_{\bar{\mathcal{H}}}(l\theta_g) \in T(\mathcal{G} \cup \{\Box\})$ *then* $Con_{\bar{\mathcal{H}}}(r\theta_g) \in T(\mathcal{G} \cup \{\Box\})$.

Proof. Suppose $Con_{\bar{\mathcal{H}}}(l\theta_g) \in T(\mathcal{G} \cup \{\Box\})$. Then, if $root(l) \notin \mathcal{H}$ then $root(l) = root(Con_{\bar{\mathcal{H}}}(l\theta_g)) \in \mathcal{G}$. Hence $root(l) \in \mathcal{H} \cup \mathcal{G}$, and so by the condition R6(b) of Definition 9, we have

(1) $\mathcal{F}(Con_{\bar{\mathcal{H}}}(r)) \subseteq \mathcal{G}$, and

(2) $\mathcal{V}(Con_{\tilde{\mathcal{H}}}(r)) \cap \mathcal{V}^L \subseteq \mathcal{V}(Con_{\tilde{\mathcal{H}}}(l))$.

Now let θ_c be a substitution defined by $\theta_c(x) = Con_{\tilde{\mathcal{H}}}(x\theta_g)$. Then by Lemma 3, we have $Con_{\tilde{\mathcal{H}}}(l\theta_g) - Con_{\tilde{\mathcal{H}}}(l)\theta_c$ and $Con_{\tilde{\mathcal{H}}}(r\theta_g) = Con_{\tilde{\mathcal{H}}}(r)\theta_c$. Since $Con_{\mathcal{H}}(l\theta_g) \in T(\mathcal{G} \cup \{\Box\})$, we have $Con_{\tilde{\mathcal{H}}}(l)\theta_c \in T(\mathcal{G} \cup \{\Box\})$. Hence $\theta_c(x) \in T(\mathcal{G} \cup \{\Box\})$ for every $x \in \mathcal{V}(Con_{\tilde{\mathcal{H}}}(l))$. From this and (2) above, we have $\theta_c(x) \in T(\mathcal{G} \cup \{\Box\})$ for every $x \in \mathcal{V}(Con_{\tilde{\mathcal{H}}}(r)) \cap \mathcal{V}^L$. On the other hand, by Lemma 6, we have $\theta_c(x) = Con_{\tilde{\mathcal{H}}}(x\theta_g) \in T(\mathcal{G} \cup \{\Box\})$ for every $x \in \mathcal{V}(Con_{\tilde{\mathcal{H}}}(r)) \cap \mathcal{V}^N$. From these and (1) above, we have $Con_{\tilde{\mathcal{H}}}(r\theta_g) = Con_{\tilde{\mathcal{H}}}(r)\theta_c \in T(\mathcal{G} \cup \{\Box\})$. □

Now we prove the announced lemma.

Lemma 9. *Let* $s_g, t_g \in T(\mathcal{F})$ *with* $s_g \to_{\mathcal{R}} t_g$. *Then,* $Con_{\tilde{\mathcal{H}}}(s_g) \in T(\mathcal{G} \cup \{\Box\})$ *implies* $Con_{\tilde{\mathcal{H}}}(t_g) \in T(\mathcal{G} \cup \{\Box\})$.

Proof. We show that for every $l \to r \in \mathcal{R}$, every context $C[\ ]$, and every ground instances $l\theta_g$ and $r\theta_g$, if $Con_{\tilde{\mathcal{H}}}(C[l\theta_g]) \in T(\mathcal{G}\cup\{\Box\})$ then $Con_{\tilde{\mathcal{H}}}(C[r\theta_g]) \in T(\mathcal{G}\cup\{\Box\})$. We prove this by induction on $C[\ ]$.

1. $C[\ ] = \Box$. Suppose $Con_{\tilde{\mathcal{H}}}(l\theta_g) \in T(\mathcal{G} \cup \{\Box\})$. We distinguish two cases.
   (a) $l \to r \in \mathcal{R}_{f_{tar}}$. Then $root(l\theta_g) = f_{tar}$, and so $Con_{\tilde{\mathcal{H}}}(l\theta_g) = \Box$. Hence by Lemma 7 and the condition R6(a) of Definition 9, we have $Con_{\tilde{\mathcal{H}}}(r\theta_g) \in T(\mathcal{G} \cup \{\Box\})$.
   (b) $l \to r \in \mathcal{R}_{N,L}$. Then by Lemma 8, we have $Con_{\tilde{\mathcal{H}}}(r\theta_g) \in T(\mathcal{G} \cup \{\Box\})$.
2. $C[\ ] = f(t_1, \ldots, C'[\ ], \ldots, t_n)$ and $f \notin \mathcal{H}$. Suppose $Con_{\tilde{\mathcal{H}}}(C[l\theta_g]) \in T(\mathcal{G}\cup\{\Box\})$. Since

$$Con_{\tilde{\mathcal{H}}}(C[l\theta_g]) = Con_{\tilde{\mathcal{H}}}(f(t_1, \ldots, C'[l\theta_g], \ldots, t_n))$$
$$= f(Con_{\tilde{\mathcal{H}}}(t_1), \ldots, Con_{\tilde{\mathcal{H}}}(C'[l\theta_g]), \ldots, Con_{\tilde{\mathcal{H}}}(t_n)),$$

we have $f \in \mathcal{G}$, $Con_{\tilde{\mathcal{H}}}(C'[l\theta_g]) \in T(\mathcal{G} \cup \{\Box\})$ and $Con_{\tilde{\mathcal{H}}}(t_i) \in T(\mathcal{G} \cup \{\Box\})$ for each i ($1 \le i \le n$). So by the induction hypothesis, $Con_{\tilde{\mathcal{H}}}(C'[r\theta_g]) \in T(\mathcal{G} \cup \{\Box\})$. Hence we have

$$Con_{\tilde{\mathcal{H}}}(C[r\theta_g]) = Con_{\tilde{\mathcal{H}}}(f(t_1, \ldots, C'[r\theta_g], \ldots, t_n))$$
$$= f(Con_{\tilde{\mathcal{H}}}(t_1), \ldots, Con_{\tilde{\mathcal{H}}}(C'[r\theta_g]), \ldots, Con_{\tilde{\mathcal{H}}}(t_n)))$$
$$\in T(\mathcal{G} \cup \{\Box\}).$$

3. $C[\ ] = f(t_1, \ldots, C'[\ ], \ldots, t_n)$ and $f \in \mathcal{H}$. Then we have $Con_{\tilde{\mathcal{H}}}(C[r\theta_g]) = Con_{\tilde{\mathcal{H}}}(f(t_1, \ldots, C'[r\theta_g], \ldots, t_n)) = \Box \in T(\mathcal{G} \cup \{\Box\})$. □

The next lemma shows that every ground term without f_{tar} has a nice property.

Lemma 10. *Let* $s_g \in T(\mathcal{F})$ *with* $f_{tar} \notin \mathcal{F}(s_g)$ *and* $Con_{\tilde{\mathcal{H}}}(s_g) \in T(\mathcal{G} \cup \{\Box\})$. *Then, there exists a ground constructor term* $u_g \in T(\mathcal{C})$ *such that* $s_g \xrightarrow{*}_{\mathcal{R}} u_g$.

Proof. By induction on the structure of s_g.

1. $s_g = x \in \mathcal{V}$. This case is impossible since $s_g \in T(\mathcal{F})$.
2. $s_g = f(s_1, \ldots, s_n)$ and $f \notin \mathcal{H}$. Then we have $Con_{\bar{\mathcal{H}}}(s_g) = f(Con_{\bar{\mathcal{H}}}(s_1), \ldots,$ $Con_{\bar{\mathcal{H}}}(s_n))$. Since $Con_{\bar{\mathcal{H}}}(s_g) \in T(\mathcal{G} \cup \{\Box\})$, we have $f \in \mathcal{G}$ and $Con_{\bar{\mathcal{H}}}(s_i) \in T(\mathcal{G} \cup \{\Box\})$ for each i $(1 \leq i \leq n)$. Also, since $f_{tar} \notin \mathcal{F}(s_g)$, we have $f_{tar} \notin Con_{\bar{\mathcal{H}}}(s_i)$ for each i $(1 \leq i \leq n)$. Hence by the induction hypothesis, for each i, there exists $\hat{s}_i \in T(\mathcal{C})$ such that $s_i \xrightarrow{*}_{\mathcal{R}} \hat{s}_i$. Now by the condition R4 of Definition 9, we have $LSC(T(\mathcal{C}), f(x_1, \ldots, x_n))$. Hence we have $s_g = f(s_1, \ldots, s_n) \xrightarrow{*}_{\mathcal{R}} f(\hat{s}_1, \ldots, \hat{s}_n) \xrightarrow{*}_{\mathcal{R}} u_g$ for some $u_g \in T(\mathcal{C})$.
3. $s_g = f(s_1, \ldots, s_n)$ and $f \in \mathcal{H}$. Since $s_g \in T(\mathcal{F})$ and $f_{tar} \notin \mathcal{F}(s_g)$, we have $f \in \mathcal{H} \setminus \{f_{tar}\}$ and $s_1, \ldots, s_n \in T(\mathcal{F} \setminus \{f_{tar}\})$. Now by the condition R5 of Definition 9, we have $LSC(T(\mathcal{F} \setminus \{f_{tar}\}), f(x_1, \ldots, x_n))$. Hence we have $s_g = f(s_1, \ldots, s_n) \xrightarrow{*}_{\mathcal{R}} u_g$ for some $u_g \in T(\mathcal{C})$. □

Now we are ready to prove the theorem on the correctness of our sufficient condition for local sufficient completeness.

Proof (of Theorem 1). It suffices to show that for every $f_{tar}(t_1, \ldots, t_n) \in T(\mathcal{F})$, there exists a ground constructor term $u_g \in T(\mathcal{C})$ such that $f_{tar}(t_1, \ldots, t_n) \xrightarrow{*}_{\mathcal{R}} u_g$. Let $s_0 = f_{tar}(t_1, \ldots, t_n)$. By the condition R1 of Definition 9, we have $SN(\mathcal{R}_{f_{tar}}/\mathcal{R}_{N,L})$, so there is a rewrite sequence $s_0 \to_{\mathcal{R}_{f_{tar}}/\mathcal{R}_{N,L}} s_1 \to_{\mathcal{R}_{f_{tar}}/\mathcal{R}_{N,L}} \cdots \to_{\mathcal{R}_{f_{tar}}/\mathcal{R}_{N,L}} s_k \in NF(\mathcal{R}_{f_{tar}}/\mathcal{R}_{N,L})$. Since $root(s_0) = f_{tar} \in \mathcal{H}$, we have $Con_{\bar{\mathcal{H}}}(s_0) = \Box \in T(\mathcal{G} \cup \{\Box\})$. Hence by Lemma 9 and $s_0 \xrightarrow{*}_{\mathcal{R}} s_k$, we have $Con_{\bar{\mathcal{H}}}(s_k) \in T(\mathcal{G} \cup \{\Box\})$. Since $s_k \in NF(\mathcal{R}_{f_{tar}}/\mathcal{R}_{N,L})$, we have $f_{tar} \notin \mathcal{F}(s_k)$ by Lemma 5. Thus by Lemma 10, we have $s_0 \xrightarrow{*}_{\mathcal{R}} s_k \xrightarrow{*}_{\mathcal{R}} u_g$ for some $u_g \in T(\mathcal{C})$. □

Observing the above proof of Theorem 1, we note that the existence of s_k such that $s_0 \xrightarrow{*}_{\mathcal{R}_{f_{tar}}/\mathcal{R}_{N,L}} s_k \in NF(\mathcal{R}_{f_{tar}}/\mathcal{R}_{N,L})$ rather than $SN(\mathcal{R}_{f_{tar}}/\mathcal{R}_{N,L})$ is sufficient. However, we adopt $SN(\mathcal{R}_{f_{tar}}/\mathcal{R}_{N,L})$ as the condition R1, since it is suitable to automated verification.

5 Applicability of the Sufficient Condition

In this section, we give some examples of applying the sufficient condition for local sufficient completeness. We also give an example where the sufficient condition cannot be applied. Furthermore, we discuss the difficulty of proving local sufficient completeness without the conditions of Definitions 3 and 9.

Example 5. Consider the TRS $\mathcal{R}$ of Example 1. With $f_{tar} = \mathsf{sum}$, $\mathcal{H} = \{\mathsf{sum}\}$ and $\mathcal{G} = \{+, \mathsf{inc}\} \cup \mathcal{C}$ where $\mathcal{C} = \{0, \mathsf{s}, [], :: \}$, we see that $\mathcal{R}$ satisfies the conditions on the signature and the conditions on the rewrite rules (cf. Example 4). Hence by Theorem 1, $\mathcal{R}$ is locally sufficiently complete for sum. □

Example 6. Consider a signature with $\mathcal{S} = \{N, L\}$ and $\mathcal{F} = \{\mathsf{take} : N \times L \to L, \mathsf{ones} : L\} \cup \mathcal{C}$. Let $\mathcal{R}$ be the following TRS where $\mathsf{take}(n, ts)$ computes the list consisting of the first n elements of a (possibly infinite) list ts of natural numbers:

$$\mathcal{R} = \begin{cases} (1)\ \mathsf{take}(0, xs) & \to [] \\ (2)\ \mathsf{take}(\mathsf{s}(x), []) & \to [] \\ (3)\ \mathsf{take}(\mathsf{s}(x), y :: ys) \to y :: \mathsf{take}(x, ys) \\ (4)\ \mathsf{ones} & \to \mathsf{s}(0) :: \mathsf{ones} \end{cases}.$$

Let $f_{tar} = \mathsf{take}$, $\mathcal{H} = \{\mathsf{take}\}$ and $\mathcal{G} = \mathcal{C}$. Then we see that $\mathcal{R}$ satisfies the conditions on the signature. Next, let $\mathcal{R} = \mathcal{R}_{\mathsf{take}} \uplus \mathcal{R}_N \uplus \mathcal{R}_L$ where $\mathcal{R}_{\mathsf{take}} = \{(1), (2), (3)\}$, $\mathcal{R}_N = \{\}$ and $\mathcal{R}_L = \{(4)\}$. We check that the conditions R1–R6 of Definition 9 are satisfied. The condition R1 can be shown by a proof method for relative termination. Also, it is easy to see that the conditions R2–R6 are satisfied. Hence by Theorem 1, $\mathcal{R}$ is locally sufficiently complete for take. □

In the next example, we apply the sufficient condition recursively in $\mathcal{H}$.

Example 7. Consider a signature with $\mathcal{S} = \{N, L\}$ and $\mathcal{F} = \{\mathsf{takeones} : N \to L, \mathsf{take} : N \times L \to L, \mathsf{ones} : L\} \cup \mathcal{C}$. Let $\mathcal{R}$ be the TRS consisting of the rules (1)–(4) of Example 6 and the following rule:

$$(5)\ \mathsf{takeones}(x) \to \mathsf{take}(x, \mathsf{ones}).$$

Let $f_{tar} = \mathsf{takeones}$, $\mathcal{H} = \{\mathsf{takeones}, \mathsf{take}\}$ and $\mathcal{G} = \mathcal{C}$. Then we see that $\mathcal{R}$ satisfies the conditions on the signature. Next, let $\mathcal{R} = \mathcal{R}_{\mathsf{takeones}} \uplus \mathcal{R}_N \uplus \mathcal{R}_L$ where $\mathcal{R}_{\mathsf{takeones}} = \{(5)\}$, $\mathcal{R}_N = \{\}$ and $\mathcal{R}_L = \{(1), (2), (3), (4)\}$. We check that the conditions R1–R6 of Definition 9 are satisfied. The condition R1 can be shown by a proof method for relative termination. It is easy to see that the conditions R2 and R4 hold. The condition R3 holds since $\mathsf{takeones}(t) \notin NF(\mathcal{R}_{\mathsf{takeones}})$ for any term t. The condition R5 holds since $LSC(T(\mathcal{F} \setminus \{\mathsf{takeones}\}), \mathsf{take}(x_1, \ldots, x_n))$ as we saw in Example 6. The condition R6 can be checked according to the forms of the rewrite rules. Hence by Theorem 1, $\mathcal{R}$ is locally sufficiently complete for $\mathsf{takeones}$. □

In the next example, the sufficient condition cannot be applied because of failure of the condition R1 of Definition 9.

Example 8. Let $\mathcal{R}$ be the TRS obtained from $\mathcal{R}$ of Example 1 by replacing the rules

$$\begin{aligned} \mathsf{nat} &\to 0 :: \mathsf{inc}(\mathsf{nat}) \\ \mathsf{inc}([]) &\to [] \\ \mathsf{inc}(x :: xs) &\to \mathsf{s}(x) :: \mathsf{inc}(xs) \end{aligned}$$

by

$$\mathsf{from}(x) \to x :: \mathsf{from}(\mathsf{s}(x))$$

where $\mathsf{from} : N \to L$. We consider the condition R1 to show that $\mathcal{R}$ is locally sufficiently complete for sum. Then we have

$$\begin{aligned} \mathsf{from}(\mathsf{sum}(0, [])) &\xrightarrow{*}_{\mathcal{R}_{N,L}} \mathsf{sum}(0, []) :: \mathsf{from}(\mathsf{s}(\mathsf{sum}(0, []))) \\ &\to_{\mathcal{R}_{\mathsf{sum}}} 0 :: \mathsf{from}(\mathsf{s}(\mathsf{sum}(0, []))) \\ &\xrightarrow{*}_{\mathcal{R}_{N,L}} 0 :: \mathsf{s}(\mathsf{sum}(0, [])) :: \mathsf{from}(\mathsf{s}(\mathsf{s}(\mathsf{sum}(0, [])))) \\ &\to_{\mathcal{R}_{\mathsf{sum}}} 0 :: \mathsf{s}(0) :: \mathsf{from}(\mathsf{s}(\mathsf{s}(\mathsf{sum}(0, [])))) \\ &\xrightarrow{*}_{\mathcal{R}_{N,L}} \cdots. \end{aligned}$$

Therefore $SN(\mathcal{R}_{\text{sum}}/\mathcal{R}_{N,L})$ does not hold. Hence we cannot apply Theorem 1 to show local sufficient completeness for sum. $\qquad\square$

Next we discuss the necessity of some conditions of Definitions 3 and 9 for proving local sufficient completeness.

Example 9. Let $\mathcal{R}$ be the TRS obtained from $\mathcal{R}$ of Example 1 by adding the following rules

$$
\begin{aligned}
\text{len}([]) &\to 0 \\
\text{len}(x :: xs) &\to +(\text{s}(0), \text{len}(xs))
\end{aligned}
$$

where len $: L \to N$. Then $\mathcal{R}$ is not locally sufficiently complete for len since $u \notin T(\mathcal{C})$ for any u with $\text{len}(\text{nat}) \xrightarrow{*}_{\mathcal{R}} u$. To make matters worse, $\mathcal{R}$ is not locally sufficiently complete for sum any more because $u \notin T(\mathcal{C})$ for any u such that $\text{sum}(\text{s}(0), \text{len}(\text{nat}) :: []) \xrightarrow{*}_{\mathcal{R}} u$.

Under the conditions S1–S3 of Definition 3, the function symbol len cannot be in $\mathcal{N}_{\mathcal{H}}$ since otherwise it contradicts the condition R5 of Definition 9. Hence len has to be in $\mathcal{N}_{\mathcal{G}}$. Then it satisfies the requirement of the condition R4, but it does not satisfy the requirement of the condition S4 of Definition 3.

This explains that the condition S4 of Definition 3 is necessary for proving local sufficient completeness for f_{tar}. $\qquad\square$

The problem above is caused by the fact that variables in rewrite rules may be instantiated by arbitrary ground terms of the same sort; Considering a case where a variable is instantiated by a ground term with its root symbol for which local sufficient completeness does not hold, it is difficult to show local sufficient completeness for a function that is defined using the variable outside functions in $\mathcal{H}$. The conditions R6(a) and R6(b) of Definition 9 are also designed carefully so that similar problems can be avoided (cf. the remark before Definition 8).

6   Comparison to Previous Work

In [10], a proof method for local sufficient completeness has been proposed, based on a derivation system. In this section, we survey the proof method to compare it to the method introduced in the present paper.

The derivation system acts on a set of *guarded terms* (Definition 11). Each guarded term is accompanied with a set of *annotated terms*, which, together with a partial order and the notion of *skeleton*, are used to check availability of an induction hypothesis in derivation rules.

First we introduce some notations used in this section. A (*strict*) *partial order* is a binary relation that is irreflexive and transitive. A partial order $\succ$ on terms is *stable* if it is closed under substitution, i.e. $s \succ t$ implies $s\theta \succ t\theta$ for every substitution θ; it is *well-founded* if there exists no infinite descending chain $t_0 \succ t_1 \succ \cdots$; it has *the subterm property* if $s \trianglelefteq t$ and $s \neq t$ implies $t \succ s$. Another ordering on terms used in our derivation system is the *subsumption ordering* $\leqslant$, which is defined by: $s \leqslant t$ iff $s\theta = t$ for some substitution θ.

Next we introduce the notions of annotation and skeleton which are heavily used in the derivation system.

Definition 10 (Annotated term, Skeleton).

1. Let $\underline{\mathcal{F}} = \{\underline{f} : \alpha_1 \times \cdots \times \alpha_n \to \alpha \mid f : \alpha_1 \times \cdots \times \alpha_n \to \alpha \in \mathcal{F}\}$ be a set of new function symbols; more precisely, for each $f \in \mathcal{F}$, prepare a new function symbol $\underline{f}$ equipped with the same sort declaration as f. The underline of $\underline{f}$ is called the *annotation* for f. The set $AT^\alpha(\mathcal{F} \cup \underline{\mathcal{F}}, \mathcal{V})$ of *annotated terms* of sort α is defined inductively as follows:
   (a) If $t \in T^\alpha(\mathcal{F}, \mathcal{V})$ then $t \in AT^\alpha(\mathcal{F} \cup \underline{\mathcal{F}}, \mathcal{V})$;
   (b) If $\underline{f} \in \underline{\mathcal{F}}$, $\underline{f} : \alpha_1 \times \cdots \times \alpha_n \to \alpha$ and $t_i \in AT^{\alpha_i}(\mathcal{F} \cup \underline{\mathcal{F}}, \mathcal{V})$ for each i $(1 \leq i \leq n)$ then $\underline{f}(t_1, \ldots, t_n) \in AT^\alpha(\mathcal{F} \cup \underline{\mathcal{F}}, \mathcal{V})$.
   We set $AT(\mathcal{F} \cup \underline{\mathcal{F}}, \mathcal{V}) = \bigcup_{\alpha \in \mathcal{S}} AT^\alpha(\mathcal{F} \cup \underline{\mathcal{F}}, \mathcal{V})$.
2. We denote by $\underline{t}$ the annotated term obtained from $t \in T(\mathcal{F}, \mathcal{V})$ by putting annotation for each function symbol occurrence in t.
3. For each annotated term $t \in AT(\mathcal{F} \cup \underline{\mathcal{F}}, \mathcal{V})$, its *skeleton skel(t)* $\in T(\mathcal{F}, \mathcal{V})$ is defined as follows: when $t \in T^\alpha(\mathcal{F}, \mathcal{V})$, $skel(t) = x$ $(\in T^\alpha(\mathcal{F}, \mathcal{V}))$; otherwise, $skel(\underline{f}(t_1, \ldots, t_n)) = f(skel(t_1), \ldots, skel(t_n))$. Here, we assume that a fresh variable x is taken for each time when a variable is required.

Clearly, we have $\underline{t} \in T(\underline{\mathcal{F}}, \mathcal{V})$ for each term t, and skeletons of annotated terms are linear terms without any annotation.

Example 10. Let $\mathcal{F} = \{0, \mathsf{s}, +\}$. Then $\underline{\mathcal{F}} = \{\underline{0}, \underline{\mathsf{s}}, \underline{+}\}$. Then, $t = \mathsf{s}(x) \underline{+} 0$ is an annotated term. Its skeleton $skel(t) = x_1 + x_2$. For $t' = \mathsf{s}(x) + 0$, we have $\underline{t'} = \underline{\mathsf{s}}(x) \underline{+} \underline{0}$.

The derivation system acts on a set of guarded terms, which are defined as follows.

Definition 11 (Guarded term). A *guarded term*, denoted by $t|H$, consists of a linear term t and a set H of linear annotated terms.

Now we are ready to define the notion of a derivation of the system.

Definition 12 (Derivation). Let $\mathcal{R}$ be a TRS, and let $\succ$ be a well-founded stable partial order with the subterm property over the set $T(\mathcal{F}, \mathcal{V})$.

1. The derivation rules of the system are listed in Fig. 1. It derives from a set of guarded terms (given at upper side) to a set of guarded terms (given at lower side) if the side condition is satisfied.
2. The relation $\succ$ between annotated terms is the same as the one after erasing all annotations.
3. We use a new unary function symbol $\hbar_t$ for each linear term t; we extend the order $\succ$ by $\hbar_t(s) \succ u$ iff $s \succ u$ or $s = u$, and the notion of skeleton by $skel(\hbar_t(u)) = t$.
4. For sets Γ, Γ' of guarded terms, we write $\Gamma \rightsquigarrow \Gamma'$ if Γ' is derived from Γ by one of the derivation rules. The reflexive transitive closure of $\rightsquigarrow$ is written as $\overset{*}{\rightsquigarrow}$.

Start $\qquad$ Decompose

$$\dfrac{\Gamma \cup \{t|H\}}{\Gamma \cup \{t|(\{\underline{t}\} \cup H)\}} \qquad\qquad \dfrac{\Gamma \cup \{f(t_1,\dots,t_n)|H\}}{\Gamma \cup \{t_1|H,\dots,t_n|H\}}\ f \in \mathcal{C}$$

Simplify $\qquad$ Delete

$$\dfrac{\Gamma \cup \{t|H\}}{\Gamma \cup \{s|H\}}\ t \to_{\mathcal{R}} s \qquad\qquad \dfrac{\Gamma \cup \{t|H\}}{\Gamma}\ \exists u \in H.\ skel(u) \leqslant t \prec u$$

Expand

$$\dfrac{\Gamma \cup \{t|H\}}{\Gamma \cup \{t\theta_i|H\theta_i\}_i}\quad \begin{array}{l} x \in \mathcal{V}(t),\ \boldsymbol{x} : \text{a sequence of fresh variables} \\ \{\theta_i\}_i = \{\{x \mapsto f(\boldsymbol{x})\} \mid f \in \mathcal{F},\ sort(x) = sort(f(\boldsymbol{x})), \\ \qquad f \in \mathcal{D} \Rightarrow \forall u \in H \setminus \mathcal{V}.\ skel(u) \not\leqslant f(\boldsymbol{x}) \vee x \notin \mathcal{V}(u)\} \end{array}$$

Abstract

$$\dfrac{\Gamma \cup \{C[t]|H\}}{\Gamma \cup \{C[x]|(\{\hbar_t(x)\} \cup H)\}}\quad x : \text{fresh},\ \exists u \in H.\ skel(u) \leqslant t \prec u$$

Lemma

$$\dfrac{\Gamma \cup \{t|H\}}{\Gamma \cup \{t|(\{\underline{s}\} \cup H), s|H\}}$$

Fig. 1. Derivation rules for proving local sufficient completeness

Theorem 2 ([10]). *Let $\mathcal{R}$ be a TRS and t a linear term. If $\{t|\emptyset\} \overset{*}{\leadsto} \{\}$ for some well-founded stable order $\succ$ with the subterm property, then $LSC(T(\mathcal{F}), t)$, i.e., $\mathcal{R}$ is locally sufficiently complete for t.*

A well-founded stable order $\succ$ with the subterm property is a particular case of a *simplification order*, and many methods for constructing such an order are known, e.g. lexicographic path order, multiset path order, Knuth-Bendix order, etc. (cf. [1,14]).

Example 11. Let $\mathcal{R}$ be the TRS given in Example 6. We show that $\mathcal{R}$ is locally sufficiently complete for $\mathsf{take}(x, \mathsf{ones})$. For this, take $\succ$ as the lexicographic path ordering based on some precedence (e.g. $\mathsf{take} > \mathsf{ones} > \mathsf{::} > \mathsf{s} > [] > 0$). In Fig. 2, we give a derivation of $\{\mathsf{take}(n, \mathsf{ones})|\emptyset\} \overset{*}{\leadsto} \{\}$. The final *Delete* step follows by

$$\begin{aligned} skel(\underline{\mathsf{take}}(\mathsf{s}(x), \underline{\mathsf{ones}})) &= \mathsf{take}(x_1, \mathsf{ones}) \\ &\leqslant \mathsf{take}(x, \mathsf{ones}) \\ &\prec \mathsf{take}(\mathsf{s}(x), \mathsf{ones}) \end{aligned}$$

Thus we conclude that $\mathcal{R}$ is locally sufficiently complete for $\mathsf{take}(n, \mathsf{ones})$. $\qquad \square$

As seen in the above example, the derivation system can deal with local sufficient completeness not only for a function symbol f (i.e. for a term of the form $f(x_1,\dots,x_n)$ where $x_1,\dots,x_n$ are distinct variables) but also for an arbitrary linear term t. This is a main reason for introducing annotations and skeletons, which would not be necessary if one treated global sufficient completeness only.

$$
\begin{array}{ll}
& \{\, \text{take}(x, \text{ones})|\emptyset \,\} \\
\rightsquigarrow_{Start} & \{\, \text{take}(x, \text{ones})|\{\underline{\text{take}(x, \text{ones})}\} \,\} \\
\rightsquigarrow_{Expand} & \{\, \text{take}(0, \text{ones})|\{\underline{\text{take}(0, \text{ones})}\}, \ \text{take}(\text{s}(x), \text{ones})|\{\underline{\text{take}(\text{s}(x), \text{ones})}\} \,\} \\
\overset{*}{\rightsquigarrow}_{Simplify} & \{\, [\,]|\{\underline{\text{take}(0, \text{ones})}\}, \ (\text{s}(0) :: \text{take}(x, \text{ones}))|\{\underline{\text{take}(\text{s}(x), \text{ones})}\} \,\} \\
\overset{*}{\rightsquigarrow}_{Decompose} & \{\, \text{take}(x, \text{ones})|\{\underline{\text{take}(\text{s}(x), \text{ones})}\} \,\} \\
\rightsquigarrow_{Delete} & \{\ \}
\end{array}
$$

Fig. 2. A derivation for $LSC(T(\mathcal{F}), \text{take}(x, \text{ones}))$ in $\mathcal{R}$ of Example 6

$$
\begin{array}{ll}
& \{\, \text{sum}(x, xs)|\emptyset \,\} \\
\rightsquigarrow_{Start} & \{\, \text{sum}(x, xs)|\{\underline{\text{sum}(x, xs)}\} \,\} \\
\rightsquigarrow_{Lemma} & \{\, \text{sum}(x, xs)|\{\underline{\text{sum}(x, xs)}, +(x, z)\} \,\} \cup \Gamma \\
\rightsquigarrow_{Expand} & \left\{ \begin{array}{l} \text{sum}(0, xs)|\{\underline{\text{sum}(0, xs)}, +(0, z)\} \\ \text{sum}(\text{s}(x'), xs)|\{\underline{\text{sum}(\text{s}(x'), xs)}, +(\text{s}(x'), z)\} \end{array} \right\} \cup \Gamma \\
\rightsquigarrow_{Simplify} & \left\{ \begin{array}{l} 0|\{\underline{\text{sum}(0, xs)}, +(0, z)\} \\ \text{sum}(\text{s}(x'), xs)|\{\underline{\text{sum}(\text{s}(x'), xs)}, +(\text{s}(x'), z)\} \end{array} \right\} \cup \Gamma \\
\rightsquigarrow_{Decompose} & \{\, \text{sum}(\text{s}(x'), xs)|\{\underline{\text{sum}(\text{s}(x'), xs)}, +(\text{s}(x'), z)\} \,\} \cup \Gamma \\
\rightsquigarrow_{Expand} & \left\{ \begin{array}{l} \text{sum}(\text{s}(x'), [\,])|\{\underline{\text{sum}(\text{s}(x'), [\,])}, +(\text{s}(x'), z)\} \\ \text{sum}(\text{s}(x'), y :: ys)|\{\underline{\text{sum}(\text{s}(x'), y :: ys)}, +(\text{s}(x'), z)\} \\ \text{sum}(\text{s}(x'), \text{from}(y))|\{\underline{\text{sum}(\text{s}(x'), \text{from}(y))}, +(\text{s}(x'), z)\} \end{array} \right\} \cup \Gamma \\
\overset{*}{\rightsquigarrow}_{Simplify} & \left\{ \begin{array}{l} 0|\{\underline{\text{sum}(\text{s}(x'), [\,])}, +(\text{s}(x'), z)\} \\ +(y, \text{sum}(x', ys))|\{\underline{\text{sum}(\text{s}(x'), y :: ys)}, +(\text{s}(x'), z)\} \\ +(y, \text{sum}(x', \text{from}(\text{s}(y))))|\{\underline{\text{sum}(\text{s}(x'), \text{from}(y))}, +(\text{s}(x'), z)\} \end{array} \right\} \cup \Gamma \\
\rightsquigarrow_{Decompose} & \left\{ \begin{array}{l} +(y, \text{sum}(x', ys))|\{\underline{\text{sum}(\text{s}(x'), y :: ys)}, +(\text{s}(x'), z)\} \\ +(y, \text{sum}(x', \text{from}(\text{s}(y))))|\{\underline{\text{sum}(\text{s}(x'), \text{from}(y))}, +(\text{s}(x'), z)\} \end{array} \right\} \cup \Gamma \\
\overset{*}{\rightsquigarrow} & \{\ \}
\end{array}
$$

Fig. 3. A derivation for $LSC(T(\mathcal{F}), \text{sum}(x, xs))$ in $\mathcal{R}$ of Example 8

The derivation system can handle the last example in the previous section, where the sufficient condition cannot be applied.

Example 12. Let $\mathcal{R}$ be the TRS given in Example 8. We show that $\mathcal{R}$ is locally sufficiently complete for sum. For this, take $\succ$ as the lexicographic path ordering based on some precedence (e.g. sum $>$ from $> + > \ :: \ > \text{s} > [\,] > 0$). In Fig. 3, we give a derivation of $\{\text{sum}(x, xs)|\emptyset\} \overset{*}{\rightsquigarrow} \{\ \}$, where $\Gamma = \{+(x, z)|\{\underline{\text{sum}(x, xs)}\}\}$ and in the last step, each of the remaining three guarded terms is removed by $\rightsquigarrow_{Start} \circ \rightsquigarrow_{Expand} \circ \overset{*}{\rightsquigarrow}_{Simplify} \circ \overset{*}{\rightsquigarrow}_{Decompose} \circ \rightsquigarrow_{Delete}$. $\square$

On the other hand, the running example in the present paper is difficult to handle by the derivation system.

Example 13. Let $\mathcal{R}$ be the TRS given in Example 1. To construct a derivation for local sufficient completeness for sum, a series of guarded terms $\text{sum}(\text{s}(x'), xs)|H$, $\text{sum}(\text{s}(x'), \text{inc}(xs'))|H', \ldots$ as seen in Fig. 4 has to be eventually removed. $\square$

$$\left\{\,\mathsf{sum}(x, xs)|\emptyset\,\right\}$$

$\rightsquigarrow_{Start} \circ \rightsquigarrow_{Lemma} \circ \rightsquigarrow_{Expand} \circ \rightsquigarrow_{Simplify} \circ$ (as in Figure 3)

$\rightsquigarrow_{Decompose} \left\{\,\mathsf{sum}(\mathsf{s}(x'), xs)|\{\underline{\mathsf{sum}}(\mathsf{s}(x'), xs), \underline{+}(\mathsf{s}(x'), z)\}\,\right\} \cup \Gamma$

$\rightsquigarrow_{Expand} \left.\begin{cases} \mathsf{sum}(\mathsf{s}(x'), [])|\{\underline{\mathsf{sum}}(\mathsf{s}(x'), []), \underline{+}(\mathsf{s}(x'), z)\} \\ \mathsf{sum}(\mathsf{s}(x'), y :: ys)|\{\underline{\mathsf{sum}}(\mathsf{s}(x'), y :: ys), \underline{+}(\mathsf{s}(x'), z)\} \\ \mathsf{sum}(\mathsf{s}(x'), \mathsf{nat})|\{\underline{\mathsf{sum}}(\mathsf{s}(x'), \mathsf{nat}), \underline{+}(\mathsf{s}(x'), z)\} \\ \mathsf{sum}(\mathsf{s}(x'), \mathsf{inc}(xs'))|\{\underline{\mathsf{sum}}(\mathsf{s}(x'), \mathsf{inc}(xs')), \underline{+}(\mathsf{s}(x'), z)\} \end{cases}\right\} \cup \Gamma$

$\overset{*}{\rightsquigarrow}_{Simplify} \left.\begin{cases} 0|\{\underline{\mathsf{sum}}(\mathsf{s}(x'), []), \underline{+}(\mathsf{s}(x'), z)\} \\ \underline{+}(y, \mathsf{sum}(x', ys))|\{\underline{\mathsf{sum}}(\mathsf{s}(x'), y :: ys), \underline{+}(\mathsf{s}(x'), z)\} \\ \mathsf{sum}(x', \mathsf{inc}(\mathsf{nat}))|\{\underline{\mathsf{sum}}(\mathsf{s}(x'), \mathsf{nat}), \underline{+}(\mathsf{s}(x'), z)\} \\ \mathsf{sum}(\mathsf{s}(x'), \mathsf{inc}(xs'))|\{\underline{\mathsf{sum}}(\mathsf{s}(x'), \mathsf{inc}(xs')), \underline{+}(\mathsf{s}(x'), z)\} \end{cases}\right\} \cup \Gamma$

$\rightsquigarrow$ $\ldots$

Fig. 4. A failing derivation for $LSC(T(\mathcal{F}), \mathsf{sum}(x, xs))$ in $\mathcal{R}$ of Example 1

The sufficient condition we proposed in the present paper successfully resolves this problem using the notions of ω-sufficient completeness, ω-quasi-reducibility and relative termination, which are all suitable to automated verification.

7 Conclusion

We have presented a sufficient condition for local sufficient completeness of TRSs that are defined on natural numbers and lists of natural numbers, and proved its correctness. The condition consists of conditions on the signature and on the rewrite rules, which are suitable to automation. Using the sufficient condition, we showed local sufficient completeness of TRSs that are non-terminating and not globally sufficiently complete. We also compared the proof abilities of the sufficient condition and the derivation system introduced in [10].

The TRSs handled by the sufficient condition have restrictions such as a sort is either one of natural numbers and lists of natural numbers. In future work, we lighten those restrictions so that the proof method will be widely applicable.

Acknowledgements. We are grateful to the anonymous referees for valuable comments. This work was partly supported by JSPS KAKENHI Grant Numbers JP19K11891, JP20H04164 and JP21K11750.

References

1. Baader, F., Nipkow, T.: Term Rewriting and All That. Cambridge University Press, Cambridge (1998)
2. Comon, H., Jacquemard, F.: Ground reducibility is EXPTIME-complete. Inf. Comput. **187**(1), 123–153 (2003)
3. Geser, A.: Relative termination. Ph.D. thesis, Universität Passau (1990). Available as technical report 91–03
4. Gnaedig, I., Kirchner, H.: Computing constructor forms with non terminating rewrite programs. In: Proceedings of the 8th PPDP, pp. 121–132. ACM (2006)

5. Gnaedig, I., Kirchner, H.: Proving weak properties of rewriting. Theoret. Comput. Sci. **412**(34), 4405–4438 (2011)
6. Guttag, J.V.: The specification and application to programming of abstract data types. Ph.D. thesis, University of Toronto (1975)
7. Guttag, J.V., Horning, J.J.: The algebraic specification of abstract data types. Acta Inf. **10**(1), 27–52 (1978)
8. Hirokawa, N., Middeldorp, A.: Decreasing diagrams and relative termination. J. Autom. Reason. **47**(4), 481–501 (2011)
9. Kapur, D., Narendran, P., Zhang, H.: On sufficient-completeness and related properties of term rewriting systems. Acta Inf. **24**(4), 395–415 (1987)
10. Kikuchi, K., Aoto, T., Sasano, I.: Inductive theorem proving in non-terminating rewriting systems and its application to program transformation. In: Proceedings of the 21st PPDP, pp. 13:1–13:14. ACM (2019)
11. Lazrek, A., Lescanne, P., Thiel, J.J.: Tools for proving inductive equalities, relative completeness, and ω-completeness. Inf. Comput. **84**(1), 47–70 (1990)
12. Lucas, S.: Context-sensitive computations in functional and functional logic programs. J. Funct. Log. Programm. **1998**(1) (1998)
13. Nakamura, M., Ogata, K., Futatsugi, K.: Reducibility of operation symbols in term rewriting systems and its application to behavioral specifications. J. Symb. Comput. **45**(5), 551–573 (2010)
14. Terese: Term Rewriting Systems. Cambridge University Press (2003)
15. Toyama, Y.: How to prove equivalence of term rewriting systems without induction. Theoret. Comput. Sci. **90**(2), 369–390 (1991)

Author Index

Printed in the United States
by Baker & Taylor Publisher Services